EVERYMAN, I will go with thee,

and be thy guide,

In thy most need to go by thy side

BEN JONSON

Believed to have been born in Westminster in
1573. Fought against the Spaniards in Flanders
returning in 1592, and took to the stage. Trial
for murder, 1598; became a Roman Catholic
for twelve years. Journey to France, 1613; to
Scotland, 1618. Died in 1637

Ben Jonson's Plays

IN TWO VOLUMES · VOLUME ONE

INTRODUCTION BY
FELIX E. SCHELLING

DENT: LONDON
EVERYMAN'S LIBRARY
DUTTON: NEW YORK

NO. *489*

3951

INTRODUCTION

THE greatest of English dramatists except Shakespeare, the first literary dictator and poet-laureate, a writer of verse, prose, satire, and criticism who most potently of all the men of his time affected the subsequent course of English letters: such was Ben Jonson, and as such his strong personality assumes an interest to us almost unparalleled, at least in his age.

Ben Jonson came of the stock that was centuries after to give to the world Thomas Carlyle; for Jonson's grandfather was of Annandale, over the Solway, whence he migrated to England. Jonson's father lost his estate under Queen Mary, "having been cast into prison and forfeited." He entered the church, but died a month before his illustrious son was born, leaving his widow and child in poverty. Jonson's birthplace was Westminster, and the time of his birth early in 1573. He was thus nearly ten years Shakespeare's junior, and less well off, if a trifle better born. But Jonson did not profit even by this slight advantage. His mother married beneath her, a wright or bricklayer, and Jonson was for a time apprenticed to the trade. As a youth he attracted the attention of the famous antiquary, William Camden, then usher at Westminster School, and there the poet laid the solid foundations of his classical learning. Jonson always held Camden in veneration, acknowledging that to him he owed,

All that I am in arts, all that I know;

and dedicating his first dramatic success, "Every Man in His Humour," to him. It is doubtful whether Jonson ever went to either university, though Fuller says that he was "statutably admitted into St. John's College, Cambridge." He tells us that he took no degree, but was later "Master of Arts in both the universities, by their favour, not his study." When a mere youth Jonson enlisted as a soldier, trailing his pike in Flanders in the protracted wars of William the Silent against the Spanish. Jonson was a large and raw-boned lad; he became by his own account in time exceedingly bulky. In chat with his friend William Drummond of Hawthornden,

vii

Jonson told how " in his service in the Low Countries he had, in the face of both the camps, killed an enemy, and taken *opima spolia* from him; " and how " since his coming to England, being appealed to the fields, he had killed his adversary which had hurt him in the arm and whose sword was ten inches longer than his." Jonson's reach may have made up for the lack of his sword; certainly his prowess lost nothing in the telling. Obviously Jonson was brave, combative, and not averse to talking of himself and his doings.

In 1592, Jonson returned from abroad penniless. Soon after he married, almost as early and quite as imprudently as Shakespeare. He told Drummond curtly that " his wife was a shrew, yet honest "; for some years he lived apart from her in the household of Lord Albany. Yet two touching epitaphs among Jonson's *Epigrams*, " On my first daughter," and " On my first son," attest the warmth of the poet's family affections. The daughter died in infancy, the son of the plague; another son grew up to manhood little credit to his father whom he survived. We know nothing beyond this of Jonson's domestic life.

How soon Jonson drifted into what we now call grandly "the theatrical profession" we do not know. In 1593, Marlowe made his tragic exit from life, and Greene, Shakespeare's other rival on the popular stage, had preceded Marlowe in an equally miserable death the year before. Shakespeare already had the running to himself. Jonson appears first in the employment of Philip Henslowe, the exploiter of several troupes of players, manager, and father-in-law of the famous actor, Edward Alleyn. From entries in *Henslowe's Diary*, a species of theatrical account book which has been handed down to us, we know that Jonson was connected with the Admiral's men; for he borrowed £4 of Henslowe, July 28, 1597, paying back 3s. 9d. on the same day on account of his " share " (in what is not altogether clear); while later, on December 3, of the same year, Henslowe advanced 20s. to him " upon a book which he showed the plot unto the company which he promised to deliver unto the company at Christmas next." In the next August Jonson was in collaboration with Chettle and Porter in a play called " Hot Anger Soon Cold." All this points to an association with Henslowe of some duration, as no mere tyro would be thus paid in advance upon mere promise. From allusions in Dekker's play, " Satiromastix," it appears that Jonson, like

Shakespeare, began life as an actor, and that he " ambled in a leather pitch by a play-wagon " taking at one time the part of Hieronimo in Kyd's famous play, " The Spanish Tragedy." By the beginning of 1598, Jonson, though still in needy circumstances, had begun to receive recognition. Francis Meres —well known for his " Comparative Discourse of our English Poets with the Greek, Latin, and Italian Poets," printed in 1598, and for his mention therein of a dozen plays of Shakespeare by title—accords to Ben Jonson a place as one of " our best in tragedy," a matter of some surprise, as no known tragedy of Jonson from so early a date has come down to us. That Jonson was at work on tragedy, however, is proved by the entries in Henslowe of at least three tragedies, now lost, in which he had a hand. These are " Page of Plymouth," " King Robert II. of Scotland," and " Richard Crookback." But all of these came later, on his return to Henslowe, and range from August 1599 to June 1602.

Returning to the autumn of 1598, an event now happened to sever for a time Jonson's relations with Henslowe. In a letter to Alleyn, dated September 26 of that year, Henslowe writes: " I have lost one of my company that hurteth me greatly; that is Gabriel [Spencer], for he is slain in Hogsden fields by the hands of Benjamin Jonson, bricklayer." The last word is perhaps Henslowe's thrust at Jonson in his displeasure rather than a designation of his actual continuance at his trade up to this time. It is fair to Jonson to remark, however, that his adversary appears to have been a notorious fire-eater who had shortly before killed one Feeke in a similar squabble. Duelling was a frequent occurrence of the time among gentlemen and the nobility; it was an impudent breach of the peace on the part of a player. This duel is the one which Jonson described years after to Drummond, and for it Jonson was duly arraigned at Old Bailey, tried, and convicted. He was sent to prison and such goods and chattels as he had " were forfeited." It is a thought to give one pause that, but for the ancient law permitting convicted felons to plead, as it was called, the benefit of clergy, Jonson might have been hanged for this deed. The circumstance that the poet could read and write saved him; and he received only a brand of the letter " T," for Tyburn, on his left thumb. While in jail Jonson became a Roman Catholic; but he returned to the faith of the Church of England a dozen years later.

On his release, in disgrace with Henslowe and his former

associates, Jonson offered his services as a playwright to Henslowe's rivals, the Lord Chamberlain's company, in which Shakespeare was a prominent shareholder. A tradition of long standing, though not susceptible of proof in a court of law, narrates that Jonson had submitted the manuscript of " Every Man in His Humour " to the Chamberlain's men and had received from the company a refusal; that Shakespeare called him back, read the play himself, and at once accepted it. Whether this story is true or not, certain it is that " Every Man in His Humour " was accepted by Shakespeare's company and acted for the first time in 1598, with Shakespeare taking a part. The evidence of this is contained in the list of actors prefixed to the comedy in the folio of Jonson's works, 1616. But it is a mistake to infer, because Shakespeare's name stands first in the list of actors and the elder Kno'well first in the *dramatis personæ*, that Shakespeare took that particular part. The order of a list of Elizabethan players was generally that of their importance or priority as shareholders in the company and seldom if ever corresponded to the list of characters.

" Every Man in His Humour " was an immediate success, and with it Jonson's reputation as one of the leading dramatists of his time was established once and for all. This could have been by no means Jonson's earliest comedy, and we have just learned that he was already reputed one of " our best in tragedy." Indeed, one of Jonson's extant comedies, " The Case is Altered," but one never claimed by him or published as his, must certainly have preceded " Every Man in His Humour " on the stage. The former play may be described as a comedy modelled on the Latin plays of Plautus. (It combines, in fact, situations derived from the " Captivi " and the " Aulularia " of that dramatist). But the pretty story of the beggar-maiden, Rachel, and her suitors, Jonson found, not among the classics, but in the ideals of romantic love which Shakespeare had already popularised on the stage. Jonson never again produced so fresh and lovable a feminine personage as Rachel, although in other respects " The Case is Altered " is not a conspicuous play, and, save for the satirising of Antony Munday in the person of Antonio Balladino and Gabriel Harvey as well, is perhaps the least characteristic of the comedies of Jonson.

" Every Man in His Humour," probably first acted late in the summer of 1598 and at the Curtain, is commonly regarded as an epoch-making play; and this view is not unjustified. As to plot, it tells little more than how an intercepted letter enabled a father to follow his supposedly studious son to London, and there observe his life with the gallants of the time. The real quality of this comedy is in its personages and in the theory upon which they are conceived. Ben Jonson had theories about poetry and the drama, and he was neither chary in talking of them nor in experimenting with them in his plays. This makes Jonson, like Dryden in his time, and Wordsworth much later, an author to reckon with; particularly when we remember that many of Jonson's notions came for a time definitely to prevail and to modify the whole trend of English poetry. First of all Jonson was a classicist, that is, he believed in restraint and precedent in art in opposition to the prevalent ungoverned and irresponsible Renaissance spirit. Jonson believed that there was a professional way of doing things which might be reached by a study of the best examples, and he found these examples for the most part among the ancients. To confine our attention to the drama, Jonson objected to the amateurishness and haphazard nature of many contemporary plays, and set himself to do something different; and the first and most striking thing that he evolved was his conception and practice of the comedy of humours.

As Jonson has been much misrepresented in this matter, let us quote his own words as to "humour." A humour, according to Jonson, was a bias of disposition, a warp, so to speak, in character by which

> Some one peculiar quality
> Doth so possess a man, that it doth draw
> All his affects, his spirits, and his powers,
> In their confluctions, all to run one way.

But continuing, Jonson is careful to add:

> But that a rook by wearing a pied feather,
> The cable hat-band, or the three-piled ruff,
> A yard of shoe-tie, or the Switzers knot
> On his French garters, should affect a humour!
> O, it is more than most ridiculous.

Jonson's comedy of humours, in a word, conceived of stage personages on the basis of a ruling trait or passion (a notable simplification of actual life be it observed in passing); and, placing these typified traits in juxtaposition in their conflict and contrast, struck the spark of comedy. Downright, as his name indicates, is "a plain squire"; Bobadill's humour is that of the braggart who is incidentally, and with delightfully comic effect, a coward; Brainworm's humour is the finding out of things to the end of fooling everybody: of course he is fooled in the end himself. But it was not Jonson's theories alone that made the success of " Every Man in His Humour." The play is admirably written and each character is vividly conceived, and with a firm touch based on observation of the men of the London of the day. Jonson was neither in this, his first great comedy (nor in any other play that he wrote), a supine classicist, urging that English drama return to a slavish adherence to classical conditions. He says as to the laws of the old comedy (meaning by " laws," such matters as the unities of time and place and the use of chorus): " I see not then, but we should enjoy the same licence, or free power to illustrate and heighten our invention as they [the ancients] did; and not be tied to those strict and regular forms which the niceness of a few, who are nothing but form, would thrust upon us." " Every Man in His Humour " is written in prose, a novel practice which Jonson had of his predecessor in comedy, John Lyly. Even the word " humour " seems to have been employed in the Jonsonian sense by Chapman before Jonson's use of it. Indeed, the comedy of humours itself is only a heightened variety of the comedy of manners which represents life, viewed at a satirical angle, and is the oldest and most persistent species of comedy in the language. None the less, Jonson's comedy merited its immediate success and marked out a definite course in which comedy long continued to run. To mention only Shakespeare's Falstaff and his rout, Bardolph, Pistol, Dame Quickly, and the rest, whether in " Henry IV." or in " The Merry Wives of Windsor," all are conceived in the spirit of humours. So are the captains, Welsh, Scotch, and Irish of " Henry V.," and Malvolio especially later; though Shakespeare never employed the method of humours for an important personage. It was not Jonson's fault that many of his successors did precisely the thing that he had reprobated, that is, degrade " the humour " into an oddity of speech, an eccentricity of manner, of dress, or cut of beard. There was an anonymous play called " Every Woman in Her Humour." Chapman wrote " A Humourous Day's Mirth," Day, " Humour Out of Breath," Fletcher later, " The Humourous Lieutenant," and Jonson, besides " Every Man Out of His Humour," returned to the title in closing the cycle of his comedies in " The Magnetic Lady or Humours Reconciled."

With the performance of " Every Man Out of His Humour "
in 1599, by Shakespeare's company once more at the Globe,
we turn a new page in Jonson's career. Despite his many real
virtues, if there is one feature more than any other that
distinguishes Jonson, it is his arrogance; and to this may
be added his self-righteousness, especially under criticism or
satire. " Every Man Out of His Humour " is the first of three
" comical satires " which Jonson contributed to what Dekker
called the *poetomachia* or war of the theatres as recent critics
have named it. This play as a fabric of plot is a very slight
affair; but as a satirical picture of the manners of the time,
proceeding by means of vivid caricature, couched in witty
and brilliant dialogue and sustained by that righteous indignation which must lie at the heart of all true satire—as a realisa-
tion, in short, of the classical ideal of comedy—there had been
nothing like Jonson's comedy since the days of Aristophanes.
" Every Man in His Humour," like the two plays that follow
it, contains two kinds of attack, the critical or generally satiric,
levelled at abuses and corruptions in the abstract; and the
personal, in which specific application is made of all this in
the lampooning of poets and others, Jonson's contemporaries.
The method of personal attack by actual caricature of a person
on the stage is almost as old as the drama. Aristophanes so
lampooned Euripides in "The Acharnians" and Socrates in
" The Clouds," to mention no other examples; and in English
drama this kind of thing is alluded to again and again. What
Jonson really did, was to raise the dramatic lampoon to an
art, and make out of a casual burlesque and bit of mimicry a
dramatic satire of literary pretensions and permanency. With
the arrogant attitude mentioned above and his uncommon
eloquence in scorn, vituperation, and invective, it is no wonder
that Jonson soon involved himself in literary and even personal
quarrels with his fellow-authors. The circumstances of the
origin of this *poetomachia* are far from clear, and those who
have written on the topic, except of late, have not helped to
make them clearer. The origin of the " war " has been
referred to satirical references, apparently to Jonson, contained
in " The Scourge of Villainy," a satire in regular form after
the manner of the ancients by John Marston, a fellow playwright, subsequent friend and collaborator of Jonson's. On
the other hand, epigrams of Jonson have been discovered
(49, 68, and 100) variously charging "playwright" (reason-
ably identified with Marston) with scurrility, cowardice, and

plagiarism; though the dates of the epigrams cannot be ascertained with certainty. Jonson's own statement of the matter to Drummond runs: "He had many quarrels with Marston, beat him, and took his pistol from him, wrote his *Poetaster* on him; the beginning[s] of them were that Marston represented him on the stage." [1]

Here at least we are on certain ground; and the principals of the quarrel are known. "Histriomastix," a play revised by Marston in 1598, has been regarded as the one in which Jonson was thus "represented on the stage"; although the personage in question, Chrisogonus, a poet, satirist, and translator, poor but proud, and contemptuous of the common herd, seems rather a complimentary portrait of Jonson than a caricature. As to the personages actually ridiculed in "Every Man Out of His Humour," Carlo Buffone was formerly thought certainly to be Marston, as he was described as "a public, scurrilous, and profane jester," and elsewhere as the grand scourge or second untruss [that is, satirist], of the time" (Joseph Hall being by his own boast the first, and Marston's work being entitled "The Scourge of Villainy"). Apparently we must now prefer for Carlo a notorious character named Charles Chester, of whom gossipy and inaccurate Aubrey relates that he was "a bold impertinent fellow . . . a perpetual talker and made a noise like a drum in a room. So one time at a tavern Sir Walter Raleigh beats him and seals up his mouth (that is his upper and his nether beard) with hard wax. From him Ben Jonson takes his Carlo Buffone [*i.e.*, jester] in 'Every Man in His Humour' [*sic*]." Is it conceivable that after all Jonson was ridiculing Marston, and that the point of the satire consisted in an intentional confusion of "the grand scourge or second untruss" with "the scurrilous and profane" Chester?

We have digressed into detail in this particular case to exemplify the difficulties of criticism in its attempts to identify the allusions in these forgotten quarrels. We are on sounder ground of fact in recording other manifestations of Jonson's enmity. In "The Case is Altered" there is clear ridicule in the character Antonio Balladino of Anthony Munday, pageant-poet of the city, translator of romances and playwright as well.

[1] The best account of this whole subject is to be found in the edition of *Poetaster* and *Satiromastrix* by J. H. Penniman in *Belles Lettres Series* shortly to appear. See also his earlier work, *The War of the Theatres*, 1892, and the excellent contributions to the subject by H. C. Hart in *Notes and Queries*, and in his edition of Jonson, 1906.

In " Every Man in His Humour " there is certainly a caricature of Samuel Daniel, accepted poet of the court, sonneteer, and companion of men of fashion. These men held recognised positions to which Jonson felt his talents better entitled him; they were hence to him his natural enemies. It seems almost certain that he pursued both in the personages of his satire through " Every Man Out of His Humour," and " Cynthia's Revels," Daniel under the characters Fastidious Brisk and Hedon, Munday as Puntarvolo and Amorphus; but in these last we venture on quagmire once more. Jonson's literary rivalry of Daniel is traceable again and again, in the entertainments that welcomed King James on his way to London, in the masques at court, and in the pastoral drama. As to Jonson's personal ambitions with respect to these two men, it is notable that he became, not pageant-poet, but chronologer to the City of London; and that, on the accession of the new king, he came soon to triumph over Daniel as the accepted entertainer of royalty.

" Cynthia's Revels," the second " comical satire," was acted in 1600, and, as a play, is even more lengthy, elaborate, and impossible than " Every Man Out of His Humour." Here personal satire seems to have absorbed everything, and while much of the caricature is admirable, especially in the detail of witty and trenchantly satirical dialogue, the central idea of a fountain of self-love is not very well carried out, and the persons revert at times to abstractions, the action to allegory. It adds to our wonder that this difficult drama should have been acted by the Children of Queen Elizabeth's Chapel, among them Nathaniel Field with whom Jonson read Horace and Martial, and whom he taught later how to make plays. Another of these precocious little actors was Salathiel Pavy, who died before he was thirteen, already famed for taking the parts of old men. Him Jonson immortalised in one of the sweetest of his epitaphs. An interesting sidelight is this on the character of this redoubtable and rugged satirist, that he should thus have befriended and tenderly remembered these little theatrical waifs, some of whom (as we know) had been literally kidnapped to be pressed into the service of the theatre and whipped to the conning of their difficult parts. To the caricature of Daniel and Munday in " Cynthia's Revels " must be added Anaides (impudence), here assuredly Marston, and Asotus (the prodigal), interpreted as Lodge or, more perilously, Raleigh. Crites, like Asper-Macilente in " Every Man Out of

His Humour," is Jonson's self-complaisant portrait of himself, the just, wholly admirable, and judicious scholar, holding his head high above the pack of the yelping curs of envy and detraction, but careless of their puny attacks on his perfections with only too mindful a neglect.

The third and last of the " comical satires " is " Poetaster," acted, once more, by the Children of the Chapel in 1601, and Jonson's only avowed contribution to the fray. According to the author's own account, this play was written in fifteen weeks on a report that his enemies had entrusted to Dekker the preparation of " Satiromastix, the Untrussing of the Humorous Poet," a dramatic attack upon himself. In this attempt to forestall his enemies Jonson succeeded, and " Poetaster " was an immediate and deserved success. While hardly more closely knit in structure than its earlier companion pieces, " Poetaster " is planned to lead up to the ludicrous final scene in which, after a device borrowed from the " Lexiphanes " of Lucian, the offending poetaster, Marston-Crispinus, is made to throw up the difficult words with which he had overburdened his stomach as well as overlarded his vocabulary. In the end Crispinus with his fellow, Dekker-Demetrius, is bound over to keep the peace and never thenceforward " malign, traduce, or detract the person or writings of Quintus Horatius Flaccus [Jonson] or any other eminent man transcending you in merit." One of the most diverting personages in Jonson's comedy is Captain Tucca. " His peculiarity " has been well described by Ward as " a buoyant blackguardism which recovers itself instantaneously from the most complete exposure, and a picturesqueness of speech like that of a walking dictionary of slang."

It was this character, Captain Tucca, that Dekker hit upon in his reply, " Satiromastix," and he amplified him, turning his abusive vocabulary back upon Jonson and adding " an immodesty to his dialogue that did not enter into Jonson's conception." It has been held, altogether plausibly, that when Dekker was engaged professionally, so to speak, to write a dramatic reply to Jonson, he was at work on a species of chronicle history, dealing with the story of Walter Terill in the reign of William Rufus. This he hurriedly adapted to include the satirical characters suggested by " Poetaster," and fashioned to convey the satire of his reply. The absurdity of placing Horace in the court of a Norman king is the result. But Dekker's play is not without its palpable hits at the arrogance, the literary pride, and self-righteousness of Jonson-Horace, whose " ningle " or pal, the absurd Asinius Bubo, has recently been shown to figure forth, in all likelihood, Jonson's friend, the poet Drayton. Slight and hastily adapted as is " Satiromastix," especially in a comparison with the better wrought and more significant satire of " Poetaster," the town awarded the palm to Dekker, not to Jonson; and Jonson gave over in consequence his practice of " comical satire." Though Jonson was cited to appear before the Lord Chief Justice to answer certain charges to the effect that he had attacked lawyers and soldiers in " Poetaster," nothing came of this complaint. It may be suspected that much of this furious clatter and give-and-take was pure playing to the gallery. The town was agog with the strife, and on no less an authority than Shakespeare (" Hamlet," ii. 2), we learn that the children's company (acting the plays of Jonson) did " so berattle the common stages . . . that many, wearing rapiers, are afraid of goose-quills, and dare scarce come thither."

Several other plays have been thought to bear a greater or less part in the war of the theatres. Among them the most important is a college play, entitled " The Return from Parnassus," dating 1601-02. In it a much-quoted passage makes Burbage, as a character, declare: " Why here's our fellow Shakespeare puts them all down; aye and Ben Jonson, too. O that Ben Jonson is a pestilent fellow; he brought up Horace, giving the poets a pill, but our fellow Shakespeare hath given him a purge that made him bewray his credit." Was Shakespeare then concerned in this war of the stages? And what could have been the nature of this " purge "? Among several suggestions, " Troilus and Cressida " has been thought by some to be the play in which Shakespeare thus " put down " his friend, Jonson. A wiser interpretation finds the " purge " in " Satiromastix," which, though not written by Shakespeare, was staged by his company, and therefore with his approval and under his direction as one of the leaders of that company.

The last years of the reign of Elizabeth thus saw Jonson recognised as a dramatist second only to Shakespeare, and not second even to him as a dramatic satirist. But Jonson now turned his talents to new fields. Plays on subjects derived from classical story and myth had held the stage from the beginning of the drama, so that Shakespeare was making no new departure when he wrote his " Julius Cæsar " about 1600

Therefore when Jonson staged " Sejanus," three years later and with Shakespeare's company once more, he was only following in the elder dramatist's footsteps. But Jonson's idea of a play on classical history, on the one hand, and Shakespeare's and the elder popular dramatists, on the other, were very different. Heywood some years before had put five straggling plays on the stage in quick succession, all derived from stories in Ovid and dramatised with little taste or discrimination. Shakespeare had a finer conception of form, but even he was contented to take all his ancient history from North's translation of Plutarch and dramatise his subject without further inquiry. Jonson was a scholar and a classical antiquarian. He reprobated this slipshod amateurishness, and wrote his " Sejanus " like a scholar, reading Tacitus, Suetonius, and other authorities, to be certain of his facts, his setting, and his atmosphere, and somewhat pedantically noting his authorities in the margin when he came to print. " Sejanus " is a tragedy of genuine dramatic power in which is told with discriminating taste the story of the haughty favourite of Tiberius with his tragical overthrow. Our drama presents no truer nor more painstaking representation of ancient Roman life than may be found in Jonson's " Sejanus " and " Catiline his Conspiracy," which followed in 1611. A passage in the address of the former play to the reader, in which Jonson refers to a collaboration in an earlier version, has led to the surmise that Shakespeare may have been that " worthier pen." There is no evidence to determine the matter.

In 1605, we find Jonson in active collaboration with Chapman and Marston in the admirable comedy of London life entitled " Eastward Hoe." In the previous year, Marston had dedicated his " Malcontent," in terms of fervid admiration, to Jonson; so that the wounds of the war of the theatres must have been long since healed. Between Jonson and Chapman there was the kinship of similar scholarly ideals. The two continued friends throughout life. " Eastward Hoe " achieved the extraordinary popularity represented in a demand for three issues in one year. But this was not due entirely to the merits of the play. In its earliest version a passage which an irritable courtier conceived to be derogatory to his nation, the Scots, sent both Chapman and Jonson to jail; but the matter was soon patched up, for by this time Jonson had influence at court.

With the accession of King James, Jonson began his long and successful career as a writer of masques. He wrote more masques than all his competitors together, and they are of an extraordinary variety and poetic excellence. Jonson did not invent the masque; for such premeditated devices to set and frame, so to speak, a court ball had been known and practised in varying degrees of elaboration long before his time. But Jonson gave dramatic value to the masque, especially in his invention of the antimasque, a comedy or farcical element of relief, entrusted to professional players or dancers. He enhanced, as well, the beauty and dignity of those portions of the masque in which noble lords and ladies took their parts to create, by their gorgeous costumes and artistic grouping and evolutions, a sumptuous show. On the mechanical and scenic side Jonson had an inventive and ingenious partner in Inigo Jones, the royal architect, who more than any one man raised the standard of stage representation in the England of his day. Jonson continued active in the service of the court in the writing of masques and other entertainments far into the reign of King Charles; but, towards the end, a quarrel with Jones embittered his life, and the two testy old men appear to have become not only a constant irritation to each other, but intolerable bores at court. In " Hymenaei," " The Masque of Queens," " Love Freed from Ignorance," " Lovers made Men," " Pleasure Reconciled to Virtue," and many more will be found Jonson's aptitude, his taste, his poetry and inventiveness in these by-forms of the drama; while in " The Masque of Christmas," and " The Gipsies Metamorphosed " especially, is discoverable that power of broad comedy which, at court as well as in the city, was not the least element of Jonson's contemporary popularity.

But Jonson had by no means given up the popular stage when he turned to the amusement of King James. In 1605 " Volpone " was produced, " The Silent Woman " in 1609, " The Alchemist " in the following year. These comedies, with " Bartholomew Fair," 1614, represent Jonson at his height, and for constructive cleverness, character successfully conceived in the manner of caricature, wit and brilliancy of dialogue, they stand alone in English drama. " Volpone, or the Fox," is, in a sense, a transition play from the dramatic satires of the war of the theatres to the purer comedy represented in the plays named above. Its subject is a struggle of wit applied to chicanery; for among its *dramatis personæ*, from the villainous Fox himself, his rascally servant Mosca, Voltore (the vulture), Corbaccio and Corvino (the big and the little raven), to Sir Politic Would-be and the rest, there is scarcely a virtuous character in the play. Question has been raised as to whether a story so forbidding can be considered a comedy, for, although the plot ends in the discomfiture and imprisonment of the most vicious, it involves no mortal catastrophe. But Jonson was on sound historical ground, for "Volpone" is conceived far more logically on the lines of the ancients' theory of comedy than was ever the romantic drama of Shakespeare, however repulsive we may find a philosophy of life that facilely divides the world into the rogues and their dupes, and, identifying brains with roguery and innocence with folly, admires the former while inconsistently punishing them.

"The Silent Woman" is a gigantic farce of the most ingenious construction. The whole comedy hinges on a huge joke, played by a heartless nephew on his misanthropic uncle, who is induced to take to himself a wife, young, fair, and warranted silent, but who, in the end, turns out neither silent nor a woman at all. In "The Alchemist," again, we have the utmost cleverness in construction, the whole fabric building climax on climax, witty, ingenious, and so plausibly presented that we forget its departures from the possibilities of life. In "The Alchemist" Jonson represented, none the less to the life, certain sharpers of the metropolis, revelling in their shrewdness and rascality and in the variety of the stupidity and wickedness of their victims. We may object to the fact that the only person in the play possessed of a scruple of honesty is discomfited, and that the greatest scoundrel of all is approved in the end and rewarded. The comedy is so admirably written and contrived, the personages stand out with such lifelike distinctness in their several kinds, and the whole is animated with such verve and resourcefulness that "The Alchemist" is a new marvel every time it is read. Lastly of this group comes the tremendous comedy, "Bartholomew Fair," less clear cut, less definite, and less structurally worthy of praise than its three predecessors, but full of the keenest and cleverest of satire and inventive to a degree beyond any English comedy save some other of Jonson's own. It is in "Bartholomew Fair" that we are presented to the immortal caricature of the Puritan, Zeal-in-the-Land Busy, and the Littlewits that group about him, and it is in this extraordinary comedy that the humour of Jonson, always open to this danger, loosens into the Rabelaisian mode that so delighted King James in " The Gipsies Metamorphosed." Another comedy of less merit is " The Devil is an Ass," acted in 1616. It was the failure of this play that caused Jonson to give over writing for the public stage for a period of nearly ten years.

" Volpone " was laid as to scene in Venice. Whether because of the success of " Eastward Hoe " or for other reasons, the other three comedies declare in the words of the prologue to " The Alchemist ":

> Our scene is London, 'cause we would make known
> No country's mirth is better than our own.

Indeed Jonson went further when he came to revise his plays for collected publication in his folio of 1616, he transferred the scene of " Every Man in His Humour " from Florence to London also, converting Signior Lorenzo di Pazzi to Old Kno'well, Prospero to Master Welborn, and Hesperida to Dame Kitely " dwelling i' the Old Jewry."

In his comedies of London life, despite his trend towards caricature, Jonson has shown himself a genuine realist, drawing from the life about him with an experience and insight rare in any generation. A happy comparison has been suggested between Ben Jonson and Charles Dickens. Both were men of the people, lowly born and hardly bred. Each knew the London of his time as few men knew it; and each represented it intimately and in elaborate detail. Both men were at heart moralists, seeking the truth by the exaggerated methods of humour and caricature; perverse, even wrong-headed at times, but possessed of a true pathos and largeness of heart, and when all has been said—though the Elizabethan ran to satire, the Victorian to sentimentality—leaving the world better for the art that they practised in it.

In 1616, the year of the death of Shakespeare, Jonson collected his plays, his poetry, and his masques for publication in a collective edition. This was an unusual thing at the time and had been attempted by no dramatist before Jonson. This volume published, in a carefully revised text, all the plays thus far mentioned, excepting " The Case is Altered," which Jonson did not acknowledge, " Bartholomew Fair," and " The Devil is an Ass," which was written too late. It included likewise a book of some hundred and thirty odd *Epigrams*, in which form of brief and pungent writing Jonson was an acknowledged master; "The Forest," a smaller collection of lyric and occasional verse and some ten *Masques* and *Entertainments*. In this same year Jonson was made poet laureate with a pension of one hundred marks a year. This, with his fees and returns from several noblemen, and the small earnings of his plays must have formed the bulk of his income. The poet appears to have done certain literary hack-work for others, as, for example, parts of the Punic Wars contributed to Raleigh's *History of the World*. We know from a story, little to the credit of either, that Jonson accompanied Raleigh's son abroad in the capacity of a tutor. In 1618 Jonson was granted the reversion of the office of Master of the Revels, a post for which he was peculiarly fitted; but he did not live to enjoy its perquisites. Jonson was honoured with degrees by both universities, though when and under what circumstances is not known. It has been said that he narrowly escaped the honour of knighthood, which the satirists of the day averred King James was wont to lavish with an indiscriminate hand. Worse men were made knights in his day than worthy Ben Jonson.

From 1616 to the close of the reign of King James, Jonson produced nothing for the stage. But he " prosecuted " what he calls " his wonted studies " with such assiduity that he became in reality, as by report, one of the most learned men of his time. Jonson's theory of authorship involved a wide acquaintance with books and "an ability," as he put it, "to convert the substance or riches of another poet to his own use." Accordingly Jonson read not only the Greek and Latin classics down to the lesser writers, but he acquainted himself especially with the Latin writings of his learned contemporaries, their prose as well as their poetry, their antiquities and curious lore as well as their more solid learning. Though a poor man, Jonson was an indefatigable collector of books. He told Drummond that " the Earl of Pembroke sent him £20 every first day of the new year to buy new books." Unhappily, in 1623, his library was destroyed by fire, an accident serio-comically described in his witty poem, "An Execration upon Vulcan." Yet even now a book turns up from time to time on which is inscribed, in fair large Italian lettering, the name, Ben Jonson. With respect to Jonson's use of his material, Dryden said memorably of him: "[He] was not only a professed imitator of Horace, but a learned plagiary of all the others; you track him everywhere in their snow. . . . But he has done his robberies so openly that one sees he fears not to be taxed by any law. He invades authors like a monarch, and what would be theft in other poets is only victory in him." And yet it is but fair to say that Jonson prided himself, and justly, on his originality. In "Catiline," he not only uses Sallust's account of the conspiracy, but he models some of the speeches of Cicero on the Roman orator's actual words. In "Poetaster," he lifts a whole satire out of Horace and dramatises it effectively for his purposes. The sophist Libanius suggests the situation of "The Silent Woman"; a Latin comedy of Giordano Bruno, "Il Candelaio," the relation of the dupes and the sharpers in "The Alchemist," the "Mostellaria" of Plautus, its admirable opening scene. But Jonson commonly bettered his sources, and putting the stamp of his sovereignty on whatever bullion he borrowed made it thenceforward to all time current and his own.

The lyric and especially the occasional poetry of Jonson has a peculiar merit. His theory demanded design and the perfection of literary finish. He was furthest from the rhapsodist and the careless singer of an idle day; and he believed that Apollo could only be worthily served in singing robes and laurel crowned. And yet many of Jonson's lyrics will live as long as the language. Who does not know "Queen and huntress, chaste and fair," "Drink to me only with thine eyes," or "Still to be neat, still to be dressed"? Beautiful in form, deft and graceful in expression, with not a word too much or one that bears not its part in the total effect, there is yet about the lyrics of Jonson a certain stiffness and formality, a suspicion that they were not quite spontaneous and unbidden, but that they were carved, so to speak, with disproportionate labour by a potent man of letters whose habitual thought is on greater things. It is for these reasons that Jonson is even better in the epigram and in occasional verse where rhetorical finish and pointed wit less interfere with the spontaneity and emotion which we usually associate with lyrical poetry. There are no such epitaphs as Ben Jonson's, witness the charming ones on his own children, on Salathiel Pavy, the child-actor, and many more; and this even though the rigid law of mine and thine must now restore to William Browne of Tavistock the famous lines beginning: "Underneath this sable hearse." Jonson is unsurpassed, too, in the difficult poetry of compliment, seldom falling into fulsome praise and disproportionate similitude, yet showing again and again a generous appreciation of worth in others, a discriminating taste and a generous personal regard. There was no man in England of his rank so well known and universally beloved as Ben Jonson. The list of his friends, of those to whom he had written verses, and those who had written verses to him, includes the name of every man of prominence in the England of King James. And the tone of many of these productions discloses an affectionate familiarity that speaks for the amiable personality and sound worth of the laureate. In 1619, growing unwieldy through inactivity, Jonson hit upon the heroic remedy of a journey afoot to Scotland. On his way thither and back he was hospitably received at the houses of many friends and by those to whom his friends had recommended him. When he arrived in Edinburgh, the burgesses met to grant him the freedom of the city, and Drummond, foremost of Scottish poets, was proud to entertain him for weeks as his guest at Hawthornden. Some of the noblest of Jonson's poems were inspired by friendship. Such is the fine " Ode to the memory of Sir Lucius Cary and Sir Henry Moryson," and that admirable piece of critical insight and filial affection, prefixed to the first Shakespeare folio, " To the memory of my beloved master, William Shakespeare, and what he hath left us," to mention only these. Nor can the earlier " Epode," beginning " Not to know vice at all," be matched in stately gravity and gnomic wisdom in its own wise and stately age.

But if Jonson had deserted the stage after the publication of his folio and up to the end of the reign of King James, he was far from inactive; for year after year his inexhaustible inventiveness continued to contribute to the masquing and entertainment at court. In " The Golden Age Restored," Pallas turns the Iron Age with its attendant evils into statues which sink out of sight; in " Pleasure Reconciled to Virtue," Atlas figures represented as an old man, his shoulders covered with snow, and Comus, " the god of cheer or the belly," is one of the characters, a circumstance which an imaginative boy of ten, named John Milton, was not to forget. " Pan's Anniversary," late in the reign of James, proclaimed that Jonson had not yet forgotten how to write exquisite lyrics, and " The Gipsies Metamorphosed " displayed the old drollery and broad humorous stroke still unimpaired and unmatchable. These, too, and the earlier years of Charles were the days of the Apollo Room of the Devil Tavern where Jonson presided,

the absolute monarch of English literary Bohemia. We hear
of a room blazoned about with Jonson's own judicious *Leges
Convivales* in letters of gold, of a company made up of the
choicest spirits of the time, devotedly attached to their veteran
dictator, his reminiscences, opinions, affections, and enmities.
And we hear, too, of valorous potations; but, in the words of
Herrick addressed to his master, Jonson, at the Devil Tavern,
as at the Dog, the Triple Tun, and at the Mermaid,

> We such clusters had
> As made us nobly wild, not mad,
> And yet each verse of thine
> Outdid the meat, outdid the frolic wine.

But the patronage of the court failed in the days of King
Charles, though Jonson was not without royal favours; and
the old poet returned to the stage, producing, between 1625
and 1633, "The Staple of News," "The New Inn," "The
Magnetic Lady," and "The Tale of a Tub," the last doubtless
revised from a much earlier comedy. None of these plays
met with any marked success, although the scathing generalisa-
tion of Dryden that designated them "Jonson's dotages" is
unfair to their genuine merits. Thus the idea of an office for
the gathering, proper dressing, and promulgation of news
(wild flight of the fancy in its time) was an excellent subject
for satire on the existing absurdities among newsmongers;
although as much can hardly be said for "The Magnetic
Lady," who, in her bounty, draws to her personages of differing
humours to reconcile them in the end according to the alter-
native title, or "Humours Reconciled." These last plays of
the old dramatist revert to caricature and the hard lines of
allegory; the moralist is more than ever present, the satire
degenerates into personal lampoon, especially of his sometime
friend, Inigo Jones, who appears unworthily to have used his
influence at court against the broken-down old poet. And now
disease claimed Jonson, and he was bedridden for months.
He had succeeded Middleton in 1628 as Chronologer to the
City of London, but lost the post for not fulfilling its duties.
King Charles befriended him, and even commissioned him to
write still for the entertainment of the court; and he was not
without the sustaining hand of noble patrons and devoted
friends among the younger poets who were proud to be "sealed
of the tribe of Ben."

Jonson died, August 6, 1637, and a second folio of his works, which he had been some time gathering, was printed in 1640, bearing in its various parts dates ranging from 1630 to 1642. It included all the plays mentioned in the foregoing paragraphs, excepting "The Case is Altered;" the masques, some fifteen, that date between 1617 and 1630; another collection of lyrics and occasional poetry called "Underwoods, including some further entertainments; a translation of "Horace's Art of Poetry" (also published in a vicesimo quarto in 1640), and certain fragments and ingatherings which the poet would hardly have included himself. These last comprise the fragment (less than seventy lines) of a tragedy called "Mortimer his Fall," and three acts of a pastoral drama of much beauty and poetic spirit, "The Sad Shepherd." There is also the exceedingly interesting *English Grammar* "made by Ben Jonson for the benefit of all strangers out of his observation of the English language now spoken and in use," in Latin and English; and *Timber, or Discoveries* "made upon men and matter as they have flowed out of his daily reading, or had their reflux to his peculiar notion of the times." The *Discoveries*, as it is usually called, is a commonplace book such as many literary men have kept, in which their reading was chronicled, passages that took their fancy translated or transcribed, and their passing opinions noted. Many passages of Jonson's *Discoveries* are literal translations from the authors he chanced to be reading, with the reference, noted or not, as the accident of the moment prescribed. At times he follows the line of Macchiavelli's argument as to the nature and conduct of princes; at others he clarifies his own conception of poetry and poets by recourse to Aristotle. He finds a choice paragraph on eloquence in Seneca the elder and applies it to his own recollection of Bacon's power as an orator; and another on facile and ready genius, and translates it, adapting it to his recollection of his fellow-playwright, Shakespeare. To call such passages—which Jonson never intended for publication—plagiarism, is to obscure the significance of words. To disparage his memory by citing them is a preposterous use of scholarship. Jonson's prose, both in his dramas, in the descriptive comments of his masques, and in the *Discoveries*, is characterised by clarity and vigorous directness, nor is it wanting in a fine sense of form or in the subtler graces of diction.

When Jonson died there was a project for a handsome monument to his memory. But the Civil War was at hand,

and the project failed. A memorial, not insufficient, was carved on the stone covering his grave in one of the aisles of Westminster Abbey:

"O rare Ben Jonson."

FELIX E. SCHELLING.

SELECT BIBLIOGRAPHY

DRAMAS. *Every Man in his Humour*, 4to, 1601; *The Case is Altered*, 4to, 1609; *Every Man out of his Humour*, 4to, 1600; *Cynthia's Revels*, 4to, 1601; *Poetaster*, 4to, 1602; *Sejanus*, 4to, 1605; *Eastward Ho* (with Chapman and Marston), 4to, 1605; *Volpone*, 4to, 1607; *Epicoene, or the Silent Woman*, 4to, 1609 (?), fol., 1616; *The Alchemist*, 4to, 1612; *Catiline, his Conspiracy*, 4to, 1611; *Bartholomew Fayre*, 4to, 1614 (?), fol., 1631; *The Divell is an Asse*, fol., 1631; *The Staple of Newes*, fol., 1631; *The New Sun*, 8vo, 1631, fol., 1692; *The Magnetic Lady, or Humours Reconcild*, fol., 1640; *A Tale of a Tub*, fol., 1640; *The Sad Shepherd, or a Tale of Robin Hood*, fol., 1641; *Mortimer his Fall* (fragment), fol., 1640.

To Jonson have also been attributed additions to Kyd's *Jeronymo*, and collaboration in *The Widow* with Fletcher and Middleton, and in the *Bloody Brother* with Fletcher.

POEMS. *Epigrams, The Forrest, Underwoods*, published in fols., 1616, 1640; Selections: *Execration against Vulcan*, and *Epigrams*, 1640; *G. Hor. Flaccus his art of Poetry, Englished by Ben Jonson*, 1640; *Leges Convivialis*, fol., 1692. Other minor poems first appeared in Gifford's edition of Works.

PROSE. *Timber, or Discoveries made upon Men and Matter*, fol., 1641; *The English Grammar, made by Ben Jonson for the benefit of strangers*, fol., 1640.

Masques and Entertainments were published in the early folios.

WORKS. Fol., 1616, vol. 2, 1640 (1631–41); fol., 1692, 1716–19, 1729; edited by P. Whalley, 7 vols., 1756; by Gifford (with Memoir), 9 vols., 1816, 1846; re-edited by F. Cunningham, 3 vols., 1871; in 9 vols., 1875; by Barry Cornwall (with Memoir), 1838; by B. Nicholson (Mermaid Series), with Introduction by C. H. Herford, 1893, etc.; *Nine Plays*, 1904; ed. H. C. Hart (Standard Library), 1906, etc.; *Plays and Poems*, with Introduction by H. Morley (Universal Library), 1885; *Plays (7) and Poems* (Newnes), 1905; *Poems*, with Memoir by H. Bennett (Carlton Classics), 1907; *Masques and Entertainments*, ed. by H. Morley, 1890.

SELECTIONS. J. A. Symonds, with Biographical and Critical Essay (Canterbury Poets), 1886; Grosart: *Brave Translunary Things*, 1895; Arber: *Jonson Anthology*, 1901; *Underwoods:* Cambridge University Press, 1905; *Lyrics* (Jonson, Beaumont and Fletcher), *The Chap Books*, No. 4, 1906; *Songs* (from Plays, Masques, etc.), with earliest known setting, Eragny Press, 1906.

BIOGRAPHY AND CRITICISM. A. C. Swinburne: *A Study of Ben Jonson*, 1884; L. C. Knights: *Drama and Society in the Age of Jonson*, 1937; G. B. Johnston: *Ben Jonson, poet*, 1945; G. E. Bentley: *Shakespeare and Jonson* 1945.

CONTENTS

EVERY MAN IN HIS HUMOUR[1]

DRAMATIS PERSONÆ

LORENZO SENIOR.	LORENZO JUNIOR.	BIANCHA.	COB.
PROSPERO.	STEPHANO.	HESPERIDA.	MATHEO.
THORELLO.	DOCTOR CLEMENT	PETO.	PISO.
GIULIANO.	BOBADILLA.	MUSCO.	TIB.

ACT I

SCENE I.—*Enter* LORENZO DI PAZZI senior, MUSCO.

Lor. se. Now trust me, here's a goodly day toward.
Musco, call up my son *Lorenzo;* bid him rise; tell him, I have some business to employ him in.

Mus. I will, sir, presently.

Lor. se. But hear you, sirrah;
If he be at study disturb him not.

Mus. Very good, sir.   [*Exit Musco.*

Lor. se. How happy would I estimate myself,
Could I by any means retire my son,
From one vain course of study he affects!
He is a scholar (if a man may trust
The liberal voice of double-tongued report)
Of dear account, in all our *Academies.*
Yet this position must not breed in me
A fast opinion that he cannot err.
Myself was once a *student*, and indeed
Fed with the self-same humour he is now,
Dreaming on nought but idle *Poetry;*
But since, Experience hath awaked my spirits,   [*Enter* STEPHANO.
And reason taught them, how to comprehend
The sovereign use of study.   What, cousin *Stephano !*
What news with you, that you are here so early?

Step. Nothing: but e'en come to see how you do, uncle.

Lor. se. That's kindly done; you are welcome, cousin.

Step. Ay, I know that, sir, I would not have come else: how doth my cousin, uncle?

Lor. se. Oh, well, well, go in and see; I doubt he's scarce stirring yet.

Step. Uncle, afore I go in, can you tell me an he have e'er a book of the sciences of hawking and hunting? I would fain borrow it.

Lor. se. Why, I hope you will not a hawking now, will you?

Step. No, wusse; but I'll practise against next year; I have

[1] The earlier version of the comedy is here for the first time placed at the head of the plays.   The later, superior, and more familiar Anglicised version, follows at the end of the volume.

bought me a hawk, and bells and all; I lack nothing but a book
to keep it by.

Lor. se. Oh, most ridiculous.

Step. Nay, look you now, you are angry, uncle, why, you know,
an a man have not skill in hawking and hunting now-a-days, I'll not
give a rush for him; he is for no gentleman's company, and (by
God's will) I scorn it, ay, so I do, to be a consort for every *hum-drum;*
hang them *scroyles,* there's nothing in them in the world, what do
you talk on it? a gentleman must shew himself like a gentleman.
Uncle, I pray you be not angry, I know what I have to do, I trow,
I am no novice.

Lor. se. Go to, you are a prodigal, and self-willed fool.
Nay, never look at me, it's I that speak,
Take't as you will, I'll not flatter you.
What? have you not means enow to waste
That which your friends have left you, but you must
Go cast away your money on a *Buzzard,*
And know not how to keep it when you have done?
Oh, it's brave, this will make you a gentleman,
Well, cousin, well, I see you are e'en past hope
Of all reclaim; ay, so, now you are told on it, you look another way.

Step. What would you have me do, trow?

Lor. What would I have you do? marry,
Learn to be wise, and practise how to thrive,
That I would have you do, and not to spend
Your crowns on every one that humours you:
I would not have you to intrude yourself
In every gentleman's society,
Till their affections or your own dessert,
Do worthily invite you to the place.
For he that's so respectless in his courses,
Oft sells his reputation vile and cheap.
Let not your carriage and behaviour taste
Of affectation, lest while you pretend
To make a blaze of gentry to the world
A little puff of scorn extinguish it,
And you be left like an unsavoury snuff,
Whose property is only to offend.
Cousin, lay by such superficial forms,
And entertain a perfect real substance;
Stand not so much on your gentility,
But moderate your expenses (now at first)
As you may keep the same proportion still:
Bear a low sail. Soft, who's this comes here?   [*Enter a* Servant.

Ser. Gentlemen, God save you.

Step. Welcome, good friend; we do not stand much upon our
gentility, yet I can assure you mine uncle is a man of a thousand
pound land a year; he hath but one son in the world; I am his
next heir, as simple as I stand here, if my cousin die. I have a
fair living of mine own too beside.

Ser. In good time, sir.

Step. In good time, sir! you do not flout me, do you?

Ser. Not I, sir.

Step. An you should, here be them can perceive it, and that quickly too. Go to; and they can give it again soundly, an need be.

Ser. Why, sir, let this satisfy you. Good faith, I had no such intent.

Step. By God, an I thought you had, sir, I would talk with you.

Ser. So you may, sir, and at your pleasure.

Step. And so I would, sir, an you were out of mine uncle's ground, I can tell you.

Lor. se. Why, how now, cousin, will this ne'er be left?

Step. Whoreson, base fellow, by God's lid, an 'twere not for shame, I would—

Lor. se. What would you do? you peremptory ass,
An you'll not be quiet, get you hence.
You see, the gentleman contains himself
In modest limits, giving no reply
To your unseason'd rude comparatives;
Yet you'll demean yourself without respect
Either of duty or humanity.
Go, get you in: 'fore God, I am asham'd   [*Exit Step.*
Thou hast a kinsman's interest in me.

Ser. I pray you, sir, is this *Pazzi* house?

Lor. se. Marry is it, sir.

Ser. I should enquire for a gentleman here, one *Signior Lorenzo di Pazzi;* do you know any such, sir, I pray you?

Lor. se. Yes, sir; or else I should forget myself.

Ser. I cry you mercy, sir, I was requested by a gentleman of Florence (having some occasion to ride this way) to deliver you this letter.

Lor. se. To me, sir? What do you mean? I pray you remember your court'sy.
To his dear and most selected friend, Signior Lorenzo di Pazzi.
What might the gentleman's name be, sir, that sent it? Nay, pray you be covered.

Ser. Signior *Prospero.*

Lor. se. Signior *Prospero?* A young gentleman of the family of *Strozzi,* is he not?

Ser. Ay, sir, the same: Signior *Thorello,* the rich Florentine merchant married his sister.   [*Enter* Musco.

Lor. se. You say very true.—*Musco.*

Mus. Sir.

Lor. se. Make this gentleman drink here.
I pray you go in, sir, an't please you.   [*Exeunt.*
Now (without doubt) this letter's to my son.
Well, all is one: I'll be so bold as read it,
Be it but for the *style's* sake, and the *phrase;*
Both which (I do presume) are excellent,
And greatly varied from the vulgar form,

If *Prospero's* invention gave them life.
How now! what stuff is here?

   Sir Lorenzo, I muse we cannot see thee at Florence: *'Sblood, I doubt,* Apollo *hath got thee to be his Ingle, that thou comest not abroad, to visit thine old friends: well, take heed of him; he may do somewhat for his household servants, or so; But for his Retainers, I am sure, I have known some of them, that have followed him, three, four, five years together, scorning the world with their bare heels, and at length been glad for a shift (though no clean shift) to lie a whole winter, in half a sheet cursing* Charles' *wain, and the rest of the stars intolerably. But* (quis contra diuos?) *well; Sir, sweet villain, come and see me; but spend one minute in my company, and 'tis enough: I think I have a world of good jests for thee: oh, sir, I can shew thee two of the most perfect, rare and absolute true* Gulls, *that ever thou saw'st, if thou wilt come. 'Sblood, invent some famous memorable lie, or other, to flap thy Father in the mouth withal: thou hast been father of a thousand, in thy days, thou could'st be no Poet else: any scurvy roguish excuse will serve; say thou com'st but to fetch wool for thine Ink-horn. And then, too, thy Father will say thy wits are a wool-gathering. But it's no matter; the worse, the better. Any thing is good enough for the old man. Sir, how if thy Father should see this now? what would he think of me? Well, (how ever I write to thee) I reverence him in my soul, for the general good all* Florence *delivers of him.* Lorenzo, *I conjure thee (by what, let me see) by the depth of our love, by all the strange sights we have seen in our days, (ay, or nights either,) to come to me to* Florence *this day. Go to, you shall come, and let your Muses go spin for once. If thou wilt not, 's hart, what's your god's name?* Apollo? *Ay,* Apollo. *If this melancholy rogue (*Lorenzo *here) do not come, grant, that he do turn Fool presently, and never hereafter be able to make a good jest, or a blank verse, but live in more penury of wit and invention, than either the* Hall-Beadle, *or Poet* Nuntius.

   Well, it is the strangest letter that ever I read.
Is this the man, my son so oft hath praised
To be the happiest, and most precious wit
That ever was familiar with Art?
Now, by our Lady's blessed son, I swear,
I rather think him most unfortunate
In the possession of such holy gifts,
Being the master of so loose a spirit.
Why, what unhallowed ruffian would have writ
With so profane a pen unto his friend?
The modest paper e'en looks pale for grief,
To feel her virgin-cheek defiled and stained
With such a black and criminal *inscription.*
Well, I had thought my son could not have strayed
So far from judgment as to mart himself
Thus cheaply in the open trade of scorn
To jeering *folly* and fantastic *humour.*
But now I see *opinion* is a fool,
And hath abused my senses.—*Musco.*

                              [*Enter* Musco.

Mus. Sir.

Lor. se. What, is the fellow gone that brought this letter?

Mus. Yes, sir, a pretty while since.

Lor. se. And where's *Lorenzo?*

Mus. In his chamber, sir.

Lor. se. He spake not with the fellow, did he?

Mus. No, sir, he saw him not.

Lor. se. Then, *Musco,* take this letter, and deliver it unto *Lorenzo:* but, sirrah, on your life take you no knowledge I have opened it.

Mus. O Lord, sir, that were a jest indeed.   [*Exit Mus.*

Lor. se. I am resolv'd I will not cross his journey,
Nor will I practise any violent means
To stay the hot and lusty course of youth.
For youth restrained straight grows impatient,
And, in condition, like an eager dog,
Who, ne'er so little from his game withheld,
Turns head and leaps up at his master's throat.
Therefore I'll study, by some milder drift,
To call my son unto a happier shrift.   [*Exit.*

SCENE II.—*Enter* LORENZO *junior, with* MUSCO.

Mus. Yes, sir, on my word he opened it, and read the contents.

Lor. ju. It scarce contents me that he did so. But, *Musco,* didst thou observe his countenance in the reading of it, whether he were angry or pleased?

Mus. Why, sir, I saw him not read it.

Lor. ju. No? how knowest thou then that he opened it?

Mus. Marry, sir, because he charg'd me on my life to tell nobody that he opened it, which, unless he had done, he would never fear to have it revealed.

Lor. ju. That's true: well, *Musco,* hie thee in again,
Lest thy protracted absence do lend light,   [*Enter* STEPHANO.
To dark suspicion: *Musco,* be assured
I'll not forget this thy respective love.

Step. Oh, *Musco,* didst thou not see a fellow here in a what-sha-call-him doublet; he brought mine uncle a letter even now?

Mus. Yes, sir, what of him?

Step. Where is he, canst thou tell?

Mus. Why, he is gone.

Step. Gone? which way? when went he? how long since?

Mus. It's almost half an hour ago since he rode hence.

Step. Whoreson scanderbag rogue; oh that I had a horse; by God's lid, I'd fetch him back again, with heave and ho.

Mus. Why, you may have my master's bay gelding, an you will.

Step. But I have no boots, that's the spite on it.

Mus. Then it's no boot to follow him. Let him go and hang, sir.

Step. Ay, by my troth; *Musco,* I pray thee help to truss me a little; nothing angers me, but I have waited such a while for him all un-lac'd and untrussed yonder; and now to see he is gone the other way.

Mus. Nay, I pray you stand still, sir.

Step. I will, I will: oh, how it vexes me.

Mus. Tut, never vex yourself with the thought of such a base fellow as he.

Step. Nay, to see he stood upon points with me too.

Mus. Like enough so; that was because he saw you had so few at your hose.

Step. What! Hast thou done? Godamercy, good *Musco.*

Mus. I marle, sir, you wear such ill-favoured coarse stockings, having so good a leg as you have.

Step. Foh! the stockings be good enough for this time of the year; but I'll have a pair of silk, e'er it be long: I think my leg would shew well in a silk hose.

Mus. Ay, afore God, would it, rarely well.

Step. In sadness I think it would: I have a reasonable good leg?

Mus. You have an excellent good leg, sir: I pray you pardon me, I have a little haste in, sir.

Step. A thousand thanks, good Musco.   [*Exit.*
What, I hope he laughs not at me; an he do—

Lor. ju. Here is a *style* indeed, for a man's senses to leap over, e'er they come at it: why, it is able to break the shins of any old man's patience in the world. My father read this with patience? Then will I be made an *Eunuch*, and learn to sing Ballads. I do not deny, but my father may have as much patience as any other man; for he used to take physic, and oft taking physic makes a man a very patient creature. But, Signior *Prospero*, had your swaggering *Epistle* here arrived in my father's hands at such an hour of his patience, I mean, when he had taken physic, it is to be doubted whether I should have read *sweet villain here*. But, what? My wise cousin; Nay then, I'll furnish our feast with one Gull more toward a mess; he writes to me of two, and here's one, that's three, i'faith. Oh for a fourth! now, *Fortune*, or never, *Fortune!*

Step. Oh, now I see who he laughed at: he laughed at somebody in that letter. By this good light, an he had laughed at me, I would have told mine uncle.

Lor. ju. Cousin Stephano: good morrow, good cousin, how fare you?

Step. The better for your asking, I will assure you. I have been all about to seek you. Since I came I saw mine uncle; and i'faith how have you done this great while? Good Lord, by my troth, I am glad you are well, cousin.

Lor. ju. And I am as glad of your coming, I protest to you, for I am sent for by a private gentleman, my most special dear friend, to come to him to *Florence* this morning, and you shall go with me, cousin, if it please you, not else, I will enjoin you no further than stands with your own consent, and the condition of a friend.

Step. Why, cousin, you shall command me an 'twere twice so far as *Florence*, to do you good; what, do you think I will not go with you? I protest—

Lor. ju. Nay, nay, you shall not protest.

Step. By God, but I will, sir, by your leave I'll protest more to my friend than I'll speak of at this time.

Lor. ju. You speak very well, sir.

Step. Nay, not so neither, but I speak to serve my turn.

Lor. ju. Your turn? why, cousin, a gentleman of so fair sort as you are, of so true carriage, so special good parts; of so dear and choice estimation; one whose lowest condition bears the stamp of a great spirit; nay more, a man so graced, gilded, or rather, to use a more fit *metaphor*, tinfoiled by nature; not that you have a leaden constitution, coz, although perhaps a little inclining to that temper, and so the more apt to melt with pity, when you fall into the fire of rage, but for your lustre only, which reflects as bright to the world as an old ale-wife's pewter again a good time; and will you now, with nice modesty, hide such real ornaments as these, and shadow their glory as a milliner's wife doth her wrought stomacher, with a smoky lawn or a black cyprus? Come, come; for shame do not wrong the quality of your dessert in so poor a kind; but let the *idea* of what you are be portrayed in your aspect, that men may read in your looks: *Here within this place is to be seen the most admirable, rare, and accomplished work of nature!* Cousin, what think you of this?

Step. Marry, I do think of it, and I will be more melancholy and gentlemanlike than I have been, I do ensure you.

Lor. ju. Why, this is well: now if I can but hold up this humour in him, as it is begun, *Catso* for *Florence*, match him an she can. Come, cousin.

Step. I'll follow you.

Lor. ju. Follow me! you must go before!

Step. Must I? nay, then I pray you shew me, good cousin.

[*Exeunt.*

SCENE III.—*Enter* Signior MATHEO, *to him* COB.

Mat. I think this be the house: what ho!

Cob. Who's there? oh, Signior *Matheo.* God give you good morrow, sir.

Mat. What? *Cob?* how doest thou, good *Cob?* dost thou inhabit here, *Cob?*

Cob. Ay, sir, I and my lineage have kept a poor house in our days.

Mat. Thy lineage, *Monsieur Cob!* what lineage, what lineage?

Cob. Why, sir, an ancient lineage, and a princely: mine ancestry came from a king's loins, no worse man; and yet no man neither, but *Herring* the king of fish, one of the monarchs of the world, I assure you. I do fetch my pedigree and name from the first red herring that was eaten in *Adam* and *Eve's* kitchen: his *Cob* was my great, great, mighty great grandfather.

Mat. Why mighty? why mighty?

Cob. Oh, it's a mighty while ago, sir, and it was a mighty great *Cob.*

Mat. How knowest thou that?

Cob. How know I? why, his ghost comes to me every night.

Mat. Oh, unsavoury jest: the ghost of a herring *Cob.*

Cob. Ay, why not the ghost of a herring *Cob*, as well as the ghost of *Rashero Bacono*, they were both broiled on the coals? you are a scholar, upsolve me that now.

Mat. Oh, rude ignorance! *Cob*, canst thou shew me of a gentleman, one Signior *Bobadilla*, where his lodging is?

Cob. Oh, my guest, sir, you mean?

Mat. Thy guest, alas! ha, ha.

Cob. Why do you laugh, sir? do you not mean Signior *Bobadilla?*

Mat. Cob, I pray thee advise thyself well: do not wrong the gentleman, and thyself too. I dare be sworn he scorns thy house; he! he lodge in such a base obscure place as thy house? Tut, I know his disposition so well, he would not lie in thy bed if thou'dst give it him.

Cob. I will not give it him. Mass, I thought somewhat was in it, we could not get him to bed all night. Well, sir, though he lie not on my bed, he lies on my bench, an't please you to go up, sir, you shall find him with two cushions under his head, and his cloak wrapt about him, as though he had neither won nor lost, and yet I warrant he ne'er cast better in his life than he hath done to-night.

Mat. Why, was he drunk?

Cob. Drunk, sir? you hear not me say so; perhaps he swallow'd a tavern token, or some such device, sir; I have nothing to do withal: I deal with water and not with wine. Give me my tankard there, ho! God be with you, sir; it's six o'clock: I should have carried two turns by this, what ho! my stopple, come.

Mat. Lie in a water-bearer's house, a gentleman of his note? Well, I'll tell him my mind.   [*Exit.*

Cob. What, *Tib*, shew this gentleman up to Signior *Bobadilla:* oh, an my house were the Brazen head now, faith it would e'en cry moe fools yet: you should have some now, would take him to be a gentleman at the least; alas, God help the simple, his father's an honest man, a good fishmonger, and so forth: and now doth he creep and wriggle into acquaintance with all the brave gallants about the town, such as my guest is, (oh, my guest is a fine man!) and they flout him invincibly. He useth every day to a merchant's house, (where I serve water) one M. *Thorello's;* and here's the jest, he is in love with my master's sister, and calls her mistress: and there he sits a whole afternoon sometimes, reading of these same abominable, vile, (a pox on them, I cannot abide them!) rascally verses, *Poetry, poetry*, and speaking of *Interludes*, 'twill make a man burst to hear him: and the wenches, they do so jeer and tihe at him; well, should they do as much to me, I'd forswear them all, by the life of Pharaoh, there's an oath: how many water-bearers shall you hear swear such an oath? oh, I have a guest, (he teacheth me) he doth swear the best of any man christened. By Phœbus, By the life of Pharaoh, By the body of me, As I am gentleman, and a soldier: such dainty oaths; and withal he doth take this same filthy roguish tobacco, the finest, and cleanliest; it would do a man good to see the fume come forth at his nostrils: well, he owes me forty shillings, (my wife lent him out of her purse; by sixpence a time,) besides his lodging; I would I had it: I shall have it, he saith, next *Action*. *Helter skelter*, hang sorrow, care will kill a cat, up-tails all, and a pox on the hangman. [*Exit*.

BOBADILLA *discovers himself: on a bench; to him* TIB.

Bob. Hostess, hostess.

Tib. What say you, sir?

Bob. A cup of your small beer, sweet hostess.

Tib. Sir, there's a gentleman below would speak with you.

Bob. A gentleman? (God's so) I am not within.

Tib. My husband told him you were, sir.

Bob. What a plague! what meant he?

Mat. Signior Bobadilla. [*Matheo within*.

Bob. Who's there? (take away the bason, good hostess) come up, sir.

Tib. He would desire you to come up, sir; you come into a cleanly house here.

Mat. God save you, sir, God save you. [*Enter* MATHEO.

Bob. Signior Matheo, is't you, sir? please you sit down.

Mat. I thank you, good Signior, you may see I am somewhat audacious.

Bob. Not so, Signior, I was requested to supper yesternight by a sort of gallants, where you were wished for, and drunk to, I assure you.

Mat. Vouchsafe me by whom, good Signior.

Bob. Marry, by Signior *Prospero*, and others; why, hostess, a stool here for this gentleman.

Mat. No haste, sir, it is very well.

Bob. Body of me, it was so late ere we parted last night, I can scarce open mine eyes yet; I was but new risen as you came: how passes the day abroad, sir? you can tell.

Mat. Faith, some half hour to seven: now trust me, you have an exceeding fine lodging here, very neat, and private.

Bob. Ay, sir, sit down. I pray you, Signior *Matheo*, in any case possess no gentlemen of your acquaintance with notice of my lodging.

Mat. Who? I, sir? no.

Bob. Not that I need to care who know it, but in regard I would not be so popular and general, as some be.

Mat. True, Signior, I conceive you.

Bob. For do you see, sir, by the heart of myself, (except it be to some peculiar and choice spirits, to whom I am extraordinarily engaged, as yourself, or so,) I could not extend thus far.

Mat. O Lord, sir! I resolve so.

Bob. What new book have you there? What? *Go by Hieronymo*.

Mat. Ay, did you ever see it acted? is't not well penned?

Bob. Well penned: I would fain see all the Poets of our time pen such another play as that was; they'll prate and swagger, and keep a stir of art and devices, when (by God's so) they are the most shallow, pitiful fellows that live upon the face of the earth again.

Mat. Indeed, here are a number of fine speeches in this book: *Oh eyes, no eyes, but fountains fraught with tears;* there's a conceit: Fountains fraught with tears. *Oh life, no life, but lively form of death:* is't not excellent? *Oh world, no world, but mass of public wrongs;* O God's me: *confused and filled with murder and misdeeds.* Is't not simply the best that ever you heard?

Ha, how do you like it?

Bob. 'Tis good.

Mat.   *To thee, the purest object to my sense,*
       The most refined essence heaven covers,
       Send I these lines, wherein I do commence
       The happy state of true deserving lovers.
       If they prove rough, unpolish'd, harsh, and rude,
       Haste made that waste; thus mildly I conclude.

Bob. Nay, proceed, proceed, where's this? where's this?

Mat. This, sir, a toy of mine own in my non-age: but when will you come and see my study? good faith, I can shew you some very good things I have done of late: that boot becomes your leg passing well, sir, methinks.

Bob. So, so, it's a fashion gentlemen use.

Mat. Mass, sir, and now you speak of the fashion, Signior *Prospero's* elder brother and I are fallen out exceedingly: this other day I happened to enter into some discourse of a hanger, which, I assure you, both for fashion and workmanship was most beautiful and gentlemanlike; yet he condemned it for the most pied and ridiculous that ever he saw.

Bob. Signior *Giuliano*, was it not? the elder brother?

Mat. Ay, sir, he.

Bob. Hang him, rook! he! why, he has no more judgment than a malt-horse. By St. *George*, I hold him the most peremptory absurd clown (one a them) in Christendom: I protest to you (as I am a gentleman and a soldier) I ne'er talk'd with the like of him: he has not so much as a good word in his belly, all iron, iron, a good commodity for a smith to make hob-nails on.

Mat. Ay, and he thinks to carry it away with his manhood still where he comes: he brags he will give me the bastinado, as I hear.

Bob. How, the bastinado? how came he by that word, trow?

Mat. Nay, indeed, he said cudgel me; I termed it so for the more grace.

Bob. That may be, for I was sure it was none of his word: but when, when said he so?

Mat. Faith, yesterday, they say, a young gallant, a friend of mine, told me so.

Bob. By the life of Pharaoh, an't were my case now, I should send him a challenge presently: the bastinado! come hither, you shall challenge him; I'll shew you a trick or two, you shall kill him at pleasure, the first *stoccado* if you will, by this air.

Mat. Indeed, you have absolute knowledge in the mystery, I have heard, sir.

Bob. Of whom? of whom, I pray?

Mat. Faith, I have heard it spoken of divers, that you have very rare skill, sir.

Bob. By heaven, no, not I, no skill in the earth: some small science, know my time, distance, or so, I have profest it more for noblemen and gentlemen's use than mine own practise, I assure you. Hostess, lend us another bed-staff here quickly: look you, sir, exalt not your point above this state at any hand, and let your poniard maintain your defence thus: give it the gentleman. So, sir, come on, oh, twine your body more about, that you may come to a more sweet comely gentlemanlike guard; so indifferent. Hollow your body more, sir, thus: now stand fast on your left leg, note your distance, keep your due proportion of time: oh, you disorder your point most vilely.

Mat. How is the bearing of it now, sir?

Bob. Oh, out of measure ill, a well-experienced man would pass upon you at pleasure.

Mat. How mean you pass upon me?

Bob. Why, thus, sir: make a thrust at me; come in upon my time; control your point, and make a full career at the body: the best-practis'd gentlemen of the time term it the *passado*, a most desperate thrust, believe it.

Mat. Well, come, sir.

Bob. Why, you do not manage your weapons with that facility and grace that you should do, I have no spirit to play with you, your dearth of judgment makes you seem tedious.

Mat. But one venue, sir.

Bob. Fie! venue, most gross denomination as ever I heard: oh, the *stoccado* while you live, Signior, not that. Come, put on your cloak, and we'll go to some private place where you are acquainted, some tavern or so, and we'll send for one of these fencers, where he shall breathe you at my direction, and then I'll teach you that trick; you shall kill him with it at the first if you please: why, I'll learn you by the true judgment of the eye, hand, and foot, to control any man's point in the world; Should your adversary confront you with a pistol, 'twere nothing, you should (by the same rule) control the bullet, most certain, by *Phœbus:* unless it were hail-shot: what money have you about you, sir?

Mat. Faith, I have not past two shillings, or so.

Bob. 'Tis somewhat with the least, but come, when we have done, we'll call up Signior *Prospero;* perhaps we shall meet with *Coridon* his brother there.   [*Exeunt.*

SCENE IV.—*Enter* Thorello, Giuliano, Piso.

Tho. Piso, come hither: there lies a note within, upon my desk; here, take my key: it's no matter neither, where's the boy?

Pis. Within, sir, in the warehouse.

Tho. Let him tell over that Spanish gold, and weigh it, and do you see the delivery of those wares to Signior *Bentivole:* I'll be there myself at the receipt of the money anon.

Pis. Very good, sir.   [*Exit Piso.*

Tho. Brother, did you see that same fellow there?

Giu. Ay, what of him?

Tho. He is e'en the honestest, faithful servant that is this day in *Florence;* (I speak a proud word now;) and one that I durst trust my life into his hands, I have so strong opinion of his love, if need were.

Giu. God send me never such need: but you said you had somewhat to tell me, what is't?

Tho. Faith, brother, I am loath to utter it,
As fearing to abuse your patience,
But that I know your judgment more direct,
Able to sway the nearest of affection.

Giu. Come, come, what needs this circumstance?

Tho. I will not say what honour I ascribe
Unto your friendship, nor in what dear state
I hold your love; let my continued zeal,
The constant and religious regard,
That I have ever carried to your name,
My carriage with your sister, all contest,
How much I stand affected to your house.

Giu. You are too tedious, come to the matter, come to the matter.

Tho. Then (without further ceremony) thus.
My brother *Prospero* (I know not how)
Of late is much declined from what he was,
And greatly alter'd in his disposition.
When he came first to lodge here in my house,
Ne'er trust me, if I was not proud of him:
Methought he bare himself with such observance,
So true election and so fair a form:
And (what was chief) it shew'd not borrow'd in him,
But all he did became him as his own,
And seem'd as perfect, proper, and innate,
Unto the mind, as colour to the blood,
But now, his course is so irregular,
So loose affected, and deprived of grace,
And he himself withal so far fallen off
From his first place, that scarce no note remains,
To tell men's judgments where he lately stood;
He's grown a stranger to all due respect,
Forgetful of his friends, and not content
To stale himself in all societies,
He makes my house as common as a *Mart*,
A *Theatre*, a public receptacle
For giddy humour, and diseased riot,
And there, (as in a tavern, or a stews,)
He, and his wild associates, spend their hours,
In repetition of lascivious jests,
Swear, leap, and dance, and revel night by night,
Control my servants: and indeed what not?

Giu. Faith, I know not what I should say to him: so God save

me, I am e'en at my wits' end, I have told him enough, one would
think, if that would serve: well, he knows what to trust to for me:
let him spend, and spend, and domineer till his heart ache: an
he get a penny more of me, I'll give him this ear.

Tho. Nay, good brother, have patience.

Giu. 'Sblood, he mads me, I could eat my very flesh for anger:
I marle you will not tell him of it, how he disquiets your house.

Tho. O, there are divers reasons to dissuade me,
But would yourself vouchsafe to travail in it,
(Though but with plain and easy circumstance,)
It would both come much better to his sense,
And savour less of grief and discontent.
You are his elder brother, and that title
Confirms and warrants your authority:
Which (seconded by your aspect) will breed
A kind of duty in him, and regard.
Whereas, if I should intimate the least,
It would but add contempt to his neglect,
Heap worse on ill, rear a huge pile of hate,
That in the building would come tottering down,
And in her ruins bury all our love.
Nay, more than this, brother; if I should speak,
He would be ready in the heat of passion,
To fill the ears of his familiars,
With oft reporting to them, what disgrace
And gross disparagement I had proposed him.
And then would they straight back him in opinion,
Make some loose comment upon every word,
And out of their distracted phantasies,
Contrive some slander, that should dwell with me.
And what would that be, think you? marry, this,
They would give out, (because my wife is fair,
Myself but lately married, and my sister
Here sojourning a virgin in my house,)
That I were jealous: nay, as sure as death,
Thus they would say: and how that I had wrong'd
My brother purposely, thereby to find
An apt pretext to banish them my house.

Giu. Mass, perhaps so.

Tho. Brother, they would, believe it: so should I
(Like one of these penurious quack-salvers)
But try experiments upon myself,
Open the gates unto mine own disgrace,
Lend bare-ribb'd envy opportunity
To stab my reputation, and good name.   [*Enter* BOBA. *and* MAT.

Mat. I will speak to him.

Bob. Speak to him? away, by the life of *Pharaoh*, you shall not,
you shall not do him that grace: the time of day to you, gentlemen:
is Signior *Prospero* stirring?

Giu. How then? what should he do?

Bob. Signior *Thorello*, is he within, sir?

Tho. He came not to his lodging to-night, sir, I assure you.

Giu. Why, do you hear? you.

Bob. This gentleman hath satisfied me, I'll talk to no Scavenger.

Giu. How, Scavenger? stay, sir, stay.   [*Exeunt.*

Tho. Nay, brother *Giuliano.*

Giu. 'Sblood, stand you away, an you love me.

Tho. You shall not follow him now, I pray you,
Good faith, you shall not.

Giu. Ha! Scavenger! well, go to, I say little, but, by this good
day, (God forgive me I should swear) if I put it up so, say I am
the rankest —— that ever pist. 'Sblood, an I swallow this, I'll
ne'er draw my sword in the sight of man again while I live; I'll
sit in a barn with Madge-owlet first. Scavenger! 'Heart, and
I'll go near to fill that huge tumbrel slop of yours with somewhat,
an I have good luck, your *Garagantua* breech cannot carry it away so.

Tho. Oh, do not fret yourself thus, never think on't.

Giu. These are my brother's consorts, these, these are his *Comrades,* his walking mates, he's a gallant, a *Cavaliero* too, right
hangman cut. God let me not live, an I could not find in my heart
to swinge the whole nest of them, one after another, and begin with
him first, I am grieved it should be said he is my brother, and take
these courses, well, he shall hear on't, and that tightly too, an I
live, i'faith.

Tho. But, brother, let your apprehension (then)
Run in an easy current, not transported
With heady rashness, or devouring choler,
And rather carry a persuading spirit,
Whose powers will pierce more gently; and allure
Th' imperfect thoughts you labour to reclaim,
To a more sudden and resolved assent.

Giu. Ay, ay, let me alone for that, I warrant you. [*Bell rings.*

Tho. How now! oh, the bell rings to breakfast.
Brother *Giuliano,* I pray you go in and bear my wife company:
I'll but give order to my servants for the dispatch of some business,
and come to you presently. [*Exit Giu.*   [*Enter* Cob.
What, Cob! our maids will have you by the back (i'faith)
For coming so late this morning.

Cob. Perhaps so, sir, take heed somebody have not them by the
belly for walking so late in the evening.   [*Exit.*

Tho. Now (in good faith) my mind is somewhat eased,
Though not reposed in that security
As I could wish; well, I must be content,
Howe'er I set a face on't to the world,
Would I had lost this finger at a vent,
So *Prospero* had ne'er lodged in my house,
Why't cannot be, where there is such resort
Of wanton gallants, and young revellers,
That any woman should be honest long.
Is't like, that factious beauty will preserve

The sovereign state of chastity unscarr'd,
When such strong motives muster, and make head
Against her single peace? no, no: beware
When mutual pleasure sways the appetite,
And spirits of one kind and quality,
Do meet to parley in the pride of blood.
Well, (to be plain) if I but thought the time
Had answer'd their affections, all the world
Should not persuade me, but I were a cuckold:
Marry, I hope they have not got that start.
For opportunity hath balk'd them yet,
And shall do still, while I have eyes and ears
To attend the imposition of my heart:
My presence shall be as an iron bar,
'Twixt the conspiring motions of desire,
Yea, every look or glance mine eye objects,
Shall check occasion, as one doth his slave,   *[Enter* BIANCHA
When he forgets the limits of prescription.   *with* HESPERIDA.

   Bia. Sister *Hesperida*, I pray you fetch down the rose-water
above in the closet: Sweet-heart, will you come in to breakfast?

   Tho. An she have overheard me now?   *[Exit Hesperida.*

   Bia. I pray thee, (good *Muss*) we stay for you.

   Tho. By Christ, I would not for a thousand crowns.

   Bia. What ail you, sweet-heart? are you not well? speak, good
Muss.

   Tho. Troth, my head aches extremely on a sudden.

   Bia. Oh Jesu!

   Tho. How now! what!

   Bia. Good Lord, how it burns! *Muss*, keep you warm; good
truth, it is this new disease, there's a number are troubled withall
for God's sake, sweet-heart, come in out of the air.

   Tho. How simple, and how subtle are her answers!
A new disease, and many troubled with it.
Why true, she heard me all the world to nothing.

   Bia. I pray thee, good sweet-heart, come in; the air will do you
harm, in troth.

   Tho. I'll come to you presently, it will away, I hope.

   Bia. Pray God it do.   *[Exit.*

   Tho. A new disease! I know not, new or old,
But it may well be call'd poor mortals' Plague;
For like a pestilence it doth infect
The houses of the brain: first it begins
Solely to work upon the phantasy,
Filling her seat with such pestiferous air,
As soon corrupts the judgment, and from thence,
Sends like contagion to the memory,
Still each of other catching the infection,
Which as a searching vapour spreads itself
Confusedly through every sensive part,
Till not a thought or motion in the mind

Be free from the black poison of suspect.
Ah, but what error is it to know this,
And want the free election of the soul
In such extremes! well, I will once more strive
(Even in despite of hell) myself to be,
And shake this fever off that thus shakes me.   *[Exit.*

ACT II

SCENE I.—*Enter* Musco, *disguised like a soldier.*

Mus. 'Sblood, I cannot choose but laugh to see myself translated thus, from a poor creature to a creator; for now must I create an intolerable sort of lies, or else my profession loses his grace, and yet the lie to a man of my coat is as ominous as the *Fico*, oh, sir, it holds for good policy to have that outwardly in vilest estimation, that inwardly is most dear to us: So much for my borrowed shape. Well, the troth is, my master intends to follow his son dry-foot to Florence, this morning: now I, knowing of this conspiracy, and the rather to insinuate with my young master, (for so must we that are blue waiters, or men of service do, or else perhaps we may wear motley at the year's end, and who wears motley you know:) I have got me afore in this disguise, determining here to lie in ambuscado, and intercept him in the midway; if I can but get his cloak, his purse, his hat, nay, any thing so I can stay his journey, *Rex Regum,* I am made for ever, i'faith: well, now must I practise to get the true garb of one of these *Lance-knights;* my arm here, and my——God's so, young master and his cousin.

    Lor. ju. So, sir, and how then?   *[Enter* Lor. ju. *and* Step.

    Step. God's foot, I have lost my purse, I think.

    Lor. ju. How? lost your purse? where? when had you it?

    Step. I cannot tell, stay.

    Mus. 'Slid, I am afraid they will know me, would I could get by them.

    Lor. ju. What! have you it?

    Step. No, I think I was bewitched, I.

    Lor. ju. Nay, do not weep, a pox on it, hang it, let it go.

    Step. Oh, it's here; nay, an it had been lost, I had not cared but for a jet ring *Marina* sent me.

    Lor. ju. A jet ring! oh, the poesie, the poesie!

    Step. Fine, i'faith: *Though fancy sleep, my love is deep:* meaning that though I did not fancy her, yet she loved me dearly.

    Lor. ju. Most excellent.

    Step. And then I sent her another, and my poesie was: *The deeper the sweeter, I'll be judged by Saint Peter.*

    Lor. ju. How, by St. *Peter?* I do not conceive that.

    Step. Marry, St. *Peter* to make up the metre.

    Lor. ju. Well, you are beholding to that Saint, he help'd you at your need; thank him, thank him.

    Mus. I will venture, come what will: Gentlemen, please you change a few crowns for a very excellent good blade here; I am a poor gentleman, a soldier, one that (in the better state of my fortunes) scorned so mean a refuge, but now it's the humour of necessity to have it so: you seem to be, gentlemen, well affected to martial men, else I should rather die with silence, than live with shame: howe'er, vouchsafe to remember it is my want speaks, not myself: this condition agrees not with my spirit.

Lor. ju. Where hast thou served?

Mus. May it please you, Signior, in all the provinces of *Bohemia, Hungaria, Dalmatia, Poland,* where not? I have been a poor servitor by sea and land, any time this xiiij. years, and follow'd the fortunes of the best Commanders in Christendom. I was twice shot at the taking of *Aleppo,* once at the relief of *Vienna;* I have been at *America* in the galleys thrice, where I was most dangerously shot in the head, through both the thighs, and yet, being thus maim'd, I am void of maintenance, nothing left me but my scars, the noted marks of my resolution.

Step. How will you sell this rapier, friend?

Mus. Faith, Signior, I refer it to your own judgment; you are a gentleman, give me what you please.

Step. True, I am a gentleman, I know that; but what though, I pray you say, what would you ask?

Mus. I assure you the blade may become the side of the best prince in *Europe.*

Lor. ju. Ay, with a velvet scabbard.

Step. Nay, an't be mine it shall have a velvet scabbard, that is flat, I'd not wear it as 'tis an you would give me an angel.

Mus. At your pleasure, Signior, nay, it's a most pure *Toledo.*

Step. I had rather it were a *Spaniard:* but tell me, what shall I give you for it? an it had a silver hilt—

Lor. ju. Come, come, you shall not buy it; hold, there's a shilling, friend, take thy rapier.

Step. Why, but I will buy it now, because you say so: what, shall I go without a rapier?

Lor. ju. You may buy one in the city.

Step. Tut, I'll buy this, so I will; tell me your lowest price.

Lor. ju. You shall not, I say.

Step. By God's lid, but I will, though I give more than 'tis worth.

Lor. ju. Come away, you are a fool.

Step. Friend, I'll have it for that word: follow me.

Mus. At you service, Signior.   [*Exeunt.*

SCENE II.—*Enter* Lorenzo *senior.*

Lor. se. My labouring spirit being late opprest
With my son's folly, can embrace no rest
Till it hath plotted by advice and skill,
How to reduce him from affected will
To reason's manage; which while I intend,
My troubled soul begins to apprehend
A farther secret, and to meditate
Upon the difference of man's estate:
Where is decipher'd to true judgment's eye

A deep, conceal'd, and precious mystery.
Yet can I not but worthily admire
At nature's art: who (when she did inspire
This heat of life) placed Reason (as a king)
Here in the head, to have the marshalling
Of our affections: and with sovereignty
To sway the state of our weak empery.
But as in divers commonwealths we see,
The form of government to disagree:
Even so in man, who searcheth soon shall find
As much or more variety of mind.
Some men's affections like a sullen wife,
Is with her husband reason still at strife.
Others (like proud arch-traitors that rebel
Against their sovereign) practise to expel
Their liege Lord Reason, and not shame to tread
Upon his holy and anointed head.
But as that land or nation best doth thrive,
Which to smooth-fronted peace is most proclive,
So doth that mind, whose fair affections ranged
By reason's rules, stand constant and unchanged,
Else, if the power of reason be not such,
Why do we attribute to him too much?
Or why are we obsequious to his law,
If he want spirit our affects to awe?
Oh no, I argue weakly, he is strong,
Albeit my son have done him too much wrong.   [_Enter_ Musco.

Mus. My master: nay, faith, have at you: I am flesh'd now I
have sped so well: Gentleman, I beseech you respect the estate of
a poor soldier; I am ashamed of this base course of life, (God's my
comfort) but extremity provokes me to't; what remedy?

Lor. se. I have not for you now.

Mus. By the faith I bear unto God, gentleman, it is no ordinary
custom, but only to preserve manhood. I protest to you, a man
I have been, a man I may be, by your sweet bounty.

Lor. se. I pray thee, good friend, be satisfied.

Mus. Good Signior: by Jesu, you may do the part of a kind
gentleman, in lending a poor soldier the price of two cans of beer, a
matter of small value, the King of heaven shall pay you, and I shall
rest thankful: sweet Signior—

Lor. se. Nay, an you be so importunate—

Mus. O Lord, sir, need will have his course: I was not made
to this vile use; well, the edge of the enemy could not have abated
me so much: it's hard when a man hath served in his Prince's
cause and be thus. Signior, let me derive a small piece of silver
from you, it shall not be given in the course of time, by this good
ground, I was fain to pawn my rapier last night for a poor supper,
I am a Pagan else: sweet Signior—

Lor. se. Believe me, I am rapt with admiration,
To think a man of thy exterior presence

Should (in the constitution of the mind)
Be so degenerate, infirm, and base.
Art thou a man? and sham'st thou not to beg?
To practise such a servile kind of life?
Why, were thy education ne'er so mean,
Having thy limbs: a thousand fairer courses
Offer themselves to thy election.
Nay, there the wars might still supply thy wants,
Or service of some virtuous gentleman,
Or honest labour; nay, what can I name,
But would become thee better than to beg?
But men of your condition feed on sloth,
As doth the *Scarab* on the dung she breeds in,
Not caring how the temper of your spirits
Is eaten with the rust of idleness.
Now, afore God, whate'er he be that should
Relieve a person of thy quality,
While you insist in this loose desperate course,
I would esteem the sin not thine, but his.

    Mus. Faith, Signior, I would gladly find some other course, if so.

    Lor. se. Ay, you'd gladly find it, but you will not seek it.

    Mus. Alas, sir, where should a man seek? in the wars, there's no ascent by desert in these days, but—and for service, would it were as soon purchased as wish'd for, (God's my comfort) I know what I would say.

    Lor. se. What's thy name?

    Mus. Please you: *Portensio.*

    Lor. se. Portensio?
Say that a man should entertain thee now,
Would thou be honest, humble, just, and true?

    Mus. Signior: by the place and honour of a soldier—

    Lor. se. Nay, nay, I like not these affected oaths;
Speak plainly, man: what thinkst thou of my words?

    Mus. Nothing, Signior, but wish my fortunes were as happy as my service should be honest.

    Lor. se. Well, follow me, I'll prove thee, if thy deeds
Will carry a proportion to thy words.   *[Exit Lor. se.*

    Mus. Yes, sir, straight, I'll but garter my hose; oh, that my belly were hoop'd now, for I am ready to burst with laughing. 'Slid, was there ever seen a fox in years to betray himself thus? now shall I be possest of all his determinations, and consequently my young master; well, he is resolved to prove my honesty: faith, and I am resolved to prove his patience: oh, I shall abuse him intolerably: this small piece of service will bring him clean out of love with the soldier for ever. It's no matter, let the world think me a bad counterfeit, if I cannot give him the slip at an instant: why, this is better than to have stayed his journey by half: well, I'll follow him. Oh, how I long to be employed.   *[Exit.*

SCENE III.—*Enter* PROSPERO, BOBADILLA, *and* MATHEO.

Mat. Yes, faith, sir, we were at your lodging to seek you too.

Pros. Oh, I came not there to-night.

Bob. Your brother delivered us as much.

Pros. Who, *Giuliano?*

Bob. Giuliano. Signior *Prospero*, I know not in what kind you value me, but let me tell you this: as sure as God, I do hold it so much out of mine honour and reputation, if I should but cast the least regard upon such a dunghill of flesh; I protest to you (as I have a soul to be saved) I ne'er saw any gentlemanlike part in him: an there were no more men living upon the face of the earth, I should not fancy him, by *Phœbus.*

Mat. Troth, nor I, he is of a rustical cut, I know not how: he doth not carry himself like a gentleman.

Pros. Oh, Signior Matheo, that's a grace peculiar but to a few; *quos œquus amavit Jupiter.*

Mat. I understand you, sir.　　　　　[*Enter* LOR. ju. *and* STEP.

Pros. No question you do, sir: Lorenzo! now on my soul, welcome; how dost thou, sweet rascal? my Genius! 'Sblood, I shall love *Apollo* and the mad Thespian girls the better while I live for this; my dear villain, now I see there's some spirit in thee: Sirrah, these be they two I writ to thee of, nay, what a drowsy humour is this now? why dost thou not speak?

Lor. ju. Oh, you are a fine gallant, you sent me a rare letter.

Pros. Why, was't not rare?

Lor. ju. Yes, I'll be sworn I was ne'er guilty of reading the like, match it in all *Pliny's* familiar Epistles, and I'll have my judgment burn'd in the ear for a rogue, make much of thy vein, for it is inimitable. But I marle what camel it was, that had the carriage of it? for doubtless he was no ordinary beast that brought it.

Pros. Why?

Lor. ju. Why, sayest thou? why, dost thou think that any reasonable creature, especially in the morning, (the sober time of the day too) would have ta'en my father for me?

Pros. 'Sblood, you jest, I hope?

Lor. ju. Indeed, the best use we can turn it to, is to make a jest on't now: but I'll assure you, my father had the proving of your copy some hour before I saw it.

Pros. What a dull slave was this! But, sirrah, what said he to it, i'faith?

Lor. ju. Nay, I know not what he said. But I have a shrewd guess what he thought.

Pro. What? what?

Lor. ju. Marry, that thou art a damn'd dissolute villain, And I some grain or two better, in keeping thee company.

Pros. Tut, that thought is like the moon in the last quarter, 'twill change shortly: but, sirrah, I pray thee be acquainted with my two *Zanies* here, thou wilt take exceeding pleasure in them if thou hear'st them once, but what strange piece of silence is this? the sign of the dumb man?

Lor. ju. Oh, sir, a kinsman of mine, one that may make our music the fuller, an he please, he hath his humour, sir.

Pros. Oh, what is't? what is't?

Lor. ju. Nay, I'll neither do thy judgment nor his folly that wrong, as to prepare thy apprehension: I'll leave him to the mercy of the time, if you can take him: so.

Pros. Well, Signior *Bobadilla*, Signior *Matheo:* I pray you know this gentleman here, he is a friend of mine, and one that will well deserve your affection, I know not your name, Signior, but I shall be glad of any good occasion to be more familiar with you.

Step. My name is Signior *Stephano*, sir, I am this gentleman's cousin, sir, his father is mine uncle; sir, I am somewhat melancholy, but you shall command me, sir, in whatsoever is incident to a gentleman.

Bob. Signior, I must tell you this, I am no general man, embrace it as a most high favour, for (by the host of Egypt) but that I conceive you to be a gentleman of some parts, I love few words: you have wit: imagine.

Step. Ay, truly, sir, I am mightily given to melancholy.

Mat. O Lord, sir, it's your only best humour, sir, your true melancholy breeds your perfect fine wit, sir: I am melancholy myself divers times, sir, and then do I no more but take your pen and paper presently, and write you your half score or your dozen of sonnets at a sitting.

Lor. ju. Mass, then he utters them by the gross.

Step. Truly, sir, and I love such things out of measure.

Lor. ju. I'faith, as well as in measure.

Mat. Why, I pray you, Signior, make use of my study, it's at your service.

Step. I thank you, sir, I shall be bold, I warrant you, have you a close stool there?

Mat. Faith, sir, I have some papers there, toys of mine own doing at idle hours, that you'll say there's some sparks of wit in them, when you shall see them.

Pros. Would they were kindled once, and a good fire made, I might see self-love burn'd for her heresy.

Step. Cousin, is it well? am I melancholy enough?

Lor. ju. Oh, ay, excellent.

Pros. Signior *Bobadilla*, why muse you so?

Lor. ju. He is melancholy too.

Bob. Faith, sir, I was thinking of a most honourable piece of service was perform'd to-morrow, being St. *Mark's* day, shall be some ten years.

Lor. ju. In what place was that service, I pray you, sir?

Bob. Why, at the beleaguering of *Ghibelletto*, where, in less than two hours, seven hundred resolute gentlemen, as any were in *Europe*, lost their lives upon the breach: I'll tell you, gentlemen, it was the first, but the best leaguer that ever I beheld with these eyes, except the taking in of *Tortosa* last year by the *Genoways*, but that (of all other) was the most fatal and dangerous exploit that ever I was ranged in, since I first bore arms before the face of the enemy, as I am a gentleman and a soldier.

Step. So, I had as lief as an angel I could swear as well as that gentleman.

Lor. ju. Then you were a servitor at both, it seems.

Bob. O Lord, sir: by *Phaeton*, I was the first man that entered the breach, and had I not effected it with resolution, I had been slain if I had had a million of lives.

Lor. ju. Indeed, sir?

Step. Nay, an you heard him discourse you would say so: how like you him?

Bob. I assure you (upon my salvation) 'tis true, and yourself shall confess.

Pros. You must bring him to the rack first.

Bob. Observe me judicially, sweet Signior: they had planted me a demi-culverin just in the mouth of the breach; now, sir, (as we were to ascend), their master gunner (a man of no mean skill and courage, you must think,) confronts me with his linstock ready to give fire; I spying his intendment, discharged my petronel in his bosom, and with this instrument, my poor rapier, ran violently upon the *Moors* that guarded the ordnance, and put them pell-mell to the sword.

Pros. To the sword? to the rapier, Signior.

Lor. ju. Oh, it was a good figure observed, sir: but did you all this, Signior, without hurting your blade?

Bob. Without any impeach on the earth: you shall perceive, sir, it is the most fortunate weapon that ever rid on a poor gentleman's thigh: shall I tell you, sir? you talk of *Morglay, Excalibur, Durindana*, or so: tut, I lend no credit to that is reported of them, I know the virtue of mine own, and therefore I dare the boldlier maintain it.

Step. I marle whether it be a *Toledo* or no?

Bob. A most perfect *Toledo*, I assure you, Signior.

Step. I have a countryman of his here.

Mat. Pray you let's see, sir: yes, faith, it is.

Bob. This a *Toledo*? pish!

Step. Why do you pish, Signior?

Bob. A Fleming, by *Phœbus!* I'll buy them for a guilder a piece, an I'll have a thousand of them.

Lor. ju. How say you, cousin? I told you thus much.

Pros. Where bought you it, Signior?

Step. Of a scurvy rogue soldier, a pox of God on him, he swore it was a *Toledo*.

Bob. A provant rapier, no better.

Mat. Mass, I think it be indeed.

Lor. ju. Tut, now it's too late to look on it, put it up, put it up.

Step. Well, I will not put it up, but by God's foot, an e'er I meet him—

Pros. Oh, it is past remedy now, sir, you must have patience.

Step. Whoreson, coney-catching rascal; oh, I could eat the very hilts for anger.

Lor. ju. A sign you have a good ostrich stomach, cousin.

Step. A stomach? would I had him here, you should see an I had a stomach.

Pros. It's better as 'tis: come, gentlemen, shall we go?

Lor. ju. A miracle, cousin, look here, look here.   [*Enter* Musco.

Step. Oh, God's lid, by your leave, do you know me, sir?

Mus. Ay, sir, I know you by sight.

Step. You sold me a rapier, did you not?

Mus. Yes, marry did I, sir.

Step. You said it was a *Toledo*, ha?

Mus. True, I did so.

Step. But it is none.

Mus. No, sir, I confess it, it is none.

Step. Gentlemen, bear witness, he has confest it. By God's lid, an you had not confest it—

Lor. ju. Oh, cousin, forbear, forbear.

Step. Nay, I have done, cousin.

Pros. Why, you have done like a gentleman, he has confest it, what would you more?

Lor. ju. Sirrah, how dost thou like him?

Pros. Oh, it's a precious good fool, make much on him: I can compare him to nothing more happily than a barber's virginals; for every one may play upon him.

Mus. Gentleman, shall I intreat a word with you?

Lor. ju. With all my heart, sir, you have not another *Toledo* to sell, have you?

Mus. You are pleasant, your name is Signior *Lorenzo*, as I take it?

Lor. ju. You are in the right: 'Sblood, he means to catechise me, I think.

Mus. No, sir, I leave that to the Curate, I am none of that coat.

Lor. ju. And yet of as bare a coat; well, say, sir.

Mus. Faith, Signior, I am but servant to God *Mars* extraordinary, and indeed (this brass varnish being washed off, and three or four other tricks sublated) I appear yours in reversion, after the decease of your good father, *Musco*.

Lor. ju. *Musco*, 'sblood, what wind hath blown thee hither in this shape?

Mus. Your easterly wind, sir, the same that blew your father hither.

Lor. ju. My father?

Mus. Nay, never start, it's true, he is come to town of purpose to seek you.

Lor. ju. Sirrah *Prospero*, what shall we do, sirrah? my father is come to the city.

Pros. Thy father: where is he?

Mus. At a gentleman's house yonder by St. *Anthony's*, where he but stays my return; and then—

Pros. Who's this? *Musco?*

Mus. The same, sir.

Pros. Why, how com'st thou transmuted thus?

Mus. Faith, a device, a device, nay, for the love of God, stand not here, gentlemen, house yourselves, and I'll tell you all.

Lor. ju. But art thou sure he will stay thy return?

Mus. Do I live, sir? what a question is that!

Pros. Well, we'll prorogue his expectation a little: *Musco*, thou shalt go with us: Come on, gentlemen: nay, I pray thee, (good rascal) droop not, 'sheart, an our wits be so gouty, that one old plodding brain can outstrip us all. Lord, I beseech thee, may they lie and starve in some miserable spittle, where they may never see the face of any true spirit again, but be perpetually haunted with some *church-yard hobgoblin* in seculo seculorum.

Mus. Amen, Amen.   [*Exeunt.*

ACT III

SCENE I.—*Enter* THORELLO, *and* PISO.

Pis. He will expect you, sir, within this half hour.

Tho. Why, what's a clock?

Pis. New striken ten.

Tho. Hath he the money ready, can you tell?

Pis. Yes, sir, *Baptista* brought it yesternight.

Tho. Oh, that's well: fetch me my cloak.   [*Exit Piso.*

Stay, let me see; an hour to go and come,
Ay, that will be the least: and then 'twill be
An hour before I can dispatch with him;
Or very near: well, I will say two hours;
Two hours? ha! things never dreamt of yet
May be contrived, ay, and effected too,
In two hours' absence: well, I will not go.
Two hours; no, fleering opportunity,
I will not give your treachery that scope.
Who will not judge him worthy to be robb'd,
That sets his doors wide open to a thief,
And shews the felon where his treasure lies?
Again, what earthy spirit but will attempt
To taste the fruit of beauty's golden tree,
When leaden sleep seals up the dragon's eyes?
Oh, beauty is a *project* of some power,
Chiefly when opportunity attends her:
She will infuse true motion in a stone,
Put glowing fire in an icy soul,
Stuff peasants' bosoms with proud *Cæsar's* spleen,
Pour rich device into an empty brain:
Bring youth to folly's gate: there train him in,
And after all, extenuate his sin.
Well, I will not go, I am resolved for that.
Go, carry it again: yet stay: yet do too,
I will defer it till some other time.   [*Enter Piso.*

Pis. Sir, Signior *Platano* will meet you there with the bond.

Tho. That's true: by Jesu, I had clean forgot it.
I must go, what's a clock?

Pis. Past ten, sir.

Tho. 'Heart, then will *Prospero* presently be here too,
With one or other of his loose consorts.
I am a Jew if I know what to say,
What course to take, or which way to resolve.
My brain (methinks) is like an hour-glass,
And my imaginations like the sands
Run dribbling forth to fill the mouth of time,
Still changed with turning in the ventricle.
What were I best to do? it shall be so.
Nay, I dare build upon his secrecy. *Piso.*

Pis. Sir.

Tho. Yet now I have bethought me too, I will not.
Is *Cob* within?

Pis. I think he be, sir.

Tho. But he'll prate too, there's no talk of him.
No, there were no course upon the earth to this,
If I durst trust him; tut, I were secure,
But there's the question now, if he should prove,
Rimarum plenus, then, 'sblood, I were *rook'd*.
The state that he hath stood in till this present
Doth promise no such change: what should I fear then?
Well, come what will, I'll tempt my fortune once.
Piso, thou mayest deceive me, but I think thou lovest me, *Piso*.

Pis. Sir, if a servant's zeal and humble duty may be term'd
love, you are possest of it.

Tho. I have a matter to impart to thee, but thou must be secret,
Piso.

Pis. Sir, for that—

Tho. Nay, hear me, man; think I esteem thee well,
To let thee in thus to my private thoughts;
Piso, it is a thing sits nearer to my crest,
Than thou art 'ware of; if thou should'st reveal it—

Pis. Reveal it, sir?

Tho. Nay, I do not think thou would'st, but if thou should'st—

Pis. Sir, then I were a villain:
Disclaim in me for ever if I do.

Tho. He will not swear: he has some meaning, sure,
Else (being urged so much) how should he choose,
But lend an oath to all this protestation?
He is no puritan, that I am certain of.
What should I think of it? urge him again,
And in some other form: I will do so.
Well, *Piso*, thou hast sworn not to disclose; ay, you did swear?

Pis. Not yet, sir, but I will, so please you.

Tho. Nay, I dare take thy word.
But if thou wilt swear, do as you think good,

I am resolved without such circumstance.

Pis. By my soul's safety, sir, I here protest,
My tongue shall ne'er take knowledge of a word
Deliver'd me in compass of your trust.

Tho. Enough, enough, these ceremonies need not,
I know thy faith to be as firm as brass.

Piso, come hither: nay, we must be close
In managing these actions: So it is,
(Now he has sworn I dare the safelier speak;)
I have of late by divers observations—
But, whether his oath be lawful, yea, or no? ha!
I will ask counsel ere I do proceed:
Piso, it will be now too long to stay,
We'll spy some fitter time soon, or to-morrow.

Pis. At your pleasure, sir.

Tho. I pray you search the books 'gainst I return
For the receipts 'twixt me and *Platano.*

Pis. I will, sir.

Tho. And hear you: if my brother *Prospero*
Chance to bring hither any gentlemen
Ere I come back, let one straight bring me word.

Pis. Very well, sir.

Tho. Forget it not, nor be not you out of the way.

Pis. I will not, sir.

Tho. Or whether he come or no, if any other,
Stranger or else: fail not to send me word.

Pis. Yes, sir.

Tho. Have care, I pray you, and remember it.

Pis. I warrant you, sir.

Tho. But, *Piso,* this is not the secret I told thee of.

Pis. No, sir, I suppose so.

Tho. Nay, believe me, it is not.

Pis. I do believe you, sir.

Tho. By heaven it is not, that's enough.
Marry, I would not thou should'st utter it to any creature living,
Yet I care not.
Well, I must hence: *Piso,* conceive thus much,
No ordinary person could have drawn
So deep a secret from me; I mean not this,
But that I have to tell thee: this is nothing, this.
Piso, remember, silence, buried here:
No greater hell than to be slave to fear.   [*Exit Tho.*

Pis. *Piso,* remember, silence, buried here:
Whence should this flow of passion (trow) take head? ha!
Faith, I'll dream no longer of this running humour,
For fear I sink, the violence of the stream
Already hath transported me so far
That I can feel no ground at all: but soft,   [*Enter* COB.
Oh, it's our water-bearer: somewhat has crost him now.

Cob. Fasting days: what tell you me of your fasting days?

would they were all on a light fire for me: they say the world shall be consumed with fire and brimstone in the latter day: but I would we had these ember weeks and these villainous Fridays burnt in the mean time, and then—

Pis. Why, how now, *Cob!* what moves thee to this choler, ha?

Cob. Collar, sir? 'swounds, I scorn your collar, I, sir, am no collier's horse, sir, never ride me with your collar, an you do, I'll shew you a jade's trick.

Pis. Oh, you'll slip your head out of the collar: why, *Cob*, you mistake me.

Cob. Nay, I have my rheum, and I be angry as well as another, sir.

Pis. Thy rheum? thy humour, man, thou mistakest.

Cob. Humour? mack, I think it be so indeed: what is this humour? it's some rare thing, I warrant.

Pis. Marry, I'll tell thee what it is (as 'tis generally received in these days): it is a monster bred in a man by self-love and affectation, and fed by folly.

Cob. How? must it be fed?

Pis. Oh ay, humour is nothing if it be not fed, why, didst thou never hear of that? it's a common phrase, *Feed my humour.*

Cob. I'll none on it: humour, avaunt, I know you not, be gone. Let who will make hungry meals for you, it shall not be I: Feed you, quoth he? 'sblood, I have much ado to feed myself, especially on these lean rascal days too, an't had been any other day but a fasting day: a plague on them all for me: by this light, one might have done God good service and have drown'd them all in the flood two or three hundred thousand years ago, oh, I do stomach them hugely: I have a maw now, an't were for Sir Bevis's horse.

Pis. Nay, but I pray thee, *Cob*, what makes thee so out of love with fasting days?

Cob. Marry, that that will make any man out of love with them, I think: their bad conditions, an you will needs know: First, they are of a Flemish breed, I am sure on't, for they raven up more butter than all the days of the week beside: next, they stink of fish miserably: thirdly, they'll keep a man devoutly hungry all day, and at night send him supperless to bed.

Pis. Indeed, these are faults, *Cob.*

Cob. Nay, an this were all, 'twere something, but they are the only known enemies to my generation. A fasting day no sooner comes, but my lineage goes to rack, poor Cobs, they smoke for it, they melt in passion, and your maids too know this, and yet would have me turn *Hannibal*, and eat my own fish and blood: my princely coz, [*pulls out a red herring.*] fear nothing; I have not the heart to devour you, an I might be made as rich as Golias: oh, that I had room for my tears, I could weep salt water enough now to preserve the lives of ten thousand of my kin: but I may curse none but these filthy Almanacks, for an 'twere not for them, these days of persecution would ne'er be known. I'll be hang'd an some fishmonger's son do not make on them, and puts in more fasting days than he should do, because he would utter his father's dried stock-fish.

Pis. 'Soul, peace, thou'lt be beaten like a stockfish else: here is Signior *Matheo.*   [*Enter* MATHEO, PROSPERO, LORENZO junior,
                                        BOBADILLA, STEPHANO, MUSCO.

Now must I look out for a messenger to my master.

                                        [*Exeunt Cob and Piso.*

SCENE II.

Pros. Beshrew me, but it was an absolute good jest, and exceedingly well carried.

Lor. ju. Ay, and our ignorance maintain'd it as well, did it not?

Pros. Yes, faith, but was't possible thou should'st not know him?

Lor. ju. 'Fore God, not I, an I might have been join'd patten with one of the nine worthies for knowing him. 'Sblood, man, he had so writhen himself into the habit of one of your poor *Dispar-view's* here, your decayed, ruinous, worm-eaten gentlemen of the round: such as have vowed to sit on the skirts of the city, let your Provost and his half dozen of halberdiers do what they can; and have translated begging out of the old hackney pace, to a fine easy amble, and made it run as smooth off the tongue as a shove-groat shilling, into the likeness of one of these lean *Pirgo's*, had he moulded himself so perfectly, observing every trick of their action, as varying the accent: swearing with an *emphasis.* Indeed, all with so special and exquisite a grace, that (hadst thou seen him) thou would'st have sworn he might have been the Tamberlane, or the Agamemnon on the rout.

Pros. Why, Musco, who would have thought thou hadst been such a gallant?

Lor. ju. I cannot tell, but (unless a man had juggled begging all his life time, and been a weaver of phrases from his infancy, for the apparelling of it) I think the world cannot produce his rival.

Pros. Where got'st thou this coat, I marle?

Mus. Faith, sir, I had it of one of the devil's near kinsmen, a broker.

Pros. That cannot be, if the proverb hold, a crafty knave needs no broker.

Mus. True, sir, but I need a broker, *ergo*, no crafty knave.

Pros. Well put off, well put off.

Lor. ju. Tut, he has more of these shifts.

Mus. And yet where I have one, the broker has ten, sir. [*Enter* PIS.

Pis. Francisco, Martino, ne'er a one to be found now: what a spite's this?

Pros. How now, *Piso?* is my brother within?

Pis. No, sir, my master went forth e'en now, but Signior *Giuliano* is within. *Cob*, what, *Cob!* Is he gone too?

Pros. Whither went thy master? *Piso*, canst thou tell?

Pis. I know not, to Doctor *Clement's*, I think, sir. *Cob.*   [*Exit* Pis.

Lor. ju. Doctor *Clement*, what's he? I have heard much speech of him.

Pros. Why, dost thou not know him? he is the *Gonfaloniere* of the state here, an excellent rare civilian, and a great scholar, but the only mad merry old fellow in Europe: I shewed him you the other day.

Lor. ju. Oh, I remember him now; Good faith, and he hath a very strange presence, methinks, it shews as if he stood out of the rank from other men. I have heard many of his jests in Padua; they say he will commit a man for taking the wall of his horse.

Pros. Ay, or wearing his cloak on one shoulder, or any thing indeed, if it come in the way of his humour.

Pis. Gaspar, Martino, Cob: 'Sheart, where should they be, trow?   [*Enter* Piso.

Bob. Signior *Thorello's* man, I pray thee vouchsafe us the lighting of this match.

Pis. A pox on your match, no time but now to vouchsafe? *Francisco, Cob.*   [*Exit.*

Bob. Body of me: here's the remainder of seven pound, since yesterday was sevennight. It's your right *Trinidado:* did you never take any, signior?

Step. No, truly, sir; but I'll learn to take it now, since you commend it so.

Bob. Signior, believe me (upon my relation) for what I tell you, the world shall not improve. I have been in the Indies, (where this herb grows) where neither myself nor a dozen gentlemen more (of my knowledge) have received the taste of any other nutriment in the world, for the space of one and twenty weeks, but tobacco only. Therefore it cannot be but 'tis most divine. Further, take it in the nature, in the true kind, so, it makes an antidote, that had you taken the most deadly poisonous simple in all Florence it should expel it, and clarify you with as much ease as I speak. And for your green wound, your *Balsamum,* and your —— are all mere gulleries, and trash to it, especially your *Trinidado*: your *Nicotian* is good too: I could say what I know of the virtue of it, for the exposing of rheums, raw humours, crudities, obstructions, with a thousand of this kind; but I profess myself no quack - salver. Only thus much; by *Hercules,* I do hold it, and will affirm it (before any Prince in Europe) to be the most sovereign and precious herb that ever the earth tendered to the use of man.

Lor. ju. Oh, this speech would have done rare in an apothecary's mouth.   [*Enter* Piso *and* Cob.

Pis. Ay; close by Saint *Anthony's:* Doctor *Clement's.*

Cob. Oh, oh.

Bob. Where's the match I gave thee?

Pis. 'Sblood, would his match, and he, and pipe, and all, were at Sancto Domingo.   [*Exit.*

Cob. By God's deins, I marle what pleasure or felicity they have in taking this roguish tobacco; it's good for nothing but to choke a man, and fill him full of smoke and embers: there were four died out of one house last week with taking of it, and two more the bell went for yesternight, one of them (they say) will ne'er escape it, he voided a bushel of soot yesterday, upward and downward. By the stocks, an there were no wiser men than I, I'd have it present death, man or woman, that should but deal with a tobacco pipe; why, it will stifle them all in the end as many as use it; it's little better than rat's-bane. [*Exit Piso.*

All. Oh, good Signior; hold, hold.

Bob. You base cullion, you.

Pis. Sir, here's your match; come, thou must needs be talking too.

Cob. Nay, he will not meddle with his match, I warrant you; well, it shall be a dear beating, an I live.

Bob. Do you prate?

Lor. ju. Nay, good Signior, will you regard the humour of a fool? Away, knave.

Pros. Piso, get him away. [*Exit Piso and Cob.*

Bob. A whoreson filthy slave, a turd, an excrement. Body of *Cæsar,* but that I scorn to let forth so mean a spirit, I'd have stabb'd him to the earth.

Pros. Marry, God forbid, sir.

Bob. By this fair heaven, I would have done it.

Step. Oh, he swears admirably: (by this fair heaven!) Body of *Cæsar :* I shall never do it, sure (upon my salvation). No, I have not the right grace.

Mat. Signior, will you any? By this air, the most divine tobacco as ever I drunk.

Lor. ju. I thank you, sir.

Step. Oh, this gentleman doth it rarely too, but nothing like the other. By this air, as I am a gentleman: By *Phœbus.* [*Exit Bob.*

Mus. Master, glance, glance: Signior *Prospero.* *and Mat.*

Step. As I have a soul to be saved, I do protest—

Pros. That you are a fool.

Lor. ju. Cousin, will you any tobacco?

Step. Ay, sir: upon my salvation.

Lor. ju. How now, cousin?

Step. I protest, as I am a gentleman, but no soldier indeed.

Pros. No, Signior, as I remember, you served on a great horse, last general muster.

Step. Ay, sir, that's true, cousin, may I swear as I am a soldier, by that?

Lor. ju. Oh yes, that you may.

Step. Then as I am a gentleman, and a soldier, it is divine tobacco.

Pros. But soft, where's Signior *Matheo?* gone?

Mus. No, sir, they went in here.

Pros. Oh, let's follow them: Signior *Matheo* is gone to salute his mistress, sirrah, now thou shalt hear some of his verses, for he never comes hither without some shreds of poetry: Come, Signior *Stephano.* *Musco.*

Step. *Musco?* where? Is this *Musco?*

Lor. ju. Ay; but peace, cousin, no words of it at any hand.

Step. Not I, by this fair heaven, as I have a soul to be saved, by *Phœbus.*

Pros. Oh rare! your cousin's discourse is simply suited, all in oaths.

Lor. ju. Ay, he lacks nothing but a little light stuff, to draw them out withal, and he were rarely fitted to the time.   [*Exeunt.*

SCENE III.—*Enter* Thorello *with* Cob.

Tho. Ha, how many are there, sayest thou?

Cob. Marry, sir, your brother, Signior *Prospero.*

Tho. Tut, beside him: what strangers are there, man?

Cob. Strangers? let me see, one, two; mass, I know not well, there's so many.

Tho. How? so many?

Cob. Ay, there's some five or six of them at the most.

Tho. A swarm, a swarm?
Spite of the devil, how they sting my heart!
How long hast thou been coming hither, *Cob?*

Cob. But a little while, sir.

Tho. Didst thou come running?

Cob. No, sir.

Tho. Tut, then I am familiar with thy haste.
Ban to my fortunes: what meant I to marry?
I that before was rank'd in such content,
My mind attired in smooth silken peace,
Being free master of mine own free thoughts,
And now become a slave? what, never sigh,
Be of good cheer, man: for thou art a cuckold,
'Tis done, 'tis done: nay, when such flowing store,
Plenty itself falls in my wife's lap,
The *Cornucopiæ* will be mine, I know. But, *Cob,*
What entertainment had they?   I am sure
My sister and my wife would bid them welcome, ha?

Cob. Like enough: yet I heard not a word of welcome.

Tho. No, their lips were seal'd with kisses, and the voice
Drown'd in a flood of joy at their arrival,
Had lost her motion, state, and faculty.
Cob, which of them was't that first kiss'd my wife?
(My sister, I should say,) my wife, alas,
I fear not her: ha? who was it, say'st thou?

Cob. By my troth, sir, will you have the truth of it?

Tho. Oh ay, good *Cob:* I pray thee.

Cob. God's my judge, I saw nobody to be kiss'd, unless they would have kiss'd the post in the middle of the warehouse; for there I left them all, at their tobacco, with a pox.

Tho. How? were they not gone in then ere thou cam'st?

Cob. Oh no, sir.

Tho. Spite of the devil, what do I stay here then?
Cob, follow me.   [*Exit Tho.*

Cob. Nay, soft and fair, I have eggs on the spit; I cannot go yet, sir: now am I for some divers reasons hammering, hammering revenge: oh, for three or four gallons of vinegar, to sharpen my wits: Revenge, vinegar revenge, russet revenge; nay, an he had not lien in my house, 'twould never have grieved me; but being my guest, one that I'll be sworn my wife has lent him her smock off her back, while his own shirt has been at washing: pawned her neckerchers for clean bands for him: sold almost all my platters to buy him tobacco; and yet to see an ingratitude wretch strike his host; well, I hope to raise up an host of furies for't: here comes M. Doctor. [*Enter* Doctor CLEMENT, LORENZO senior, PETO.

Clem. What's Signior *Thorello* gone?

Pet. Ay, sir.

Clem. Heart of me, what made him leave us so abruptly? How now, sirrah; what make you here? what would you have, ha?

Cob. An't please your worship, I am a poor neighbour of your worship's.

Clem. A neighbour of mine, knave?

Cob. Ay, sir, at the sign of the Water-tankard, hard by the Green Lattice: I have paid scot and lot there any time this eighteen years.

Clem. What, at the Green Lattice?

Cob. No, sir: to the parish: marry, I have seldom scaped scot-free at the Lattice.

Clem. So: but what business hath my neighbour?

Cob. An't like your worship, I am come to crave the peace of your worship.

Clem. Of me, knave? peace of me, knave? did I e'er hurt thee? did I ever threaten thee? or wrong thee? ha?

Cob. No, God's my comfort, I mean your worship's warrant, for one that hath wrong'd me, sir: his arms are at too much liberty, I would fain have them bound to a treaty of peace, an I could by any means compass it.

Lor. Why, dost thou go in danger of thy life for him?

Cob. No, sir; but I go in danger of my death every hour by his means; an I die within a twelve-month and a day, I may swear, by the laws of the land, that he kill'd me.

Clem. How? how, knave? swear he kill'd thee? what pretext? what colour hast thou for that?

Cob. Marry, sir, both black and blue, colour enough, I warrant you, I have it here to shew your worship.

Clem. What is he that gave you this, sirrah?

Cob. A gentleman in the city, sir.

Clem. A gentleman? what call you him?

Cob. Signior *Bobadilla.*

Clem. Good: But wherefore did he beat you, sirrah? how began the quarrel 'twixt you? ha: speak truly, knave, I advise you.

Cob. Marry, sir, because I spake against their vagrant tobacco, as I came by them: for nothing else.

Clem. Ha, you speak against tobacco?   *Peto,* his name.

Pet. What's your name, sirrah?

Cob. Oliver Cob, sir, set Oliver Cob, sir.

Clem. Tell *Oliver Cob* he shall go to the jail.

Pet. *Oliver Cob,* master Doctor says you shall go to the jail.

Cob. Oh, I beseech your worship, for God's love, dear master Doctor.

Clem. Nay, God's precious! an such drunken knaves as you are come to dispute of tobacco once, I have done: away with him.

Cob. Oh, good master Doctor, sweet gentleman.

Lor. se. Sweet *Oliver,* would I could do thee any good; master Doctor, let me intreat, sir.

Clem. What? a tankard-bearer, a thread-bare rascal, a beggar, a slave that never drunk out of better than piss-pot metal in his life, and he to deprave and abuse the virtue of an herb so generally received in the courts of princes, the chambers of nobles, the bowers of sweet ladies, the cabins of soldiers: *Peto,* away with him, by God's passion, I say, go to.

Cob. Dear master Doctor.

Lor. se. Alas, poor *Oliver.*

Clem. *Peto:* ay: and make him a warrant, he shall not go, I but fear the knave.

Cob. O divine Doctor, thanks, noble Doctor, most dainty Doctor, delicious Doctor.　　　　　　　　　　　　[*Exeunt Peto with Cob.*

Clem. Signior *Lorenzo :* God's pity, man,
Be merry, be merry, leave these dumps.

Lor. se. Troth, would I could, sir: but enforced mirth
(In my weak judgment) has no happy birth.
The mind, being once a prisoner unto cares,
The more it dreams on joy, the worse it fares.
A smiling look is to a heavy soul
As a gilt bias to a leaden bowl,
Which (in itself) appears most vile, being spent
To no true use; but only for ostent.

Clem. Nay, but, good Signior, hear me a word, hear me a word, your cares are nothing; they are like my cap, soon put on, and as soon put off. What? your son is old enough to govern himself; let him run his course, it's the only way to make him a staid man: if he were an unthrift, a ruffian, a drunkard, or a licentious liver, then you had reason: you had reason to take care: but being none of these, God's passion, an I had twice so many cares as you have, I'd drown them all in a cup of sack: come, come, I muse your parcel of a soldier returns not all this while.　　　　[*Exeunt.*

SCENE IV.—*Enter* GIULIANO, *with* BIANCHA.

Giu. Well, sister, I tell you true: and you'll find it so in the end.

Bia. Alas, brother, what would you have me to do? I cannot help it; you see, my brother *Prospero* he brings them in here, they are his friends.

Giu. His friends? his friends? 'sblood, they do nothing but haunt him up and down like a sort of unlucky sprites, and tempt him to all manner of villainy that can be thought of; well, by this

light, a little thing would make me play the devil with some of them;
an't were not more for your husband's sake than any thing else,
I'd make the house too hot for them; they should say and swear,
hell were broken loose, ere they went. But by God's bread, 'tis
nobody's fault but yours; for an you had done as you might have
done, they should have been damn'd ere they should have come in,
e'er a one of them.

Bia. God's my life; did you ever hear the like? what a strange
man is this! could I keep out all them, think you? I should put
myself against half a dozen men, should I? Good faith, you'd
mad the patient'st body in the world, to hear you talk so, without
any sense or reason. [*Enter* Matheo *with* Hesperida, Bobadilla,
              Stephano, Lorenzo junior, Prospero, Musco.

Hesp. Servant, (in troth) you are too prodigal of your wits'
treasure, thus to pour it forth upon so mean a subject as my worth.

Mat. You say well, you say well.

Giu. Hoyday, here is stuff.

Lor. ju. Oh, now stand close; pray God she can get him to read it.

Pros. Tut, fear not: I warrant thee he will do it of himself with
much impudency.

Hes. Servant, what is that same, I pray you?

Mat. Marry, an *Elegy*, an *Elegy*, an odd toy.

Giu. Ay, to mock an ape withal. O Jesu.

Bia. Sister, I pray you let's hear it.

Mat. Mistress, I'll read it, if you please.

Hes. I pray you do, *servant*.

Giu. Oh, here's no foppery. 'Sblood, it frets me to the gall to
think on it.   [*Exit.*

Pros. Oh ay, it is his condition, peace: we are fairly rid of him.

Mat. Faith, I did it in an humour: I know not how it is, but
please you come near, signior: this gentleman hath judgment, he
knows how to censure of a——I pray you, sir, you can judge.

Step. Not I, sir: *as I have a soul to be saved, as I am a gentleman.*

Lor. ju. Nay, it's well; so long as he doth not forswear himself.

Bob. Signior, you abuse the excellency of your mistress and her
fair sister. Fie, while you live avoid this prolixity.

Mat. I shall, sir; well, *incipere dulce.*

Lor. ju. How, *incipere dulce?* a sweet thing to be a fool indeed.

Pros. What, do you take *incipere* in that sense?

Lor. ju. You do not, you? 'Sblood, this was your villainy to
gull him with a motte.

Pros. Oh, the benchers' phrase: *pauca verba, pauca verba.*

Mat. *Rare creature, let me speak without offence,*
Would God my rude words had the influence
To rule thy thoughts, as thy fair looks do mine,
Then shouldst thou be his prisoner, who is thine.

Lor. ju. 'Sheart, this is in *Hero* and *Leander* !

Pros. Oh ay: peace, we shall have more of this.

Mat. *Be not unkind and fair: misshapen stuff*
Is of behaviour boisterous and rough :

How like you that, Signior? 'sblood, he shakes his head like a
bottle, to feel an there be any brain in it.

Mat. But observe the *catastrophe* now,
And I in duty will exceed all other,
As you in beauty do excel love's mother.

Lor. ju. Well, I'll have him free of the brokers, for he utters
nothing but stolen remnants.

Pros. Nay, good *critic*, forbear.

Lor. ju. A pox on him, hang him, filching rogue, steal from the
dead? it's worse than sacrilege.

Pros. Sister, what have you here? *verses?* I pray you let's see.

Bia. Do you let them go so lightly, sister?

Hes. Yes, faith, when they come lightly.

Bia. Ay, but if your *servant* should hear you, he would take it
heavily.

Hes. No matter, he is able to bear.

Bia. So are *asses.*

Hes. So is he.

Pros. Signior *Matheo*, who made these verses? they are excellent
good.

Mat. O God, sir, it's your pleasure to say so, sir.
Faith, I made them *extempore* this morning.

Pros. How *extempore?*

Mat. Ay, would I might be damn'd else; ask Signior *Bobadilla.*
He saw me write them, at the—(pox on it) the *Mitre* yonder.

Mus. Well, an the Pope knew he cursed the *Mitre* it were enough
to have him excommunicated all the taverns in the town.

Step. Cousin, how do you like this gentleman's verses?

Lor. ju. Oh, admirable, the best that ever I heard.

Step. By this fair heavens, they are admirable,
The best that ever I heard.   *[Enter* GIULIANO.

Giu. I am vext I can hold never a bone of me still,
'Sblood, I think they mean to build a *Tabernacle* here, well?

Pros. Sister, you have a simple servant here, that crowns your
beauty with such *encomiums* and *devices*, you may see what it is to
be the mistress of a wit that can make your perfections so transparent, that every blear eye may look through them, and see him
drowned over head and ears in the deep well of desire. Sister
Biancha, I marvel you get you not a servant that can rhyme and
do *tricks* too.

Giu. O monster! impudence itself! *tricks!*

Bia. Tricks, brother? what *tricks?*

Hes. Nay, speak, I pray you, what *tricks?*

Bia. Ay, never spare any body here: but say, what *tricks?*

Hes. Passion of my heart! do *tricks?*

Pros. 'Sblood, here's a *trick* vied, and revied: why, you monkeys, you! what a cater-wauling do you keep! has he not given
you *rhymes*, and *verses*, and *tricks?*

Giu. Oh, see the devil!

Pros. Nay, you lamp of virginity, that take it in snuff so: come and cherish this tame poetical fury in your *servant*, you'll be begg'd else shortly for a concealment: go to, reward his muse, you cannot give him less than a shilling in conscience, for the book he had it out of cost him a teston at the least. How now, gallants, *Lorenzo*, Signior *Bobadilla!* what, all sons of silence? no spirit.

Giu. Come, you might practise your ruffian tricks somewhere else, and not here, I wiss: this is no tavern, nor no place for such exploits.

Pros. 'Sheart, how now !

Giu. Nay, boy, never look askance at me for the matter; I'll tell you of it, by God's bread, ay, and you and your companions mend yourselves when I have done.

Pros. My companions?

Giu. Ay, your companions, sir, so I say! 'Sblood, I am not afraid of you nor them neither, you must have your poets, and your cavaliers, and your fools follow you up and down the city, and here they must come to domineer and swagger? sirrah, you *ballad-singer*, and *slops*, your fellow there, get you out; get you out: or (by the will of God) I'll cut off your ears, go to.

Pros. 'Sblood, stay, let's see what he dare do: cut off his ears; you are an ass, touch any man here, and by the Lord I'll run my rapier to the hilts in thee.

Giu. Yea, that would I fain see, boy.

Bia. O Jesu ! *Piso ! Matheo !* murder !

Hes. Help, help, *Piso !*

[*They all draw, enter Piso and some more of the house to part them, the women make a great cry.*

Lor. ju. Gentlemen, *Prospero*, forbear, I pray you.

Bob. Well, sirrah, you *Holofernes :* by my hand, I will pink thy flesh full of holes with my rapier for this, I will, by this good heaven: nay, let him come, let him come, gentlemen, by the body of St. *George*, I'll not kill him. [*They offer to fight again, and are parted.*

Pis. Hold, hold, forbear.

Giu. You whoreson, bragging coistril.   [*Enter* THORELLO.

Tho. Why, how now? what's the matter? what stir is here? Whence springs this quarrel? *Piso*, where is he? Put up your weapons, and put off this rage. My wife and sister, they are cause of this. What, *Piso?* where is this knave?

Pis. Here, sir.

Pros. Come, let's go: this is one of my brother's ancient humours, this.

Step. I am glad nobody was hurt by this ancient humour.

[*Exit Prospero, Lorenzo ju., Musco, Stephano, Bobadilla, Matheo.*

Tho. Why, how now, brother, who enforced this brawl?

Giu. A sort of lewd rake-hells, that care neither for God nor the devil. And they must come here to read *ballads* and *roguery*, and *trash*. I'll mar the knot of them ere I sleep, perhaps; especially Signior *Pithagoras*, he that's all manner of shapes: and *songs and sonnets*, his fellow there.

Hes. Brother, indeed you are too violent,
Too sudden in your courses, and you know
My brother *Prospero's* temper will not bear
Any reproof, chiefly in such a presence,
Where every slight disgrace he should receive,
Would wound him in opinion and respect.

Giu. Respect? what talk you of respect 'mongst such
As had neither spark of manhood nor good manners?
By God I am ashamed to hear you: respect?   [*Exit.*

Hes. Yes, there was one a civil gentleman,
And very worthily demeaned himself.

Tho. Oh, that was some love of yours, sister.

Hes. A love of mine? i'faith, I would he were
No other's love but mine.

Bia. Indeed, he seem'd to be a gentleman of an exceeding fair
disposition, and of very excellent good parts.

[*Exit Hesperida, Biancha.*

Tho. Her love, by Jesu: my wife's minion,
Fair disposition? excellent good parts?
'Sheart, these phrases are intolerable,
Good parts? how should she know his parts? well, well,
It is too plain, too clear: *Piso*, come hither.
What, are they gone?

Pis. Ay, sir, they went in.

Tho. Are any of the gallants within?

Pis. No, sir, they are all gone.

Tho. Art thou sure of it?

Pis. Ay, sir, I can assure you.

Tho. Piso, what gentleman was that they praised so?

Piso. One they call him Signior *Lorenzo*, a fair young gentleman,
sir.

Tho. Ay, I thought so: my mind gave me as much:
'Sblood, I'll be hang'd if they have not hid him in the house,
Some where, I'll go search, *Piso*, go with me,
Be true to me and thou shalt find me bountiful.   [*Exeunt.*

SCENE V.—*Enter* COB, *to him* TIB.

Cob. What, *Tib, Tib*, I say.

Tib. How now, what cuckold is that knocks so hard? Oh,
husband, is't you? What's the news?

Cob. Nay, you have stunn'd me, i'faith; you have given me a
knock on the forehead will stick by me: cuckold? 'Swounds,
cuckold?

Tib. Away, you fool, did I know it was you that knock'd?
Come, come, you may call me as bad when you list.

Cob. May I? 'swounds, *Tib*, you are a whore.

Tib. 'Sheart, you lie in your throat.

Cob. How, the lie? and in my throat too? do you long to be
stabb'd, ha?

Tib. Why, you are no soldier?

Cob. Mass, that's true, when was *Bobadilla* here? that *rogue,*
that *slave,* that fencing *Burgullion?* I'll tickle him, i'faith.

Tib. Why, what's the matter?

Cob. Oh, he hath basted me rarely, sumptuously: but I have it
here will sauce him, oh, the *doctor,* the honestest old *Trojan* in
all *Italy,* I do honour the very flea of his dog: a plague on him, he
put me once in a villainous filthy fear: marry, it vanish'd away like
the smoke of *tobacco:* but I was smok'd soundly first, I thank the
devil, and his good *angel* my guest: well, wife, or Tib, (which you
will) get you in, and lock the door, I charge you; let nobody into
you, not *Bobadilla* himself, nor the devil in his likeness; you are a
woman; you have flesh and blood enough in you; therefore be not
tempted; keep the door shut upon all comers.

Tib. I warrant you there shall nobody enter here without my
consent.

Cob. Nor with your consent, sweet *Tib,* and so I leave you.

Tib. It's more than you know, whether you leave me so.

Cob. How?

Tib. Why, sweet.

Cob. Tut, sweet or sour, thou art a flower.
Keep close thy door, I ask no more.　　　　　　　　　[*Exeunt.*

SCENE VI.—*Enter* Lorenzo jun., Prospero, Stephano, Musco.

Lor. ju. Well, *Musco,* perform this business happily,
And thou makest a conquest of my love for ever.

Pros. I'faith, now let thy spirits put on their best habit,
But at any hand remember thy message to my brother,
For there's no other means to start him.

Mus. I warrant you, sir, fear nothing; I have a nimble soul that
hath waked all my imaginative forces by this time, and put them
in true motion: what you have possest me withal, I'll discharge
it amply, sir. Make no question.　　　　　　　　　[*Exit Musco.*

Pros. That's well said, *Musco:* faith, sirrah, how dost thou
approve my wit in this device?

Lor. ju. Troth, well, howsoever; but excellent if it take.

Pros. Take, man: why, it cannot choose but take, if the circumstances miscarry not, but tell me zealously: dost thou affect my
sister *Hesperida,* as thou pretendest?

Lor. ju. Prospero, by Jesu.

Pros. Come, do not protest, I believe thee: i'faith, she is a virgin
of good ornament, and much modesty, unless I conceived very
worthily of her, thou shouldest not have her.

Lor. ju. Nay, I think it a question whether I shall have her for
all that.

Pros. 'Sblood, thou shalt have her, by this light, thou shalt!

Lor. ju. Nay, do not swear.

Pros. By St. *Mark,* thou shalt have her: I'll go fetch her presently, 'point but where to meet, and by this hand, I'll bring her!

Lor. ju. Hold, hold, what, all policy dead? no prevention of
mischiefs stirring.

Pros. Why, by—what shall I swear by? thou shalt have her, by my soul.

Lor. ju. I pray thee have patience, I am satisfied: *Prospero*, omit no offered occasion that may make my desires complete, I beseech thee.

Pros. I warrant thee.   [*Exeunt.*

ACT IV

SCENE I.—*Enter* LORENZO sen., PETO, *meeting* MUSCO.

Peto. Was your man a soldier, sir?

Lor. se. Ay, a knave, I took him up begging upon the way,
This morning as I was coming to the city.
Oh! here he is; come on, you make fair speed:
Why, where in God's name have you been so long?

Mus. Marry, (God's my comfort) where I thought I should have had little comfort of your worship's service.

Lor. se. How so?

Mus. O God, sir! your coming to the city, and your entertainment of men, and your sending me to watch; indeed, all the circumstances are as open to your son as to yourself.

Lor. se. How should that be? unless that villain *Musco*
Have told him of the letter, and discovered
All that I strictly charged him to conceal? 'tis so.

Mus. I'faith, you have hit it: 'tis so indeed.

Lor. se. But how should he know thee to be my man?

Mus. Nay, sir, I cannot tell; unless it were by the black art? is not your son a scholar, sir?

Lor. se. Yes; but I hope his soul is not allied
To such a devilish practice: if it were,
I had just cause to weep my part in him,
And curse the time of his creation.
But where didst thou find them, *Portensio?*

Mus. Nay, sir, rather you should ask where they found me? for I'll be sworn I was going along in the street, thinking nothing, when (of a sudden) one calls, *Signior Lorenzo's man:* another, he cries, *soldier:* and thus half a dozen of them, till they had got me within doors, where I no sooner came, but out flies their rapiers and all bent against my breast, they swore some two or three hundred oaths, and all to tell me I was but a dead man, if I did not confess where you were, and how I was employed, and about what; which, when they could not get out of me, (as God's my judge, they should have kill'd me first,) they lock'd me up into a room in the top of a house, where, by great miracle, (having a light heart) I slid down by a bottom of packthread into the street, and so scaped: but, master, thus much I can assure you, for I heard it while I was lock'd up: there were a great many merchants and rich citizens' wives with them at a banquet, and your son, Signior *Lorenzo,* has 'pointed one of them to meet anon at one *Cob's* house, a water-bearer's, that dwells by the wall: now there you shall be sure to take him: for fail he will not.

Lor. se. Nor will I fail to break this match, I doubt not;
Well, go thou along with master Doctor's man,
And stay there for me; at one *Cob's* house, say'st thou?   [*Exit.*

Mus. Ay, sir, there you shall have him: when can you tell? Much wench, or much son: 'sblood, when he has stay'd there three or four hours, travelling with the expectation of somewhat; and at the length be delivered of nothing: oh, the sport that I should then take to look on him if I durst; but now I mean to appear no more afore him in this shape: I have another trick to act yet; oh, that I were so happy as to light upon an ounce now of this Doctor's clerk: God save you, sir.

Peto. I thank you, good sir.

Mus. I have made you stay somewhat long, sir.

Peto. Not a whit, sir, I pray you what, sir, do you mean? you have been lately in the wars, sir, it seems.

Mus. Ay, marry have I, sir.

Peto. Troth, sir, I would be glad to bestow a bottle of wine on you, if it please you to accept it.

Mus. O Lord, sir.

Peto. But to hear the manner of your services, and your devices in the wars, they say they be very strange, and not like those a man reads in the Roman histories.

Mus. O God, no, sir, why, at any time when it please you, I shall be ready to discourse to you what I know: and more too somewhat.

Peto. No better time than now, sir, we'll go to the *Mermaid:* there we shall have a cup of neat wine, I pray you, sir, let me request you.

Mus. I'll follow you, sir, he is mine own, i'faith.   [*Exeunt.*

Enter BOBADILLA, LORENZO jun., MATHEO, STEPHANO.

Mat. Signior, did you ever see the like clown of him where we were to-day: Signior *Prospero's* brother? I think the whole earth cannot shew his like, by Jesu.

Lor. ju. We were now speaking of him, Signior *Bobadillo* tells me he is fallen foul of you too.

Mat. Oh ay, sir, he threatened me with the bastinado.

Bob. Ay, but I think I taught you a trick this morning for that. You shall kill him without all question, if you be so minded.

Mat. Indeed, it is a most excellent trick.

Bob. Oh, you do not give spirit enough to your motion; you are too dull, too tardy: oh, it must be done like lightning, hay!

Mat. Oh, rare.

Bob. Tut, 'tis nothing an't be not done in a—

Lor. ju. Signior, did you never play with any of our masters here?

Mat. Oh, good sir.

Bob. Nay, for a more instance of their preposterous humour, there came three or four of them to me, at a gentleman's house, where it was my chance to be resident at that time, to intreat my presence at their schools, and withal so much importuned me, that (I protest to you as I am a gentleman) I was ashamed of their rude demeanour out of all measure: well, I told them that to come to a public school they should pardon me, it was opposite to my humour, but if so they would attend me at my lodging, I protested to do them what right or favour I could, as I was a gentleman, etc.

Lor. ju. So, sir, then you tried their skill.

Bob. Alas, soon tried: you shall hear, sir, within two or three days after they came, and by Jesu, good Signior, believe me, I graced them exceedingly, shewed them some two or three tricks of prevention hath got them since admirable credit, they cannot deny this; and yet now they hate me, and why? because I am excellent, and for no other reason on the earth.

Lor. ju. This is strange and vile as ever I heard.

Bob. I will tell you, sir, upon my first coming to the city, they assaulted me some three, four, five, six of them together, as I have walk'd alone in divers places of the city; as upon the Exchange, at my lodging, and at my ordinary, where I have driven them afore me the whole length of a street, in the open view of all our gallants, pitying to hurt them, believe me; yet all this lenity will not depress their spleen; they will be doing with the pismire, raising a hill a man may spurn abroad with his foot at pleasure: by my soul, I could have slain them all, but I delight not in murder: I am loth to bear any other but a bastinado for them, and yet I hold it good policy not to go disarm'd, for though I be skilful, I may be suppressed with multitudes.

Lor. ju. Ay, by Jesu, may you, sir, and (in my conceit) our whole nation should sustain the loss by it, if it were so.

Bob. Alas, no: what's a peculiar man to a nation? not seen.

Lor. ju. Ay, but your skill, sir.

Bob. Indeed, that might be some loss, but who respects it? I will tell you, Signior, (in private) I am a gentleman, and live here obscure, and to myself; but were I known to the Duke (observe me) I would undertake (upon my head and life) for the public benefit of the state, not only to spare the entire lives of his subjects in general, but to save the one half, nay, three parts of his yearly charges, in holding wars generally against all his enemies; and how will I do it, think you?

Lor. ju. Nay, I know not, nor can I conceive.

Bob. Marry, thus, I would select nineteen more to myself, throughout the land, gentlemen they should be of good spirit; strong and able constitution, I would choose them by an instinct, a trick that I have, and I would teach these nineteen the special tricks, as your *punto*, your *reverso*, your *stoccato*, your *imbroccato*, your *passado*, your *montanto*, till they could all play very near or altogether as well as myself. This done, say the enemy were forty thousand strong: we twenty would come into the field the tenth of *March*, or thereabouts, and would challenge twenty of the enemy; they could not in their honour refuse the combat: well, we would kill them: challenge twenty more, kill them; twenty more, kill them; twenty more, kill them too; and thus would we kill every man his twenty a day, that's twenty score; twenty score, that's two hundred; two hundred a day, five days a thousand: forty thousand; forty times five, five times forty, two hundred days kills them all, by computation, and this will I venture my life to perform: provided there be no treason practised upon us.

Lor. ju. Why, are you so sure of your hand at all times?

Bob. Tut, never mistrust, upon my soul.

Lor. ju. Mass, I would not stand in Signior *Giuliano's* state, then, an you meet him, for the wealth of *Florence*.

Bob. Why, Signior, by Jesu, if he were here now, I would not draw my weapon on him, let this gentleman do his mind, but I will bastinado him (by heaven) an ever I meet him.

Enter GIULIANO *and goes out again.*

Mat. Faith, and I'll have a fling at him.

Lor. ju. Look, yonder he goes, I think.

Giu. 'Sblood, what luck have I, I cannot meet with these bragging rascals.

Bob. It's not he: is it?

Lor. ju. Yes, faith, it is he.

Mat. I'll be hang'd then if that were he.

Lor. ju. Before God, it was he: you make me swear.

Step. Upon my salvation, it was he.

Bob. Well, had I thought it had been he, he could not have gone so, but I cannot be induced to believe it was he yet.   [*Enter* GIU.

Giu. Oh, gallant, have I found you? draw to your tools; draw, or by God's will I'll thrash you.

Bob. Signior, hear me.

Giu. Draw your weapons then.

Bob. Signior, I never thought it till now: body of St. *George*, I have a warrant of the peace served on me even now, as I came along, by a water-bearer, this gentleman saw it, Signior *Matheo*.

Giu. The peace! 'Sblood, you will not draw?

[*Matheo runs away. He beats him and disarms him.*

Lor. ju. Hold, Signior, hold, under thy favour forbear.

Giu. Prate again as you like this, you whoreson cowardly rascal, you'll control the point, you? your consort he is gone; had he staid he had shared with you, in faith.   [*Exit Giuliano.*

Bob. Well, gentlemen, bear witness, I was bound to the peace, by Jesu.

Lor. ju. Why, and though you were, sir, the law allows you to defend yourself; that's but a poor excuse.

Bob. I cannot tell; I never sustained the like disgrace (by heaven); sure I was struck with a planet then, for I had no power to touch my weapon.   [*Exit.*

Lor. ju. Ay, like enough; I have heard of many that have been beaten under a planet; go, get you to the surgeon's, 'sblood, an these be your tricks, your passados, and your montantos, I'll none of them: O God, that this age should bring forth such creatures! come, cousin.

Step. Mass, I'll have this cloak.

Lor. ju. God's will: it's *Giuliano's.*

Step. Nay, but 'tis mine now, another might have ta'en it up as well as I, I'll wear it, so I will.

Lor. ju. How an he see it? he'll challenge it, assure yourself.

Step. Ay, but he shall not have it; I'll say I bought it.

Lor. ju. Advise you, cousin, take heed he give not you as much.

[*Exeunt.*

Enter THORELLO, PROSPERO, BIANCHA, HESPERIDA.

Tho. Now trust me, *Prospero*, you were much to blame,
T' incense your brother and disturb the peace
Of my poor house, for there be sentinels,
That every minute watch to give alarms
Of civil war, without adjection
Of your assistance and occasion.

Pros. No harm done, brother, I warrant you: since there is no harm done, anger costs a man nothing: and a tall man is never his own man till he be angry, to keep his valour in obscurity, is to keep himself as it were in a cloak-bag: what's a musician unless he play? what's a tall man unless he fight? for indeed, all this my brother stands upon absolutely, and that made me fall in with him so resolutely.

Bia. Ay, but what harm might have come of it?

Pros. Might? so might the good warm clothes your husband wears be poison'd for any thing he knows, or the wholesome wine he drunk even now at the table.

Tho. Now, God forbid: O me! now I remember,
My wife drunk to me last; and changed the cup,
And bade me wear this cursed suit to-day,
See if God suffer murder undiscover'd!
I feel me ill; give me some mithridate,
Some mithridate and oil; good sister, fetch me,
Oh, I am sick at heart: I burn, I burn;
If you will save my life, go fetch it me.

Pros. Oh, strange humour, my very breath hath poison'd him.

Hes. Good brother, be content, what do you mean?
The strength of these extreme conceits will kill you.

Bia. Beshrew your heart-blood, brother *Prospero*,
For putting such a toy into his head.

Pros. Is a fit simile a toy? will he be poison'd with a simile?
Brother *Thorello*, what a strange and vain imagination is this?
For shame be wiser, on my soul there's no such matter.

Tho. Am I not sick? how am I then not poison'd?
Am I not poison'd? how am I then so sick?

Bia. If you be sick, your own thoughts make you sick.

Pros. His jealousy is the poison he hath taken.

Enter MUSCO *like the doctor's man.*

Mus. Signior *Thorello*, my master, Doctor *Clement*, salutes you, and desires to speak with you, with all speed possible.

Tho. No time but now? well, I'll wait upon his worship, *Piso*,

Cob, I'll seek them out, and set them sentinels till I return. *Piso,
Cob, Piso.*   [*Exit.*

Pros. *Musco*, this is rare, but how got'st thou this apparel of the
Doctor's man?

Mus. Marry, sir. My youth would needs bestow the wine on me
to hear some martial discourse; where I so marshall'd him, that I
made him monstrous drunk, and because too much heat was the
cause of his distemper, I stript him stark naked as he lay along
asleep, and borrowed his suit to deliver this counterfeit message in,
leaving a rusty armour and an old brown bill to watch him till my
return: which shall be when I have pawn'd his apparel, and spent
the money perhaps.

Pros. Well, thou art a mad knave, *Musco*, his absence will be a
good subject for more mirth: I pray thee return to thy young
master *Lorenzo*, and will him to meet me and *Hesperida* at the
Friary presently: for here, tell him, the house is so stored with
jealousy, that there is no room for love to stand upright in: but
I'll use such means she shall come thither, and that I think will meet
best with his desires: Hie thee, good *Musco*.

Mus. I go, sir.   [*Exit.*

Enter THORELLO, *to him* PISO.

Tho. Ho, *Piso, Cob*, where are these villains, trow?
Oh, art thou there? *Piso*, hark thee here:
Mark what I say to thee, I must go forth;
Be careful of thy promise, keep good watch,
Note every gallant and observe him well,
That enters in my absence to thy mistress;
If she would shew him rooms, the jest is stale,
Follow them, *Piso*, or else hang on him,
And let him not go after, mark their looks;
Note if she offer but to see his band,
Or any other amorous toy about him,
But praise his leg, or foot, or if she say,
The day is hot, and bid him feel her hand,
How hot it is, oh, that's a monstrous thing:
Note me all this, sweet *Piso;* mark their sighs,
And if they do but whisper, break them off,
I'll bear thee out in it: wilt thou do this?
Wilt thou be true, sweet *Piso?*

Pis. Most true, sir.

Tho. Thanks, gentle *Piso:* where is *Cob?* now: *Cob?*
        [*Exit Thorello.*

Bia. He's ever calling for *Cob*, I wonder how he employs *Cob* so.

Pros. Indeed, sister, to ask how he employs *Cob* is a necessary
question for you that are his wife, and a thing not very easy for
you to be satisfied in: but this I'll assure you, *Cob's* wife is an
excellent bawd indeed, and oftentimes your husband haunts her
house, marry, to what end I cannot altogether accuse him, imagine
you what you think convenient: but I have known fair hides have
foul hearts ere now, I can tell you.

Bia. Never said you truer than that, brother! *Piso*, fetch your cloke, and go with me, I'll after him presently: I would to Christ I could take him there, i'faith.   [*Exeunt Piso and Biancha.*

Pros. So let them go: this may make sport anon, now, my fair sister *Hesperida:* ah, that you knew how happy a thing it were to be fair and beautiful!

Hes. That toucheth not me, brother.

Pros. That's true: that's even the fault of it, for indeed beauty stands a woman in no stead, unless it procure her touching: but, sister, whether it touch you or no, it touches your beauties, and I am sure they will abide the touch, an they do not, a plague of all ceruse, say I! and it touches me too in part, though not in thee. Well, there's a dear and respected friend of mine, sister, stands very strongly affected towards you, and hath vowed to inflame whole bonfires of zeal in his heart, in honour of your perfections.   I have already engaged my promise to bring you where you shall hear him confirm much more than I am able to lay down for him: Signior *Lorenzo* is the man: what say you, sister; shall I intreat so much favour of you for my friend, as to direct and attend you to his meeting? upon my soul, he loves you extremely, approve it, sweet *Hesperida*, will you?

Hes. Faith, I had very little confidence in mine own constancy, if I durst not meet a man: but, brother *Prospero*, this motion of yours savours of an old knight adventurer's servant, methinks.

Pros. What's that, sister?

Hes. Marry, of the squire.

Pros. No matter, *Hesperida*, if it did, I would be such an one for my friend, but say, will you go?

Hes. Brother, I will, and bless my happy stars.

Enter CLEMENT *and* THORELLO.

Clem. Why, what villainy is this? my man gone on a false message, and run away when he has done, why, what trick is there in it, trow? 1, 2, 3, 4, and 5.

Tho. How! is my wife gone forth, where is she, sister?

Hes. She's gone abroad with *Piso*.

Tho. Abroad with *Piso*? Oh, that villain dors me,
He hath discovered all unto my wife,
Beast that I was to trust him: whither went she?

Hes. I know not, sir.

Pros. I'll tell you, brother, whither I suspect she's gone.

Tho. Whither, for God's sake?

Pros. To *Cob's* house, I believe: but keep my counsel.

Tho. I will, I will, to *Cob's* house? doth she haunt *Cob's*?
She's gone a purpose now to cuckold me,
With that lewd rascal, who to win her favour,
Hath told her all.   [*Exit.*

Clem. But did your mistress see my man bring him a message?

Pros. That we did, master Doctor.

Clem. And whither went the knave?

Pros. To the tavern, I think, sir.

Clem. What, did *Thorello* give him any thing to spend for the message he brought him? if he did I should commend my man's wit exceedingly if he would make himself drunk with the joy of it, farewell, lady, keep good rule, you two, I beseech you now: by God's—; marry, my man makes me laugh. [*Exit.*

Pros. What a mad doctor is this! come, sister, let's away.
[*Exeunt.*

Enter MATHEO *and* BOBADILLA.

Mat. I wonder, Signior, what they will say of my going away, ha?

Bob. Why, what should they say? but as of a discreet gentleman. Quick, wary, respectful of natures,
Fair lineaments, and that's all.

Mat. Why so, but what can they say of your beating?

Bob. A rude part, a touch with soft wood, a kind of gross battery used, laid on strongly: borne most patiently, and that's all.

Mat. Ay, but would any man have offered it in *Venice?*

Bob. Tut, I assure you no: you shall have there your *Nobilis,* your *Gentilezza,* come in bravely upon your reverse, stand you close, stand you firm, stand you fair, save your retricato with his left leg, come to the assaulto with the right, thrust with brave steel, defy your base wood. But wherefore do I awake this remembrance? I was bewitch'd, by Jesu: but I will be revenged.

Mat. Do you hear, is't not best to get a warrant and have him arrested, and brought before Doctor *Clement?*

Bob. It were not amiss, would we had it. [*Enter* MUSCO.

Mat. Why, here comes his man, let's speak to him.

Bob. Agreed, do you speak.

Mat. God save you, sir.

Mus. With all my heart, sir.

Mat. Sir, there is one *Giuliano* hath abused this gentleman and me, and we determine to make our amends by law, now if you would do us the favour to procure us a warrant, for his arrest, of your master, you shall be well considered, I assure i'faith, sir.

Mus. Sir, you know my service is my living, such favours as these gotten of my master is his only preferment, and therefore you must consider me as I may make benefit of my place.

Mat. How is that?

Mus. Faith, sir, the thing is extraordinary, and the gentleman may be of great account: yet be what he will, if you will lay me down five crowns in my hand, you shall have it, otherwise not.

Mat. How shall we do, Signior? you have no money.

Bob. Not a cross, by Jesu.

Mat. Nor I, before God, but two pence, left of my two shillings in the morning for wine and cakes, let's give him some pawn.

Bob. Pawn? we have none to the value of his demand.

Mat. O Lord, man, I'll pawn this jewel in my ear, and you may pawn your silk stockings, and pull up your boots, they will ne'er be mist.

Bob. Well, an there be no remedy, I'll step aside and put them off.

Mat. Do you hear, sir? we have no store of money at this time, but you shall have good pawns, look you, sir, this jewel and this gentleman's silk stockings, because we would have it dispatch'd ere we went to our chambers.

Mus. I am content, sir, I will get you the warrant presently. What's his name, say you, *Giuliano ?*

Mat. Ay, ay, *Giuliano.*

Mus. What manner of man is he ?

Mat. A tall, big man, sir; he goes in a cloak most commonly of silk russet, laid about with russet lace.

Mus. 'Tis very good, sir.

Mat. Here, sir, here's my jewel.

Bob. And here are stockings.

Mus. Well, gentlemen, I'll procure this warrant presently, and appoint you a varlet of the city to serve it, if you'll be upon the Realto anon, the varlet shall meet you there.

Mat. Very good, sir, I wish no better.   [*Exeunt Boba. and Mat.*

Mus. This is rare, now will I go pawn this cloak of the doctor's man's at the broker's for a varlet's suit, and be the varlet myself, and get either more pawns, or more money of *Giuliano* for my arrest.   [*Exit.*

ACT V

SCENE I.—*Enter* LORENZO *senior.*

Lor. se. Oh, here it is, I am glad I have found it now.
Ho! who is within here?   [*Enter* TIB.

Tib. I am within, sir, what's your pleasure?

Lor. se. To know who is within besides yourself.

Tib. Why, sir, you are no constable, I hope?

Lor. se. Oh, fear you the constable? then I doubt not,
You have some guests within deserve that fear;
I'll fetch him straight.

Tib. O' God's name, sir.

Lor. se. Go to, tell me is not the young *Lorenzo* here?

Tib. Young *Lorenzo*, I saw none such, sir, of mine honesty.

Lor. se. Go to, your honesty flies too lightly from you:
There's no way but fetch the constable.

Tib. The constable, the man is mad, I think. [*Claps to the door.*
Enter PISO *and* BIANCHA.

Piso. Ho, who keeps house here?

Lor. se. Oh, this is the female copes-mate of my son.
Now shall I meet him straight.

Bia. Knock, *Piso,* pray thee.

Pis. Ho, good wife.   [*Enter* TIB.

Tib. Why, what's the matter with you?

Bia. Why, woman, grieves it you to ope your door?
Belike you get something to keep it shut.

Tib. What mean these questions, pray ye?

Bia. So strange you make it! is not *Thorello,* my tried husband, here?

Lor. se. Her husband?

Tib. I hope he needs not be tried here.

Bia. No, dame: he doth it not for need but pleasure.

Tib. Neither for need nor pleasure is he here.

Lor. se. This is but a device to balk me withal; Soft, who's this?   [*Enter* THORELLO.

Bia. Oh, sir, have I forestall'd your honest market?
Found your close walks? you stand amazed now, do you?
I'faith (I am glad) I have smoked you yet at last;
What's your jewel, trow? In: come, let's see her;
Fetch forth your housewife, dame; if she be fairer
In any honest judgment than myself,
I'll be content with it: but she is change,
She feeds you fat; she soothes your appetite,
And you are well: your wife, an honest woman,
Is meat twice sod to you, sir; Oh, you treachour.

Lor. se. She cannot counterfeit this palpably.

Tho. Out on thee, more than strumpet's impudency,
Steal'st thou thus to thy haunts? and have I taken
Thy bawd and thee, and thy companion,
This hoary-headed letcher, this old goat,
Close at your villainy, and would'st thou 'scuse it,
With this stale harlot's jest, accusing me?
Oh, old incontinent, dost thou not shame,
When all thy powers in chastity are spent,
To have a mind so hot? and to entice
And feed the enticements of a lustful woman?

Bia. Out, I defy thee, I, dissembling wretch!

Tho. Defy me, strumpet? ask thy pander here,
Can he deny it? or that wicked elder.

Lor. se. Why, hear you, Signior?

Tho. Tut, tut, never speak,
Thy guilty conscience will discover thee.

Lor. se. What lunacy is this that haunts this man?   [*Enter* GIU.

Giu. Oh, sister, did you see my cloak?

Bia. Not I, I see none.

Giu. God's life, I have lost it then, saw you *Hesperida?*

Tho. Hesperida? is she not at home?

Giu. No, she is gone abroad, and nobody can tell me of it at home.   [*Exit.*

Tho. O heaven! abroad? what light! a harlot too!
Why? why? hark you, hath she, hath she not a brother?
A brother's house to keep, to look unto?
But she must fling abroad, my wife hath spoil'd her,
She takes right after her, she does, she does,
Well, you goody bawd and—   [*Enter* COB.
That make your husband such a hoddy-doddy;
And you, young apple squire, and old cuckold-maker,
I'll have you every one before the Doctor,
Nay, you shall answer it, I charge you go.

Lor. se. Marry, with all my heart, I'll go willingly: how have I wrong'd myself in coming here.

Bia. Go with thee? I'll go with thee to thy shame, I warrant thee.

Cob. Why, what's the matter? what's here to do?

Tho. What, *Cob*, art thou here? oh, I am abused, And in thy house, was never man so wrong'd.

Cob. 'Slid, in my house? who wrong'd you in my house?

Tho. Marry, young lust in old, and old in young here, Thy wife's their bawd, here have I taken them.

Cob. Do you hear? did I not charge you keep your doors shut here, and do you let them lie open for all comers, do you scratch?

         [*Cob beats his wife.*

Lor. se. Friend, have patience; if she have done wrong in this, let her answer it afore the Magistrate.

Cob. Ay, come, you shall go afore the Doctor.

Tib. Nay, I will go, I'll see an you may be allowed to beat your poor wife thus at every cuckoldly knave's pleasure, the devil and the pox take you all for me: why do you not go now?

Tho. A bitter quean, come, we'll have you tamed.   [*Exeunt.*

        Enter Musco *alone.*

Mus. Well, of all my disguises yet, now am I most like myself, being in this varlet's suit, a man of my present profession never counterfeits till he lay hold upon a debtor, and says he rests him, for then he brings him to all manner of unrest. A kind of little kings we are, bearing the diminutive of a mace, made like a young artichoke, that always carries pepper and salt in itself, well, I know not what danger I undergo by this exploit, pray God I come well off.   [*Enter* Bobadilla *and* Matheo.

Mat. See, I think yonder is the varlet.

Bob. Let's go in quest of him.

Mat. God save you, friend, are not you here by the appointment of Doctor *Clement's* man?

Mus. Yes, an't please you, sir; he told me two gentlemen had will'd him to procure an arrest upon one Signior *Giuliano* by a warrant from his master, which I have about me.

Mat. It is honestly done of you both; and see where he comes you must arrest; upon him, for God's sake, before he be 'ware.

Bob. Bear back, *Matheo!*   [*Enter* Stephano.

Mus. Signior *Giuliano*, I arrest you, sir, in the Duke's name.

Step. Signior *Giuliano!* am I Signior *Giuliano?* I am one Signior *Stephano*, I tell you, and you do not well, by God's lid, to arrest me, I tell you truly; I am not in your master's books, I would you should well know; ay, and a plague of God on you for making me afraid thus.

Mus. Why, how are you deceived, gentlemen?

Bob. He wears such a cloak, and that deceived us, But see, here a comes, officer, this is he.   [*Enter* Giuliano.

Giu. Why, how now, signior gull: are you a turn'd filcher of late? come, deliver my cloak.

Step. Your cloak, sir? I bought it even now in the market.

Mus. Signior *Giuliano*, I must arrest you, sir.

Giu. Arrest me, sir, at whose suit?

Mus. At these two gentlemen's.

Giu. I obey thee, varlet; but for these villains—

Mus. Keep the peace, I charge you, sir, in the Duke's name, sir.

Giu. What's the matter, varlet?

Mus. You must go before master Doctor *Clement*, sir, to answer what these gentlemen will object against you, hark you, sir, I will use you kindly.

Mat. We'll be even with you, sir, come, Signior *Bobadilla*, we'll go before and prepare the Doctor: varlet, look to him.

[*Exeunt Bobadilla and Matheo.*

Bob. The varlet is a tall man, by Jesu.

Giu. Away, you rascals, Signior, I shall have my cloak.

Step. Your cloak? I say once again, I bought it, and I'll keep it.

Giu. You will keep it?

Step. Ay, that I will.

Giu. Varlet, stay, here's thy fee, arrest him.

Mus. Signior *Stephano*, I arrest you.

Step. Arrest me! there, take your cloak: I'll none of it.

Giu. Nay, that shall not serve your turn, varlet, bring him away, I'll go with thee now to the Doctor's, and carry him along.

Step. Why, is not here your cloak? what would you have?

Giu. I care not for that.

Mus. I pray you, sir.

Giu. Never talk of it; I will have him answer it.

Mus. Well, sir, then I'll leave you, I'll take this gentleman's word for his appearance, as I have done yours.

Giu. Tut, I'll have no words taken, bring him along to answer it.

Mus. Good sir, I pity the gentleman's case, here's your money again.

Giu. God's bread, tell not me of my money, bring him away, I say.

Mus. I warrant you, he will go with you of himself.

Giu. Yet more ado?

Mus. I have made a fair mash of it.

Step. Must I go?   [*Exeunt.*

Enter Doctor CLEMENT, THORELLO, LORENZO senior, BIANCHA, PISO, TIB, *a Servant or two of the* Doctor's.

Clem. Nay, but stay, stay, give me leave; my chair, sirrah; you, Signior *Lorenzo*, say you went thither to meet your son.

Lor. se. Ay, sir.

Clem. But who directed you thither?

Lor. se. That did my man, sir.

Clem. Where is he?

Lor. se. Nay, I know not now, I left him with your clerk, And appointed him to stay here for me.

Clem. About what time was this?

Lor. se. Marry, between one and two, as I take it.

Clem. So, what time came my man with the message to you, Signior *Thorello ?*

Tho. After two, sir.

Clem. Very good, but, lady, how that you were at *Cob's,* ha ?

Bia. An't please you, sir, I'll tell you: my brother *Prospero* told me that *Cob's* house was a suspected place.

Clem. So it appears, methinks; but on.

Bia. And that my husband used thither daily.

Clem. No matter, so he use himself well.

Bia. True, sir, but you know what grows by such haunts often-times.

Clem. Ay, rank fruits of a jealous brain, lady: but did you find your husband there in that case, as you suspected ?

Tho. I found her there, sir.

Clem. Did you so ? that alters the case; who gave you know-ledge of your wife's being there ?

Tho. Marry, that did my brother *Prospero.*

Clem. How, *Prospero* first tell her, then tell you after ?   Where is *Prospero ?*

Tho. Gone with my sister, sir, I know not whither.

Clem. Why, this is a mere trick, a device; you are gulled in this most grossly: alas, poor wench, wert thou beaten for this ? how now, sirrah, what's the matter ?   [*Enter one of the* Doctor's *men.*

Ser. Sir, there's a gentleman in the court without desires to speak with your worship.

Clem. A gentleman ? what's he ?

Ser. A soldier, sir, he sayeth.

Clem. A soldier ? fetch me my armour, my sword, quickly; a soldier speak with me, why, when, knaves ?—come on, come on, hold my cap there, so; give me my gorget, my sword; stand by, I will end your matters anon; let the soldier enter, now, sir, what have you to say to me ?   [*Enter* BOBADILLA *and* MATHEO.

Bob. By your worship's favour.

Clem. Nay, keep out, sir, I know not your pretence, you send me word, sir, you are a soldier, why, sir, you shall be answered here, here be them have been amongst soldiers.   Sir, your pleasure.

Bob. Faith, sir, so it is: this gentleman and myself have been most violently wronged by one Signior *Giuliano:* a gallant of the city here; and for my own part, I protest, being a man in no sort given to this filthy humour of quarrelling, he hath assaulted me in the way of my peace, despoiled me of mine honour, disarmed me of my weapons, and beaten me in the open streets: when I not so much as once offered to resist him.

Clem. Oh, God's precious, is this the soldier ? here, take my armour quickly, 'twill make him swoon, I fear; he is not fit to look on't that will put up a blow.   [*Enter* Servant.

Mat. An't please your worship, he was bound to the peace.

Clem. Why, an he were, sir, his hands were not bound, were they ?

Ser. There is one of the varlets of the city has brought two gentlemen here upon arrest, sir.

Clem. Bid him come in, set by the picture.

Enter Musco *with* Giuliano *and* Stephano.

Now, sir, what! Signior *Giuliano?* is't you that are arrested at signior freshwater's suit here?

Giu. I'faith, master Doctor, and here's another brought at my suit.

Clem. What are you, sir?

Step. A gentleman, sir; oh, uncle?

Clem. Uncle? who, *Lorenzo?*

Lor. se. Ay, sir.

Step. God's my witness, my uncle, I am wrong'd here monstrously; he chargeth me with stealing of his cloak, and would I might never stir, if I did not find it in the street by chance.

Giu. Oh, did you find it now? you said you bought it erewhile.

Step. And you said I stole it, nay, now my uncle is here I care not.

Clem. Well, let this breathe awhile; you that have cause to complain there, stand forth; had you a warrant for this arrest?

Bob. Ay, an't please your worship.

Clem. Nay, do not speak in passion so, where had you it?

Bob. Of your clerk, sir.

Clem. That's well, an my clerk can make warrants, and my hand not at them; where is the warrant? varlet, have you it?

Mus. No, sir, your worship's man bid me do it for these gentlemen, and he would be my discharge.

Clem. Why, Signior *Giuliano,* are you such a novice to be arrested and never see the warrant?

Giu. Why, sir, he did not arrest me.

Clem. No? how then?

Giu. Marry, sir, he came to me and said he must arrest me, and he would use me kindly, and so forth.

Clem. Oh, God's pity, was it so, sir? he must arrest you. Give me my long sword there; help me off, so; come on, sir varlet, I must cut off your legs, sirrah; nay, stand up, I'll use you kindly; I must cut off your legs, I say.

Mus. Oh, good sir, I beseech you, nay, good master Doctor. Oh, good sir.

Clem. I must do it; there is no remedy;
I must cut off your legs, sirrah.
I must cut off your ears, you rascal, I must do it;
I must cut off your nose, I must cut off your head.

Mus. Oh, for God's sake, good master Doctor.

Clem. Well, rise; how dost thou now? dost thou feel thyself well? hast thou no harm?

Mus. No, I thank God, sir, and your good worship.

Clem. Why so? I said I must cut off thy legs, and I must cut off thy arms, and I must cut off thy head; but I did not do it so: you said you must arrest this gentleman, but you did not arrest him, you knave, you slave, you rogue, do you say you must arrest sirrah? away with him to the jail, I'll teach you a trick for your must.

Mus. Good master Doctor, I beseech you be good to me.

Clem. Marry o' God: away with him, I say.

Mus. Nay, 'sblood, before I go to prison, I'll put on my old brazen face, and disclaim in my vocation: I'll discover, that's flat, an I be committed, it shall be for the committing of more villainies than this, hang me an I lose the least grain of my fame.

Clem. Why? when, knave? by God's marry, I'll clap thee by the heels too.

Mus. Hold, hold, I pray you.

Clem. What's the matter? stay there.

Mus. Faith, sir, afore I go to this house of bondage, I have a case to unfold to your worship: which (that it may appear more plain unto your worship's view) I do thus first of all uncase, and appear in mine own proper nature, servant to this gentleman: and known by the name of *Musco*.

Lor. se. Ha, *Musco!*

Step. Oh, uncle, *Musco* has been with my cousin and I all this day.

Clem. Did not I tell you there was some device?

Mus. Nay, good master Doctor, since I have laid myself thus open to your worship, now stand strong for me, till the progress of my tale be ended, and then if my wit do not deserve your countenance, 'slight, throw it on a dog, and let me go hang myself.

Clem. Body of me, a merry knave, give me a bowl of sack. Signior *Lorenzo*, I bespeak your patience in particular, marry, your ears in general, here, knave, Doctor *Clement* drinks to thee.

Mus. I pledge master Doctor an't were a sea to the bottom.

Clem. Fill his bowl for that, fill his bowl: so, now speak freely.

Mus. Indeed, this is it will make a man speak freely. But to the point, know then that I, *Musco*, (being somewhat more trusted of my master than reason required, and knowing his intent to *Florence*,) did assume the habit of a poor soldier in wants, and minding by some means to intercept his journey in the midway, 'twixt the grange and the city, I encountered him, where begging of him in the most accomplished and true garb, (as they term it) contrary to all expectation, he reclaimed me from that bad course of life; entertained me into his service, employed me in his business, possest me with his secrets, which I no sooner had received, but (seeking my young master, and finding him at this gentleman's house) I revealed all most amply: this done, by the device of Signior *Prospero* and him together, I returned (as the raven did to the ark) to mine old master again, told him he should find his son in what manner he knows, at one *Cob's* house, where indeed he never meant to come; now my master, he to maintain the jest, went thither, and left me with your worship's clerk, who, being of a most fine supple disposition, (as most of your clerks are) proffers me the wine, which I had the grace to accept very easily, and to the tavern we went: there after much ceremony, I made him drunk in kindness, stript him to his shirt, and leaving him in that cool vein, departed, frolick, courtier-like, having obtained a suit: which suit fitting me exceedingly well, I put on, and usurping your man's phrase and action, carried a message to Signior *Thorello* in your name; which message was merely devised but to procure his absence, while Signior *Prospero* might make a conveyance of *Hesperida* to my master.

Clem. Stay, fill me the bowl again, here; 'twere pity of his life would not cherish such a spirit: I drink to thee, fill him wine, why, now do you perceive the trick of it?

Tho. Ay, ay, perceive well we were all abused.

Lor. se. Well, what remedy?

Clem. Where is *Lorenzo* and *Prospero*, canst thou tell?

Mus. Ay, sir, they are at supper at the *Mermaid*, where I left your man.

Clem. Sirrah, go warn them hither presently before me, and if the hour of your fellow's resurrection be come, bring him too. But forward, forward, when thou hast been at *Thorello's*. [*Exit Servant.*

Mus. Marry, sir, coming along the street, these two gentlemen meet me, and very strongly supposing me to be your worship's scribe, entreated me to procure them a warrant for the arrest of Signior *Giuliano*, I promised them, upon some pair of silk stockings or a jewel, or so, to do it, and to get a varlet of the city to serve it, which varlet I appointed should meet them upon the Realto at such an hour, they no sooner gone, but I, in a mere hope of more gain by Signior *Giuliano*, went to one of *Satan's* old ingles, a broker, and there pawned your man's livery for a varlet's suit, which here, with myself, I offer unto your worship's consideration.

Clem. Well, give me thy hand; *Proh. superi ingenium magnum quis noscit Homerum. Illias æternum si latuisset opus?* I admire thee, I honour thee, and if thy master or any man here be angry with thee, I shall suspect his wit while I know him for it: do you hear, Signior *Thorello*, Signior *Lorenzo*, and the rest of my good friends, I pray you let me have peace when they come, I have sent for the two gallants and *Hesperida*, God's marry, I must have you, friends, how now? what noise is there?

Enter Servant, *then* Peto.

Ser. Sir, it is *Peto* is come home.

Clem. Peto, bring him hither, bring him hither, what, how now, signior drunkard, in arms against me, ha? your reason, your reason for this.

Pet. I beseech your worship to pardon me.

Clem. Well, sirrah, tell him I do pardon him.

Pet. Truly, sir, I did happen into bad company by chance, and they cast me in a sleep and stript me of all my clothes.

Clem. Tut, this is not to the purpose touching your armour, what might your armour signify?

Pet. Marry, sir, it hung in the room where they stript me, and I borrowed it of one of the drawers, now in the evening, to come home in, because I was loth to come through the street in my shirt.

Enter LORENZO junior, PROSPERO, HESPERIDA.

Clem. Well, disarm him, but it's no matter, let him stand by: who be these? oh, young gallants; welcome, welcome, and you, lady, nay, never scatter such amazed looks amongst us, *Qui nil potest sperare desperet nihil.*

Pros. Faith, master Doctor, that's even I, my hopes are small, and my despair shall be as little. Brother, sister, brother, what, cloudy, cloudy? *and will no sunshine on these looks appear?* well, since there is such a tempest toward, I'll be the porpoise, I'll dance: wench, be of good cheer, thou hast a cloak for the rain yet, where is he? 'Sheart, how now, the picture of the prodigal, go to, I'll have the calf drest for you at my charges.

Lor. se. Well, son *Lorenzo*, this day's work of yours hath much deceived my hopes, troubled my peace, and stretch'd my patience further than became the spirit of duty.

Clem. Nay, God's pity, Signior *Lorenzo*, you shall urge it no more: come, since you are here, I'll have the disposing of all, but first, Signior *Giuliano*, at my request take your cloak again.

Giu. Well, sir, I am content.

Clem. Stay, now let me see, oh, signior snow-liver, I had almost forgotten him, and your *Genius* there, what, doth he suffer for a good conscience too? doth he bear his cross with patience?

Mus. Nay, they have scarce one cross between them both to bear.

Clem. Why, dost thou know him? what is he? what is he?

Mus. Marry, search his pocket, sir, and he'll shew you he is an author, sir.

Clem. *Dic mihi musa virum:* are you an author, sir? give me leave a little, come on, sir, I'll make verses with you now in honour of the gods and the goddesses for what you dare *extempore;* and now I begin.

> *Mount thee my Phlegon muse, and testify,*
> *How* Saturn *sitting in an ebon cloud,*
> *Disrobed his podex, white as ivory,*
> *And through the welkin thunder'd all aloud.*

There's for you, sir.

Pros. Oh, he writes not in that height of style.

Clem. No: we'll come a step or two lower then.

> *From Catadupa and the banks of Nile,*
> *Where only breeds your monstrous crocodile,*
> *Now are we purposed for to fetch our style.*

Pros. Oh, too far-fetch'd for him still, master Doctor.

Clem. Ay, say you so? let's intreat a sight of his vein then.

Pros. Signior, master Doctor desires to see a sight of your vein, nay, you must not deny him.

Clem. What, all this verse, body of me, he carries a whole realm; a commonwealth of paper in his hose, let's see some of his subjects.

> *Unto the boundless ocean of thy beauty,*
> *Runs this poor river, charg'd with streams of zeal,*

  Returning thee the tribute of my duty:
   Which here my youth, my plaints, my love reveal.

Good! is this your own invention?

 Mat. No, sir, I translated that out of a book, called *Delia.*

 Clem. Oh, but I would see some of your own, some of your own.

 Mat. Sir, here's the beginning of a sonnet I made to my mistress.

 Clem. That, that: who? to *Madonna Hesperida*, is she your mistress?

 Pros. It pleaseth him to call her so, sir.

 Clem. In summer time, when Phœbus' *golden rays.*
You translated this too, did you not?

 Pros. No, this is invention; he found it in a ballad.

 Mat. Faith, sir, I had most of the conceit of it out of a ballad indeed.

 Clem. Conceit, fetch me a couple of torches, sirrah,
I may see the conceit: quickly! it's very dark!

 Giu. Call you this poetry?

 Lor. ju. Poetry? nay, then call blasphemy, religion;
Call devils, angels; and sin, piety:
Let all things be preposterously transchanged.

 Lor. se. Why, how now, son! what, are you startled now?
Hath the brize prick'd you, ha? go to; you see
How abjectly your poetry is rank'd in general opinion.

 Lor. ju. Opinion, O God, let gross opinion sink and be damn'd
As deep as *Barathrum*,
If it may stand with your most wish'd content,
I can refell opinion and approve
The state of poesy, such as it is,
Blessed, eternal, and most truly divine:
Indeed, if you will look on Poesy
As she appears in many, poor and lame,
Patch'd up in remnants and old worn rags,
Half starved for want of her peculiar food:
Sacred invention, then I must confirm
Both your conceit and censure of her merit,
But view her in her glorious ornaments,
Attired in the majesty of art,
Set high in spirit, with the precious taste
Of sweet philosophy, and which is most,
Crown'd with the rich traditions of a soul
That hates to have her dignity profaned
With any relish of an earthly thought:
Oh, then how proud a presence doth she bear.
Then is she like herself, fit to be seen
Of none but grave and consecrated eyes:
Nor is it any blemish to her fame,
That such lean, ignorant, and blasted wits,
Such brainless gulls, should utter their stol'n wares
With such applauses in our vulgar ears:
Or that their slubber'd lines have current pass

From the fat judgments of the multitude,
But that this barren and infected age
Should set no difference 'twixt these empty spirits
And a true poet: than which reverend name
Nothing can more adorn humanity.   [*Enter with torches.*

Clem. Ay, *Lorenzo*, but election is now governed altogether by
the influence of humour, which, instead of those holy flames that
should direct and light the soul to eternity, hurls forth nothing but
smoke and congested vapours, that stifle her up, and bereave her
of all sight and motion.   But she must have store of *hellebore* given
her to purge these gross obstructions: oh, that's well said, give me
thy torch, come, lay this stuff together.   So, give fire! there, see,
see, how our poet's glory shines brighter and brighter, still, still it
increaseth, oh, now it's at the highest, and now it declines as fast:
you may see, gallants, *sic transit gloria mundi.*   Well now, my two
signior outsides, stand forth, and lend me your large ears, to a
sentence, to a sentence: first, you, Signior, shall this night to the
cage, and so shall you, sir, from thence to-morrow morning, you,
Signior, shall be carried to the market cross, and be there bound;
and so shall you, sir, in a large motley coat, with a rod at your
girdle; and you in an old suit of sackcloth, and the ashes of your
papers (save the ashes, sirrah) shall mourn all day, and at night
both together sing some ballad of repentance very piteously, which
you shall make to the tune of *Who list to lead and a soldier's life.*
Sirrah bill-man, embrace you this torch, and light the gentlemen to
their lodgings, and because we tender their safety, you shall watch
them to-night, you are provided for the purpose, away, and look
to your charge with an open eye, sirrah.

Bob. Well, I am arm'd in soul against the worst of fortune.

Mat. Faith, so should I be, an I had slept on it.

Pet. I am arm'd too, but I am not like to sleep on it.

Mus. Oh, how this pleaseth me.   [*Exeunt.*

Clem. Now, Signior *Thorello, Giuliano, Prospero, Biancha.*

Step. And not me, sir.

Clem. Yes, and you, sir: I had lost a sheep an he had not bleated,
I must have you all friends: but first a word with you, young
gallant, and you, lady.

Giu. Well, brother *Prospero*, by this good light that shines here,
I am loth to kindle fresh coals, but an you had come in my walk
within these two hours I had given you that you should not have
clawed off again in haste, by Jesus, I had done it, I am the arrant'st
rogue that ever breathed else, but now beshrew my heart if I
bear you any malice in the earth.

Pros. Faith, I did it but to hold up a jest, and help my sister to
a husband, but, brother *Thorello*, and sister, you have a spice of the
jealous yet, both of you, (in your hose, I mean,) come, do not dwell
upon your anger so much, let's all be smooth foreheaded once again.

Thor. He plays upon my forehead, brother *Giuliano*, I pray you
tell me one thing I shall ask you: is my forehead any thing rougher
than it was wont to be?

Giu. Rougher? your forehead is smooth enough, man.

Tho. Why should he then say, be smooth foreheaded,
Unless he jested at the smoothness of it?
And that may be, for horn is very smooth;
So are my brows, by Jesu, smooth as horn!

Bia. Brother, had he no haunt thither, in good faith?

Pros. No, upon my soul.

Bia. Nay, then, sweet-heart: nay, I pray thee, be not angry, good faith, I'll never suspect thee any more, nay, kiss me, sweet muss.

Tho. Tell me, *Biancha*, do not you play the woman with me.

Bia. What's that, sweet-heart?

Tho. Dissemble.

Bia. Dissemble?

Tho. Nay, do not turn away: but say i'faith was it not a match appointed 'twixt this old gentleman and you?

Bia. A match?

Tho. Nay, if it were not, I do not care: do not weep, I pray thee, sweet *Biancha*, nay, so now! by Jesus, I am not jealous, but resolved I have the faithful'st wife in *Italy*.

> *For this I find, where jealousy is fed,*
> *Horns in the mind are worse than on the head.*
> *See what a drove of horns fly in the air,*
> *Wing'd with my cleansed and my credulous breath:*
> *Watch them, suspicious eyes, watch where they fall,*
> *See, see, on heads that think they have none at all.*
> *Oh, what a plenteous world of this will come,*
> *When air rains horns, all men be sure of some.*

Clem. Why, that's well, come then: what say you, are all agreed? doth none stand out?

Pros. None but this gentleman: to whom in my own person I owe all duty and affection; but most seriously intreat pardon, for whatsoever hath past in these occurrants that might be contrary to his most desired content.

Lor. se. Faith, sir, it is a virtue that pursues
Any save rude and uncomposed spirits,
To make a fair construction, and indeed
Not to stand off, when such respective means
Invite a general content in all.

Clem. Well, then I conjure you all here to put off all discontentment, first, you, Signior *Lorenzo*, your cares; you, and you, your jealousy; you, your anger, and you, your wit, sir; and for a peace-offering, here's one willing to be sacrificed upon this altar: say, do you approve my motion?

Pros. We do, I'll be mouth for all.

Clem. Why, then I wish them all joy, and now, to make our evening happiness more full: this night you shall be all my guests: where we'll enjoy the very spirit of mirth, and carouse to the health of this *heroic* spirit, whom to honour the more I do invest in my own robes, desiring you two, *Giuliano* and *Prospero*, to be his supporters, the train to follow, myself will lead, ushered by my page here with this honourable verse—*Claudite jam rivos pueri sat prata biberunt.*

EVERY MAN OUT OF HIS HUMOUR

TO THE NOBLEST NURSERIES OF HUMANITY AND LIBERTY IN
THE KINGDOM

THE INNS OF COURT

I UNDERSTAND you, Gentlemen, not your houses: and a worthy succession
of you, to all time, as being born the judges of these studies. When I
wrote this poem, I had friendship with divers in your societies; who, as
they were great names in learning, so they were no less examples of living.
Of them, and then, that I say no more, it was not despised. Now that
the printer, by a doubled charge, thinks it worthy a longer life than
commonly the air of such things doth promise, I am careful to put it a
servant to their pleasures, who are the inheritors of the first favour born
it. Yet, I command it lie not in the way of your more noble and useful
studies to the public: for so I shall suffer for it. But when the gown and
cap is off, and the lord of liberty reigns, then, to take it in your hands,
perhaps may make some bencher, tincted with humanity, read and not
repent him.　　　　By your true honourer,　　　　BEN JONSON.

DRAMATIS PERSONÆ

ASPER, *the Presenter.*	SAVIOLINA.
MACILENTE.	SORDIDO.—*His Hind.*
PUNTARVOLO,—*his Lady.*—*Waiting Gent.*— *Huntsman.*— *Servingmen.* —*Dog and Cat.*	FUNGOSO. — *Tailor, Haberdasher, Shoemaker.*
CARLO BUFFONE.	SOGLIARDO.
FASTIDIOUS BRISK,—Cinedo, *his Page.*	SHIFT.—*Rustics.* NOTARY.
DELIRO, FALLACE, —Fido, *their Servant.*—*Musicians.*	CLOVE, ORANGE. — *A Groom. — Drawers.*—*Constable, and Officers.*
	GREX.—CORDATUS—MITIS.

THE CHARACTERS OF THE PERSONS

ASPER, he is of an ingenious and free spirit, eager and constant in reproof,
without fear controlling the world's abuses. One whom no servile hope
of gain, or frosty apprehension of danger, can make to be a parasite, either
to time, place, or opinion.

MACILENTE, a man well parted, a sufficient scholar, and travelled; who,
wanting that place in the world's account which he thinks his merit
capable of, falls into such an envious apoplexy, with which his judgment
is so dazzled and distasted, that he grows violently impatient of any
opposite happiness in another.

PUNTARVOLO, a vain-glorious knight, over-englishing his travels, and
wholly consecrated to singularity; the very Jacob's staff of compliment;
a sir that hath lived to see the revolution of time in most of his apparel.
Of presence good enough, but so palpably affected to his own praise, that
for want of flatterers he commends himself, to the floutage of his own
family. He deals upon returns, and strange performances, resolving, in
despite of public derision, to stick to his own fashion, phrase, and gesture.

CARLO BUFFONE, a public, scurrilous, and profane jester, that more
swift than Circe, with absurd similes, will transform any person into
deformity. A good feast-hound or banquet-beagle, that will scent you
out a supper some three miles off, and swear to his patrons, damn him!
he came in oars, when he was but wafted over in a sculler. A slave that
hath an extraordinary gift in pleasing his palate, and will swill up more
sack at a sitting than would make all the guard a posset. His religion is
railing, and his discourse ribaldry.

FASTIDIOUS BRISK, a neat, spruce, affecting courtier, one that wears clothes well, and in fashion; practiseth by his glass how to salute; speaks good remnants, notwithstanding the base viol and tobacco; swears tersely, and with variety; cares not what lady's favour he belies, or great man's familiarity: a good property to perfume the boot of a coach. He will borrow another man's horse to praise, and backs him as his own. Or, for a need, on foot can post himself into credit with his merchant, only with the gingle of his spur, and the jerk of his wand.

DELIRO, a good doting citizen, who, it is thought, might be of the common-council for his wealth; a fellow sincerely besotted on his own wife, and so wrapt with a conceit of her perfections, that he simply holds himself unworthy of her. And, in that hood-wink'd humour, lives more like a suitor than a husband; standing in as true dread of her displeasure, as when he first made love to her. He doth sacrifice two-pence in juniper to her every morning before she rises, and wakes her with villainous-out-of-tune music, which she out of her contempt (though not out of her judgment) is sure to dislike.

FALLACE, Deliro's wife, and idol; a proud mincing peat, and as perverse as he is officious. She dotes as perfectly upon the courtier, as her husband doth on her, and only wants the face to be dishonest.

SAVIOLINA, a court-lady, whose weightiest praise is a light wit, admired by herself, and one more, her servant Brisk.

SORDIDO, a wretched hob-nailed chuff, whose recreation is reading of almanacks; and felicity, foul weather. One that never pray'd but for a lean dearth, and ever wept in a fat harvest.

FUNGOSO, the son of Sordido, and a student; one that has revelled in his time, and follows the fashion afar off, like a spy. He makes it the whole bent of his endeavours to wring sufficient means from his wretched father, to put him in the courtiers' cut; at which he earnestly aims, but so unluckily, that he still lights short a suit.

SOGLIARDO, an essential clown, brother to Sordido, yet so enamoured of the name of a gentleman, that he will have it, though he buys it. He comes up every term to learn to take tobacco, and see new motions. He is in his kingdom when in company where he may be well laughed at.

SHIFT, a thread-bare shark; one that never was a soldier, yet lives upon lendings. His profession is skeldring and odling, his bank Paul's, and his warehouse Picthatch. Takes up single testons upon oaths, till doomsday. Falls under executions of three shillings, and enters into five-groat bonds. He way-lays the reports of services, and cons them without book, damning himself he came new from them, when all the while he was taking the diet in the bawdy-house, or lay pawned in his chamber for rent and victuals. He is of that admirable and happy memory, that he will salute one for an old acquaintance that he never saw in his life before. He usurps upon cheats, quarrels, and robberies, which he never did, only to get him a name. His chief exercises are, taking the whiff, squiring a cockatrice, and making privy searches for imparters.

CLOVE and ORANGE, an inseparable case of coxcombs, city born; the Gemini, or twins of foppery; that like a pair of wooden foils, are fit for nothing but to be practised upon. Being well flattered they'll lend money, and repent when they have done. Their glory is to invite players, and make suppers. And in company of better rank, to avoid the suspect of insufficiency, will inforce their ignorance most desperately, to set upon the understanding of any thing. Orange is the most humorous of the two, (whose small portion of juice being squeezed out,) Clove serves to stick him with commendations.

CORDATUS, the author's friend; a man inly acquainted with the scope and drift of his plot; of a discreet and understanding judgment; and has the place of a moderator.

MITIS, is a person of no action, and therefore we afford him no character.

THE STAGE. *After the second sounding.*

Enter CORDATUS, ASPER, *and* MITIS.

Cor. *Nay, my dear Asper.*

Mit. *Stay your mind.*

Asp. *Away!*
Who is so patient of this impious world,
That he can check his spirit, or rein his tongue?
Or who hath such a dead unfeeling sense,
That heaven's horrid thunders cannot wake?
To see the earth crack'd with the weight of sin,
Hell gaping under us, and o'er our heads
Black, ravenous ruin, with her sail-stretch'd wings,
Ready to sink us down, and cover us.
Who can behold such prodigies as these,
And have his lips seal'd up? Not I: my soul
Was never ground into such oily colours,
To flatter vice, and daub iniquity:
But, with an armed and resolved hand,
I'll strip the ragged follies of the time
Naked as at their birth—

Cor. *Be not too bold.*

Asp. *You trouble me—and with a whip of steel,*
Print wounding lashes in their iron ribs.
I fear no mood stamp'd in a private brow,
When I am pleased t'unmask a public vice.
I fear no strumpet's drugs, nor ruffian's stab,
Should I detect their hateful luxuries:
No broker's, usurer's, or lawyer's gripe,
Were I disposed to say, they are all corrupt.
I fear no courtier's frown, should I applaud
The easy flexure of his supple hams.
Tut, these are so innate and popular,
That drunken custom would not shame to laugh,
In scorn, at him, that should but dare to tax 'em:
And yet, not one of these, but knows his works,
Knows what damnation is, the devil, and hell;
Yet hourly they persist, grow rank in sin,
Puffing their souls away in perjurous air,
To cherish their extortion, pride, or lusts.

Mit. *Forbear, good Asper; be not like your name.*

Asp. *O, but to such whose faces are all zeal,*
And, with the words of Hercules, invade
Such crimes as these! that will not smell of sin,
But seem as they were made of sanctity!
Religion in their garments, and their hair
Cut shorter than their eye-brows! when the conscience
Is vaster than the ocean, and devours
More wretches than the counters.

Mit. *Gentle Asper,*
Contain your spirits in more stricter bounds,
And be not thus transported with the violence
Of your strong thoughts.

Cor. *Unless your breath had power,*
To melt the world, and mould it new again,
It is in vain to spend it in these moods.

Asp. [*turning to the stage.*] *I not observed this thronged round till now!*
Gracious and kind spectators, you are welcome;
Apollo and the Muses feast your eyes

With graceful objects, and may our Minerva
Answer your hopes, unto their largest strain!
Yet here mistake me not, judicious friends ;
I do not this, to beg your patience,
Or servilely to fawn on your applause,
Like some dry brain, despairing in his merit.
Let me be censured by the austerest brow,
Where I want art or judgment, tax me freely.
Let envious censors, with their broadest eyes,
Look through and through me, I pursue no favour ;
Only vouchsafe me your attentions,
And I will give you music worth your ears.
O, how I hate the monstrousness of time,
Where every servile imitating spirit,
Plagued with an itching leprosy of wit,
In a mere halting fury, strives to fling
His ulcerous body in the Thespian spring,
And straight leaps forth a poet! but as lame
As Vulcan, or the founder of Cripplegate.

    Mit. *In faith this humour will come ill to some,*
You will be thought to be too peremptory.

    Asp. *This humour? good! and why this humour, Mitis?*
Nay, do not turn, but answer.

    Mit. *Answer, what?*

    Asp. *I will not stir your patience, pardon me,*
I urged it for some reasons, and the rather
To give these ignorant well-spoken days
Some taste of their abuse of this word humour.

    Cor. *O, do not let your purpose fall, good Asper ;*
It cannot but arrive most acceptable,
Chiefly to such as have the happiness
Daily to see how the poor innocent word
Is rack'd and tortured.

    Mit. *Ay, I pray you proceed.*

    Asp. *Ha, what? what is't?*

    Cor. *For the abuse of humour.*

    Asp. *O, I crave pardon, I had lost my thoughts.*
Why, humour, as 'tis ens, we thus define it,
To be a quality of air, or water,
And in itself holds these two properties,
Moisture and fluxure : as, for demonstration,
Pour water on this floor, 'twill wet and run :
Likewise the air, forced through a horn or trumpet,
Flows instantly away, and leaves behind
A kind of dew ; and hence we do conclude,
That whatsoe'er hath fluxure and humidity,
As wanting power to contain itself,
Is humour. So in every human body,
The choler, melancholy, phlegm, and blood,
By reason that they flow continually
In some one part, and are not continent,
Receive the name of humours. Now thus far
It may, by metaphor, apply itself
Unto the general disposition :
As when some one peculiar quality
Doth so possess a man, that it doth draw
All his affects, his spirits, and his powers,
In their confluctions, all to run one way,
This may be truly said to be a humour.

But that a rook, by wearing a pyed feather,
The cable hat-band, or the three-piled ruff,
A yard of shoe-tye, or the Switzer's knot
On his French garters, should affect a humour!
O, it is more than most ridiculous.
  Cor. *He speaks pure truth; now if an idiot*
Have but an apish or fantastic strain,
It is his humour.
  Asp. *Well, I will scourge those apes,*
And to these courteous eyes oppose a mirror,
As large as is the stage whereon we act;
Where they shall see the time's deformity
Anatomised in every nerve, and sinew,
With constant courage, and contempt of fear.
  Mit. *Asper, (I urge it as your friend,) take heed,*
The days are dangerous, full of exception,
And men are grown impatient of reproof.
  Asp. *Ha, ha!*
You might as well have told me, yond' is heaven,
This earth, these men, and all had moved alike.—
Do not I know the time's condition?
Yes, Mitis, and their souls; and who they be
That either will or can except against me.
None but a sort of fools, so sick in taste,
That they contemn all physic of the mind,
And, like gall'd camels, kick at every touch.
Good men, and virtuous spirits, that loath their vices,
Will cherish my free labours, love my lines,
And with the fervour of their shining grace
Make my brain fruitful, to bring forth more objects,
Worthy their serious and intentive eyes.
But why enforce I this? as fainting? no.
If any here chance to behold himself,
Let him not dare to challenge me of wrong;
For, if he shame to have his follies known,
First he should shame to act 'em: my strict hand
Was made to seize on vice, and with a gripe
Squeeze out the humour of such spongy souls,
As lick up every idle vanity.
  Cor. *Why, this is right furor poeticus!*
Kind gentlemen, we hope your patience
Will yet conceive the best, or entertain
This supposition, that a madman speaks.
  Asp. *What, are you ready there? Mitis, sit down,*
And my Cordatus. Sound ho! and begin.
I leave you two, as censors, to sit here:
Observe what I present, and liberally
Speak your opinions upon every scene,
As it shall pass the view of these spectators.
Nay, now y'are tedious, sirs; for shame begin.
And, Mitis, note me; if in all this front
You can espy a gallant of this mark,
Who, to be thought one of the judicious,
Sits with his arms thus wreath'd, his hat pull'd here,
Cries mew, and nods, then shakes his empty head,
Will shew more several motions in his face
Than the new London, Rome, or Niniveh,
And, now and then, breaks a dry biscuit jest,
Which, that it may more easily be chew'd,

He steeps in his own laughter.
  Cor. *Why, will that*
Make it be sooner swallowed?
  Asp. *O, assure you.*
Or if it did not, yet as Horace sings,
Mean cates are welcome still to hungry guests.
    Cor. *'Tis true; but why should we observe them, Asper?*
  Asp. *O, I would know 'em; for in such assemblies*
They are more infectious than the pestilence:
And therefore I would give them pills to purge,
And make them fit for fair societies.
How monstrous and detested is't to see
A fellow that has neither art nor brain,
Sit like an Aristarchus, or stark ass,
Taking men's lines with a tobacco face,
In snuff still spitting, using his wry'd looks,
In nature of a vice, to wrest and turn
The good aspect of those that shall sit near him,
From what they do behold! O, 'tis most vile.
  Mit. *Nay, Asper.*
  Asp. *Peace, Mitis, I do know your thought;*
You'll say, your guests here will except at this:
Pish! you are too timorous, and full of doubt.
Then he, a patient, shall reject all physic,
'Cause the physician tells him, you are sick:
Or, if I say, that he is vicious,
You will not hear of virtue. Come, you are fond.
Shall I be so extravagant, to think,
That happy judgments, and composed spirits,
Will challenge me for taxing such as these?
I am ashamed.
  Cor. *Nay, but good, pardon us;*
We must not bear this peremptory sail,
But use our best endeavours how to please.
  Asp. *Why, therein I commend your careful thoughts,*
And I will mix with you in industry
To please: but whom? attentive auditors,
Such as will join their profit with their pleasure,
And come to feed their understanding parts:
For these I'll prodigally spend myself,
And speak away my spirit into air;
For these, I'll melt my brain into invention,
Coin new conceits, and hang my richest words
As polish'd jewels in their bounteous ears?
But stay, I lose myself, and wrong their patience:
If I dwell here, they'll not begin, I see.
Friends, sit you still, and entertain this troop
With some familiar and by-conference,
I'll haste them sound. Now, gentlemen, I go
To turn an actor, and a humorist,
Where, ere I do resume my present person,
We hope to make the circles of your eyes
Flow with distilled laughter: if we fail,
We must impute it to this only chance,
Art hath an enemy call'd ignorance.   [Exit.
    Cor. *How do you like his spirit, Mitis?*
    Mit. *I should like it much better, if he were less confident.*
    Cor. *Why, do you suspect his merit?*
    Mit. *No; but I fear this will procure him much envy.*

Cor. O, that sets the stronger seal on his desert: if he had no enemies, I should esteem his fortunes most wretched at this instant.

Mit. You have seen his play, Cordatus: pray you, how is it?

Cor. Faith, sir, I must refrain to judge; only this I can say of it, 'tis strange, and of a particular kind by itself, somewhat like Vetus Comœdia; a work that hath bounteously pleased me; how it will answer the general expectation, I know not.

Mit. Does he observe all the laws of comedy in it?

Cor. What laws mean you?

Mit. Why, the equal division of it into acts and scenes, according to the Terentian manner; his true number of actors; the furnishing of the scene with Grex or Chorus, and that the whole argument fall within compass of a day's business.

Cor. O no, these are too nice observations.

Mit. They are such as must be received, by your favour, or it cannot be authentic.

Cor. Troth, I can discern no such necessity.

Mit. No!

Cor. No, I assure you, signior. If those laws you speak of had been delivered us ab initio, and in their present virtue and perfection, there had been some reason of obeying their powers; but 'tis extant, that that which we call Comœdia, was at first nothing but a simple and continued song, sung by one only person, till Susario invented a second; after him, Epicharmus a third; Phormus and Chionides devised to have four actors, with a prologue and chorus; to which Cratinus, long after, added a fifth and sixth: Eupolis, more; Aristophanes, more than they; every man in the dignity of his spirit and judgment supplied something. And, though that in him this kind of poem appeared absolute, and fully perfected, yet how is the face of it changed since, in Menander, Philemon, Cecilius, Plautus, and the rest! who have utterly excluded the chorus, altered the property of the persons, their names, and natures, and augmented it with all liberty, according to the elegancy and disposition of those times wherein they wrote. I see not then, but we should enjoy the same license, or free power to illustrate and heighten our invention, as they did; and not be tied to those strict and regular forms which the niceness of a few, who are nothing but form, would thrust upon us.

Mit. Well, we will not dispute of this now; but what's his scene?

Cor. Marry, Insula Fortunata, sir.

Mit. O, the Fortunate Island: mass, he has bound himself to a strict law there.

Cor. Why so?

Mit. He cannot lightly alter the scene, without crossing the seas.

Cor. He needs not, having a whole island to run through, I think.

Mit. No! how comes it then, that in some one play we see so many seas, countries, and kingdoms, passed over with such admirable dexterity?

Cor. O, that but shews how well the authors can travel in their vocation, and outrun the apprehension of their auditory. But, leaving this, I would they would begin at once: this protraction is able to sour the best-settled patience in the theatre. [*The third sounding.*

Mit. They have answered your wish, sir; they sound.

Cor. O, here comes the Prologue.

Enter Prologue.

Now, sir, if you had staid a little longer, I meant to have spoke your prologue for you, i'faith.

Prol. Marry, with all my heart, sir, you shall do it yet, and I thank you.
[*Going.*

Cor. Nay, nay, stay, stay; hear you?

Prol. You could not have studied to have done me a greater benefit at the instant; for I protest to you, I am unperfect, and, had I spoke it, I must of necessity have been out.

Cor. *Why, but do you speak this seriously?*

Prol. *Seriously! ay, wit's my help, do I; and esteem myself indebted to your kindness for it.*

Cor. *For what?*

Prol. *Why, for undertaking the prologue for me.*

Cor. *How! did I undertake it for you?*

Prol. *Did you! I appeal to all these gentlemen, whether you did or no. Come, come, it pleases you to cast a strange look on't now; but 'twill not serve.*

Cor. *'Fore me, but it must serve; and therefore speak your prologue.*

Prol. *An I do, let me die poisoned with some venomous hiss, and never live to look as high as the two-penny room again.* [*Exit.*

Mit. *He has put you to it, sir.*

Cor. *'Sdeath, what a humorous fellow is this! Gentlemen, good faith I can speak no prologue, howsoever his weak wit has had the fortune to make this strong use of me here before you: but I protest—*

Enter CARLO BUFFONE, followed by a Boy with wine.

Car. *Come, come, leave these fustian protestations; away, come, I cannot abide these grey-headed ceremonies. Boy, fetch me a glass quickly, I may bid these gentlemen welcome; give them a health here.* [*Exit Boy.*] *I mar'le whose wit it was to put a prologue in yond' sackbut's mouth; they might well think he'd be out of tune, and yet you'd play upon him too.*

Cor. *Hang him, dull block!*

Car. *O, good words, good words; a well-timber'd fellow, he would have made a good column, an he had been thought on, when the house was a building—*

Re-enter Boy with glasses.

O, art thou come? Well said; give me, boy; fill so! Here's a cup of wine sparkles like a diamond. Gentlewomen (I am sworn to put them in first) and gentlemen, around, in place of a bad prologue, I drink this good draught to your health here, Canary, the very elixir and spirit of wine. [*Drinks.*] *This is that our poet calls Castalian liquor, when he comes abroad now and then, once in a fortnight, and makes a good meal among players, where he has* caninum appetitum; *marry, at home he keeps a good philosophical diet, beans and butter-milk; an honest pure rogue, he will take you off three, four, five of these, one after another, and look villainously when he has done, like a one-headed Cerberus.—He does not hear me, I hope.—And then, when his belly is well ballaced, and his brain rigged a little, he sails away withal, as though he would work wonders when he comes home. He has made a play here, and he calls it,* Every Man out of his Humour: *but an he get me out of the humour he has put me in, I'll trust none of his tribe again while I live. Gentles, all I can say for him is, you are welcome. I could wish my bottle here amongst you; but there's an old rule, No pledging your own health. Marry, if any here be thirsty for it, their best way (that I know) is, sit still, seal up their lips, and drink so much of the play in at their ears.* [*Exit.*

Mit. *What may this fellow be, Cordatus?*

Cor. *Faith, if the time will suffer his description, I'll give it you. He is one, the author calls him Carlo Buffone, an impudent common jester, a violent railer, and an incomprehensible epicure; one whose company is desired of all men, but beloved of none; he will sooner lose his soul than a jest, and profane even the most holy things, to excite laughter: no honourable or reverend personage whatsoever can come within the reach of his eye, but is turned into all manner of variety, by his adulterate similes.*

Mit. *You paint forth a monster.*

Cor. *He will prefer all countries before his native, and thinks he can never sufficiently, or with admiration enough, deliver his affectionate conceit of foreign atheistical policies. But stay—*

Enter MACILENTE.

Observe these: he'll appear himself anon.

Mit. *O, this is your envious man, Macilente, I think.*

Cor. *The same, sir.*

ACT I

SCENE I.—*The Country.*

Enter MACILENTE, *with a book.*

Maci. Viri est, fortunæ cœcitatem facilè ferre.
'Tis true; but, Stoic, where, in the vast world,
Doth that man breathe, that can so much command
His blood and his affection? Well, I see
I strive in vain to cure my wounded soul;
For every cordial that my thoughts apply
Turns to a corsive and doth eat it farther.
There is no taste in this philosophy;
'Tis like a potion that a man should drink,
But turns his stomach with the sight of it.
I am no such pill'd Cynick to believe,
That beggary is the only happiness;
Or with a number of these patient fools,
To sing: *My mind to me a kingdom is,*
When the lank hungry belly barks for food,
I look into the world, and there I meet
With objects, that do strike my blood-shot eyes
Into my brain: where, when I view myself,
Having before observ'd this man is great,
Mighty and fear'd; that lov'd and highly favour'd:
A third thought wise and learn'd; a fourth rich,
And therefore honour'd; a fifth rarely featur'd;
A sixth admired for his nuptial fortunes:
When I see these, I say, and view myself,
I wish the organs of my sight were crack'd;
And that the engine of my grief could cast
Mine eyeballs, like two globes of wildfire, forth,
To melt this unproportion'd frame of nature.
Oh, they are thoughts that have transfix'd my heart,
And often, in the strength of apprehension,
Made my cold passion stand upon my face,
Like drops of dew on a stiff cake of ice.

Cor. *This alludes well to that of the poet,*
          Invidus suspirat, gemit, incutitque dentes,
          Sudat frigidus, intuens quod odit.
Mit. *O, peace, you break the scene.*

          Enter SOGLIARDO *and* CARLO BUFFONE.
Maci. Soft, who be these?
I'll lay me down awhile till they be past.   [*Lies down.*

Cor. *Signior, note this gallant, I pray you.*
Mit. *What is he?*
Cor. *A tame rook, you'll take him presently; list.*

Sog. Nay, look you, Carlo; this is my humour now! I have land and money, my friends left me well, and I will be a gentleman whatsoever it cost me.

Car. A most gentlemanlike resolution.

Sog. Tut! an I take an humour of a thing once, I am like your tailor's needle, I go through: but, for my name, signior, how think you? will it not serve for a gentleman's name, when the signior is put to it, ha?

Car. Let me hear; how is it?

Sog. Signior Insulso Sogliardo: methinks it sounds well.

Car. O excellent! tut! an all fitted to your name, you might very well stand for a gentleman: I know many Sogliardos gentlemen.

Sog. Why, and for my wealth I might be a justice of peace.

Car. Ay, and a constable for your wit.

Sog. All this is my lordship you see here, and those farms you came by.

Car. Good steps to gentility too, marry: but, Sogliardo, if you affect to be a gentleman indeed, you must observe all the rare qualities, humours, and compliments of a gentleman.

Sog. I know it, signior, and if you please to instruct, I am not too good to learn, I'll assure you.

Car. Enough, sir.—I'll make admirable use in the projection of my medicine upon this lump of copper here. [*Aside.*]—I'll bethink me for you, sir.

Sog. Signior, I will both pay you, and pray you, and thank you, and think on you.

Cor. *Is this not purely good?*

Maci. S'blood, why should such a prick-ear'd hind as this
Be rich, ha? a fool! such a transparent gull
That may be seen through! wherefore should he have land,
Houses, and lordships? O, I could eat my entrails,
And sink my soul into the earth with sorrow.

Car. First, to be an accomplished gentleman, that is, a gentleman of the time, you must give over housekeeping in the country, and live altogether in the city amongst gallants: where, at your first appearance, 'twere good you turn'd four or five hundred acres of your best land into two or three trunks of apparel—you may do it without going to a conjurer—and be sure you mix yourself still with such as flourish in the spring of the fashion, and are least popular; study their carriage and behaviour in all; learn to play at primero and passage, and ever (when you lose) have two or three peculiar oaths to swear by, that no man else swears: but, above all, protest in your play, and affirm, *Upon your credit, As you are a true gentleman,* at every cast; you may do it with a safe conscience, I warrant you.

Sog. O admirable rare! he cannot choose but be a gentleman that has these excellent gifts: more, more, I beseech you.

Car. You must endeavour to feed cleanly at your ordinary, sit melancholy, and pick your teeth when you cannot speak: and when you come to plays, be humorous, look with a good starch'd face, and ruffle your brow like a new boot, laugh at nothing but your own jests, or else as the noblemen laugh. That's a special grace you must observe.

Sog. I warrant you, sir.

Car. Ay, and sit on the stage and flout, provided you have a good suit.

Sog. O, I'll have a suit only for that, sir.

Car. You must talk much of your kindred and allies.

Sog. Lies! no, signior, I shall not need to do so, I have kindred in the city to talk of: I have a niece is a merchant's wife; and a nephew, my brother Sordido's son, of the Inns of court.

Car. O, but you must pretend alliance with courtiers and great persons: and ever when you are to dine or sup in any strange presence, hire a fellow with a great chain, (though it be copper, it's no matter,) to bring you letters, feign'd from such a nobleman, or such a knight, or such a lady, *To their worshipful, right rare, and nobly qualified friend and kinsman, signior Insulso Sogliardo :* give yourself style enough. And there, while you intend circumstances of news, or enquiry of their health, or so, one of your familiars, whom you must carry about you still, breaks it up, as 'twere in a jest, and reads it publicly at the table: at which you must seem to take as unpardonable offence, as if he had torn your mistress's colours, or breath'd upon her picture, and pursue it with that hot grace, as if you would advance a challenge upon it presently.

Sog. Stay, I do not like that humour of challenge, it may be accepted; but I'll tell you what's my humour now, I will do this: I will take occasion of sending one of my suits to the tailor's, to have the pocket repaired, or so; and there such a letter as you talk of, broke open and all shall be left; O, the tailor will presently give out what I am, upon the reading of it, worth twenty of your gallants.

Car. But then you must put on an extreme face of discontentment at your man's negligence.

Sog. O, so I will, and beat him too: I'll have a man for the purpose.

Mac. You may; you have land and crowns: O partial fate!

Car. Mass, well remember'd, you must keep your men gallant at the first, fine pied liveries laid with good gold lace; there's no loss in it, they may rip it off and pawn it when they lack victuals.

Sog. By 'r Lady, that is chargeable, signior, 'twill bring a man in debt.

Car. Debt! why that's the more for your credit, sir: it's an excellent policy to owe much in these days, if you note it.

Sog. As how, good signior? I would fain be a politician.

Car. O! look where you are indebted any great sum, your creditor observes you with no less regard, than if he were bound to you for some huge benefit, and will quake to give you the least cause of offence, lest he lose his money. I assure you, in these times, no man has his servant more obsequious and pliant, than gentlemen their creditors: to whom, if at any time you pay but a moiety, or a fourth part, it comes more acceptably than if you gave them a new-year's gift.

Sog. I perceive you, sir: I will take up, and bring myself in credit, sure.

Car. Marry this, always beware you commerce not with bankrupts, or poor needy Ludgathians; they are impudent creatures, turbulent spirits, they care not what violent tragedies they stir, nor how they play fast and loose with a poor gentleman's fortunes, to get their own. Marry, these rich fellows that have the world, or the better part of it, sleeping in their counting-houses, they are ten times more placable, they; either fear, hope, or modesty, restrains them from offering any outrages: but this is nothing to your followers, you shall not run a penny more in arrearage for them, an you list, yourself.

Sog. No! how should I keep 'em then?

Car. Keep 'em! 'sblood, let them keep themselves, they are no sheep, are they? what, you shall come in houses, where plate, apparel, jewels, and divers other pretty commodities lie negligently scattered, and I would have those Mercuries follow me, I trow, should remember they had not their fingers for nothing.

Sog. That's not so good, methinks.

Car. Why, after you have kept them a fortnight, or so, and shew'd them enough to the world, you may turn them away, and keep no more but a boy, it's enough.

Sog. Nay, my humour is not for boys, I'll keep men, an I keep any; and I'll give coats, that's my humour: but I lack a cullisen.

Car. Why, now you ride to the city, you may buy one; I'll bring you where you shall have your choice for money.

Sog. Can you, sir?

Car. O, ay: you shall have one take measure of you, and make you a coat of arms to fit you, of what fashion you will.

Sog. By word of mouth, I thank you, signior; I'll be once a little prodigal in a humour, i'faith, and have a most prodigious coat.

Mac. Torment and death! break head and brain at once,
To be deliver'd of your fighting issue.
Who can endure to see blind Fortune dote thus?
To be enamour'd on this dusty turf,
This clod, a whoreson puck-fist! O G——!
I could run wild with grief now, to behold
The rankness of her bounties, that doth breed
Such bulrushes; these mushroom gentlemen,
That shoot up in a night to place and worship.

Car. [*seeing Macilente.*] Let him alone; some stray, some stray.

Sog. Nay, I will examine him before I go, sure.

Car. The lord of the soil has all wefts and strays here, has he not?

Sog. Yes, sir.

Car. Faith then I pity the poor fellow, he's fallen into a fool's hands.   [*Aside.*

Sog. Sirrah, who gave you a commission to lie in my lordship?

Mac. Your lordship!

Sog. How! my lordship? do you know me, sir?

Mac. I do know you, sir.

Car. He answers him like an echo.   [*Aside.*

Sog. Why, Who am I, sir?

Mac. One of those that fortune favours.

Car. The periphrasis of a fool. I'll observe this better. [*Aside.*

Sog. That fortune favours! how mean you that, friend?

Mac. I mean simply: that you are one that lives not by your wits.

Sog. By my wits! no, sir, I scorn to live by my wits, I. I have better means, I tell thee, than to take such base courses, as to live by my wits. What, dost thou think I live by my wits?

Mac. Methinks, jester, you should not relish this well.

Car. Ha! does he know me?

Mac. Though yours be the worst use a man can put his wit to, of thousands, to prostitute it at every tavern and ordinary; yet, methinks, you should have turn'd your broadside at this, and have been ready with an apology, able to sink this hulk of ignorance into the bottom and depth of his contempt.

Car. Oh, 'tis Macilente! Signior, you are well encountered; how is it? O, we must not regard what he says, man, a trout, a shallow fool, he has no more brain than a butterfly, a mere stuft suit; he looks like a musty bottle new wicker'd, his head's the cork, light, light! [*Aside to Macilente.*]—I am glad to see you so well return'd, signior.

Mac. You are! gramercy, good Janus.

Sog. Is he one of your acquaintance? I love him the better for that.

Car. Od's precious, come away, man, what do you mean? an you knew him as I do, you'd shun him as you would do the plague.

Sog. Why, sir?

Car. O, he's a black fellow, take heed of him.

Sog. Is he a scholar, or a soldier?

Car. Both, both; a lean mongrel, he looks as if he were chopfallen, with barking at other men's good fortunes: 'ware how you offend him; he carries oil and fire in his pen, will scald where it drops: his spirit is like powder, quick, violent; he'll blow a man up with a jest: I fear him worse than a rotten wall does the cannon; shake an hour after at the report. Away, come not near him.

Sog. For God's sake let's be gone; an he be a scholar, you know I cannot abide him; I had as lieve see a cockatrice, specially as cockatrices go now.

Car. What, you'll stay, signior? this gentleman Sogliardo, and I, are to visit the knight Puntarvolo, and from thence to the city; we shall meet there.   [*Exit with Sogliardo.*

Mac. Ay, when I cannot shun you, we will meet.
'Tis strange! of all the creatures I have seen,

I envy not this Buffone, for indeed
Neither his fortunes nor his parts deserve it:
But I do hate him, as I hate the devil,
Or that brass-visaged monster Barbarism.
O, 'tis an open-throated, black-mouth'd cur,
That bites at all, but eats on those that feed him.
A slave, that to your face will, serpent-like,
Creep on the ground, as he would eat the dust,
And to your back will turn the tail, and sting
More deadly than the scorpion: stay, who's this?
Now, for my soul, another minion
Of the old lady Chance's! I'll observe him.

Enter SORDIDO *with an Almanack in his hand.*

Sord. O rare! good, good, good, good, good!
I thank my stars, I thank my stars for it.
Mac. Said I not true? doth not his passion speak
Out of my divination? O my senses,
Why lose you not your powers, and become
Dull'd, if not deaded, with this spectacle?
I know him, it is Sordido, the farmer,
A boor, and brother to that swine was here.   [*Aside.*
Sord. Excellent, excellent, excellent! as I would wish, as I
would wish.
Mac. See how the strumpet fortune tickles him,
And makes him swoon with laughter, O, O, O!
Sord. Ha, ha, ha! I will not sow my grounds this year.   Let me
see, what harvest shall we have?   *June, July?*
Mac. What, is't a prognostication raps him so?
Sord. The 20, 21, 22 *days, rain and wind.* O good, good! *the* 23,
and 24, *rain and some wind,* good! *the* 25, *rain,* good still! 26, 27,
28, *wind and some rain;* would it had been rain and some wind!
well, 'tis good, when it can be no better.   29, *inclining to rain:*
inclining to rain! that's not so good now: 30, *and* 31, *wind and no
rain:* no rain! 'slid, stay: this is worse and worse: What says he
of St. Swithin's? turn back, look, *saint Swithin's: no rain!*
Mac. O, here's a precious, dirty, damned rogue,
That fats himself with expectation
Of rotten weather, and unseason'd hours;
And he is rich for it, an elder brother!
His barns are full, his ricks and mows well trod,
His garners crack with store! O, 'tis well; ha, ha, ha!
A plague consume thee, and thy house!
Sord. O here, *St. Swithin's,* the 15 *day, variable weather, for the
most part rain,* good! *for the most part rain:* why, it should rain
forty days after, now, more or less, it was a rule held, afore I was
able to hold a plough, and yet here are two days no rain; ha! it
makes me muse.   We'll see how the next month begins, if that be
better.   August 1, 2, 3, *and* 4, *days, rainy and blustering:* this is well

now: 5, 6, 7, 8, *and* 9, *rainy, with some thunder ;* Ay marry, this is
excellent; the other was false printed sure: *the* 10 *and* 11, *great
store of rain ;* O good, good, good, good, good! *the* 12, 13, *and* 14
days, rain ; good still: 15, *and* 16, *rain ;* good still: 17 *and* 18, *rain,*
good still: 19 *and* 20, good still, good still, good still, good still, good
still! 21, *some rain ;* some rain! well, we must be patient, and attend
the heaven's pleasure, would it were more though: *the* 22, 23, *great
tempests of rain, thunder and lightning.*
O good again, past expectation good!
I thank my blessed angel; never, never
Laid I [a] penny better out than this,
To purchase this dear book: not dear for price,
And yet of me as dearly prized as life,
Since in it is contain'd the very life,
Blood, strength, and sinews, of my happiness.
Blest be the hour wherein I bought this book;
His studies happy that composed the book,
And the man fortunate that sold the book!
Sleep with this charm, and be as true to me,
As I am joy'd and confident in thee.   *[Puts it up.*

Enter a Hind, *and gives* Sordido *a paper to read.*

  Mac. Ha, ha, ha!
Is not this good ? Is it not pleasing this ?
Ha, ha, ha! God pardon me! ha, ha!
Is't possible that such a spacious villain
Should live, and not be plagued ? or lies he hid
Within the wrinkled bosom of the world,
Where Heaven cannot see him ? S'blood! methinks
'Tis rare, and strange, that he should breathe and walk,
Feed with digestion, sleep, enjoy his health,
And, like a boisterous whale swallowing the poor,
Still swim in wealth and pleasure! is't not strange ?
Unless his house and skin were thunder proof,
I wonder at it! Methinks, now, the hectic,
Gout, leprosy, or some such loath'd disease,
Might light upon him; or that fire from heaven
Might fall upon his barns; or mice and rats
Eat up his grain; or else that it might rot
Within the hoary ricks, even as it stands:
Methinks this might be well; and after all
The devil might come and fetch him.   Ay, 'tis true!
Meantime he surfeits in prosperity,
And thou, in envy of him, gnaw'st thyself:
Peace, fool, get hence, and tell thy vexed spirit,
Wealth in this age will scarcely look on merit.   *[Rises and exit.*
  Sord. Who brought this same, sirrah ?
  Hind. Marry, sir, one of the justice's men; he says 'tis a precept,
and all their hands be at it.

   Sord. Ay, and the prints of them stick in my flesh,
Deeper than in their letters: they have sent me
Pills wrapt in paper here, that, should I take them,
Would poison all the sweetness of my book,
And turn my honey into hemlock-juice.
But I am wiser than to serve their precepts,
Or follow their prescriptions. Here's a device,
To charge me bring my grain unto the markets:
Ay, much! when I have neither barn nor garner,
Nor earth to hide it in, I'll bring 't; till then,
Each corn I send shall be as big as Paul's.
O, but (say some) the poor are like to starve.
Why, let 'em starve, what's that to me? are bees
Bound to keep life in drones and idle moths? no:
Why such are these that term themselves the poor,
Only because they would be pitied,
But are indeed a sort of lazy beggars,
Licentious rogues, and sturdy vagabonds,
Bred by the sloth of a fat plenteous year,
Like snakes in heat of summer, out of dung;
And this is all that these cheap times are good for:
Whereas a wholesome and penurious dearth
Purges the soil of such vile excrements,
And kills the vipers up.
   Hind. O, but master,
Take heed they hear you not.
   Sord. Why so?
   Hind. They will exclaim against you.
   Sord. Ay, their exclaims
Move me as much, as thy breath moves a mountain.
Poor worms, they hiss at me, whilst I at home
Can be contented to applaud myself,
To sit and clap my hands, and laugh, and leap,
Knocking my head against my roof, with joy
To see how plump my bags are, and my barns.
Sirrah, go hie you home, and bid your fellows
Get all their flails ready again I come.
   Hind. I will, sir.   *[Exit.*
   Sord. I'll instantly set all my hinds to thrashing
Of a whole rick of corn, which I will hide
Under the ground; and with the straw thereof
I'll stuff the outsides of my other mows:
That done, I'll have them empty all my garners,
And in the friendly earth bury my store,
That, when the searchers come, they may suppose
All's spent, and that my fortunes were belied.
And to lend more opinion to my want,
And stop that many-mouthed vulgar dog,
Which else would still be baying at my door,

Each market-day I will be seen to buy
Part of the purest wheat, as for my household;
Where when it comes, it shall increase my heaps:
'Twill yield me treble gain at this dear time,
Promised in this dear book: I have cast all.
Till then I will not sell an ear, I'll hang first.
O, I shall make my prices as I list;
My house and I can feed on peas and barley.
What though a world of wretches starve the while;
He that will thrive must think no courses vile.   [*Exit.*

Cor. Now, signior, how approve you this? have the humourists exprest themselves truly or no?

Mit. Yes, if it be well prosecuted, 'tis hitherto happy enough: but methinks Macilente went hence too soon; he might have been made to stay, and speak somewhat in reproof of Sordido's wretchedness now at the last.

Cor. O, no, that had been extremely improper; besides, he had continued the scene too long with him, as 'twas, being in no more action.

Mit. You may inforce the length as a necessary reason; but for propriety, the scene would very well have borne it, in my judgment.

Cor. O, worst of both; why, you mistake his humour utterly then.

Mit. How do I mistake it? Is it not envy?

Cor. Yes, but you must understand, signior, he envies him not as he is a villain, a wolf in the commonwealth, but as he is rich and fortunate; for the true condition of envy is, *dolor alienæ felicitatis,* to have our eyes continually fixed upon another man's prosperity that is, his chief happiness, and to grieve at that. Whereas, if we make his monstrous and abhorr'd actions our object, the grief we take then comes nearer the nature of hate than envy, as being bred out of a kind of contempt and loathing in ourselves.

Mit. So you'll infer it had been hate, not envy in him, to reprehend the humour of Sordido?

Cor. Right, for what a man truly envies in another, he could always love and cherish in himself; but no man truly reprehends in another, what he loves in himself; therefore reprehension is out of his hate. And this distinction hath he himself made in a speech there, if you marked it, where he says, I envy not this Buffone, but I hate him.

Mit. Stay, sir: I envy not this Buffone, but I hate him. Why might he not as well have hated Sordido as him?

Cor. No, sir, there was subject for his envy in Sordido, his wealth: so was there not in the other. He stood possest of no one eminent gift, but a most odious and fiend-like disposition, that would turn charity itself into hate, much more envy, for the present.

Mit. You have satisfied me, sir. O, here comes the fool, and the jester again, methinks.

Cor. 'Twere pity they should be parted, sir.

Mit. What bright-shining gallant's that with them? the knight they went to?

Cor. No, sir, this is one monsieur Fastidious Brisk, otherwise called the fresh Frenchified courtier.

Mit. A humourist too?

Cor. As humorous as quicksilver; do but observe him; the scene is the country still, remember.

ACT II

SCENE I.—*The Country; before* PUNTARVOLO'S *House.*

Enter FASTIDIOUS BRISK, CINEDO, CARLO BUFFONE,
and SOGLIARDO.

Fast. Cinedo, watch when the knight comes, and give us word.

Cin. I will, sir.   [*Exit.*

Fast. How lik'st thou my boy, Carlo?

Car. O, well, well. He looks like a colonel of the Pigmies horse, or one of these motions in a great antique clock; he would shew well upon a haberdasher's stall, at a corner shop, rarely.

Fast. 'Sheart, what a damn'd witty rogue's this! How he confounds with his similes!

Car. Better with similes than smiles: and whither were you riding now, signior?

Fast. Who, I? What a silly jest's that! Whither should I ride but to the court?

Car. O, pardon me, sir, twenty places more; your hot-house, or your whore-house—

Fast. By the virtue of my soul, this knight dwells in Elysium here.

Car. He's gone now, I thought he would fly out presently. These be our nimble-spirited catsos, that have their evasions at pleasure, will run over a bog like your wild Irish; no sooner started, but they'll leap from one thing to another, like a squirrel, heigh! dance and do tricks in their discourse, from fire to water, from water to air, from air to earth, as if their tongues did but e'en lick the four elements over, and away.

Fast. Sirrah, Carlo, thou never saw'st my gray hobby yet, didst thou?

Car. No; have you such a one?

Fast. The best in Europe, my good villain, thou'lt say when thou seest him.

Car. But when shall I see him?

Fast. There was a nobleman in the court offered me a hundred pound for him, by this light: a fine little fiery slave, he runs like a—oh, excellent, excellent!—with the very sound of the spur.

Car. How! the sound of the spur?

Fast. O, it's your only humour now extant, sir; a good gingle, a good gingle.

Car. S'blood! you shall see him turn morrice-dancer, he has got him bells, a good suit, and a hobby-horse.

Sog. Signior, now you talk of a hobby-horse, I know where one is will not be given for a brace of angels.

Fast. How is that, sir?

Sog. Marry, sir, I am telling this gentleman of a hobby-horse; it was my father's indeed, and, though I say it—

Car. That should not say it—on, on.

Sog. He did dance in it, with as good humour and as good regard as any man of his degree whatsoever, being no gentleman: I have danc'd in it myself too.

Car. Not since the humour of gentility was upon you, did you?

Sog. Yes, once; marry, that was but to shew what a gentleman might do in a humour.

Car. O, very good.

Mit. *Why, this fellow's discourse were nothing but for the word humour.*

Cor. *O bear with him ; an he should lack matter and words too, 'twere pitiful.*

Sog. Nay, look you, sir, there's ne'er a gentleman in the country has the like humours, for the hobby-horse, as I have; I have the method for the threading of the needle and all, the—

Car. How, the method?

Sog. Ay, the leigerity for that, and the whighhie, and the daggers in the nose, and the travels of the egg from finger to finger, and all the humours incident to the quality. The horse hangs at home in my parlour. I'll keep it for a monument as long as I live, sure.

Car. Do so; and when you die, 'twill be an excellent trophy to hang over your tomb.

Sog. Mass, and I'll have a tomb, now I think on't; 'tis but so much charges.

Car. Best build it in your lifetime then, your heirs may hap to forget it else.

Sog. Nay, I mean so, I'll not trust to them.

Car. No, for heirs and executors are grown damnable careless, 'specially since the ghosts of testators left walking.—How like you him, signior?

Fast. 'Fore heavens, his humour arrides me exceedingly.

Car. Arrides you!

Fast. Ay, pleases me: a pox on't! I am so haunted at the court, and at my lodging, with your refined choice spirits, that it makes me clean of another garb, another sheaf, I know not how! I cannot frame me to your harsh vulgar phrase, 'tis against my genius.

Sog. Signior Carlo!   [*Takes him aside.*

Cor. *This is right to that of Horace,* Dum vitant stulti vitia, in contraria currunt; *so this gallant, labouring to avoid popularity, falls into a habit of affectation, ten thousand times hatefuller than the former.*

Car. [*pointing to Fastidious.*] Who, he? a gull, a fool, no salt in him i' the earth, man; he looks like a fresh salmon kept in a tub;

he'll be spent shortly. His brain's lighter than his feather already, and his tongue more subject to lye, than that is to wag; he sleeps with a musk-cat every night, and walks all day hang'd in pomander chains for penance; he has his skin tann'd in civet, to make his complexion strong, and the sweetness of his youth lasting in the sense of his sweet lady; a good empty puff, he loves you well, signior.

Sog. There shall be no love lost, sir, I'll assure you.

Fast. [*advancing to them.*] Nay, Carlo, I am not happy in thy love, I see: pray thee suffer me to enjoy thy company a little, sweet mischief: by this air, I shall envy this gentleman's place in thy affections, if you be thus private, i'faith.

Enter CINEDO.

How now! Is the knight arrived?

Cin. No, sir, but 'tis guess'd he will arrive presently, by his fore-runners.

Fast. His hounds! by Minerva, an excellent figure; a good boy.

Car. You should give him a French crown for it; the boy would find two better figures in that, and a good figure of your bounty beside.

Fast. Tut, the boy wants no crowns.

Car. No crown; speak in the singular number, and we'll believe you.

Fast. Nay, thou art so capriciously conceited now. Sirrah damnation, I have heard this knight Puntarvolo reported to be a gentleman of exceeding good humour, thou know'st him; prithee, how is his disposition? I never was so favoured of my stars, as to see him yet. Boy, do you look to the hobby?

Cin. Ay, sir, the groom has set him up.

[*As Cinedo is going out, Sogliardo takes him aside.*

Fast. 'Tis well: I rid out of my way of intent to visit him, and take knowledge of his—— Nay, good Wickedness, his humour, his humour.

Car. Why, he loves dogs, and hawks, and his wife well; he has a good riding face, and he can sit a great horse; he will taint a staff well at tilt; when he is mounted he looks like the sign of the George, that's all I know; save, that instead of a dragon, he will brandish against a tree, and break his sword as confidently upon the knotty bark, as the other did upon the scales of the beast.

Fast. O, but this is nothing to that's delivered of him. They say he has dialogues and discourses between his horse, himself, and his dog; and that he will court his own lady, as she were a stranger never encounter'd before.

Car. Ay, that he will, and make fresh love to her every morning; this gentleman has been a spectator of it, Signior Insulso.

Sog. I am resolute to keep a page.—Say you, sir?

[*Leaps from whispering with Cinedo.*

Car. You have seen Signior Puntarvolo accost his lady?

Sog. O, ay, sir.

Fast. And how is the manner of it, prithee, good signior?

Sog. Faith, sir, in very good sort; he has his humours for it, sir; as first, (suppose he were now to come from riding or hunting, or so,) he has his trumpet to sound, and then the waiting-gentlewoman she looks out, and then he speaks, and then she speaks,——very pretty, i'faith, gentlemen.

Fast. Why, but do you remember no particulars, signior?

Sog. O, yes, sir, first, the gentlewoman, she looks out at the window.

Car. After the trumpet has summon'd a parle, not before?

Sog. No, sir, not before; and then says he,—ha, ha, ha, ha!

Car. What says he? be not rapt so.

Sog. Says he,—ha, ha, ha, ha!

Fast. Nay, speak, speak.

Sog. Ha, ha, ha!—says he, God save you, says he;—ha, ha!

Car. Was this the ridiculous motive to all this passion?

Sog. Nay, that that comes after is,—ha, ha, ha, ha!

Car. Doubtless he apprehends more than he utters, this fellow; or else—   *[A cry of hounds within.*

Sog. List, list, they are come from hunting; stand by, close under this terras, and you shall see it done better than I can show it.

Car. So it had need, 'twill scarce poise the observation else.

Sog. Faith, I remember all, but the manner of it is quite out of my head.

Fast. O, withdraw, withdraw, it cannot be but a most pleasing object.   *[They stand aside.*

      Enter PUNTARVOLO, *followed by his Huntsman leading a greyhound.*

Punt. Forester, give wind to thy horn.—Enough; by this the sound hath touch'd the ears of the inclos'd: depart, leave the dog, and take with thee what thou hast deserved, the horn and thanks.

                                     [Exit Huntsman.

Car. Ay, marry, there is some taste in this.

Fast. Is't not good?

Sog. Ah, peace; now above, now above!

             [A Waiting-gentlewoman appears at the window.

Punt. Stay; mine eye hath, on the instant, through the bounty of the window, received the form of a nymph. I will step forward three paces; of the which, I will barely retire one; and, after some little flexure of the knee, with an erected grace salute her; one, two, and three! Sweet lady, God save you!

Gent. [*above.*] No, forsooth; I am but the waiting-gentlewoman.

Car. He knew that before.

Punt. Pardon me: *humanum est errare.*

Car. He learn'd that of his chaplain.

Punt. To the perfection of compliment (which is the dial of the thought, and guided by the sun of your beauties,) are required these three specials; the gnomon, the puntilios, and the superficies: the superficies is that we call place; the puntilios, circumstance; and the gnomon, ceremony; in either of which, for a stranger to err, 'tis easy and facile; and such am I.

Car. True, not knowing her horizon, he must needs err; which I fear he knows too well.

Punt. What call you the lord of the castle, sweet face?

Gent. [*above.*] The lord of the castle is a knight, sir; signior Puntarvolo.

Punt. Puntarvolo! O—

Car. Now must he ruminate.

Fast. Does the wench know him all this while, then?

Car. O, do you know me, man? why, therein lies the syrup of the jest; it's a project, a designment of his own, a thing studied, and rehearst as ordinarily at his coming from hawking or hunting, as a jig after a play.

Sog. Ay, e'en like your jig, sir.

Punt. 'Tis a most sumptuous and stately edifice! Of what years is the knight, fair damsel?

Gent. Faith, much about your years, sir.

Punt. What complexion, or what stature bears he?

Gent. Of your stature, and very near upon your complexion.

Punt. Mine is melancholy,—

Car. So is the dog's, just.

Punt. And doth argue constancy, chiefly in love. What are his endowments? is he courteous?

Gent. O, the most courteous knight in Christian land, sir.

Punt. Is he magnanimous?

Gent. As the skin between your brows, sir.

Punt. Is he bountiful?

Car. 'Slud, he takes an inventory of his own good parts.

Gent. Bountiful! ay, sir, I would you should know it; the poor are served at his gate, early and late, sir.

Punt. Is he learned?

Gent. O, ay, sir, he can speak the French and Italian.

Punt. Then he has travelled?

Gent. Ay, forsooth, he hath been beyond seas once or twice.

Car. As far as Paris, to fetch over a fashion, and come back again.

Punt. Is he religious?

Gent. Religious! I know not what you call religious, but he goes to church, I am sure.

Fast. 'Slid, methinks these answers should offend him.

Car. Tut, no; he knows they are excellent, and to her capacity that speaks them.

Punt. Would I might but see his face!

Car. She should let down a glass from the window at that word, and request him to look in't.

Punt. Doubtless the gentleman is most exact, and absolutely qualified; doth the castle contain him?

Gent. No, sir, he is from home, but his lady is within.

Punt. His lady! what, is she fair, splendidious, and amiable?

Gent. O, Lord, sir.

Punt. Prithee, dear nymph, intreat her beauties to shine on this side of the building.   [*Exit Waiting-gentlewoman from the window.*

Car. That he may erect a new dial of compliment, with his gnomons and his puntilios.

Fast. Nay, thou art such another cynic now, a man had need walk uprightly before thee.

Car. Heart, can any man walk more upright than he does? Look, look; as if he went in a frame, or had a suit of wainscot on: and the dog watching him, lest he should leap out on't.

Fast. O, villain!

Car. Well, an e'er I meet him in the city, I'll have him jointed, I'll pawn him in Eastcheap, among the butchers, else.

Fast. Peace; who be these, Carlo?

Enter Sordido *and* Fungoso.

Sord. Yonder's your godfather; do your duty to him, son.

Sog. This, sir? a poor elder brother of mine, sir, a yeoman, may dispend some seven or eight hundred a year; that's his son, my nephew, there.

Punt. You are not ill come, neighbour Sordido, though I have not yet said, well-come; what, my godson is grown a great proficient by this.

Sord. I hope he will grow great one day, sir.

Fast. What does he study? the law?

Sog. Ay, sir, he is a gentleman, though his father be but a yeoman.

Car. What call you your nephew, signior?

Sog. Marry, his name is Fungoso.

Car. Fungoso! O, he look'd somewhat like a sponge in that pink'd yellow doublet, methought; well, make much of him; I see he was never born to ride upon a mule.

Gent. [*reappears at the window.*] My lady will come presently, sir.

Sog. O, now, now!

Punt. Stand by, retire yourselves a space; nay, pray you, forget not the use of your hat; the air is piercing.

[*Sordido and Fungoso withdraw.*

Fast. What! will not their presence prevail against the current of his humour?

Car. O, no; it's a mere flood, a torrent carries all afore it.

[*Lady Puntarvolo appears at the window.*

Punt. What more than heavenly pulchritude is this,
What magazine, or treasury of bliss?
Dazzle, you organs to my optic sense,
To view a creature of such eminence:
O, I am planet-struck, and in yon sphere
A brighter star than Venus doth appear!

Fast. How! in verse!

Car. An extacy, an extacy, man.

Lady P. [*above.*] Is your desire to speak with me, sir knight?

Car. He will tell you that anon; neither his brain nor his body are yet moulded for an answer.

Punt. Most debonair, and luculent lady, I decline me as low as the basis of your altitude.

Cor. *He makes congies to his wife in geometrical proportions.*

Mit. *Is it possible there should be any such humourist?*

Cor. *Very easily possible, sir, you see there is.*

Punt. I have scarce collected my spirits, but lately scattered in the admiration of your form; to which, if the bounties of your mind be any way responsible, I doubt not but my desires shall find a smooth and secure passage. I am a poor knight-errant, lady, that hunting in the adjacent forest, was, by adventure, in the pursuit of a hart, brought to this place; which hart, dear madam, escaped by enchantment: the evening approaching, myself and servant wearied, my suit is, to enter your fair castle and refresh me.

Lady. Sir knight, albeit it be not usual with me, chiefly in the absence of a husband, to admit any entrance to strangers, yet in the true regard of those innated virtues, and fair parts, which so strive to express themselves, in you; I am resolved to entertain you to the best of my unworthy power; which I acknowledge to be nothing, valued with what so worthy a person may deserve. Please you but stay while I descend.   [*Exit from the window.*

Punt. Most admired lady, you astonish me.

[*Walks aside with Sordido and his son.*

Car. What! with speaking a speech of your own penning?

Fast. Nay, look; prithee, peace.

Car. Pox on't! I am impatient of such foppery.

Fast. O let us hear the rest.

Car. What! a tedious chapter of courtship, after sir Lancelot and queen Guenever? Away! I marle in what dull cold nook he found this lady out; that, being a woman, she was blest with no more copy of wit but to serve his humour thus. 'Slud, I think he feeds her with porridge, I: she could never have such a thick brain else.

Sog. Why, is porridge so hurtful, signior?

Car. O, nothing under heaven more prejudicial to those ascending subtle powers, or doth sooner abate that which we call *acumen ingenii,* than your gross fare: Why, I'll make you an instance; your city-wives, but observe 'em, you have not more perfect true fools in the world bred than they are generally; and yet you see, by the fineness and delicacy of their diet, diving into the fat capons, drinking your rich wines, feeding on larks, sparrows, potato-pies, and such good unctuous meats, how their wits are refined and rarified; and sometimes a very quintessence of conceit flows from them, able to drown a weak apprehension.

Enter Lady PUNTARVOLO *and her Waiting-woman.*

Fast. Peace, here comes the lady.

Lady. Gad's me, here's company! turn in again.

[*Exit with her woman.*

Fast. 'Slight, our presence has cut off the convoy of the jest.

Car. All the better, I am glad on't; for the issue was very perspicuous.   Come let's discover, and salute the knight.

[*They come forward.*

Punt. Stay; who be these that address themselves towards us?
What Carlo!   Now by the sincerity of my soul, welcome; welcome,
gentlemen: and how dost thou, thou *Grand Scourge*, or *Second
Untruss of the time?*

Car. Faith, spending my metal in this reeling world (here and
there), as the sway of my affection carries me, and perhaps stumble
upon a yeoman-feuterer, as I do now; or one of fortune's mules,
laden with treasure, and an empty cloak-bag, following him, gaping
when a bag will untie.

Punt. Peace, you bandog, peace!   What brisk Nymphadoro is
that in the white virgin-boot there?

Car. Marry, sir, one that I must intreat you to take a very particular knowledge of, and with more than ordinary respect; monsieur
Fastidious.

Punt. Sir, I could wish, that for the time of your vouchsafed
abiding here, and more real entertainment, this my house stood on
the Muses hill, and these my orchards were those of the Hesperides.

Fast. I possess as much in your wish, sir, as if I were made lord
of the Indies; and I pray you believe it.

Car. I have a better opinion of his faith, than to think it will be
so corrupted.

Sog. Come, brother, I'll bring you acquainted with gentlemen,
and good fellows, such as shall do you more grace than—

Sord. Brother, I hunger not for such acquaintance: Do you take
heed, lest—   [*Carlo comes toward them.*

Sog. Husht!   My brother, sir, for want of education, sir, somewhat nodding to the boor, the clown; but I request you in private,
sir.

Fung. [*looking at Fastidious Brisk.*] By heaven, it is a very fine
suit of clothes.   [*Aside.*

Cor. *Do you observe that, signior?   There's another humour has
new-crack'd the shell.*

Mit. *What! he is enamour'd of the fashion, is he?*

Cor. *O, you forestall the jest.*

Fung. I marle what it might stand him in.   [*Aside.*

Sog. Nephew!

Fung. 'Fore me, it's an excellent suit, and as neatly becomes
him. [*Aside.*]—What said you, uncle?

Sog. When saw you my niece?

Fung. Marry, yesternight I supp'd there.—That kind of boot does very rare too. [*Aside.*

Sog. And what news hear you?

Fung. The gilt spur and all! Would I were hang'd, but 'tis exceeding good. [*Aside.*]—Say you, uncle?

Sog. Your mind is carried away with somewhat else: I ask what news you hear?

Fung. Troth, we hear none.—In good faith [*looking at Fastidious Brisk*] I was never so pleased with a fashion, days of my life. O an I might have but my wish, I'd ask no more of heaven now, but such a suit, such a hat, such a band, such a doublet, such a hose, such a boot, and such a— [*Aside.*

Sog. They say, there's a new motion of the city of Nineveh, with Jonas and the whale, to be seen at Fleet-bridge. You can tell, cousin?

Fung. Here's such a world of questions with him now!—Yes, I think there be such a thing, I saw the picture.—Would he would once be satisfied! Let me see, the doublet, say fifty shillings the doublet, and between three or four pound the hose; then boots, hat, and band: some ten or eleven pound will do it all, and suit me for the heavens! [*Aside.*

Sog. I'll see all those devices an I come to London once.

Fung. Ods 'slid, an I could compass it, 'twere rare. [*Aside.*]— Hark you, uncle.

Sog. What says my nephew?

Fung. Faith, uncle, I would have desired you to have made a motion for me to my father, in a thing that—— Walk aside, and I'll tell you, sir; no more but this: there's a parcel of law books (some twenty pounds worth) that lie in a place for a little more than half the money they cost; and I think, for some twelve pound, or twenty mark, I could go near to redeem them; there's Plowden, Dyar, Brooke, and Fitz-Herbert, divers such as I must have ere long; and you know, I were as good save five or six pound, as not, uncle. I pray you, move it for me.

Sog. That I will: when would you have me do it? presently?

Fung. O, ay, I pray you, good uncle: [*Sogliardo takes Sordido aside.*]—send me good luck, Lord, an't be thy will, prosper it! O my stars, now, now, if it take now, I am made for ever.

Fast. Shall I tell you, sir? by this air, I am the most beholden to that lord, of any gentleman living; he does use me the most honourably, and with the greatest respect, more indeed than can be utter'd with any opinion of truth.

Punt. Then have you the count Gratiato?

Fast. As true noble a gentleman too as any breathes; I am exceedingly endear'd to his love: By this hand, I protest to you, signior, I speak it not gloriously, nor out of affectation, but there's he and the count Frugale, signior Illustre, signior Luculento, and a sort of 'em, that when I am at court, they do share me amongst them; happy is he can enjoy me most private. I do wish myself sometime an ubiquitary for their love, in good faith.

Car. There's ne'er a one of these but might lie a week on the rack, ere they could bring forth his name; and yet he pours them out as familiarly, as if he had seen them stand by the fire in the presence, or ta'en tobacco with them over the stage, in the lord's room.

Punt. Then you must of necessity know our court-star there, that planet of wit, madona Saviolina?

Fast. O Lord, sir, my mistress.

Punt. Is she your mistress?

Fast. Faith, here be some slight favours of hers, sir, that do speak it, she is; as this scarf, sir, or this ribbon in my ear, or so; this feather grew in her sweet fan sometimes, though now it be my poor fortune to wear it, as you see, sir: slight, slight, a foolish toy.

Punt. Well, she is the lady of a most exalted and ingenious spirit.

Fast. Did you ever hear any woman speak like her? or enriched with a more plentiful discourse?

Car. O villainous! nothing but sound, sound, a mere echo; she speaks as she goes tired, in cobweb-lawn, light, thin; good enough to catch flies withal.

Punt. O manage your affections.

Fast. Well, if thou be'st not plagued for this blasphemy one day—

Punt. Come, regard not a jester: It is in the power of my purse to make him speak well or ill of me.

Fast. Sir, I affirm it to you upon my credit and judgment, she has the most harmonious and musical strain of wit that ever tempted a true ear; and yet to see!—a rude tongue would profane heaven, if it could.

Punt. I am not ignorant of it, sir.

Fast. Oh, it flows from her like nectar, and she doth give it that sweet quick grace, and exornation in the composure, that by this good air, as I am an honest man, would I might never stir, sir, but— she does observe as pure a phrase, and use as choice figures in her ordinary conferences, as any be in the *Arcadia.*

Car. Or rather in Green's works, whence she may steal with more security.

Sord. Well, if ten pound will fetch 'em, you shall have it; but I'll part with no more.

Fung. I'll try what that will do, if you please.

Sord. Do so; and when you have them, study hard.

Fung. Yes, sir. An I could study to get forty shillings more now! Well, I will put myself into the fashion, as far as this will go, presently.

Sord. I wonder it rains not: the almanack says, we should have a store of rain to-day.   [*Aside.*

Punt. Why, sir, to-morrow I will associate you to court myself, and from thence to the city about a business, a project I have; I will expose it to you, sir; Carlo, I am sure, has heard of it.

Car. What's that, sir?

Punt. I do intend, this year of jubilee coming on, to travel: and because I will not altogether go upon expense, I am determined to put forth some five thousand pound, to be paid me five for one, upon the return of myself, my wife, and my dog from the Turk's court in Constantinople. If all or either of us miscarry in the journey, 'tis gone: if we be successful, why, there will be five and twenty thousand pound to entertain time withal. Nay, go not, neighbour Sordido; stay to-night, and help to make our society the fuller. Gentlemen, frolic: Carlo! what! dull now?

Car. I was thinking on your project, sir, an you call it so. Is this the dog goes with you?

Punt. This is the dog, sir.

Car. He does not go barefoot, does he?

Punt. Away, you traitor, away!

Car. Nay, afore God, I speak simply; he may prick his foot with a thorn, and be as much as the whole venture is worth. Besides, for a dog that never travell'd before, it's a huge journey to Constantinople. I'll tell you now, an he were mine, I'd have some present conference with a physician, what antidotes were good to give him, preservatives against poison; for assure you, if once your money be out, there'll be divers attempts made against the life of the poor animal.

Punt. Thou art still dangerous.

Fast. Is signior Deliro's wife your kinswoman?

Sog. Ay, sir, she is my niece, my brother's daughter here, and my nephew's sister.

Sord. Do you know her, sir?

Fast. O Lord, sir! signior Deliro, her husband, is my merchant.

Fung. Ay, I have seen this gentleman there often.

Fast. I cry you mercy, sir; let me crave your name, pray you.

Fung. Fungoso, sir.

Fast. Good signior Fungoso, I shall request to know you better, sir.

Fung. I am her brother, sir.

Fast. In fair time, sir.

Punt. Come, gentlemen, I will be your conduct.

Fast. Nay, pray you, sir; we shall meet at signior Deliro's often.

Sog. You shall have me at the herald's office, sir, for some week or so at my first coming up. Come, Carlo.   [*Exeunt.*

Mit. *Methinks, Cordatus, he dwelt somewhat too long on this scene; it hung in the hand.*

Cor. *I see not where he could have insisted less, and to have made the humours perspicuous enough.*

Mit. *True, as his subject lies; but he might have altered the shape of his argument, and explicated them better in single scenes.*

Cor. *That had been single indeed. Why, be they not the same persons in this, as they would have been in those? and is it not an*

*object of more state, to behold the scene full, and relieved with variety
of speakers to the end, than to see a vast empty stage, and the actors
come in one by one, as if they were dropt down with a feather into the
eye of the spectators?*

Mit. *Nay, you are better traded with these things than I, and therefore
I'll subscribe to your judgment; marry, you shall give me leave to
make objections.*

Cor. *O, what else? it is the special intent of the author you should
do so; for thereby others, that are present, may as well be satisfied,
who haply would object the same you would do.*

Mit. *So, sir; but when appears Macilente again?*

Cor. *Marry, he stays but till our silence give him leave: here he
comes, and with him signior Deliro, a merchant at whose house he is
come to sojourn: make your own observation now, only transfer your
thoughts to the city, with the scene: where suppose they speak.*

SCENE II.   *A Room in* Deliro's *House.*

Enter Deliro, Macilente, *and* Fido *with flowers and perfumes.*

Deli. I'll tell you by and by, sir,—
Welcome, good Macilente, to my house,
To sojourn even for ever; if my best
In cates, and every sort of good entreaty,
May move you stay with me.   [*He censeth: the boy strews flowers.*

Maci. I thank you, sir.—
And yet the muffled Fates, had it pleased them,
Might have supplied me from their own full store,
Without this word, *I thank you,* to a fool.
I see no reason why that dog call'd Chance,
Should fawn upon this fellow more than me;
I am a man, and I have limbs, flesh, blood,
Bones, sinews, and a soul, as well as he:
My parts are every way as good as his;
If I said better, why, I did not lie.
Nath'less, his wealth, but nodding on my wants,
Must make me bow, and cry, *I thank you, sir.*   [*Aside.*

Deli. Dispatch! take heed your mistress see you not.

Fido. I warrant you, sir, I'll steal by her softly.   [*Exit.*

Deli. Nay, gentle friend, be merry; raise your looks
Out of your bosom: I protest, by heaven,
You are the man most welcome in the world.

Maci. I thank you, sir.—I know my cue, I think.   [*Aside.*

Re-enter Fido, *with more perfumes and flowers.*

Fido. Where will you have them burn, sir?

Deli. Here, good Fido.
What, she did not see thee?

Fido. No, sir.

Deli. That is well.

Strew, strew, good Fido, the freshest flowers; so!

Maci. What means this, signior Deliro? all this censing?

Deli. Cast in more frankincense, yet more; well said.—
O Macilente, I have such a wife!
So passing fair! so passing-fair-unkind!
But of such worth, and right to be unkind,
Since no man can be worthy of her kindness—

Maci. What, can there not?

Deli. No, that is as sure as death,
No man alive. I do not say, is not,
But cannot possibly be worth her kindness,
Nay, it is certain, let me do her right.
How, said I? do her right! as though I could,
As though this dull, gross tongue of mine could utter
The rare, the true, the pure, the infinite rights,
That sit, as high as I can look, within her!

Maci. This is such dotage as was never heard.

Deli. Well, this must needs be granted.

Maci. Granted, quoth you?

Deli. Nay, Macilente, do not so discredit
The goodness of your judgment to deny it.
For I do speak the very least of her:
And I would crave, and beg no more of Heaven,
For all my fortunes here, but to be able
To utter first in fit terms, what she is,
And then the true joys I conceive in her.

Maci. Is't possible she should deserve so well,
As you pretend?

Deli. Ay, and she knows so well
Her own deserts, that, when I strive t'enjoy them,
She weighs the things I do, with what she merits;
And, seeing my worth out-weigh'd so in her graces,
She is so solemn, so precise, so froward,
That no observance I can do to her
Can make her kind to me: if she find fault,
I mend that fault; and then she says, I faulted,
That I did mend it. Now, good friend, advise me,
How I may temper this strange spleen in her.

Maci. You are too amorous, too obsequious,
And make her too assured she may command you.
When women doubt most of their husbands' loves,
They are most loving. Husbands must take heed
They give no gluts of kindness to their wives,
But use them like their horses; whom they feed
Not with a mangerful of meat together,
But half a peck at once; and keep them so
Still with an appetite to that they give them.
He that desires to have a loving wife,
Must bridle all the show of that desire:

Be kind, not amorous; nor bewraying kindness,
As if love wrought it, but considerate duty.
Offer no love rites, but let wives still seek them,
For when they come unsought, they seldom like them.

   Deli. Believe me, Macilente, this is gospel.
O, that a man were his own man so much,
To rule himself thus. I will strive, i'faith,
To be more strange and careless; yet I hope
I have now taken such a perfect course,
To make her kind to me, and live contented,
That I shall find my kindness well return'd,
And have no need to fight with my affections.
She late hath found much fault with every room
Within my house; one was too big, she said,
Another was not furnish'd to her mind,
And so through all; all which, now, I have alter'd.
Then here, she hath a place, on my back-side,
Wherein she loves to walk; and that, she said,
Had some ill smells about it: now, this walk
Have I, before she knows it, thus perfumed
With herbs, and flowers; and laid in divers places,
As 'twere on altars consecrate to her,
Perfumed gloves, and delicate chains of amber,
To keep the air in awe of her sweet nostrils:
This have I done, and this I think will please her.
Behold, she comes.

Enter FALLACE.

   Fal. Here's a sweet stink indeed!
What, shall I ever be thus crost and plagued,
And sick of husband? O, my head doth ache,
As it would cleave asunder, with these savours!
All my rooms alter'd, and but one poor walk
That I delighted in, and that is made
So fulsome with perfumes, that I am fear'd,
My brain doth sweat so, I have caught the plague!

   Deli. Why, gentle wife, is now thy walk too sweet?
Thou said'st of late, it had sour airs about it,
And found'st much fault that I did not correct it.

   Fal. Why, an I did find fault, sir?

   Deli. Nay, dear wife,
I know thou hast said thou hast loved perfumes,
No woman better.

   Fal. Ay, long since, perhaps;
But now that sense is alter'd: you would have me,
Like to a puddle, or a standing pool,
To have no motion, nor no spirit within me.
No, I am like a pure and sprightly river,
That moves for ever, and yet still the same;

Or fire, that burns much wood, yet still one flame.

   Deli. But yesterday, I saw thee at our garden,
Smelling on roses, and on purple flowers;
And since, I hope, the humour of thy sense
Is nothing changed.

   Fal. Why, those were growing flowers,
And these within my walk are cut and strewed.

   Deli. But yet they have one scent.

   Fal. Ay! have they so?
In your gross judgment. If you make no difference
Betwixt the scent of growing flowers and cut ones,
You have a sense to taste lamp oil, i'faith:
And with such judgment have you changed the chambers,
Leaving no room, that I can joy to be in,
In all your house; and now my walk, and all,
You smoke me from, as if I were a fox,
And long, belike, to drive me quite away:
Well, walk you there, and I'll walk where I list.

   Deli. What shall I do? O, I shall never please her.

   Maci. Out on thee, dotard! what star ruled his birth,
That brought him such a Star? blind Fortune still
Bestows her gifts on such as cannot use them:
How long shall I live, ere I be so happy
To have a wife of this exceeding form?   [*Aside.*

   Deli. Away with 'em! would I had broke a joint
When I devised this, that should so dislike her.
Away, bear all away.   [*Exit Fido, with flowers, etc.*

   Fal. Ay, do; for fear
Aught that is there should like her. O, this man,
How cunningly he can conceal himself,
As though he loved, nay, honour'd and ador'd!—

   Deli. Why, my sweet heart?

   Fal. Sweet heart! O, better still!
And asking, why? wherefore? and looking strangely,
As if he were as white as innocence!
Alas, you're simple, you: you cannot change,
Look pale at pleasure, and then red with wonder;
No, no, not you! 'tis pity o' your naturals.
I did but cast an amorous eye, e'en now,
Upon a pair of gloves that somewhat liked me,
And straight he noted it, and gave command
All should be ta'en away.

   Deli. Be they my bane then!
What, sirrah, Fido, bring in those gloves again
You took from hence.

   Fal. 'Sbody, sir, but do not:
Bring in no gloves to spite me; if you do—

   Deli. Ay me, most wretched; how am I misconstrued!

   Maci. O, how she tempts my heart-strings with her eye,

To knit them to her beauties, or to break!
What mov'd the heavens, that they could not make
Me such a woman! but a man, a beast,
That hath no bliss like others? Would to heaven,
In wreak of my misfortunes, I were turn'd
To some fair water-nymph, that, set upon
The deepest whirl-pit of the rav'nous seas,
My adamantine eyes might headlong hale
This iron world to me, and drown it all.   [*Aside.*

   Cor. Behold, behold, the translated gallant.
   Mit. O, he *is* welcome.

Enter FUNGOSO, *apparelled like* FASTIDIOUS BRISK.

   Fung. Save you, brother and sister; save you, sir! I have commendations for you out o' the country. I wonder they take no knowledge of my suit: [*Aside.*]—Mine uncle Sogliardo is in town. Sister, methinks you are melancholy; why are you so sad? I think you took me for Master Fastidious Brisk, sister, did you not?
   Fal. Why should I take you for him?
   Fung. Nay, nothing.—I was lately in Master Fastidious's company, and methinks we are very like.
   Deli. You have a fair suit, brother, 'give you joy on't.
   Fung. Faith, good enough to ride in, brother; I made it to ride in.
   Fal. O, now I see the cause of his idle demand was his new suit.
   Deli. Pray you, good brother, try if you can change her mood.
   Fung. I warrant you, let me alone: I'll put her out of her dumps. Sister, how like you my suit!
   Fal. O, you are a gallant in print now, brother.
   Fung. Faith, how like you the fashion? it is the last edition, I assure you.
   Fal. I cannot but like it to the desert.
   Fung. Troth, sister, I was fain to borrow these spurs, I have left my gown in gage for them, pray you lend me an angel.
   Fal. Now, beshrew my heart then.
   Fung. Good truth, I'll pay you again at my next exhibition. I had but bare ten pound of my father, and it would not reach to put me wholly into the fashion.
   Fal. I care not.
   Fung. I had spurs of mine own before, but they were not ginglers. Monsieur Fastidious will be here anon, sister.
   Fal. You jest!
   Fung. Never lend me penny more while you live then; and that I'd be loth to say, in truth.
   Fal. When did you see him?
   Fung. Yesterday; I came acquainted with him at Sir Puntarvolo's: nay, sweet sister.
   Maci. I fain would know of heaven now, why yond fool
Should wear a suit of satin? he? that rook,

That painted jay, with such a deal of outside:
What is his inside, trow? ha, ha, ha, ha, ha!
Good heaven, give me patience, patience, patience.
A number of these popinjays there are,
Whom, if a man confer, and but examine
Their inward merit, with such men as want;
Lord, lord, what things they are!   [*Aside.*

Fal. [*Gives him money.*] Come, when will you pay me again, now?
Fung. O lord, sister!
Maci. Here comes another.

Enter FASTIDIOUS BRISK, *in a new suit.*

Fast. Save you, signior Deliro! How dost thou, sweet lady? let
me kiss thee.
Fung. How! a new suit? ah me!
Deli. And how does master Fastidious Brisk?
Fast. Faith, live in court, signior Deliro; in grace, I thank God,
both of the noble masculine and feminine. I must speak with you
in private by and by.
Deli. When you please, sir.
Fal. Why look you so pale, brother?
Fung. 'Slid, all this money is cast away now.
Maci. Ay, there's a newer edition come forth.
Fung. 'Tis but my hard fortune! well, I'll have my suit changed,
I'll go fetch my tailor presently but first, I'll devise a letter to my
father. Have you any pen and ink, sister?
Fal. What would you do withal?
Fung. I would use it. 'Slight, an it had come but four days
sooner, the fashion.   [*Exit.*
Fast. There was a countess gave me her hand to kiss to-day,
i' the presence: did me more good by that light than——and
yesternight sent her coach twice to my lodging, to intreat me accompany her, and my sweet mistress, with some two or three nameless
ladies more: O, I have been graced by them beyond all aim of
affection: this is her garter my dagger hangs in: and they do so
commend and approve my apparel, with my judicious wearing of it,
it's above wonder.
Fal. Indeed, sir, 'tis a most excellent suit, and you do wear it as
extraordinary.
Fast. Why, I'll tell you now, in good faith, and by this chair,
which, by the grace of God, I intend presently to sit in, I had three
suits in one year made three great ladies in love with me: I had
other three, undid three gentlemen in imitation: and other three
gat three other gentlemen widows of three thousand pound a year.
Deli. Is't possible?
Fast. O, believe it, sir; your good face is the witch, and your
apparel the spells, that bring all the pleasures of the world into
their circle.
Fal. Ah, the sweet grace of a courtier!

Maci. Well, would my father had left me but a good face for my portion yet! though I had shared the unfortunate wit that goes with it, I had not cared; I might have passed for somewhat in the world then.

Fast. Why, assure you, signior, rich apparel has strange virtues: it makes him that hath it without means, esteemed for an excellent wit: he that enjoys it with means, puts the world in remembrance of his means: it helps the deformities of nature, and gives lustre to her beauties; makes continual holiday where it shines; sets the wits of ladies at work, that otherwise would be idle; furnisheth your two-shilling ordinary; takes possession of your stage at your new play; and enricheth your oars, as scorning to go with your scull.

Maci. Pray you, sir, add this; it gives respect to your fools, makes many thieves, as many strumpets, and no fewer bankrupts.

Fal. Out, out! unworthy to speak where he breatheth.

Fast. What's he, signior?

Deli. A friend of mine, sir.

Fast. By heaven I wonder at you citizens, what kind of creatures you are!

Deli. Why, sir?

Fast. That you can consort yourselves with such poor seam-rent fellows.

Fal. He says true.

Deli. Sir, I will assure you, however you esteem of him, he's a man worthy of regard.

Fast. Why, what has he in him of such virtue to be regarded, ha?

Deli. Marry, he is a scholar, sir.

Fast. Nothing else!

Deli. And he is well travell'd.

Fast. He should get him clothes; I would cherish those good parts of travel in him, and prefer him to some nobleman of good place.

Deli. Sir, such a benefit should bind me to you for ever, in my friend's right; and I doubt not, but his desert shall more than answer my praise.

Fast. Why, an he had good clothes, I'd carry him to court with me to-morrow.

Deli. He shall not want for those, sir, if gold and the whole city will furnish him.

Fast. You say well, sir: faith, signior Deliro, I am come to have you play the alchemist with me, and change the species of my land into that metal you talk of.

Deli. With all my heart, sir; what sum will serve you?

Fast. Faith, some three or four hundred.

Deli. Troth, sir, I have promised to meet a gentleman this morning in Paul's, but upon my return I'll dispatch you.

Fast. I'll accompany you thither.

Deli. As you please, sir; but I go not thither directly.

Fast. 'Tis no matter, I have no other designment in hand, and therefore as good go along.

Deli. I were as good have a quartain fever follow me now, for I shall ne'er be rid of him. Bring me a cloak there, one. Still, upon his grace at court, I am sure to be visited; I was a beast to give him any hope. Well, would I were in, that I am out with him once, and——Come, signior Macilente, I must confer with you, as we go. Nay, dear wife, I beseech thee, forsake these moods: look not like winter thus. Here, take my keys, open my counting-houses, spread all my wealth before thee, choose any object that delights thee: if thou wilt eat the spirit of gold, and drink dissolved pearl in wine, 'tis for thee.

Fal. So, sir!

Deli. Nay, my sweet wife.

Fal. Good lord, how you are perfumed in your terms and all! pray you leave us.

Deli. Come, gentlemen.

Fast. Adieu, sweet lady.   [*Exeunt all but Fallace.*

Fal. Ay, ay! let thy words ever sound in mine ears, and thy graces disperse contentment through all my senses! O, how happy is that lady above other ladies, that enjoys so absolute a gentleman to her servant! *A countess gives him her hand to kiss:* ah, foolish countess! he's a man worthy, if a woman may speak of a man's worth, to kiss the lips of an empress.

Re-enter FUNGOSO, *with his* Tailor.

Fung. What's master Fastidious gone, sister?

Fal. Ay, brother.—He has a face like a cherubin!   [*Aside.*

Fung. 'Ods me, what luck's this? I have fetch'd my tailor and all: which way went he, sister, can you tell?

Fal. Not I, in good faith—and he has a body like an angel!
                                                      [*Aside.*

Fung. How long is't since he went?

Fal. Why, but e'en now; did you not meet him?—and a tongue able to ravish any woman in the earth.   [*Aside.*

Fung. O, for God's sake—I'll please you for your pains, [*to his Tailor.*]—But e'en now, say you? Come, good sir: 'slid, I had forgot it too: if any body ask for mine uncle Sogliardo, they shall have him at the herald's office yonder, by Paul's.
                                            [*Exit with his Tailor.*

Fal. Well, I will not altogether despair: I have heard of a citizen's wife has been beloved of a courtier; and why not I? heigh, ho! well, I will into my private chamber, lock the door to me, and think over all his good parts one after another.   [*Exit.*

Mit. *Well, I doubt, this last scene will endure some grievous torture.*

Cor. *How? you fear 'twill be rack'd by some hard construction?*

Mit. *Do not you?*

Cor. *No, in good faith: unless mine eyes could light me beyond sense. I see no reason why this should be more liable to the rack than the rest : you'll say, perhaps, the city will not take it well that the merchant is made here to doat so perfectly upon his wife ; and she again to be so Fastidiously affected as she is.*

Mit. *You have utter'd my thought, sir, indeed.*

Cor. *Why, by that proportion, the court might as well take offence at him we call the courtier, and with much more pretext, by how much the place transcends, and goes before in dignity and virtue : but can you imagine that any noble or true spirit in court, whose sinewy and altogether unaffected graces, very worthily express him a courtier, will make any exception at the opening of such an empty trunk as this Brisk is ? or think his own worth impeached, by beholding his motley inside ?*

Mit. *No, sir, I do not.*

Cor. *No more, assure you, will any grave, wise citizen, or modest matron, take the object of this folly in Deliro and his wife ; but rather apply it as the foil to their own virtues. For that were to affirm, that a man writing of Nero, should mean all emperors ; or speaking of Machiavel, comprehend all statesmen ; or in our Sordido, all farmers ; and so of the rest : than which nothing can be uttered more malicious or absurd. Indeed there are a sort of these narrow-eyed decypherers, I confess, that will extort strange and abstruse meanings out of any subject, be it never so conspicuous and innocently delivered. But to such, where'er they sit concealed, let them know, the author defies them and their writing-tables ; and hopes no sound or safe judgment will infect itself with their contagious comments, who, indeed, come here only to pervert and poison the sense of what they hear, and for nought else.*

Enter Cavalier SHIFT, *with two Si-quisses (bills) in his hand.*

Mit. *Stay, what new mute is this, that walks so suspiciously ?*

Cor. *O, marry, this is one, for whose better illustration, we must desire you to presuppose the stage, the middle aisle in Paul's, and that, the west end of it.*

Mit. *So, sir, and what follows ?*

Cor. *Faith, a whole volume of humour, and worthy the unclasping.*

Mit. *As how ? What name do you give him first ?*

Cor. *He hath shift of names, sir : some call him Apple-John, some signior Whiffe ; marry, his main standing name is cavalier Shift : the rest are but as clean shirts to his natures.*

Mit. *And what makes he in Paul's now ?*

Cor. *Troth, as you see, for the advancement of a si quis, or two ; wherein he has so varied himself, that if any of 'em take, he may hull up and down in the humorous world a little longer.*

Mit. *It seems then he bears a very changing sail ?*

Cor. *O, as the wind, sir : here comes more.*

ACT III

SCENE I.—*The Middle Aisle of* St. Paul's.

Shift. [*coming forward.*] This is rare, I have set up my bills without discovery.

Enter Orange.

Orange. What, signior Whiffe! what fortune has brought you into these west parts?

Shift. Troth, signior, nothing but your rheum; I have been taking an ounce of tobacco hard by here, with a gentleman, and I am come to spit private in Paul's. 'Save you, sir.

Orange. Adieu, good signior Whiffe.   [*Passes onward.*

Enter Clove.

Clove. Master Apple-John! you are well met; when shall we sup together, and laugh, and be fat with those good wenches, ha?

Shift. Faith, sir, I must now leave you, upon a few humours and occasions; but when you please, sir.   [*Exit.*

Clove. Farewell, sweet Apple-John! I wonder there are no more store of gallants here.

Mit. *What be these two, signior?*

Cor. *Marry, a couple, sir, that are mere strangers to the whole scope of our play; only come to walk a turn or two in this scene of Paul's, by chance.*

Orange. Save you, good master Clove!

Clove. Sweet master Orange.

Mit. *How! Clove and Orange?*

Cor. *Ay, and they are well met, for 'tis as dry an Orange as ever grew: nothing but salutation, and O lord, sir! and, It pleases you to say so, sir! one that can laugh at a jest for company with a most plausible and extemporal grace; and some hour after in private ask you what it was. The other monsieur, Clove, is a more spiced youth; he will sit you a whole afternoon sometimes in a bookseller's shop, reading the Greek, Italian, and Spanish, when he understands not a word of either; if he had the tongues to his suits, he were excellent linguist.*

Clove. Do you hear this reported for certainty?

Orange. O lord, sir.

Enter Puntarvolo *and* Carlo, *followed by two* Serving-men, *one leading a dog, the other bearing a bag.*

Punt. Sirrah, take my cloak; and you, sir knave, follow me closer. If thou losest my dog, thou shalt die a dog's death; I will hang thee.

Car. Tut, fear him not, he's a good lean slave; he loves a dog well, I warrant him; I see by his looks, I:—Mass, he's somewhat like him. 'Slud [*to the Servant.*] poison him, make him away with a crooked pin, or somewhat, man; thou may'st have more security of thy life; and—So, sir; what! you have not put out your whole venture yet, have you?

Punt. No, I do want yet some fifteen or sixteen hundred pounds; but my lady, my wife, is *Out of her Humour*, she does not now go.

Car. No! how then?

Punt. Marry, I am now enforced to give it out, upon the return of myself, my dog, and my cat.

Car. Your cat! where is she?

Punt. My squire has her there, in the bag; sirrah, look to her. How lik'st thou my change, Carlo?

Car. Oh, for the better, sir; your cat has nine lives, and your wife has but one.

Punt. Besides, she will never be sea-sick, which will save me so much in conserves. When saw you signior Sogliardo?

Car. I came from him but now; he is at the herald's office yonder; he requested me to go afore, and take up a man or two for him in Paul's, against his cognisance was ready.

Punt. What, has he purchased arms, then?

Car. Ay, and rare ones too; of as many colours as e'er you saw any fool's coat in your life. I'll go look among yond' bills, an I can fit him with legs to his arms.

Punt. With legs to his arms! Good! I will go with you, sir.

[*They go to read the bills.*

Enter FASTIDIOUS, DELIRO, *and* MACILENTE.

Fast. Come, let's walk in Mediterraneo: I assure you, sir, I am not the least respected among ladies; but let that pass: do you know how to go into the presence, sir?

Maci. Why, on my feet, sir.

Fast. No, on your head, sir; for 'tis that must bear you out, I assure you; as thus, sir. You must first have an especial care so to wear your hat, that it oppress not confusedly this your predominant, or foretop; because, when you come at the presence-door, you may with once or twice stroking up your forehead, thus, enter with your predominant perfect; that is, standing up stiff.

Maci. As if one were frighted?

Fast. Ay, sir.

Maci. Which, indeed, a true fear of your mistress should do, rather than gum-water, or whites of eggs; is't not so, sir?

Fast. An ingenious observation. Give me leave to crave your name, sir?

Deli. His name is Macilente, sir.

Fast. Good signior Macilente, if this gentleman, signior Deliro, furnish you, as he says he will, with clothes, I will bring you, to-morrow by this time, into the presence of the most divine and acute lady in court; you shall see sweet silent rhetorick, and dumb eloquence speaking in her eye, but when she speaks herself, such an anatomy of wit, so sinewised and arterised, that 'tis the goodliest model of pleasure that ever was to behold. Oh! she strikes the world into admiration of her; O, O, O! I cannot express them, believe me.

Maci. O, your only admiration is your silence, sir.

Punt. 'Fore God, Carlo, this is good! let's read them again.

[Reads the bill.

If there be any lady or gentlewoman of good carriage that is desirous to entertain to her private uses, a young, straight, and upright gentleman, of the age of five or six and twenty at the most ; who can serve in the nature of a gentleman-usher, and hath little legs of purpose, and a black satin suit of his own, to go before her in ; which suit, for the more sweetening, now lies in lavender ; and can hide his face with her fan, if need require ; or sit in the cold at the stair foot for her, as well as another gentleman : let her subscribe her name and place, and diligent respect shall be given.

Punt. This is above measure excellent, ha!

Car. No, this, this! here's a fine slave. *[Reads.*

If this city, or the suburbs of the same, do afford any young gentleman of the first, second, or third head, more or less, whose friends are but lately deceased, and whose lands are but new come into his hands, that, to be as exactly qualified as the best of our ordinary gallants are, is affected to entertain the most gentleman-like use of tobacco ; as first, to give it the most exquisite perfume ; then, to know all the delicate sweet forms for the assumption of it ; as also the rare corollary and practice of the Cuban ebolition, euripus and whiff, which he shall receive or take in here at London, and evaporate at Uxbridge, or farther, if it please him. If there be any such generous spirit, that is truly enamoured of these good faculties ; may it please him, but by a note of his hand to specify the place or ordinary where he uses to eat and lie ; and most sweet attendance, with tobacco and pipes of the best sort, shall be ministered. Stet, quæso, candide Lector.

Punt. Why, this is without parallel, this.

Car. Well, I'll mark this fellow for Sogliardo's use presently.

Punt. Or rather, Sogliardo, for his use.

Car. Faith, either of them will serve, they are both good properties: I'll design the other a place too, that we may see him.

Punt. No better place than the Mitre, that we may be spectators with you, Carlo. Soft, behold who enters here:

Enter SOGLIARDO.

Signior Sogliardo! save you.

Sog. Save you, good sir Puntarvolo; your dog's in health, sir, I see: How now, Carlo?

Car. We have ta'en simple pains, to choose you out followers here. *[Shews him the bills.*

Punt. Come hither, signior.

Clove. Monsieur Orange, yon gallants observe us; prithee let's talk fustian a little, and gull them; make them believe we are great scholars.

Orange. O lord, sir!

Clove. Nay, prithee let us, believe me,—you have an excellent habit in discourse.

Orange. It pleases you to say so, sir.

Clove. By this church, you have, la; nay, come, begin—Aristotle, in his dæmonologia, approves Scaliger for the best navigator in his time; and in his hypercritics, he reports him to be Heautontimorumenos:—you understand the Greek, sir?

Orange. O, good sir!

Maci. For society's sake he does. O, here be a couple of fine tame parrots!

Clove. Now, sir, whereas the ingenuity of the time and the soul's synderisis are but embrions in nature, added to the panch of Esquiline, and the inter-vallum of the zodiac, besides the ecliptic line being optic, and not mental, but by the contemplative and theoric part thereof, doth demonstrate to us the vegetable circumference, and the ventosity of the tropics, and whereas our intellectual, or mincing capreal (according to the metaphysicks) as you may read in Plato's Histriomastix——You conceive me, sir?

Orange. O lord, sir!

Clove. Then coming to the pretty animal, as reason long since is fled to animals, you know, or indeed for the more modelising, or enamelling, or rather diamondising of your subject, you shall perceive the hypothesis, or galaxia, (whereof the meteors long since had their initial inceptions and notions,) to be merely Pythagorical, mathematical, and aristocratical——For, look you, sir, there is ever a kind of concinnity and species——Let us turn to our former discourse, for they mark us not.

Fast. Mass, yonder's the knight Puntarvolo.

Deli. And my cousin Sogliardo, methinks.

Maci. Ay, and his familiar that haunts him, the devil with the shining face.

Deli. Let 'em alone, observe 'em not.

[*Sogliardo, Puntarvolo, and Carlo, walk together.*

Sog. Nay, I will have him, I am resolute for that. By this parchment, gentlemen, I have been so toiled among the harrots yonder, you will not believe! they do speak in the strangest language, and give a man the hardest terms for his money, that ever you knew.

Car. But have you arms, have you arms?

Sog. I'faith, I thank them; I can write myself gentleman now; here's my patent, it cost me thirty pound, by this breath.

Punt. A very fair coat, well charged, and full of armory.

Sog. Nay, it has as much variety of colours in it, as you have seen a coat have; how like you the crest, sir?

Punt. I understand it not well, what is't?

Sog. Marry, sir, it is your boar without a head, rampant. A boar without a head, that's very rare!

Car. Ay, and rampant too! troth, I commend the herald's wit, he has decyphered him well: a swine without a head, without brain, wit, anything indeed, ramping to gentility. You can blazon the rest, signior, can you not?

Sog. O, ay, I have it in writing here of purpose; it cost me two shillings the tricking.

Car. Let's hear, let's hear.

Punt. It is the most vile, foolish, absurd, palpable, and ridiculous escutcheon that ever this eye survised.—Save you, good monsieur Fastidious.   [*They salute as they meet in the walk.*

Car. Silence, good knight; on, on.

Sog. [Reads.] *Gyrony of eight pieces; azure and gules; between three plates, a chevron engrailed checquy, or, vert, and ermins; on a chief argent, between two ann'lets sable, a boar's head, proper.*

Car. How's that! on a chief argent?

Sog. [Reads.] *On a chief argent, a boar's head proper, between two ann'lets sable.*

Car. 'Slud, it's a hog's cheek and puddings in a pewter field, this.
    [*Here they shift. Fastidious mixes with Puntarvolo; Carlo and Sogliardo; Deliro and Macilente; Clove and Orange; four couple.*

Sog. How like you them, signior?

Punt. Let the word be, *Not without mustard:* your crest is very rare, sir.

Car. A frying-pan to the crest, had had no fellow.

Fast. Intreat your poor friend to walk off a little, signior, I will salute the knight.

Car. Come, lap it up, lap it up.

Fast. You are right well encounter'd, sir; how does your fair dog?

Punt. In reasonable state, sir; what citizen is that you were consorted with? A merchant of any worth?

Fast. 'Tis signior Deliro, sir.

Punt. Is it he?—Save you, sir!   [*They salute.*

Deli. Good sir Puntarvolo!

Maci. O what copy of fool would this place minister, to one endued with patience to observe it!

Car. Nay, look you, sir, now you are a gentleman, you must carry a more exalted presence, change your mood and habit to a more austere form; be exceeding proud, stand upon your gentility, and scorn every man; speak nothing humbly, never discourse under a nobleman, though you never saw him but riding to the star-chamber, it's all one. Love no man: trust no man: speak ill of no man to his face; nor well of any man behind his back. Salute fairly on the front, and wish them hanged upon the turn. Spread yourself upon his bosom publicly, whose heart you would eat in private. These be principles, think on them; I'll come to you again presently. [*Exit.*

Punt. [*to his servant.*] Sirrah, keep close; yet not so close: thy breath will thaw my ruff.

Sog. O, good cousin, I am a little busy, how does my niece? I am to walk with a knight, here.

Enter Fungoso *with his* Tailor.

Fung. O, he is here; look you, sir, that's the gentleman.

Tai. What, he in the blush-coloured satin?

Fung. Ay, he, sir; though his suit blush, he blushes not, look you, that's the suit, sir: I would have mine such a suit without difference, such stuff, such a wing, such a sleeve, such a skirt, belly and all; therefore, pray you observe it. Have you a pair of tables?

Fast. Why, do you see, sir, they say I am fantastical; why, true, I know it, and I pursue my humour still, in contempt of this censorious age. 'Slight, an a man should do nothing but what a sort of stale judgments about this town will approve in him, he were a sweet ass: I'd beg him, i'faith. I ne'er knew any more find fault with a fashion, than they that knew not how to put themselves into it. For mine own part, so I please mine own appetite, I am careless what the fusty world speaks of me. Puh!

Fung. Do you mark, how it hangs at the knee there?

Tai. I warrant you, sir.

Fung. For God's sake do, note all; do you see the collar, sir?

Tai. Fear nothing, it shall not differ in a stitch, sir.

Fung. Pray heaven it do not! you'll make these linings serve, and help me to a chapman for the outside, will you?

Tai. I'll do my best, sir: you'll put it off presently.

Fung. Ay, go with me to my chamber you shall have it——but make haste of it, for the love of a customer; for I'll sit in my old suit, or else lie a bed, and read the *Arcadia* till you have done.

[*Exit with his Tailor.*

Re-enter Carlo.

Car. O, if ever you were struck with a jest, gallants, now, now, now, I do usher the most strange piece of military profession that ever was discovered in *Insula Paulina*.

Fast. Where? where?

Punt. What is he for a creature?

Car. A pimp, a pimp, that I have observed yonder, the rarest superficies of a humour; he comes every morning to empty his lungs in Paul's here; and offers up some five or six hecatombs of faces and sighs, and away again. Here he comes; nay, walk, walk, be not seen to note him, and we shall have excellent sport.

Enter Shift; *and walks by, using action to his rapier.*

Punt. 'Slid, he vented a sigh e'en now, I thought he would have blown up the church.

Car. O, you shall have him give a number of those false fires ere he depart.

Fast. See, now he is expostulating with his rapier: look, look!

Car. Did you ever in your days observe better passion over a hilt?

Punt. Except it were in the person of a cutler's boy, or that the fellow were nothing but vapour, I should think it impossible.

Car. See again, he claps his sword o' the head, as who should say, well, go to.

Fast. O violence! I wonder the blade can contain itself, being so provoked.

Car. *With that the moody squire thumpt his breast,*
And rear'd his eyen to heaven for revenge.

Sog. Troth, an you be good gentlemen, let's make them friends, and take up the matter between his rapier and him.

Car. Nay, if you intend that, you must lay down the matter; for this rapier, it seems, is in the nature of a hanger-on, and the good gentleman would happily be rid of him.

Fast. By my faith, and 'tis to be suspected; I'll ask him.

Maci. O, here's rich stuff! for life's sake, let us go:
A man would wish himself a senseless pillar,
Rather than view these monstrous prodigies:
Nil habet infelix paupertas durius in se,
Quam quod ridiculos homines facit—   [*Exit with Deliro.*

Fast. Signior.

Shift. At your service.

Fast. Will you sell your rapier?

Car. He is turn'd wild upon the question; he looks as he had seen a serjeant.

Shift. Sell my rapier! now fate bless me!

Punt. Amen.

Shift. You ask'd me if I would sell my rapier, sir?

Fast. I did indeed.

Shift. Now, lord have mercy upon me!

Punt. Amen, I say still.

Shift. 'Slid, sir, what should you behold in my face, sir, that should move you, as they say, sir, to ask me, sir, if I would sell my rapier?

Fast. Nay, let me pray you, sir, be not moved: I protest, I would rather have been silent, than any way offensive, had I known your nature.

Shift. Sell my rapier? 'ods lid!—Nay, sir, for mine own part, as I am a man that has serv'd in causes, or so, so I am not apt to injure any gentleman in the degree of falling foul, but—sell my rapier! I will tell you, sir, I have served with this foolish rapier, where some of us dare not appear in haste; I name no man; but let that pass. Sell my rapier!—death to my lungs! This rapier, sir, has travell'd by my side, sir, the best part of France, and the Low Country: I have seen Flushing, Brill, and the Hague, with this rapier, sir, in my Lord of Leicester's time; and by God's will, he that should offer to disrapier me now, I would——Look you, sir, you presume to be a gentleman of sort, and so likewise your friends here; if you have any disposition to travel for the sight of service, or so, one, two, or all of you, I can lend you letters to divers officers and commanders in the Low Countries, that shall for my cause do you all the good offices, that shall pertain or belong to gentleman of your——— [*lowering his voice.*] Please you to shew the bounty of your mind, sir, to impart some ten groats, or half a crown to our use, till our ability be of growth to return it, and we shall think ourself——— 'Sblood! sell my rapier!

Sog. I pray you, what said he, signior? he's a proper man.

Fast. Marry, he tells me, if I please to shew the bounty of my mind, to impart some ten groats to his use, or so———

Punt. Break his head, and give it him.

Car. I thought he had been playing o' the Jew's trump, I.

Shift. My rapier! no, sir; my rapier is my guard, my defence, my revenue, my honour;—if you cannot impart, be secret, I beseech you—and I will maintain it, where there is a grain of dust, or a drop of water. [*Sighs.*] Hard is the choice when the valiant must eat their arms, or clem. Sell my rapier! no, my dear, I will not be divorced from thee, yet; I have ever found thee true as steel, and———You cannot impart, sir?—Save you, gentlemen;— nevertheless, if you have a fancy to it, sir—

Fast. Prithee away: Is signior Deliro departed?

Car. Have you seen a pimp outface his own wants better?

Sog. I commend him that can dissemble them so well.

Punt. True, and having no better a cloak for it than he has neither.

Fast. Od's precious, what mischievous luck is this! adieu, gentlemen.

Punt. Whither in such haste, monsieur Fastidious?

Fast. After my merchant, signior Deliro, sir.   [*Exit.*

Car. O hinder him not, he may hap lose his tide; a good flounder, i'faith.

Orange. Hark you, signior Whiffe, a word with you.

                                        [*Orange and Clove call Shift aside.*

Car. How! signior Whiffe?

Orange. What was the difference between that gallant that's gone and you, sir?

Shift. No difference; he would have given me five pound for my rapier, and I refused it; that's all.

Clove. O, was it no otherwise? we thought you had been upon some terms.

Shift. No other than you saw, sir.

Clove. Adieu, good master Apple-John.   [*Exit with Orange.*

Car. How! Whiffe, and Apple-John too? Heart, what will you say if this be the appendix or label to both yon indentures?

Punt. It may be.

Car. Resolve us of it, Janus, thou that look'st every way; or thou, Hercules, that hast travelled all countries.

Punt. Nay, Carlo, spend not time in invocations now, 'tis late.

Car. Signior, here's a gentleman desirous of your name, sir.

Shift. Sir, my name is cavalier Shift: I am known sufficiently in this walk, sir.

Car. Shift! I heard your name varied even now, as I take it.

Shift. True, sir, it pleases the world, as I am her excellent tobacconist, to give me the style of signior Whiffe; as I am a poor esquire about the town here, they call me master Apple-John. Variety of good names does well, sir.

Car. Ay, and good parts, to make those good names; out of which I imagine yon bills to be yours.

Shift. Sir, if I should deny the manuscripts, I were worthy to be banish'd the middle aisle for ever.

Car. I take your word, sir: this gentleman has subscribed to them, and is most desirous to become your pupil. Marry, you must use expedition. Signior Insulso Sogliardo, this is the professor.

Sog. In good time, sir: nay, good sir, house your head; do you profess these sleights in tobacco?

Shift. I do more than profess, sir, and, if you please to be a practitioner, I will undertake in one fortnight to bring you, that you shall take it plausibly in any ordinary, theatre, or the Tilt-yard, if need be, in the most popular assembly that is.

Punt. But you cannot bring him to the whiffe so soon?

Shift. Yes, as soon, sir; he shall receive the first, second, and third whiffe, if it please him, and, upon the receipt, take his horse, drink his three cups of canary, and expose one at Hounslow, a second at Stains, and a third at Bagshot.

Car. Baw-waw!

Sog. You will not serve me, sir, will you? I'll give you more than countenance.

Shift. Pardon me, sir, I do scorn to serve any man.

Car. Who! he serve? 'sblood, he keeps high men, and low men, he! he has a fair living at Fullam.

Shift. But in the nature of a fellow, I'll be your follower, if you please.

Sog. Sir, you shall stay, and dine with me, and if we can agree, we'll not part in haste: I am very bountiful to men of quality. Where shall we go, signior?

Punt. Your Mitre is your best house.

Shift. I can make this dog take as many whiffes as I list, and he shall retain, or effume them, at my pleasure.

Punt. By your patience, follow me, fellows.

Sog. Sir Puntarvolo!

Punt. Pardon me, my dog shall not eat in his company for a million.   [*Exit with his Servants.*

Car. Nay, be not you amazed, signior Whiffe, whatever that stiff-necked gentleman says.

Sog. No, for you do not know the humour of the dog, as we do: Where shall we dine, Carlo? I would fain go to one of these ordinaries, now I am a gentleman.

Car. So you may; were you never at any yet?

Sog. No, faith; but they say there resorts your most choice gallants.

Car. True, and the fashion is, when any stranger comes in amongst 'em, they all stand up and stare at him, as he were some unknown beast, brought out of Africk; but that will be helped with a good adventurous face. You must be impudent enough, sit down, and use no respect: when anything's propounded above your capacity, smile at it, make two or three faces, and 'tis excellent; they'll think you have travell'd; though you argue, a whole day, in silence thus, and discourse in nothing but laughter, 'twill pass. Only, now and then, give fire, discharge a good full oath, and offer a great wager; 'twill be admirable.

Sog. I warrant you, I am resolute; come, good signior, there's a poor French crown for your ordinary.

Shift. It comes well, for I had not so much as the least portcullis of coin before.

Mit. I travail with another objection, signior, which I fear will be enforced against the author, ere I can be deliver'd of it.

Cor. What's that, sir?

Mit. That the argument of his comedy might have been of some other nature, as of a duke to be in love with a countess, and that countess to be in love with the duke's son, and the son to love the lady's waiting-maid; some such cross wooing, with a clown to their servingman, better than to be thus near, and familiarly allied to the time.

Cor. You say well, but I would fain hear one of these autumn-judgments define once, Quid sit comœdia? if he cannot, let him content himself with Cicero's definition, till he have strength to propose to himself a better, who would have a comedy to be imitatio vitæ, speculum consuetudinis, imago veritatis; a thing throughout pleasant and ridiculous, and accommodated to the correction of manners: if the maker have fail'd in any particle of this, they may worthily tax him; but if not, why——be you, that are for them, silent, as I will be for him; and give way to the actors.

SCENE II.—*The Country.*

Enter SORDIDO, *with a halter about his neck.*

Sord. Nay, God's precious, if the weather and season be so respectless, that beggars shall live as well as their betters; and that my hunger and thirst for riches shall not make them hunger and thirst with poverty; that my sleep shall be broken, and their hearts not broken; that my coffers shall be full, and yet care; their's empty, and yet merry;—'tis time that a cross should bear flesh and blood, since flesh and blood cannot bear this cross.

Mit. What, will he hang himself?

Cor. Faith, ay; it seems his prognostication has not kept touch with him, and that makes him despair.

Mit. Beshrew me, he will be OUT OF HIS HUMOUR *then indeed.*

Sord. Tut, these star-monger knaves, who would trust them?
One says dark and rainy, when 'tis as clear as chrystal; another
says, tempestuous blasts and storms, and 'twas as calm as a milk-
bowl; here be sweet rascals for a man to credit his whole fortunes
with! You sky-staring coxcombs you, you fat-brains, out upon you;
you are good for nothing but to sweat night-caps, and make rug-
gowns dear! you learned men, and have not a legion of devils *à
vostre service! à vostre service!* by heaven, I think I shall die a
better scholar than they: but soft—

Enter a Hind, *with a letter.*

How now, sirrah?

Hind. Here's a letter come from your son, sir.

Sord. From my son, sir! what would my son, sir? some good
news, no doubt.   [*Reads.*

*Sweet and dear father, desiring you first to send me your blessing,
which is more worth to me than gold or silver, I desire you likewise to
be advertised, that this Shrove-tide, contrary to custom, we use always
to have revels ; which is indeed dancing, and makes an excellent shew
in truth ; especially if we gentlemen be well attired, which our seniors
note, and think the better of our fathers, the better we are maintained,
and that they shall know if they come up, and have anything to do in
the law ; therefore, good father, these are, for your own sake as well as
mine, to re-desire you, that you let me not want that which is fit for the
setting up of our name, in the honourable volume of gentility, that I
may say to our calumniators, with Tully, Ego sum ortus domus meæ,
tu occasus tuæ. And thus, not doubting of your fatherly benevolence,
I humbly ask your blessing, and pray God to bless you.*

Yours, if his own, [Fungoso.]

How's this! *Yours, if his own!* Is he not my son, except he be
his own son? belike this is some new kind of subscription the
gallants use. Well! wherefore dost thou stay, knave? away; go.
[*Exit Hind.*] Here's a letter, indeed! revels? and benevolence?
is this a weather to send benevolence? or is this a season to revel
in? 'Slid, the devil and all takes part to vex me, I think! this
letter would never have come now else, now, now, when the sun
shines, and the air thus clear. Soul! if this hold, we shall shortly
have an excellent crop of corn spring out of the high ways: the
streets and houses of the town will be hid with the rankness of the
fruits, that grow there in spite of good husbandry. Go to, I'll
prevent the sight of it, come as quickly as it can, I will prevent the
sight of it. I have this remedy, heaven. [*Clambers up, and suspends
the halter to a tree.*] Stay; I'll try the pain thus a little. O, nothing,
nothing. Well now! shall my son gain a benevolence by my death?
or anybody be the better for my gold, or so forth? no; alive I kept
it from them, and dead, my ghost shall walk about it, and preserve
it. My son and daughter shall starve ere they touch it; I have
hid it as deep as hell from the sight of heaven, and to it I go now.
[*Flings himself off.*

Enter five or six Rustics, *one after another.*

1 *Rust.* Ah me, what pitiful sight is this! help, help, help!

2 *Rust.* How now! what's the matter?

1 *Rust.* O, here's a man has hang'd himself, help to get him again.

2 *Rust.* Hang'd himself! 'Slid, carry him afore a justice, 'tis chance-medley, o' my word.

3 *Rust.* How now, what's here to do?

4 *Rust.* How comes this?

2 *Rust.* One has executed himself, contrary to order of law, and by my consent he shall answer it.   [*They cut him down.*

5 *Rust.* Would he were in case to answer it!

1 *Rust.* Stand by, he recovers, give him breath.

Sord. Oh!

5 *Rust.* Mass, 'twas well you went the footway, neighbour.

1 *Rust.* Ay, an I had not cut the halter—

Sord. How! cut the halter! ah me, I am undone, I am undone!

2 *Rust.* Marry, if you had not been undone, you had been hang'd, I can tell you.

Sord. You thread-bare, horse-bread-eating rascals, if you would needs have been meddling, could you not have untied it, but you must cut it; and in the midst too! ah me!

1 *Rust.* Out on me, 'tis the caterpillar Sordido! how curst are the poor, that the viper was blest with this good fortune!

2 *Rust.* Nay, how accurst art thou, that art cause to the curse of the poor?

3 *Rust.* Ay, and to save so wretched a caitiff?

4 *Rust.* Curst be thy fingers that loos'd him!

2 *Rust.* Some desperate fury possess thee, that thou may'st hang thyself too!

5 *Rust.* Never may'st thou be saved, that saved so damn'd a monster!

Sord. What curses breathe these men! how have my deeds
Made my looks differ from another man's,
That they should thus detest and loath my life!
Out on my wretched humour! it is that
Makes me thus monstrous in true humane eyes.
Pardon me, gentle friends, I'll make fair 'mends
For my foul errors past, and twenty-fold
Restore to all men, what with wrong I robb'd them:
My barns and garners shall stand open still
To all the poor that come, and my best grain
Be made alms-bread, to feed half-famish'd mouths.
Though hitherto amongst you I have lived,
Like an unsavoury muck-hill to myself,
Yet now my gather'd heaps being spread abroad,
Shall turn to better and more fruitful uses.
Bless then this man, curse him no more for saving
My life and soul together.   O how deeply

The bitter curses of the poor do pierce!
I am by wonder changed; come in with me
And witness my repentance: now I prove,
No life is blest, that is not graced with love.   [*Exit.*

2 Rust. O miracle! see when a man has grace!

3 Rust. Had it not been pity so good a man should have been cast away?

2 Rust. Well, I'll get our clerk put his conversion in the *Acts and Monuments.*

4 Rust. Do, for I warrant him he's a martyr.

2 Rust. O God, how he wept, if you mark'd it! did you see how the tears trill'd?

5 Rust. Yes, believe me, like master vicar's bowls upon the green, for all the world.

3 Rust. O neighbour, God's blessing o' your heart, neighbour, 'twas a good grateful deed.   [*Exeunt.*

Cor. How now, Mitis! what's that you consider so seriously?

Mit. Troth, that which doth essentially please me, the warping condition of this green and soggy multitude; but in good faith, signior, your author hath largely outstript my expectation in this scene, I will liberally confess it. For when I saw Sordido so desperately intended, I thought I had had a hand of him, then.

Cor. What! you supposed he should have hung himself indeed?

Mit. I did, and had framed my objection to it ready, which may yet be very fitly urged, and with some necessity; for though his purposed violence lost the effect, and extended not to death, yet the intent and horror of the object was more than the nature of a comedy will in any sort admit.

Cor. Ay! what think you of Plautus, in his comedy called Cistellaria? there, where he brings in Alcesimarchus with a drawn sword ready to kill himself, and as he is e'en fixing his breast upon it, to be restrained from his resolved outrage, by Silenium and the bawd? Is not his authority of power to give our scene approbation?

Mit. Sir, I have this only evasion left me, to say, I think it be so indeed; your memory is happier than mine: but I wonder, what engine he will use to bring the rest out of their humours!

Cor. That will appear anon, never pre-occupy your imagination withal. Let your mind keep company with the scene still, which now removes itself from the country to the court. Here comes Macilente, and signior Brisk freshly suited; lose not yourself, for now the epitasis, or busy part of our subject, is in act.

SCENE III.—*An Apartment at the Court.*

Enter MACILENTE, FASTIDIOUS, *both in a new suit, and* CINEDO, *with tobacco.*

Fast. Well, now, signior Macilente, you are not only welcome to the court, but also to my mistress's withdrawing chamber.—Boy, get me some tobacco. I'll but go in, and shew I am here, and come to you presently, sir.   [*Exit.*

Maci. What's that he said? by heaven, I mark'd him not:
My thoughts and I were of another world.
I was admiring mine own outside here,
To think what privilege and palm it bears
Here, in the court! be a man ne'er so vile,
In wit, in judgment, manners, or what else;
If he can purchase but a silken cover,
He shall not only pass, but pass regarded:
Whereas, let him be poor, and meanly clad,
Though ne'er so richly parted, you shall have
A fellow that knows nothing but his beef,
Or how to rince his clammy guts in beer,
Will take him by the shoulders, or the throat,
And kick him down the stairs. Such is the state
Of virtue in bad clothes!—ha, ha, ha, ha!
That raiment should be in such high request!
How long should I be, ere I should put off
To the lord chancellor's tomb, or the shrives' posts?
By heav'n, I think, a thousand, thousand year.
His gravity, his wisdom, and his faith
To my dread sovereign, graces that survive him,
These I could well endure to reverence,
But not his tomb; no more than I'd commend
The chapel organ for the gilt without,
Or this base-viol, for the varnish'd face.

Re-enter FASTIDIOUS.

Fast. I fear I have made you stay somewhat long, sir; but is my tobacco ready, boy?

Cin. Ay, sir.

Fast. Give me; my mistress is upon coming, you shall see her presently, sir. [*Puffs.*] You'll say you never accosted a more piercing wit.—This tobacco is not dried, boy, or else the pipe is defective.—Oh, your wits of Italy are nothing comparable to her: her brain's a very quiver of jests, and she does dart them abroad with that sweet, loose, and judicial aim, that you would——here she comes, sir.   [SAVIOLINA *looks in, and draws back again.*

Maci. 'Twas time, his invention had been bogged else.

Sav. [*within.*] Give me my fan there.

Maci. How now, monsieur Brisk?

Fast. A kind of affectionate reverence strikes me with a cold shivering, methinks.

Maci. I like such tempers well, as stand before their mistresses with fear and trembling; and before their Maker, like impudent mountains!

Fast. By this hand, I'd spend twenty pound my vaulting horse stood here now, she might see me do but one trick.

Maci. Why, does she love activity?

Cin. Or, if you had but your long stockings on, to be dancing a galliard as she comes by.

Fast. Ay, either. O, these stirring humours make ladies mad with desire; she comes. My good genius embolden me: boy, the pipe quickly.

Enter SAVIOLINA.

Maci. What! will he give her music?

Fast. A second good morrow to my fair mistress.

Sav. Fair servant, I'll thank you a day hence, when the date of your salutation comes forth.

Fast. How like you that answer? is't not admirable?

Maci. I were a simple courtier, if I could not admire trifles, sir.

Fast. [*Talks and takes tobacco between the breaks.*] Troth, sweet lady, I shall [*puffs*]——be prepared to give you thanks for those thanks, and——study more officious, and obsequious regards——to your fair beauties.——Mend the pipe, boy.

Maci. I never knew tobacco taken as a parenthesis before.

Fast. 'Fore God, sweet lady, believe it, I do honour the meanest rush in this chamber for your love.

Sav. Ay, you need not tell me that, sir; I do think you do prize a rush before my love.

Maci. Is this the wonder of nations!

Fast. O, by this air, pardon me, I said *for* your love, by this light: but it is the accustomed sharpness of your ingenuity, sweet mistress, to [*takes down the viol, and plays*]——mass, your viol's new strung, methinks.

Maci. Ingenuity! I see his ignorance will not suffer him to slander her, which he had done most notably, if he had said wit for ingenuity, as he meant it.

Fast. By the soul of music, lady—*hum, hum.*

Sav. Would we might hear it once.

Fast. I do more adore and admire your—*hum, hum*—predominant perfections, than—*hum, hum*—ever I shall have power and faculty to express—*hum.*

Sav. Upon the viol de gambo, you mean?

Fast. It's miserably out of tune, by this hand.

Sav. Nay, rather by the fingers.

Maci. It makes good harmony with her wit.

Fast. Sweet lady, tune it. [*Saviolina tunes the viol.*]—Boy, some tobacco.

Maci. Tobacco again! he does court his mistress with very exceeding good changes.

Fast. Signior Macilente, you take none, sir?

Maci. No, unless I had a mistress, signior, it were a great indecorum for me to take tobacco.

Fast. How like you her wit?

[*Talks and takes tobacco between again.*

Maci. Her ingenuity is excellent, sir.

Fast. You see the subject of her sweet fingers there——Oh, she tickles it so, that——She makes it laugh most divinely;——I'll tell you a good jest now, and yourself shall say it's a good one: I have wished myself to be that instrument, I think, a thousand times, and not so few, by heaven!—

Maci. Not unlike, sir; but how? to be cased up and hung by on the wall?

Fast. O, no, sir, to be in use, I assure you; as your judicious eyes may testify.—

Sav. Here, servant, if you will play, come.

Fast. Instantly, sweet lady.——In good faith, here's most divine tobacco!

Sav. Nay, I cannot stay to dance after your pipe.

Fast. Good! Nay, dear lady, stay; by this sweet smoke, I think your wit be all fire.—

Maci. And he's the salamander belongs to it.

Sav. Is your tobacco perfumed, servant, that you swear by the sweet smoke?

Fast. Still more excellent! Before heaven, and these bright lights, I think——you are made of ingenuity, I—

Maci. True, as your discourse is. O abominable!

Fast. Will your ladyship take any?

Sav. O peace, I pray you; I love not the breath of a woodcock's head.

Fast. Meaning my head, lady?

Sav. Not altogether so, sir; but, as it were fatal to their follies that think to grace themselves with taking tobacco, when they want better entertainment, you see your pipe bears the true form of a woodcock's head.

Fast. O admirable simile!

Sav. 'Tis best leaving of you in admiration, sir.   [*Exit.*

Maci. Are these the admired lady-wits, that having so good a plain song, can run no better division upon it? All her jests are of the stamp March was fifteen years ago. Is this the comet, monsieur Fastidious, that your gallants wonder at so?

Fast. Heart of a gentleman, to neglect me afore the presence thus! Sweet sir, I beseech you be silent in my disgrace. By the muses, I was never in so vile a humour in my life, and her wit was at the flood too! Report it not for a million, good sir; let me be so far endeared to your love.   [*Exeunt.*

Mit. *What follows next, signior Cordatus? this gallant's humour is almost spent; methinks it ebbs apace, with this contrary breath of his mistress.*

Cor. *O, but it will flow again for all this, till there come a general drought of humour among all our actors, and then I fear not but his will fall as low as any. See who presents himself here!*

Mit. *What, in the old case?*

Cor. *Ay, faith, which makes it the more pitiful; you understand where the scene is?*

ACT IV

SCENE I.—*A Room in* DELIRO'S *House.*

Enter FUNGOSO, FALLACE *following him.*

Fal. Why are you so melancholy, brother?

Fung. I am not melancholy, I thank you, sister.

Fal. Why are you not merry then? there are but two of us in all the world, and if we should not be comforts one to another, God help us!

Fung. Faith, I cannot tell, sister; but if a man had any true melancholy in him, it would make him melancholy to see his yeomanly father cut his neighbours' throats, to make his son a gentleman; and yet, when he has cut them, he will see his son's throat cut too, ere he make him a true gentleman indeed, before death cut his own throat. I must be the first head of our house, and yet he will not give me the head till I be made so. Is any man termed a gentleman, that is not always in the fashion? I would know but that.

Fal. If you be melancholy for that, brother, I think I have as much cause to be melancholy as any one: for I'll be sworn, I live as little in the fashion as any woman in London. By the faith of a gentlewoman, beast that I am to say it! I have not one friend in the world besides my husband. When saw you master Fastidious Brisk, brother?

Fung. But a while since, sister, I think: I know not well in truth. By this hand I could fight with all my heart, methinks.

Fal. Nay, good brother, be not resolute.

Fung. I sent him a letter, and he writes me no answer neither.

Fal. Oh, sweet Fastidious Brisk! O fine courtier! thou art he makest me sigh, and say, how blessed is that woman that hath a courtier to her husband, and how miserable a dame she is, that hath neither husband, nor friend in the court! O sweet Fastidious! O fine courtier! How comely he bows him in his court'sy! how full he hits a woman between the lips when he kisses! how upright he sits at the table! how daintily he carves! how sweetly he talks, and tells news of this lord and of that lady! how cleanly he wipes his spoon at every spoonful of any whitemeat he eats! and what a neat case of pick-tooths he carries about him still! O sweet Fastidious! O fine courtier!

Enter DELIRO *at a distance, with* Musicians.

Deli. See, yonder she is, gentlemen. Now, as ever you'll bear the name of musicians, touch your instruments sweetly; she has a delicate ear, I tell you: play not a false note, I beseech you.

Musi. Fear not, signior Deliro.

Deli. O, begin, begin, some sprightly thing: lord, how my imagination labours with the success of it! [*They strike up a lively tune.*] Well said, good i'faith! Heaven grant it please her. I'll not be seen, for then she'll be sure to dislike it.

Fal. Hey——da! this is excellent! I'll lay my life this is my husband's dotage. I thought so; nay, never play bo-peep with me; I know you do nothing but study how to anger me, sir.

Deli. [*coming forward.*] Anger thee, sweet wife! why, didst thou not send for musicians at supper last night thyself?

Fal. To supper, sir! now, come up to supper, I beseech you: as though there were no difference between supper-time, when folks should be merry, and this time when they should be melancholy. I would never take upon me to take a wife, if I had no more judgment to please her.

Deli. Be pleased, sweet wife, and they shall have done; and would to fate my life were done, if I can never please thee!

[*Exeunt Musicians.*

Enter MACILENTE.

Maci. Save you, lady; where is master Deliro?

Deli. Here, master Macilente: you are welcome from court, sir; no doubt you have been graced exceedingly of master Brisk's mistress, and the rest of the ladies for his sake.

Maci. Alas, the poor fantastic! he's scarce known
To any lady there; and those that know him,
Know him the simplest man of all they know:
Deride, and play upon his amorous humours,
Though he but apishly doth imitate
The gallant'st courtiers, kissing ladies' pumps,
Holding the cloth for them, praising their wits,
And servilely observing every one
May do them pleasure: fearful to be seen
With any man, though he be ne'er so worthy,
That's not in grace with some that are the greatest.
Thus courtiers do, and these he counterfeits,
But sets no such a sightly carriage
Upon their vanities, as they themselves;
And therefore they despise him: for indeed
He's like the zany to a tumbler,
That tries tricks after him, to make men laugh.

Fal. Here's an unthankful spiteful wretch! the good gentleman vouchsafed to make him his companion, because my husband put him into a few rags, and now see how the unrude rascal backbites him! [*Aside.*

Deli. Is he no more graced amongst them then, say you?

Maci. Faith, like a pawn at chess: fills up a room, that's all.

Fal. O monster of men! can the earth bear such an envious caitiff? [*Aside.*

Deli. Well, I repent me I ever credited him so much: but now I see what he is, and that his masking vizor is off, I'll forbear him no longer. All his lands are mortgaged to me, and forfeited; besides, I have bonds of his in my hand, for the receipt of now fifty pounds now a hundred, now two hundred; still, as he has had a fan but wagged at him, he would be in a new suit. Well, I'll salute him by a serjeant, the next time I see him i'faith, I'll suit him.

Maci. Why, you may soon see him, sir, for he is to meet signior Puntarvolo at a notary's by the Exchange, presently; where he means to take up, upon return.

Fal. Now, out upon thee, Judas! canst thou not be content to backbite thy friend, but thou must betray him! Wilt thou seek the undoing of any man? and of such a man too? and will you, sir, get your living by the counsel of traitors?

Deli. Dear wife, have patience.

Fal. The house will fall, the ground will open and swallow us: I'll not bide here for all the gold and silver in heaven.

                                    [Exit with Fungoso.

Deli. O, good Macilente, let's follow and appease her, or the peace of my life is at an end.   *[Exit.*

Maci. Now pease, and not peace, feed that life, whose head hangs so heavily over a woman's manger!   *[Exit.*

SCENE II.—*Another Room in the same.*

Enter FALLACE *and* FUNGOSO *running ; she claps to the door.*

Fal. Help me, brother! Ods body, an you come here I'll do myself a mischief.

Deli. [*within.*] Nay, hear me, sweet wife; unless thou wilt have me go, I will not go.

Fal. Tut, you shall never have that vantage of me, to say, you are undone by me. I'll not bid you stay, I. Brother, sweet brother, here's four angels, I'll give you towards your suit: for the love of gentry, and as ever you came of Christian creature, make haste to the water side, (you know where master Fastidious uses to land,) and give him warning of my husband's malicious intent; and tell him of that lean rascal's treachery. O heavens, how my flesh rises at him! Nay, sweet brother, make haste: you may say, I would have writ to him, but that the necessity of the time would not permit. He cannot choose but take it extraordinarily from me: and commend me to him, good brother; say, I sent you. [*Exit.*

Fung. Let me see, these four angels, and then forty shillings more I can borrow on my gown in Fetter Lane.—Well, I will go presently, say on my suit, pay as much money as I have, and swear myself into credit with my tailor for the rest.   *[Exit.*

SCENE III.—*Another Room in the same.*

Enter DELIRO *and* MACILENTE.

Deli. O, on my soul you wrong her, Macilente. Though she be froward, yet I know she is honest.

Maci. Well, then have I no judgment. Would any woman, but one that were wild in her affections, have broke out into that immodest and violent passion against her husband? or is't possible—

Deli. If you love me, forbear; all the arguments i' the world shall never wrest my heart to believe it.   [*Exeunt.*

Cor. How like you the deciphering of his dotage?

Mit. O, strangely: and of the other's envy too, that labours so seriously to set debate betwixt a man and his wife. Stay, here comes the knight adventurer.

Cor. Ay, and his scrivener with him.

SCENE IV.—PUNTARVOLO'S *Lodgings.*

Enter PUNTARVOLO, Notary, *and* Servants *with the dog and cat.*

Punt. I wonder monsieur Fastidious comes not! But, notary, if thou please to draw the indentures the while, I will give thee thy instructions.

Not. With all my heart, sir; and I'll fall in hand with them presently.

Punt. Well then, first the sum is to be understood.

Not. [*writes.*] Good, sir.

Punt. Next, our several appellations, and character of my dog and cat, must be known. Shew him the cat, sirrah.

Not. So, sir.

Punt. Then, that the intended bound is the Turk's court in Constantinople; the time limited for our return, a year; and that if either of us miscarry, the whole venture is lost. These are general, conceiv'st thou? or if either of us turn Turk.

Not. Ay, sir.

Punt. Now, for particulars: that I may make my travels by sea or land, to my best liking; and that hiring a coach for myself, it shall be lawful for my dog or cat, or both, to ride with me in the said coach.

Not. Very good, sir.

Punt. That I may choose to give my dog or cat, fish, for fear of bones; or any other nutriment that, by the judgment of the most authentical physicians where I travel, shall be thought dangerous.

Not. Well, sir.

Punt. That, after the receipt of his money, he shall neither, in his own person, nor any other, either by direct or indirect means, as magic, witchcraft, or other such exotic arts, attempt, practise, or complot any thing to the prejudice of me, my dog, or my cat: neither shall I use the help of any such sorceries or enchantments, as unctions to make our skins impenetrable, or to travel invisible by virtue of a powder, or a ring, or to hang any three-forked charm about my dog's neck, secretly conveyed into his collar; (understand you?) but that all be performed sincerely, without fraud or imposture.

Not. So, sir.

Punt. That, for testimony of the performance, myself am to bring thence a Turk's mustachio, my dog a Grecian hare's lips, and my cat the train or tail of a Thracian rat.

Not. [*writes.*] 'Tis done, sir.

Punt. 'Tis said, sir; not done, sir.   But forward; that, upon my return, and landing on the Tower - wharf, with the aforesaid testimony, I am to receive five for one, according to the proportion of the sums put forth.

Not. Well, sir.

Punt. Provided, that if before our departure, or setting forth, either myself or these be visited with sickness, or any other casual event, so that the whole course of the adventure be hindered thereby, that then he is to return, and I am to receive the pre-nominated proportion upon fair and equal terms.

Not. Very good, sir; is this all?

Punt. It is all, sir; and dispatch them, good notary.

Not. As fast as is possible, sir.   [*Exit.*

Enter CARLO.

Punt. O Carlo! welcome: saw you monsieur Brisk?

Car. Not I: did he appoint you to meet here?

Punt. Ay, and I muse he should be so tardy; he is to take an hundred pounds of me in venture, if he maintain his promise.

Car. Is his hour past?

Punt. Not yet, but it comes on apace.

Car. Tut, be not jealous of him; he will sooner break all the commandments, than his hour; upon my life, in such a case trust him.

Punt. Methinks, Carlo, you look very smooth, ha!

Car. Why, I came but now from a hot-house; I must needs look smooth.

Punt. From a hot-house!

Car. Ay, do you make a wonder on't? why, it is your only physic. Let a man sweat once a week in a hot-house, and be well rubb'd, and froted, with a good plump juicy wench, and sweet linen, he shall ne'er have the pox.

Punt. What, the French pox?

Car. The French pox! our pox: we have them in as good a form as they, man; what?

Punt. Let me perish, but thou art a salt one! was your new-created gallant there with you, Sogliardo?

Car. O porpoise! hang him, no: he's a leiger at Horn's ordinary, yonder; his villainous Ganymede and he have been droning a tobacco-pipe there ever since yesterday noon.

Punt. Who? signior Tripartite, that would give my dog the whiffe?

Car. Ay, he.   They have hired a chamber and all, private, to practise in, for the making of the patoun, the receipt reciprocal, and a number of other mysteries not yet extant.   I brought some dozen or twenty gallants this morning to view them, as you'd do a piece of perspective, in at a key-hole; and there we might see Sogliardo sit in a chair, holding his snout up like a sow under an apple-tree, while the other open'd his nostrils with a poking-stick, to give the smoke a more free delivery. They had spit some three or four-score ounces between 'em, afore we came away.

Punt. How! spit three or fourscore ounces?

Car. Ay, and preserv'd it in porrengers, as a barber does his blood, when he opens a vein.

Punt. Out, pagan! how dost thou open the vein of thy friend?

Car. Friend! is there any such foolish thing in the world, ha? 'slid, I never relished it yet.

Punt. Thy humour is the more dangerous.

Car. No, not a whit, signior. Tut, a man must keep time in all; I can oil my tongue when I meet him next, and look with a good sleek forehead; 'twill take away all soil of suspicion, and that's enough: what Lynceus can see my heart? Pish, the title of a friend! it's a vain, idle thing, only venerable among fools; you shall not have one that has any opinion of wit affect it.

Enter DELIRO *and* MACILENTE.

Deli. Save you, good sir Puntarvolo.

Punt. Signior Deliro! welcome.

Deli. Pray you, sir, did you see master Fastidious Brisk? I heard he was to meet your worship here.

Punt. You heard no figment, sir; I do expect him at every pulse of my watch.

Deli. In good time, sir.

Car. There's a fellow now looks like one of the patricians of Sparta; marry, his wit's after ten i' the hundred: a good blood-hound, a close-mouthed dog, he follows the scent well; marry, he's at a fault now, methinks.

Punt. I should wonder at that creature is free from the danger of thy tongue.

Car. O, I cannot abide these limbs of satin, or rather Satan indeed, that will walk, like the children of darkness, all day in a melancholy shop, with their pockets full of blanks, ready to swallow up as many poor unthrifts as come within the verge.

Punt. So! and what hast thou for him that is with him, now?

Car. O, d——n me! immortality! I'll not meddle with him; the pure element of fire, all spirit, extraction.

Punt. How, Carlo! ha, what is he, man?

Car. A scholar, Macilente; do you not know him? a rank, raw-boned anatomy, he walks up and down like a charged musket, no man dares encounter him: that's his rest there.

Punt. His rest! why, has he a forked head?

Car. Pardon me, that's to be suspended; you are too quick, too apprehensive.

Deli. Troth, now I think on't, I'll defer it till some other time.

Maci. Not by any means, signior, you shall not lose this opportunity, he will be here presently now.

Deli. Yes, faith, Macilente, 'tis best. For, look you, sir, I shall so exceedingly offend my wife in't, that—

Maci. Your wife! now for shame lose these thoughts, and become the master of your own spirits. Should I, if I had a wife, suffer myself to be thus passionately carried to and fro with the stream of her humour, and neglect my deepest affairs, to serve her affections? 'Slight, I would geld myself first.

Deli. O, but signior, had you such a wife as mine is, you would—

Maci. Such a wife! Now hate me, sir, if ever I discern'd any wonder in your wife yet, with all the speculation I have: I have seen some that have been thought fairer than she, in my time; and I have seen those, have not been altogether so tall, esteem'd properer women; and I have seen less noses grow upon sweeter faces, that have done very well too, in my judgment. But, in good faith, signior, for all this, the gentlewoman is a good, pretty, proud, hard-favour'd thing, marry not so peerlessly to be doted upon, I must confess: nay, be not angry.

Deli. Well, sir, however you please to forget yourself, I have not deserv'd to be thus played upon; but henceforth, pray you forbear my house, for I can but faintly endure the savour of his breath, at my table, that shall thus jade me for my courtesies.

Maci. Nay, then, signior, let me tell you, your wife is no proper woman, and by my life, I suspect her honesty, that's more, which you may likewise suspect, if you please, do you see? I'll urge you to nothing against your appetite, but if you please, you may suspect it.

Deli. Good, sir.   [*Exit.*

Maci. Good, sir! now horn upon horn pursue thee, thou blind, egregious dotard!

Car. O, you shall hear him speak like envy.—Signior Macilente, you saw monsieur Brisk lately: I heard you were with him at court.

Maci. Ay, Buffone, I was with him.

Car. And how is he respected there? I know you'll deal ingenuously with us; is he made much of amongst the sweeter sort of gallants?

Maci. Faith, ay; his civet and his casting-glass
Have helpt him to a place amongst the rest:
And there, his seniors give him good slight looks,
After their garb, smile, and salute in French
With some new compliment.

Car. What, is this all?

Maci. Why say, that they should shew the frothy fool
Such grace as they pretend comes from the heart,
He had a mighty windfall out of doubt!
Why, all their graces are not to do grace
To virtue or desert; but to ride both
With their gilt spurs quite breathless, from themselves.
'Tis now esteem'd precisianism in wit,
And a disease in nature, to be kind

Toward desert, to love or seek good names.
Who feeds with a good name? who thrives with loving?
Who can provide feast for his own desires,
With serving others?—ha, ha, ha!
'Tis folly, by our wisest worldlings proved,
If not to gain by love, to be beloved.

Car. How like you him? is't not a good spiteful slave, ha?

Punt. Shrewd, shrewd.

Car. D—n me! I could eat his flesh now; divine sweet villain!

Maci. Nay, prithee leave: What's he there?

Car. Who? this in the starched beard? it's the dull stiff knight Puntarvolo, man; he's to travel now presently: he has a good knotty wit; marry, he carries little on't out of the land with him.

Maci. How then?

Car. He puts it forth in venture, as he does his money upon the return of a dog and cat.

Maci. Is this he?

Car. Ay, this is he; a good tough gentleman: he looks like a shield of brawn at Shrove-tide, out of date, and ready to take his leave; or a dry pole of ling upon Easter-eve, that has furnish'd the table all Lent, as he has done the city this last vacation.

Maci. Come, you'll never leave your stabbing similes: I shall have you aiming at me with 'em by and by; but—

Car. O, renounce me then! pure, honest, good devil, I love thee above the love of women: I could e'en melt in admiration of thee, now. Ods so, look here, man; Sir Dagonet and his squire!

Enter SOGLIARDO *and* SHIFT.

Sog. Save you, my dear gallantos: nay, come, approach, good cavalier: prithee, sweet knight, know this gentleman, he's one that it pleases me to use as my good friend and companion; and therefore do him good offices: I beseech you, gentles, know him, I know him all over.

Punt. Sir, for signior Sogliardo's sake, let it suffice, I know you.

Sog. Why, as I am a gentleman, I thank you, knight, and it shall suffice. Hark you, sir Puntarvolo, you'd little think it; he's as resolute a piece of flesh as any in the world.

Punt. Indeed, sir!

Sog. Upon my gentility, sir: Carlo, a word with you; do you see that same fellow, there?

Car. What, cavalier Shift?

Sog. O, you know him; cry you mercy: before me, I think him the tallest man living within the walls of Europe.

Car. The walls of Europe! take heed what you say, signior, Europe's a huge thing within the walls.

Sog. Tut, an 'twere as huge again, I'd justify what I speak. 'Slid, he swagger'd even now in a place where we were—I never saw a man do it more resolute.

Car. Nay, indeed, swaggering is a good argument of resolution. Do you hear this, signior?

Maci. Ay, to my grief.   O, that such muddy flags,
For every drunken flourish should achieve
The name of manhood, whilst true perfect valour,
Hating to shew itself, goes by despised!
Heart! I do know now, in a fair just cause,
I dare do more than he, a thousand times:
Why should not they take knowledge of this, ha!
And give my worth allowance before his?
Because I cannot swagger.—Now, the pox
Light on your Pickt-hatch prowess!

Sog. Why, I tell you, sir; he has been the only *Bid-stand* that ever kept New-market, Salisbury-plain, Hockley i' the Hole, Gads-hill, and all the high places of any request: he has had his mares and his geldings, he, have been worth forty, threescore, a hundred pound a horse, would ha' sprung you over hedge and ditch like your greyhound: he has done five hundred robberies in his time, more or less, I assure you.

Punt. What, and scaped?

Sog. Scaped! i' faith, ay: he has broken the gaol when he has been in irons and irons; and been out and in again; and out, and in; forty times, and not so few, he.

Maci. A fit trumpet, to proclaim such a person.

Car. But can this be possible?

Shift. Why, 'tis nothing, sir, when a man gives his affections to it.

Sog. Good Pylades, discourse a robbery or two, to satisfy these gentlemen of thy worth.

Shift. Pardon me, my dear Orestes; causes have their quiddits, and 'tis ill jesting with bell-ropes.

Car. How! Pylades and Orestes?

Sog. Ay, he is my Pylades, and I am his Orestes: how like you the conceit?

Car. O, 'tis an old stale interlude device: no, I'll give you names myself, look you; he shall be your Judas, and you shall be his elder-tree to hang on.

Maci. Nay, rather let him be captain Pod, and this his motion: for he does nothing but shew him.

Car. Excellent: or thus; you shall be Holden, and he your camel.

Shift. You do not mean to ride, gentlemen?

Punt. Faith, let me end it for you, gallants: you shall be his Countenance, and he your Resolution.

Sog. Troth, that's pretty: how say you, cavalier, shall it be so?

Car. Ay, ay, most voices.

Shift. Faith, I am easily yielding to any good impressions.

Sog. Then give hands, good Resolution.

Car. Mass, he cannot say, good Countenance, now, properly, to him again.

Punt. Yes, by an irony.

Maci. O, sir, the countenance of Resolution should, as he is, be altogether grim and unpleasant.

Enter FASTIDIOUS BRISK.

Fast. Good hours make music with your mirth, gentlemen, and keep time to your humours!—How now, Carlo?

Punt. Monsieur Brisk? many a long look have I extended for you, sir.

Fast. Good faith, I must crave pardon: I was invited this morning, ere I was out of my bed, by a bevy of ladies, to a banquet: whence it was almost one of Hercules's labours for me to come away, but that the respect of my promise did so prevail with me. I know they'll take it very ill, especially one, that gave me this bracelet of her hair but over night, and this pearl another gave me from her forehead, marry she——what! are the writings ready?

Punt. I will send my man to know. Sirrah, go you to the notary's, and learn if he be ready: leave the dog, sir. [*Exit Servant.*

Fast. And how does my rare qualified friend, Sogliardo? Oh, signior Macilente! by these eyes, I saw you not; I had saluted you sooner else, o' my troth. I hope, sir, I may presume upon you, that you will not divulge my late check, or disgrace, indeed, sir.

Maci. You may, sir.

Car. He knows some notorious jest by this gull, that he hath him so obsequious.

Sog. Monsieur Fastidious, do you see this fellow there? does he not look like a clown? would you think there were any thing in him?

Fast. Any thing in him! beshrew me, ay; the fellow hath a good ingenious face.

Sog. By this element he is as ingenious a tall man as ever swagger'd about London: he, and I, call Countenance and Resolution; but his name is cavalier Shift.

Punt. Cavalier, you knew signior Clog, that was hang'd for the robbery at Harrow on the hill?

Sog. Knew him, sir! why, 'twas he gave all the directions for the action.

Punt. How! was it your project, sir?

Shift. Pardon me, Countenance, you do me some wrong to make occasions public, which I imparted to you in private.

Sog. God's will! here are none but friends, Resolution.

Shift. That's all one; things of consequence must have their respects; where, how, and to whom.—Yes, sir, he shewed himself a true Clog in the coherence of that affair, sir; for, if he had managed matters as they were corroborated to him, it had been better for him by a forty or fifty score of pounds, sir; and he himself might have lived, in despight of fates, to have fed on woodcocks, with the rest: but it was his heavy fortune to sink, poor Clog! and therefore talk no more of him.

Punt. Why, had he more aiders then?

Sog. O lord, sir! ay, there were some present there, that were the Nine Worthies to him, i'faith.

Shift. Ay, sir, I can satisfy you at more convenient conference: but, for mine own part, I have now reconciled myself to other courses, and profess a living out of my other qualities.

Sog. Nay, he has left all now, I assure you, and is able to live like a gentleman, by his qualities. By this dog, he has the most rare gift in tobacco that ever you knew.

Car. He keeps more ado with this monster, than ever Banks did with his horse, or the fellow with the elephant.

Maci. He will hang out his picture shortly, in a cloth, you shall see.

Sog. O, he does manage a quarrel the best that ever you saw, for terms and circumstances.

Fast. Good faith, signior, now you speak of a quarrel, I'll acquaint you with a difference that happened between a gallant and myself; sir Puntarvolo, you know him if I should name him, signior Luculento.

Punt. Luculento! what inauspicious chance interposed itself to your two loves?

Fast. Faith, sir, the same that sundered Agamemnon and great Thetis' son; but let the cause escape, sir: he sent me a challenge, mixt with some few braves, which I restored, and in fine we met. Now, indeed, sir, I must tell you, he did offer at first very desperately, but without judgment: for, look you, sir, I cast myself into this figure; now he comes violently on, and withal advancing his rapier to strike, I thought to have took his arm, for he had left his whole body to my election, and I was sure he could not recover his guard. Sir, I mist my purpose in his arm, rash'd his doublet-sleeve, ran him close by the left cheek, and through his hair. He again lights me here,—I had on a gold cable hatband, then new come up, which I wore about a murey French hat I had,—cuts my hatband, and yet it was massy goldsmith's work, cuts my brims, which by good fortune, being thick embroidered with gold twist and spangles, disappointed the force of the blow: nevertheless, it grazed on my shoulder, takes me away six purls of an Italian cut-work band I wore, cost me three pound in the Exchange but three days before.

Punt. This was a strange encounter.

Fast. Nay, you shall hear, sir: with this we both fell out, and breath'd. Now, upon the second sign of his assault, I betook me to the former manner of my defence; he, on the other side, abandon'd his body to the same danger as before, and follows me still with blows: but I being loth to take the deadly advantage that lay before me of his left side, made a kind of stramazoun, ran him up to the hilts through the doublet, through the shirt, and yet miss'd the skin. He, making a reverse blow,—falls upon my emboss'd girdle, I had thrown off the hangers a little before—strikes off a skirt of a thick-laced satin doublet I had, lined with four taffatas, cuts off two panes embroidered with pearl, rends through the drawings-out of tissue, enters the linings, and skips the flesh.

Car. I wonder he speaks not of his wrought shirt.

Fast. Here, in the opinion of mutual damage, we paused; but, ere I proceed, I must tell you, signior, that, in this last encounter, not having leisure to put off my silver spurs, one of the rowels catch'd hold of the ruffle of my boot, and, being Spanish leather, and subject to tear, overthrows me, rends me two pair of silk stockings, that I put on, being somewhat a raw morning, a peach colour and another, and strikes me some half inch deep into the side of the calf: he, seeing the blood come, presently takes horse, and away: I, having bound up my wound with a piece of my wrought shirt——

Car. O! comes it in there?

Fast. Rid after him, and, lighting at the court gate both together, embraced, and march'd hand in hand up into the presence. Was not this business well carried?

Maci. Well! yes, and by this we can guess what apparel the gentleman wore.

Punt. 'Fore valour, it was a designment begun with much resolution, maintain'd with as much prowess, and ended with more humanity.——

Re-enter Servant.

How now, what says the notary?

Serv. He says, he is ready, sir; he stays but your worship's pleasure.

Punt. Come, we will go to him, monsieur. Gentlemen, shall we entreat you to be witnesses?

Sog. You shall entreat me, sir.—Come, Resolution.

Shift. I follow you, good Countenance.

Car. Come, signior, come, come.   [*Exeunt all but Macilente.*

Maci. O, that there should be fortune
To clothe these men, so naked in desert!
And that the just storm of a wretched life
Beats them not ragged for their wretched souls,
And, since as fruitless, even as black, as coals!   [*Exit.*

Mit. Why, but signior, how comes it that Fungoso appeared not with his sister's intelligence to Brisk?

Cor. Marry, long of the evil angels that she gave him, who have indeed tempted the good simple youth to follow the tail of the fashion, and neglect the imposition of his friends. Behold, here he comes, very worshipfully attended, and with good variety.

SCENE V.—*A Room in* DELIRO'S *House.*

Enter FUNGOSO *in a new suit, followed by his* Tailor, Shoemaker,
and Haberdasher.

Fung. Gramercy, good shoemaker, I'll put to strings myself.
[*Exit Shoemaker.*]—Now, sir, let me see, what must you have for
this hat?

Habe. Here's the bill, sir.

Fung. How does it become me, well?

Tai. Excellent, sir, as ever you had any hat in your life.

Fung. Nay, you'll say so all.

Habe. In faith, sir, the hat's as good as any man in this town can
serve you, and will maintain fashion as long; never trust me for a
groat else.

Fung. Does it apply well to my suit?

Tai. Exceeding well, sir.

Fung. How lik'st thou my suit, haberdasher?

Habe. By my troth, sir, 'tis very rarely well made; I never saw
a suit sit better, I can tell on.

Tai. Nay, we have no art to please our friends, we!

Fung. Here, haberdasher, tell this same.   [*Gives him money.*

Habe. Good faith, sir, it makes you have an excellent body.

Fung. Nay, believe me, I think I have as good a body in clothes
as another.

Tai. You lack points to bring your apparel together, sir.

Fung. I'll have points anon. How now! Is't right?

Habe. Faith, sir, 'tis too little; but upon farther hopes——Good
morrow to you, sir.   [*Exit.*

Fung. Farewell, good haberdasher. Well, now, master Snip, let
me see your bill.

Mit. Me thinks he discharges his followers too thick.

*Cor. O, therein he saucily imitates some great man. I warrant you,
though he turns off them, he keeps this tailor, in place of a page, to
follow him still.*

Fung. This bill is very reasonable, in faith: hark you, master
Snip—Troth, sir, I am not altogether so well furnished at this
present, as I could wish I were; but——if you'll do me the favour
to take part in hand, you shall have all I have, by this hand.

Tai. Sir——

Fung. And but give me credit for the rest, till the beginning of
the next term.

Tai. O lord, sir——

Fung. 'Fore God, and by this light, I'll pay you to the utmost,
and acknowledge myself very deeply engaged to you by the courtesy.

Tai. Why, how much have you there, sir?

Fung. Marry, I have here four angels, and fifteen shillings of
white money: it's all I have, as I hope to be blest.

Tai. You will not fail me at the next term with the rest?

Fung. No, an I do, pray heaven I be hang'd. Let me never breathe again upon this mortal stage, as the philosopher calls it! By this air, and as I am a gentleman, I'll hold.

Cor. He were an iron-hearted fellow, in my judgment, that would not credit him upon this volley of oaths.

Tai. Well, sir, I'll not stick with any gentleman for a trifle: you know what 'tis remains?

Fung. Ay, sir, and I give you thanks in good faith. O fate, how happy I am made in this good fortune! Well, now I'll go seek out monsieur Brisk. 'Ods so, I have forgot riband for my shoes, and points. 'Slid, what luck's this! how shall I do? Master Snip, pray let me reduct some two or three shillings for points and ribands: as I am an honest man, I have utterly disfurnished myself, in the default of memory; pray let me be beholding to you; it shall come home in the bill, believe me.

Tai. Faith, sir, I can hardly depart with ready money; but I'll take up, and send you some by my boy presently. What coloured riband would you have?

Fung. What you shall think meet in your judgment, sir, to my suit.

Tai. Well, I'll send you some presently.

Fung. And points too, sir?

Tai. And points too, sir.

Fung. Good lord, how shall I study to deserve this kindness of you, sir! Pray let your youth make haste, for I should have done a business an hour since, that I doubt I shall come too late. [*Exit Tailor.*] Now, in good faith, I am exceeding proud of my suit.

Cor. Do you observe the plunges that this poor gallant is put to, signior, to purchase the fashion?

Mit. Ay, and to be still a fashion behind with the world, that's the sport.

Cor. Stay: O, here they come from seal'd and deliver'd.

SCENE VI.—PUNTARVOLO'S *Lodgings.*

Enter PUNTARVOLO, FASTIDIOUS BRISK *in a new suit, and* Servants *with the dog.*

Punt. Well, now my whole venture is forth, I will resolve to depart shortly.

Fast. Faith, sir Puntarvolo, go to the court, and take leave of the ladies first.

Punt. I care not, if it be this afternoon's labour. Where is Carlo?

Fast. Here he comes.

Enter CARLO, SOGLIARDO, SHIFT, *and* MACILENTE.

Car. Faith, gallants, I am persuading this gentleman [*points to Sogliardo*] to turn courtier. He is a man of fair revenue, and his estate will bear the charge well. Besides, for his other gifts of the mind, or so, why they are as nature lent him them, pure, simple, without any artificial drug or mixture of these two threadbare beggarly qualities, learning and knowledge, and therefore the more accommodate and genuine. Now, for the life itself——

Fast. O, the most celestial, and full of wonder and delight, that can be imagined, signior, beyond thought and apprehension of pleasure! A man lives there in that divine rapture, that he will think himself i' the ninth heaven for the time, and lose all sense of 'mortality whatsoever, when he shall behold such glorious, and almost immortal beauties; hear such angelical and harmonious voices, discourse with such flowing and ambrosial spirits, whose wits are as sudden as lightning, and humorous as nectar; oh, it makes a man all quintessence and flame, and lifts him up, in a moment, to the very crystal crown of the sky, where, hovering in the strength of his imagination, he shall behold all the delights of the Hesperides, the Insulæ Fortunatæ, Adonis' Gardens, Tempe, or what else, confined within the amplest verge of poesy, to be mere umbræ, and imperfect figures, conferred with the most essential felicity of your court.

Maci. Well, this ecomium was not extemporal, it came too perfectly off.

Car. Besides, sir, you shall never need to go to a hot-house, you shall sweat there with courting your mistress, or losing your money at primero, as well as in all the stoves in Sweden. Marry, this, sir, you must ever be sure to carry a good strong perfume about you, that your mistress's dog may smell you out amongst the rest; and, in making love to her, never fear to be out; for you may have a pipe of tobacco, or a bass viol shall hang o' the wall, of purpose, will put you in presently. The tricks your Resolution has taught you in tobacco, the whiffe, and those sleights, will stand you in very good ornament there.

Fast. Ay, to some, perhaps; but, an he should come to my mistress with tobacco (this gentleman knows) she'd reply upon him, i'faith. O, by this bright sun, she has the most acute, ready, and facetious wit that——tut, there's no spirit able to stand her. You can report it, signior, you have seen her.

Punt. Then can he report no less, out of his judgment, I assure him.

Maci. Troth, I like her well enough, but she's too self-conceited, methinks.

Fast. Ay, indeed, she's a little too self-conceited; an 'twere not for that humour, she were the most-to-be-admired lady in the world.

Punt. Indeed, it is a humour that takes from her other excellences.

Maci. Why, it may easily be made to forsake her, in my thought.

Fast. Easily, sir! then are all impossibilities easy.

Maci. You conclude too quick upon me, signior. What will you say, if I make it so perspicuously appear now, that yourself shall confess nothing more possible?

Fast. Marry, I will say, I will both applaud and admire you for it.

Punt. And I will second him in the admiration.

Maci. Why, I'll show you, gentlemen.—Carlo, come hither.

　　　　　　　　　　[Maci., Car., Punt., and Fast. whisper together.

Sog. Good faith, I have a great humour to the court. What thinks my Resolution? shall I adventure?

Shift. Troth, Countenance, as you please; the place is a place of good reputation and capacity.

Sog. O, my tricks in tobacco, as Carlo says, will show excellent there.

Shift. Why, you may go with these gentlemen now, and see fashions; and after, as you shall see correspondence.

Sog. You say true. You will go with me, Resolution?

Shift. I will meet you, Countenance, about three or four o'clock; but, to say to go with you, I cannot; for, as I am Apple-John, I am to go before the cockatrice you saw this morning, and therefore pray, present me excused, good Countenance.

Sog. Farewell, good Resolution, but fail not to meet.

Shift. As I live.　　　　　　　　　　　　　　　　　*[Exit.*

Punt. Admirably excellent!

Maci. If you can but persuade Sogliardo to court, there's all now.

Car. O, let me alone, that's my task.　　　*[Goes to Sogliardo.*

Fast. Now, by wit, Macilente, it's above measure excellent; 'twill be the only court-exploit that ever proved courtier ingenious.

Punt. Upon my soul, it puts the lady quite out of her humour, and we shall laugh with judgment.

Car. Come, the gentleman was of himself resolved to go with you, afore I moved it.

Maci. Why, then, gallants, you two and Carlo go afore to prepare the jest; Sogliardo and I will come some while after you.

Car. Pardon me, I am not for the court.

Punt. That's true; Carlo comes not at court, indeed. Well, you shall leave it to the faculty of monsieur Brisk, and myself; upon our lives, we will manage it happily. Carlo shall bespeak supper at the Mitre, against we come back: where we will meet and dimple our cheeks with laughter at the success.

Car. Ay, but will you promise to come?

Punt. Myself shall undertake for them; he that fails, let his reputation lie under the lash of thy tongue.

Car. Ods so, look who comes here!

　　　　　　　　　　　Enter FUNGOSO.

Sog. What, nephew!

Fung. Uncle, God save you; did you see a gentleman, one monsieur Brisk, a courtier? he goes in such a suit as I do.

Sog. Here is the gentleman, nephew, but not in such a suit.

Fung. Another suit!

Sog. How now, nephew?

Fast. Would you speak with me, sir?

Car. Ay, when he has recovered himself, poor Poll!

Punt. Some rosa-solis.

Maci. How now, signior?

Fung. I am not well, sir.

Maci. Why, this it is to dog the fashion.

Car. Nay, come, gentlemen, remember your affairs; his disease is nothing but the flux of apparel.

Punt. Sirs, return to the lodging, keep the cat safe; I'll be the dog's guardian myself.   [*Exeunt Servants.*

Sog. Nephew, will you go to court with us? these gentlemen and I are for the court; nay, be not so melancholy.

Fung. 'Slid, I think no man in Christendom has that rascally fortune that I have.

Maci. Faith, you suit is well enough, signior.

Fung. Nay, not for that, I protest; but I had an errand to monsieur Fastidious, and I have forgot it.

Maci. Why, go along to court with us, and remember it; come, gentlemen, you three take one boat, and Sogliardo and I will take another; we shall be there instantly.

Fast. Content: good sir, vouchsafe us your pleasance.

Punt. Farewell, Carlo: remember.

Car. I warrant you: would I had one of Kemp's shoes to throw after you.

Punt. Good fortune will close the eyes of our jest, fear not: and we shall frolick.   [*Exeunt.*

Mit. This Macilente, signior, begins to be more sociable on a sudden, methinks, than he was before : there's some portent in it, I believe.

Cor. O, he's a fellow of a strange nature. Now does he, in this calm of his humour, plot, and store up a world of malicious thoughts in his brain, till he is so full with them, that you shall see the very torrent of his envy break forth like a land-flood : and, against the course of all their affections, oppose itself so violently, that you will almost have wonder to think, how 'tis possible the current of their dispositions shall receive so quick and strong an alteration.

Mit. Ay, marry, sir, this is that, on which my expectation has dwelt all this while ; for I must tell you, signior, though I was loth to interrupt the scene, yet I made it a question in mine own private discourse, how he should properly call it Every Man out of his Humour, *when I saw all his actors so strongly pursue, and continue their humours ?*

Cor. Why, therein his art appears most full of lustre, and approacheth nearest the life ; especially when in the flame and height of their humours, they are laid flat, it fills the eye better, and with more contentment. How tedious a sight were it to behold a proud exalted tree lopt, and cut down by degrees, when it might be fell'd in a moment! and to set the axe to it before it came to that pride and fulness, were, as not to have it grow.

Mit. *Well, I shall long till I see this fall, you talk of.*

Cor. *To help your longing, signior, let your imagination be swifter than a pair of oars : and by this, suppose Puntarvolo, Brisk, Fungoso, and the dog, arrived at the court-gate, and going up to the great chamber. Macilente and Sogliardo, we'll leave them on the water, till possibility and natural means may land them. Here come the gallants, now prepare your expectation.*

ACT V

SCENE I.—*The Palace Stairs.*

Enter Puntarvolo, *with his dog, followed by* Fastidious Brisk *and* Fungoso.

Punt. Come, gentles, Signior, you are sufficiently instructed.

Fast. Who, I, sir?

Punt. No, this gentleman. But stay, I take thought how to bestow my dog; he is no competent attendant for the presence.

Fast. Mass, that's true, indeed, knight; you must not carry him into the presence.

Punt. I know it, and I, like a dull beast, forgot to bring one of my cormorants to attend me.

Fast. Why, you were best leave him at the porter's lodge.

Punt. Not so; his worth is too well known amongst them, to be forth-coming.

Fast. 'Slight, how will you do then?

Punt. I must leave him with one that is ignorant of his quality, if I will have him to be safe. And see! here comes one that will carry coals, ergo, will hold my dog.

Enter a Groom, *with a basket.*

My honest friend, may I commit the tuition of this dog to thy prudent care?

Groom. You may, if you please, sir.

Punt. Pray thee let me find thee here at my return; it shall not be long, till I will ease thee of thy employment, and please thee. Forth, gentles.

Fast. Why, but will you leave him with so slight command, and infuse no more charge upon the fellow?

Punt. Charge! no; there were no policy in that; that were to let him know the value of the gem he holds, and so to tempt frail nature against her disposition. No, pray thee let thy honesty be sweet, as it shall be short.

Groom. Yes, sir.

Punt. But hark you, gallants, and chiefly monsieur Brisk: when we come in eye-shot, or presence of this lady, let not other matters carry us from our project; but, if we can, single her forth to some place——

Fast. I warrant you.

Punt. And be not too sudden, but let the device induce itself with good circumstance. On.

Fung. Is this the way? good truth, here be fine hangings.

                         [*Exeunt Punt., Fast., and Fungoso.*

Groom. Honesty! *sweet,* and *short!* Marry, it shall, sir, doubt you not; for even at this instant if one would give me twenty pounds, I would not deliver him; there's for the *sweet :* but now, if any man come offer me but two-pence, he shall have him; there's for the *short* now. 'Slid, what a mad humorous gentleman is this to leave his dog with me! I could run away with him now, an he were worth any thing.

Enter MACILENTE *and* SOGLIARDO.

Maci. Come on, signior, now prepare to court this all-witted lady, most naturally, and like yourself.

Sog. Faith, an you say the word, I'll begin to her in tobacco.

Maci. O, fie on't! no; you shall begin with, *How does my sweet lady,* or, *Why are you so melancholy, madam?* though she be very merry, it's all one. Be sure to kiss your hand often enough; pray for her health, and tell her, how *more than most fair she is.* Screw your face at one side thus, and protest: let her fleer, and look askance, and hide her teeth with her fan, when she laughs a fit, to bring her into more matter, that's nothing: you must talk forward, (though it be without sense, so it be without blushing,) 'tis most court-like and well.

Sog. But shall I not use tobacco at all?

Maci. O, by no means; 'twill but make your breath suspected, and that you use it only to confound the rankness of that.

Sog. Nay, I'll be advised, sir, by my friends.

Maci. Od's my life, see where sir Puntarvolo's dog is.

Groom. I would the gentleman would return for his follower here, I'll leave him to his fortunes else.

Maci. 'Twere the only true jest in the world to poison him now; ha! by this hand I'll do it, if I could but get him of the fellow. [*Aside.*] Signior Sogliardo, walk aside, and think upon some device to entertain the lady with.

    Sog. So I do, sir.   [*Walks off in a meditating posture.*

Maci. How now, mine honest friend! whose dog-keeper art thou?

Groom. Dog-keeper, sir! I hope I scorn that, i'faith.

Maci. Why, dost thou not keep a dog?

Groom. Sir, now I do, and now I do not: [*throws off the dog.*] I think this be *sweet* and *short.* Make me his dog-keeper!   [*Exit.*

Maci. This is excellent, above expectation! nay, stay, sir; [*seizing the dog.*] you'd be travelling; but I'll give you a dram shall shorten your voyage, here. [*Gives him poison.*] So, sir, I'll be bold to take my leave of you. Now to the Turk's court in the devil's name, for you shall never go o' God's name. [*Kicks him out.*]—Sogliardo, come.

Sog. I have it i'faith now, will sting it.

Maci. Take heed you leese it not, signior, ere you come there; preserve it.   [*Exeunt.*

Cor. How like you this first exploit of his?

Mit. O, a piece of true envy; but I expect the issue of the other device.

Cor. Here they come will make it appear.

SCENE II.—*An Apartment in the Palace.*

Enter SAVIOLINA, PUNTARVOLO, FASTIDIOUS BRISK, *and* FUNGOSO.

Sav. Why, I thought, sir Puntarvolo, you had been gone your voyage?

Punt. Dear and most amiable lady, your divine beauties do bind me to those offices, that I cannot depart when I would.

Sav. 'Tis most court-like spoken, sir; but how might we do to have a sight of your dog and cat?

Fast. His dog is in the court, lady.

Sav. And not your cat? how dare you trust her behind you, sir.

Punt. Troth, madam, she hath sore eyes, and she doth keep her chamber; marry, I have left her under sufficient guard, there are two of my followers to attend her.

Sav. I'll give you some water for her eyes. When do you go, sir?

Punt. Certes, sweet lady, I know not.

Fast. He doth stay the rather, madam, to present your acute judgment with so courtly and well parted a gentleman as yet your ladyship hath never seen.

Sav. What is he, gentle monsieur Brisk? not that gentleman?
                                                          [*Points to Fungoso.*

Fast. No, lady, this is a kinsman to justice Silence.

Punt. Pray, sir, give me leave to report him. He's a gentleman, lady, of that rare and admirable faculty, as, I protest, I know not his like in Europe; he is exceedingly valiant, an excellent scholar, and so exactly travelled, that he is able, in discourse, to deliver you a model of any prince's court in the world; speaks the languages with that purity of phrase, and facility of accent, that it breeds astonishment; his wit, the most exuberant, and, above wonder, pleasant, of all that ever entered the concave of this ear.

Fast. 'Tis most true, lady; marry, he is no such excellent proper man.

Punt. His travels have changed his complexion, madam.

Sav. O, sir Puntarvolo, you must think every man was not born to have my servant Brisk's feature.

Punt. But that which transcends all, lady; he doth so peerlessly imitate any manner of person for gesture, action, passion, or whatever——

Fast. Ay, especially a rustic or a clown, madam, that it is not possible for the sharpest-sighted wit in the world to discern any sparks of the gentleman in him, when he does it.

Sav. O, monsieur Brisk, be not so tyrannous to confine all wits within the compass of your own; not find the sparks of a gentleman in him, if he be a gentleman!

Fung. No, in truth, sweet lady, I believe you cannot.

Sav. Do you believe so? why, I can find sparks of a gentleman in you, sir.

Punt. Ay, he is a gentleman, madam, and a reveller.

Fung. Indeed, I think I have seen your ladyship at our revels.

Sav. Like enough, sir; but would I might see this wonder you talk of; may one have a sight of him for any reasonable sum?

Punt. Yes, madam, he will arrive presently.

Sav. What, and shall we see him clown it?

Fast. I'faith, sweet lady, that you shall; see, here he comes.

Enter MACILENTE and SOGLIARDO.

Punt. This is he! pray observe him, lady.

Sav. Beshrew me, he clowns it properly indeed.

Punt. Nay, mark his courtship.

Sog. How does my sweet lady? *hot and moist? beautiful and lusty?* ha!

Sav. Beautiful, an it please you, sir, but not lusty.

Sog. O ho, lady, it pleases you to say so, in truth: And *how does my sweet lady?* in health? *Bona roba, quæso, que novelles? que novelles?* sweet creature!

Sav. O excellent! why, gallants, is this he that cannot be deciphered? they were very blear-witted, i'faith, that could not discern the gentleman in him.

Punt. But you do, in earnest, lady?

Sav. Do I, sir! why, if you had any true court-judgment in the carriage of his eye, and that inward power that forms his countenance, you might perceive his counterfeiting as clear as the noonday; alas——nay, if you would have tried my wit, indeed, you should never have told me he was a gentleman, but presented him for a true clown indeed; and then have seen if I could have deciphered him.

Fast. 'Fore God, her ladyship says true, knight: but does he not affect the clown most naturally, mistress?

Punt. O, she cannot but affirm that, out of the bounty of her judgment.

Sav. Nay, out of doubt he does well, for a gentleman to imitate: but I warrant you, he becomes his natural carriage of the gentleman, much better than his clownery.

Fast. 'Tis strange, in truth, her ladyship should see so far into him!

Punt. Ay, is it not?

Sav. Faith, as easily as may be; not decipher him, quoth you!

Fung. Good sadness, I wonder at it.

Maci. Why, has she deciphered him, gentlemen?

Punt. O, most miraculously, and beyond admiration.

Maci. Is it possible?

Fast. She hath gather'd most infallible signs of the gentleman in him, that's certain.

Sav. Why, gallants, let me laugh at you a little: was this your device, to try my judgment in a gentleman?

Maci. Nay, lady, do not scorn us, though you have this gift of perspicacy above others. What if he should be no gentleman now, but a clown indeed, lady?

Punt. How think you of that? would not your ladyship be Out of your Humour?

Fast. O, but she knows it is not so.

Sav. What if he were not a man, ye may as well say? Nay, if your worships could gull me so, indeed, you were wiser than you are taken for.

Maci. In good faith, lady, he is a very perfect clown, both by father and mother; that I'll assure you.

Sav. O, sir, you are very pleasurable.

Maci. Nay, do but look on his hand, and that shall resolve you; look you, lady, what a palm here is.

Sog. Tut, that was with holding the plough.

Maci. The plough! did you discern any such thing in him, madam?

Fast. Faith no, she saw the gentleman as bright as noon-day, she; she deciphered him at first.

Maci. Troth, I am sorry your ladyship's sight should be so suddenly struck.

Sav. O, you are goodly beagles!

Fast. What, is she gone?

Sog. Nay, stay, sweet lady: *que novelles? que novelles?*

Sav. Out, you fool, you!   [*Exit in anger.*

Fung. She's Out of her Humour, i'faith.

Fast. Nay, let's follow it while 'tis hot, gentlemen.

Punt. Come, on mine honour we shall make her blush in the presence; my spleen is great with laughter.

Maci. Your laughter will be a child of a feeble life, I believe, sir. [*Aside.*]—Come, signior, your looks are too dejected, methinks; why mix you not mirth with the rest?

Fung. Od's will, this suit frets me at the soul. I'll have it alter'd to-morrow, sure.   [*Exeunt*

SCENE III.—*The Palace Stairs.*

Enter SHIFT.

Shift. I am come to the court, to meet with my Countenance, Sogliardo; poor men must be glad of such countenance, when they can get no better. Well, need may insult upon a man, but it shall never make him despair of consequence. The world will say, 'tis base: tush, base! 'tis base to live under the earth, not base to live above it by any means.

Enter FASTIDIOUS, PUNTARVOLO, SOGLIARDO, FUNGOSO,
and MACILENTE.

Fast. The poor lady is most miserably out of her humour, i'faith.

Punt. There was never so witty a jest broken, at the tilt of all the court wits christen'd.

Maci. O, this applause taints it foully.

Sog. I think I did my part in courting.—O, Resolution!

Punt. Ay me, my dog!

Maci. Where is he?

Fast. 'Sprecious, go seek for the fellow, good signior.

[*Exit Fungoso.*

Punt. Here, here I left him.

Maci. Why, none was here when we came in now, but cavalier Shift; enquire of him.

Fast. Did you see sir Puntarvolo's dog here, cavalier, since you came?

Shift. His dog, sir! he may look his dog, sir; I saw none of his dog, sir.

Maci. Upon my life, he has stolen your dog, sir, and been hired to it by some that have ventured with you; you may guess by his peremptory answers.

Punt. Not unlike; for he hath been a notorious thief by his own confession. Sirrah, where is my dog?

Shift. Charge me with your dog, sir! I have none of your dog, sir.

Punt. Villain, thou liest.

Shift. Lie, sir! s'blood,—you are but a man, sir.

Punt. Rogue and thief, restore him.

Sog. Take heed, sir Puntarvolo, what you do; he'll bear no coals, I can tell you, o' my word.

Maci. This is rare.

Sog. It's marle he stabs you not: By this light, he hath stabbed forty, for forty times less matter, I can tell you of my knowledge.

Punt. I will make thee stoop, thou abject.

Sog. Make him stoop, sir! Gentlemen, pacify him, or he'll be kill'd.

Maci. Is he so tall a man?

Sog. Tall a man! if you love his life, stand betwixt them. Make him stoop!

Punt. My dog, villain, or I will hang thee; thou hast confest robberies, and other felonious acts, to this gentleman, thy Countenance——

Sog. I'll bear no witness.

Punt. And without my dog, I will hang thee, for them.

[*Shift kneels.*

Sog. What! kneel to thine enemies!

Shift. Pardon me, good sir; God is my witness, I never did robbery in all my life.

Re-enter FUNGOSO.

Fung. O, sir Puntarvolo, your dog lies giving up the ghost in the wood-yard.

Maci. Heart, is he not dead yet! [*Aside.*

Punt. O, my dog, born to disastrous fortune! pray you conduct me, sir. [*Exit with Fungoso.*

Sog. How! did you never do any robbery in your life?

Maci. O, this is good! so he swore, sir.

Sog. Ay, I heard him: and did you swear true, sir?

Shift. Ay, as I hope to be forgiven, sir, I never robbed any man; I never stood by the highwayside, sir, but only said so, because I would get myself a name, and be counted a tall man.

Sog. Now out, base viliaco! thou my Resolution! I thy Countenance! By this light, gentlemen, he hath confest to me the most inexorable company of robberies, and damn'd himself that he did 'em: you never heard the like. Out, scoundrel, out! follow me no more, I command thee; out of my sight, go, hence, speak not; I will not hear thee: away, camouccio! [*Exit Shift.*

Maci. O, how I do feed upon this now, and fat myself! here were a couple unexpectedly dishumour'd. Well, by this time, I hope, sir Puntarvolo and his dog are both out of humour to travel. [*Aside.*]—Nay, gentlemen, why do you not seek out the knight, and comfort him? our supper at the Mitre must of necessity hold to-night, if you love your reputations.

Fast. 'Fore God, I am so melancholy for his dog's disaster—but I'll go.

Sog. Faith, and I may go too, but I know I shall be so melancholy.

Maci. Tush, melancholy! you must forget that now, and remember you lie at the mercy of a fury: Carlo will rack your sinews asunder, and rail you to dust, if you come not. [*Exeunt.*

Mit. O, then their fear of Carlo, belike, makes them hold their meeting.

Cor. Ay, here he comes; conceive him but to be enter'd the Mitre, and 'tis enough.

SCENE IV.—*A Room at the Mitre.*

Enter CARLO.

Car. Holla! where be these shot-sharks?

Enter Drawer.

Draw. By and by; you are welcome, good master Buffone.

Car. Where's George? call me George hither, quickly.

Draw. What wine please you have, sir? I'll draw you that's neat, master Buffone.

Car. Away, neophite, do as I bid thee, bring my dear George to me:—

Enter GEORGE.

Mass, here he comes.

George. Welcome, master Carlo.

Car. What, is supper ready, George?

George. Ay, sir, almost: Will you have the cloth laid, master Carlo?

Car. O, what else? Are none of the gallants come yet?

George. None yet, sir.

Car. Stay, take me with you, George; let me have a good fat loin of pork laid to the fire, presently.

George. It shall, sir.

Car. And withal, hear you, draw me the biggest shaft you have out of the butt you wot of; away, you know my meaning, George; quick!

George. Done, sir.   [*Exit.*

Car. I never hungered so much for anything in my life, as I do to know our gallants' success at court; now is that lean, bald-rib Macilente, that salt villain, plotting some mischievous device, and lies a soaking in their frothy humours like a dry crust, till he has drunk 'em all up: Could the pummice but hold up his eyes at other men's happiness, in any reasonable proportion, 'slid, the slave were to be loved next heaven, above honour, wealth, rich fare, apparel, wenches, all the delights of the belly and the groin, whatever.

Re-enter GEORGE *with two jugs of wine.*

George. Here, master Carlo.

Car. Is it right, boy?

George. Ay, sir, I assure you 'tis right.

Car. Well said, my dear George, depart: [*Exit George.*]—Come, my small gimblet, you in the false scabbard, away, so! [*Puts forth the Drawer, and shuts the door.*] Now to you, sir Burgomaster, let's taste of your bounty.

Mit. *What, will he deal upon such quantities of wine, alone?*

Cor. *You will perceive that, sir.*

Car. [*drinks.*] Ay, marry, sir, here's purity; O, George—I could bite off his nose for this now, sweet rogue, he has drawn nectar, the very soul of the grape! I'll wash my temples with some on't presently, and drink some half a score draughts; 'twill heat the brain, kindle my imagination, I shall talk nothing but crackers and fire-works to-night. So, sir! please you to be here, sir, and I here: so.

    [*Sets the two cups asunder, drinks with the one, and pledges with the other, speaking for each of the cups, and drinking alternately.*

Cor. *This is worth the observation, signior.*

Car. 1 *Cup.* Now, sir, here's to you; and I present you with so much of my love.

2 Cup. I take it kindly from you, sir [*drinks*], and will return you the like proportion; but withal, sir, remembering the merry night we had at the countess's, you know where, sir.

1 Cup. By heaven, you put me in mind now of a very necessary office, which I will propose in your pledge, sir; the health of that honourable countess, and the sweet lady that sat by her, sir.

2 Cup. I do vail to it with reverence [*drinks*]. And now, signior, with these ladies, I'll be bold to mix the health of your divine mistress.

1 Cup. Do you know her, sir?

2 Cup. O lord, sir, ay; and in the respectful memory and mention of her, I could wish this wine were the most precious drug in the world.

1 Cup. Good faith, sir, you do honour me in't exceedingly. [*Drinks.*]

Mit. *Whom should he personate in this, signior?*
Cor. *Faith, I know not, sir; observe, observe him.*

2 Cup. If it were the basest filth, or mud that runs in the channel, I am bound to pledge it respectively, sir. [*Drinks.*] And now, sir, here is a replenish'd bowl, which I will reciprocally turn upon you, to the health of the count Frugale.

1 Cup. The count Frugale's health, sir? I'll pledge it on my knees, by this light.   [*Kneels.*

2 Cup. Will you, sir? I'll drink it on my knees, then, by the light.

Mit. *Why this is strange.*
Cor. *Have you heard a better drunken dialogue?*

2 Cup. Nay, do me right, sir.

1 Cup. So I do, in faith.

2 Cup. Good faith you do not; mine was fuller.

1 Cup. Why, believe me, it was not.

2 Cup. Believe me it was; and you do lie.

1 Cup. Lie, sir!

2 Cup. Ay, sir.

1 Cup. 'Swounds! you rascal!

2 Cup. O, come, stab if you have a mind to it.

1 Cup. Stab! dost thou think I dare not?

Car. [*speaks in his own person.*] Nay, I beseech you, gentlemen, what means this? nay, look, for shame respect your reputations.
    [*Overturns wine, pot, cups, and all.*

Enter MACILENTE.

Maci. Why, how now, Carlo! what humour's this?

Car. O, my good mischief! art thou come? where are the rest, where are the rest?

Maci. Faith, three of our ordnance are burst.

Car. Burst! how comes that?

Maci. Faith, overcharged, overcharged.

Car. But did not the train hold?

Maci. O, yes, and the poor lady is irrecoverably blown up.

Car. Why, but which of the munition is miscarried, ha?

Maci. Imprimis, sir Puntarvolo; next, the Countenance and Resolution.

Car. How, how, for the love of wit?

Maci. Troth, the Resolution is proved recreant; the Countenance hath changed his copy; and the passionate knight is shedding funeral tears over his departed dog.

Car. What! is his dog dead?

Maci. Poison'd, 'tis thought; marry, how, or by whom, that's left for some cunning woman here o' the Bank-side to resolve. For my part, I know nothing more than that we are like to have an exceeding melancholy supper of it.

Car. 'Slife, and I had purposed to be extraordinarily merry, I had drunk off a good preparative of old sack here; but will they come, will they come?

Maci. They will assuredly come; marry, Carlo, as thou lov'st me, run over 'em all freely to-night, and especially the knight; spare no sulphurous jest that may come out of that sweaty forge of thine; but ply them with all manner of shot, minion, saker, culverin, or anything, what thou wilt.

Car. I warrant thee, my dear case of petronels; so I stand not in dread of thee, but that thou'lt second me.

Maci. Why, my good German tapster, I will.

Car. What George! *Lomtero, Lomtero, etc.*   [*Sings and dances.*

Re-enter GEORGE.

George. Did you call, master Carlo?

Car. More nectar, George: *Lomtero, etc.*

George. Your meat's ready, sir, an your company were come.

Car. Is the loin of pork enough?

George. Ay, sir, it is enough.   [*Exit.*

Maci. Pork! heart, what dost thou with such a greasy dish? I think thou dost varnish thy face with the fat on't, it looks so like a glue-pot.

Car. True, my raw-boned rogue, and if thou wouldst farce thy lean ribs with it too, they would not, like ragged laths, rub out so many doublets as they do; but thou know'st not a good dish, thou. O, it's the only nourishing meat in the world. No marvel though that saucy, stubborn generation, the Jews, were forbidden it; for what would they have done, well pamper'd with fat pork, that durst murmur at their Maker out of garlick and onions? 'Slight! fed with it, the whoreson strummel-patch'd, goggled-eyed grumble-dories, would have gigantomachised—

Re-enter GEORGE *with wine.*

Well said, my sweet George, fill, fill.

Mit. This savours too much of profanation.

Cor. O ——————— —————— Servetur ad imum,
Qualis ab incœpto processerit, et sibi constet.
*The necessity of his vein compels a toleration, for ; bar this, and dash
him out of humour before his time.*

Car. 'Tis an axiom in natural philosophy, what comes nearest the
nature of that it feeds, converts quicker to nourishment, and doth sooner
essentiate.   Now nothing in flesh and entrails assimilates or resembles
man more than a hog or swine.   [*Drinks.*
Maci. True; and he, to requite their courtesy, oftentimes doffeth
his own nature, and puts on theirs; as when he becomes as churlish
as a hog, or as drunk as a sow; but to your conclusion.   [*Drinks.*
Car. Marry, I say, nothing resembling man more than a swine,
it follows, nothing can be more nourishing; for indeed (but that it
abhors from our nice nature) if we fed upon one another, we should
shoot up a great deal faster, and thrive much better; I refer me
to your usurous cannibals, or such like; but since it is so contrary,
pork, pork, is your only feed.
Maci. I take it, your devil be of the same diet; he would never
have desired to have been incorporated into swine else.—O, here
comes the melancholy mess; upon 'em, Carlo, charge, charge!

Enter PUNTARVOLO, FASTIDIOUS BRISK, SOGLIARDO, *and*
FUNGOSO.

Car. 'Fore God, sir Puntarvolo, I am sorry for your heaviness:
body o' me, a shrew'd mischance! why, had you no unicorn's horn,
nor bezoar's stone about you, ha?
Punt. Sir, I would request you to be silent.
Maci. Nay, to him again.
Car. Take comfort, good knight, if your cat have recovered her
catarrh, fear nothing; your dog's mischance may be holpen.
Fast. Say how, sweet Carlo; for, so God mend me, the poor
knight's moans draw me into fellowship of his misfortunes.   But
be not discouraged, good sir Puntarvolo, I am content your adventure shall be performed upon your cat.
Maci. I believe you, musk-cod, I believe you; for rather than
thou would'st make present repayment, thou would'st take it upon
his own bare return from Calais.   [*Aside.*
Car. Nay, 'slife, he'd be content, so he were well rid out of his
company, to pay him five for one, at his next meeting him in Paul's.
[*Aside to Macilente.*]—But for your dog, sir Puntarvolo, if he be not
out-right dead, there is a friend of mine, a quack-salver, shall put
life in him again, that's certain.
Fung. O, no, that comes too late.
Maci. 'Sprecious! knight, will you suffer this?
Punt. Drawer, get me a candle and hard wax presently.
                                                    [*Exit George.*
Sog. Ay, and bring up supper; for I am so melancholy.
Car. O, signior, where's your Resolution?

Sog. Resolution! hang him, rascal: O, Carlo, if you love me, do not mention him.

Car. Why, how so?

Sog. O, the arrantest crocodile that ever Christian was acquainted with. By my gentry, I shall think the worse of tobacco while I live, for his sake: I did think him to be as tall a man——

Maci. Nay, Buffone, the knight, the knight.   [*Aside to Carlo.*

Car. 'Slud, he looks like an image carved out of box, full of knots; his face is, for all the world, like a Dutch purse, with the mouth downward, his beard the tassels; and he walks—let me see—as melancholy as one o' the master's side in the Counter.—Do you hear, sir Puntarvolo?

Punt. Sir, I do entreat you, no more, but enjoin you to silence, as you affect your peace.

Car. Nay, but dear knight, understand here are none but friends, and such as wish you well, I would have you do this now; flay me your dog presently (but in any case keep the head) and stuff his skin well with straw, as you see these dead monsters at Bartholomew fair.

Punt. I shall be sudden, I tell you.

Car. O, if you like not that, sir, get me somewhat a less dog, and clap into the skin; here's a slave about the town here, a Jew, one Yohan: or a fellow that makes perukes will glue it on artificially, it shall never be discern'd; besides, 'twill be so much the warmer for the hound to travel in, you know.

Maci. Sir Puntarvolo, death, can you be so patient!

Car. Or thus, sir; you may have, as you come through Germany, a familiar for little or nothing, shall turn itself into the shape of your dog, or any thing, what you will, for certain hours——[*Puntarvolo strikes him*]——Ods my life, knight, what do you mean? you'll offer no violence, will you? hold, hold!

        Re-enter GEORGE, *with wax, and a lighted candle.*

Punt. 'Sdeath, you slave, you ban-dog, you!

Car. As you love wit, stay the enraged knight, gentlemen.

Punt. By my knighthood, he that stirs in his rescue, dies.— Drawer, begone!   [*Exit George.*

Car. Murder, murder, murder!

Punt. Ay, are you howling, you wolf?—Gentlemen, as you tender your lives, suffer no man to enter till my revenge be perfect. Sirrah, Buffone, lie down; make no exclamations, but down; down, you cur, or I will make thy blood flow on my rapier hilts.

Car. Sweet knight, hold in thy fury, and 'fore heaven I'll honour thee more than the Turk does Mahomet.

Punt. Down, I say! [*Carlo lies down.*]—Who's there?

                                [*Knocking within.*

Cons. [*within.*] Here's the constable, open the doors.

Car. Good Macilente——

Punt. Open no door; if the Adalantado of Spain were here he should not enter: one help me with the light, gentlemen; you knock in vain, sir officer.

Car. *Et tu, Brute!*

Punt. Sirrah, close your lips, or I will drop it in thine eyes, by heaven.

Car. O! O!

Cons. [*within.*] Open the door, or I will break it open.

Maci. Nay, good constable, have patience a little; you shall come in presently; we have almost done.

[*Puntarvolo seals up Carlo's lips.*

Punt. So, now, are you Out of your Humour, sir? Shift, gentlemen.

[*They all draw, and run out, except Fungoso, who conceals himself beneath the table.*

Enter Constable *and Officers, and seize* FASTIDIOUS *as he is rushing by.*

Cons. Lay hold upon this gallant, and pursue the rest.

Fast. Lay hold on me, sir, for what?

Cons. Marry, for your riot here, sir, with the rest of your companions.

Fast. My riot! master constable, take heed what you do. Carlo, did I offer any violence?

Cons. O, sir, you see he is not in case to answer you, and that makes you so peremptory.

Re-enter GEORGE *and* Drawer.

Fast. Peremptory! 'Slife, I appeal to the drawers, if I did him any hard measure.

George. They are all gone, there's none of them will be laid any hold on.

Cons. Well, sir, you are like to answer till the rest can be found out.

Fast. 'Slid, I appeal to George here.

Cons. Tut, George was not here: away with him to the Counter, sirs.—Come, sir, you were best get yourself drest somewhere.

[*Exeunt Const. and Officers, with Fast. and Car.*

George. Good lord, that master Carlo could not take heed, and knowing what a gentleman the knight is, if he be angry.

Drawer. A pox on 'em, they have left all the meat on our hands; would they were choaked with it for me!

Re-enter MACILENTE.

Maci. What, are they gone, sirs?

George. O, here's master Macilente.

Maci. [*pointing to Fungoso.*] Sirrah, George, do you see that concealment there, that napkin under the table?

George. 'Ods so, signior Fungoso!

Maci. He's good pawn for the reckoning; be sure you keep him here, and let him not go away till I come again, though he offer to discharge all; I'll return presently.

George. Sirrah, we have a pawn for the reckoning.

Draw. What, of Macilente?

George. No; look under the table.

Fung. [*creeping out.*] I hope all be quiet now; if I can get but forth of this street, I care not: masters, I pray you tell me, is the constable gone?

George. What, master Fungoso!

Fung. Was't not a good device this same of me, sirs?

George. Yes, faith; have you been here all this while?

Fung. O lord, ay; good sir, look an the coast be clear, I'd fain be going.

George. All's clear, sir, but the reckoning; and that you must clear and pay before you go, I assure you.

Fung. I pay! 'Slight, I eat not a bit since I came into the house, yet.

Draw. Why, you may when you please, 'tis all ready below that was bespoken.

Fung. Bespoken! not by me, I hope?

George. By you, sir! I know not that; but 'twas for you and your company, I am sure.

Fung. My company! 'Slid, I was an invited guest, so I was.

Draw. Faith we have nothing to do with that, sir: they are all gone but you, and we must be answered; that's the short and the long on't.

Fung. Nay, if you will grow to extremities, my masters, then would this pot, cup, and all were in my belly, if I have a cross about me.

George. What, and have such apparel! do not say so, signior; that mightily discredits your clothes.

Fung. As I am an honest man, my tailor had all my money this morning, and yet I must be fain to alter my suit too. Good sirs, let me go, 'tis Friday night, and in good truth I have no stomach in the world to eat any thing.

Draw. That's no matter, so you pay, sir.

Fung. 'Slight, with what conscience can you ask me to pay that I never drank for?

George. Yes, sir, I did see you drink once.

Fung. By this cup, which is silver, but you did not; you do me infinite wrong: I looked in the pot once, indeed, but I did not drink.

Draw. Well, sir, if you can satisfy our master, it shall be all one to us.

Within. George!

George. By and by.   [*Exeunt.*

Cor. *Lose not yourself now, signior.*

SCENE V.—*A Room in* DELIRO'S *House.*

Enter MACILENTE *and* DELIRO.

Maci. Tut, sir, you did bear too hard a conceit of me in that; but I will now make my love to you most transparent, in spite of any dust of suspicion that may be raised to cloud it; and henceforth, since I see it is so against your humour, I will never labour to persuade you.

Deli. Why, I thank you, signior; but what is that you tell me may concern my peace so much?

Maci. Faith, sir, 'tist hus. Your wife's brother, signior Fungoso, being at supper to-night at a tavern, with a sort of gallants, there happened some division amongst them, and he is left in pawn for the reckoning. Now, if ever you look that time shall present you with an happy occasion to do your wife some gracious and acceptable service, take hold of this opportunity, and presently go and redeem him; for, being her brother, and his credit so amply engaged as now it is, when she shall hear, (as he cannot himself, but he must out of extremity report it,) that you came, and offered yourself so kindly, and with that respect of his reputation; why, the benefit cannot but make her dote, and grow mad of your affections.

Deli. Now, by heaven, Macilente, I acknowledge myself exceedingly indebted to you, by this kind tender of your love; and I am sorry to remember that I was ever so rude, to neglect a friend of your importance.—Bring me shoes and a cloak here.—I was going to bed, if you had not come. What tavern is it?

Maci. The Mitre, sir.

Deli. O! Why, Fido! my shoes.—Good faith, it cannot but please her exceedingly.

Enter FALLACE.

Fal. Come, I marle what piece of night-work you have in hand now, that you call for a cloak, and your shoes: What, is this your pander?

Deli. O, sweet wife, speak lower, I would not he should hear thee for a world——

Fal. Hang him, rascal, I cannot abide him for his treachery, with his wild quick-set beard there. Whither go you now with him?

Deli. No, whither with him, dear wife; I go alone to a place, from whence I will return instantly.—Good Macilente, acquaint not her with it by any means, it may come so much the more accepted; frame some other answer.—I'll come back immediately. [*Exit.*

Fal. Nay, an I be not worthy to know whither you go, stay till I take knowledge of your coming back.

Maci. Hear you, mistress Deliro.

Fal. So, sir, and what say you?

Maci. Faith, lady, my intents will not deserve this slight respect, when you shall know them.

Fal. Your intents! why, what may your intents be, for God's sake?

Maci. Troth, the time allows no circumstance, lady, therefore know this was but a device to remove your husband hence, and bestow him securely, whilst, with more conveniency, I might report to you a misfortune that hath happened to monsieur Brisk——Nay, comfort, sweet lady. This night, being at supper, a sort of young gallants committed a riot, for the which he only is apprehended and carried to the Counter, where, if your husband, and other creditors, should but have knowledge of him, the poor gentleman were undone for ever.

Fal. Ah me! that he were.

Maci. Now, therefore, if you can think upon any present means for his delivery, do not foreslow it. A bribe to the officer that committed him will do it.

Fal. O lord, sir! he shall not want for a bribe; pray you, will you commend me to him, and say I'll visit him presently.

Maci. No, lady, I shall do you better service, in protracting your husband's return, that you may go with more safety.

Fal. Good truth, so you may; farewell, good sir. [*Exit Maci.*]— Lord, how a woman may be mistaken in a man! I would have sworn upon all the Testaments in the world he had not loved master Brisk. Bring me my keys there, maid. Alas, good gentleman, if all I have in this earthly world will pleasure him, it shall be at his service. [*Exit.*

Mit. *How Macilente sweats in this business, if you mark him!*

Cor. *Ay, you shall see the true picture of spite, anon : here comes the pawn and his redeemer.*

SCENE VI.—*A Room at the* MITRE.

Enter DELIRO, FUNGOSO, *and* GEORGE.

Deli. Come, brother, be not discouraged for this, man; what!

Fung. No, truly, I am not discouraged; but I protest to you, brother, I have done imitating any more gallants either in purse or apparel, but as shall become a gentleman, for good carriage, or so.

Deli. You say well.—This is all in the bill here, is it not?

George. Ay, sir.

Deli. There's your money, tell it: and, brother, I am glad I met with so good occasion to shew my love to you.

Fung. I will study to deserve it in good truth an I live.

Deli. What, is it right?

George. Ay, sir, and I thank you.

Fung. Let me have a capon's leg saved, now the reckoning is paid.

George. You shall, sir. [*Exit.*

Enter MACILENTE.

Maci. Where's signior Deliro?

Deli. Here, Macilente.

Maci. Hark you, sir, have you dispatch'd this same?

Deli. Ay, marry have I.

Maci. Well then, I can tell you news; Brisk is in the Counter.

Deli. In the Counter!

Maci. 'Tis true, sir, committed for the stir here to-night. Now would I have you send your brother home afore him, with the report of this your kindness done him, to his sister, which will so pleasingly possess her, and out of his mouth too, that in the mean-time you may clap your action on Brisk, and your wife, being in so happy a mood, cannot entertain it ill, by any means.

Deli. 'Tis very true, she cannot, indeed, I think.

Maci. Think! why 'tis past thought; you shall never meet the like opportunity, I assure you.

Deli. I will do it.—Brother, pray you go home afore (this gentle-man and I have some private business), and tell my sweet wife I'll come presently.

Fung. I will, brother.

Maci. And, signior, acquaint your sister, how liberally, and out of his bounty, your brother has used you (do you see?), made you a man of good reckoning; redeem'd that you never were possest of, credit; gave you as gentlemanlike terms as might be; found no fault with your coming behind the fashion; nor nothing.

Fung. Nay, I am out of those humours now.

Maci. Well, if you be out, keep your distance, and be not made a shot-clog any more.—Come, signior, let's make haste.   [*Exeunt.*

SCENE VII.—*The Counter.*

Enter FALLACE *and* FASTIDIOUS BRISK.

Fal. O, master Fastidious, what pity is it to see so sweet a man as you are, in so sour a place!   [*Kisses him.*

Cor. *As upon her lips, does she mean ?*

Mit. *O, this is to be imagined the Counter, belike.*

Fast. Troth, fair lady, 'tis first the pleasure of the fates, and next of the constable, to have it so: but I am patient, and indeed com-forted the more in your kind visit.

Fal. Nay, you shall be comforted in me more than this, if you please, sir. I sent you word by my brother, sir, that my husband laid to 'rest you this morning; I know not whether you received it or no.

Fast. No, believe it, sweet creature, your brother gave me no such intelligence.

Fal. O, the lord!

Fast. But has your husband any such purpose?

Fal. O, sweet master Brisk, yes: and therefore be presently dis-charged, for if he come with his actions upon you, Lord deliver you! you are in for one half-a-score year; he kept a poor man in Ludgate once twelve year for sixteen shillings. Where's your keeper? for love's sake call him, let him take a bribe, and despatch you. Lord, how my heart trembles! here are no spies, are there?

Fast. No, sweet mistress. Why are you in this passion?

Fal. O lord, master Fastidious, if you knew how I took up my husband to-day, when he said he would arrest you; and how I railed at him that persuaded him to it, the scholar there (who, on my conscience, loves you now), and what care I took to send you intelligence by my brother; and how I gave him four sovereigns for his pains: and now, how I came running out hither without man or boy with me, so soon as I heard on't; you'd say I were in a passion indeed. Your keeper, for God's sake! O, master Brisk, as 'tis in *Euphues, Hard is the choice, when one is compelled either by silence to die with grief, or by speaking to live with shame.*

Fast. Fair lady, I conceive you, and may this kiss assure you, that where adversity hath, as it were, contracted, prosperity shall not——Od's me! your husband.

Enter DELIRO *and* MACILENTE.

Fal. O me!

Deli. Ay! Is it thus?

Maci. Why, how now, signior Deliro! has the wolf seen you, ha? Hath Gorgon's head made marble of you?

Deli. Some planet strike me dead!

Maci. Why, look you, sir, I told you, you might have suspected this long afore, had you pleased, and have saved this labour of admiration now, and passion, and such extremities as this frail lump of flesh is subject unto. Nay, why do you not doat now, signior? methinks you should say it were some enchantment, *deceptio visus*, or so, ha! If you could persuade yourself it were a dream now, 'twere excellent: faith, try what you can do, signior: it may be your imagination will be brought to it in time; there's nothing impossible.

Fal. Sweet husband!

Deli. Out, lascivious strumpet!   [*Exit.*

Maci. What! did you see how ill that stale vein became him afore, of *sweet wife*, and *dear heart ;* and are you fallen just into the same now, with *sweet husband !* Away, follow him, go, keep state: what! remember you are a woman, turn impudent; give him not the head, though you give him the horns. Away. And yet, methinks, you should take your leave of *enfant perdu* here, your forlorn hope. [*Exit Fal.*]—How now, monsieur Brisk? what! Friday night, and in affliction too, and yet your pulpamenta, your delicate morsels! I perceive the affection of ladies and gentle-women pursues you wheresoever you go, monsieur.

Fast. Now, in good faith, and as I am gentle, there could not have come a thing in this world to have distracted me more, than the wrinkled fortunes of this poor dame.

Maci. O yes, sir; I can tell you a thing will distract you much better, believe it: Signior Deliro has entered three actions against you, three actions, monsieur! marry, one of them (I'll put you in comfort) is but three thousand, and the other two, some five thousand pound together: trifles, trifles.

Fast. O, I am undone.

Maci. Nay, not altogether so, sir; the knight must have his hundred pound repaid, that will help too; and then six score pounds for a diamond, you know where. These be things will weigh, monsieur, they will weigh.

Fast. O heaven!

Maci. What! do you sigh? this is to *kiss the hand of a countess, to have her coach sent for you, to hang poniards in ladies' garters, to wear bracelets of their hair,* and for every one of these great favours to *give some slight jewel of five hundred crowns, or so ;* why, 'tis nothing. Now, monsieur, you see the plague that treads on the heels o' your foppery: well, go your ways in, remove yourself to the two-penny ward quickly, to save charges, and there set up your rest to spend sir Puntarvolo's hundred pound for him. Away, good pomander, go!   [*Exit Fastidious.*

Why, here's a change! now is my soul at peace:
I am as empty of all envy now,
As they of merit to be envied at.
My humour, like a flame, no longer lasts
Than it hath stuff to feed it; and their folly
Being now raked up in their repentant ashes,
Affords no ampler subject to my spleen.
I am so far from malicing their states,
That I begin to pity them.   It grieves me
To think they have a being.   I could wish
They might turn wise upon it, and be saved now,
So heaven were pleased; but let them vanish, vapours!——
Gentlemen, how like you it? has't not been tedious?

Cor. Nay, we have done censuring now.
Mit. Yes, faith.

Maci. How so?

Cor. Marry, because we'll imitate your actors, and be out of our humours.   Besides, here are those round about you of more ability in censure than we, whose judgments can give it a more satisfying allowance ;   we'll refer you to them.   [Exeunt Cordatus and Mitis.

Maci. [*coming forward.*] Ay, is it even so?—Well, gentlemen, I should have gone in, and return'd to you as I was Asper at the first; but by reason the shift would have been somewhat long, and we are loth to draw your patience farther, we'll entreat you to imagine it.   And now, that you may see I will be out of humour for company, I stand wholly to your kind approbation, and indeed am nothing so peremptory as I was in the beginning: marry, I will not do as Plautus in his *Amphytrio*, for all this, *summi Jovis causâ plaudite ;* beg a plaudite for God's sake; but if you, out of the bounty of your good-liking, will bestow it, why, you may in time make lean Macilente as fat as sir John Falstaff.   [*Exit.*

THE EPILOGUE

AT THE

PRESENTATION BEFORE QUEEN ELIZABETH

BY MACILENTE.

Never till now did object greet mine eyes
With any light content: but in her graces
All my malicious powers have lost their stings.
Envy is fled from my soul at sight of her,
And she hath chased all black thoughts from my bosom,
Like as the sun doth darkness from the world,
My stream of humour is run out of me,
And as our city's torrent, bent t'infect
The hallow'd bowels of the silver Thames,
Is check'd by strength and clearness of the river,
Till it hath spent itself even at the shore;
So in the ample and unmeasured flood
Of her perfections, are my passions drown'd;
And I have now a spirit as sweet and clear
As the more rarefied and subtle air:—
With which, and with a heart as pure as fire,
Yet humble as the earth, do I implore,   [*Kneels.*
O heaven, that She, whose presence hath effected
This change in me, may suffer most late change
In her admired and happy government:
May still this Island be call'd Fortunate,
And rugged Treason tremble at the sound,
When Fame shall speak it with an emphasis.
Let foreign polity be dull as lead,
And pale Invasion come with half a heart,
When he but looks upon her blessed soil.
The throat of War be stopt within her land,
And turtle-footed Peace dance fairy rings
About her court; where never may there come
Suspect or danger, but all trust and safety.
Let Flattery be dumb, and Envy blind
In her dread presence; Death himself admire her;
And may her virtues make him to forget
The use of his inevitable hand.
Fly from her, Age; sleep, Time, before her throne;
Our strongest wall falls down, when she is gone.

CYNTHIA'S REVELS.

OR, THE FOUNTAIN OF SELF-LOVE

TO THE SPECIAL FOUNTAIN OF MANNERS

THE COURT

THOU art a bountiful and brave spring, and waterest all the noble plants of this island. In thee the whole kingdom dresseth itself, and is ambitious to use thee as her glass. Beware then thou render men's figures truly, and teach them no less to hate their deformities, than to love their forms: for, to grace, there should come reverence; and no man can call that lovely, which is not also venerable. It is not powdering, perfuming, and every day smelling of the tailor, that converteth to a beautiful object: but a mind shining through any suit, which needs no false light, either of riches or honours, to help it. Such shalt thou find some here, even in the reign of Cynthia,—a Crites and an Arete. Now, under thy Phœbus, it will be thy province to make more; except thou desirest to have thy source mix with the spring of self-love, and so wilt draw upon thee as welcome a discovery of thy days, as was then made of her nights.

Thy servant, but not slave, BEN JONSON.

DRAMATIS PERSONÆ

CYNTHIA.	ECHO.
MERCURY.	ARETE.
HESPERUS.	PHANTASTE.
CRITES.	ARGURION.
AMORPHUS.	PHILAUTIA.
ASOTUS.	MORIA.
HEDON.	COS.
ANAIDES.	GELAIA.
MORPHIDES	PHRONESIS,
PROSAITES.	THAUMA, } *Mutes.*
MORUS.	TIME,
CUPID.	

SCENE,—GARGAPHIE

INDUCTION.

THE STAGE.

After the second sounding.

Enter three of the *Children*, struggling.

1 Child. *Pray you away; why, fellows! Gods so, what do you mean?*

2 Child. *Marry, that you shall not speak the prologue, sir.*

3 Child. *Why, do you hope to speak it?*

2 *Child.* *Ay, and I think I have most right to it : I am sure I studied it first.*

3 *Child.* *That's all one, if the author think I can speak it better.*

1 *Child.* *I plead possession of the cloak : gentles, your suffrages, I pray you.*

[*Within.*] *Why, children ! are you not ashamed ? come in there.*

3 *Child.* *Slid, I'll play nothing in the play, unless I speak it.*

1 *Child.* *Why, will you stand to most voices of the gentlemen ? let that decide it.*

3 *Child.* *O, no, sir gallant ; you presume to have the start of us there, and that makes you offer so prodigally.*

1 *Child.* *No, would I were whipped if I had any such thought ; try it by lots either.*

2 *Child.* *Faith, I dare tempt my fortune in a greater venture than this.*

3 *Child.* *Well said, resolute Jack ! I am content too, so we draw first. Make the cuts.*

1 *Child.* *But will you not snatch my cloak while I am stooping ?*

3 *Child.* *No, we scorn treachery.*

2 *Child.* *Which cut shall speak it ?*

3 *Child.* *The shortest.*

1 *Child.* *Agreed : draw.* [*They draw cuts.*] *The shortest is come to the shortest. Fortune was not altogether blind in this. Now, sir, I hope I shall go forward without your envy.*

2 *Child.* *A spite of all mischievous luck ! I was once plucking at the other.*

3 *Child.* *Stay, Jack : 'slid, I'll do somewhat now afore I go in, though it be nothing but to revenge myself on the author : since I speak not his prologue, I'll go tell all the argument of his play afore-hand, and so stale his invention to the auditory, before it come forth.*

1 *Child.* *O, do not so.*

2 *Child.* *By no means.*

3 *Child.* [*Advancing to the front of the Stage.*] *First, the title of his play is* Cynthia's Revels, *as any man that hath hope to be saved by his book can witness ; the scene* Gargaphie, *which I do vehemently suspect for some fustian country ; but let that vanish. Here is the court of* Cynthia, *whither he brings* Cupid *travelling on foot, resolved to turn page. By the way* Cupid *meets with* Mercury *(as that's a thing to be noted) ; take any of our play-books without a* Cupid *or a* Mercury *in it, and burn it for an heretic in poetry.*—[*In these and the subsequent speeches, at every break, the other two interrupt, and endeavour to stop him.*] *Pray thee, let me alone.* Mercury, *he in the nature of a conjuror, raises up* Echo, *who weeps over her love, or daffodil,* Narcissus, *a little ; sings ; curses the spring wherein the pretty foolish gentleman melted himself away : and there's an end of her.*——*Now I am to inform you, that* Cupid *and* Mercury *do both become pages.* Cupid *attends on* Philautia, *or Self-love, a court lady :* Mercury *follows* Hedon, *the Voluptuous, and a courtier ; one that ranks himself even with* Anaides, *or the Impudent, a gallant, and that's*

my part; one that keeps Laughter, Gelaia, the daughter of Folly, a wench in boy's attire, to wait on him.——These, in the court, meet with Amorphus, or the deformed, a traveller that hath drunk of the fountain, and there tells the wonders of the water. They presently dispatch away their pages with bottles to fetch of it, and themselves go to visit the ladies. But I should have told you—Look, these emmets put me out here—that with this Amorphus, there comes along a citizen's heir, Asotus, or the Prodigal, who, in imitation of the traveller, who hath the Whetstone following him, entertains the Beggar, to be his attendant——Now, the nymphs who are mistresses to these gallants, are Philautia, Self-love; Phantaste, a light Wittiness; Argurion, Money; and their guardian, mother Moria, or mistress Folly.

1 Child. *Pray thee, no more.*

3 Child. *There Cupid strikes Money in love with the Prodigal, makes her dote upon him, give him jewels, bracelets, carcanets, etc. All which he most ingeniously departs withal to be made known to the other ladies and gallants ; and in the heat of this, increases his train with the Fool to follow him, as well as the Beggar——By this time, your Beggar begins to wait close, who is returned with the rest of his fellow bottlemen.——There they all drink, save Argurian, who is fallen into a sudden apoplexy——*

1 Child. *Stop his mouth.*

3 *Child. And then, there's a retired scholar there, you would not wish a thing to be better contemn'd of a society of gallants, than it is ; and he applies his service, good gentleman, to the lady Arete, or Virtue, a poor nymph of Cynthia's train, that's scarce able to buy herself a gown ; you shall see her play in a black robe anon : a creature that, I assure you, is no less scorn'd than himself. Where am I now ? at a stand !*

2 Child. *Come, leave at last, yet.*

3 Child. *O, the night is come ('twas somewhat dark, methought), and Cynthia intends to come forth ; that helps it a little yet. All the courtiers must provide for revels ; they conclude upon a masque, the device of which is——What, will you ravish me ?——that each of these Vices, being to appear before Cynthia, would seem other than indeed they are ; and therefore assume the most neighbouring Virtues as their masking habit——I'd cry a rape, but that you are children.*

2 Child. *Come, we'll have no more of this anticipation ; to give them the inventory of their cates aforehand, were the discipline of a tavern, and not fitting this presence.*

1 Child. *Tut, this was but to shew us the happiness of his memory. I thought at first he would have plaid the ignorant critic with everything along as he had gone ; I expected some such device.*

3 Child. *O, you shall see me do that rarely ; lend me thy cloak.*

1 Child. *Soft, sir, you'll speak my prologue in it.*

3 Child. *No, would I might never stir then.*

2 Child. *Lend it him, lend it him.*

1 Child. *Well, you have sworn.* [Gives him the cloak.

3 Child. *I have. Now, sir, suppose I am one of your genteel*

auditors, that am come in, having paid my money at the door, with much ado, and here I take my place and sit down : I have my three sorts of tobacco in my pocket, my light by me, and thus I begin. [At the breaks he takes his tobacco.] *By this light, I wonder that any man is so mad, to come to see these rascally tits play here——They do act like so many wrens or pismires——not the fifth part of a good face amongst them all.——And then their music is abominable——able to stretch a man's ears worse than ten——pillories and their ditties—— most lamentable things, like the pitiful fellows that make them——poets. By this vapour, an 'twere not for tobacco——I think——the very stench of 'em would poison me, I should not dare to come in at their gates——A man were better visit fifteen jails——or a dozen or two of hospitals——than once adventure to come near them. How is't ? well ?*

1 Child. *Excellent ; give me my cloak.*

3 Child. *Stay ; you shall see me do another now, but a more sober, or better-gather'd gallant ; that is, as it may be thought, some friend, or well-wisher to the house : and here I enter.*

1 Child. *What, upon the stage too ?*

2 Child. *Yes ; and I step forth like one of the children, and ask you. Would you have a stool, sir ?*

3 Child. *A stool, boy !*

2 Child. *Ay, sir, if you'll give me sixpence I'll fetch you one.*

3 Child. *For what, I pray thee ? what shall I do with it ?*

2 Child. *O lord, sir ! will you betray your ignorance so much ? why throne yourself in state on the stage, as other gentlemen use, sir.*

3 Child. *Away, wag ; what, would'st thou make an implement of me ? 'Slid, the boy takes me for a piece of perspective, I hold my life, or some silk curtain, come to hang the stage here ! Sir crack, I am none of your fresh pictures, that use to beautify the decayed dead arras in a public theatre.*

2 Child. *'Tis a sign, sir, you put not that confidence in your good clothes, and your better face, that a gentleman should do, sir. But I pray you, sir, let me be a suitor to you, that you will quit our stage then, and take a place ; the play is instantly to begin.*

3 Child. *Most willingly, my good wag ; but I would speak with your author : where is he ?*

2 Child. *Not this way, I assure you, sir ; we are not so officiously befriended by him, as to have his presence in the tiring-house, to prompt us aloud, stamp at the book-holder, swear for our properties, curse the poor tireman, rail the music out of tune, and sweat for every venial trespass we commit, as some author would, if he had such fine enghles as we. Well, 'tis but our hard fortune !*

3 Child. *Nay, crack, be not dishearten'd.*

2 Child. *Not I, sir ; but if you please to confer with our author, by attorney, you may, sir ; our proper self here, stands for him.*

3 Child. *Troth, I have no such serious affair to negotiate with him, but what may very safely be turn'd upon thy trust. It is in the general behalf of this fair society here that I am to speak, at least the more judicious part of it, which seems much distasted with the immodest and*

*obscene writing of many in their plays. Besides, they could wish
your poets would leave to be promoters of other men's jests, and to
way-lay all the stale apothegms, or old books they can hear of, in print,
or otherwise, to farce their scenes withal. That they would not so
penuriously glean wit from every laundress or hackney-man, or derive
their best grace, with servile imitation, from common stages, or observation of the company they converse with; as if their invention lived
wholly upon another man's trencher. Again, that feeding their
friends with nothing of their own, but what they have twice or thrice
cooked, they should not wantonly give out how soon they had drest it;
nor how many coaches came to carry away the broken meat, besides
hobby-horses and foot-cloth nags.*

2 Child. *So, sir, this is all the reformation you seek?*

3 Child. *It is; do not you think it necessary to be practised, my
little wag?*

2 Child. *Yes, where any such ill-habited custom is received.*

3 Child. *O (I had almost forgot it too), they say, the* umbræ *or
ghosts of some three or four plays departed a dozen years since, have
been seen walking on your stage here; take heed, boy, if your house
be haunted with such hobgoblins, 'twill fright away all your spectators
quickly.*

2 Child. *Good, sir; but what will you say now, if a poet, untouch'd
with any breath of this disease, find the tokens upon you, that are of
the auditory? As some one civet-wit among you, that knows no other
learning, than the price of satin and velvets: nor other perfection than
the wearing of a neat suit; and yet will censure as desperately as the
most profess'd critic in the house, presuming his clothes should bear
him out in it. Another, whom it hath pleased nature to furnish with
more beard than brain, prunes his mustaccio, lisps, and, with some
score of affected oaths, swears down all that sit about him; " That the
old Hieronimo, as it was first acted, was the only best, and judiciously
penn'd play of Europe." A third great-bellied juggler talks of twenty
years since, and when Monsieur was here, and would enforce all wits
to be of that fashion, because his doublet is still so. A fourth miscalls
all by the name of fustian, that his grounded capacity cannot aspire
to. A fifth only shakes his bottle head, and out of his corky brain
squeezeth out a pitiful learned face, and is silent.*

3 Child. *By my faith, Jack, you have put me down: I would I
knew how to get off with any indifferent grace! here, take your cloak,
and promise some satisfaction in your prologue, or, I'll be sworn we
have marr'd all.*

2 Child. *Tut, fear not, child, this will never distaste a true sense:
be not out, and good enough. I would thou hadst some sugar candied
to sweeten thy mouth.*

The Third Sounding.

PROLOGUE.

If gracious silence, sweet attention,
Quick sight, and quicker apprehension,
The lights of judgment's throne, shine any where,
Our doubtful author hopes this is their sphere ;
And therefore opens he himself to those,
To other weaker beams his labours close,
As loth to prostitute their virgin-strain,
To every vulgar and adulterate brain,
In this alone, his Muse her sweetness hath,
She shuns the print of any beaten path ;
And proves new ways to come to learned ears :
Pied ignorance she neither loves nor fears.
Nor hunts she after popular applause,
Or foamy praise, that drops from common jaws :
The garland that she wears, their hands must twine,
Who can both censure, understand, define
What merit is : then cast those piercing rays,
Round as a crown, instead of honour'd bays,
About his poesy ; which, he knows, affords
Words, above action ; matter, above words.

ACT I

SCENE I.—*A Grove and Fountain.*

Enter CUPID, *and* MERCURY *with his caduceus, on different sides.*

Cup. Who goes there?

Mer. 'Tis I, blind archer.

Cup. Who, Mercury?

Mer. Ay.

Cup. Farewell.

Mer. Stay, Cupid.

Cup. Not in your company, Hermes, except your hands were riveted at your back.

Mer. Why so, my little rover?

Cup. Because I know you have not a finger, but is as long as my quiver, cousin Mercury, when you please to extend it.

Mer. Whence derive you this speech, boy?

Cup. O! 'tis your best polity to be ignorant. You did never steal Mars his sword out of the sheath, you! nor Neptune's trident! nor Apollo's bow! no, not you! Alas, your palms, Jupiter knows, they are as tender as the foot of a foundered nag, or a lady's face new mercuried, they'll touch nothing.

Mer. Go to, infant, you'll be daring still.

Cup. Daring! O Janus! what a word is there? why, my light feather-heel'd coz, what are you any more than my uncle Jove's pander? a lacquey that runs on errands for him, and can whisper a light message to a loose wench with some round volubility? wait mannerly at a table with a trencher, warble upon a crowd a little, and fill out nectar when Ganymede's away? one that sweeps the gods' drinking-room every morning, and sets the cushions in order again, which they threw one at another's head over night; can brush the carpets, call the stools again to their places, play the crier of the court with an audible voice, and take state of a president upon you at wrestlings, pleadings, negociations, etc. Here's the catalogue of your employments, now! O, no, I err; you have the marshalling of all the ghosts too that pass the Stygian ferry, and I suspect you for a share with the old sculler there, if the truth were known; but let that scape. One other peculiar virtue you possess, in lifting, or *leiger-du-main*, which few of the house of heaven have else besides, I must confess. But, methinks, that should not make you put that extreme distance 'twixt yourself and others, that we should be said to "over-dare" in speaking to your nimble deity. So Hercules might challenge priority of us both, because he can throw the bar farther, or lift more join'd stools at the arm's end, than we. If this might carry it, then we, who have made the whole body of divinity tremble at the twang of our bow, and enforc'd Saturnius himself to lay by his curled front, thunder, and three-fork'd fires, and put on a masking suit, too light for a reveller of eighteen to be seen in——

Mer. How now! my dancing braggart in *decimo sexto!* charm your skipping tongue, or I'll——

Cup. What! use the virtue of your snaky tip-staff there upon us?

Mer. No, boy, but the smart vigour of my palm about your ears. You have forgot since I took your heels up into air, on the very hour I was born, in sight of all the bench of deities, when the silver roof of the Olympian palace rung again with applause of the fact.

Cup. O no, I remember it freshly, and by a particular instance; for my mother Venus, at the same time, but stoop'd to embrace you, and, to speak by metaphor, you borrow'd a girdle of her's, as you did Jove's sceptre while he was laughing; and would have done his thunder too, but that 'twas too hot for your itching fingers.

Mer. 'Tis well, sir.

Cup. I heard, you but look'd in at Vulcan's forge the other day, and entreated a pair of his new tongs along with you for company: 'tis joy on you, i' faith, that you will keep your hook'd talons in practice with any thing. 'Slight, now you are on earth, we shall have you filch spoons and candlesticks rather than fail: pray Jove the perfum'd courtiers keep their casting-bottles, pick-tooths, and shittle-cocks from you, or our more ordinary gallants their tobacco-boxes; for I am strangely jealous of your nails.

Mer. Never trust me, Cupid, but you are turn'd a most acute gallant of late! the edge of my wit is clean taken off with the fine and subtile stroke of your thin-ground tongue; you fight with too poignant a phrase, for me to deal with.

Cup. O Hermes, your craft cannot make me confident. I know my own steel to be almost spent, and therefore entreat my peace with you, in time: you are too cunning for me to encounter at length, and I think it my safest ward to close.

Mer. Well, for once, I'll suffer you to win upon me, wag; but use not these strains too often, they'll stretch my patience. Whither might you march, now?

Cup. Faith, to recover thy good thoughts, I'll discover my whole project. The huntress and queen of these groves, Diana, in regard of some black and envious slanders hourly breathed against her, for her divine justice on Acteon, as she pretends, hath here in the vale of Gargaphie, proclaim'd a solemn revels, which (her godhead put off) she will descend to grace, with the full and royal expense of one of her clearest moons: in which time it shall be lawful for all sorts of ingenious persons to visit her palace, to court her nymphs, to exercise all variety of generous and noble pastimes; as well to intimate how far she treads such malicious imputations beneath her, as also to shew how clear her beauties are from the least wrinkle of austerity they may be charged with.

Mer. But, what is all this to Cupid?

Cup. Here do I mean to put off the title of a god, and take the habit of a page, in which disguise, during the interim of these revels, I will get to follow some one of Diana's maids, where, if my bow hold, and my shafts fly but with half the willingness and aim they are directed, I doubt not but I shall really redeem the minutes I have lost, by their so long and over nice proscription of my deity from their court.

Mer. Pursue it, divine Cupid, it will be rare.

Cup. But will Hermes second me?

Mer. I am now to put in act an especial designment from my father Jove; but, that perform'd, I am for any fresh action that offers itself.

Cup. Well, then we part.   [*Exit.*

Mer. Farewell, good wag.

Now to my charge.—Echo, fair Echo, speak,
'Tis Mercury that calls thee; sorrowful nymph,
Salute me with thy repercussive voice,
That I may know what cavern of the earth
Contains thy airy spirit, how, or where
I may direct my speech, that thou may'st hear.

Echo. [*below.*] Here.

Mer. So nigh!

Echo. Ay.

Mer. Know, gentle soul, then, I am sent from Jove,
Who, pitying the sad burthen of thy woes,
Still growing on thee, in thy want of words
To vent thy passion for Narcissus' death,

Commands, that now, after three thousand years,
Which have been exercised in Juno's spite,
Thou take a corporal figure and ascend,
Enrich'd with vocal and articulate power.
Make haste, sad nymph, thrice shall my winged rod
Strike the obsequious earth, to give thee way.
Arise, and speak thy sorrows, Echo, rise,
Here, by this fountain, where thy love did pine,
Whose memory lives fresh to vulgar fame,
Shrined in this yellow flower, that bears his name.

    Echo. [*ascends.*] His name revives, and lifts me up from earth,
O, which way shall I first convert myself,
Or in what mood shall I essay to speak,
That, in a moment, I may be deliver'd
Of the prodigious grief I go withal?
See, see, the mourning fount, whose springs weep yet
Th' untimely fate of that too beauteous boy,
That trophy of self-love, and spoil of nature,
Who, now transform'd into this drooping flower,
Hangs the repentant head, back from the stream,
As if it wish'd, *Would I had never look'd*
In such a flattering mirror! O Narcissus,
Thou that wast once, and yet art, my Narcissus,
Had Echo but been private with thy thoughts,
She would have dropt away herself in tears,
Till she had all turn'd water; that in her,
As in a truer glass, thou might'st have gazed
And seen thy beauties by more kind reflection,
But self-love never yet could look on truth
But with blear'd beams; slick flattery and she
Are twin-born sisters, and so mix their eyes,
As if you sever one, the other dies.
Why did the gods give thee a heavenly form,
And earthly thoughts to make thee proud of it?
Why do I ask? 'Tis now the known disease
That beauty hath, to bear too deep a sense
Of her own self-conceived excellence.
O, hadst thou known the worth of heaven's rich gift,
Thou wouldst have turn'd it to a truer use,
And not with starv'd and covetous ignorance,
Pined in continual eyeing that bright gem,
The glance whereof to others had been more,
Than to thy famish'd mind the wide world's store:
So wretched is it to be merely rich!
Witness thy youth's dear sweets here spent untasted,
Like a fair taper, with his own flame wasted.

    Mer. Echo, be brief, Saturnia is abroad,
And if she hear, she'll storm at Jove's high will.

    Echo. I will, kind Mercury, be brief as time.

Vouchsafe me, I may do him these last rites,
But kiss his flower, and sing some mourning strain
Over his wat'ry hearse.
   Mer. Thou dost obtain;
I were no son to Jove, should I deny thee,
Begin, and more to grace thy cunning voice,
The humorous air shall mix her solemn tunes
With thy sad words: strike, music, from the spheres,
And with your golden raptures swell our ears.

Echo [*accompanied*].

Slow, slow, fresh fount, keep time with my salt tears :
  Yet, slower, yet ; O faintly, gentle springs :
    List to the heavy part the music bears,
  Woe weeps out her division, when she sings.
      Droop herbs and flowers,
      Fall grief and showers,
      Our beauties are not ours ;
        O, I could still,
  Like melting snow upon some craggy hill,
    Drop, drop, drop, drop,
Since nature's pride is now a wither'd daffodil.—

   Mer. Now, have you done?
   Echo. Done presently, good Hermes: bide a little;
Suffer my thirsty eye to gaze awhile,
But e'en to taste the place, and I am vanish'd.
   Mer. Forego thy use and liberty of tongue,
And thou mayst dwell on earth, and sport thee there.
   Echo. Here young Acteon fell, pursued and torn
By Cynthia's wrath, more eager than his hounds;
And here—ah me, the place is fatal!—see
The weeping Niobe, translated hither
From Phrygian mountains; and by Phœbe rear'd,
As the proud trophy of her sharp revenge.
   Mer. Nay, but hear—
   Echo. But here, O here, the fountain of self-love,
In which Latona, and her careless nymphs,
Regardless of my sorrows, bathe themselves
In hourly pleasures.
   Mer. Stint thy babbling tongue!
Fond Echo, thou profan'st the grace is done thee.
So idle worldlings merely made of voice,
Censure the powers above them. Come, away,
Jove calls thee hence; and his will brooks no stay.
   Echo. O, stay: I have but one poor thought to clothe
In airy garments, and then, faith, I go.
Henceforth, thou treacherous and murdering spring,
Be ever call'd the FOUNTAIN OF SELF-LOVE:

And with thy water let this curse remain,
As an inseparate plague, that who but taste
A drop thereof, may, with the instant touch,
Grow dotingly enamour'd on themselves.
Now, Hermes, I have finish'd.

Mer. Then thy speech
Must here forsake thee, Echo, and thy voice,
As it was wont, rebound but the last words.
Farewell.

Echo. [*retiring.*] Well.

Mer. Now, Cupid, I am for you, and your mirth,
To make me light before I leave the earth.

Enter AMORPHUS, *hastily.*

Amo. Dear spark of beauty, make not so fast away.

Echo. Away.

Mer. Stay, let me observe this portent yet.

Amo. I am neither your Minotaur, nor your Centaur, nor your satyr, nor your hyæna, nor your babion, but your mere traveller, believe me.

Echo. Leave me.

Mer. I guess'd it should be some travelling motion pursued Echo so.

Amo. Know you from whom you fly? or whence?

Echo. Hence.   [*Exit.*

Amo. This is somewhat above strange: A nymph of her feature and lineament, to be so preposterously rude! well, I will but cool myself at yon spring, and follow her.

Mer. Nay, then, I am familiar with the revels: I'll leave you too.
                                                                  [*Exit.*

Amor. I am a rhinoceros, if I had thought a creature of her symmetry could have dared so improportionable and abrupt a digression.—Liberal and divine fount, suffer my profane hand to take of thy bounties. [*Takes up some of the water.*] By the purity of my taste, here is most ambrosiac water; I will sup of it again. By thy favour, sweet fount. See, the water, a more running, subtile, and humorous nymph than she, permits me to touch, and handle her. What should I infer? if my behaviours had been of a cheap or customary garb; my accent or phrase vulgar; my garments trite; my countenance illiterate, or unpractised in the encounter of a beautiful and brave attired piece; then I might, with some change of colour, have suspected my faculties: But, knowing myself an essence so sublimated and refined by travel; of so studied and well exercised a gesture; so alone in fashion; able to render the face of any statesman living; and to speak the mere extraction of language, one that hath now made the sixth return upon venture; and was your first that ever enrich'd his country with the true laws of the duello; whose optics have drunk the spirit of beauty in some eight score and eighteen prince's courts, where I have resided, and been there fortunate in the amours of three hundred and forty and five ladies, all nobly, if not princely descended; whose names I have in catalogue: To conclude, in all so happy, as even admiration herself doth seem to fasten her kisses upon me:—certes, I do neither see, nor feel, nor taste, nor savour the least steam or fume of a reason, that should invite this foolish, fastidious nymph, so peevishly to abandon me. Well, let the memory of her fleet into air; my thoughts and I am for this other element, water.

Enter CRITES *and* ASOTUS.

Cri. What, the well dieted Amorphus become a water drinker! I see he means not to write verses then.

Aso. No, Crites! why?

Cri. Because——

Nulla placere diu, nec vivere carmina possunt,
Quæ scribuntur aquæ potoribus.

Amo. What say you to your Helicon?

Cri. O, the Muses' well! that's ever excepted.

Amo. Sir, your Muses have no such water, I assure you; your nectar, or the juice of your nepenthe, is nothing to it; 'tis above your metheglin, believe it.

Aso. Metheglin; what's that, sir? may I be so audacious to demand?

Amo. A kind of Greek wine I have met with, sir, in my travels; it is the same that Demosthenes usually drunk, in the composure of all his exquisite and mellifluous orations.

Cri. That's to be argued, Amorphus, if we may credit Lucian, who, in his *Encomio Demosthenis*, affirms, he never drunk but water in any of his compositions.

Amo. Lucian is absurd, he knew nothing: I will believe mine own travels before all the Lucians of Europe. He doth feed you with fittons, figments, and leasings.

Cri. Indeed, I think, next a traveller, he does prettily well.

Amo. I assure you it was wine, I have tasted it, and from the hand of an Italian antiquary, who derives it authentically from the duke of Ferrara's bottles. How name you the gentleman you are in rank there with, sir?

Cri. 'Tis Asotus, son to the late deceased Philargyrus, the citizen.

Amo. Was his father of any eminent place or means?

Cri. He was to have been prætor next year.

Amo. Ha! a pretty formal young gallant, in good sooth; pity he is not more genteelly propagated. Hark you, Crites, you may say to him what I am, if you please; though I affect not popularity, yet I would loth to stand out to any, whom you shall vouchsafe to call friend.

Cri. Sir, I fear I may do wrong to your sufficiencies in the reporting them, by forgetting or misplacing some one: yourself can best inform him of yourself, sir; except you had some catalogue or list

of your faculties ready drawn, which you would request me to show
him for you, and him to take notice of.

Amo. This Crites is sour: [*Aside.*]—I will think, sir.

Cri. Do so, sir.—O heaven! that anything in the likeness of man
should suffer these rack'd extremities, for the uttering of his
sophisticate good parts. [*Aside.*

Aso. Crites, I have a suit to you; but you must not deny me;
pray you make this gentleman and I friends.

Cri. Friends! why, is there any difference between you?

Aso. No; I mean acquaintance, to know one another.

Cri. O, now I apprehend you; your phrase was without me
before.

Aso. In good faith, he's a most excellent rare man, I warrant him.

Cri. 'Slight, they are mutually enamour'd by this time. [*Aside.*

Aso. Will you, sweet Crites?

Cri. Yes, yes.

Aso. Nay, but when? you'll defer it now, and forget it.

Cri. Why, is it a thing of such present necessity, that it requires
so violent a dispatch!

Aso. No, but would I might never stir, he's a most ravishing man!
Good Crites, you shall endear me to you, in good faith; la!

Cri. Well, your longing shall be satisfied, sir.

Aso. And withal, you may tell him what my father was, and how
well he left me, and that I am his heir.

Cri. Leave it to me, I'll forget none of your dear graces, I warrant
you.

Aso. Nay, I know you can better marshal these affairs than I
can——O gods! I'd give all the world, if I had it, for abundance of
such acquaintance.

Cri. What ridiculous circumstance might I devise now to bestow
this reciprocal brace of butterflies one upon another? [*Aside.*

Amo. Since I trod on this side the Alps, I was not so frozen
in my invention. Let me see: to accost him with some choice
remnant of Spanish, or Italian! that would indifferently express
my languages now: marry, then, if he shall fall out to be ignorant,
it were both hard and harsh. How else? step into some *ragioni del
stato*, and so make my induction! that were above him too; and
out of his element, I fear. Feign to have seen him in Venice or
Padua! or some face near his in similitude! 'tis too pointed and
open. No, it must be a more quaint and collateral device, as——
stay: to frame some encomiastic speech upon this our metropolis,
or the wise magistrates thereof, in which politic number, 'tis odds
but his father fill'd up a room? descend into a particular admiration
of their justice, for the due measuring of coals, burning of cans, and
such like? as also their religion, in pulling down a superstitious
cross, and advancing a Venus, or Priapus, in place of it? ha! 'twill
do well. Or to talk of some hospital, whose walls record his father
a benefactor? or of so many buckets bestow'd on his parish church
in his lifetime, with his name at length, for want of arms, trickt upon

them? any of these. Or to praise the cleanness of the street wherein he dwelt? or the provident painting of his posts, against he should have been prætor? or, leaving his parent, come to some special ornament about himself, as his rapier, or some other of his accoutrements? I have it: thanks, gracious Minerva!

Aso. Would I had but once spoke to him, and then——He comes to me!

Amo. 'Tis a most curious and neatly wrought band this same, as I have seen, sir.

Aso. O lord, sir!

Amo. You forgive the humour of mine eye, in observing it.

Cri. His eye waters after it, it seems.   [*Aside.*

Aso. O lord, sir! there needs no such apology, I assure you.

Cri. I am anticipated; they'll make a solemn deed of gift of themselves, you shall see.   [*Aside.*

Amo. Your riband too does most gracefully in troth.

Aso. 'Tis the most genteel and received wear now, sir.

Amo. Believe me, sir, I speak it not to humour you—I have not seen a young gentleman, generally, put on his clothes with more judgment.

Aso. O, 'tis your pleasure to say so, sir.

Amo. No, as I am virtuous, being altogether untravell'd, it strikes me into wonder.

Aso. I do purpose to travel, sir, at spring.

Amo. I think I shall affect you, sir. This last speech of yours hath begun to make you dear to me.

Aso. O lord, sir! I would there were any thing in me, sir, that might appear worthy the least worthiness of your worth, sir. I protest, sir, I should endeavour to shew it, sir, with more than common regard, sir.

Cri. O, here's rare motley, sir.   [*Aside.*

Amo. Both your desert, and your endeavours are plentiful, suspect them not: but your sweet disposition to travel, I assure you, hath made you another myself in mine eye, and struck me enamour'd on your beauties.

Aso. I would I were the fairest lady of France for your sake, sir! and yet I would travel too.

Amo. O, you should digress from yourself else: for, believe it, your travel is your only thing that rectifies, or, as the Italian says, *vi rendi pronto all' attioni*, makes you fit for action.

Aso. I think it be great charge though, sir.

Amo. Charge! why 'tis nothing for a gentleman that goes private, as yourself, or so; my intelligence shall quit my charge at all time. Good faith, this hat hath possest mine eye exceedingly; 'tis so pretty and fantastic: what! is it a beaver?

Aso. Ay, sir, I'll assure you 'tis a beaver, it cost me eight crowns but this morning.

Amo. After your French account?

Aso. Yes, sir.

Cri. And so near his head! beshrew me, dangerous.   [*Aside.*

Amo. A very pretty fashion, believe me, and a most novel kind of trim: your band is conceited too!

Aso. Sir, it is all at your service.

Amo. O, pardon me.

Aso. I beseech you, sir, if you please to wear it, you shall do me a most infinite grace.

Cri. 'Slight, will he be prais'd out of his clothes?

Aso. By heaven, sir, I do not offer it you after the Italian manner; I would you should conceive so of me.

Amo. Sir, I shall fear to appear rude in denying your courtesies, especially being invited by so proper a distinction: May I pray your name, sir?

Aso. My name is Asotus, sir.

Amo. I take your love, gentle Asotus; but let me win you to receive this, in exchange—   [*They exchange beavers.*

Cri. Heart! they'll change doublets anon.   [*Aside.*

Amo. And, from this time esteem yourself in the first rank of those few whom I profess to love. What make you in company of this scholar here? I will bring you known to gallants, as Anaides of the ordinary, Hedon the courtier, and others, whose society shall render you graced and respected: this is a trivial fellow, too mean, too cheap, too coarse for you to converse with.

Aso. 'Slid, this is not worth a crown, and mine cost me eight but this morning.

Cri. I looked when he would repent him, he has begun to be sad a good while.

Amo. Sir, shall I say to you for that hat? Be not so sad, be not so sad: It is a relic I could not so easily have departed with, but as the hieroglyphic of my affection; you shall alter it to what form you please, it will take any block; I have received it varied on record to the three thousandth time, and not so few: It hath these virtues beside: your head shall not ache under it, nor your brain leave you, without license; it will preserve your complexion to eternity; for no beam of the sun, should you wear it under *zona torrida*, hath power to approach it by two ells. It is proof against thunder, and enchantment; and was given me by a great man in Russia, as an especial prized present; and constantly affirm'd to be the hat that accompanied the politic Ulysses in his tedious and ten years' travels.

Aso. By Jove, I will not depart withal, whosoever would give me a million.

Enter Cos *and* Prosaites.

Cos. Save you, sweet bloods! does any of you want a creature, or a dependent?

Cri. Beshrew me, a fine blunt slave!

Amo. A page of good timber! it will now be my grace to entertain him first, though I cashier him again in private.—How art thou call'd?

Cos. Cos, sir, Cos.

Cri. Cos! how happily hath fortune furnish'd him with a whetstone?

Amo. I do entertain you, Cos; conceal your quality till we be
private; if your parts be worthy of me, I will countenance you; if
not, catechise you.—Gentles, shall we go?

Aso. Stay, sir: I'll but entertain this other fellow, and then——
I have a great humour to taste of this water too, but I'll come again
alone for that——mark the place.—What's your name, youth?

Pros. Prosaites, sir.

Aso. Prosaites! a very fine name; Crites, is it not?

Cri. Yes, and a very ancient one, sir, the Beggar.

Aso. Follow me, good Prosaites; let's talk. [*Exeunt all but Crites.*

Cri. He will rank even with you, ere't be long,
If you hold on your course. O, vanity,
How are thy painted beauties doted on,
By light and empty idiots! how pursued
With open and extended appetite!
How they do sweat, and run themselves from breath,
Raised on their toes, to catch thy airy forms,
Still turning giddy, till they reel like drunkards,
That buy the merry madness of one hour
With the long irksomeness of following time!
O, how despised and base a thing is man,
If he not strive t'erect his grovelling thoughts
Above the strain of flesh! but how more cheap,
When, ev'n his best and understanding part,
The crown and strength of all his faculties,
Floats, like a dead drown'd body, on the stream
Of vulgar humour, mixt with common'st dregs!
I suffer for their guilt now, and my soul,
Like one that looks on ill-affected eyes,
Is hurt with mere intention on their follies.
Why will I view them then, my sense might ask me?
Or is't a rarity, or some new object,
That strains my strict observance to this point?
O, would it were! therein I could afford
My spirit should draw a little near to theirs,
To gaze on novelties; so vice were one.
Tut, she is stale, rank, foul; and were it not
That those that woo her greet her with lock'd eyes,
In spight of all th' impostures, paintings, drugs,
Which her bawd, Custom, dawbs her cheeks withal,
She would betray her loth'd and leprous face,
And fright the enamour'd dotards from themselves:
But such is the perverseness of our nature,
That if we once but fancy levity,
How antic and ridiculous soe'er
It suit with us, yet will our muffled thought

Choose rather not to see it, than avoid it:
And if we can but banish our own sense,
We act our mimic tricks with that free license,
That lust, that pleasure, that security,
As if we practised in a paste-board case,
And no one saw the motion, but the motion.
Well, check thy passion, lest it grow too loud:
While fools are pitied, they wax fat and proud.

ACT II

SCENE I.—*The Court.*

Enter Cupid *and* Mercury, *disguised as Pages.*

Cup. Why, this was most unexpectedly followed, my divine delicate Mercury; by the beard of Jove, thou art a precious deity.

Mer. Nay, Cupid, leave to speak improperly; since we are turn'd cracks, let's study to be like cracks; practise their language and behaviours, and not with a dead imitation: Act freely, carelessly, and capriciously, as if our veins ran with quicksilver, and not utter a phrase, but what shall come forth steep'd in the very brine of conceit, and sparkle like salt in fire.

Cup. That's not every one's happiness, Hermes: Though you can presume upon the easiness and dexterity of your wit, you shall give me leave to be a little jealous of mine; and not desperately to hazard it after your capering humour.

Mer. Nay, then, Cupid, I think we must have you hood-wink'd again; for you are grown too provident since your eyes were at liberty.

Cup. Not so, Mercury, I am still blind Cupid to thee.

Mer. And what to the lady nymph you serve?

Cup. Troth, page, boy, and sirrah: these are all my titles.

Mer. Then thou hast not altered thy name, with thy disguise?

Cup. O, no, that had been supererogation; you shall never hear your courtier call but by one of these three.

Mer. Faith, then both our fortunes are the same.

Cup. Why, what parcel of man hast thou lighted on for a master?

Mer. Such a one as, before I begin to decipher him, I dare not affirm to be any thing less than a courtier. So much he is during this open time of revels, and would be longer, but that his means are to leave him shortly after. His name is Hedon, a gallant wholly consecrated to his pleasures.

Cup. Hedon! he uses much to my lady's chamber, I think.

Mer. How is she call'd, and then I can shew thee?

Cup. Madam Philautia.

Mer. O ay, he affects her very particularly indeed. These are his graces. He doth (besides me) keep a barber and a monkey; he has a rich wrought waistcoat to entertain his visitants in, with a cap almost suitable. His curtains and bedding are thought to be his own; his bathing-tub is not suspected. He loves to have a fencer, a pedant, and a musician seen in his lodging a-mornings.

Cup. And not a poet?

Mer. Fie, no: himself is a rhymer, and that's thought better than a poet. He is not lightly within to his mercer, no, though he come when he takes physic, which is commonly after his play. He beats a tailor very well, but a stocking-seller admirably: and so consequently any one he owes money to, that dares not resist him. He never makes general invitement, but against the publishing of a new suit; marry, then you shall have more drawn to his lodging, than come to the launching of some three ships; especially if he be furnish'd with supplies for the retiring of his old wardrobe from pawn: if not, he does hire a stock of apparel, and some forty or fifty pound in gold, for that forenoon, to shew. He is thought a very necessary perfume for the presence, and for that only cause welcome thither: six milliners' shops afford you not the like scent. He courts ladies with how many great horse he hath rid that morning, or how oft he hath done the whole, or half the pommado in a seven-night before: and sometime ventures so far upon the virtue of his pomander, that he dares tell 'em how many shirts he has sweat at tennis that week; but wisely conceals so many dozen of balls he is on the score. Here he cames, that is all this.

Enter HEDON, ANAIDES, *and* GELAIA.

Hed. Boy!

Mer. Sir.

Hed. Are any of the ladies in the presence?

Mer. None yet, sir.

Hed. Give me some gold,—more.

Ana. Is that thy boy, Hedon?

Hed. Ay, what think'st thou of him?

Ana. I'd geld him; I warrant he has the philosopher's stone.

Hed. Well said, my good melancholy devil: sirrah, I have devised one or two of the prettiest oaths, this morning in my bed, as ever thou heard'st, to protest withal in the presence.

Ana. Prithee, let's hear them.

Hed. Soft, thou'lt use them afore me.

Ana. No, d—mn me then—I have more oaths than I know how to utter, by this air.

Hed. Faith, one is, *By the tip of your ear, sweet lady.* Is it not pretty, and genteel?

Ana. Yes, for the person 'tis applied to, a lady. It should be light and—

Hed. Nay, the other is better, exceeds it much: the invention is farther fet too. *By the white valley that lies between the alpine hills of your bosom, I protest.*—

Ana. Well, you travell'd for that, Hedon.

Mer. Ay, in a map, where his eyes were but blind guides to his understanding, it seems.

Hed. And then I have a salutation will nick all, by this caper: hay!

Ana. How is that?

Hed. You know I call madam Philautia, my Honour; and she calls me, her Ambition. Now, when I meet her in the presence anon, I will come to her, and say, *Sweet Honour, I have hitherto contented my sense with the lilies of your hand, but now I will taste the roses of your lip;* and, withal, kiss her: to which she cannot but blushing answer, *Nay, now you are too ambitious.* And then do I reply: *I cannot be too Ambitious of Honour, sweet lady.* Will't not be good? ha? ha?

Ana. O, assure your soul.

Hed. By heaven, I think 'twill be excellent: and a very politic achievement of a kiss.

Ana. I have thought upon one for Moria of a sudden too, if it take.

Hed. What is't, my dear Invention?

Ana. Marry, I will come to her, (and she always wears a muff, if you be remembered,) and I will tell her, *Madam, your whole self cannot but be perfectly wise; for your hands have wit enough to keep themselves warm.*

Hed. Now, before Jove, admirable! [*Gelaia laughs.*] Look, thy page takes it, too. By Phœbus, my sweet facetious rascal, I could eat water-gruel with thee a month for this jest, my dear rogue.

Ana. O, Hercules, 'ti. your only dish; above all your potatoes or oyster-pies in the world.

Hed. I have ruminated upon a most rare wish too, and the prophecy to it; but I'll have some friend to be the prophet; as thus: I do wish myself one of my mistress's cioppini. Another demands, Why would he be one of his mistress's cioppini? a third answers, Because he would make her higher: a fourth shall say, That will make her proud: and a fifth shall conclude, Then do I prophesy pride will have a fall;—and he shall give it her.

Ana. I will be your prophet. Gods so, it will be most exquisite; thou art a fine inventious rogue, sirrah.

Hed. Nay, and I have posies for rings, too, and riddles that they dream not of.

Ana. Tut, they'll do that, when they come to sleep on them, time enough: But were thy devices never in the presence yet, Hedon?

Hed. O, no, I disdain that.

Ana. 'Twere good we went afore then, and brought them acquainted with the room where they shall act, lest the strangeness of it put them out of countenance, when they should come forth.

[*Exeunt Hedon and Anaides.*

Cup. Is that a courtier, too?

Mer. Troth, no; he has two essential parts of the courtier, pride and ignorance; marry, the rest come somewhat after the ordinary gallant. 'Tis Impudence itself, Anaides; one that speaks all that comes in his cheeks, and will blush no more than a sackbut. He lightly occupies the jester's room at the table, and keeps laughter, Gelaia, a wench in page's attire, following him in place of a squire, whom he now and then tickles with some strange ridiculous stuff, utter'd as his land came to him, by chance. He will censure or discourse of any thing, but as absurdly as you would wish. His fashion is not to take knowledge of him that is beneath him in clothes. He never drinks below the salt. He does naturally admire his wit that wears gold lace, or tissue: stabs any man that speaks more contemptibly of the scholar than he. He is a great proficient in all the illiberal sciences, as cheating, drinking, swaggering, whoring, and such like: never kneels but to pledge healths, nor prays but for a pipe of pudding-tobacco. He will blaspheme in his shirt. The oaths which he vomits at one supper would maintain a town of garrison in good swearing a twelvemonth. One other genuine quality he has which crowns all these, and that is this: to a friend in want, he will not depart with the weight of a soldered groat, lest the world might censure him prodigal, or report him a gull: marry, to his cockatrice or punquetto, half a dozen taffata gowns or satin kirtles in a pair or two of months, why, they are nothing.

Cup. I commend him, he is one of my clients.

[*They retire to the back of the stage.*

Enter AMORPHUS, ASOTUS, *and* COS.

Amo. Come, sir. You are now within regard of the presence, and see, the privacy of this room how sweetly it offers itself to our retired intendments.—Page, cast a vigilant and enquiring eye about, that we be not rudely surprised by the approach of some ruder stranger.

Cos. I warrant you, sir. I'll tell you when the wolf enters, fear nothing.

Mer. O what a mass of benefit shall we possess, in being the invisible spectators of this strange show now to be acted!

Amo. Plant yourself there, sir; and observe me. You shall now, as well be the ocular, as the ear-witness, how clearly I can refel that paradox, or rather pseudodox, of those, which hold the face to be the index of the mind, which, I assure you, is not so in any politic creature: for instance; I will now give you the particular and distinct face of every your most noted species of persons, as your merchant, your scholar, your soldier, your lawyer, courtier, etc., and each of these so truly, as you would swear, but that your eye shall see the variation of the lineament, it were my most proper and genuine aspect. First, for your merchant, or city-face, 'tis thus; a dull, plodding-face, still looking in a direct line, forward: there is no great matter in this face. Then have you your student's, or academic face, which is here an honest, simple, and methodical face; but somewhat more spread than the former. The third is your soldier's face, a menacing and astounding face, that looks broad and big: the grace of his face consisteth much in a beard. The anti-face to this, is your lawyer's face, a contracted, subtile, and intricate face, full of quirks and turnings, a labyrinthean face, now angularly, now circularly, every way aspected. Next is your statist's face, a serious, solemn, and supercilious face, full of formal and square gravity; the eye, for the most part, deeply and artificially shadow'd: there is great judgment required in the making of this face. But now, to come to your face of faces, or courtier's face; 'tis of three sorts, according to our subdivision of a courtier, elementary, practic, and theoric. Your courtier theoric, is he that hath arrived to his farthest, and doth now know the court rather by speculation than practice; and this is his face: a fastidious and oblique face; that looks as it went with a vice, and were screw'd thus. Your courtier practic, is he that is yet in his path, his course, his way, and hath not touch'd the punctilio or point of his hopes; his face is here: a most promising, open, smooth, and overflowing face, that seems as it would run and pour itself into you: somewhat a northerly face. Your courtier elementary, is one but newly enter'd, or as it were in the alphabet, or *ut-re-mi-fa-sol-la* of courtship. Note well this face, for it is this you must practise.

Aso. I'll practise them all, if you please, sir.

Amo. Ay, hereafter you may: and it will not be altogether an ungrateful study. For, let your soul be assured of this, in any rank or profession whatever, the more general or major part of opinion goes with the face and simply respects nothing else. Therefore, if that can be made exactly, curiously, exquisitely, thoroughly, it is enough: but for the present you shall only apply yourself to this face of the elementary courtier, a light, revelling, and protesting face, now blushing, now smiling, which you may help much with a wanton wagging of your head, thus, (a feather will teach you,) or with kissing your finger that hath the ruby, or playing with some string of your band, which is a most quaint kind of melancholy besides: or, if among ladies, laughing loud, and crying up your own wit, though perhaps borrow'd, it is not amiss. Where is your page? call for your casting-bottle, and place your mirror in your hat, as I told you: so! Come, look not pale, observe me, set your face, and enter.

Mer. O, for some excellent painter, to have taken the copy of all these faces!   [*Aside.*

Aso. Prosaites!

Amo. Fie! I premonish you of that: in the court, boy, lacquey, or sirrah.

Cos. Master, *lupus in*——O, 'tis Prosaites.

Enter PROSAITES.

Aso. Sirrah, prepare my casting-bottle; I think I must be enforced to purchase me another page; you see how at hand Cos waits here.   [*Exeunt Amorphus, Asotus, Cos, and Prosaites.*

Mer. So will he too, in time.

Cup. What's he, Mercury?

Mer. A notable smelt. One that hath newly entertain'd the beggar to follow him, but cannot get him to wait near enough. 'Tis Asotus, the heir of Philargyrus; but first I'll give ye the other's character, which may make his the clearer. He that is with him is Amorphus, a traveller, one so made out of the mixture of shreds of forms, that himself is truly deform'd. He walks most commonly with a clove or pick-tooth in his mouth, he is the very mint of compliment, all his behaviours are printed, his face is another volume of essays, and his beard is an Aristarchus. He speaks all cream skimm'd, and more affected than a dozen waiting women. He is his own promoter in every place. The wife of the ordinary gives him his diet to maintain her table in discourse; which, indeed, is a mere tyranny over her other guests, for he will usurp all the talk: ten constables are not so tedious. He is no great shifter; once a year his apparel is ready to revolt. He doth use much to arbitrate quarrels, and fights himself, exceeding well, out at a window. He will lie cheaper than any beggar, and louder than most clocks; for which he is right properly accommodated to the Whetstone, his page. The other gallant is his zany, and doth most of these tricks after him; sweats to imitate him in every thing to a hair, except a beard, which is not yet extant. He doth learn to make strange sauces, to eat anchovies, maccaroni, bovoli, fagioli, and caviare, because he loves them; speaks as he speaks, looks, walks, goes so in clothes and fashion: is in all as if he were moulded of him. Marry, before they met, he had other very pretty sufficiencies, which yet he retains some light impression of; as frequenting a dancing-school, and grievously torturing strangers with inquisition after his grace in his galliard. He buys a fresh acquaintance at any rate. His eyes and his raiment confer much together as he goes in the street. He treads nicely like the fellow that walks upon ropes, especially the first Sunday of his silk stockings; and when he is most neat and new, you shall strip him with commendations.

Cup. Here comes another.   [*Crites passes over the stage.*

Mer. Ay, but one of another strain, Cupid; this fellow weighs somewhat.

Cup. His name, Hermes?

Mer. Crites. A creature of a most perfect and divine temper: one, in whom the humours and elements are peaceably met, without emulation of precedency; he is neither too fantastically melancholy, too slowly phlegmatic, too lightly sanguine, or too rashly choleric; but in all so composed and ordered, as it is clear Nature went about some full work, she did more than make a man when she made him. His discourse is like his behaviour, uncommon, but not unpleasing; he is prodigal of neither. He strives rather to be that which men call judicious, than to be thought so; and is so truly learned, that he affects not to shew it. He will think and speak his thought both freely; but as distant from depraving another man's merit, as proclaiming his own. For his valour, 'tis such, that he dares as little to offer any injury as receive one. In sum, he hath a most ingenuous and sweet spirit, a sharp and season'd wit, a straight judgment and a strong mind. Fortune could never break him, nor make him less. He counts it his pleasure to despise pleasures, and is more delighted with good deeds than goods. It is a competency to him that he can be virtuous. He doth neither covet nor fear; he hath too much reason to do either; and that commends all things to him.

Cup. Not better than Mercury commends him.

Mer. O, Cupid, 'tis beyond my deity to give him his due praises: I could leave my place in heaven to live among mortals, so I were sure to be no other than he.

Cup. 'Slight, I believe he is your minion, you seem to be so ravish'd with him.

Mer. He's one I would not have a wry thought darted against, willingly.

Cup. No, but a straight shaft in his bosom I'll promise him, if I am Cytherea's son.

Mer. Shall we go, Cupid?

Cup. Stay, and see the ladies now: they'll come presently. I'll help to paint them.

Mer. What, lay colour upon colour! that affords but an ill blazon.

Cup. Here comes metal to help it, the lady Argurion.

[Argurion passes over the stage.

Mer. Money, money.

Cup. The same. A nymph of a most wandering and giddy disposition, humorous as the air, she'll run from gallant to gallant, as they sit at primero in the presence, most strangely, and seldom stays with any. She spreads as she goes. To-day you shall have her look as clear and fresh as the morning, and to-morrow as melancholic as midnight. She takes special pleasure in a close obscure lodging, and for that cause visits the city so often, where she has many secret true concealing favourites. When she comes abroad, she's more loose and scattering than dust, and will fly from place to place, as she were wrapped with a whirlwind. Your young student, for the most part, she affects not, only salutes him, and away: a poet, nor a philosopher, she is hardly brought to take any notice of; no, though he be some part of an alchemist. She loves a player well, and a lawyer infinitely; but your fool above all. She can do much in court for the obtaining of any suit whatsoever, no door but flies open to her, her presence is above a charm. The worst in her is want of keeping state, and too much descending into inferior and base offices; she's for any coarse employment you will put upon her, as to be your procurer, or pander.

Mer. Peace, Cupid, here comes more work for you, another character or two.

Enter PHANTASTE, MORIA, *and* PHILAUTIA.

Pha. Stay, sweet Philautia, I'll but change my fan, and go presently.

Mor. Now, in very good serious, ladies, I will have this order revers'd, the presence must be better maintain'd from you: a quarter past eleven, and ne'er a nymph in prospective! Beshrew my hand, there must be a reform'd discipline. Is that your new ruff, sweet lady-bird? By my troth, 'tis most intricately rare.

Mer. Good Jove, what reverend gentlewoman in years might this be?

Cup. 'Tis madam Moria, guardian of the nymphs; one that is not now to be persuaded of her wit; she will think herself wise against all the judgments that come. A lady made all of voice and air, talks any thing of any thing. She is like one of your ignorant poetasters of the time, who, when they have got acquainted with a strange word, never rest till they have wrung it in, though it loosen the whole fabric of their sense.

Mer. That was pretty and sharply noted, Cupid.

Cup. She will tell you, Philosophy was a fine reveller, when she was young, and a gallant, and that then, though she say it, she was thought to be the dame Dido and Helen of the court: as also, what a sweet dog she had this time four years, and how it was called Fortune; and that, if the Fates had not cut his thread, he had been a dog to have given entertainment to any gallant in this kingdom; and unless she had whelp'd it herself, she could not have loved a thing better in this world.

Mer. O, I prithee no more; I am full of her.

Cup. Yes, I must needs tell you she composes a sack-posset well; and would court a young page sweetly, but that her breath is against it.

Mer. Now, her breath or something more strong protect me from her! The other, the other, Cupid?

Cup. O, that's my lady and mistress, madam Philautia. She admires not herself for any one particularity, but for all: she is fair, and she knows it; she has a pretty light wit too, and she knows it; she can dance, and she knows that too; play at shuttle-cock, and that too: no quality she has, but she shall take a very particular knowledge of, and most lady-like commend it to you. You shall have her at any time read you the history of herself, and very subtilely run over another lady's sufficiencies to come to her own. She has a good superficial judgment in painting, and would seem to have so in poetry. A most complete lady in the opinion of some three beside herself.

Phi. Faith, how liked you my quip to Hedon, about the garter? Was't not witty?

Mor. Exceeding witty and integrate: you did so aggravate the jest withal.

Phi. And did I not dance movingly the last night?

Mor. Movingly! out of measure, in troth, sweet charge.

Mer. A happy commendation, to dance out of measure!

Mor. Save only you wanted the swim in the turn: O! when I was at fourteen——

Phi. Nay, that's mine own from any nymph in the court, I'm sure on't; therefore you mistake me in that, guardian: both the swim and the trip are properly mine; every body will affirm it that has any judgment in dancing, I assure you.

Pha. Come now, Philautia, I am for you; shall we go?

Phi. Ay, good Phantaste: What! have you changed your head-tire?

Pha. Yes, faith, the other was so near the common, it had no extraordinary grace; besides, I had worn it almost a day, in good troth.

Phi. I'll be sworn, this is most excellent for the device, and rare; 'tis after the Italian print we look'd on t'other night.

Pha. 'Tis so: by this fan, I cannot abide any thing that savours the poor over-worn cut, that has any kindred with it; I must have variety, I: this mixing in fashion, I hate it worse than to burn juniper in my chamber, I protest.

Phi. And yet we cannot have a new peculiar court-tire, but these retainers will have it; these suburb Sunday-waiters; these courtiers for high days; I know not what I should call 'em——

Pha. O, ay, they do most pitifully imitate; but I have a tire a coming, i'faith, shall——

Mor. In good certain, madam, it makes you look most heavenly; but, lay your hand on your heart, you never skinn'd a new beauty more prosperously in your life, nor more metaphysically: look, good lady; sweet lady, look.

Phi. 'Tis very clear and well, believe me. But if you had seen mine yesterday, when 'twas young, you would have——Who's your doctor, Phantaste?

Pha. Nay, that's counsel, Philautia; you shall pardon me: yet I'll assure you he's the most dainty, sweet, absolute, rare man of the whole college. O! his very looks, his discourse, his behaviour, all he does is physic, I protest.

Phi. For heaven's sake, his name, good dear Phantaste?

Pha. No, no, no, no, no, no, believe me, not for a million of heavens: I will not make him cheap. Fie——

[*Exeunt Phantaste, Moria, and Philautia.*

Cup. There is a nymph too of a most curious and elaborate strain, light, all motion, an ubiquitary, she is every where, Phantaste——

Mer. Her very name speaks her, let her pass. But are these, Cupid, the stars of Cynthia's court? Do these nymphs attend upon Diana?

Cup. They are in her court, Mercury, but not as stars; these never come in the presence of Cynthia. The nymphs that make her train are the divine Arete, Timè, Phronesis, Thauma, and others of that high sort. These are privately brought in by Moria in this licentious time, against her knowledge: and, like so many meteors, will vanish when she appears.

Enter PROSAITES *singing, followed by* GELAIA *and* COS, *with bottles.*

> *Come follow me, my wags, and say, as I say,*
> *There's no riches but in rags, hey day, hey day :*
> *You that profess this art, come away, come away,*
> *And help to bear a part. Hey day, hey day, etc.*

>   [*Mercury and Cupid come forward.*

Mer. What, those that were our fellow pages but now, so soon preferr'd to be yeomen of the bottles! The mystery, the mystery, good wags?

Cup. Some diet-drink they have the guard of.

Pro. No, sir, we are going in quest of a strange fountain, lately found out.

Cup. By whom?

Cos. My master, or the great discoverer, Amorphus.

Mer. Thou hast well entitled him, Cos, for he will discover all he knows.

Gel. Ay, and a little more too, when the spirit is upon him.

Pro. O, the good travelling gentleman yonder has caused such a drought in the presence, with reporting the wonders of this new water, that all the ladies and gallants lie languishing upon the rushes, like so many pounded cattle in the midst of harvest, sighing one to another, and gasping, as if each of them expected a cock from the fountain to be brought into his mouth; and without we return quickly, they are all, as a youth would say, no better than a few trouts cast ashore, or a dish of eels in a sand-bag.

Mer. Well then, you were best dispatch, and have a care of them. Come, Cupid, thou and I'll go peruse this dry wonder. [*Exeunt.*

ACT III

SCENE I.—*An Apartment at the Court.*

Enter AMORPHUS *and* ASOTUS.

Amo. Sir, let not this discountenance or disgallant you a whit; you must not sink under the first disaster. It is with your young grammatical courtier, as with your neophyte player, a thing usual to be daunted at the first presence or interview: you saw, there was Hedon, and Anaides, far more practised gallants than yourself, who were both out, to comfort you. It is no disgrace, no more than for your adventurous reveller to fall by some inauspicious chance in his galliard, or for some subtile politic to undertake the bastinado, that the state might think worthily of him, and respect him as a man well beaten to the world. What! hath your tailor provided the property we spake of at your chamber, or no?

Aso. I think he has.

Amo. Nay, I entreat you, be not so flat and melancholic. Erect your mind: you shall redeem this with the courtship I will teach you against the afternoon. Where eat you to-day?

Aso. Where you please, sir; any where, I.

Amo. Come, let us go and taste some light dinner, a dish of sliced caviare, or so; and after, you shall practise an hour at your lodging some few forms that I have recall'd. If you had but so far gathered your spirits to you, as to have taken up a rush when you were out, and wagg'd it thus, or cleansed your teeth with it; or but turn'd aside, and feign'd some business to whisper with your page, till you had recovered yourself, or but found some slight stain in your stocking, or any other pretty invention, so it had been sudden, you might have come off with a most clear and courtly grace.

Aso. A poison of all! I think I was forespoke, I.

Amo. No, I must tell you, you are not audacious enough; you must frequent ordinaries a month more, to initiate yourself: in which time, it will not be amiss, if, in private, you keep good your acquaintance with Crites, or some other of his poor coat; visit his lodging secretly and often; become an earnest suitor to hear some of his labours.

Aso. O Jove! sir, I could never get him to read a line to me.

Amo. You must then wisely mix yourself in rank with such as you know can; and, as your ears do meet with a new phrase, or an acute jest, take it in: a quick nimble memory will lift it away, and, at your next public meal, it is your own.

Aso. But I shall never utter it perfectly, sir.

Amo. No matter, let it come lame. In ordinary talk you shall play it away, as you do your light crowns at primero: it will pass.

Aso. I shall attempt, sir.

Amo. Do. It is your shifting age for wit, and, I assure you, men must be prudent. After this you may to court, and there fall in, first with the waiting-woman, then with the lady. Put case they do retain you there, as a fit property, to hire coaches some pair of months, or so; or to read them asleep in afternoons upon some pretty pamphlet, to breathe you; why, it shall in time embolden you to some farther achievement: in the interim, you may fashion yourself to be careless and impudent.

Aso. How if they would have me to make verses? I heard Hedon spoke to for some.

Amo. Why, you must prove the aptitude of your genius; if you find none, you must hearken out a vein, and buy; provided you pay for the silence as for the work, then you may securely call it your own.

Aso. Yes, and I'll give out my acquaintance with all the best writers, to countenance me the more.

Amo. Rather seem not to know them, it is your best. Ay, be wise, that you never so much as mention the name of one, nor remember it mentioned; but if they be offer'd to you in discourse, shake your light head, make between a sad and a smiling face, pity some, rail at all, and commend yourself: 'tis your only safe and unsuspected course. Come, you shall look back upon the court again to-day, and be restored to your colours: I do now partly aim at the cause of your repulse—which was ominous indeed —for as you enter at the door, there is opposed to you the frame of a wolf in the hangings, which, surprising your eye suddenly, gave a false alarm to the heart; and that was it called your blood out of your face, and so routed the whole rank of your spirits: I beseech you labour to forget it. And remember, as I inculcated to you before, for your comfort, Hedon and Anaides.   [*Exeunt.*

SCENE II.—*Another Apartment in the same.*

Enter HEDON *and* ANAIDES.

Hedon. Heart, was there ever so prosperous an invention thus unluckily perverted and spoiled by a whoreson book-worm, a candle-waster?

Ana. Nay, be not impatient, Hedon.

Hed. 'Slight, I would fain know his name.

Ana. Hang him, poor grogan rascal! prithee think not of him: I'll send for him to my lodging, and have him blanketed when thou wilt, man.

Hed. Ods so, I would thou couldst. Look, here he comes.

Enter CRITES, *and walks in a musing posture at the back of the stage.*

Laugh at him, laugh at him; ha, ha, ha!

Ana. Fough! he smells all lamp-oil with studying by candle-light.

Hed. How confidently he went by us, and carelessly! Never moved, nor stirred at any thing! Did you observe him?

Ana. Ay, a pox on him, let him go, dormouse: he is in a dream now. He has no other time to sleep, but thus when he walks abroad to take the air.

Hed. 'Sprecious, this afflicts me more than all the rest, that we should so particularly direct our hate and contempt against him, and he to carry it thus without wound or passion! 'tis insufferable.

Ana. 'Slid, my dear Envy, if thou but say'st the word now, I'll undo him eternally for thee.

Hed. How, sweet Anaides?

Ana. Marry, half a score of us get him in, one night, and make him pawn his wit for a supper.

Hed. Away, thou hast such unseasonable jests! By this heaven, I wonder at nothing more than our gentlemen ushers, that will suffer a piece of serge or perpetuana to come into the presence: methinks they should, out of their experience, better distinguish the silken disposition of courtiers, than to let such terrible coarse rags mix with us, able to fret any smooth or gentle society to the threads with their rubbing devices.

Ana. Unless 'twere Lent, Ember-weeks, or fasting days, when the place is most penuriously empty of all other good outsides. D——n me, if I should adventure on his company once more, without a suit of buff to defend my wit! he does nothing but stab, the slave! How mischievously he cross'd thy device of the prophecy, there? and Moria, she comes without her muff too, and there my invention was lost.

Hed. Well, I am resolved what I'll do.

Ana. What, my good spirituous spark?

Hed. Marry, speak all the venom I can of him; and poison his reputation in every place where I come.

Ana. 'Fore God, most courtly.

Hed. And if I chance to be present where any question is made of his sufficiencies, or of any thing he hath done private or public, I'll censure it slightly and ridiculously.

Ana. At any hand beware of that; so thou may'st draw thine own judgment in suspect. No, I'll instruct thee what thou shalt do, and by a safer means: approve any thing thou hearest of his, to the received opinion of it; but if it be extraordinary, give it from him to some other whom thou more particularly affect'st; that's the way to plague him, and he shall never come to defend himself. 'Slud, I'll give out all he does is dictated from other men, and swear it too, if thou'lt have me, and that I know the time and place where he stole it, though my soul be guilty of no such thing; and that I think, out of my heart, he hates such barren shifts: yet to do thee a pleasure, and him a disgrace, I'll damn myself, or do any thing.

Hed. Grammercy, my dear devil; we'll put it seriously in practice, i'faith.   [*Exeunt Hedon and Anaides.*

Cri. [*coming forward.*] Do, good Detraction, do, and I the while
Shall shake thy spight off with a careless smile.
Poor piteous gallants! what lean idle slights
Their thoughts suggest to flatter their starv'd hopes!
As if I knew not how to entertain
These straw-devices; but, of force must yield
To the weak stroke of their calumnious tongues.
What should I care what every dor doth buz
In credulous ears? It is a crown to me
That the best judgments can report me wrong'd;
Them liars, and their slanders impudent.
Perhaps, upon the rumour of their speeches,
Some grieved friend will whisper to me; Crites,
Men speak ill of thee. So they be ill men,
If they spake worse, 'twere better: for of such
To be dispraised, is the most perfect praise.
What can his censure hurt me, whom the world
Hath censured vile before me! If good Chrestus,

Euthus, or Phronimus, had spoke the words,
They would have moved me, and I should have call'd
My thoughts and actions to a strict account
Upon the hearing: but when I remember,
'Tis Hedon and Anaides, alas, then
I think but what they are, and am not stirr'd.
The one a light voluptuous reveller,
The other, a strange arrogating puff,
Both impudent, and ignorant enough;
That talk as they are wont, not as I merit;
Traduce by custom, as most dogs do bark,
Do nothing out of judgment, but disease,
Speak ill, because they never could speak well.
And who'd be angry with this race of creatures?
What wise physician have we ever seen
Moved with a frantic man? the same affects
That he doth bear to his sick patient,
Should a right mind carry to such as these;
And I do count it a most rare revenge,
That I can thus, with such a sweet neglect,
Pluck from them all the pleasure of their malice;
For that's the mark of all their enginous drifts,
To wound my patience, howsoe'er they seem
To aim at other objects; which if miss'd,
Their envy's like an arrow shot upright,
That, in the fall, endangers their own heads.

Enter ARETE.

Are. What, Crites! where have you drawn forth the day,
You have not visited your jealous friends?
    Cri. Where I have seen, most honour'd Arete,
The strangest pageant, fashion'd like a court,
(At least I dreamt I saw it) so diffused,
So painted, pied, and full of rainbow strains,
As never yet, either by time, or place,
Was made the food to my distasted sense;
Nor can my weak imperfect memory
Now render half the forms unto my tongue,
That were convolved within this thrifty room.
Here stalks me by a proud and spangled sir,
That looks three handfuls higher than his foretop;
Savours himself alone, is only kind
And loving to himself; one that will speak
More dark and doubtful than six oracles!
Salutes a friend, as if he had a stitch;
Is his own chronicle, and scarce can eat
For regist'ring himself; is waited on
By mimics, jesters, panders, parasites,
And other such like prodigies of men.

He past, appears some mincing marmoset
Made all of clothes and face; his limbs so set
As if they had some voluntary act
Without man's motion, and must move just so
In spight of their creation: one that weighs
His breath between his teeth, and dares not smile
Beyond a point, for fear t'unstarch his look;
Hath travell'd to make legs, and seen the cringe
Of several courts, and courtiers; knows the time
Of giving titles, and of taking walls;
Hath read court common-places; made them his:
Studied the grammar of state, and all the rules
Each formal usher in that politic school
Can teach a man. A third comes, giving nods
To his repenting creditors, protests
To weeping suitors, takes the coming gold
Of insolent and base ambition,
That hourly rubs his dry and itchy palms;
Which griped, like burning coals, he hurls away
Into the laps of bawds, and buffoons' mouths.
With him there meets some subtle Proteus, one
Can change, and vary with all forms he sees;
Be any thing but honest; serves the time;
Hovers betwixt two factions, and explores
The drifts of both; which, with cross face, he bears
To the divided heads, and is received
With mutual grace of either: one that dares
Do deeds worthy the hurdle or the wheel,
To be thought somebody; and is in sooth
Such as the satirist points truly forth,
That only to his crimes owes all his worth.
    Are. You tell us wonders, Crites.
    Cri. This is nothing.
There stands a neophite glazing of his face,
Pruning his clothes, perfuming of his hair,
Against his idol enters; and repeats,
Like an unperfect prologue, at third music,
His part of speeches, and confederate jests,
In passion to himself. Another swears
His scene of courtship over; bids, believe him,
Twenty times ere they will; anon, doth seem
As he would kiss away his hand in kindness;
Then walks off melancholic, and stands wreath'd,
As he were pinn'd up to the arras, thus.
A third is most in action, swims and frisks,
Plays with his mistress's paps, salutes her pumps,
Adores her hems, her skirts, her knots, her curls,
Will spend his patrimony for a garter,
Or the least feather in her bounteous fan.

A fourth, he only comes in for a mute;
Divides the act with a dumb show, and exit.
Then must the ladies laugh, straight comes their scene,
A sixth times worse confusion than the rest.
Where you shall hear one talk of this man's eye,
Another of his lip, a third, his nose,
A fourth commend his leg, a fifth, his foot,
A sixth, his hand, and every one a limb;
That you would think the poor distorted gallant
Must there expire.   Then fall they in discourse
Of tires and fashions, how they must take place,
Where they may kiss, and whom, when to sit down,
And with what grace to rise; if they salute,
What court'sy they must use: such cobweb stuff
As would enforce the common'st sense abhor
Th' Arachnean workers.
    Are. Patience, gentle Crites.
This knot of spiders will be soon dissolved,
And all their webs swept out of Cynthia's court,
When once her glorious deity appears,
And but presents itself in her full light:
'Till when, go in, and spend your hours with us,
Your honour'd friends, Time and Phronesis,
In contemplation of our goddess' name.
Think on some sweet and choice invention now,
Worthy her serious and illustrious eyes,
That from the merit of it we may take
Desired occasion to prefer your worth,
And make your service known to Cynthia.
It is the pride of Arete to grace
Her studious lovers; and, in scorn of time,
Envy, and ignorance, to lift their state
Above a vulgar height.   True happiness
Consists not in the multitude of friends,
But in their worth and choice.   Nor would I have
Virtue a popular regard pursue:
Let them be good that love me, though but few.
    Cri. I kiss thy hands, divinest Arete,
And vow myself to thee, and Cynthia.   [*Exeunt.*

SCENE III.—*Another Apartment in the same.*

Enter AMORPHUS, *followed by* ASOTUS *and his* Tailor.

Amo. A little more forward: so, sir. Now go in, discloak yourself, and come forth. [*Exit Asotus.*] Tailor, bestow thy absence
upon us; and be not prodigal of this secret, but to a dear customer.
                                                        [*Exit Tailor.*

Re-enter Asotus.

'Tis well enter'd, sir. Stay, you come on too fast; your pace is too impetuous. Imagine this to be the palace of your pleasure, or place where your lady is pleased to be seen. First, you present yourself, thus: and spying her, you fall off, and walk some two turns; in which time, it is to be supposed, your passion hath sufficiently whited your face, then, stifling a sigh or two, and closing your lips, with a trembling boldness, and bold terror, you advance yourself forward. Prove thus much, I pray you.

Aso. Yes, sir;—pray Jove I can light on it! Here, I come in, you say, and present myself?

Amo. Good.

Aso. And then I spy her, and walk off?

Amo. Very good.

Aso. Now, sir, I stifle, and advance forward?

Amo. Trembling.

Aso. Yes, sir, trembling; I shall do it better when I come to it. And what must I speak now?

Amo. Marry, you shall say; *Dear Beauty*, or *sweet Honour* (or by what other title you please to remember her), *methinks you are melancholy.* This is, if she be alone now, and discompanied.

Aso. Well, sir, I'll enter again; her title shall be, *My dear Lindabrides.*

Amo. Lindabrides!

Aso. Ay, sir, the emperor Alicandroe's daughter, and the prince Meridian's sister, in *the Knight of the Sun ;* she should have been married to him, but that the princess Claridiana——

Amo. O, you betray your reading.

Aso. Nay, sir, I have read history, I am a little humanitian. Interrupt me not, good sir. *My dear Lindabrides,—my dear Lindabrides,—my dear Lindabrides, methinks you are melancholy.*

Amo. Ay, and take her by the rosy finger'd hand.

Aso. Must I so: O!—*My dear Lindabrides, methinks you are melancholy.*

Amo. Or thus, sir. *All variety of divine pleasures, choice sports, sweet music, rich fare, brave attire, soft beds, and silken thoughts, attend this dear beauty.*

Aso. Believe me, that's pretty. *All variety of divine pleasures, choice sports, sweet music, rich fare, brave attire, soft beds, and silken thoughts, attend this dear beauty.*

Amo. And then, offering to kiss her hand, if she shall coily recoil, and signify your repulse, you are to re-enforce yourself with, *More than most fair lady,*
Let not the rigour of your just disdain
Thus coarsely censure of your servant's zeal.
And withal, protest her to be the only and absolute unparallel'd creature you do adore, and admire, and respect, and reverence, in this court, corner of the world, or kingdom.

Aso. This is hard, by my faith. I'll begin it all again.

Amo. Do so, and I will act it for your lady.

Aso. Will you vouchsafe, sir? *All variety of divine pleasures, choice sports, sweet music, rich fare, brave attire, soft beds, and silken thoughts, attend this dear beauty.*

Amo. So, sir, pray you, away.

Aso. *More than most fair lady,*
Let not the rigour of your just disdain
Thus coarsely censure of your servant's zeal ;
I protest you are the only, and absolute, unapparell'd——

Amo. Unparallel'd.

Aso. *Unparallel'd creature, I do adore, and admire, and respect, and reverence, in this corner of the world or kingdom.*

Amo. This is, if she abide you. But now, put the case she should be passant when you enter, as thus: you are to frame your gait thereafter, and call upon her, *lady, nymph, sweet refuge, star of our court.* Then, if she be guardant, here; you are to come on, and, laterally disposing yourself, swear by her blushing and well-coloured cheek, the bright dye of her hair, her ivory teeth, though they be ebony), or some such white and innocent oath, to induce you. If regardant, then maintain your station, brisk and irpe, show the supple motion of your pliant body, but in chief of your knee, and hand, which cannot but arride her proud humour exceedingly.

Aso. I conceive you, sir. I shall perform all these things in good time, I doubt not, they do so hit me.

Amo. Well, sir, I am your lady; make use of any of these beginnings, or some other out of your own invention; and prove how you can hold up, and follow it. Say, say.

Aso. Yes, sir. *My dear Lindabrides.*

Amo. No, you affect that Lindabrides too much; and let me tell you it is not so courtly. Your pedant should provide you some parcels of French, or some pretty commodity of Italian, to commence with, if you would be exotic and exquisite.

Aso. Yes, sir, he was at my lodging t'other morning, I gave him a doublet.

Amo. Double your benevolence, and give him the hose too; clothe you his body, he will help to apparel your mind. But now, see what your proper genius can perform alone, without adjection of any other Minerva.

Aso. I comprehend you, sir.

Amo. I do stand you, sir; fall back to your first place. Good, passing well: very properly pursued.

Aso. *Beautiful, ambiguous, and sufficient lady, what! are you all alone ?*

Amo. *We would be, sir, if you would leave us.*

Aso. *I am at your beauty's appointment, bright angel ; but——*

Amo. *What but ?*

Aso. *No harm, more than most fair feature.*

Amo. That touch relish'd well.

Aso. *But, I protest——*

Amo. *And why should you protest?*

Aso. *For good will, dear esteem'd madam, and I hope your ladyship will so conceive of it :*
And will, in time, return from your disdain,
And rue the suff'rance of our friendly pain.

Amo. O, that piece was excellent! If you could pick out more of these play-particles, and, as occasion shall salute you, embroider or damask your discourse with them, persuade your soul, it would most judiciously commend you. Come, this was a well-discharged and auspicious bout. Prove the second.

Aso. *Lady, I cannot ruffle it in red and yellow.*

Amo. *Why, if you can revel it in white, sir, 'tis sufficient.*

Aso. *Say you so, sweet lady! Lan, tede, de, de, de, dant, dant, dant, dante.* [Sings and dances.] *No, in good faith, madam, whosoever told your ladyship so, abused you ; but I would be glad to meet your ladyship in a measure.*

Amo. *Me, sir ! Belike you measure me by yourself, then ?*

Aso. *Would I might, fair feature.*

Amo. *And what were you the better, if you might ?*

Aso. *The better it please you to ask, fair lady.*

Amo. Why, this was ravishing, and most acutely continued. Well, spend not your humour too much, you have now competently exercised your conceit: this, once or twice a day, will render you an accomplish'd, elaborate, and well-levell'd gallant. Convey in your courting-stock, we will in the heat of this go visit the nymphs' chamber. [*Exeunt.*

ACT IV

SCENE I.—*An Apartment in the Palace.*

Enter Phantaste, Philautia, Argurion, Moria, *and* Cupid.

Pha. I would this water would arrive once, our travelling friend so commended to us.

Arg. So would I, for he has left all us in travail with expectation of it.

Pha. Pray Jove, I never rise from this couch, if ever I thirsted more for a thing in my whole time of being a courtier.

Phi. Nor I, I'll be sworn: the very mention of it sets my lips in a worse heat, than if he had sprinkled them with mercury. Reach me the glass, sirrah.

Cup. Here, lady.

Mor. They do not peel, sweet charge, do they?

Phi. Yes, a little, guardian.

Mor. O, 'tis an eminent good sign. Ever when my lips do so, I am sure to have some delicious good drink or other approaching.

Arg. Marry, and this may be good for us ladies, for it seems 'tis far fet by their stay.

Mor. My palate for yours, dear Honour, it shall prove most elegant, I warrant you. O, I do fancy this gear that's long a coming, with an unmeasurable strain.

Pha. Pray thee sit down, Philautia; that rebatu becomes thee singularly.

Phi. Is it not quaint?

Pha. Yes, faith. Methinks, thy servant Hedon is nothing so obsequious to thee, as he was wont to be: I know not how, he is grown out of his garb a-late, he's warp'd.

Mor. In trueness, and so methinks too; he is much converted.

Phi. Tut, let him be what he will, 'tis an animal I dream not of. This tire, methinks, makes me look very ingeniously, quick, and spirited; I should be some Laura, or some Delia, methinks.

Mor. As I am wise, fair Honours, that title she gave him, to be her Ambition, spoil'd him: before, he was the most propitious and observant young novice—

Pha. No, no, you are the whole heaven awry, guardian; 'tis the swaggering coach-horse Anaides draws with him there, has been the diverter of him.

Phi. For Cupid's sake speak no more of him; would I might never dare to look in a mirror again, if I respect ever a marmoset of 'em all, otherwise than I would a feather, or my shuttle-cock, to make sport with now and then.

Pha. Come, sit down; troth, an you be good beauties, let's run over them all now: Which is the properest man amongst them? I say, the traveller, Amorphus.

Phi. O, fie on him, he looks like a Venetian trumpeter in the battle of Lepanto, in the gallery yonder; and speaks to the tune of a country lady that comes ever in the rearward or train of a fashion.

Mor. I should have judgment in a feature, sweet beauties.

Pha. A body would think so, at these years.

Mor. And I prefer another now, far before him, a million, at least.

Pha. Who might that be, guardian?

Mor. Marry, fair charge, Anaides.

Pha. Anaides! you talk'd of a tune, Philautia; there's one speaks in a key, like the opening of some justice's gate, or a postboy's horn, as if his voice feared an arrest for some ill words it should give, and were loth to come forth.

Phi. Ay, and he has a very imperfect face.

Pha. Like a sea-monster, that were to ravish Andromeda from the rock.

Phi. His hands too great too, by at least a straw's breadth.

Pha. Nay, he has a worse fault than that too.

Phi. A long heel?

Pha. That were a fault in a lady, rather than him: no, they say he puts off the calves of his legs, with his stockings, every night.

Phi. Out upon him! Turn to another of the pictures, for love's sake. What says Argurion? Whom does she commend afore the rest?

Cup. I hope I have instructed her sufficiently for an answer.

[Aside.

Mor. Troth, I made the motion to her ladyship for one to-day, i'the presence, but it appear'd she was otherways furnished before: she would none.

Pha. Who was that, Argurion?

Mor. Marry, the poor plain gentleman in the black there.

Pha. Who, Crites?

Arg. Ay, ay, he: a fellow that nobody so much as look'd upon, or regarded; and she would have had me done him particular grace.

Pha. That was a true trick of yourself, Moria, to persuade Argurion to affect the scholar.

Arg. Tut, but she shall be no chooser for me. In good faith, I like the citizen's son there, Asotus; methinks none of them all come near him.

Pha. Not Hedon?

Arg. Hedon! In troth, no. Hedon's a pretty slight courtier, and he wears his clothes well, and sometimes in fashion; marry, his face is but indifferent, and he has no such excellent body. No, the other is a most delicate youth; a sweet face, a straight body, a well-proportion'd leg and foot, a white hand, a tender voice.

Phi. How now, Argurion!

Pha. O, you should have let her alone, she was bestowing a copy of him upon us. Such a nose were enough to make me love a man, now.

Phi. And then his several colours he wears; wherein he flourisheth changeably, every day.

Pha. O, but his short hair, and his narrow eyes!

Phi. Why she doats more palpably upon him than ever his father did upon her.

Pha. Believe me, the young gentleman deserves it. If she could doat more, 'twere not amiss. He is an exceeding proper youth, and would have made a most neat barber surgeon, if he had been put to it in time.

Phi. Say you so! Methinks he looks like a tailor already.

Pha. Ay, that had sayed on one of his customer's suits. His face is like a squeezed orange, or—

Arg. Well, ladies, jest on: the best of you both would be glad of such a servant.

Mor. Ay, I'll be sworn would they, though he be a little shame-faced.

Pha. Shame-faced, Moria! out upon him. Your shame-faced servant is your only gull.

Mor. Go to, beauties, make much of time, and place, and occasion, and opportunity, and favourites, and things that belong to them, for I'll ensure you they will all relinquish; they cannot endure above another year; I know it out of future experience; and therefore take exhibition and warning. I was once a reveller myself, and though I speak it, as mine own trumpet, I was then esteem'd—

Phi. The very march-pane of the court, I warrant you.

Pha. And all the gallants came about you like flies, did they not?

Mor. Go to, they did somewhat; that's no matter now.

Pha. Nay, good Moria, be not angry. Put case, that we four now had the grant from Juno, to wish ourselves into what happy estate we could, what would you wish to be, Moria?

Mor. Who, I! let me see now. I would wish to be a wise woman, and know all the secrets of court, city, and country. I would know what were done behind the arras, what upon the stairs, what in the garden, what in the nymphs' chamber, what by barge, and what by coach. I would tell you which courtier were scabbed and which not; which lady had her own face to lie with her a-nights and which not; who put off their teeth with their clothes in court, who their hair, who their complexion; and in which box they put it. There should not a nymph, or a widow, be got with child in the verge, but I would guess, within one or two, who was the right father, and in what month it was gotten; with what words, and which way. I would tell you which madam loved a monsieur, which a player, which a page; who slept with her husband, who with her friend, who with her gentleman-usher, who with her horse-keeper, who with her monkey, and who with all; yes, and who jigg'd the cock too.

Pha. Fie, you'd tell all, Moria! If I should wish now, it should be to have your tongue out. But what says Philautia? Who should she be?

Phi. Troth, the very same I am. Only I would wish myself a little more command and sovereignty; that all the court were subject to my absolute beck, and all things in it depending on my look; as if there were no other heaven but in my smile, nor other hell but in my frown; that I might send for any man I list, and have his head cut off when I have done with him, or made an eunuch if he denied me; and if I saw a better face than mine own, I might have my doctor to poison it. What would you wish, Phantaste?

Pha. Faith, I cannot readily tell you what: but methinks I should wish myself all manner of creatures. Now I would be an empress, and by and by a duchess; then a great lady of state, then one of your miscellany madams, then a waiting-woman, then your citizen's wife, then a coarse country gentlewoman, then a dairy-maid, then a shepherd's lass, then an empress again, or the queen of fairies: and thus I would prove the vicissitudes and whirl of pleasures about and again. As I were a shepherdess, I would be piped and sung to; as a dairy-wench, I would dance at maypoles, and make syllabubs; as a country gentlewoman, keep a good house, and come up to term to see motions; as a citizen's wife, to be troubled with a jealous husband, and put to my shifts; others' miseries should be my pleasures. As a waiting-woman, I would taste my lady's delights to her; as a miscellany madam, invent new tires, and go visit courtiers; as a great lady, lie a-bed, and have courtiers visit me; as a duchess, I would keep my state; and as an empress, I would do any thing. And, in all these shapes, I would ever be follow'd with the affections of all that see me. Marry, I myself would affect none; or if I did, it should not be heartily, but so as I might save myself in them still, and take pride in tormenting the poor wretches. Or, now I think on't, I would, for one year, wish myself one woman; but the richest, fairest, and delicatest in a kingdom, the very centre of wealth and beauty, wherein all lines of love should meet; and in that person I would prove all manner of suitors, of all humours, and of all complexions, and never have any two of a sort. I would see how love, by the power of his object, could work inwardly alike, in a choleric man and a sanguine, in a melancholic and a phlegmatic, in a fool and a wise man, in a clown and a courtier, in a valiant man and a coward; and how he could vary outward, by letting this gallant express himself in dumb gaze; another with sighing and rubbing his fingers; a third with play-ends and pitiful verses; a fourth, with stabbing himself, and drinking healths, or writing languishing letters in his blood; a fifth, in colour'd ribands and good clothes; with this lord to smile, and that lord to court, and the t'other lord to dote, and one lord to hang himself. And, then, I to have a book made of all this, which I would call the *Book of Humours*, and every night read a little piece ere I slept, and laugh at it.—Here comes Hedon.

Enter HEDON, ANAIDES, *and* MERCURY, *who retires with* CUPID
to the back of the stage, where they converse together.

Hed. Save you sweet and clear beauties! By the spirit that moves in me, you are all most pleasingly bestow'd, ladies. Only I can take it for no good omen, to find mine Honour so dejected.

Phi. You need not fear, sir; I did of purpose humble myself against your coming, to decline the pride of my Ambition.

Hed. Fair Honour, Ambition dares not stoop; but if it be your sweet pleasure I shall lose that title, I will, as I am Hedon, apply myself to your bounties.

Phi. That were the next way to dis-title myself of honour. O, no, rather be still Ambitious, I pray you.

Hed. I will be any thing that you please, whilst it pleaseth you to be yourself, lady. Sweet Phantaste, dear Moria, most beautiful Argurion—

Ana. Farewell, Hedon.

Hed. Anaides, stay, whither go you?

Ana. 'Slight, what should I do here? an you engross them all for your own use, 'tis time for me to seek out.

Hed. I engross them! Away, mischief; this is one of your extravagant jests now, because I began to salute them by their names.

Ana. Faith, you might have spared us madam Prudence, the guardian there, though you had more covetously aim'd at the rest.

Hed. 'Sheart, take them all, man: what speak you to me of aiming or covetous?

Ana. Ay, say you so! nay, then, have at them:—Ladies, here's one hath distinguish'd you by your names already: It shall only become me to ask how you do.

Hed. Ods so, was this the design you travail'd with?

Pha. Who answers the brazen head? it spoke to somebody.

Ana. Lady Wisdom, do you interpret for these puppets?

Mor. In truth and sadness, honours, you are in great offence for this. Go to; the gentleman (I'll undertake with him) is a man of fair living, and able to maintain a lady in her two coaches a day, besides pages, monkeys, and paraquettoes, with such attendants as she shall think meet for her turn; and therefore there is more respect requirable, howsoe'er you seem to connive. Hark you, sir, let me discourse a syllable with you. I am to say to you, these ladies are not of that close and open behaviour as haply you may suspend; their carriage is well known to be such as it should be, both gentle and extraordinary.

Mer. O, here comes the other pair.

Enter AMORPHUS *and* ASOTUS.

Amo. That was your father's love, the nymph Argurion. I would have you direct all your courtship thither; if you could but endear yourself to her affection, you were eternally engallanted.

Aso. In truth, sir! pray Phœbus I prove favoursome in her fair eyes.

Amo. All divine mixture, and increase of beauty to this bright bevy of ladies; and to the male courtiers, compliment and courtesy.

Hed. In the behalf of the males, I gratify you, Amorphus.

Pha. And I of the females.

Amo. Succinctly return'd. I do vail to both your thanks, and kiss them; but primarily to yours, most ingenious, acute, and polite lady.

Phi. Ods my life, how he does all-to-bequalify her! *ingenious, acute,* and *polite!* as if there was not others in place as ingenious, acute, and polite as she.

Hed. Yes, but you must know, lady, he cannot speak out of a dictionary method.

Pha. Sit down, sweet Amorphus. When will this water come, think you?

Amo. It cannot now be long, fair lady.

Cup. Now observe, Mercury.

Aso. How, most ambiguous beauty! love you? that I will, by this handkerchief.

Mer. 'Slid, he draws his oaths out of his pocket.

Arg. But will you be constant?

Aso. Constant, madam! I will not say for constantness; but by this purse, which I would be loth to swear by, unless it were embroidered, I protest, more than most fair lady, you are the only absolute, and unparallel'd creature, I do adore, and admire, and respect, and reverence in this court, corner of the world, or kingdom. Methinks you are melancholy.

Arg. Does your heart speak all this?

Aso. Say you?

Mer. O, he is groping for another oath.

Aso. Now by this watch—I marle how forward the day is—I do unfeignedly avow myself—'slight, 'tis deeper than I took it, past five—yours entirely addicted, madam.

Arg. I require no more, dearest Asotus; henceforth let me call you mine, and in remembrance of me, vouchsafe to wear this chain and this diamond.

Aso. O lord, sweet lady!

Cup. There are new oaths for him. What! doth Hermes taste no alteration in all this?

Mer. Yes, thou hast strook Argurion enamour'd on Asotus, methinks.

Cup. Alas, no; I am nobody, I; I can do nothing in this disguise.

Mer. But thou hast not wounded any of the rest, Cupid.

Cup. Not yet; it is enough that I have begun so prosperously.

Arg. Nay, these are nothing to the gems I will hourly bestow upon thee; be but faithful and kind to me, and I will lade thee with my richest bounties: behold, here my bracelets from mine arms.

Aso. Not so, good lady, by this diamond.

Arg. Take 'em, wear 'em; my jewels, chain of pearl pendants, all I have.

Aso. Nay then, by this pearl you make me a wanton.

Cup. Shall she not answer for this, to maintain him thus in swearing?

Mer. O no, there is a way to wean him from this, the gentleman may be reclaim'd.

Cup. Ay, if you had the airing of his apparel, coz, I think.

Aso. Loving! 'twere pity an I should be living else, believe me. Save you, sir, save you, sweet lady, save you, monsieur Anaides, save you, dear madam.

Ana. Dost thou know him that saluted thee, Hedon?

Hed. No, some idle Fungoso, that hath got above the cupboard since yesterday.

Ana. 'Slud, I never saw him till this morning, and he salutes me as familiarly as if we had known together since the deluge, or the first year of Troy action.

Amo. A most right-handed and auspicious encounter. Confine yourself to your fortunes.

Phi. For sport's sake let's have some Riddles or Purposes, ho!

Pha. No, faith, your Prophecies are best, the t'other are stale.

Phi. Prophecies! we cannot all sit in at them; we shall make a confusion. No; what call'd you that we had in the forenoon?

Pha. Substantives and adjectives, is it not, Hedon?

Phi. Ay, that. Who begins?

Pha. I have thought; speak your adjectives, sirs.

Phi. But do not you change then.

Pha. Not I. Who says?

Mor. Odoriferous.

Phi. Popular.

Arg. Humble.

Ana. White-liver'd.

Hed. Barbarous.

Amo. Pythagorical.

Hed. Yours, signior.

Aso. What must I do, sir?

Amo. Give forth your adjective with the rest; as prosperous, good, fair, sweet, well—

Hed. Any thing that hath not been spoken.

Aso. Yes, sir, well spoken shall be mine.

Pha. What, have you all done?

All. Ay.

Pha. Then the substantive is Breeches. Why *odoriferous* breeches, guardian?

Mor. Odoriferous,—because odoriferous: that which contains most variety of savour and smell we say is most odoriferous; now breeches, I presume, are incident to that variety, and therefore odoriferous breeches.

Pha. Well, we must take it howsoever. Who's next? Philautia?

Phi. Popular.

Pha. Why *popular* breeches?

Pha. Marry, that is, when they are not content to be generally noted in court, but will press forth on common stages and brokers' stalls, to the public view of the world.

Pha. Good. Why *humble* breeches, Argurion?

Arg. Humble! because they use to be sat upon; besides, if you tie them not up, their property is to fall down about your heels.

Mer. She has worn the breeches, it seems, which have done so.

Pha. But why *white-liver'd?*

Ana. Why! are not their linings white? Besides, when they come in swaggering company, and will pocket up any thing, may they not properly be said to be white-liver'd?

Pha. O yes, we must not deny it. And why *barbarous*, Hedon?

Hed. Barbarous! because commonly, when you have worn your breeches sufficiently, you give them to your barber.

Amo. That's good; but how *Pythagorical?*

Phi. Ay, Amorphus, why Pythagorical breeches?

Amo. O most kindly of all; 'tis a conceit of that fortune, I am bold to hug my brain for.

Pha. How is it, exquisite Amorphus?

Amo. O, I am rapt with it, 'tis so fit, so proper, so happy—

Phi. Nay, do not rack us thus.

Amo. I never truly relish'd myself before. Give me your ears.

Breeches Pythagorical, by reason of their transmigration into several shapes.

Mor. Most rare, in sweet troth. Marry this young gentleman, for his well-spoken—

Pha. Ay, why *well-spoken* breeches?

Aso. Well-spoken! Marry, well - spoken, because — whatsoever they speak is well-taken; and whatsoever is well-taken is well-spoken.

Mor. Excellent! believe me.

Aso. Not so, ladies, neither.

Hed. But why breeches, now?

Pha. Breeches, *quasi* bear-riches; when a gallant bears all his riches in his breeches.

Amo. Most fortunately etymologised.

Pha. 'Nay, we have another sport afore this, of A thing done, and who did it, etc.

Phi. Ay, good Phantaste, let's have that: distribute the places.

Pha. Why, I imagine, A thing done; Hedon thinks, who did it; Moria, with what it was done; Anaides, where it was done; Argurion, when it was done; Amorphus, for what cause was it done; you, Philautia, what followed upon the doing of it; and this gentleman, who would have done it better. What? is it conceived about?

All. Yes, yes.

Pha. Then speak you, sir, *Who would have done it better?*

Aso. How! does it begin at me?

Pha. Yes, sir: this play is called the Crab, it goes backward.

Aso. May I not name myself?

Phi. If you please, sir, and dare abide the venture of it.

Aso. Then I would have done it better, whatever it is.

Pha. No doubt on't, sir: a good confidence. *What followed upon the act,* Philautia?

Phi. A few heat drops, and a month's mirth.

Pha. *For what cause,* Amorphus?

Amo. For the delight of ladies.

Pha. *When,* Argurion?

Arg. Last progress.

Pha. *Where,* Anaides?

Ana. Why, in a pair of pain'd slops.

Pha. *With what,* Moria?

Mor. With a glyster.

Pha. *Who,* Hedon?

Hed. A traveller.

Pha. Then the thing done was, *An oration was made.* Rehearse. An oration was made—

Hed. By a traveller—

Mor. With a glyster—

Ana. In a pair of pain'd slops—

Arg. Last progress—

Amo. For the delight of ladies—

Phi. A few heat drops, and a month's mirth followed.

Pha. And, this silent gentleman would have done it better.

Aso. This was not so good, now.

Phi. In good faith, these unhappy pages would be whipp'd for staying thus.

Mor. Beshrew my hand and my heart else.

Amo. I do wonder at their protraction.

Ana. Pray Venus my whore have not discover'd herself to the rascally boys, and that be the cause of their stay.

Aso. I must suit myself with another page: this idle Prosaites will never be brought to wait well.

Mor. Sir, I have a kinsman I could willingly wish to your service, if you will deign to accept of him.

Aso. And I shall be glad, most sweet lady, to embrace him: Where is he?

Mor. I can fetch him, sir, but I would be loth to make you to turn away your other page.

Aso. You shall not, most sufficient lady; I will keep both: pray you let's go see him.

Arg. Whither goes my love?

Aso. I'll return presently, I go but to see a page with this lady.

[*Exeunt Asotus and Moria.*

Ana. As sure as fate, 'tis so: she has opened all: a pox of all cockatrices! D—n me, if she have play'd loose with me, I'll cut her throat, within a hair's breadth, so it may be heal'd again.

Mer. What, is he jealous of his hermaphrodite?

Cup. O, ay, this will be excellent sport.

Phi. Phantaste, Argurion! what, you are suddenly struck, methinks! For love's sake let's have some music till they come: Ambition, reach the lyra, I pray you.

Hed. Anything to which my Honour shall direct me.

Phi. Come, Amorphus, cheer up Phantaste.

Amo. It shall be my pride, fair lady, to attempt all that is in my power. But here is an instrument that alone is able to infuse soul into the most melancholic and dull-disposed creature upon earth. O, let me kiss thy fair knees. Beauteous ears, attend it.

Hed. Will you have " *the Kiss,* " Honour?

Phi. Ay, good Ambition.

HEDON *sings.*

O, that joy so soon should waste !
Or so sweet a bliss
As a kiss
Might not for ever last !
So sugar'd, so melting, so soft, so delicious,
The dew that lies on roses,
When the morn herself discloses,
Is not so precious.

O rather than I would it smother,
Were I to taste such another ;
It should be my wishing
That I might die with kissing.

Hed. I made this ditty, and the note to it, upon a kiss that my Honour gave me; how like you it, sir?

Amo. A pretty air; in general, I like it well: but in particular, your long die-note did arride me most, but it was somewhat too long. I can show one almost of the same nature, but much before it, and not so long, in a composition of mine own. I think I have both the note and ditty about me.

Hed. Pray you, sir, see.

Amo. Yes, there is the note; and all the parts, if I misthink not. I will read the ditty to your beauties here; but first I am to make you familiar with the occasion, which presents itself thus. Upon a time, going to take my leave of the emperor, and kiss his great hands, there being then present the kings of France and Arragon, the dukes of Savoy, Florence, Orleans, Bourbon, Brunswick, the Landgrave, count Palatine; all which had severally feasted me; besides infinite more of inferior persons, as counts and others; it was my chance (the emperor detained by some exorbitant affair) to wait him the fifth part of an hour, or much near it. In which time, retiring myself into a bay-window, the beauteous lady Annabel, niece to the empress, and sister to the king of Arragon, who having never before eyed me, but only heard the common report of my virtue, learning, and travel, fell into that extremity of passion for my love, that she there immediately swooned: physicians were sent for, she had to her chamber, so to her bed; where, languishing some few days, after many times calling upon me, with my name in her lips, she expired. As that (I must mourningly say) is the only fault of my fortune, that, as it hath ever been my hap to be sued to, by all ladies and beauties, where I have come; so I never yet sojourn'd or rested in that place or part of the world, where some high-born, admirable, fair feature died not for my love.

Mer. O, the sweet power of travel!—Are you guilty of this, Cupid?

Cup. No, Mercury, and that his page Cos knows, if he were here present to be sworn.

Phi. But how doth this draw on the ditty, sir?

Mer. O, she is too quick with him; he hath not devised that yet.

Amo. Marry, some hour before she departed, she bequeath'd to me this glove: which golden legacy, the emperor himself took care to send after me, in six coaches, cover'd all with black velvet, attended by the state of his empire; all which he freely presented me with: and I reciprocally (out of the same bounty) gave to the lords that brought it: only reserving the gift of the deceased lady, upon which I composed this ode, and set it to my most affected instrument, the lyra.

> *Thou more than most sweet glove,*
> *Unto my more sweet love,*
> *Suffer me to store with kisses*
> *This empty lodging, that now misses*
> *The pure rosy hand, that wear thee,*
> *Whiter than the kid that bare thee.*
> *Thou art soft, but that was softer ;*
> *Cupid's self hath kiss'd it ofter*
> *Than e'er he did his mother's doves.*
> *Supposing her the queen of loves,*
> *That was thy mistress,* BEST OF GLOVES.

Mer. Blasphemy, blasphemy, Cupid!

Cup. I'll revenge it time enough, Hermes.

Phi. Good Amorphus, let's hear it sung.

Amo. I care not to admit that, since it pleaseth Philautia to request it.

Hed. Here, sir.

Amo. Nay, play it, I pray you; you do well, you do well.—[*He sings it.*]—How like you it, sir?

Hed. Very well, in troth.

Amo. But very well! O, you are a mere mammothrept in judgment, then. Why, do you not observe how excellently the ditty is affected in every place? that I do not marry a word of short quantity to a long note? nor an ascending syllable to a descending tone? Besides, upon the word *best* there, you see how I do enter with an odd minum, and drive it through the brief; which no intelligent musician, I know, but will affirm to be very rare, extraordinary, and pleasing.

Mer. And yet not fit to lament the death of a lady, for all this.

Cup. Tut, here be they will swallow anything.

Pha. Pray you, let me have a copy of it, Amorphus.

Phi. And me too; in troth, I like it exceedingly.

Amo. I have denied it to princes; nevertheless, to you, the true female twins of perfection, I am won to depart withal.

Hed. I hope, I shall have my Honour's copy.

Pha. You are Ambitious in that, Hedon.

Re-enter ANAIDES.

Amo. How now, Anaides! what is it hath conjured up this distemperature in the circle of your face?

Ana. Why, what have you to do? A pox upon your filthy travelling face! hold your tongue.

Hed. Nay, dost hear, Mischief?

Ana. Away, musk-cat!

Amo. I say to thee thou art rude, debauch'd, impudent, coarse, unpolish'd, a frapler, and base.

Hed. Heart of my father, what a strange alteration has half a year's haunting of ordinaries wrought in this fellow! that came with a tufftaffata jerkin to town but the other day, and a pair of penny-less hose, and now he is turn'd Hercules, he wants but a club.

Ana. Sir, you with the pencil on your chin; I will garter my hose with your guts, and that shall be all. [*Exit.*

Mer. 'Slid, what rare fireworks be here? flash, flash.

Pha. What's the matter, Hedon? can you tell?

Hed. Nothing, but that he lacks crowns, and thinks we'll lend him some to be friends.

Re-enter ASOTUS *and* MORIA, *with* MORUS.

Aso. Come, sweet lady, in good truth I'll have it, you shall not deny me. Morus, persuade your aunt I may have her picture, by any means.

Morus. Yea, Sir: good aunt now, let him have it, he will use me the better; if you love me do, good aunt.

Mor. Well, tell him he shall have it.

Morus. Master, you shall have it, she says.

Aso. Shall I? thank her, good page.

Cup. What, has he entertain'd the fool?

Mer. Ay, he'll wait close, you shall see, though the beggar hang off a while.

Morus. Aunt, my master thanks you.

Mor. Call him hither.

Morus. Yes; master.

Mor. Yes, in verity, and gave me this purse, and he has promised me a most fine dog; which he will have drawn with my picture, he says: and desires most vehemently to be known to your ladyships.

Pha. Call him hither, 'tis good groping such a gull.

Morus. Master Asotus, master Asotus!

Aso. For love's sake, let me go: you see I am call'd to the ladies.

Arg. Wilt thou forsake me, then?

Aso. Od so! what would you have me do?

Mor. Come hither, master Asotus.—I do ensure your ladyships, he is a gentleman of a very worthy desert: and of a most bountiful nature.—You must shew and insinuate yourself responsible, and equivalent now to my commendment.—Good honours grace him.

Aso. I protest, more than most fair ladies, *I do wish all variety of divine pleasures, choice sports, sweet music, rich fare, brave attire, soft beds, and silken thoughts, attend these fair beauties.* Will it please your ladyship to wear this chain of pearl, and this diamond, for my sake?

Arg. O!

Aso. And you, madam, this jewel and pendants?

Arg. O!

Pha. We know not how to deserve these bounties, out of so slight

Pha. And soon after the revels, I will bestow a garter on you.
merit, Asotus.

Phi. No, in faith, but there's my glove for a favour.

Aso. O lord, ladies! it is more grace than ever I could have hoped, but that it pleaseth your ladyships to extend. I protest it is enough, that you but take knowledge of my——if your ladyships want embroider'd gowns, tires of any fashion, rebatues, jewels, or carcanets, any thing whatsoever, if you vouchsafe to accept—

Cup. And for it they will help you to shoe-ties, and devices.

Aso. I cannot utter myself, dear beauties, but you can conceive—

Arg. O!

Pha. Sir, we will acknowledge your service, doubt not—henceforth, you shall be no more Asotus to us, but our goldfinch, and we your cages.

Aso. O Venus! madams! how shall I deserve this? if I were but made acquainted with Hedon, now,—I'll try: pray you, away.

[*To Argurion.*

Mer. How he prays money to go away from him.

Aso. Amorphus, a word with you; here's a watch I would bestow upon you, pray you make me known to that gallant.

Amo. That I will, sir.—Monsieur Hedon, I must entreat you to exchange knowledge with this gentleman.

Hed. 'Tis a thing, next to the water, we expect, I thirst after, sir. Good monsieur Asotus.

Aso. Good monsieur Hedon, I would be glad to be loved of men of your rank and spirit, I protest. Please you to accept this pair of bracelets, sir; they are not worth the bestowing—

Mer. O Hercules, how the gentleman purchases, this must needs bring Argurion to a consumption.

Hed. Sir, I shall never stand in the merit of such bounty, I fear.

Aso. O Venus, sir; your acquaintance shall be sufficient. And, if at any time you need my bill, or my bond—

Arg. O! O! [*Swoons.*

Amo. Help the lady there!

Mor. Gods-dear, Argurion! madam, how do you?

Arg. Sick.

Pha. Have her forth, and give her air.

Aso. I come again straight, ladies.

[*Exeunt Asotus, Morus, and Argurion.*

Mer. Well, I doubt all the physic he has will scarce recover her; she's too far spent.

Re-enter ANAIDES *with* GELAIA, PROSAITES, *and* COS, *with the bottles.*

Phi. O here's the water come; fetch glasses, page.

Gel. Heart of my body, here's a coil, indeed, with your jealous humours! nothing but whore and bitch, and all the villainous swaggering names you can think on! 'Slid, take your bottle, and put it in your guts for me, I'll see you pox'd ere I follow you any longer.

Ana. Nay, good punk, sweet rascal; d——n me, if I am jealous now.

Gel. That's true, indeed; pray let's go.

Mor. What's the matter there?

Gel. 'Slight, he has me upon interrogatories, (nay, my mother shall know how you use me,) where I have been? and why I should stay so long, and, how is't possible? and withal calls me at his pleasure I know not how many cockatrices, and things.

Mor. In truth and sadness, these are no good epitaphs, Anaides, to bestow upon any gentlewoman; and I'll ensure you if I had known you would have dealt thus with my daughter, she should never have fancied you so deeply as she has done. Go to.

Ana. Why, do you hear, mother Moria? heart!

Mor. Nay, I pray you, sir, do not swear.

Ana. Swear! why? 'sblood, I have sworn afore now, I hope. Both you and your daughter mistake me. I have not honour'd Arete, that is held the worthiest lady in court, next to Cynthia, with half that observance and respect, as I have done her in private, howsoever outwardly I have carried myself careless, and negligent. Come, you are a foolish punk, and know not when you are well employed. Kiss me, come on; do it, I say.

Mor. Nay, indeed, I must confess, she is apt to misprision. But I must have you leave it, minion.

Re-enter ASOTUS.

Amo. How now, Asotus! how does the lady?

Aso. Faith, ill. I have left my page with her, at her lodging.

Hed. O, here's the rarest water that ever was tasted: fill him some.

Pro. What! has my master a new page?

Mer. Yes, a kinsman of the lady Moria's: you must wait better now, or you are cashiered, Prosaites.

Ana. Come, gallants, you must pardon my foolish humour; when I am angry, that any thing crosses me, I grow impatient straight. Here, I drink to you.

Phi. O, that we had five or six bottles more of this liquor!

Pha. Now I commend your judgment, Amorphus:—[*knocking within.*] Who's that knocks? look, page. [*Exit Cos.*

Mor. O, most delicious; a little of this would make Argurion well.

Pha. O, no, give her no cold drink, by any means.

Ana. 'Sblood, this water is the spirit of wine, I'll be hang'd else.

Re-enter COS *with* ARETE.

Cos. Here's the lady Arete, madam.

Are. What, at your bever, gallants?

Mor. Will't please your ladyship to drink? 'tis of the New Fountain water.

Are. Not I, Moria, I thank you.—Gallants, you are for this night free to your peculiar delights; Cynthia will have no sports: when she is pleased to come forth, you shall have knowledge. In the mean time, I could wish you did provide for solemn revels, and some unlooked for device of wit, to entertain her, against she should vouchsafe to grace your pastimes with her presence.

Amo. What say you to a masque?

Hed. Nothing better, if the project were new and rare.

Are. Why, I'll send for Crites, and have his advice: be you ready in your endeavours: he shall discharge you of the inventive part.

Pha. But will not your ladyship stay?

Are. Not now, Phantaste.   [*Exit.*

Phi. Let her go, I pray you, good lady Sobriety, I am glad we are rid of her.

Pha. What a set face the gentlewoman has, as she were still going to a sacrifice!

Phi. O, she is the extraction of a dozen of Puritans, for a look.

Mor. Of all nymphs i' the court, I cannot away with her; 'tis the coarsest thing!

Phi. I wonder how Cynthia can affect her so above the rest. Here be they are every way as fair as she, and a thought fairer, I trow.

Pha. Ay, and as ingenious and conceited as she.

Mor. Ay, and as politic as she, for all she sets such a forehead on't.

Phi. Would I were dead, if I would change to be Cynthia.

Pha. Or I.

Mor. Or I.

Amo. And there's her minion, Crites: why his advice more than Amorphus? Have not I invention afore him? learning to better that invention above him? and infanted with pleasant travel—

Ana. Death, what talk you of his learning? he understands no more than a schoolboy; I have put him down myself a thousand times, by this air, and yet I never talk'd with him but twice in my life: you never saw his like. I could never get him to argue with me but once; and then because I could not construe an author I quoted at first sight, he went away, and laughed at me. By Hercules, I scorn him, as I do the sodden nymph that was here even now, his mistress, Arete: and I love myself for nothing else.

Hed. I wonder the fellow does not hang himself, being thus scorn'd and contemn'd of us that are held the most accomplish'd society of gallants.

Mer. By yourselves, none else.

Hed. I protest, if I had no music in me, no courtship, that I were not a reveller and could dance, or had not those excellent qualities that give a man life and perfection, but a mere poor scholar as he is, I think I should make some desperate way with myself; whereas now,—would I might never breathe more, if I do know that creature in this kingdom with whom I would change.

Cup. This is excellent! Well, I must alter all this soon.

Mer. Look you do, Cupid. The bottles have wrought, it seems.

Aso. O, I am sorry the revels are crost. I should have tickled it soon. I did never appear till then. 'Slid, I am the neatliest-made gallant i' the company, and have the best presence; and my dancing——well, I know what our usher said to me last time I was at the school: Would I might have led Philautia in the measures, an it had been the gods' will! I am most worthy, I am sure.

Re-enter MORUS.

Morus. Master, I can tell you news; the lady kissed me yonder, and played with me, and says she loved you once as well as she does me, but that you cast her off.

Aso. Peace, my most esteemed page.

Morus. Yes.

Aso. What luck is this, that our revels are dash'd, now was I beginning to glister in the very highway of preferment. An Cynthia had but seen me dance a strain, or do but one trick, I had been kept in court, I should never have needed to look towards my friends again.

Amo. Contain yourself, you were a fortunate young man, if you knew your own good; which I have now projected, and will presently multiply upon you. Beauties and valours, your vouchsafed applause to a motion. The humorous Cynthia hath, for this night, withdrawn the light of your delight.

Pha. 'Tis true, Amorphus; what may we do to redeem it?

Amo. Redeem that we cannot, but to create a new flame is in our power. Here is a gentleman, my scholar, whom, for some private reasons me specially moving, I am covetous to gratify with title of master in the noble and subtile science of courtship: for which grace, he shall this night, in court, and in the long gallery, hold his public act, by open challenge, to all masters of the mystery whatsoever, to play at the four choice and principal weapons thereof, viz., *the Bare Accost, the Better Regard, the Solemn Address,* and *the Perfect Close.* What say you?

All. Excellent, excellent, Amorphus.

Amo. Well, let us then take our time by the forehead: I will instantly have bills drawn, and advanced in every angle of the court.—Sir, betray not your too much joy.—Anaides, we must mix this gentleman with you in acquaintance, monsieur Asotus.

Ana. I am easily entreated to grace any of your friends, Amorphus.

Aso. Sir, and his friends shall likewise grace you, sir. Nay, I begin to know myself now.

Amo. O, you must continue your bounties.

Aso. Must I? Why, I'll give him this ruby on my finger. Do you hear, sir? I do heartily wish your acquaintance, and I partly know myself worthy of it; please you, sir, to accept this poor ruby in a ring, sir. The poesy is of my own device, *Let this blush for me,* sir.

Ana. So it must for me too, for I am not asham'd to take it.

Morus. Sweet man! By my troth, master, I love you; will you love me too, for my aunt's sake? I'll wait well, you shall see. I'll still be here. Would I might never stir, but you are a fine man in these clothes; master, shall I have them when you have done with them?

Aso. As for that, Morus, thou shalt see more hereafter; in the mean time, by this air, or by this feather, I'll do as much for thee, as any gallant shall do for his page, whatsoever, in this court, corner of the world, or kingdom. [*Exeunt all but the Pages.*

Mer. I wonder this gentleman should affect to keep a fool: methinks he makes sport enough with himself.

Cup. Well, Prosaites, 'twere good you did wait closer.

Pro. Ay, I'll look to it; 'tis time.

Cos. The revels would have been most sumptuous to-night, if they had gone forward. [*Exit.*

Mer. They must needs, when all the choicest singularities of the court were up in pantofles; ne'er a one of them but was able to make a whole show of itself.

Aso. [*within.*] Sirrah, a torch, a torch!

Pro. O, what a call is there! I will have a canzonet made, with nothing in it but sirrah; and the burthen shall be, I come. [*Exit.*

Mer. How now, Cupid, how do you like this change?

Cup. Faith, the thread of my device is crack'd, I may go sleep till the revelling music awake me.

Mer. And then, too, Cupid, without you had prevented the fountain. Alas, poor god, that remembers not self-love to be proof against the violence of his quiver! Well, I have a plot against these prizers, for which I must presently find out Crites, and with his assistance pursue it to a high strain of laughter, or Mercury hath lost of his metal. [*Exeunt.*

ACT V

SCENE I.—*The same.*

Enter MERCURY *and* CRITES.

Mer. It is resolved on, Crites, you must do it.

Cri. The grace divinest Mercury hath done me,
In this vouchsafed discovery of himself,
Binds my observance in the utmost term
Of satisfaction to his godly will:
Though I profess, without the affectation
Of an enforced and form'd austerity,
I could be willing to enjoy no place
With so unequal natures.

Mer. We believe it.
But for our sake, and to inflict just pains
On their prodigious follies, aid us now:
No man is presently made bad with ill.
And good men, like the sea, should still maintain

Their noble taste, in midst of all fresh humours
That flow about them, to corrupt their streams,
Bearing no season, much less salt of goodness.
It is our purpose, Crites, to correct,
And punish, with our laughter, this night's sport,
Which our court-dors so heartily intend:
And by that worthy scorn, to make them know
How far beneath the dignity of man
Their serious and most practised actions are.

Cri. Ay, but though Mercury can warrant out
His undertakings, and make all things good,
Out of the powers of his divinity,
Th' offence will be return'd with weight on me,
That am a creature so despised and poor;
When the whole court shall take itself abused
By our ironical confederacy.

Mer. You are deceived. The better race in court,
That have the true nobility call'd virtue,
Will apprehend it, as a grateful right
Done to their separate merit; and approve
The fit rebuke of so ridiculous heads,
Who, with their apish customs and forced garbs,
Would bring the name of courtier in contempt,
Did it not live unblemish'd in some few,
Whom equal Jove hath loved, and Phœbus form'd
Of better metal, and in better mould.

Cri. Well, since my leader-on is Mercury,
I shall not fear to follow. If I fall,
My proper virtue shall be my relief,
That follow'd such a cause, and such a chief.   [*Exeunt.*

SCENE II.—*Another Room in the same.*

Enter ASOTUS *and* AMORPHUS.

Aso. No more, if you love me, good master; you are incompatible to live withal: send me for the ladies!

Amo. Nay, but intend me.

Aso. Fear me not; I warrant you, sir.

Amo. Render not yourself a refractory on the sudden. I can allow, well, you should repute highly, heartily, and to the most, of your own endowments; it gives you forth to the world the more assured: but with reservation of an eye, to be always turn'd dutifully back upon your teacher.

Aso. Nay, good sir, leave it to me. Trust me with trussing all the points of this action, I pray. 'Slid, I hope we shall find wit to perform the science as well as another.

Amo. I confess you to be of an apted and docible humour. Yet there are certain punctilios, or (as I may more nakedly insinuate them) certain intrinsecate strokes and wards, to which your activity is not yet amounted, as your gentle dor in colours. For supposition, your mistress appears here in prize, ribanded with green and yellow; now, it is the part of every obsequious servant, to be sure to have daily about him copy and variety of colours, to be presently answerable to any hourly or half-hourly change in his mistress's revolution—

Aso. I know it, sir.

Amo. Give leave, I pray you—which, if your antagonist, or player against you, shall ignorantly be without, and yourself can produce, you give him the dor.

Aso. Ay, ay, sir.

Amo. Or, if you can possess your opposite, that the green your mistress wears, is her rejoicing or exultation in his service; the yellow, suspicion of his truth, from her height of affection: and that he, greenly credulous, shall withdraw thus, in private, and from the abundance of his pocket (to displace her jealous conceit) steal into his hat the colour, whose blueness doth express trueness, she being not so, nor so affected; you give him the dor.

Aso. Do not I know it, sir?

Amo. Nay, good——swell not above your understanding. There is yet a third dor in colours.

Aso. I know it too, I know it.

Amo. Do you know it too? what is it? make good your knowledge.

Aso. Why it is——no matter for that.

Amo. Do it, on pain of the dor.

Aso. Why; what is't, say you?

Amo. Lo, you have given yourself the dor. But I will remonstrate to you the third dor, which is not, as the two former dors, indicative, but deliberative: as how? as thus. Your rival is, with a dutiful and serious care, lying in his bed, meditating how to observe his mistress, dispatcheth his lacquey to the chamber early, to know what her colours are for the day, with purpose to apply his wear that day accordingly: you lay wait before, preoccupy the chambermaid, corrupt her to return false colours; he follows the fallacy, comes out accoutred to his believed instructions; your mistress smiles, and you give him the dor.

Aso. Why, so I told you, sir, I knew it.

Amo. Told me! It is a strange outrecuidance, your humour too much redoundeth.

Aso. Why, sir, what, do you think you know more?

Amo. I know that a cook may as soon and properly be said to smell well, as you to be wise. I know these are most clear and clean strokes. But then, you have your passages and imbrocatas in courtship; as the bitter bob in wit; the reverse in face or wrymouth; and these more subtile and secure offenders. I will example unto you: Your opponent makes entry as you are engaged with your mistress. You seeing him, close in her ear with this whisper, *Here comes your baboon, disgrace him;* and withal stepping off, fall on his bosom, and turning to her, politicly, aloud say, Lady, regard this noble gentleman, a man rarely parted, second to none in this court; and then, stooping over his shoulder, your hand on his breast, your mouth on his backside, you give him the reverse stroke, with this sanna, or stork's-bill, which makes up your wit's bob most bitter.

Aso. Nay, for heaven's sake, teach me no more. I know all as well——'Slid, if I did not, why was I nominated? why did you choose me? why did the ladies prick out me? I am sure there were other gallants. But me of all the rest! By that light, and, as I am a courtier, would I might never stir, but 'tis strange. Would to the lord the ladies would come once!

Enter MORPHIDES.

Morp. Signior, the gallants and ladies are at hand. Are you ready, sir?

Amo. Instantly. Go, accomplish your attire: [*Exit Asotus.*] Cousin Morphides, assist me to make good the door with your officious tyranny.

Citizen. [*within.*] By your leave, my masters there, pray you let's come by.

Pages. [*within.*] You by! why should you come by more than we?

Citizen's Wife. [*within.*] Why, sir! because he is my brother that plays the prizes.

Morp. Your brother!

Citizen. [*within.*] Ay, her brother, sir, and we must come in.

Tailor. [*within.*] Why, what are you?

Citizen. [*within.*] I am her husband, sir.

Tailor. [*within.*] Then thrust forward your head.

Amo. What tumult is there?

Morp. Who's there? bear back there! Stand from the door!

Amo. Enter none but the ladies and their hang-byes.——

Enter PHANTASTE, PHILAUTIA, ARGURION, MORIA, HEDON, *and* ANAIDES, *introducing two* Ladies.

Welcome beauties, and your kind shadows.

Hed. This country lady, my friend, good signior Amorphus.

Ana. And my cockatrice here.

Amo. She is welcome.

The Citizen, *and his* Wife, Pages, *etc., appear at the door.*

Morp. Knock those same pages there; and, goodman coxcomb the citizen, who would you speak withal?

Wife. My brother.

Amo. With whom? your brother!

Morp. Who is your brother?

Wife. Master Asotus.

Amo. Master Asotus! is he your brother? he is taken up with great persons; he is not to know you to-night.

Re-enter ASOTUS *hastily.*

Aso. O Jove, master! an there come e'er a citizen gentlewoman in my name, let her have entrance, I pray you: it is my sister.

Wife. Brother!

Cit. [*thrusting in.*] Brother, master Asotus!

Aso. Who's there?

Wife. 'Tis I, brother.

Aso. Gods me, there she is! good master, intrude her.

Morp. Make place! bear back there!

Enter Citizen's Wife.

Amo. Knock that simple fellow there.

Wife. Nay, good sir, it is my husband.

Morp. The simpler fellow he.—Away! back with your head, sir!
[*Pushes the Citizen back.*

Aso. Brother, you must pardon your non-entry: husbands are not allow'd here, in truth. I'll come home soon with my sister; pray you meet us with a lantern, brother. Be merry, sister; I shall make you laugh anon. [*Exit.*

Pha. Your prizer is not ready, Amorphus.

Amo. Apprehend your places; he shall be soon, and at all points.

Ana. Is there any body come to answer him? shall we have any sport?

Amo. Sport of importance; howsoever, give me the gloves.

Hed. Gloves! why gloves, signior?

Phi. What's the ceremony?

Amo. [*distributing gloves.*] Beside their received fitness, at all prizes, they are here properly accommodate to the nuptials of my scholar's 'haviour to the lady Courtship. Please you apparel your hands. Madam Phantaste, madam Philautia, guardian, signior Hedon, signior Anaides, gentlemen all, ladies.

All. Thanks, good Amorphus.

Amo. I will now call forth my provost, and present him. [*Exit.*

Ana. Heart! why should not we be masters as well as he?

Hed. That's true, and play our masters' prizes as well as the t'other?

Mor. In sadness, for using your court-weapons, methinks you may.

Pha. Nay, but why should not we ladies play our prizes, I pray? I see no reason but we should take them down at their own weapons.

Phi. Troth, and so we may, if we handle them well.

Wife. Ay, indeed, forsooth, madam, if 'twere in the city, we would think foul scorn but we would, forsooth.

Pha. Pray you, what should we call your name?

Wife. My name is Downfall.

Hed. Good mistress Downfall! I am sorry your husband could not get in.

Wife. 'Tis no matter for him, sir.

Ana. No, no, she has the more liberty for herself.   [*A flourish.*
Pha. Peace, peace! they come.

Re-enter AMORPHUS, *introducing* ASOTUS *in a full-dress suit.*

Amo. So, keep up your ruff; the tincture of your neck is not all so pure, but it will ask it.   Maintain your sprig upright; your cloke on your half-shoulder falling; so: I will read your bill, advance it, and present you.—Silence!

Be it known to all that profess courtship, by these presents (from the white satin reveller, to the cloth of tissue and bodkin) that we, Ulysses-Polytropus-Amorphus, master of the noble and subtile science of courtship, do give leave and licence to our provost, Acolastus-Polypragmon-Asotus, to play his master's prize, against all masters whatsoever, in this subtile mystery, at these four, the choice and most cunning weapons of court-compliment, viz. the BARE ACCOST; the BETTER REGARD; the SOLEMN ADDRESS; and the PERFECT CLOSE. These are therefore to give notice to all comers, that he, the said Acolastus-Polypragmon-Asotus, is here present (by the help of his mercer, tailor, milliner, sempster, and so forth) at his designed hour, in this fair gallery, the present day of this present month, to perform and do his uttermost for the achievement and bearing away of the prizes, which are these : viz. For the Bare Accost, two wall-eyes in a face forced : for the Better Regard, a face favourably simpering, with a fan waving : for the Solemn Address, two lips wagging, and never a wise word : for the Perfect Close, a wring by the hand, with a banquet in a corner. And Phœbus save Cynthia !

Appeareth no man yet, to answer the prizer? no voice?—Music, give them their summons.   [*Music.*
Pha. The solemnity of this is excellent.
Amo. Silence!   Well, I perceive your name is their terror, and keepeth them back.
Aso. I'faith, master, let's go;   no body comes.   *Victus, victa, victum ; victi, victæ, victi*——let's be retrograde.
Amo. Stay.   That were dispunct to the ladies.   Rather ourself shall be your encounter.   Take your state up to the wall; and, lady, [*leading Moria to the state.*] may we implore you to stand forth, as first term or bound to our courtship.
Hed. 'Fore heaven, 'twill shew rarely.
Amo. Sound a charge.   [*A charge.*
Ana. A pox on't!   Your vulgar will count this fabulous and impudent now: by that candle, they'll never conceit it.
  [*They act their Accost severally to Moria.*
Pha. Excellent well! admirable!
Phi. Peace!
Hed. Most fashionably, believe it.
Phi. O, he is a well-spoken gentleman.
Pha. Now the other.
Phi. Very good.

Hed. For a scholar, Honour.

Ana. O, 'tis too Dutch. He reels too much.   [*A flourish.*

Hed. This weapon is done.

Amo. No, we have our two bouts at every weapon; expect.

Cri. [*within.*] Where be these gallants, and their brave prizer here?

Morp. Who's there? bear back; keep the door.

Enter CRITES, *introducing* MERCURY *fantastically dressed.*

Amo. What are you, sir?

Cri. By your license, grand-master.—Come forward, sir.
                                        [*To Mercury.*

Ana. Heart! who let in that rag there amongst us? Put him out, an impecunious creature.

Hed. Out with him.

Morp. Come, sir.

Amo. You must be retrograde.

Cri. Soft, sir, I am truchman, and do flourish before this monsieur, or French-behaved gentleman, here; who is drawn hither by report of your chartels, advanced in court, to prove his fortune with your prizer, so he may have fair play shewn him, and the liberty to choose his stickler.

Amo. Is he a master?

Cri. That, sir, he has to shew here; and confirmed under the hands of the most skilful and cunning complimentaries alive: Please you read, sir.   [*Gives him a certificate.*

Amo. What shall we do?

Ana. Death! disgrace this fellow in the black stuff, whatever you do.

Amo. Why, but he comes with the stranger.

Hed. That's no matter: he is our own countryman.

Ana. Ay, and he is a scholar besides. You may disgrace him here with authority.

Amo. Well, see these first.

Aso. Now shall I be observed by yon scholar, till I sweat again; I would to Jove it were over.

Cri. [*to Mercury.*] Sir, this is the wight of worth, that dares you to the encounter. A gentleman of so pleasing and ridiculous a carriage; as, even standing, carries meat in the mouth, you see; and, I assure you, although no bred courtling, yet a most particular man, of goodly havings, well-fashion'd 'haviour, and of as hardened and excellent a bark as the most naturally qualified amongst them, inform'd, reform'd, and transform'd, from his original citycism; by this elixir, or mere magazine of man. And, for your spectators, you behold them what they are: the most choice particulars in court: this tells tales well; this provides coaches; this repeats jests; this presents gifts; this holds up the arras; this takes down from horse; this protests by this light; this swears by that candle; this delighteth; this adoreth: yet all but three men. Then, for your ladies, the most proud, witty creatures, all things apprehending, nothing understanding, perpetually laughing, curious maintainers of fools, mercers, and minstrels, costly to be kept, miserably keeping, all disdaining but their painter and apothecary, 'twixt whom and them there is this reciprock commerce, their beauties maintain their painters, and their painters their beauties.

Mer. Sir, you have plaid the painter yourself, and limn'd them to the life. I desire to deserve before them.

Amo. [*returning the certificate.*] This is authentic. We must resolve to entertain the monsieur, howsoever we neglect him.

Hed. Come, let's all go together, and salute him.

Ana. Content, and not look on the other.

Amo. Well devised; and a most punishing disgrace.

Hed. On.

Amo. Monsieur, we must not so much betray ourselves to discourtship, as to suffer you to be longer unsaluted: please you to use the state ordain'd for the opponent; in which nature, without envy, we receive you.

Hed. And embrace you.

Ana. And commend us to you, sir.

Phi. Believe it, he is a man of excellent silence.

Pha. He keeps all his wit for action.

Ana. This hath discountenanced our scholaris, most richly.

Hed. Out of all emphasis. The monsieur sees we regard him not.

Amo. Hold on; make it known how bitter a thing it is not to be look'd on in court.

Hed. 'Slud, will he call him to him yet! Does not monsieur perceive our disgrace?

Ana. Heart! he is a fool, I see. We have done ourselves wrong to grace him.

Hed. 'Slight, what an ass was I to embrace him!

Cri. Illustrious and fearful judges—

Hed. Turn away, turn away.

Cri. It is the suit of the strange opponent (to whom you ought not to turn your tails, and whose noses I must follow) that he may have the justice, before he encounter his respected adversary, to see some light stroke of his play, commenced with some other.

Hed. Answer not him, but the stranger; we will not believe him.

Amo. I will demand him, myself.

Cri. O dreadful disgrace, if a man were so foolish to feel it.

Amo. Is it your suit, monsieur, to see some prelude of my scholar? Now, sure the monsieur wants language—

Hed. And take upon him to be one of the accomplished! 'Slight, that's a good jest; would we could take him with that nullity.— *Non sapete voi parlar' Italiano?*

Ana. 'Sfoot, the carp has no tongue.

Cri. Signior, in courtship, you are to bid your abettors forbear, and satisfy the monsieur's request.

Amo. Well, I will strike him more silent with admiration, and terrify his daring hither. He shall behold my own play with my scholar. Lady, with the touch of your white hand, let me reinstate you. [*Leads Moria back to the state.*] Provost, [*to Asotus.*] begin to me at the *Bare Accost.* [*A charge.*] Now, for the honour of my discipline.

Hed. Signior Amorphus, reflect, reflect; what means he by that mouthed wave?

Cri. He is in some distaste of your fellow disciple.

Mer. Signior, your scholar might have played well still, if he could have kept his seat longer; I have enough of him, now. He is a mere piece of glass, I see through him by this time.

Amo. You come not to give us the scorn, monsieur?

Mer. Nor to be frighted with a face, signior. I have seen the lions. You must pardon me. I shall be loth to hazard a reputation with one that has not a reputation to lose.

Amo. How!

Cri. Meaning your pupil, sir.

Ana. This is that black devil there.

Amo. You do offer a strange affront, monsieur.

Cri. Sir, he shall yield you all the honour of a competent adversary, if you please to undertake him.

Mer. I am prest for the encounter.

Amo. Me! challenge me!

Aso. What, my master, sir! 'Slight, monsieur, meddle with me, do you hear: but do not meddle with my master.

Mer. Peace, good squib, go out.

Cri. And stink, he bids you.

Aso. Master!

Amo. Silence! I do accept him. Sit you down and observe. Me! he never profest a thing at more charges.—Prepare yourself, sir.—Challenge me! I will prosecute what disgrace my hatred can dictate to me.

Cri. How tender a traveller's spleen is! Comparison to men that deserve least, is ever most offensive.

Amo. You are instructed in our chartel, and know our weapons?

Mer. I appear not without their notice, sir.

Aso. But must I lose the prizes, master?

Amo. I will win them for you; be patient.—Lady, [*to Moria.*] vouchsafe the tenure of this ensign.—Who shall be your stickler?

Mer. Behold him. [*Points to Crites.*

Amo. I would not wish you a weaker.—Sound, musics.—I provoke you at the Bare Accost. [*A charge.*

Pha. Excellent comely!

Cri. And worthily studied. This is the exalted foretop.

Hed. O, his leg was too much produced.

Ana. And his hat was carried scurvily.

Phi. Peace; let's see the monsieur's Accost: Rare!

Pha. Sprightly and short.

Ana. True, it is the French courteau: he lacks but to have his nose slit.

Hed. He does hop. He does bound too much.   *[A flourish.*

Amo. The second bout, to conclude this weapon.   *[A charge.*

Pha. Good, believe it!

Phi. An excellent offer!

Cri. This is called the solemn band-string.

Hed. Foh, that cringe was not put home.

Ana. He makes a face like a stabb'd Lucrece.

Aso. Well, he would needs take it upon him, but would I had done it for all this. He makes me sit still here, like a baboon as I am.

Cri. Making villainous faces.

Phi. See, the French prepares it richly.

Cri. Ay, this is ycleped the Serious Trifle.

Ana. 'Slud, 'tis the horse-start out o' the brown study.

Cri. Rather the bird-eyed stroke, sir. Your observance is too blunt, sir.   *[A flourish.*

Amo. Judges, award the prize. Take breath, sir. This bout hath been laborious.

Aso. And yet your critic, or your besogno, will think these things foppery, and easy, now!

Cri. Or rather mere lunacy. For would any reasonable creature make these his serious studies and perfections, much less, only live to these ends? to be the false pleasure of a few, the true love of none, and the just laughter of all?

Hed. We must prefer the monsieur, we courtiers must be partial.

Ana. Speak, guardian. Name the prize, at the Bare Accost.

Mor. A pair of wall-eyes in a face forced.

Ana. Give the monsieur. Amorphus hath lost his eyes.

Amo. I! Is the palate of your judgment down? Gentles, I do appeal.

Aso. Yes, master, to me: the judges be fools.

Ana. How now, sir! tie up your tongue, mungrel. He cannot appeal.

Aso. Say, you sir?

Ana. Sit you still, sir.

Aso. Why, so I do; do not I, I pray you?

Mer. Remercie, madame, and these honourable censors.

Amo. Well, to the second weapon, the *Better Regard*. I will encounter you better. Attempt.

Hed. Sweet Honour.

Phi. What says my good Ambition?

Hed. Which take you at this next weapon? I lay a Discretion with you on Amorphus's head.

Phi. Why, I take the French-behaved gentleman.

Hed. 'Tis done, a Discretion.

Cri. A Discretion! A pretty court-wager! Would any discreet person hazard his wit so?

Pha. I'll lay a Discretion with you, Anaides.

Ana. Hang 'em, I'll not venture a doit of Discretion on either of their heads.

Cri. No, he should venture all then.

Ana. I like none of their plays.   [*A charge.*

Hed. See, see! this is strange play!

Ana. 'Tis too full of uncertain motion. He hobbles too much.

Cri. 'Tis call'd your court-staggers, sir.

Hed. That same fellow talks so now he has a place!

Ana. Hang him! neglect him.

Mer. *Your good ladyship's affectioned.*

Wife. Ods so! they speak at this weapon, brother.

Aso. They must do so, sister; how should it be the Better Regard, else?

Pha. Methinks he did not this respectively enough.

Phi. Why, the monsieur but dallies with him.

Hed. Dallies! 'Slight, see! he'll put him to't in earnest.—Well done, Amorphus!

Ana. That puff was good indeed.

Cri. Ods me! this is desperate play: he hits himself o' the shins.

Hed. An he make this good through, he carries it, I warrant him.

Cri. Indeed he displays his feet rarely.

Hed. See, see! he does the respective leer damnably well.

Amo. *The true idolater of your beauties shall never pass their deities unadored : I rest your poor knight.*

Hed. See, now the oblique leer, or the Janus: he satisfies all with that aspect most nobly.   [*A flourish.*

Cri. And most terribly he comes off; like your rodomontado.

Pha. How like you this play, Anaides?

Ana. Good play; but 'tis too rough and boisterous.

Amo. I will second it with a stroke easier, wherein I will prove his language.   [*A charge.*

Ana. This is filthy, and grave, now.

Hed. O, 'tis cool and wary play. We must not disgrace our own camerade too much.

Amo. *Signora, ho tanto obligo per le favore resciuto da lei ; che veramente desidero con tutto il core, à remunerarla in parte : e sicurative, signora mea cara, chè io sera sempre pronto à servirla, e honorarla. Bascio le mane de vo' signoria.*

Cri. The Venetian dop this.

Pha. Most unexpectedly excellent! The French goes down certain.

Aso. *As buckets are put down into a well ;*
Or as a school-boy—

Cri. Truss up your simile, jack-daw, and observe.

Hed. Now the monsieur is moved.

Ana. Bo-peep!

Hed. O, most antick.

Cri. The French quirk, this sir.

Ana. Heart, he will over-run her.

Mer. *Madamoyselle, Je voudroy que pouvoy monstrer mon affection, mais je suis tant malheureuse, ci froid, ci layd, ci—— Je ne scay qui de dire——excuse moi, Je suis tout vostre.*   [*A flourish.*

Phi. O brave and spirited! he's a right Jovialist.

Pha. No, no: Amorphus's gravity outweighs it.

Cri. And yet your lady, or your feather, would outweigh both.

Ana. What's the prize, lady, at this Better Regard?

Mor. A face favourably simpering, and a fan waving.

Ana. They have done doubtfully. Divide. Give the favourable face to the signior, and the light wave to the monsieur.

Amo. You become the simper well, lady.

Mer. And the wag better.

Amo. Now, to our *Solemn Address.* Please the well-graced Philautia to relieve the lady sentinel; she hath stood long.

Phi. With all my heart; come, guardian, resign your place.
[*Moria comes from the state.*

Amo. Monsieur, furnish yourself with what solemnity of ornament you think fit for this third weapon; at which you are to shew all the cunning of stroke your devotion can possibly devise.

Mer. Let me alone, sir. I'll sufficiently decipher your amorous solemnities.—Crites, have patience. See, if I hit not all their practic observance, with which they lime twigs to catch their fantastic lady-birds.

Cri. Ay, but you should do more charitably to do it more openly, that they might discover themselves mock'd in these monstrous affections.   [*A charge.*

Mer. Lackey, where's the tailor?

Enter Tailor, Barber, Perfumer, Milliner, Jeweller, *and* Feather-maker.

Tai. Here, sir.

Hed. See, they have their tailor, barber, perfumer, milliner, jeweller, feather-maker, all in common!
[*They make themselves ready on the stage.*

Ana. Ay, this is pretty.

Amo. Here is a hair too much, take it off. Where are thy mullets?

Mer. Is this pink of equal proportion to this cut, standing off this distance from it?

Tai. That it is, sir.

Mer. Is it so, sir? You impudent poltroon, you slave, you list, you shreds, you——   [*Beats the Tailor.*

Hed. Excellent! This was the best yet.

Ana. Why, we must use our tailors thus: this is our true magnanimity.

Mer. Come, go to, put on; we must bear with you for the times' sake.

Amo. Is the perfume rich in this jerkin?

Per. Taste, smell; I assure you, sir, pure benjamin, the only spirited scent that ever awaked a Neapolitan nostril. You would wish yourself all nose for the love on't. I frotted a jerkin for a new-revenued gentleman yielded me three-score crowns but this morning, and the same titillation.

Amo. I savour no sampsuchine in it.

Per. I am a Nulli-fidian, if there be not three-thirds of a scruple more of sampsuchinum in this confection, than ever I put in any. I'll tell you all the ingredients, sir.

Amo. You shall be simple to discover your simples.

Per. Simple! why, sir? What reck I to whom I discover? I have in it musk, civet, amber, Phœnicobalanus, the decoction of turmerick, sesana, nard, spikenard, calamus odoratus, stacte, opobalsamum, amomum, storax, ladanum, aspalathum, opoponax, œnanthe. And what of all these now? what are you the better? Tut, it is the sorting, and the dividing, and the mixing, and the tempering, and the searching, and the decocting, that makes the fumigation and the suffumigation.

Amo. Well, indue me with it.

Per. I will, sir.

Hed. An excellent confection.

Cri. And most worthy a true voluptuary, Jove! what a coil these musk-worms take to purchase another's delight? for themselves, who bear the odours, have ever the least sense of them. Yet I do like better the prodigality of jewels and clothes, whereof one passeth to a man's heirs; the other at least wears out time. This presently expires, and, without continual riot in reparation, is lost: which whoso strives to keep, it is one special argument to me, that, affecting to smell better than other men, he doth indeed smell far worse.

Mer. I know you will say, it sits well, sir.

Tai. Good faith, if it do not, sir, let your mistress be judge.

Mer. By heaven, if my mistress do not like it, I'll make no more conscience to undo thee, than to undo an oyster.

Tai. Believe it, there's ne'er a mistress in the world can mislike it.

Mer. No, not goodwife tailor, your mistress; that has only the judgment to heat your pressing-tool. But for a court-mistress that studies these decorums, and knows the proportion of every cut to a hair, knows why such a colour is cut upon such a colour, and when a satin is cut upon six taffataes, will look that we should dive into the depth of the cut——Give me my scarf. Shew some ribands, sirrah. Have you the feather?

Feat. Ay, sir.

Mer. Have you the jewel?|

Jew. Yes, sir.

Mer. What must I give for the hire on't?

Jew. You shall give me six crowns, sir.

Mer. Six crowns! By heaven, 'twere a good deed to borrow it of thee to shew, and never let thee have it again.

Jew. I hope your worship will not do so, sir.

Mer. By Jove, sir, there be such tricks stirring, I can tell you, and worthily too. Extorting knaves, that live by these court-decorums, and yet——What's your jewel worth, I pray?

Jew. A hundred crowns, sir.

Mer. A hundred crowns, and six for the loan on't an hour! what's that in the hundred for the year? These impostors would not be hang'd! Your thief is not comparable to them, by Hercules. Well, put it in, and the feather; you will have it and you shall, and the pox give you good on't!

Amo. Give me my confects, my moscadini, and place those colours in my hat.

Mer. These are Bolognian ribands, I warrant you.

Mil. In truth, sir, if they be not right Granado silk—

Mer. A pox on you, you'll all say so.

Mil. You give me not a penny, sir.

Mer. Come, sir, perfume my devant;
  May it ascend, like solemn sacrifice,
  Into the nostrils of the Queen of Love !

Hed. Your French ceremonies are the best.

Ana. Monsieur, signior, your Solemn Address is too long; the ladies long to have you come on.

Amo. Soft, sir, our coming on is not so easily prepared. Signior Fig!

Per. Ay, sir.

Amo. Can you help my complexion, here?

Per. O yes, sir, I have an excellent mineral fucus for the purpose. The gloves are right, sir; you shall bury them in a muck-hill, a draught, seven years, and take them out and wash them, they shall still retain their first scent, true Spanish. There's ambre in the umbre.

Mer. Your price, sweet Fig?

Per. Give me what you will, sir; the signior pays me two crowns a pair; you shall give me your love, sir.

Mer. My love! with a pox to you, goodman Sassafras.

Per. I come, sir. There's an excellent diapasm in a chain, too, if you like it.

Amo. Stay, what are the ingredients to your fucus?

Per. Nought but sublimate and crude mercury, sir, well prepared and dulcified, with the jaw-bones of a sow, burnt, beaten, and searced.

Amo. I approve it. Lay it on.

Mer. I'll have your chain of pomander, sirrah; what's your price?

Per. We'll agree, monsieur; I'll assure you it was both decocted and dried where no sun came, and kept in an onyx ever since it was balled.

Mer. Come, invert my mustachio, and we have done.

Amo. 'Tis good.

Bar. Hold still, I pray you, sir.

Per. Nay, the fucus is exorbitant, sir.

Mer. Death, dost thou burn me, harlot!

Bar. I beseech you, sir.

Mer. Beggar, varlet, poltroon.   [*Beats him.*

Hed. Excellent, excellent!

Ana. Your French beat is the most natural beat of the world.

Aso. O that I had played at this weapon.   [*A charge.*

Pha. Peace, now they come on; the second part.

Amo. Madam, your beauties being so attractive, I muse you are left thus alone.

Phi. Better be alone, sir, than ill accompanied.

Amo. Nought can be ill, lady, that can come near your goodness.

Mer. Sweet madam, on what part of you soever a man casts his eye, he meets with perfection ; you are the lively image of Venus throughout ; all the graces smile in your cheeks ; your beauty nourishes as well as delights ; you have a tongue steeped in honey, and a breath like a panther ; your breasts and forehead are whiter than goats' milk, or May blossoms ; a cloud is not so soft as your skin—

Hed. Well strook, monsieur! He charges like a Frenchman indeed, thick and hotly.

Mer. Your cheeks are Cupid's baths, wherein he uses to steep himself in milk and nectar : he does light all his torches at your eyes, and instructs you how to shoot and wound with their beams. Yet I love nothing in you more than your innocence ; you retain so native a simplicity, so unblamed a behaviour ! Methinks, with such a love, I should find no head, nor foot of my pleasure : you are the very spirit of a lady.

Ana. Fair play, monsieur, you are too hot on the quarry; give your competitor audience.

Amo. Lady, how stirring soever the monsieur's tongue is, he will lie by your side more dull than your eunuch.

Ana. A good stroke; that mouth was excellently put over.

Amo. You are fair, lady—

Cri. You offer foul, signior, to close; keep your distance; for all your bravo rampant here.

Amo. I say you are fair, lady, let your choice be fit, as you are fair.

Mer. I say ladies do never believe they are fair, till some fool begins to doat upon them.

Phi. You play too rough, gentlemen.

Amo. Your frenchified fool is your only fool, lady : I do yield to this honourable monsieur in all civil and humane courtesy.

                             [*A flourish.*

Mer. Buz!

Ana. Admirable. Give him the prize, give him the prize: that mouth again was most courtly hit, and rare.

Amo. I knew I should pass upon him with the bitter bob.

Hed. O, but the reverse was singular.

Pha. It was most subtile, Amorphus.

Aso. If I had done't, it should have been better.

Mer. How heartily they applaud this, Crites!

Cri. You suffer them too long.

Mer. I'll take off their edge instantly.

Ana. Name the prize, at the *Solemn Address*.

Phi. Two lips wagging.

Cri. And never a wise word, I take it.

Ana. Give to Amorphus. And, upon him again; let him not draw free breath.

Amo. Thanks, fair deliverer, and my honourable judges. Madam Phantaste, you are our worthy object at this next weapon.

Pha. Most covetingly ready, Amorphus.

[*She takes the state instead of Philautia.*

Hed. Your monsieur is crest-fallen.

Ana. So are most of them once a year.

Amo. You will see, I shall now give him the gentle Dor presently, he forgetting to shift the colours, which are now changed with alteration of the mistress. At your last weapon, sir. *The Perfect Close.* Set forward. [*A charge.*] Intend your approach, monsieur.

Mer. 'Tis yours, signior.

Amo. With your example, sir.

Mer. Not I, sir.

Amo. It is your right.

Mer. By no possible means.

Amo. You have the way.

Mer. As I am noble—

Amo. As I am virtuous—

Mer. Pardon me, sir.

Amo. I will die first.

Mer. You are a tyrant in courtesy.

Amo. He is removed.—[*Stays Mercury on his moving.*]—Judges, bear witness.

Mer. What of that, sir?

Amo. You are removed, sir.

Mer. Well.

Amo. I challenge you; you have received the Dor. Give me the prize.

Mer. Soft, sir. How, the Dor?

Amo. The common mistress, you see, is changed.

Mer. Right, sir.

Amo. And you have still in your hat the former colours.

Mer. You lie, sir, I have none: I have pulled them out. I meant to play discoloured. [*A flourish.*

Cri. The Dor, the Dor, the Dor, the Dor, the Dor, the palpable Dor!

Ana. Heart of my blood, Amorphus, what have you done? stuck a disgrace upon us all, and at your last weapon!

Aso. I could have done no more.

Hed. By heaven, it was most unfortunate luck.

Ana. Luck! by that candle, it was mere rashness, and oversight;

would any man have ventured to play so open, and forsake his ward? D——n me, if he have not eternally undone himself in court, and discountenanced us that were his main countenance, by it.

Amo. Forgive it now : it was the solecism of my stars.

Cri. The wring by the hand, and the banquet, is ours.

Mer. O, here's a lady feels like a wench of the first year; you would think her hand did melt in your touch; and the bones of her fingers ran out at length when you prest 'em, they are so gently delicate! He that had the grace to print a kiss on these lips, should taste wine and rose-leaves. O, she kisses as close as a cockle. Let's take them down, as deep as our hearts, wench, till our very souls mix. Adieu, signior: good faith I shall drink to you at supper, sir.

Ana. Stay, monsieur. Who awards you the prize?

Cri. Why, his proper merit, sir; you see he has played down your grand garb-master, here.

Ana. That's not in your logic to determine, sir: you are no courtier. This is none of your seven or nine beggarly sciences, but a certain mystery above them, wherein we that have skill must pronounce, and not such fresh men as you are.

Cri. Indeed, I must declare myself to you no profest courtling; nor to have any excellent stroke at your subtile weapons; yet if you please, I dare venture a hit with you, or your fellow, sir Dagonet, here.

Ana. With me!

Cri. Yes, sir.

Ana. Heart, I shall never have such a fortune to save myself in a fellow again, and your two reputations, gentlemen, as in this. I'll undertake him.

Hed. Do, and swinge him soundly, good Anaides.

Ana. Let me alone; I'll play other manner of play, than has been seen yet. I would the prize lay on't.

Mer. It shall if you will, I forgive my right.

Ana. Are you so confident! what's your weapon?

Cri. At any, I, sir.

Mer. The Perfect Close, that's now the best.

Ana. Content, I'll pay your scholarity. Who offers?

Cri. Marry, that will I: I dare give you that advantage too.

Ana. You dare! well, look to your liberal sconce.

Amo. Make your play still, upon the answer, sir.

Ana. Hold your peace, you are a hobby-horse.

Aso. Sit by me, master.

Mer. Now, Crites, strike home.   *[A charge.*

Cri. You shall see me undo the assured swaggerer with a trick, instantly: I will play all his own play before him; court the wench in his garb, in his phrase, with his face; leave him not so much as a look, an eye, a stalk, or an imperfect oath, to express himself by, after me.   *[Aside to Mercury.*

Mer. Excellent, Crites.

Ana. When begin you, sir? have you consulted?

Cri. To your cost, sir. Which is the piece stands forth to be courted? O, are you she? [*To Philautia.*] *Well, madam, or sweet lady, it is so, I do love you in some sort, do you conceive? and though I am no monsieur, nor no signior, and do want, as they say, logic and sophistry, and good words, to tell you why it is so; yet by this hand and by that candle it is so: and though I be no book-worm, nor one that deals by art, to give you rhetoric and causes, why it should be so, or make it good it is so? yet, d——n me, but I know it is so, and am assured it is so, and I and my sword shall make it appear it is so, and give you reason sufficient how it can be no otherwise but so—*

Hed. 'Slight, Anaides, you are mocked, and so we are all.

Mer. How now, signior! what, suffer yourself to be cozened of your courtship before your face?

Hed. This is plain confederacy to disgrace us: let's be gone, and plot some revenge.

Amo. *When men disgraces share,*
  The lesser is the care.

Cri. Nay, stay, my dear Ambition, [*to Hedon.*] I can do you over too. You that tell your mistress, her beauty is all composed of theft; her hair stole from Apollo's goldy-locks; her white and red, lilies and roses stolen out of paradise; her eyes two stars, pluck'd from the sky; her nose the gnomon of Love's dial, that tells you how the clock of your heart goes: and for her other parts, as you cannot reckon them, they are so many; so you cannot recount them, they are so manifest. Yours, if his own, unfortunate Hoyden, instead of Hedon. [*A flourish.*

Aso. Sister, come away, I cannot endure them longer.
  [*Exeunt all but Mercury and Crites.*

Mer. Go, Dors, and you, my madam Courting-stocks,
Follow your scorned and derided mates;
Tell to your guilty breasts, what mere gilt blocks
You are, and how unworthy human states.

Cri. Now, sacred God of Wit, if you can make
Those, whom our sports tax in these apish graces,
Kiss, like the fighting snakes, your peaceful rod,
These times shall canonise you for a god.

Mer. Why, Crites, think you any noble spirit,
Or any, worth the title of a man,
Will be incensed to see the enchanted veils
Of self-conceit, and servile flattery,
Wrapt in so many folds by time and custom,
Drawn from his wronged and bewitched eyes?
Who sees not now their shape and nakedness,
Is blinder than the son of earth, the mole;
Crown'd with no more humanity, nor soul.

Cri. Though they may see it, yet the huge estate
Fancy, and form, and sensual pride have gotten,

Will make them blush for anger, not for shame,
And turn shewn nakedness to impudence.
Humour is now the test we try things in:
All power is just: nought that delights is sin.
And yet the zeal of every knowing man
Opprest with hills of tyranny, cast on virtue
By the light fancies of fools, thus transported,
Cannot but vent the Ætna of his fires,
T'inflame best bosoms with much worthier love
Than of these outward and effeminate shades;
That these vain joys, in which their wills consume
Such powers of wit and soul as are of force
To raise their beings to eternity,
May be converted on works fitting men:
And, for the practice of a forced look,
An antic gesture, or a fustian phrase,
Study the native frame of a true heart,
An inward comeliness of bounty, knowledge,
And spirit that may conform them actually
To God's high figures, which they have in power;
Which to neglect for a self-loving neatness,
Is sacrilege of an unpardon'd greatness.

   Mer. Then let the truth of these things strengthen thee,
In thy exempt and only man-like course;
Like it the more, the less it is respected:
Though men fail, virtue is by gods protected.—
See, here comes Arete; I'll withdraw myself.   *[Exit.*

Enter ARETE.

   Are. Crites, you must provide straight for a masque,
'Tis Cynthia's pleasure.
   Cri. How, bright Arete!
Why, 'twere a labour more for Hercules:
Better and sooner durst I undertake
To make the different seasons of the year,
The winds, or elements, to sympathise,
Than their unmeasurable vanity
Dance truly in a measure.   They agree!
What though all concord's born of contraries;
So many follies will confusion prove,
And like a sort of jarring instruments,
All out of tune; because, indeed, we see
There is not that analogy 'twixt discords,
As between things but merely opposite.
   Are. There is your error: for as Hermes' wand
Charms the disorders of tumultuous ghosts;
And as the strife of Chaos then did cease,
When better light than Nature's did arrive:
So, what could never in itself agree,

Forgetteth the eccentric property,
And at her sight turns forthwith regular,
Whose sceptre guides the flowing ocean:
And though it did not, yet the most of them
Being either courtiers, or not wholly rude,
Respect of majesty, the place, and presence,
Will keep them within ring, especially
When they are not presented as themselves,
But masqued like others: for, in troth, not so
To incorporate them, could be nothing else,
Than like a state ungovern'd, without laws,
Or body made of nothing but diseases:
The one, through impotency, poor and wretched;
The other, for the anarchy, absurd.

Cri. But, lady, for the revellers themselves,
It would be better, in my poor conceit,
That others were employ'd; for such as are
Unfit to be in Cynthia's court, can seem
No less unfit to be in Cynthia's sports.

Are. That, Crites, is not purposed without
Particular knowledge of the goddess' mind;
Who holding true intelligence, what follies
Had crept into her palace, she resolved
Of sports and triumphs, under that pretext,
To have them muster in their pomp and fulness,
That so she might more strictly, and to root,
Effect the reformation she intends.

Cri. I now conceive her heavenly drift in all,
And will apply my spirits to serve her will.
O thou, the very power by which I am,
And but for which it were in vain to be,
Chief next Diana, virgin heavenly fair,
Admired Arete, of them admired
Whose souls are not enkindled by the sense,
Disdain not my chaste fire, but feed the flame
Devoted truly to thy gracious name.

Are. Leave to suspect us: Crites well shall find,
As we are now most dear, we'll prove most kind.

[*Within.*] Arete!

Are. Hark, I am call'd.   [*Exit.*

Cri. I follow instantly.
Phœbus Apollo, if with ancient rites,
And due devotions, I have ever hung
Elaborate Pæans on thy golden shrine,
Or sung thy triumphs in a lofty strain,
Fit for a theatre of gods to hear:
And thou, the other son of mighty Jove,
Cyllenian Mercury, sweet Maia's joy,
If in the busy tumults of the mind

My path thou ever hast illumined,
For which thine altars I have oft perfumed.
And deck'd thy statues with discolour'd flowers:
Now thrive invention in this glorious court,
That not of bounty only, but of right,
Cynthia may grace, and give it life by sight.   [*Exit.*

SCENE III.

Enter HESPERUS, CYNTHIA, ARETE, TIME, PHRONESIS, *and*
THAUMA.

Music accompanied. HESPERUS *sings.*

Queen and huntress, chaste and fair,
Now the sun is laid to sleep,
Seated in thy silver chair,
State in wonted manner keep:
        Hesperus entreats thy light,
        Goddess, excellently bright.

Earth, let not thy envious shade
Dare itself to interpose;
Cynthia's shining orb was made
Heav'n to clear, when day did close:
        Bless us then with wished sight,
        Goddess excellently bright.

Lay thy bow of pearl apart,
And thy crystal shining quiver;
Give unto the flying hart
Space to breathe, how short soever:
        Thou that mak'st a day of night,
        Goddess excellently bright.

Cyn. When hath Diana, like an envious wretch,
That glitters only to his soothed self,
Denying to the world the precious use
Of hoarded wealth, withheld her friendly aid?
Monthly we spend our still-repaired shine,
And not forbid our virgin-waxen torch
To burn and blaze, while nutriment doth last:
That once consumed, out of Jove's treasury
A new we take, and stick it in our sphere,
To give the mutinous kind of wanting men
Their look'd-for light.   Yet what is their desert?
Bounty is wrong'd, interpreted as due;
Mortals can challenge not a ray, by right,
Yet do expect the whole of Cynthia's light.
But if that deities withdrew their gifts
For human follies, what could men deserve
But death and darkness?   It behoves the high,

For their own sakes, to do things worthily.
   Are. Most true, most sacred goddess; for the heavens
Receive no good of all the good they do:
Nor Jove, nor you, nor other heavenly Powers,
Are fed with fumes which do from incense rise,
Or sacrifices reeking in their gore;
Yet, for the care which you of mortals have,
(Whose proper good it is that they be so,)
You well are pleased with odours redolent:
But ignorant is all the race of men,
Which still complains, not knowing why, or when.
   Cyn. Else, noble Arete, they would not blame,
And tax, or for unjust, or for as proud,
Thy Cynthia, in the things which are indeed
The greatest glories in our starry crown;
Such is our chastity, which safely scorns,
Not love, for who more fervently doth love
Immortal honour, and divine renown?
But giddy Cupid, Venus' frantic son.
Yet, Arete, if by this veiled light
We but discover'd (what we not discern)
Any the least of imputations stand
Ready to sprinkle our unspotted fame
With note of lightness, from these revels near;
Not, for the empire of the universe,
Should night, or court, this whatsoever shine,
Or grace of ours, unhappily enjoy.
Place and occasion are two privy thieves,
And from poor innocent ladies often steal
The best of things, an honourable name;
To stay with follies, or where faults may be,
Infers a crime, although the party free.
   Are. How Cynthianly, that is, how worthily
And like herself, the matchless Cynthia speaks!
Infinite jealousies, infinite regards,
Do watch about the true virginity:
But Phœbe lives from all, not only fault,
But as from thought, so from suspicion free.
Thy presence broad-seals our delights for pure;
What's done in Cynthia's sight, is done secure.
   Cyn. That then so answer'd, dearest Arete,
What th' argument, or of what sort our sports
Are like to be this night, I not demand.
Nothing which duty, and desire to please,
Bears written in the forehead, comes amiss.
But unto whose invention must we owe
The complement of this night's furniture?
   Are. Excellent goddess, to a man's, whose worth,
Without hyperbole, I thus may praise;

One at least studious of deserving well,
And, to speak truth, indeed deserving well.
Potential merit stands for actual,
Where only opportunity doth want,
Not will, nor power; both which in him abound.
One whom the Muses and Minerva love;
For whom should they, than Crites, more esteem,
Whom Phœbus, though not Fortune, holdeth dear?
And, which convinceth excellence in him,
A principal admirer of yourself.
Even through the ungentle injuries of Fate,
And difficulties, which do virtue choke,
Thus much of him appears. What other things
Of farther note do lie unborn in him,
Them I do leave for cherishment to shew,
And for a goddess graciously to judge.

    Cyn. We have already judged him, Arete,
Nor are we ignorant how noble minds
Suffer too much through those indignities
Which times and vicious persons cast on them.
Ourself have ever vowed to esteem
As virtue for itself, so fortune, base;
Who's first in worth, the same be first in place.
Nor farther notice, Arete, we crave
Than thine approval's sovereign warranty:
Let 't be thy care to make us known to him;
Cynthia shall brighten what the world made dim.   [*Exit Arete.*

The First Masque.

Enter Cupid, *disguised as* Anteros, *followed by* Storgé, Aglaia, Euphantaste, *and* Apheleia.

    Cup. Clear pearl of heaven, and, not to be farther ambitious in titles, Cynthia! the fame of this illustrious night, among others, hath also drawn these four fair virgins from the palace of their queen Perfection, (a word which makes no sufficient difference betwixt her's and thine,) to visit thy imperial court: for she, their sovereign, not finding where to dwell among men, before her return to heaven, advised them wholly to consecrate themselves to thy celestial service, as in whose clear spirit (the proper element and sphere of virtue) they should behold not her alone, their ever-honoured mistress, but themselves (more truly themselves) to live enthronised. Herself would have commended them unto thy favour more particularly, but that she knows no commendation is more available with thee, than that of proper virtue. Nevertheless she willed them to present this crystal mound, a note of monarchy, and symbol of perfection, to thy more worthy deity; which, as here by me they most humbly do, so amongst the rarities thereof, that is the chief, to shew whatsoever the world hath excellent, howsoever remote and various. But your irradiate judgment will soon discover the secrets of this little crystal world. Themselves, to appear more plainly, because they know nothing more odious than false pretexts, have chosen to express their several qualities thus in several colours.

The first, in citron colour, is natural affection, which, given us to procure our good, is sometime called Storgé ; and as every one is nearest to himself, so this handmaid of reason, allowable Self-love, as it is without harm, so are none without it : her place in the court of Perfection was to quicken minds in the pursuit of honour. Her device is a perpendicular level, upon a cube or square ; the word, se suo modulo; *alluding to that true measure of one's self, which, as every one ought to make, so is it most conspicuous in thy divine example.*

The second, in green, is Aglaia, delectable and pleasant conversation, whose property is to move a kindly delight, and sometime not without laughter : her office to entertain assemblies, and keep societies together with fair familiarity. Her device, within a ring of clouds, a heart with shine about it ; the word, curarum nubila pello : *an allegory of Cynthia's light, which no less clears the sky than her fair mirth the heart.*

The third, in the discoloured mantle spangled all over, is Euphantaste, a well-conceited Wittiness, and employed in honouring the court with the riches of her pure invention. Her device, upon a Petasus, or Mercurial hat, a crescent ; the word, sic laus ingenii; *inferring that the praise and glory of wit doth ever increase, as doth thy growing moon.*

The fourth, in white, is Apheleia, a nymph as pure and simple as the soul, or as an abrase table, and is therefore called Simplicity ; without folds, without plaits, without colour, without counterfeit ; and (to speak plainly) plainness itself. Her device is no device. The word under her silver shield, omnis abest fucus; *alluding to thy spotless self, who art as far from impurity as from mortality.*

Myself, celestial goddess, more fit for the court of Cynthia than the arbours of Cytherea, am called Anteros, or Love's enemy ; the more welcome therefore to thy court, and the fitter to conduct this quaternion, who, as they are thy professed votaries, and for that cause adversaries to Love, yet thee, perpetual virgin, they both love, and vow to love eternally.

Re-enter ARETE, with CRITES.

Cyn. Not without wonder, nor without delight,
Mine eyes have view'd, in contemplation's depth,
This work of wit, divine and excellent:
What shape, what substance, or what unknown power,
In virgin's habit, crown'd with laurel leaves,
And olive-branches woven in between,
On sea-girt rocks, like to a goddess shines!
O front! O face! O all celestial, sure,
And more than mortal! Arete, behold
Another Cynthia, and another queen,
Whose glory, like a lasting plenilune,
Seems ignorant of what it is to wane.

Nor under heaven an object could be found
More fit to please.   Let Crites make approach.
Bounty forbids to pall our thanks with stay,
Or to defer our favour, after view:
The time of grace is, when the cause is new.
    Are. Lo, here the man, celestial Delia,
Who (like a circle bounded in itself)
Contains as much as man in fulness may.
Lo, here the man, who not of usual earth,
But of that nobler and more precious mould
Which Phœbus' self doth temper, is composed;
And who, though all were wanting to reward,
Yet to himself he would not wanting be:
Thy favour's gain is his ambition's most,
And labour's best; who (humble in his height)
Stands fixed silent in thy glorious sight.
    Cyn. With no less pleasure than we have beheld
This precious crystal work of rarest wit,
Our eye doth read thee, now instiled, our Crites;
Whom learning, virtue, and our favour last,
Exempteth from the gloomy multitude.
With common eye the Supreme should not see:
Henceforth be ours, the more thyself to be.
    Cri. Heaven's purest light, whose orb may be eclipsed,
But not thy praise; divinest Cynthia!
How much too narrow for so high a grace,
Thine (save therein) the most unworthy Crites
Doth find himself! for ever shine thy fame;
Thine honours ever, as thy beauties do.
In me they must, my dark world's chiefest lights,
By whose propitious beams my powers are raised
To hope some part of those most lofty points,
Which blessed Arete hath pleased to name,
As marks, to which my endeavour's steps should bend:
Mine, as begun at thee, in thee must end.

THE SECOND MASQUE.

Enter MERCURY *as a page, introducing* Eucosmos, Eupathes,
Eutolmos, *and* Eucolos.

    Mer. *Sister of Phœbus, to whose bright orb we owe, that we not
complain of his absence ; these four brethren (for they are brethren,
and sons of Eutaxia, a lady known, and highly beloved of your re-
splendent deity) not able to be absent, when Cynthia held a solemnity,
officiously insinuate themselves into thy presence : for, as there are
four cardinal virtues, upon which the whole frame of the court doth
move, so are these the four cardinal properties, without which the body
of compliment moveth not. With these four silver javelins, (which they
bear in their hands) they support in princes' courts the state of the*

presence, as by office they are obliged: which, though here they may seem superfluous, yet, for honour's sake, they thus presume to visit thee, having also been employed in the palace of queen Perfection. And though to them that would make themselves gracious to a goddess, sacrifices were fitter than presents, or impresses, yet they both hope thy favour, and (in place of either) use several symbols, containing the titles of thy imperial dignity.

First, the hithermost, in the changeable blue and green robe, is the commendably-fashioned gallant, Eucosmos; whose courtly habit is the grace of the presence, and delight of the surveying eye; whom ladies understand by the names of Neat and Elegant. His symbol is, divæ virgini, in which he would express thy deity's principal glory, which hath ever been virginity.

The second, in the rich accoutrement, and robe of purple, empaled with gold, is Eupathes; who entertains his mind with an harmless, but not incurious variety; all the objects of his senses are sumptuous, himself a gallant, that, without excess, can make use of superfluity, go richly in embroideries, jewels, and what not, without vanity, and fare delicately without gluttony; and therefore (not without cause) is universally thought to be of fine humour. His symbol is, divæ optimæ; an attribute to express thy goodness, in which thou so resemblest Jove thy father.

The third, in the blush-coloured suit, is Eutolmos, as duly respecting others, as never neglecting himself; commonly known by the title of good Audacity; to courts and courtly assemblies a guest most acceptable. His symbol is, divæ viragini; to express thy hardy courage in chase of savage beasts, which harbour in woods and wildernesses.

The fourth, in watchet tinsel, is the kind and truly benefique Eucolos, who imparteth not without respect, but yet without difficulty, and hath the happiness to make every kindness seem double, by the timely and freely bestowing thereof. He is the chief of them, who by the vulgar are said to be of good nature. His symbol is, divæ maximæ; an adjunct to signify thy greatness, which in heaven, earth, and hell, is formidable.

Music. A Dance by the two Masques joined, during which
CUPID *and* MERCURY *retire to the side of the stage.*

Cup. Is not that Amorphus, the traveller?

Mer. As though it were not! do you not see how his legs are in travail with a measure?

Cup. Hedon, thy master is next.

Mer. What, will Cupid turn nomenclator, and cry them?

Cup. No, faith, but I have a comedy toward, that would not be lost for a kingdom.

Mer. In good time, for Cupid will prove the comedy.

Cup. Mercury, I am studying how to match them.

Mer. How to mismatch them were harder.

Cup. They are the nymphs must do it; I shall sport myself with their passions above measure.

Mer. Those nymphs would be tamed a little indeed, but I fear thou hast not arrows for the purpose.

Cup. O yes, here be of all sorts, flights, rovers, and butt-shafts. But I can wound with a brandish, and never draw bow for the matter.

Mer. I cannot but believe it, my invisible archer, and yet methinks you are tedious.

Cup. It behoves me to be somewhat circumspect, Mercury; for if Cynthia hear the twang of my bow, she'll go near to whip me with the string; therefore, to prevent that, I thus discharge a brandish upon——it makes no matter which of the couples. Phantaste and Amorphus, at you. [*Waves his arrow at them.*

Mer. Will the shaking of a shaft strike them into such a fever of affection?

Cup. As well as the wink of an eye: but, I pray thee, hinder me not with thy prattle.

Mer. Jove forbid I hinder thee; Marry, all that I fear is Cynthia's presence, which, with the cold of her chastity, casteth such an antiperistasis about the place, that no heat of thine will tarry with the patient.

Cup. It will tarry the rather, for the antiperistasis will keep it in.

Mer. I long to see the experiment.

Cup. Why, their marrow boils already, or they are all turn'd eunuchs.

Mer. Nay, an't be so, I'll give over speaking, and be a spectator only. [*The first dance ends.*

Amo. Cynthia, by my bright soul, is a right exquisite and splendidious lady; yet Amorphus, I think, hath seen more fashions, I am sure more countries; but whether I have or not, what need we gaze on Cynthia, that have ourself to admire?

Pha. O, excellent Cynthia! yet if Phantaste sat where she does, and had such attire on her head, (for attire can do much,) I say no more—but goddesses are goddesses, and Phantaste is as she is! I would the revels were done once, I might go to my school of glass again, and learn to do myself right after all this ruffling.

[*Music; they begin the second dance.*

Mer. How now, Cupid? here's a wonderful change with your brandish! do you not hear how they dote?

Cup. What prodigy is this? no word of love, no mention, no motion!

Mer. Not a word, my little ignis fatue, not a word.

Cup. Are my darts enchanted? is their vigour gone? is their virtue—

Mer. What! Cupid turned jealous of himself? ha, ha, ha!

Cup. Laughs Mercury?

Mer. Is Cupid angry?

Cup. Hath he not cause, when his purpose is so deluded?

Mer. A rare comedy, it shall be entitled Cupid's?

Cup. Do not scorn us, Hermes.

Mer. Choler and Cupid are two fiery things; I scorn them not. But I see that come to pass which I presaged in the beginning.

Cup. You cannot tell: perhaps the physic will not work so soon upon some as upon others. It may be the rest are not so resty.

Mer. *Ex ungue ;* you know the old adage, as these so are the remainder.

Cup. I'll try: this is the same shaft with which I wounded Argurion. [*Waves his arrow again.*

Mer. Ay, but let me save you a labour, Cupid: there were certain bottles of water fetch'd, and drunk off since that time, by these gallants.

Cup. Jove strike me into the earth! the Fountain of Self-love!

Mer. Nay, faint not, Cupid.

Cup. I remember'd it not.

Mer. Faith, it was ominous to take the name of Anteros upon you; you know not what charm or enchantment lies in the word: you saw, I durst not venture upon any device in our presentment, but was content to be no other than a simple page. Your arrows' properties, (to keep decorum,) Cupid, are suited, it should seem, to the nature of him you personate.

Cup. Indignity not to be borne!

Mer. Nay rather, an attempt to have been forborne.

[*The second dance ends.*

Cup. How might I revenge myself on this insulting Mercury? there's Crites, his minion, he has not tasted of this water. [*Waves his arrow at Crites.*] It shall be so. Is Crites turn'd dotard on himself too?

Mer. That follows not, because the venom of your shafts cannot pierce him, Cupid.

Cup. As though there were one antidote for these, and another for him.

Mer. As though there were not; or, as if one effect might not arise of divers causes? What say you to Cynthia, Arete, Phronesis, Time, and others there?

Cup. They are divine.

Mer. And Crites aspires to be so.

[*Music; they begin the third dance.*

Cup. But that shall not serve him.

Mer. 'Tis like to do it, at this time. But Cupid is grown too covetous, that will not spare one of a multitude.

Cup. One is more than a multitude.

Mer. Arete's favour makes any one shot-proof against thee, Cupid. I pray thee, light honey-bee, remember thou art not now in Adonis' garden, but in Cynthia's presence, where thorns lie in garrison about the roses. Soft, Cynthia speaks.

Cyn. Ladies and gallants of our court, to end,
And give a timely period to our sports,
Let us conclude them with declining night;
Our empire is but of the darker half.

And if you judge it any recompence
For your fair pains, t' have earn'd Diana's thanks,
Diana grants them, and bestows their crown
To gratify your acceptable zeal.
For you are they, that not, as some have done,
Do censure us, as too severe and sour,
But as, more rightly, gracious to the good;
Although we not deny, unto the proud,
Or the profane, perhaps indeed austere:
For so Actæon, by presuming far,
Did, to our grief, incur a fatal doom;
And so, swoln Niobe, comparing more
Than he presumed, was trophæed into stone.
But are we therefore judged too extreme?
Seems it no crime to enter sacred bowers,
And hallow'd places, with impure aspéct,
Most lewdly to pollute? Seems it no crime
To brave a deity? Let mortals learn
To make religion of offending heaven.
And not at all to censure powers divine.
To men this argument should stand for firm,
A goddess did it, therefore it was good:
We are not cruel, nor delight in blood.—
But what have serious repetitions
To do with revels, and the sports of court?
We not intend to sour your late delights
With harsh expostulation. Let it suffice
That we take notice, and can take revenge
Of these calumnious and lewd blasphemies.
For we are no less Cynthia than we were,
Nor is our power, but as ourself, the same:
Though we have now put on no tire of shine,
But mortal eyes undazzled may endure.
Years are beneath the spheres, and time makes weak
Things under heaven, not powers which govern heaven.
And though ourself be in ourself secure,
Yet let not mortals challenge to themselves
Immunity from thence. Lo, this is all:
Honour hath store of spleen, but wanteth gall.
Once more we cast the slumber of our thanks
On your ta'en toil, which here let take an end.
And that we not mistake your several worths,
Nor you our favour, from yourselves remove
What makes you not yourselves, those clouds of masque;
Particular pains particular thanks do ask.   [*The dancers unmask.*
How! let me view you. Ha! are we contemn'd?
Is there so little awe of our disdain,
That any (under trust of their disguise)
Should mix themselves with others of the court,

And, without forehead, boldly press so far,
As farther none?   How apt is lenity
To be abused! severity to be loath'd!
And yet, how much more doth the seeming face
Of neighbour virtues, and their borrow'd names,
Add of lewd boldness to loose vanities!
Who would have thought that Philautia durst
Or have usurped noble Storgé's name,
Or with that theft have ventured on our eyes?
Who would have thought, that all of them should hope
So much of our connivence, as to come
To grace themselves with titles not their own?
Instead of med'cines, have we maladies?
And such imposthumes as Phantaste is
Grow in our palace?   We must lance these sores,
Or all will putrify.   Nor are these all,
For we suspect a farther fraud than this:
Take off our veil, that shadows many depart,
And shapes appear, beloved Arete——So,
Another face of things presents itself,
Than did of late.   What! feather'd Cupid masqued,
And masked like Anteros?   And stay! more strange!
Dear Mercury, our brother, like a page,
To countenance the ambush of the boy!
Nor endeth our discovery as yet:
Gelaia, like a nymph, that, but erewhile,
In male attire, did serve Anaides?—
Cupid came hither to find sport and game,
Who heretofore hath been too conversant
Among our train, but never felt revenge;
And Mercury bare Cupid company.
Cupid, we must confess, this time of mirth,
Proclaim'd by us, gave opportunity
To thy attempts, although no privilege:
Tempt us no farther; we cannot endure
Thy presence longer; vanish hence, away!   [*Exit Cupid.*
You, Mercury, we must entreat to stay,
And hear what we determine of the rest;
For in this plot we well perceive your hand.
But, (for we mean not a censorian task,
And yet to lance these ulcers grown so ripe,)
Dear Arete, and Crites, to you two
We give the charge; impose what pains you please:
Th' incurable cut off, the rest reform,
Remembering ever what we first decreed,
Since revels were proclaim'd, let now none bleed.

   Are. How well Diana can distinguish times,
And sort her censures, keeping to herself
The doom of gods, leaving the rest to us!

Come, cite them, Crites, first, and then proceed.

Cri. First, Philautia, for she was the first,
Then light Gelaia in Aglaia's name,
Thirdly, Phantaste, and Moria next,
Main Follies all, and of the female crew:
Amorphus, or Eucosmos' counterfeit,
Voluptuous Hedon ta'en for Eupathes,
Brazen Anaides, and Asotus last,
With his two pages, Morus and Prosaites;
And thou, the traveller's evil, Cos, approach,
Impostors all, and male deformities—

Are. Nay, forward, for I delegate my power,
And will that at thy mercy they do stand,
Whom they so oft, so plainly scorn'd before.
'Tis virtue which they want, and wanting it,
Honour no garment to their backs can fit.
Then, Crites, practise thy discretion.

Cri. Adored Cynthia, and bright Arete,
Another might seem fitter for this task,
Than Crites far, but that you judge not so:
For I (not to appear vindicative,
Or mindful of contempts, which I contemn'd,
As done of impotence) must be remiss:
Who, as I was the author, in some sort,
To work their knowledge into Cynthia's sight,
So should be much severer to revenge
The indignity hence issuing to her name:
But there's not one of these who are unpain'd,
Or by themselves unpunished; for vice
Is like a fury to the vicious mind,
And turns delight itself to punishment.
But we must forward, to define their doom.
You are offenders, that must be confess'd;
Do you confess it?

All. We do.

Cri. And that you merit sharp correction?

All. Yes.

Cri. Then we (reserving unto Delia's grace
Her farther pleasure, and to Arete
What Delia granteth) thus do sentence you:
That from this place (for penance known of all,
Since you have drunk so deeply of Self-love)
You, two and two, singing a Palinode,
March to your several homes by Niobe's stone,
And offer up two tears a-piece thereon,
That it may change the name, as you must change,
And of a stone be called Weeping-cross:
Because it standeth cross of Cynthia's way,
One of whose names is sacred Trivia.

And after penance thus perform'd you pass
In like set order, not as Midas did,
To wash his gold off into Tagus' stream;
   But to the well of knowledge, Helicon;
Where, purged of your present maladies,
Which are not few, nor slender, you become
Such as you fain would seem, and then return,
Offering your service to great Cynthia.
This is your sentence, if the goddess please
To ratify it with her high consent;
The scope of wise mirth unto fruit is bent.
   Cyn. We do approve thy censure, belov'd Crites;
Which Mercury, thy true propitious friend,
(A deity next Jove beloved of us,)
Will undertake to see exactly done.
And for this service of discovery,
Perform'd by thee, in honour of our name,
We vow to guerdon it with such due grace
As shall become our bounty, and thy place.
Princes that would their people should do well,
Must at themselves begin, as at the head;
For men, by their example, pattern out
Their imitations, and regard of laws:
A virtuous court, a world to virtue draws.

    [Exeunt Cynthia and her Nymphs, followed by Arete and Crites:—
     Amorphus, Phantaste, etc., go off the stage in pairs, singing
     the following

PALINODE.

Amo. From Spanish shrugs, French faces, smirks, irpes, and all
affected humours,

       Chorus. Good Mercury defend us.
   Pha. From secret friends, sweet servants, loves, doves, and such
fantastic humours,

       Chorus. Good Mercury defend us.
   Amo. From stabbing of arms, flap-dragons, healths, whiffs, and
all such swaggering humours,

       Chorus. Good Mercury defend us.
   Pha. From waving fans, coy glances, glicks, cringes, and all such
simpering humours,

       Chorus. Good Mercury defend us.
   Amo. From making love by attorney, courting of puppets, and
paying for new acquaintance,

       Chorus. Good Mercury defend us.
   Pha. From perfumed dogs, monkies, sparrows, dildoes, and
paraquettoes,

       Chorus. Good Mercury defend us.
   Amo. From wearing bracelets of hair, shoe-ties, gloves, garters,
and rings with poesies,

       Chorus. Good Mercury defend us.

Pha. From pargetting, painting, slicking, glazing, and renewing old rivelled faces,

                      Chorus. Good Mercury defend us.

Amo. From 'squiring to tilt yards, play-houses, pageants, and all such public places,

                      Chorus. Good Mercury defend us.

Pha. From entertaining one gallant to gull another, and making fools of either,

                      Chorus. Good Mercury defend us.

Amo. From belying ladies' favours, noblemen's countenance, coining counterfeit employments, vain-glorious taking to them other men's services, and all self-loving humours,

                      Chorus. Good Mercury defend us.

Mercury *and* Crites *sing.*

Now each one dry his weeping eyes,
   And to the Well of Knowledge haste;
Where, purged of your maladies,
   You may of sweeter waters taste:
And, with refined voice, report
   The grace of Cynthia, and her court.

                                   [*Exeunt.*

THE EPILOGUE.

Gentles, be't known to you, since I went in
I am turn'd rhymer, and do thus begin.
The author (jealous how your sense doth take
His travails) hath enjoined me to make
Some short and ceremonious epilogue;
But if I yet know what, I am a rogue:
He ties me to such laws as quite distract
My thoughts, and would a year of time exact.
I neither must be faint, remiss, nor sorry,
Sour, serious, confident, nor peremptory;
But betwixt these. Let's see; to lay the blame
Upon the children's action, that were lame.
To crave your favour, with a begging knee,
Were to distrust the writer's faculty.
To promise better at the next we bring,
Prorogues disgrace, commends not any thing.
Stiffly to stand on this, and proudly approve
The play, might tax the maker of Self-love.
I'll only speak what I have heard him say,
" By —— 'tis good, and if you like't, you may."

Ecce rubet quidam, pallet, stupet, oscitat, odit
  Hoc volo: nunc nobis carmina nostra placent.

THE POETASTER : OR, HIS
ARRAIGNMENT

то THE VIRTUOUS, AND MY WORTHY FRIEND
MR. RICHARD MARTIN

SIR,—A thankful man owes a courtesy ever; the unthankful but when he needs it. To make mine own mark appear, and shew by which of these seals I am known, I send you this piece of what may live of mine; for whose innocence, as for the author's, you were once a noble and timely undertaker, to the greatest justice of this kingdom. Enjoy now the delight of your goodness, which is, to see that prosper you preserved, and posterity to owe the reading of that, without offence, to your name, which so much ignorance and malice of the times then conspired to have supprest.

Your true lover, BEN JONSON.

DRAMATIS PERSONÆ

AUGUSTUS CÆSAR.	HERMOGENES TIGELLIUS.
MECÆNAS.	DEMETRIUS FANNIUS.
MARC. OVID.	ALBIUS.
COR. GALLUS.	MINOS.
SEX. PROPERTIUS.	HISTRIO.
FUS. ARISTIUS.	ÆSOP.
PUB. OVID.	PYRGI.
VIRGIL.	*Lictors, Equitis, etc.*
HORACE.	
TREBATIUS.	JULIA.
ASINIUS LUPUS.	CYTHERIS.
PANTILIUS TUCCA.	PLAUTIA.
LUSCUS.	CHLOE.
RUF. LAB. CRISPINUS.	*Maids.*

SCENE,—ROME

After the second sounding.

ENVY arises in the midst of the stage.

Light, I salute thee, but with wounded nerves,
Wishing the golden splendor pitchy darkness.
What's here ? THE ARRAIGNMENT! *ay; this, this is it,*
That our sunk eyes have waked for all this while:
Here will be subject for my snakes and me.
Cling to my neck and wrists, my loving worms,
And cast you round in soft and amorous folds,
Till I do bid uncurl; then, break your knots,
Shoot out yourselves at length, as your forced stings

233

Would hide themselves within his maliced sides,
To whom I shall apply you.   Stay ! the shine
Of this assembly here offends my sight;
I'll darken that first, and outface their grace.
Wonder not, if I stare: these fifteen weeks,
So long as since the plot was but an embrion,
Have I, with burning lights mixt vigilant thoughts,
In expectation of this hated play,
To which at last I am arrived as Prologue.
Nor would I you should look for other looks,
Gesture, or compliment from me, than what
The infected bulk of Envy can afford:
For I am risse here with a covetous hope,
To blast your pleasures and destroy your sports,
With wrestings, comments, applications,
Spy-like suggestions, privy whisperings,
And thousand such promoting sleights as these.
Mark how I will begin: The scene is, ha !
Rome ? Rome ? and Rome ?   Crack, eye-strings, and your balls
Drop into earth: let me be ever blind.
I am prevented; all my hopes are crost,
Check'd, and abated; fie, a freezing sweat
Flows forth at all my pores, my entrails burn:
What should I do ?   Rome ! Rome !   O my vext soul,
How might I force this to the present state ?
Are there no players here ? no poet apes,
That come with basilisk's eyes, whose forked tongues
Are steeped in venom, as their hearts in gall ?
Either of these would help me; they could wrest,
Pervert, and poison all they hear or see,
With senseless glosses, and allusions.
Now, if you be good devils, fly me not.
You know what dear and ample faculties
I have endowed you with: I'll lend you more.
Here, take my snakes among you, come and eat,
And while the squeez'd juice flows in your black jaws,
Help me to damn the author.   Spit it forth
Upon his lines, and shew your rusty teeth
At every word, or accent: or else choose
Out of my longest vipers, to stick down
In your deep throats; and let the heads come forth
At your rank mouths; that he may see you arm'd
With triple malice, to hiss, sting, and tear
His work and him; to forge, and then declaim,
Traduce, corrupt, apply, inform, suggest;
O, these are gifts wherein your souls are blest.
What ? do you hide yourselves ? will none appear ?
None answer ? what, doth this calm troop affright you ?
Nay, then I do despair; down, sink again:

This travail is all lost with my dead hopes.
If in such bosoms spite have left to dwell,
Envy is not on earth, nor scarce in hell.   [*Descends slowly.*

The third sounding.

As she disappears, enter PROLOGUE hastily, in armour.

Stay, monster, ere thou sink—thus on thy head
Set we our bolder foot; with which we tread
Thy malice into earth: so Spite should die,
Despised and scorn'd by noble industry.
If any muse why I salute the stage,
An armed Prologue; know, 'tis a dangerous age:
Wherein who writes, had need present his scenes
Forty-fold proof against the conjuring means
Of base detractors, and illiterate apes,
That fill up rooms in fair and formal shapes.
'Gainst these, have we put on this forced defence:
Whereof the allegory and hid sense
Is, that a well erected confidence
Can fright their pride, and laugh their folly hence.
Here now, put case our author should, once more,
Swear that his play were good; he doth implore,
You would not argue him of arrogance:
Howe'er that common spawn of ignorance,
Our fry of writers, may beslime his fame,
And give his action that adulterate name.
Such full-blown vanity he more doth loth,
Than base dejection; there's a mean 'twixt both,
Which with a constant firmness he pursues,
As one that knows the strength of his own Muse.
And this he hopes all free souls will allow:
Others that take it with a rugged brow,
Their moods he rather pities than enviés:
His mind it is above their injuries.

ACT I

SCENE I.—*Scene draws, and discovers* OVID *in his study.*

Ovid. Then, when this body falls in funeral fire,
My name shall live, and my best part aspire.
It shall go so.

Enter LUSCUS, *with a gown and cap.*

Lusc. Young master, master Ovid, do you hear? Gods a'me!
away with your songs and sonnets, and on with your gown and cap
quickly: here, here, your father will be a man of this room presently.
Come, nay, nay, nay, nay, be brief. These verses too, a poison on
'em! I cannot abide them, they make me ready to cast, by the

banks of Helicon! Nay, look, what a rascally untoward thing this poetry is; I could tear them now.

Ovid. Give me; how near is my father?

Lusc. Heart a'man: get a law book in your hand, I will not answer you else. [*Ovid puts on his cap and gown.*] Why so! now there's some formality in you. By Jove, and three or four of the gods more, I am right of mine old master's humour for that; this villainous poetry will undo you, by the welkin.

Ovid. What, hast thou buskins on, Luscus, that thou swearest so tragically and high?

Lusc. No, but I have boots on, sir, and so has your father too by this time; for he call'd for them ere I came from the lodging.

Ovid. Why, was he no readier?

Lusc. O no; and there was the mad skeldering captain, with the velvet arms, ready to lay hold on him as he comes down: he that presses every man he meets, with an oath to lend him money, and cries, *Thou must do't, old boy, as thou art a man, a man of worship.*

Ovid. Who, Pantilius Tucca?

Lus. Ay, he; and I met little master Lupus, the tribune, going thither too.

Ovid. Nay, an he be under their arrest, I may with safety enough read over my elegy before he come.

Lus. Gods a'me! what will you do? why, young master, you are not Castalian mad, lunatic, frantic, desperate, ha!

Ovid. What ailest thou, Luscus?

Lus. God be with you, sir; I'll leave you to your poetical fancies, and furies. I'll not be guilty, I.   [*Exit.*

Ovid. Be not, good ignorance. I'm glad th'art gone;
For thus alone, our ear shall better judge
The hasty errors of our morning muse.

> *Envy, why twit'st thou me my time's spent ill,*
> *And call'st my verse, fruits of an idle quill?*
> *Or that, unlike the line from whence I sprung,*
> *War's dusty honours I pursue not young?*
> *Or that I study not the tedious laws,*
> *And prostitute my voice in every cause?*
> *Thy scope is mortal; mine eternal fame,*
> *Which through the world shall ever chaunt my name.*
> *Homer will live whilst Tenedos stands, and Ide,*
> *Or, to the sea, fleet Simois doth slide:*
> *And so shall Hesiod too, while vines do bear,*
> *Or crooked sickles crop the ripen'd ear.*
> *Callimachus, though in invention low,*
> *Shall still be sung, since he in art doth flow.*
> *No loss shall come to Sophocles' proud vein;*
> *With sun and moon, Aratus shall remain.*
> *While slaves be false, fathers hard, and bawds be whorish*
> *Whilst harlots flatter, shall Menander flourish.*

Ennius, though rude, and Accius's high-rear'd strain,
A fresh applause in every age shall gain,
Of Varro's name, what ear shall not be told,
Of Jason's Argo and the fleece of gold ?
Then shall Lucretius' lofty numbers die,
When earth and seas in fire and flame shall fry.
Tityrus, Tillage, Ænee shall be read,
Whilst Rome of all the conquered world is head !
Till Cupid's fires be out, and his bow broken,
Thy verses, neat Tibullus, shall be spoken.
Our Gallus shall be known from east to west;
So shall Lycoris, whom he now loves best.
The suffering plough-share or the flint may wear;
But heavenly Poesy no death can fear.
Kings shall give place to it, and kingly shows,
The banks o'er which gold-bearing Tagus flows.
Kneel hinds to trash: me let bright Phœbus swell
With cups full flowing from the Muses' well.
Frost-fearing myrtle shall impale my head,
And of sad lovers I be often read.
Envy the living, not the dead, doth bite !
For after death all men receive their right.
Then, when this body falls in funeral fire,
My name shall live, and my best part aspire.

Enter OVID *senior, followed by* LUSCUS, TUCCA, *and* LUPUS.

Ovid se. Your *name shall live*, indeed, sir! you say true: but how infamously, how scorn'd and contemn'd in the eyes and ears of the best and gravest Romans, that you think not on; you never so much as dream of that. Are these the fruits of all my travail and expenses? Is this the scope and aim of thy studies? Are these the hopeful courses, wherewith I have so long flattered my expectation from thee? Verses! Poetry! Ovid, whom I thought to see the pleader, become Ovid the play-maker!

Ovid ju. No, sir.

Ovid se. Yes, sir; I hear of a tragedy of yours coming forth for the common players there, call'd Medea. By my household gods, if I come to the acting of it, I'll add one tragic part more than is yet expected to it: believe me, when I promise it. What! shall I have my son a stager now? an enghle for players? a gull, a rook, a shot-clog, to make suppers, and be laugh'd at? Publius, I will set thee on the funeral pile first.

Ovid ju. Sir, I beseech you to have patience.

Lus. Nay, this 'tis to have your ears damn'd up to good counsel. I did augur all this to him beforehand, without poring into an ox's paunch for the matter, and yet he would not be scrupulous.

Tuc. How now, goodman slave! what, rowly-powly? all rivals, rascal? Why, my master of worship, dost hear? are these thy best projects? is this thy designs and thy discipline, to suffer knaves to be competitors with commanders and gentlemen? Are we parallels, rascal, are we parallels?

Ovid se. Sirrah, go get my horses ready. You'll still be prating.

Tuc. Do, you perpetual stinkard, do, go; talk to tapsters and ostlers, you slave; they are in your element, go; here be the emperor's captains, you raggamuffin rascal, and not your comrades.

[*Exit Luscus.*

Lup. Indeed, Marcus Ovid, these players are an idle generation, and do much harm in a state, corrupt young gentry very much, I know it; I have not been a tribune thus long and observed nothing: besides, they will rob us, us, that are magistrates, of our respect, bring us upon their stages, and make us ridiculous to the plebeians; they will play you or me, the wisest men they can come by still, only to bring us in contempt with the vulgar, and make us cheap.

Tur. Thou art in the right, my venerable cropshin, they will indeed; the tongue of the oracle never twang'd truer. Your courtier cannot kiss his mistress's slippers in quiet for them; nor your white innocent gallant pawn his revelling suit to make his punk a supper. An honest decayed commander cannot skelder, cheat, nor be seen in a bawdy-house, but he shall be straight in one of their wormwood comedies. They are grown licentious, the rogues; libertines, flat libertines. They forget they are in the statute, the rascals; they are blazon'd there; there they are trick'd, they and their pedigrees; they need no other heralds, I wiss.

Ovid se. Methinks, if nothing else, yet this alone, the very reading of the public edicts, should fright thee from commerce with them, and give thee distaste enough of their actions. But this betrays what a student you are, this argues your proficiency in the law!

Ovid ju. They wrong me, sir, and do abuse you more,
That blow your ears with these untrue reports.
I am not known unto the open stage,
Nor do I traffic in their theatres:
Indeed, I do acknowledge, at request
Of some near friends, and honourable Romans,
I have begun a poem of that nature.

Ovid se. You have, sir, a poem! and where is it? That's the law you study.

Ovid ju. Cornelius Gallus borrowed it to read.

Ovid se. Cornelius Gallus! there's another gallant too hath drunk of the same poison, and Tibullus and Propertius. But these are gentlemen of means and revenues now. Thou art a younger brother, and hast nothing but they bare exhibition; which I protest shall be bare indeed, if thou forsake not these unprofitable by-courses, and that timely too. Name me a profest poet, that his poetry did ever afford him so much as a competency. Ay, your god of poets there, whom all of you admire and reverence so much, Homer, he whose worm-eaten statue must not be spewed against, but with hallow'd lips and groveling adoration, what was he? what was he?

Tuc. Marry, I'll tell thee, old swaggerer; he was a poor blind, rhyming rascal, that lived obscurely up and down in booths and tap-houses, and scarce ever made a good meal in his sleep, the whoreson hungry beggar.

Ovid se. He says well:—nay, I know this nettles you now; but answer me, is it not true? You'll tell me his name shall live; and that now being dead his works have eternised him, and made him divine: but could this divinity feed him while he lived? could his name feast him?

Tuc. Or purchase him a senator's revenue, could it?

Ovid se. Ay, or give him place in the commonwealth? worship, or attendants? make him be carried in his litter?

Tuc. Thou speakest sentences, old Bias.

Lup. All this the law will do, young sir, if you'll follow it.

Ovid se. If he be mine, he shall follow and observe what I will apt him to, or I profess here openly and utterly to disclaim him.

Ovid ju. Sir, let me crave you will forego these moods;
I will be any thing, or study any thing;
I'll prove the unfashion'd body of the law
Pure elegance, and make her rugged'st strains
Run smoothly as Propertius' elegies.

Ovid se. Propertius' elegies? good!

Lup. Nay, you take him too quickly, Marcus.

Ovid se. Why, he cannot speak, he cannot think out of poetry; he is bewitch'd with it.

Lup. Come, do not misprise him.

Ovid se. Misprise ! ay, marry, I would have him use some such words now; they have some touch, some taste of the law. He should make himself a style out of these, and let his Propertius' elegies go by.

Lup. Indeed, young Publius, he that will now hit the mark, must shoot through the law; we have no other planet reigns, and in that sphere you may sit and sing with angels. Why, the law makes a man happy, without respecting any other merit; a simple scholar, or none at all, may be a lawyer.

Tuc. He tells thee true, my noble neophyte; my little grammaticaster, he does: it shall never put thee to thy mathematics, metaphysics, philosophy, and I know not what supposed sufficiencies; if thou canst but have the patience to plod enough, talk, and make a noise enough, be impudent enough, and 'tis enough.

Lup. Three books will furnish you.

Tuc. And the less art the better: besides, when it shall be in the power of thy chevril conscience, to do right or wrong at thy pleasure, my pretty Alcibiades.

Lup. Ay, and to have better men than himself, by many thousand degrees, to observe him, and stand bare.

Tuc. True, and he to carry himself proud and stately, and have the law on his side for't, old boy.

Ovid se. Well, the day grows old, gentlemen, and I must leave you. Publius, if thou wilt hold my favour, abandon these idle, fruitless studies, that so bewitch thee. Send Janus home his back face again, and look only forward to the law: intend that. I will allow thee what shall suit thee in the rank of gentlemen, and maintain thy society with the best; and under these conditions I leave thee. My blessings light upon thee, if thou respect them; if not, mine eyes may drop for thee, but thine own heart will ache for itself; and so farewell! What, are my horses come?

Lus. Yes, sir, they are at the gate without.

Ovid se. That's well.—Asinius Lupus, a word. Captain, I shall take my leave of you?

Tuc. No, my little old boy, dispatch with Cothurnus there: I'll attend thee, I—

Lus. To borrow some ten drachms: I know his project. [*Aside.*

Ovid se. Sir, you shall make me beholding to you. Now, captain Tucca, what say you?

Tuc. Why, what should I say, or what can I say, my flower o' the order? Should I say thou art rich, or that thou art honourable, or wise, or valiant, or learned, or liberal? why, thou art all these, and thou knowest it, my noble Lucullus, thou knowest it. Come, be not ashamed of thy virtues, old stump: honour's a good brooch to wear in a man's hat at all times. Thou art the man of war's Mecænas, old boy. Why shouldst not thou be graced then by them, as well as he is by his poets?—

Enter PYRGUS *and whispers* TUCCA.

How now, my carrier, what news?

Lus. The boy has stayed within for his cue this half-hour. [*Aside.*

Tuc. Come, do not whisper to me, but speak it out: what; it is no treason against the state I hope, is it?

Lus. Yes, against the state of my master's purse. [*Aside, and exit.*

Pyr. [*aloud.*] Sir, Agrippa desires you to forbear him till the next week; his mules are not yet come up.

Tuc. His mules! now the bots, the spavin, and the glanders, and some dozen diseases more, light on him and his mules! What, have they the yellows, his mules, that they come no faster? or are they foundered, ha? his mules have the staggers belike, have they?

Pyr. O no, sir;—then your tongue might be suspected for one of his mules. [*Aside.*

Tuc. He owes me almost a talent, and he thinks to bear it away with his mules, does he? Sirrah, you nut-cracker, go your ways to him again, and tell him I must have money, I: I cannot eat stones and turfs, say. What, will he clem me and my followers? ask him an he will clem me; do, go. He would have me fry my jerkin, would he? Away, setter, away. Yet, stay, my little tumbler, this old boy shall supply now. I will not trouble him, I cannot be importunate, I; I cannot be impudent.

Pyr. Alas, sir, no; you are the most maidenly blushing creature upon the earth. [*Aside.*

Tuc. Dost thou hear, my little six and fifty, or thereabouts? thou art not to learn the humours and tricks of that old bald cheater, Time; thou hast not this chain for nothing. Men of worth have their chimeras, as well as other creatures; and they do see monsters sometimes, they do, they do, brave boy.

Pyr. Better cheap than he shall see you, I warrant him. [*Aside.*

Tuc. Thou must let me have six—six drachms, I mean, old boy: thou shalt do it; I tell thee, old boy, thou shalt, and in private too, dost thou see?—Go, walk off: [*to the* Boy]—There, there. Six is the sum. Thy son's a gallant spark and must not be put out of a sudden. Come hither, Callimachus; thy father tells me thou art too poetical, boy: thou must not be so; thou must leave them, young novice, thou must; they are a sort of poor starved rascals, that are ever wrapt up in foul linen; and can boast of nothing but a lean visage, peering out of a seam-rent suit, the very emblems of beggary. No, dost hear, turn lawyer, thou shalt be my solicitor.— 'Tis right, old boy, is't?

Ovid se. You were best tell it, captain.

Tuc. No; fare thou well, mine honest horseman; and thou, old beaver. [*To Lupus*]—Pray thee, Roman, when thou comest to town, see me at my lodging, visit me sometimes? thou shalt be welcome, old boy. Do not balk me, good swaggerer. Jove keep thy chain from pawning; go thy ways, if thou lack money I'll lend thee some; I'll leave thee to thy horse now. Adieu.

Ovid se. Farewell, good captain.

Tuc. Boy, you can have but half a share now, boy.

[*Exit, followed by Pyrgus.*

Ovid se. 'Tis a strange boldness that accompanies this fellow.— Come.

Ovid ju. I'll give attendance on you to your horse, sir, please you.

Ovid se. No; keep your chamber, and fall to your studies; do so: The gods of Rome bless thee! [*Exit with Lupus.*

Ovid ju. And give me stomach to digest this law:
That should have follow'd sure, had I been he.
O, sacred Poesy, thou spirit of arts,
The soul of science, and the queen of souls;
What profane violence, almost sacrilege,
Hath here been offered thy divinities!
That thine own guiltless poverty should arm
Prodigious ignorance to wound thee thus!
For thence is all their force of argument
Drawn forth against thee; or, from the abuse
Of thy great powers in adulterate brains:
When, would men learn but to distinguish spirits
And set true difference 'twixt those jaded wits
That run a broken pace for common hire,
And the high raptures of a happy muse,
Borne on the wings of her immortal thought,
That kicks at earth with a disdainful heel,

And beats at heaven gates with her bright hoofs;
They would not then, with such distorted faces,
And desperate censures, stab at Poesy.
They would admire bright knowledge, and their minds
Should ne'er descend on so unworthy objects
As gold, or titles; they would dread far more
To be thought ignorant, than be known poor.
The time was once, when wit drown'd wealth; but now,
Your only barbarism is t'have wit, and want.
No matter now in virtue who excels,
He that hath coin, hath all perfection else.

    Tib. [*within.*] Ovid!
    Ovid. Who's there? Come in.

Enter TIBULLUS.

    Tib. Good morrow, lawyer.
    Ovid. Good morrow, dear Tibullus; welcome: sit down.
    Tib. Not I. What, so hard at it? Let's see, what's here?
Numa in decimo nono ! Nay, I will see it—
    Ovid. Prithee away—
    Tib. *If thrice in field a man vanquish his foe,*
    'Tis after in his choice to serve or no.
How, now, Ovid! Law cases in verse?
    Ovid. In truth, I know not; they run from my pen unwittingly
if they be verse. What's the news abroad?
    Tib. Off with this gown; I come to have thee walk.
    Ovid. No, good Tibullus, I'm not now in case.
Pray let me alone.
    Tib. How! not in case?
Slight, thou'rt in too much case, by all this law.
    Ovid. Troth, if I live, I will new dress the law
In sprightly Poesy's habiliments.
    Tib. The hell thou wilt! What! turn law into verse?
Thy father has school'd thee, I see. Here, read that same;
There's subject for you; and, if I mistake not,
A *supersedeas* to your melancholy.
    Ovid. How! subscribed *Julia !* O my life, my heaven!
    Tib. Is the mood changed?
    Ovid. Music of wit! note for th' harmonious spheres!
Celestial accents, how you ravish me!
    Tib. What is it, Ovid?
    Ovid. That I must meet my Julia, the princess Julia.
    Tib. Where?
    Ovid. Why, at ——
Heart, I've forgot; my passion so transports me.
    Tib. I'll save your pains: it is at Albius' house,
The jeweller's, where the fair Lycoris lies.
    Ovid. Who? Cytheris, Cornelius Gallus' love?
    Tib. Ay, he'll be there too, and my Plautia.

Ovid. And why not your Delia?

Tib. Yes, and your Corinna.

Ovid. True; but, my sweet Tibullus, keep that secret?
I would not, for all Rome, it should be thought
I veil bright Julia underneath that name:
Julia, the gem and jewel of my soul,
That takes her honours from the golden sky,
As beauty doth all lustre from her eye.
The air respires the pure Elysian sweets
In which she breathes, and from her looks descend
The glories of the summer.   Heaven she is,
Praised in herself above all praise; and he
Which hears her speak, would swear the tuneful orbs
Turn'd in his zenith only.

Tib. Publius, thou'lt lose thyself.

Ovid. O, in no labyrinth can I safelier err,
Than when I lose myself in praising her.
Hence, law, and welcome Muses, though not rich,
Yet are you pleasing: let's be reconciled,
And new made one.   Henceforth, I promise faith
And all my serious hours to spend with you;
With you, whose music striketh on my heart,
And with bewitching tones steals forth my spirit,
In Julia's name; fair Julia: Julia's love
Shall be a law, and that sweet law I'll study,
The law and art of sacred Julia's love:
All other objects will but abjects prove.

Tib. Come, we shall have thee as passionate as Propertius, anon.

Ovid. O, how does my Sextus?

Tib. Faith, full of sorrow for his Cynthia's death.

Ovid. What, still?

Tib. Still, and still more, his griefs do grow upon him
As do his hours.   Never did I know
An understanding spirit so take to heart
The common work of Fate.

Ovid. O, my Tibullus,
Let us not blame him; for against such chances
The heartiest strife of virtue is not proof.
We may read constancy and fortitude
To other souls; but had ourselves been struck
With the like planet, had our loves, like his,
Been ravish'd from us by injurious death,
And in the height and heat of our best days,
It would have crack'd our sinews, shrunk our veins,
And made our very heart-strings jar, like his.
Come, let's go take him forth, and prove if mirth
Or company will but abate his passion.

Tib. Content, and I implore the gods it may.   [*Exeunt.*

ACT II

SCENE I.—*A Room in* ALBIUS's *House.*

Enter ALBIUS *and* CRISPINUS.

Alb. Master Crispinus, you are welcome: pray use a stool, sir. Your cousin Cytheris will come down presently. We are so busy for the receiving of these courtiers here, that I can scarce be a minute with myself, for thinking of them: Pray you sit, sir; pray you sit, sir.

Crisp. I am very well, sir. Never trust me, but your are most delicately seated here, full of sweet delight and blandishment! an excellent air, an excellent air!

Alb. Ay, sir, 'tis a pretty air. These courtiers run in my mind still; I must look out. For Jupiter's sake, sit, sir; or please you walk into the garden? There's a garden on the back-side.

Crisp. I am most strenuously well, I thank you, sir.

Alb. Much good do you, sir.

Enter CHLOE, *with two* Maids.

Chloe. Come, bring those perfumes forward a little, and strew some roses and violets here: Fie! here be rooms savour the most pitifully rank that ever I felt. I cry the gods mercy, [*sees Albius.*] my husband's in the wind of us!

Alb. Why, this is good, excellent, excellent! well said, my sweet Chloe; trim up your house most obsequiously.

Chloe. For Vulcan's sake, breathe somewhere else; in troth you overcome our perfumes exceedingly; you are too predominant.

Alb. Hear but my opinion, sweet wife.

Chloe. A pin for your pinion! In sincerity, if you be thus fulsome to me in every thing, I'll be divorced. Gods my body! you know what you were before I married you; I was a gentlewoman born, I; I lost all my friends to be a citizen's wife, because I heard, indeed, they kept their wives as fine as ladies; and that we might rule our husbands like ladies, and do what we listed; do you think I would have married you else?

Alb. I acknowledge, sweet wife:—she speaks the best of any woman in Italy, and moves as mightily; which makes me, I had rather she should make bumps on my head, as big as my two fingers, than I would offend her.—But, sweet wife—

Chloe. Yet again! Is it not grace enough for you, that I call you husband, and you call me wife; but you must still be poking me, against my will, to things?

Alb. But you know, wife, here are the greatest ladies, and gallantest gentlemen of Rome, to be entertained in our house now; and I would fain advise thee to entertain them in the best sort, i'faith, wife.

Chloe. In sincerity, did you ever hear a man talk so idly? You would seem to be master! you would have your spoke in my cart! you would advise me to entertain ladies and gentlemen! Because you can marshal your pack-needles, horse-combs, hobby-horses, and wall-candlesticks in your warehouse better than I, therefore you can tell how to entertain ladies and gentlefolks better than I?

Alb. O, my sweet wife, upbraid me not with that; gain savours sweetly from any thing; he that respects to get, must relish all commodities alike, and admit no difference between oade and frankincense, or the most precious balsamum and a tar-barrel.

Chloe. Marry, foh! you sell snuffers too, if you be remember'd; but I pray you let me buy them out of your hand; for, I tell you true, I take it highly in snuff, to learn how to entertain gentlefolks of you, at these years, i'faith. Alas, man, there was not a gentleman came to your house in your t'other wife's time, I hope! nor a lady, nor music, nor masques! Nor you nor your house were so much as spoken of, before I disbased myself, from my hood and my farthingal, to these bum-rowls and your whale-bone bodice.

Alb. Look here, my sweet wife; I am mum, my dear mummia, my balsamum, my spermaceti, and my very city of—— She has the most best, true, feminine wit in Rome!

Cris. I have heard so, sir; and do most vehemently desire to participate the knowledge of her fair features.

Alb. Ah, peace; you shall hear more anon: be not seen yet, I pray you; not yet: observe.   [*Exit.*

Chloe. 'Sbody! give husbands the head a little more, and they'll be nothing but head shortly: What's he there?

1 Maid. I know not, forsooth.

2 Maid. Who would you speak with, sir?

Cris. I would speak with my cousin Cytheris.

2 Maid. He is one, forsooth, would speak with his cousin Cytheris.

Chloe. Is she your cousin, sir?

Cris. [*coming forward.*] Yes, in truth, forsooth, for fault of a better.

Chloe. She is a gentlewoman.

Cris. Or else she should not be my cousin, I assure you.

Chloe. Are you a gentleman born?

Cris. That I am, lady; you shall see mine arms, if it please you.

Chloe. No, your legs do sufficiently shew you are a gentleman born, sir; for a man borne upon little legs, is always a gentleman born.

Cris. Yet, I pray you, vouchsafe the sight of my arms, mistress; for I bear them about me, to have them seen: My name is *Crispinus*, or *Crispinas* indeed; which is well expressed in my arms; a face crying *in chief;* and beneath it a bloody toe, between three thorns *pungent.*

Chloe. Then you are welcome, sir: now you are a gentleman born, I can find in my heart to welcome you; for I am a gentlewoman born too, and will bear my head high enough, though 'twere my fortune to marry a tradesman.

Cris. No doubt of that, sweet feature; your carriage shews it in any man's eye, that is carried upon you with judgment.

Re-enter ALBIUS.

Alb. Dear wife, be not angry.

Chloe. Gods my passion!

Alb. Hear me but one thing; let not your maids set cushions in the parlour windows, nor in the dining-chamber windows; nor upon stools, in either of them, in any case; for 'tis tavern-like: but lay them one upon another, in some out-room or corner of the dining-chamber.

Chloe. Go, go; meddle with your bed-chamber only; or rather with your bed in your chamber only; or rather with your wife in your bed only; or on my faith I'll not be pleased with you only.

Alb. Look here, my dear wife, entertain that gentleman kindly, I prithee——mum. [*Exit.*

Chloe. Go, I need your instructions indeed! anger me no more, I advise you. Citi-sin, quotha! she's a wise gentlewoman, i'faith, will marry herself to the sin of the city.

Alb. [*re-entering.*] But this time, and no more, by heav'n, wife: hang no pictures in the hall, nor in the dining-chamber, in any case, but in the gallery only; for 'tis not courtly else, o' my word, wife.

Chloe. 'Sprecious, never have done!

Alb. Wife— [*Exit.*

Chloe. Do I not bear a reasonable corrigible hand over him, Crispinus?

Cris. By this hand, lady, you hold a most sweet hand over him.

Alb. [*re-entering.*] And then, for the great gilt andirons—

Chloe. Again! Would the andirons were in your great guts for me!

Alb. I do vanish, wife. [*Exit.*

Chloe. How shall I do, master Crispinus? here will be all the bravest ladies in court presently to see your cousin Cytheris: O the gods! how might I behave myself now, as to entertain them most courtly?

Cris. Marry, lady, if you will entertain them most courtly, you must do thus: as soon as ever your maid or your man brings you word they are come, you must say, *A pox on 'em! what do they here?* And yet, when they come, speak them as fair, and give them the kindest welcome in words that can be.

Chloe. Is that the fashion of courtiers, Crispinus?

Cris. I assure you it is, lady; I have observed it.

Chloe. For your pox, sir, it is easily hit on; but it is not so easy to speak fair after, methinks.

Alb. [*re-entering.*] O, wife, the coaches are come, on my word; a number of coaches and courtiers.

Chloe. *A pox on them! what do they here?*

Alb. How now, wife! would'st thou not have them come?

Chloe. Come! come, you are a fool, you.—He knows not the

trick on't. Call Cytheris, I pray you: and, good master Crispinus, you can observe, you say; let me entreat you for all the ladies' behaviours, jewels, jests, and attires, that you marking, as well as I, we may put both our marks together, when they are gone, and confer of them.

Cris. I warrant you, sweet lady; let me alone to observe till I turn myself to nothing but observation.—

Enter CYTHERIS.

Good morrow, cousin Cytheris.

Cyth. Welcome, kind cousin. What! are they come?

Alb. Ay, your friend Cornelius Gallus, Ovid, Tibullus, Propertius, with Julia, the emperor's daughter, and the lady Plautia, are 'lighted at the door; and with them Hermogenes Tigellius, the excellent musician.

Cyth. Come, let us go meet them, Chloe.

Chloe. Observe, Crispinus.

Crisp. At a hair's breadth, lady, I warrant you.

As they are going out, enter CORNELIUS GALLUS, OVID, TIBULLUS, PROPERTIUS, HERMOGENES, JULIA, *and* PLAUTIA.

Gal. Health to the lovely Chloe! you must pardon me, mistress, that I prefer this fair gentlewoman.

Cyth. I pardon and praise you for it, sir; and I beseech your excellence, receive her beauties into your knowledge and favour.

Jul. Cytheris, she hath favour and behaviour, that commands as much of me: and, sweet Chloe, know I do exceedingly love you, and that I will approve in any grace my father the emperor may shew you. Is this your husband?

Alb. For fault of a better, if it please your highness.

Chloe. Gods my life, how he shames me!

Cyth. Not a whit, Chloe, they all think you politic and witty; wise women choose not husbands for the eye, merit, or birth, but wealth and sovereignty.

Ovid. Sir, we all come to gratulate, for the good report of you.

Tib. And would be glad to deserve your love, sir.

Alb. My wife will answer you all, gentlemen; I'll come to you again presently.   [*Exit.*

Plau. You have chosen you a most fair companion here, Cytheris, and a very fair house.

Cyth. To both which, you and all my friends are very welcome, Plautia.

Chloe. With all my heart, I assure your ladyship.

Plau. Thanks, sweet mistress Chloe.

Jul. You must needs come to court, lady, i'faith, and there be sure your welcome shall be as great to us.

Ovid. She will deserve it, madam; I see, even in her looks, gentry, and general worthiness.

Tib. I have not seen a more certain character of an excellent disposition.

Alb. [*re-entering.*] Wife!

Chloe. O, they do so commend me here, the courtiers! what's the matter now?

Alb. For the banquet, sweet wife.

Chloe. Yes; and I must needs come to court, and be welcome, the princess says.   [*Exit with Albius.*

Gal. Ovid and Tibullus, you may be bold to welcome your mistress here.

Ovid. We find it so, sir.

Tib. And thank Cornelius Gallus.

Ovid. Nay, my sweet Sextus, in faith thou art not sociable.

Prop. In faith I am not, Publius; nor I cannot.
Sick minds are like sick men that burn with fevers,
Who when they drink, please but a present taste,
And after bear a more impatient fit.
Pray let me leave you; I offend you all,
And myself most.

Gal. Stay, sweet Propertius.

Tib. You yield too much unto your griefs and fate,
Which never hurts, but when we say it hurts us.

Prop. O peace, Tibullus; your philosophy
Lends you too rough a hand to search my wounds.
Speak they of griefs, that know to sigh and grieve:
The free and unconstrained spirit feels
No weight of my oppression.   [*Exit.*

Ovid. Worthy Roman!
Methinks I taste his misery, and could
Sit down, and chide at his malignant stars.

Jul. Methinks I love him, that he loves so truly.

Cyth. This is the perfect'st love, lives after death.

Gal. Such is the constant ground of virtue still.

Plau. It puts on an inseparable face.

Re-enter CHLOE.

Chloe. Have you mark'd every thing, Crispinus?

Cris. Every thing, I warrant you.

Chloe. What gentlemen are these? do you know them?

Cris. Ay, they are poets, lady.

Chloe. Poets! they did not talk of me since I went, did they?

Cris. O yes, and extolled your perfections to the heavens.

Chloe. Now in sincerity they be the finest kind of men that ever I knew: Poets! Could not one get the emperor to make my husband a poet, think you?

Cris. No, lady, 'tis love and beauty make poets: and since you like poets so well, your love and beauties shall make me a poet.

Chloe. What! shall they? and such a one as these?

Cris. Ay, and a better than these: I would be sorry else.

Chloe. And shall your looks change, and your hair change, and all, like these?

Cris. Why, a man may be a poet, and yet not change his hair, lady.

Chloe. Well, we shall see your cunning: yet, if you can change your hair, I pray do.

Re-enter ALBIUS.

Alb. Ladies, and lordlings, there's a slight banquet stays within for you; please you draw near, and accost it.

Jul. We thank you, good Albius: but when shall we see those excellent jewels you are commended to have?

Alb. At your ladyship's service.—I got that speech by seeing a play last day, and it did me some grace now: I see, 'tis good to collect sometimes; I'll frequent these plays more than I have done, now I come to be familiar with courtiers. [*Aside.*

Gal. Why, how now, Hermogenes? what ailest thou, trow?

Her. A little melancholy; let me alone, prithee.

Gal. Melancholy! how so?

Her. With riding: a plague on all coaches for me!

Chloe. Is that hard-favour'd gentleman a poet too, Cytheris?

Cyth. No, this is Hermogenes: as humorous as a poet, though: he is a musician.

Chloe. A musician! then he can sing.

Cyth. That he can, excellently; did you never hear him?

Chloe. O no: will he be entreated, think you?

Cyth. I know not.—Friend, mistress Chloe would fain hear Hermogenes sing: are you interested in him?

Gal. No doubt, his own humanity will command him so far, to the satisfaction of so fair a beauty; but rather than fail, we'll all be suitors to him.

Her. 'Cannot sing.

Gal. Prithee, Hermogenes.

Her. 'Cannot sing.

Gal. For honour of this gentlewoman, to whose house I know thou mayest be ever welcome.

Chloe. That he shall, in truth, sir, if he can sing.

Ovid. What's that?

Gal. This gentlewoman is wooing Hermogenes for a song.

Ovid. A song! come, he shall not deny her. Hermogenes!

Her. 'Cannot sing.

Gal. No, the ladies must do it; he stays but to have their thanks acknowledged as a debt to his cunning.

Jul. That shall not want; ourself will be the first shall promise to pay him more than thanks, upon a favour so worthily vouchsafed.

Her. Thank you, madam; but 'will not sing.

Tib. Tut, the only way to win him, is to abstain from entreating him.

Cris. Do you love singing, lady?

Chloe. O, passingly.

Cris. Entreat the ladies to entreat me to sing then, I beseech you.

Chloe. I beseech your grace, entreat this gentleman to sing.

Jul. That we will, Chloe; can he sing excellently?

Chloe. I think so, madam; for he entreated me to entreat you to entreat him to sing.

Cris. Heaven and earth! would you tell that?

Jul. Good, sir, let's entreat you to use your voice.

Cris. Alas, madam, I cannot, in truth.

Pla. The gentleman is modest: I warrant you he sings excellently.

Ovid. Hermogenes, clear your throat: I see by him, here's a gentleman will worthily challenge you.

Cris. Not I, sir, I'll challenge no man.

Tib. That's your modesty, sir; but we, out of an assurance of your excellency, challenge him in your behalf.

Cris. I thank you, gentlemen, I'll do my best.

Her. Let that best be good, sir, you were best.

Gal. O, this contention is excellent! What is't you sing, sir?

Cris. *If I freely may discover,* sir; I'll sing that.

Ovid. One of your own compositions, Hermogenes. He offers you vantage enough.

Cris. Nay, truly, gentlemen, I'll challenge no man.—I can sing but one staff of the ditty neither.

Gal. The better: Hermogenes himself will be entreated to sing the other.

CRISPINUS *sings.*

> If I freely may discover
> What would please me in my lover,
> I would have her fair and witty,
> Savouring more of court than city;
> A little proud, but full of pity:
> Light and humorous in her toying,
> Oft building hopes, and soon destroying,
> Long, but sweet in the enjoying;
> Neither too easy nor too hard:
> All extremes I would have barr'd.

Gal. Believe me, sir, you sing most excellently.

Ovid. If there were a praise above excellence, the gentleman highly deserves it.

Her. Sir, all this doth not yet make me envy you; for I know I sing better than you.

Tib. Attend Hermogenes, now.

HERMOGENES, *accompanied.*

> She should be allow'd her passions,
> So they were but used as fashions;
> Sometimes froward, and then frowning,
> Sometimes sickish and then swowning,

Every fit with change still crowning.
Purely jealous I would have her,
Then only constant when I crave her:
'Tis a virtue should not save her.
Thus, nor her delicates would cloy me,
Neither her peevishness annoy me.

Jul. Nay, Hermogenes, your merit hath long since been both known and admired of us.

Her. You shall hear me sing another. Now will I begin.

Gal. We shall do this gentleman's banquet too much wrong, that stays for us, ladies.

Jul. 'Tis true; and well thought on, Cornelius Gallus.

Her. Why, 'tis but a short air, 'twill be done presently, pray stay: strike, music.

Ovid. No, good Hermogenes; we'll end this difference within.

Jul. 'Tis the common disease of all your musicians, that they know no mean, to be entreated either to begin or end.

Alb. Please you lead the way, gentles.

All. Thanks, good Albius.   *[Exeunt all but Albius.*

Alb. O, what a charm of thanks was here put upon me! O Jove, what a setting forth it is to a man to have many courtiers come to his house! Sweetly was it said of a good old housekeeper, *I had rather want meat, than want guests ;* especially, if they be courtly guests. For, never trust me, if one of their good legs made in a house be not worth all the good cheer a man can make them. He that would have fine guests, let him have a fine wife! he that would have a fine wife, let him come to me.

Re-enter CRISPINUS.

Cris. By your kind leave, master Albius.

Alb. What, you are not gone, master Crispinus?

Cris. Yes, faith, I have a design draws me hence: pray, sir, fashion me an excuse to the ladies.

Alb. Will you not stay and see the jewels, sir? I pray you stay.

Cris. Not for a million, sir, now. Let it suffice, I must relinquish; and so, in a word, please you to expiate this compliment.

Alb. Mum.   *[Exit.*

Cris. I'll presently go and enghle some broker for a poet's gown, and bespeak a garland: and then, jeweller, look to your best jewel, i'faith.   *[Exit.*

ACT III

SCENE I.—*The Via Sacra (or Holy Street).*

Enter HORACE, CRISPINUS *following.*

Hor. Umph! yes, I will begin an ode so; and it shall be to Mecænas.

Cris. 'Slid, yonder's Horace! they say he's an excellent poet: Mecænas loves him. I'll fall into his acquaintance, if I can; I think he be composing as he goes in the street! ha! 'tis a good humour, if he be: I'll compose too.

Hor.   *Swell me a bowl with lusty wine,*
       Till I may see the plump Lyæus swim
                Above the brim:
    I drink as I would write,
      In flowing measure fill'd with flame and sprite.

Cris. Sweet Horace, Minerva and the Muses stand auspicious to thy designs! How farest thou, sweet man? frolic? rich? gallant? ha!

Hor. Not greatly gallant, sir; like my fortunes, well: I am bold to take my leave, sir; you'll nought else, sir, would you?

Cris. Troth, no, but I could wish thou didst know us, Horace; we are a scholar, I assure thee.

Hor. A scholar, sir! I shall be covetous of your fair knowledge.

Cris. Gramercy, good Horace. Nay, we are new turn'd poet too, which is more; and a satirist too, which is more than that: I write just in thy vein, I. I am for your odes, or your sermons, or any thing indeed; we are a gentleman besides: our name is Rufus Laberius Crispinus; we are a pretty Stoic too.

Hor. To the proportion of your beard, I think it, sir.

Cris. By Phœbus, here's a most neat, fine street, is't not? I protest to thee, I am enamoured of this street now, more than of half the streets of Rome again; 'tis so polite and terse! there's the front of a building now! I study architecture too: if ever I should build, I'd have a house just of that prospective.

Hor. Doubtless, this gallant's tongue has a good turn, when he sleeps.   [*Aside.*

Cris. I do make verses, when I come in such a street as this: O, your city ladies, you shall have them sit in every shop like the Muses—offering you the Castalian dews, and the Thespian liquors, to as many as have but the sweet grace and audacity to——sip of their lips. Did you never hear any of my verses?

Hor. No, sir;—but I am in some fear I must now.   [*Aside.*

Cris. I'll tell thee some, if I can but recover them, I composed even now of a dressing I saw a jeweller's wife wear, who indeed was a jewel herself: I prefer that kind of tire now; what's thy opinion, Horace?

Hor. With your silver bodkin, it does well, sir.

Cris. I cannot tell; but it stirs me more than all your court-curls,

or your spangles, or your tricks: I affect not these high gable-ends,
these Tuscan tops, nor your coronets, nor your arches, nor your
pyramids; give me a fine, sweet—little delicate dressing with a
bodkin, as you say; and a mushroom for all your other ornatures!

Hor. Is it not possible to make an escape from him?   *[Aside.*

Cris. I have remitted my verses all this while; I think I have
forgot them.

Hor. Here's he could wish you had else.   *[Aside.*

Cris. Pray Jove I can entreat them of my memory!

Hor. You put your memory to too much trouble, sir.

Cris. No, sweet Horace, we must not have thee think so.

Hor. I cry you mercy; then they are my ears
That must be tortured: well, you must have patience, ears.

Cris. Pray thee, Horace, observe.

Hor. Yes, sir; your satin sleeve begins to fret at the rug that is
underneath it, I do observe: and your ample velvet bases are not
without evident stains of a hot disposition naturally.

Cris. O—I'll dye them into another colour, at pleasure: How
many yards of velvet dost thou think they contain?

Hor. 'Heart! I have put him now in a fresh way
To vex me more:—faith, sir, your mercer's book
Will tell you with more patience than I can:—
For I am crost, and so's not that, I think.

Cris. 'Slight, these verses have lost me again!
I shall not invite them to mind, now.

Hor. Rack not your thoughts, good sir; rather defer it
To a new time; I'll meet you at your lodging,
Or where you please: 'till then, Jove keep you, sir!

Cris. Nay, gentle Horace, stay; I have it now.

Hor. Yes, sir. Apollo, Hermes, Jupiter,
Look down upon me.   *[Aside.*

   Cris. Rich was thy hap, sweet dainty cap,
       There to be placed;
Where thy smooth black, sleek white may smack,
       And both be graced.

White is there usurp'd for her brow; her forehead: and then sleek,
as the parallel to smooth, that went before. A kind of paranomasie,
or agnomination: do you conceive, sir?

Hor. Excellent. Troth, sir, I must be abrupt, and leave you.

Cris. Why, what haste hast thou? prithee, stay a little; thou
shalt not go yet, by Phœbus.

Hor. I shall not! what remedy? fie, how I sweat with suffering!

Cris. And then—

Hor. Pray, sir, give me leave to wipe my face a little.

Cris. Yes, do, good Horace.

Hor. Thank you, sir.
Death! I must crave his leave to p— anon;
Or that I may go hence with half my teeth:
I am in some such fear. This tyranny

Is strange, to take mine ears up by commission,
(Whether I will or no,) and make them stalls
To his lewd solecisms, and worded trash.
Happy thou, bold Bolanus, now I say;
Whose freedom, and impatience of this fellow,
Would, long ere this, have call'd him fool, and fool,
And rank and tedious fool! and have flung jests
As hard as stones, till thou hadst pelted him
Out of the place; whilst my tame modesty
Suffers my wit be made a solemn ass,
To bear his fopperies—   [*Aside.*

  Cris. Horace, thou art miserably affected to be gone, I see. But
—prithee let's prove to enjoy thee a while. Thou hast no business,
I assure me. Whither is thy journey directed, ha?

  Hor. Sir, I am going to visit a friend that's sick.

  Cris A friend! what is he; do not I know him?

  Hor. No, sir, you do not know him; and 'tis not the worse for him.

  Cris. What's his name? where is he lodged?

  Hor. Where I shall be fearful to draw you out of your way, sir;
a great way hence; pray, sir, let's part.

  Cris. Nay, but where is't? I prithee say.

  Hor. On the far side of all Tyber yonder, by Cæsar's gardens.

  Cris. O, that's my course directly; I am for you. Come, go;
why stand'st thou?

  Hor. Yes, sir: marry, the plague is in that part of the city; I
had almost forgot to tell you, sir.

  Cris. Foh! it is no matter, I fear no pestilence; I have not
offended Phœbus.

  Hor. I have, it seems, or else this heavy scourge
Could ne'er have lighted on me.

  Cris. Come along.

  Hor. I am to go down some half mile this way, sir, first, to speak
with his physician; and from thence to his apothecary, where I
shall stay the mixing of divers drugs.

  Cris. Why, it's all one, I have nothing to do, and I love not to
be idle; I'll bear thee company. How call'st thou the apothecary?

  Hor. O that I knew a name would fright him now!—
Sir, Rhadamanthus, Rhadamanthus, sir.
There's one so called, is a just judge in hell,
And doth inflict strange vengeance on all those
That here on earth torment poor patient spirits.

  Cris. He dwells at the Three Furies, by Janus's temple.

  Hor. Your pothecary does, sir.

  Cris. Heart, I owe him money for sweetmeats, and he has laid
to arrest me, I hear: but—

  Hor. Sir, I have made a most solemn vow, I will never bail any
man.

  Cris. Well then, I'll swear, and speak him fair, if the worst come.
But his name is Minos, not Rhadamanthus, Horace.

Hor. That may be, sir, I but guess'd at his name by his sign. But your Minos is a judge too, sir.

Cris. I protest to thee, Horace, (do but taste me once,) if I do know myself, and mine own virtues truly, thou wilt not make that esteem of Varius, or Virgil, or Tibullus, or any of 'em indeed, as now in thy ignorance thou dost; which I am content to forgive: I would fain see which of these could pen more verses in a day, or with more facility, than I; or that could court his mistress, kiss her hand, make better sport with her fan or her dog—

Hor. I cannot bail you yet, sir.

Cris. Or that could move his body more gracefully, or dance better; you should see me, were it not in the street—

Hor. Nor yet.

Cris. Why, I have been a reveller, and at my cloth of silver suit and my long stocking, in my time, and will be again—

Hor. If you may be trusted, sir.

Cris. And then, for my singing, Hermogenes himself envies me, that is your only master of music you have in Rome.

Hor. Is your mother living, sir?

Cris. Au! convert thy thoughts to somewhat else, I pray thee.

Hor. You have much of the mother in you, sir:
Your father is dead?

Cris. Ay, I thank Jove, and my grandfather too, and all my kinsfolks, and well composed in their urns.

Hor. The more their happiness, that rest in peace,
Free from the abundant torture of thy tongue:
Would I were with them too!

Cris. What's that, Horace?

Hor. I now remember me, sir, of a sad fate
A cunning woman, one Sabella, sung,
When in her urn she cast my destiny,
I being but a child.

Cris. What was it, I pray thee?

Hor. She told me I should surely never perish
By famine, poison, or the enemy's sword;
The hectic fever, cough, or pleurisy,
Should never hurt me, nor the tardy gout:
But in my time, I should be once surprised
By a strong tedious talker, that should vex
And almost bring me to consumption:
Therefore, if I were wise, she warn'd me shun
All such long-winded monsters as my bane;
For if I could but 'scape that one discourser,
I might no doubt prove an old aged man.—
By your leave, sir. *[Going.*

Cris. Tut, tut; abandon this idle humour, 'tis nothing but melancholy. 'Fore Jove, now I think on't, I am to appear in court here, to answer to one that has me in suit: sweet Horace, go with me, this is my hour; if I neglect it, the law proceeds against me.

Thou art familiar with these things; prithee, if thou lov'st me, go.

Hor. Now, let me die, sir, if I know your laws,
Or have the power to stand still half so long
In their loud courts, as while a case is argued.
Besides, you know, sir, where I am to go.
And the necessity—

Cris. 'Tis true.

Hor. I hope the hour of my release be come: he will, upon this consideration, discharge me, sure.

Cris. Troth, I am doubtful what I may best do, whether to leave thee or my affairs, Horace.

Hor. O Jupiter! me, sir, me, by any means; I beseech you, me, sir.

Cris. No, faith, I'll venture those now; thou shalt see I love thee—come, Horace.

Hor. Nay, then I am desperate: I follow you, sir. 'Tis hard contending with a man that overcomes thus.

Cris. And how deals Mecænas with thee? liberally, ha? is he open handed? bountiful?

Hor. He's still himself, sir.

Cris. Troth, Horace, thou art exceeding happy in thy friends and acquaintance; they are all most choice spirits, and of the first rank of Romans: I do not know that poet, I protest, has used his fortune more prosperously than thou hast. If thou wouldst bring me known to Mecænas, I should second thy desert well; thou shouldst find a good sure assistant of me, one that would speak all good of thee in thy absence, and be content with the next place, not envying thy reputation with thy patron. Let me not live, but I think thou and I, in a small time, should lift them all out of favour, both Virgil, Varius, and the best of them, and enjoy him wholly to ourselves.

Hor. Gods, you do know it, I can hold no longer;
This brize has prick'd my patience. Sir, your silkness
Clearly mistakes Mecænas and his house,
To think there breathes a spirit beneath his roof,
Subject unto those poor affections
Of undermining envy and detraction,
Moods only proper to base grovelling minds.
That place is not in Rome, I dare affirm,
More pure or free from such low common evils.
There's no man griev'd, that this is thought more rich,
Or this more learned; each man hath his place,
And to his merit his reward of grace,
Which, with a mutual love, they all embrace.

Cris. You report a wonder: 'tis scarce credible, this.

Hor. I am no torturer to enforce you to believe it; but it is so.

Cris. Why, this inflames me with a more ardent desire to be his, than before; but I doubt I shall find the entrance to his familiarity somewhat more than difficult, Horace.

Hor. Tut, you'll conquer him, as you have done me; there's no standing out against you, sir, I see that: either your importunity, or the intimation of your good parts, or—

Cris. Nay, I'll bribe his porter, and the grooms of his chamber; make his doors open to me that way first, and then I'll observe my times. Say he should extrude me his house to-day, shall I therefore desist, or let fall my suit to-morrow? No; I'll attend him, follow him, meet him in the street, the highways, run by his coach, never leave him. What! man hath nothing given him in this life without much labour—

Hor. And impudence.
Archer of heaven, Phœbus, take thy bow,
And with a full-drawn shaft nail to the earth
This Python, that I may yet run hence and live:
Or, brawny Hercules, do thou come down,
And, tho' thou mak'st it up thy thirteenth labour,
Rescue me from this hydra of discourse here.

Enter FUSCUS ARISTIUS.

Ari. Horace, well met.
Hor. O welcome, my reliever;
Aristius, as thou lov'st me, ransom me.
Ari. What ail'st thou, man?
Hor. 'Death, I am seized on here
By a land remora; I cannot stir,
Nor move, but as he pleases.
Cris. Wilt thou go, Horace?
Hor. Heart! he cleaves to me like Alcides' shirt,
Tearing my flesh and sinews: O, I've been vex'd
And tortured with him beyond forty fevers.
For Jove's sake, find some means to take me from him.
Ari. Yes, I will:—but I'll go first and tell Mecænas.   [*Aside.*
Cris. Come, shall we go?
Ari. The jest will make his eyes run, i'faith.   [*Aside.*
Hor. Nay, Aristius!
Ari. Farewell, Horace.   [*Going.*
Hor. 'Death! will he leave me? Fuscus Aristius! do you hear? Gods of Rome! You said you had somewhat to say to me in private.
Ari. Ay, but I see you are now employed with that gentleman; 'twere offence to trouble you; I'll take some fitter opportunity: farewell.   [*Exit.*
Hor. Mischief and torment! O my soul and heart,
How are you cramp'd with anguish! Death itself
Brings not the like convulsions. O, this day!
That ever I should view thy tedious face.—
Cris. Horace, what passion, what humour is this?
Hor. Away, good prodigy, afflict me not.—

A friend, and mock me thus! Never was man
So left under the axe.—

Enter MINOS *with two* Lictors.

How now?

Min. That's he in the embroidered hat, there, with the ash-
colour'd feather: his name is Laberius Crispinus.

Lict. Laberius Crispinus, I arrest you in the emperor's name.

Cris. Me, sir! do you arrest me?

Lict. Ay, sir, at the suit of master Minos the apothecary.

Hor. Thanks, great Apollo, I will not slip thy favour offered me
in my escape, for my fortunes. [*Exit hastily.*

Cris. Master Minos! I know no master Minos. Where's Horace?
Horace! Horace!

Min. Sir, do not you know me?

Cris. O yes, I know you, master Minos; cry you mercy. But
Horace? God's me, is he gone?

Min. Ay, and so would you too, if you knew how.—Officer, look
to him.

Cris. Do you hear, master Minos? pray let us be used like a man
of our own fashion. By Janus and Jupiter, I meant to have paid
you next week every drachm. Seek not to eclipse my reputation
thus vulgarly.

Min. Sir, your oaths cannot serve you; you know I have forborne you long.

Cris. I am conscious of it, sir. Nay, I beseech you, gentlemen,
do not exhale me thus, remember 'tis but for sweetmeats—

Lict. Sweet meat must have sour sauce, sir. Come along.

Cris. Sweet master Minos, I am forfeited to eternal disgrace, if
you do not commiserate. Good officer, be not so officious.

Enter TUCCA *and* Pyrgi.

Tuc. Why, how now, my good brace of bloodhounds, whither do
you drag the gentleman? You mongrels, you curs, you ban-dogs!
we are captain Tucca that talk to you, you inhuman pilchers.

Min. Sir, he is their prisoner.

Tuc. Their pestilence! What are you, sir?

Min. A citizen of Rome, sir.

Tuc. Then you are not far distant from a fool, sir.

Min. A pothecary, sir.

Tuc. I knew thou wast not a physician: foh! out of my nostrils,
thou stink'st of lotium and the syringe; away, quack-salver!—
Follower, my sword.

1 *Pyr.* Here, noble leader; you'll do no harm with it, I'll trust
you. [*Aside.*

Tuc. Do you hear, you goodman, slave? Hook, ram, rogue,
catchpole, loose the gentleman, or by my velvet arms—

Lict. What will you do, sir?
[*Strikes up his heels, and seizes his sword.*

Tuc. Kiss thy hand, my honourable active varlet, and embrace thee thus.

1 *Pyr.* O patient metamorphosis!

Tuc. My sword, my tall rascal.

Lict. Nay, soft, sir; some wiser than some.

Tuc. What! and a wit too? By Pluto, thou must be cherish'd, slave; here's three drachms for thee; hold.

2 *Pyr.* There's half his lendings gone.

Tuc. Give me.

Lict. No, sir, your first word shall stand; I'll hold all.

Tuc. Nay, but rogue—

Lict. You would make a rescue of our prisoner, sir, you.

Tuc. I a rescue! Away, inhuman varlet. Come, come, I never relish above one jest at most; do not disgust me, sirrah; do not, rogue! I tell thee, rogue, do not.

Lict. How, sir! rogue?

Tuc. Ay; why, thou art not angry, rascal, art thou?

Lict. I cannot tell, sir; I am little better upon these terms.

Tuc. Ha, gods and fiends! why, dost hear, rogue, thou? give me thy hand; I say unto thee, thy hand, rogue. What, dost not thou know me? not me, rogue? not captain Tucca, rogue?

Min. Come, pray surrender the gentleman his sword, officer; we'll have no fighting here.

Tuc. What's thy name?

Min. Minos, an't please you.

Tuc. Minos! Come hither, Minos; thou art a wise fellow, it seems; let me talk with thee.

Cris. Was ever wretch so wretched as unfortunate I!

Tuc. Thou art one of the centumviri, old boy, art not?

Min. No indeed, master captain.

Tuc. Go to, thou shalt be then; I'll have thee one, Minos. Take my sword from these rascals, dost thou see! go, do it; I cannot attempt with patience. What does this gentleman owe thee, little Minos?

Min. Fourscore sesterties, sir.

Tuc. What, no more! Come, thou shalt release him, Minos: what, I'll be his bail, thou shalt take my word, old boy, and cashier these furies: thou shalt do't, I say, thou shalt, little Minos, thou shalt.

Cris. Yes; and as I am a gentleman and a reveller, I'll make a piece of poetry, and absolve all, within these five days.

Tuc. Come, Minos is not to learn how to use a gentleman of quality, I know.—My sword: If he pay thee not, I will, and I must, old boy. Thou shalt be my pothecary too. Hast good eringos, Minos?

Min. The best in Rome, sir.

Tuc. Go to, then——Vermin, know the house.

1 *Pyr.* I warrant you, colonel.

Tuc For this gentleman, Minos—

Min. I'll take your word, captain.

Tuc. Thou hast it. My sword.

Min. Yes, sir: But you must discharge the arrest, master Crispinus.

Tuc. How, Minos! Look in the gentleman's face, and but read his silence. Pay, pay; 'tis honour, Minos.

Cris. By Jove, sweet captain, you do most infinitely endear and oblige me to you.

Tuc. Tut, I cannot compliment, by Mars; but, Jupiter love me, as I love good words and good clothes, and there's an end. Thou shalt give my boy that girdle and hangers, when thou hast worn them a little more.

Cris. O Jupiter! captain, he shall have them now, presently:— Please you to be acceptive, young gentleman.

1 *Pyr.* Yes, sir, fear not; I shall accept; I have a pretty foolish humour of taking, if you knew all. [*Aside.*

Tuc. Not now, you shall not take, boy.

Cris. By my truth and earnest, but he shall, captain, by your leave.

Tuc. Nay, an he swear by his truth and earnest, take it, boy: do not make a gentleman forsworn.

Lict. Well, sir, there's your sword; but thank master Minos; you had not carried it as you do else.

Tuc. Minos is just, and you are knaves, and—

Lict. What say you, sir?

Tuc. Pass on, my good scoundrel, pass on, I honour thee: [*Exeunt Lictors.*] But that I hate to have action with such base rogues as these, you should have seen me unrip their noses now, and have sent them to the next barber's to stitching; for do you see— I am a man of humour, and I do love the varlets, the honest varlets, they have wit and valour, and are indeed good profitable,—errant rogues, as any live in an empire. Dost thou hear, poetaster? [*To Crispinus.*] second me. Stand up, Minos, close, gather, yet, so! Sir, (thou shalt have a quarter-share, be resolute) you shall, at my request, take Minos by the hand here, little Minos, I will have it so; all friends, and a health; be not inexorable. And thou shalt impart the wine, old boy, thou shalt do it, little Minos, thou shalt; make us pay it in our physic. What! we must live, and honour the gods sometimes; now Bacchus, now Comus, now Priapus; every god a little. [*Histrio passes by.*] What's he that stalks by there, boy, Pyrgus? You were best let him pass, sirrah; do, ferret, let him pass, do—

2 *Pyr.* 'Tis a player, sir.

Tuc. A player! call him, call the lousy slave hither; what, will he sail by and not once strike, or vail to a man of war? ha!—Do you hear, you player, rogue, stalker, come back here!—

Enter HISTRIO.

No respect to men of worship, you slave! what, you are proud, you rascal, are you proud, ha? you grow rich, do you, and purchase, you twopenny tear-mouth? you have FORTUNE, and the good year on your side, you stinkard, you have, you have!

Hist. Nay, sweet captain, be confined to some reason; I protest I saw you not, sir.

Tuc. You did not? where was your sight, Œdipus? you walk with hare's eyes, do you? I'll have them glazed, rogue; an you say the word, they shall be glazed for you: come we must have you turn fiddler again, slave, get a base viol at your back, and march in a tawny coat, with one sleeve, to Goose-fair; then you'll know us, you'll see us then, you will, gulch, you will. Then, *Will't please your worship to have any music, captain?*

Hist. Nay, good captain.

Tuc. What, do you laugh, Howleglas! death, you perstemptuous varlet, I am none of your fellows; I have commanded a hundred and fifty such rogues, I.

2 Pyr. Ay, and most of that hundred and fifty have been leaders of a legion. [*Aside.*

Hist. If I have exhibited wrong, I'll tender satisfaction, captain.

Tuc. Say'st thou so, honest vermin! Give me thy hand; thou shalt make us a supper one of these nights.

Hist. When you please, by Jove, captain, most willingly.

Tuc. Dost thou swear! To-morrow then; say and hold, slave. There are some of you players honest gentlemen-like scoundrels, and suspected to have some wit, as well as your poets, both at drinking and breaking of jests, and are companions for gallants. A man may skelder ye, now and then, of half a dozen shillings, or so. Dost thou not know that Pantalabus there?

Hist. No, I assure you, captain.

Tuc. Go; and be acquainted with him then; he is a gentleman, parcel poet, you slave; his father was a man of worship, I tell thee. Go, he pens high, lofty, in a new stalking strain, bigger than half the rhymers in the town again; he was born to fill thy mouth, Minotaurus, he was, he will teach thee to tear and rand. Rascal, to him, cherish his muse, go; thou hast forty—forty shillings, I mean, stinkard; give him in earnest, do, he shall write for thee, slave! If he pen for thee once, thou shalt not need to travel with thy pumps full of gravel any more, after a blind jade and a hamper, and stalk upon boards and barrel heads to an old crack'd trumpet.

Hist. Troth, I think I have not so much about me, captain.

Tuc. It's no matter; give him what thou hast, stiff-toe, I'll give my word for the rest; though it lack a shilling or two, it skills not: go, thou art an honest shifter; I'll have the statute repeal'd for thee.—Minos, I must tell thee, Minos, thou hast dejected yon gentleman's spirit exceedingly; dost observe, dost note, little Minos?

Min. Yes, sir.

Tuc. Go to then, raise, recover, do; suffer him not to droop in prospect of a player, a rogue, a stager: put twenty into his hand—twenty sesterces I mean,—and let nobody see; go, do it—the work shall commend itself; ye Minos, I'll pay.

Min. Yes, forsooth, captain.

2 *Pyr.* Do not we serve a notable shark? [*Aside.*

Tuc. And what new matters have you now afoot, sirrah, ha? I would fain come with my cockatrice one day, and see a play, if I knew when there were a good bawdy one; but they say you have nothing but HUMOURS, REVELS, and SATIRES, that gird and f—t at the time, you slave.

Hist. No, I assure you, captain, not we. They are on the other side of Tyber: we have as much ribaldry in our plays as can be, as you would wish, captain: all the sinners in the suburbs come and applaud our action daily.

Tuc. I hear you'll bring me o' the stage there; you'll play me, they say; I shall be presented by a sort of copper-laced scoundrels of you: life of Pluto! an you stage me, stinkard, your mansions shall sweat for't, your tabernacles, varlets, your Globes, and your Triumphs.

Hist. Not we, by Phœbus, captain; do not do us imputation without desert.

Tuc. I will not, my good twopenny rascal; reach me thy neuf. Dost hear? what wilt thou give me a week for my brace of beagles here, my little point-trussers? you shall have them act among ye.— Sirrah, you, pronounce.—Thou shalt hear him speak in King Darius' doleful strain.

1 Pyr. *O doleful days! O direful deadly dump!*
O wicked world, and worldly wickedness!
How can I hold my fist from crying, thump,
In rue of this right rascal wretchedness!

Tuc. In an amorous vein now, sirrah: peace!

1 Pyr. *O, she is wilder, and more hard, withal,*
Than beast, or bird, or tree, or stony wall.
Yet might she love me, to uprear her state:
Ay, but perhaps she hopes some nobler mate.
Yet might she love me, to content her fire:
Ay, but her reason masters her desire.
Yet might she love me as her beauty's thrall:
Ay, but I fear she cannot love at all.

Tuc. Now, the horrible, fierce soldier, you, sirrah.

2 Pyr. *What! will I brave thee? ay, and beard thee too;*
A Roman spirit scorns to bear a brain
So full of base pusillanimity.

Hist. Excellent!

Tuc. Nay, thou shalt see that shall ravish thee anon; prick up thine ears, stinkard.—The ghost, boys!

1 Pyr. *Vindicta.*
2 Pyr. *Timoria!*
1 Pyr. *Vindicta!*
2 Pyr. *Timoria!*
1 Pyr. *Veni!*
2 Pyr. *Veni!*

Tuc. Now thunder, sirrah, you, the rumbling player.

2 *Pyr.* Ay, but somebody must cry, *Murder!* then, in a small voice.

Tuc. Your fellow-sharer there shall do't: Cry, sirrah, cry.

1 Pyr. *Murder, murder!*

2 Pyr. *Who calls out murder? lady, was it you?*

Hist. O, admirable good, I protest.

Tuc. Sirrah, boy, brace your drum a little straiter, and do the t'other fellow there, he in the—what sha' call him—and yet stay too.

2 Pyr. *Nay, an thou dalliest, then I am thy foe,*
And fear shall force what friendship cannot win;
Thy death shall bury what thy life conceals.
Villain! thou diest for more respecting her—

1 Pyr. *O stay, my lord.*

2 Pyr. *Than me:*
Yet speak the truth, and I will guerdon thee;
But if thou dally once again, thou diest.

Tuc. Enough of this, boy.

2 Pyr. *Why, then lament therefore: d—n'd be thy guts*
Unto king Pluto's Hell, and princely Erebus;
For sparrows must have food—

Hist. Pray, sweet captain, let one of them do a little of a lady.

Tuc. O! he will make thee eternally enamour'd of him, there: do, sirrah, do; 'twill allay your fellow's fury a little.

1 Pyr. *Master, mock on; the scorn thou givest me,*
Pray Jove some lady may return on thee.

2 *Pyr.* Now you shall see me do the Moor: master, lend me your scarf a little.

Tuc. Here, 'tis at thy service, boy.

2 *Pyr.* You, master Minos, hark hither a little.

[*Exit with Minos, to make himself ready.*

Tuc. How dost like him? art not rapt, art not tickled now? dost not applaud, rascal? dost not applaud?

Hist. Yes: what will you ask for them a week, captain?

Tuc. No, you mangonising slave, I will not part from them; you'll sell them for enghles, you: let's have good cheer to-morrow night at supper, stalker, and then we'll talk; good capon and plover, do you hear, sirrah? and do not bring your eating player with you there; I cannot away with him: he will eat a leg of mutton while I am in my porridge, the lean Poluphagus, his belly is like Barathrum; he looks like a midwife in man's apparel, the slave: nor the villanous out-of-tune fiddler, Ænobarbus, bring not him. What hast thou there? six and thirty, ha?

Hist. No, here's all I have, captain, some five and twenty: pray, sir, will you present and accommodate it unto the gentleman? for mine own part, I am a mere stranger to his humour; besides, I have some business invites me hence, with master Asinius Lupus, the tribune.

Tuc. Well, go thy ways, pursue thy projects, let me alone with this design; my Poetaster shall make thee a play, and thou shalt be a man of good parts in it. But stay, let me see; do not bring your Æsop, your politician, unless you can ram up his mouth with cloves; the slave smells ranker than some sixteen dunghills, and is seventeen times more rotten. Marry, you may bring Frisker, my zany; he's a good skipping swaggerer; and your fat fool there, my mango, bring him too; but let him not beg rapiers nor scarfs, in his over-familiar playing face, nor roar out his barren bold jests with a tormenting laughter, between drunk and dry. Do you hear, stiff-toe? give him warning, admonition, to forsake his saucy glavering grace, and his goggle eye; it does not become him, sirrah: tell him so. I have stood up and defended you, I, to gentlemen, when you have been said to prey upon puisnes, and honest citizens, for socks or buskins; or when they have call'd you usurers or brokers, or said you were able to help to a piece of flesh—I have sworn, I did not think so, nor that you were the common retreats for punks decayed in their practice; I cannot believe it of you.

Hist. Thank you, captain. Jupiter and the rest of the gods confine your modern delights without disgust.

Tuc. Stay, thou shalt see the Moor ere thou goest.—

Enter DEMETRIUS *at a distance.*

What's he with the half arms there, that salutes us out of his cloak, like a motion, ha?

Hist. O, sir, his doublet's a little decayed; he is otherwise a very simple honest fellow, sir, one Demetrius, a dresser of plays about the town here; we have hired him to abuse Horace, and bring him in, in a play, with all his gallants, as Tibullus, Mecænas, Cornelius Gallus, and the rest.

Tuc. And why so, stinkard?

Hist. O, it will get us a huge deal of money, captain, and we have need on`t; for this winter has made us all poorer than so many starved snakes: nobody comes at us, not a gentleman, nor a—

Tuc. But you know nothing by him, do you, to make a play of?

Hist. Faith, not much, captain; but our author will devise that that shall serve in some sort.

Tuc. Why, my Parnassus here shall help him, if thou wilt. Can thy author do it impudently enough?

Hist. O, I warrant you, captain, and spitefully enough too; he has one of the most overflowing rank wits in Rome; he will slander any man that breathes, if he disgust him.

Tuc. I'll know the poor, egregious, nitty rascal; an he have these commendable qualities, I'll cherish him — stay, here comes the Tartar—I'll make a gathering for him, I, a purse, and put the poor slave in fresh rags; tell him so to comfort him.—

[*Demetrius comes forward.*

Re-enter MINOS, *with* 2 Pyrgus *on his shoulders, and stalks backward and forward, as the boy acts.*

Well said, boy.

2 *Pyr.* Where art thou, boy? where is Calipolis?
Fight earthquakes in the entrails of the earth,
And eastern whirlwinds in the hellish shades;
Some foul contagion of the infected heavens
Blast all the trees, and in their cursed tops
The dismal night raven and tragic owl
Breed and become forerunners of my fall!

Tuc. Well, now fare thee well, my honest penny-biter: commend me to seven shares and a half, and remember to-morrow.—If you lack a service, you shall play in my name, rascals; but you shall buy your own cloth, and I'll have two shares for my countenance. Let thy author stay with me. [*Exit Histrio.*

Dem. Yes, sir.

Tuc. 'Twas well done, little Minos, thou didst stalk well: forgive me that I said thou stunk'st, Minos; 'twas the savour of a poet I met sweating in the street, hangs yet in my nostrils.

Cris. Who, Horace?

Tuc. Ay, he; dost thou know him?

Cris. O, he forsook me most barbarously, I protest.

Tuc. Hang him, fusty satyr, he smells all goat; he carries a ram under his arm-holes, the slave: I am the worse when I see him.— Did not Minos impart? [*Aside to Crispinus.*

Cris. Yes, here are twenty drachms he did convey.

Tuc. Well said, keep them, we'll share anon; come, little Minos.

Cris. Faith, captain, I'll be bold to shew you a mistress of mine, a jeweller's wife, a gallant, as we go along.

Tuc. There spoke my genius. Minos, some of thy eringos, little Minos; send. Come hither, Parnassus, I must have thee familiar with my little locust here; 'tis a good vermin, they say.—[*Horace and Trebatius pass over the stage.*]—See, here's Horace, and old Trebatius, the great lawyer, in his company; let's avoid him now, he is too well seconded. [*Exeunt.*

ACT IV

SCENE I.—*A Room in* ALBIUS'S *House.*

Enter CHLOE, CYTHERIS, *and* Attendants.

Chloe. But, sweet lady, say; am I well enough attired for the court, in sadness?

Cyth. Well enough! excellent well, sweet mistress Chloe; this strait-bodied city attire, I can tell you, will stir a courtier's blood, more than the finest loose sacks the ladies use to be put in; and then you are as well jewell'd as any of them; your ruff and linen about you is much more pure than theirs; and for your beauty, I can tell you, there's many of them would defy the painter, if they could change with you. Marry, the worst is, you must look to be envied, and endure a few court-frumps for it.

Chloe. O Jove, madam, I shall buy them too cheap!—Give me my muff, and my dog there.—And will the ladies be any thing familiar with me, think you?

Cyth. O Juno! why you shall see them flock about you with their puff-wings, and ask you where you bought your lawn, and what you paid for it? who starches you? and entreat you to help 'em to some pure laundresses out of the city.

Chloe. O Cupid!—Give me my fan, and my mask too.—And will the lords, and the poets there, use one well too, lady?

Cyth. Doubt not of that; you shall have kisses from them, go pit-pat, pit-pat, pit-pat, upon your lips, as thick as stones out of slings at the assault of a city. And then your ears will be so furr'd with the breath of their compliments, that you cannot catch cold of your head, if you would, in three winters after.

Chloe. Thank you, sweet lady. O heaven! and how must one behave herself amongst 'em? You know all.

Cyth. Faith, impudently enough, mistress Chloe, and well enough. Carry not too much under thought betwixt yourself and them; nor your city-mannerly word, *forsooth*, use it not too often in any case; but plain, *Ay, madam,* and *no, madam:* nor never say, *your lordship,* nor *your honour;* but, *you,* and *you, my lord,* and *my lady:* the other they count too simple and minsitive. And though they desire to kiss heaven with their titles, yet they will count them fools that give them too humbly.

Chloe. O intolerable, Jupiter! by my troth, lady, I would not for a world but you had lain in my house; and, i'faith, you shall not pay a farthing for your board, nor your chambers.

Cyth. O, sweet mistress Chloe!

Chloe. I'faith you shall not, lady; nay, good lady, do not offer it.

Enter GALLUS *and* TIBULLUS.

Gal. Come, where be these ladies? By your leave, bright stars, this gentleman and I are come to man you to court; where your late kind entertainment is now to be requited with a heavenly banquet.

Cyth. A heavenly banquet, Gallus!

Gal. No less, my dear Cytheris.

Tib. That were not strange, lady, if the epithet were only given for the company invited thither; your self, and this fair gentle-woman.

Chloe. Are we invited to court, sir?

Tib. You are, lady, by the great princess Julia; who longs to greet you with any favours that may worthily make you an often courtier.

Chloe. In sincerity, I thank her, sir. You have a coach, have you not?

Tib. The princess hath sent her own, lady.

Chloe. O Venus! that's well: I do long to ride in a coach most vehemently.

Cyth. But, sweet Gallus, pray you resolve me why you give that heavenly praise to this earthly banquet?

Gal. Because, Cytheris, it must be celebrated by the heavenly powers: all the gods and goddesses will be there; to two of which you two must be exalted.

Chloe. A pretty fiction, in truth.

Cyth. A fiction, indeed, Chloe, and fit for the fit of a poet.

Gal. Why, Cytheris, may not poets (from whose divine spirits all the honours of the gods have been deduced) entreat so much honour of the gods, to have their divine presence at a poetical banquet?

Cyth. Suppose that no fiction; yet, where are your habilities to make us two goddesses at your feast?

Gal. Who knows not, Cytheris, that the sacred breath of a true poet can blow any virtuous humanity up to deity?

Tib. To tell you the female truth, which is the simple truth, ladies; and to shew that poets, in spite of the world, are able to deify themselves; at this banquet, to which you are invited, we intend to assume the figures of the gods; and to give our several loves the forms of goddesses. Ovid will be Jupiter; the princess Julia, Juno; Gallus here, Apollo; you, Cytheris, Pallas; I will be Bacchus; and my love Plautia, Ceres: and to install you and your husband, fair Chloe, in honours equal with ours, you shall be a goddess, and your husband a god.

Chloe. A god!—O my gods!

Tib. A god, but a lame god, lady; for he shall be Vulcan, and you Venus: and this will make our banquet no less than heavenly.

Chloe. In sincerity, it will be sugared. Good Jove, what a pretty foolish thing it is to be a poet! but, hark you, sweet Cytheris, could they not possibly leave out my husband? methinks a body's husband does not so well at court; a body's friend, or so—but, husband! 'tis like your clog to your marmoset, for all the world, and the heavens.

Cyth. Tut, never fear, Chloe! your husband will be left without in the lobby, or the great chamber, when you shall be put in, i'the closet, by this lord, and by that lady.

Chloe. Nay, then I am certified; he shall go.

Enter HORACE.

Gal. Horace! welcome.

Hor. Gentlemen, hear you the news?

Tib. What news, my Quintus!

Hor. Our melancholic friend, Propertius,
Hath closed himself up in his Cynthia's tomb;
And will by no entreaties be drawn thence.

Enter ALBIUS, *introducing* CRISPINUS *and* DEMETRIUS, *followed by* TUCCA.

Alb. Nay, good Master Crispinus, pray you bring near the gentleman.

Hor. Crispinus! Hide me, good Gallus; Tibullus, shelter me.
[*Going.*

Cris. Make your approach, sweet captain.

Tib. What means this, Horace?

Hor. I am surprised again; farewell.

Gal. Stay, Horace.

Hor. What, and be tired on by yond' vulture! No: Phœbus defend me! [*Exit hastily.*

Tib. 'Slight, I hold my life
This same is he met him in Holy-street.

Gal. Troth, 'tis like enough.—This act of Propertius relisheth very strange with me.

Tuc. By thy leave, my neat scoundrel: what, is this the mad boy you talk'd on?

Cris. Ay, this is master Albius, captain.

Tuc. Give me thy hand, Agamemnon; we hear abroad thou art the Hector of citizens: What sayest thou? are we welcome to thee, noble Neoptolemus?

Alb. Welcome, captain, by Jove and all the gods in the Capitol—

Tuc. No more, we conceive thee. Which of these is thy wedlock, Menelaus? thy Helen, thy Lucrece? that we may do her honour, mad boy.

Cris. She in the little fine dressing, sir, is my mistress.

Alb. For fault of a better, sir.

Tuc. A better! profane rascal: I cry thee mercy, my good scroyle, was't thou?

Alb. No harm, captain.

Tuc. She is a Venus, a Vesta, a Melpomene: come hither, Penelope; what's thy name, Iris?

Chloe. My name is Chloe, sir; I am a gentlewoman.

Tuc. Thou art in merit to be an empress, Chloe, for an eye and a lip; thou hast an emperor's nose: kiss me again: 'tis a virtuous punk; so! Before Jove, the gods were a sort of goslings, when they suffered so sweet a breath to perfume the bed of a stinkard: thou hadst ill fortune, Thisbe; the Fates were infatuate, they were, punk, they were.

Chloe. That's sure, sir: let me crave your name, I pray you, sir.

Tuc. I am known by the name of captain Tucca, punk; the noble Roman, punk: a gentleman, and a commander, punk.

Chloe. In good time: a gentleman, and a commander! that's as good as a poet, methinks. [*Walks aside.*

Cris. A pretty instrument! It's my cousin Cytheris' viol this, is it not?

Cyth. Nay, play, cousin; it wants but such a voice and hand to grace it, as yours is.

Cris. Alas, cousin, you are merrily inspired.

Cyth. Pray you play, if you love me.

Cris. Yes, cousin; you know I do not hate you.

Tib. A most subtile wench! how she hath baited him with a viol yonder, for a song!

Cris. Cousin, 'pray you call mistress Chloe! she shall hear an essay of my poetry.

Tuc. I'll call her.—Come hither, cockatrice: here's one will set thee up, my sweet punk, set thee up.

Chloe. Are you a poet so soon, sir?

Alb. Wife, mum.

CRISPINUS *plays and sings.*

Love is blind, and a wanton;
In the whole world, there is scant one
  —Such another:
  No, not his mother.
He hath pluck'd her doves and sparrows,
To feather his sharp arrows,
  And alone prevaileth,
  While sick Venus waileth.
But if Cypris once recover
The wag; it shall behove her
  To look better to him:
  Or she will undo him.

Alb. O, most odoriferous music!

Tuc. Aha, stinkard! Another Orpheus, you slave, another Orpheus! an Arion riding on the back of a dolphin, rascal!

Gal. Have you a copy of this ditty, sir?

Cris. Master Albius has.

Alb. Ay, but in truth they are my wife's verses; I must not shew them.

Tuc. Shew them, bankrupt, shew them; they have salt in them, and will brook the air, stinkard.

Gal. How! *To his bright mistress Canidia!*

Cris. Ay, sir, that's but a borrowed name; as Ovid's Corinna, or Propertius his Cynthia, or your Nemesis, or Delia, Tibullus.

Gal. It's the name of Horace his witch, as I remember.

Tib. Why, the ditty's all borrowed; 'tis Horace's: hang him, plagiary!

Tuc. How! he borrow of Horace? he shall pawn himself to ten brokers first. Do you hear, Poetasters? I know you to be men of worship—He shall write with Horace, for a talent! and let Mecænas and his whole college of critics take his part: thou shalt do't, young Phœbus; thou shalt, Phaeton, thou shalt.

Dem. Alas, sir, Horace! he is a mere sponge; nothing but Humours and observation; he goes up and down sucking from every society, and when he comes home squeezes himself dry again. I know him, I.

Tuc. Thou say'st true, my poor poetical fury, he will pen all he knows. A sharp thorny-tooth'd satirical rascal, fly him; he carries hay in his horn: he will sooner lose his best friend, than his least jest. What he once drops upon paper, against a man, lives eternally to upbraid him in the mouth of every slave, tankard-bearer, or waterman; not a bawd, or a boy that comes from the bake-house, but shall point at him: 'tis all dog, and scorpion; he carries poison in his teeth, and a sting in his tail. Fough! body of Jove! I'll have the slave whipt one of these days for his Satires and his Humours, by one cashier'd clerk or another.

Cris. We'll undertake him, captain.

Dem. Ay, and tickle him i'faith, for his arrogancy and his impudence, in commending his own things; and for his translating, I can trace him, i'faith. O, he is the most open fellow living; I had as lieve as a new suit I were at it.

Tuc. Say no more then, but do it; 'tis the only way to get thee a new suit; sting him, my little neufts; I'll give you instructions: I'll be your intelligencer; we'll all join, and hang upon him like so many horse-leeches, the players and all. We shall sup together, soon; and then we'll conspire, i'faith.

Gal. O that Horace had stayed still here!

Tib. So would not I; for both these would have turn'd Pythagoreans then.

Gal. What, mute?

Tib. Ay, as fishes, i'faith: come, ladies, shall we go?

Cyth. We wait you, sir. But mistress Chloe asks, if you have not a god to spare for this gentleman.

Gal. Who, captain Tucca?

Cyth. Ay, he.

Gal. Yes, if we can invite him along, he shall be Mars.

Chloe. Has Mars any thing to do with Venus?

Tib. O, most of all, lady.

Chloe. Nay, then I pray let him be invited: And what shall Crispinus be?

Tib. Mercury, mistress Chloe.

Chloe. Mercury! that's a poet, is it?

Gal. No, lady, but somewhat inclining that way; he is a herald at arms.

Chloe. A herald at arms! good; and Mercury! pretty: he has to do with Venus too?

Tib. A little with her face, lady; or so.

Chloe. 'Tis very well; pray let us go, I long to be at it.

Cyth. Gentlemen, shall we pray your companies along?

Cris. You shall not only pray, but prevail, lady.—Come, sweet captain.

Tuc. Yes, I follow: but thou must not talk of this now, my little bankrupt.

Alb. Captain, look here, mum.

Dem. I'll go write, sir.

Tuc. Do, do: stay, there's a drachm to purchase ginger-bread for thy muse.   [*Exeunt.*

SCENE II.—*A Room in* LUPUS's *House.*

Enter LUPUS, HISTRIO, *and* Lictors.

Lup. Come, let us talk here; here we may be private; shut the door, lictor. You are a player, you say.

Hist. Ay, an't please your worship.

Lup. Good; and how are you able to give this intelligence?

Hist. Marry, sir, they directed a letter to me and my fellow-sharers.

Lup. Speak lower, you are not now in your theatre, stager:—my sword, knave. They directed a letter to you, and your fellow-sharers: forward.

Hist. Yes, sir, to hire some of our properties; as a sceptre and crown for Jove; and a caduceus for Mercury; and a petasus—

Lup. Caduceus and petasus! let me see your letter. This is a conjuration: a conspiracy, this. Quickly, on with my buskins: I'll act a tragedy, i'faith. Will nothing but our gods serve these poets to profane? dispatch! Player, I thank thee. The emperor shall take knowledge of thy good service. [*A knocking within.*] Who's there now? Look, knave. [*Exit Lictor.*] *A crown and a sceptre!* this is good rebellion, now.

Re-enter Lictor.

Lic. 'Tis your pothecary, sir, master Minos.

Lup. What tell'st thou me of pothecaries, knave! Tell him, I have affairs of state in hand; I can talk to no apothecaries now. Heart of me! Stay the pothecary there. [*Walks in a musing posture.*] You shall see, I have fish'd out a cunning piece of plot now: they have had some intelligence, that their project is discover'd, and now have they dealt with my apothecary, to poison me; 'tis so; knowing that I meant to take physic to-day: as sure as death, 'tis there. Jupiter, I thank thee, that thou hast yet made me so much of a politician.

Enter MINOS.

You are welcome, sir; take the potion from him there; I have an antidote more than you wot of, sir; throw it on the ground there: so! Now fetch in the dog; and yet we cannot tarry to try experiments now: arrest him; you shall go with me, sir; I'll tickle you, pothecary; I'll give you a glister, i'faith. Have I the letter? ay, 'tis here.—Come, your fasces, lictors: the half pikes and the halberds, take them down from the Lares there. Player, assist me.

As they are going out, enter MECÆNAS *and* HORACE.

Mec. Whither now, Asinius Lupus, with this armory?

Lup. I cannot talk now; I charge you assist me: treason! treason!

Hor. How! treason?

Lup. Ay: if you love the emperor, and the state, follow me.

[*Exeunt.*

SCENE III.—*An Apartment in the Palace.*

Enter OVID, JULIA, GALLUS, CYTHERIS, TIBULLUS, PLAUTIA, ALBIUS, CHLOE, TUCCA, CRISPINUS, HERMOGENES, PYRGUS, *characteristically habited, as gods and goddesses.*

Ovid. Gods and goddesses, take your several seats. Now, Mercury, move your caduceus, and, in Jupiter's name, command silence.

Cris. In the name of Jupiter, silence.

Her. The crier of the court hath too clarified a voice.

Gal. Peace, Momus.

Ovid. Oh, he is the god of reprehension; let him alone: 'tis his office. Mercury, go forward, and proclaim, after Phœbus, our high pleasure, to all the deities that shall partake this high banquet.

Cris. Yes, sir.

Gal. The great god, Jupiter,—[Here, and at every break in the line, Crispinus repeats aloud the words of Gallus.]——*Of his licentious goodness,*——*Willing to make this feast no fast*——*From any manner of pleasure;*——*Nor to bind any god or goddess*——*To be any thing the more god or goddess, for their names:*——*He gives them all free license*——*To speak no wiser than persons of baser titles;*—— *And to be nothing better, than common men, or women.*——*And therefore no god*——*Shall need to keep himself more strictly to his goddess*——*Than any man does to his wife:*——*Nor any goddess*—— *Shall need to keep herself more strictly to her god*——*Than any woman does to her husband.*——*But, since it is no part of wisdom,*——*In these days, to come into bonds;*——*It shall be lawful for every lover*—— *To break loving oaths,*——*To change their lovers, and make love to others,*——*As the heat of every one's blood,*——*And the spirit of our nectar, shall inspire.*——*And Jupiter save Jupiter!*

Tib. So; now we may play the fools by authority.

Her. To play the fool by authority is wisdom.

Jul. Away with your mattery sentences, Momus; they are too grave and wise for this meeting.

Ovid. Mercury, give our jester a stool, let him sit by; and reach him one of our cates.

Tuc. Dost hear, mad Jupiter? we'll have it enacted, he that speaks the first wise word, shall be made cuckold. What say'st thou? Is it not a good motion?

Ovid. Deities, are you all agreed?

All. Agreed, great Jupiter.

Alb. I have read in a book, that to play the fool wisely, is high wisdom.

Gal. How now, Vulcan! will you be the first wizard?

Ovid. Take his wife, Mars, and make him cuckold quickly.

Tuc. Come, cockatrice.

Chloe. No, let me alone with him, Jupiter: I'll make you take heed, sir, while you live again; if there be twelve in a company, that you be not the wisest of 'em.

Alb. No more; I will not indeed, wife, hereafter; I'll be here: mum.

Ovid. Fill us a bowl of nectar, Ganymede: we will drink to our daughter Venus.

Gal. Look to your wife, Vulcan: Jupiter begins to court her.

Tib. Nay, let Mars look to it: Vulcan must do as Venus does, bear.

Tuc. Sirrah, boy; catamite: Look you play Ganymede well now, you slave. Do not spill your nectar; carry your cup even: so! You should have rubbed your face with whites of eggs, you rascal; till your brows had shone like our sooty brother's here, as sleek as a horn-book: or have steept your lips in wine, till you made them so plump, that Juno might have been jealous of them. Punk, kiss me, punk.

Ovid. Here, daughter Venus, I drink to thee.

Chloe. Thank you, good father Jupiter.

Tuc. Why, mother Juno! gods and fiends! what, wilt thou suffer this ocular temptation?

Tib. Mars is enraged, he looks big, and begins to stut for anger.

Her. Well played, captain Mars.

Tuc. Well said, minstrel Momus: I must put you in, must I? when will you be in good fooling of yourself, fidler, never?

Her. O, 'tis our fashion to be silent, when there is a better fool in place ever.

Tuc. Thank you, rascal.

Ovid. Fill to our daughter Venus, Ganymede, who fills her father with affection.

Jul. Wilt thou be ranging, Jupiter, before my face?

Ovid. Why not, Juno? why should Jupiter stand in awe of thy face, Juno?

Jul. Because it is thy wife's face, Jupiter.

Ovid. What, shall a husband be afraid of his wife's face? will she paint it so horribly? we are a king, cotquean; and we will reign in our pleasures; and we will cudgel thee to death, if thou find fault with us.

Jul. I will find fault with thee, king cuckold-maker: What, shall the king of gods turn the king of good-fellows, and have no fellow in wickedness? This makes our poets, that know our profaneness, live as profane as we: By my godhead, Jupiter, I will join with all the other gods here, bind thee hand and foot, throw thee down into the earth and make a poor poet of thee, if thou abuse me thus.

Gal. A good smart-tongued goddess, a right Juno!

Ovid. Juno, we will cudgel thee, Juno: we told thee so yesterday, when thou wert jealous of us for Thetis.

Pyr. Nay, to-day she had me in inquisition too.

Tuc. Well said, my fine Phrygian fry; inform, inform. Give me some wine, king of heralds, I may drink to my cockatrice.

Ovid. No more, Ganymede; we will cudgel thee, Juno; by Styx we will.

Jul. Ay, 'tis well; gods may grow impudent in iniquity, and they must not be told of it—

Ovid. Yea, we will knock our chin against our breast, and shake thee out of Olympus into an oyster-boat, for thy scolding.

Jul. Your nose is not long enough to do it, Jupiter, if all thy strumpets thou hast among the stars took thy part. And there is never a star in thy forehead but shall be a horn, if thou persist to abuse me.

Cris. A good jest, i'faith.

Ovid. We tell thee thou angerest us, cotquean; and we will thunder thee in pieces for thy cotqueanity.

Cris. Another good jest.

Alb. O, my hammers and my Cyclops! This boy fills not wine enough to make us kind enough to one another.

Tuc. Nor thou hast not collied thy face enough, stinkard.

Alb. I'll ply the table with nectar, and make them friends.

Her. Heaven is like to have but a lame skinker, then.

Alb. Wine and good livers make true lovers: I'll sentence them together. Here, father, here, mother, for shame, drink yourselves drunk, and forget this dissension; you two should cling together before our faces, and give us example of unity.

Gal. O, excellently spoken, Vulcan, on the sudden!

Tib. Jupiter may do well to prefer his tongue to some office for his eloquence.

Tuc. His tongue shall be gentleman-usher to his wit, and still go before it.

Alb. An excellent fit office!

Cris. Ay, and an excellent good jest besides.

Her. What, have you hired Mercury to cry your jests you make?

Ovid. Momus, you are envious.

Tuc. Why, ay, you whoreson blockhead, 'tis your only block of wit in fashion now-a-days, to applaud other folks' jests.

Her. True; with those that are not artificers themselves. Vulcan, you nod, and the mirth of the jest droops.

Pyr. He has filled nectar so long, till his brain swims in it.

Gal. What, do we nod, fellow-gods! Sound startle our spirits with a song.

Tuc. Do, Apollo, thou art a good musician.

Gal. What says Jupiter?

Ovid. Ha! ha!

Gal. A song.

Ovid. Why, do, do, sing.

Pla. Bacchus, what say you?

Tib. Ceres?

Pla. But, to this song?

Tib. Sing, for my part.

Jul. Your belly weighs down your head, Bacchus; here's a song toward.

Tib. Begin, Vulcan.

Alb. What else, what else?

Tuc. Say, Jupiter—

Ovid. Mercury—

Cris. Ay, say, say.   [*Music.*

Alb. *Wake! our mirth begins to die;*
   Quicken it with tunes and wine.
  Raise your notes; you're out; fie, fie!
  This drowsiness is an ill sign.
  We banish him the quire of gods,
   That droops agen:
   Then all are men,
  For here's not one but nods.

Ovid. I like not this sudden and general heaviness amongst our godheads; 'tis somewhat ominous. Apollo, command us louder music, and let Mercury and Momus contend to please and revive our senses.   [*Music.*

Herm. *Then, in a free and lofty strain.*
   Our broken tunes we thus repair;
Cris. *And we answer them again,*
   Running division on the panting air;
Ambo.   *To celebrate this feast of sense,*
   As free from scandal as offence.
Herm. *Here is beauty for the eye;*
Cris. *For the ear sweet melody.*
Herm. *Ambrosiac odours, for the smell;*
Cris. *Delicious nectar, for the taste;*
Ambo. *For the touch, a lady's waist;*
  Which doth all the rest excel.

Ovid. Ay, this has waked us. Mercury, our herald; go from ourself, the great god Jupiter, to the great emperor Augustus Cæsar, and command him from us, of whose bounty he hath received the sirname of Augustus, that, for a thank-offering to our beneficence, he presently sacrifice, as a dish to this banquet, his beautiful and wanton daughter Julia: she's a curst quean, tell him, and plays the scold behind his back; therefore let her be sacrificed. Command him this, Mercury, in our high name of Jupiter Altitonans.

Jul. Stay, feather-footed Mercury, and tell Augustus, from us, the great Juno Saturnia; if he think it hard to do as Jupiter hath commanded him, and sacrifice his daughter, that he had better do so ten times, than suffer her to love the well-nosed poet, Ovin; whom he shall do well to whip or cause to be whipped, about the capitol, for soothing her in her follies.

Enter Augustus Cæsar, Mecænas, Horace, Lupus, Histrio, Minus, *and* Lictors.

Cæs. What sight is this? Mecænas! Horace! say?
Have we our senses? do we hear and see?
Or are these but imaginary objects
Drawn by our phantasy! Why speak you not?
Let us do sacrifice. Are they the gods?   [*Ovid and the rest kneel.*
Reverence, amaze, and fury fight in me.
What, do they kneel! Nay, then I see 'tis true
I thought impossible: O, impious sight!
Let me divert mine eyes; the very thought
Everts my soul with passion: Look not, man,
There is a panther, whose unnatural eyes
Will strike thee dead: turn, then, and die on her
With her own death.   [*Offers to kill his daughter.*
  Mec. Hor. What means imperial Cæsar?
  Cæs. What would you have me let the strumpet live
That, for this pageant, earns so many deaths?
  Tuc. Boy, slink, boy.
  Pyr. Pray Jupiter we be not followed by the scent, master.
                       [*Exeunt Tucca and Pyrgus.*

  Cæs. Say, sir, what are you?
  Alb. I play Vulcan, sir.
  Cæs. But what are you, sir?
  Alb. Your citizen and jeweller, sir.
  Cæs. And what are you, dame?
  Chloe. I play Venus, forsooth.
  Cæs. I ask not what you play, but what you are.
  Chloe. Your citizen and jeweller's wife, sir.
  Cæs. And you, good sir?
  Cris. Your gentleman parcel-poet, sir.   [*Exit.*
  Cæs. O, that profaned name!—
And are these seemly company for thee,   [*To Julia.*
Degenerate monster? All the rest I know,
And hate all knowledge for their hateful sakes.
Are you, that first the deities inspired
With skill of their high natures and their powers,
The first abusers of their useful light;
Profaning thus their dignities in their forms,
And making them, like you, but counterfeits?
O, who shall follow Virtue and embrace her,
When her false bosom is found nought but air!
And yet of those embraces centaurs spring,
That war with human peace, and poison men.—
Who shall, with greater comforts comprehend

Her unseen being and her excellence;
When you, that teach, and should eternise her,
Live as she were no law unto your lives,
Nor lived herself, but with your idle breaths?
If you think gods but feign'd, and virtue painted,
Know we sustain an actual residence,
And with the title of an emperor,
Retain his spirit and imperial power;
By which, in imposition too remiss,
Licentious Naso, for thy violent wrong,
In soothing the declined affections
Of our base daughter, we exile thy feet
From all approach to our imperial court,
On pain of death; and thy misgotten love
Commit to patronage of iron doors;
Since her soft-hearted sire cannot contain her.

   Mec. O, good my lord, forgive! be like the gods.

   Hor. Let royal bounty, Cæsar, mediate.

   Cæs. There is no bounty to be shew'd to such
As have no real goodness: bounty is
A spice of virtue; and what virtuous act
Can take effect on them, that have no power
Of equal habitude to apprehend it,
But live in worship of that idol, vice,
As if there were no virtue, but in shade
Of strong imagination, merely enforced?
This shews their knowledge is mere ignorance,
Their far-fetch'd dignity of soul a fancy,
And all their square pretext of gravity
A mere vain-glory; hence, away with them!
I will prefer for knowledge, none but such
As rule their lives by it, and can becalm
All sea of Humour with the marble trident
Of their strong spirits: others fight below
With gnats and shadows; others nothing know.   [*Exeunt.*

SCENE V.—*A Street before the Palace.*

Enter TUCCA, CRISPINUS, *and* PYRGUS.

   Tuc. What's become of my little punk, Venus, and the poult-foot stinkard, her husband, ha?

   Cris. O, they are rid home in the coach, as fast as the wheels can run.

   Tuc. God Jupiter is banished, I hear, and his cockatrice Juno lock'd up. 'Heart, an all the poetry in Parnassus get me to be a player again, I'll sell 'em my share for a sesterce. But this is Humours, Horace, that goat-footed envious slave; he's turn'd fawn now; an informer, the rogue! 'tis he has betray'd us all. Did you not see him with the emperor crouching?

Cris. Yes.

Tuc. Well, follow me. Thou shalt libel, and I'll cudgel the rascal. Boy, provide me a truncheon. Revenge shall gratulate him, *tam Marti, quam Mercurio.*

Pyr. Ay, but master, take heed how you give this out; Horace is a man of the sword.

Cris. 'Tis true, in troth; they say he's valiant.

Tuc. Valiant? so is mine a—. Gods and fiends! I'll blow him into air when I meet him next: he dares not fight with a puck-fist.

[Horace passes over the stage.

Pyr. Master, he comes!

Tuc. Where? Jupiter save thee, my good poet, my noble prophet, my little fat Horace.—I scorn to beat the rogue in the court; and I saluted him thus fair, because he should suspect nothing, the rascal. Come, we'll go see how far forward our journeyman is toward the untrussing of him.

Cris. Do you hear, captain? I'll write nothing in it but innocence, because I may swear I am innocent. *[Exeunt.*

SCENE VI.

Enter HORACE, MECÆNAS, LUPUS, HISTRIO, *and* Lictors.

Hor. Nay, why pursue you not the emperor for your reward now, Lupus?

Mec. Stay, Asinius;
You and your stager, and your band of lictors:
I hope your service merits more respect,
Than thus, without a thanks, to be sent hence.

His. Well, well, jest on, jest on.

Hor. Thou base, unworthy groom!

Lup. Ay, ay, 'tis good.

Hor. Was this the treason, this the dangerous plot,
Thy clamorous tongue so bellow'd through the court?
Hadst thou no other project to encrease
Thy grace with Cæsar, but this wolfish train,
To prey upon the life of innocent mirth
And harmless pleasures, bred of noble wit?
Away! I loath thy presence; such as thou,
They are the moths and scarabs of a state,
The bane of empires, and the dregs of courts;
Who, to endear themselves to an employment,
Care not whose fame they blast, whose life they endanger;
And, under a disguised and cobweb mask
Of love unto their sovereign, vomit forth
Their own prodigious malice; and pretending
To be the props and columns of their safety,
The guards unto his person and his peace,
Disturb it most, w th their false, lapwing-cries.

Lup. Good! Cæsar shall know of this, believe it.

Mec. Cæsar doth know it, wolf, and to his knowledge,
He will, I hope, reward your base endeavours.
Princes that will but hear, or give access
To such officious spies, can ne'er be safe:
They take in poison with an open ear,
And, free from danger, become slaves to fear.   [*Exeunt.*

SCENE VII.—*An open Space before the Palace.*

Enter OVID.

Banish'd the court! Let me be banish'd life,
Since the chief end of life is there concluded:
Within the court is all the kingdom bounded,
And as her sacred sphere doth comprehend
Ten thousand times so much, as so much place
In any part of all the empire else;
So every body, moving in her sphere,
Contains ten thousand times as much in him,
As any other her choice orb excludes.
As in a circle, a magician then
Is safe against the spirit he excites;
But, out of it, is subject to his rage,
And loseth all the virtue of his art:
So I, exiled the circle of the court,
Lose all the good gifts that in it I 'joy'd.
No virtue current is, but with her stamp,
And no vice vicious, blanch'd with her white hand.
The court's the abstract of all Rome's desert,
And my dear Julia the abstract of the court.
Methinks, now I come near her, I respire
Some air of that late comfort I received;
And while the evening, with her modest veil,
Gives leave to such poor shadows as myself
To steal abroad, I, like a heartless ghost,
Without the living body of my love,
Will here walk and attend her: for I know
Not far from hence she is imprisoned,
And hopes, of her strict guardian, to bribe
So much admittance, as to speak to me,
And cheer my fainting spirits with her breath.
    Julia. [*appears above at her chamber window.*] Ovid? my love?
    Ovid. Here, heavenly Julia.
    Jul. Here! and not here! O, how that word doth play
With both our fortunes, differing, like ourselves,
Both one; and yet divided, as opposed!
I high, thou low: O, this our plight of place
Doubly presents the two lets of our love,
Local and ceremonial height, and lowness:
Both ways, I am too high, and thou too low,

Our minds are even yet; O, why should our bodies,
That are their slaves, be so without their rule?
I'll cast myself down to thee; if I die,
I'll ever live with thee: no height of birth,
Of place, of duty, or of cruel power,
Shall keep me from thee; should my father lock
This body up within a tomb of brass,
Yet I'll be with thee.   If the forms I hold
Now in my soul, be made one substance with it;
That soul immortal, and the same 'tis now;
Death cannot raze the affects she now retaineth:
And then, may she be any where she will.
The souls of parents rule not children's souls,
When death sets both in their dissolv'd estates;
Then is no child nor father; then eternity
Frees all from any temporal respect.
I come, my Ovid; take me in thine arms,
And let me breathe my soul into thy breast.

  Ovid. O stay, my love; the hopes thou dost conceive
Of thy quick death, and of thy future life,
Are not authentical.   Thou choosest death,
So thou might'st 'joy thy love in the other life:
But know, my princely love, when thou art dead,
Thou only must survive in perfect soul;
And in the soul are no affections.
We pour out our affections with our blood,
And, with our blood's affections, fade our loves.
No life hath love in such sweet state as this;
No essence is so dear to moody sense
As flesh and blood, whose quintessence is sense.
Beauty, composed of blood and flesh, moves more,
And is more plausible to blood and flesh,
Than spiritual beauty can be to the spirit.
Such apprehension as we have in dreams,
When, sleep, the bond of senses, locks them up,
Such shall we have, when death destroys them quite.
If love be then thy object, change not life;
Live high and happy still: I still below,
Close with my fortunes, in thy height shall joy.

  Jul. Ay me, that virtue, whose brave eagle's wings,
With every stroke blow stars in burning heaven,
Should, like a swallow, preying towards storms,
Fly close to earth, and with an eager plume,
Pursue those objects which none else can see,
But seem to all the world the empty air!
Thus thou, poor Ovid, and all virtuous men,
Must prey, like swallows, on invisible food,
Pursuing flies, or nothing: and thus love,
And every worldly fancy, is transposed

By worldly tyranny to what plight it list.
O father, since thou gav'st me not my mind,
Strive not to rule it; take but what thou gav'st
To thy disposure: thy affections
Rule not in me; I must bear all my griefs,
Let me use all my pleasures; virtuous love
Was never scandal to a goddess' state.—
But he's inflexible! and, my dear love,
Thy life may chance be shorten'd by the length
Of my unwilling speeches to depart.
Farewell, sweet life; though thou be yet exiled
The officious court, enjoy me amply still:
My soul, in this my breath, enters thine ears,
And on this turret's floor will I lie dead,
Till we may meet again: In this proud height,
I kneel beneath thee in my prostrate love,
And kiss the happy sands that kiss thy feet.
Great Jove submits a sceptre to a cell,
And lovers, ere they part, will meet in hell.

    Ovid. Farewell all company, and, if I could,
All light with thee! hell's shade should hide my brows,
Till thy dear beauty's beams redeem'd my vows.   *[Going*

    Jul. Ovid, my love; alas! may we not stay
A little longer, think'st thou, undiscern'd?

    Ovid. For thine own good, fair goddess, do not stay.
Who would engage a firmament of fires
Shining in thee, for me, a falling star?
Be gone, sweet life-blood; if I should discern
Thyself but touch'd for my sake, I should die.

    Jul. I will begone, then; and not heaven itself
Shall draw me back.

    Ovid. Yet, Julia, if thou wilt,
A little longer stay.

    Jul. I am content.

    Ovid. O, mighty Ovid! what the sway of heaven
Could not retire, my breath hath turned back.

    Jul. Who shall go first, my love? my passionate eyes
Will not endure to see thee turn from me.

    Ovid. If thou go first, my soul will follow thee.

    Jul. Then we must stay.

    Ovid. Ay me, there is no stay
In amorous pleasures; if both stay, both die.
I hear thy father; hence, my deity.   *[Julia retires from the window.*
Fear forgeth sounds in my deluded ears;
I did not hear him; I am mad with love.
There is no spirit under heaven, that works
With such illusion; yet such witchcraft kill me,
Ere a sound mind, without it, save my life!
Here, on my knees, I worship the blest place

That held my goddess; and the loving air,
That closed her body in his silken arms.
Vain Ovid! kneel not to the place, nor air;
She's in thy heart; rise then, and worship there.
The truest wisdom silly men can have,
Is dotage on the follies of their flesh. [*Exit.*

ACT V

SCENE I.—*An Apartment in the Palace.*

Enter CÆSAR, MECÆNAS, GALLUS, TIBULLUS, HORACE, *and*
Equites Romani.

Cæs. We, that have conquer'd still, to save the conquer'd,
And loved to make inflictions fear'd, not felt;
Grieved to reprove, and joyful to reward;
More proud of reconcilement than revenge;
Resume into the late state of our love,
Worthy Cornelius Gallus, and Tibullus:
You both are gentlemen: and, you, Cornelius,
A soldier of renown, and the first provost
That ever let our Roman eagles fly
On swarthy Ægypt, quarried with her spoils.
Yet (not to bear cold forms, nor men's out-terms,
Without the inward fires, and lives of men)
You both have virtues shining through your shapes;
To shew, your titles are not writ on posts,
Or hollow statues which the best men are,
Without Promethean stuffings reach'd from heaven!
Sweet poesy's sacred garlands crown your gentry:
Which is, of all the faculties on earth,
The most abstract and perfect; if she be
True-born, and nursed with all the sciences.
She can so mould Rome, and her monuments,
Within the liquid marble of her lines,
That they shall stand fresh and miraculous,
Even when they mix with innovating dust;
In her sweet streams shall our brave Roman spirits
Chase, and swim after death, with their choice deeds
Shining on their white shoulders; and therein
Shall Tyber, and our famous rivers fall
With such attraction, that the ambitious line
Of the round world shall to her centre shrink,
To hear their music: and, for these high parts,
Cæsar shall reverence the Pierian arts.
　Mec. Your majesty's high grace to poesy,
Shall stand 'gainst all the dull detractions
Of leaden souls; who, for the vain assumings

Of some, quite worthless of her sovereign wreaths,
Contain her worthiest prophets in contempt.

Gal. Happy is Rome of all earth's other states,
To have so true and great a president,
For her inferior spirits to imitate,
As Cæsar is; who addeth to the sun
Influence and lustre; in increasing thus
His inspirations, kindling fire in us.

Hor. Phœbus himself shall kneel at Cæsar's shrine,
And deck it with bay garlands dew'd with wine,
To quit the worship Cæsar does to him:
Where other princes, hoisted to their thrones
By Fortune's passionate and disorder'd power,
Sit in their height, like clouds before the sun,
Hindering his comforts; and, by their excess
Of cold in virtue, and cross heat in vice,
Thunder and tempest on those learned heads,
Whom Cæsar with such honour doth advance.

Tib. All human business fortune doth command
Without all order; and with her blind hand,
She, blind, bestows blind gifts, that still have nurst,
They see not who, nor how, but still, the worst.

Cæs. Cæsar, for his rule, and for so much stuff
As Fortune puts in his hand, shall dispose it,
As if his hand had eyes and soul in it,
With worth and judgment. Hands, that part with gifts
Or will restrain their use, without desert,
Or with a misery numb'd to virtue's right,
Work, as they had no soul to govern them,
And quite reject her; severing their estates
From human order. Whosoever can,
And will not cherish virtue, is no man.

Enter some of the Equestrian Order.

Eques. Virgil is now at hand, imperial Cæsar.

Cæs. Rome's honour is at hand then. Fetch a chair,
And set it on our right hand, where 'tis fit
Rome's honour and our own should ever sit.
Now he is come out of Campania,
I doubt not he hath finish'd all his Æneids.
Which, like another soul, I long to enjoy.
What think you three of Virgil, gentlemen,
That are of his profession, though rank'd higher;
Or, Horace, what say'st thou, that art the poorest,
And likeliest to envy, or to detract?

Hor. Cæsar speaks after common men in this,
To make a difference of me for my poorness;
As if the filth of poverty sunk as deep
Into a knowing spirit, as the bane

Of riches doth into an ignorant soul.
No, Cæsar, they be pathless, moorish minds
That being once made rotten with the dung
Of damned riches, ever after sink
Beneath the steps of any villainy.
But knowledge is the nectar that keeps sweet
A perfect soul, even in this grave of sin;
And for my soul, it is as free as Cæsar's,
For what I know is due I'll give to all.
He that detracts or envies virtuous merit,
Is still the covetous and the ignorant spirit.

Cæs. Thanks, Horace, for thy free and wholesome sharpness,
Which pleaseth Cæsar more than servile fawns.
A flatter'd prince soon turns the prince of fools.
And for thy sake, we'll put no difference more
Between the great and good for being poor.
Say then, loved Horace, thy true thought of Virgil.

Hor. I judge him of a rectified spirit,
By many revolutions of discourse,
(In his bright reason's influence,) refined
From all the tartarous moods of common men;
Bearing the nature and similitude
Of a right heavenly body; most severe
In fashion and collection of himself;
And, then, as clear and confident as Jove.

Gal. And yet so chaste and tender is his ear,
In suffering any syllable to pass,
That he thinks may become the honour'd name
Of issue to his so examined self,
That all the lasting fruits of his full merit,
In his own poems, he doth still distaste;
And if his mind's piece, which he strove to paint,
Could not with fleshly pencils have her right.

Tib. But to approve his works of sovereign worth,
This observation, methinks, more than serves,
And is not vulgar. That which he hath writ
Is with such judgment labour'd, and distill'd
Through all the needful uses of our lives,
That could a man remember but his lines,
He should not touch at any serious point,
But he might breathe his spirit out of him.

Cæs. You mean, he might repeat part of his works,
As fit for any conference he can use?

Tib. True, royal Cæsar.

Cæs. Worthily observed;
And a most worthy virtue in his works.
What thinks material Horace of his learning?

Hor. His learning savours not the school-like gloss,
That most consists in echoing words and terms,

And soonest wins a man an empty name;
Nor any long or far-fetch'd circumstance
Wrapp'd in the curious generalities of arts;
But a direct and analytic sum
Of all the worth and first effects of arts.
And for his poesy, 'tis so ramm'd with life,
That it shall gather strength of life, with being,
And live hereafter more admired than now.

Cæs. This one consent in all your dooms of him,
And mutual loves of all your several merits,
Argues a truth of merit in you all.—

Enter VIRGIL.

See, here comes Virgil; we will rise and greet him.
Welcome to Cæsar, Virgil! Cæsar and Virgil
Shall differ but in sound; to Cæsar, Virgil,
Of his expressed greatness, shall be made
A second sirname, and to Virgil, Cæsar.
Where are thy famous Æneids? do us grace
To let us see, and surfeit on their sight.

Virg. Worthless they are of Cæsar's gracious eyes,
If they were perfect; much more with their wants,
Which are yet more than my time could supply.
And, could great Cæsar's expectation
Be satisfied with any other service,
I would not shew them.

Cæs. Virgil is too modest;
Or seeks, in vain, to make our longings more:
Shew them, sweet Virgil.

Virg. Then, in such due fear
As fits presenters of great works to Cæsar,
I humbly shew them.

Cæs. Let us now behold
A human soul made visible in life;
And more refulgent in a senseless paper
Than in the sensual complement of kings.
Read, read thyself, dear Virgil; let not me
Profane one accent with an untuned tongue:
Best matter, badly shewn, shews worse than bad.
See then this chair, of purpose set for thee
To read thy poem in; refuse it not.
Virtue, without presumption, place may take
Above best kings, whom only she should make.

Virg. It will be thought a thing ridiculous
To present eyes, and to all future times
A gross untruth, that any poet, void
Of birth, or wealth, or temporal dignity,
Should, with decorum, transcend Cæsar's chair.
Poor virtue raised, high birth and wealth set under,

Crosseth heaven's courses, and makes worldlings wonder.

Cæs. The course of heaven, and fate itself, in this,
Will Cæsar cross; much more all worldly custom.

Hor. Custom, in course of honour, ever errs;
And they are best whom fortune least prefers.

Cæs. Horace hath but more strictly spoke our thoughts.
The vast rude swing of general confluence
Is, in particular ends, exempt from sense:
And therefore reason (which in right should be
The special rector of all harmony)
Shall shew we are a man distinct by it,
From those, whom custom rapteth in her press.
Ascend then, Virgil; and where first by chance
We here have turn'd thy book, do thou first read.

Virg. Great Cæsar hath his will; I will ascend.
'Twere simple injury to his free hand,
That sweeps the cobwebs from unused virtue,
And makes her shine proportion'd to her worth,
To be more nice to entertain his grace,
Than he is choice, and liberal to afford it.

Cæs. Gentlemen of our chamber, guard the doors,
And let none enter; [*Exeunt Equites.*] peace.   Begin, good Virgil.

    Virg. Meanwhile the skies 'gan thunder, and in tail
Of that, fell pouring storms of sleet and hail:
The Tyrian lords and Trojan youth, each where
With Venus' Dardane nephew, now, in fear,
Seek out for several shelter through the plain,
Whilst floods come rolling from the hills amain.
Dido a cave, the Trojan prince the same
Lighted upon.   There earth and heaven's great dame,
That hath the charge of marriage, first gave sign
Unto his contract; fire and air did shine,
As guilty of the match; and from the hill
The nymphs with shriekings do the region fill.
Here first began their bane; this day was ground
Of all their ills; for now, nor rumour's sound,
Nor nice respect of state, moves Dido ought;
Her love no longer now by stealth is sought:
She calls this wedlock, and with that fair name
Covers her fault.   Forthwith the bruit and fame,
Through all the greatest Lybian towns is gone;
Fame, a fleet evil, than which is swifter none,
That moving grows, and flying gathers strength;
Little at first, and fearful; but at length
She dares attempt the skies, and stalking proud
With feet on ground, her head doth pierce a cloud !
This child, our parent earth, stirr'd up with spite
Of all the gods, brought forth; and, as some write,
She was last sister of that giant race

That thought to scale Jove's court; right swift of pace,
And swifter far of wing; a monster vast,
And dreadful. Look, how many plumes are placed
On her huge corps, so many waking eyes
Stick underneath; and, which may stranger rise
In the report, as many tongues she bears,
As many mouths, as many listening ears.
Nightly, in midst of all the heaven, she flies,
And through the earth's dark shadow shrieking cries;
Nor do her eyes once bend to taste sweet sleep;
By day on tops of houses she doth keep,
Or on high towers; and doth thence affright
Cities and towns of most conspicuous site:
As covetous she is of tales and lies,
As prodigal of truth: this monster—

Lup. [*within.*] Come, follow me, assist me, second me! Where's the emperor?

1 *Eques.* [*within.*] Sir, you must pardon us.

2 *Eques.* [*within.*] Cæsar is private now; you may not enter.

Tuc. [*within.*] Not enter! Charge them upon their allegiance, cropshin.

1 *Eques.* [*within.*] We have a charge to the contrary, sir.

Lup. [*within.*] I pronounce you all traitors, horrible traitors: What! do you know my affairs? I have matter of danger and state to impart to Cæsar.

Cæs. What noise is there? who's that names Cæsar?

Lup. [*within.*] A friend to Cæsar.
One that, for Cæsar's good, would speak with Cæsar.

Cæs. Who is it? look, Cornelius.

1 *Eques.* [*within.*] Asinius Lupus.

Cæs. O, bid the turbulent informer hence;
We have no vacant ear now, to receive
The unseason'd fruits of his officious tongue.

Mec. You must avoid him there.

Lup. [*within.*] I conjure thee, as thou art Cæsar, or respectest thine own safety, or the safety of the state, Cæsar, hear me, speak with me, Cæsar; 'tis no common business I come about, but such, as being neglected, may concern the life of Cæsar.

Cæs. The life of Cæsar! Let him enter. Virgil, keep thy seat.

Equites. [*within.*] Bear back, there: whither will you? keep back!

Enter LUPUS, TUCCA, *and* Lictors.

Tuc. By thy leave, goodman usher: mend thy peruke; so.

Lup. Lay hold on Horace there; and on Mecænas, lictors. Romans, offer no rescue, upon your allegiance: read, royal Cæsar. [*Gives a paper.*] I'll tickle you, Satyr.

Tuc. He will, Humours, he will; he will squeeze you, poet puck-fist.

Lup. I'll lop you off for an unprofitable branch, you satirical varlet.

Tuc. Ay, and Epaminondas your patron here, with his flagon chain; come, resign: [*takes off Mecœnas' chain,*] though 'twere your great grandfather's, the law has made it mine now, sir. Look to him, my party-coloured rascals; look to him.

Cœs. What is this, Asinius Lupus? I understand it not.

Lup. Not understand it! A libel, Cæsar; a dangerous, seditious libel; a libel in picture.

Cœs. A libel!

Lup. Ay, I found it in this Horace his study, in Mecænas his house, here; I challenge the penalty of the laws against them.

Tuc. Ay, and remember to beg their land betimes; before some of these hungry court-hounds scent it out.

Cœs. Shew it to Horace: ask him if he know it.

Lup. Know it! his hand is at it, Cæsar.

Cœs. Then 'tis no libel.

Hor. It is the imperfect body of an emblem, Cæsar, I began for Mecænas.

Lup. An emblem! right: that's Greek for a libel. Do but mark how confident he is.

Hor. A just man cannot fear, thou foolish tribune;
Not, though the malice of traducing tongues,
The open vastness of a tyrant's ear,
The senseless rigour of the wrested laws,
Or the red eyes of strain'd authority,
Should, in a point, meet all to take his life:
His innocence is armour 'gainst all these.

Lup. Innocence! O impudence! let me see, let me see! Is not here an eagle! and is not that eagle meant by Cæsar, ha? Does not Cæsar give the eagle? answer me; what sayest thou?

Tuc. Hast thou any evasion, stinkard?

Lup. Now he's turn'd dumb. I'll tickle you, Satyr.

Hor. Pish: ha, ha!

Lup. Dost thou pish me? Give me my long sword.

Hor. With reverence to great Cæsar, worthy Romans,
Observe but this ridiculous commenter;
The soul to my device was in this distich:

> Thus oft, the base and ravenous multitude
> Survive, to share the spoils of fortitude.

Which in this body I have figured here,
A vulture—

Lup. A vulture! Ay, now, 'tis a vulture. O abominable! monstrous! monstrous! has not your vulture a beak? has it not legs, and talons, and wings, and feathers?

Tuc. Touch him, old buskins.

Hor. And therefore must it be an eagle?

Mec. Respect him not, good Horace: say your device.

Hor. A vulture and a wolf—

Lup. A wolf! good: that's I; I am the wolf: my name's Lupus;
I am meant by the wolf. On, on; a vulture and a wolf—

Hor. Preying upon the carcass of an ass—

Lup. An ass! good still: that's I too; I am the ass. You mean
me by the ass.

Mec. Prithee, leave braying then.

Hor. If you will needs take it, I cannot with modesty give it
from you.

Mec. But, by that beast, the old Egyptians
Were wont to figure, in their hieroglyphics,
Patience, frugality, and fortitude;
For none of which we can suspect you, tribune.

Cæs. Who was it, Lupus, that inform'd you first,
This should be meant by us? Or was't your comment?

Lup. No, Cæsar; a player gave me the first light of it indeed.

Tuc. Ay, an honest sycophant-like slave, and a politician besides.

Cæs. Where is that player?

Tuc. He is without here.

Cæs. Call him in.

Tuc. Call in the player there: master Æsop, call him.

Equites. [*within.*] Player! where is the player? bear back: none
but the player enter.

Enter ÆSOP, *followed by* CRISPINUS *and* DEMETRIUS.

Tuc. Yes, this gentleman and his Achates must.

Cris. Pray you, master usher:—we'll stand close, here.

Tuc. 'Tis a gentleman of quality, this; though he be somewhat
out of clothes, I tell ye.—Come, Æsop, hast a bay-leaf in thy mouth?
Well said; be not out, stinkard. Thou shalt have a monopoly of
playing confirm'd to thee, and thy covey, under the emperor's
broad seal, for this service.

Cæs. Is this he?

Lup. Ay, Cæsar, this is he.

Cæs. Let him be whipped. Lictors, go take him hence.
And, Lupus, for your fierce credulity,
One fit him with a pair of larger ears:
'Tis Cæsar's doom, and must not be revoked.
We hate to have our court and peace disturb'd
With these quotidian clamours. See it done.

Lup. Cæsar! [*Exeunt some of the Lictors, with Lupus and Æsop.*

Cæs. Gag him, [that] we may have his silence.

Virg. Cæsar hath done like Cæsar. Fair and just
Is his award, against these brainless creatures.
'Tis not the wholesome sharp morality,
Or modest anger of a satiric spirit,
That hurts or wounds the body of the state;
But the sinister application
Of the malicious, ignorant, and base
Interpreter; who will distort, and strain

The general scope and purpose of an author
To his particular and private spleen.

   Cæs. We know it, our dear Virgil, and esteem it
A most dishonest practice in that man,
Will seem too witty in another's work.
What would Cornelius Gallus, and Tibullus?   [*They whisper Cæsar.*

   Tuc. [*to Mecænas.*] Nay, but as thou art a man, dost hear! a
man of worship and honourable: hold, here, take thy chain again.
Resume, mad Mecænas. What! dost thou think I meant to have
kept it, old boy? no: I did it but to fright thee, I, to try how
thou would'st take it. What! will I turn shark upon my friends, or
my friends' friends? I scorn it with my three souls. Come, I love
bully Horace as well as thou dost, I: 'tis an honest hieroglyphic.
Give me thy wrist, Helicon. Dost thou think I'll second e'er a
rhinoceros of them all, against thee, ha? or thy noble Hippocrene,
here? I'll turn stager first, and be whipt too: dost thou see, bully?

   Cæs. You have your will of Cæsar: use it, Romans.
Virgil shall be your prætor: and ourself
Will here sit by, spectator of your sports;
And think it no impeach of royalty.
Our ear is now too much profaned, grave Maro,
With these distastes, to take thy sacred lines;
Put up thy book, till both the time and we
Be fitted with more hallow'd circumstance
For the receiving of so divine a work.
Proceed with your design.

   Mec. Gal. Tib. Thanks to great Cæsar.

   Gal. Tibullus, draw you the indictment then, whilst Horace
arrests them on the statute of Calumny. Mecænas and I will take
our places here. Lictors, assist him.

   Hor. I am the worst accuser under heaven.

   Gal. Tut, you must do it; 'twill be noble mirth.

   Hor. I take no knowledge that they do malign me.

   Tib. Ay, but the world takes knowledge.

   Hor. Would the world knew
How heartily I wish a fool should hate me!

   Tuc. Body of Jupiter! what! will they arraign my brisk Poetaster
and his poor journeyman, ha? Would I were abroad skeldering for
a drachm, so I were out of this labyrinth again! I do feel myself
turn stinkard already: but I must set the best face I have upon't
now. [*Aside.*]—Well said, my divine, deft Horace, bring the
whoreson detracting slaves to the bar, do; make them hold up their
spread golls: I'll give in evidence for thee, if thou wilt. Take
courage, Crispinus; would thy man had a clean band!

   Cris. What must we do, captain?

   Tuc. Thou shalt see anon: do not make division with thy legs so.

   Cæs. What's he, Horace?

   Hor. I only know him for a motion, Cæsar.

   Tuc. I am one of thy commanders, Cæsar; a man of service and action: my name is Pantilius Tucca; I have served in thy wars against Mark Antony, I.

Cæs. Do you know him, Cornelius?

Gal. He's one that hath had the mustering, or convoy of a company now and then: I never noted him by any other employment.

Cæs. We will observe him better.

Tib. Lictor, proclaim silence in the court.

Lict. In the name of Cæsar, silence!

Tib. Let the parties, the accuser and the accused, present themselves.

Lict. The accuser and the accused, present yourselves in court.

Cris. Dem. Here.

Virg. Read the indictment.

Tib. Rufus Laberius Crispinus, and Demetrius Fannius, hold up your hands. You are, before this time, jointly and severally indicted, and here presently to be arraigned upon the statute of calumny, or Lex Remmia, *the one by the name of Rufus Laberius Crispinus, alias Cri-spinas, poetaster and plagiary; the other by the name of Demetrius Fannius, play-dresser and plagiary. That you (not having the fear of Phœbus, or his shafts, before your eyes) contrary to the peace of our liege lord, Augustus Cæsar, his crown and dignity, and against the form of a statute, in that case made and provided, have most ignorantly, foolishly, and, more like yourselves, maliciously, gone about to deprave, and calumniate the person and writings of Quintus Horatius Flaccus, here present, poet, and priest to the Muses; and to that end have mutually conspired and plotted, at sundry times, as by several means, and in sundry places, for the better accomplishing your base and envious purpose; taxing him falsely, of self-love, arrogancy, impudence, railing, filching by translation, etc. Of all which calumnies, and every of them, in manner and form aforesaid; what answer you? Are you guilty, or not guilty?*

Tuc. Not guilty, say.

Cris. Dem. Not guilty.

Tib. How will you be tried?

Tuc. By the Roman Gods, and the noblest Romans.

[*Aside to Crispinus.*

Cris. Dem. By the Roman gods, and the noblest Romans.

Virg. Here sits Mecænas, and Cornelius Gallus, are you contented to be tried by these?

Tuc. Ay, so the noble captain may be joined with them in commission, say. [*Aside.*

Cris. Dem. Ay, so the noble captain may be joined with them in commission.

Virg. What says the plaintiff?

Hor. I am content.

Virg. Captain, then take your place.

Tuc. Alas, my worshipful prætor! 'tis more of thy gentleness than of my deserving, I wusse. But since it hath pleased the court to make choice of my wisdom and gravity, come, my calumnious

varlets; let's hear you talk for yourselves, now, an hour or two.
What can you say? Make a noise. Act, act!

Virg. Stay, turn, and take an oath first. *You shall swear,*
By thunder-darting Jove, the king of gods,
And by the genius of Augustus Cæsar;
By your own white and uncorrupted souls,
And the deep reverence of our Roman justice;
To judge this case, with truth and equity:
As bound by your religion, and your laws.
Now read the evidence: but first demand
Of either prisoner, if that writ be theirs. [*Gives him two papers.*

Tib. Shew this unto Crispinus. Is it yours?

Tuc. Say, ay. [*Aside.*]—What! dost thou stand upon it, pimp?
Do not deny thine own Minerva, thy Pallas, the issue of thy brain.

Cris. Yes it is mine.

Tib. Shew that unto Demetrius. Is it yours?

Dem. It is.

Tuc. There's a father will not deny his own bastard now, I
warrant thee.

Virg. Read them aloud.

Tib. *Ramp up my genius, be not retrograde;*
But boldly nominate a spade a spade
What, shall thy lubrical and glibbery muse
Live, as she were defunct, like punk in stews!

Tuc. Excellent!

Alas! that were no modern consequence,
To have cothurnal buskins frighted hence.
No, teach thy Incubus to poetise;
And throw abroad thy spurious snotteries,
Upon that puft-up lump of balmy froth,

Tuc. Ah, Ah!

Or clumsy chilblain'd judgment; that with oath
Magnificates his merit; and bespawls
The conscious time, with humorous foam and brawls,
As if his organons of sense would crack
The sinews of my patience. Break his back,
O poets all and some! for now we list
Of strenuous vengeance to clutch the fist. CRISPINUS.

Tuc. Ay, marry, this was written like a Hercules in poetry, now.

Cæs. Excellently well threaten'd!

Virg. And as strangely worded, Cæsar.

Cæs. We observe it.

Virg. The other now.

Tuc. This is a fellow of a good prodigal tongue too, this will do
well.

Tib. *Our Muse is in mind for th' untrussing a poet;*
I slip by his name, for most men do know it:
A critic, that all the world bescumbers
With satirical humours and lyrical numbers:

Tuc. Art thou there, boy?
And for the most part, himself doth advance
With much self-love, and more arrogance.

Tuc. Good again!
And, but that I would not be thought a prater,
I could tell you he were a translator.
I know the authors from whence he has stole,
And could trace him too, but that I understand them not full and whole.

Tuc. That line is broke loose from all his fellows: chain him up shorter, do.
The best note I can give you to know him by,
Is, that he keeps gallants' company;
Whom I could wish, in time should him fear,
Lest after they buy repentance too dear. DEME. FANNIUS.

Tuc. Well said! This carries palm with it.

Hor. And why, thou motley gull, why should they fear?
When hast thou known us wrong or tax a friend?
I dare thy malice to betray it. Speak.
Now thou curl'st up, thou poor and nasty snake,
And shrink'st thy poisonous head into thy bosom:
Out, viper! thou that eat'st thy parents, hence!
Rather, such speckled creatures, as thyself,
Should be eschew'd, and shunn'd; such as will bite
And gnaw their absent friends, not cure their fame;
Catch at the loosest laughters, and affect
To be thought jesters; such as can devise
Things never seen, or head, t'impair men's names,
And gratify their credulous adversaries;
Will carry tales, do basest offices,
Cherish divided fires, and still encrease
New flames, out of old embers; will reveal
Each secret that's committed to their trust:
These be black slaves; Romans, take heed of these.

Tuc. Thou twang'st right, little Horace: they be indeed a couple of chap-fall'n curs. Come, we of the bench, let's rise to the urn, and condemn them quickly.

Virg. Before you go together, worthy Romans,
We are to tender our opinion;
And give you those instructions, that may add
Unto your even judgment in the cause:
Which thus we do commence. First, you must know,
That where there is a true and perfect merit,
There can be no dejection; and the scorn
Of humble baseness, oftentimes so works
In a high soul, upon the grosser spirit,
That to his bleared and offended sense,
There seems a hideous fault blazed in the object;
When only the disease is in his eyes.
Here-hence it comes our Horace now stands tax'd

Of impudence, self-love, and arrogance,
By those who share no merit in themselves;
And therefore think his portion is as small.
For they, from their own guilt, assure their souls,
If they should confidently praise their works,
In them it would appear inflation:
Which, in a full and well digested man,
Cannot receive that foul abusive name,
But the fair title of erection.
And, for his true use of translating men,
It still hath been a work of as much palm,
In clearest judgments, as to invent or make,
His sharpness,—that is most excusable;
As being forced out of a suffering virtue,
Oppressed with the license of the time:
And howsoever fools or jerking pedants,
Players, or such-like buffoon barking wits,
May with their beggarly and barren trash
Tickle base vulgar ears, in their despite;
This, like Jove's thunder, shall their pride control,
" The honest satire hath the happiest soul."
Now, Romans, you have heard our thoughts; withdraw when you
please.

  Tib. Remove the accused from the bar.

  Tuc. Who holds the urn to us, ha? Fear nothing, I'll quit you,
mine honest pitiful stinkards; I'll do't.

  Cris. Captain, you shall eternally girt me to you, as I am generous.

  Tuc. Go to.

  Cæs. Tibullus, let there be a case of vizards privately provided;
we have found a subject to bestow them on.

  Tib. It shall be done, Cæsar.

  Cæs. Here be words, Horace, able to bastinado a man's ears.

  Hor. Ay.
Please it, great Cæsar, I have pills about me,
Mixt with the whitest kind of hellebore,
Would give him a light vomit, that should purge
His brain and stomach of those tumorous heats:
Might I have leave to minister unto him.

  Cæs. O, be his Æsculapius, gentle Horace!
You shall have leave, and he shall be your patient.
Virgil,
Use your authority, command him forth.

  Virg. Cæsar is careful of your health, Crispinus;
And hath himself chose a physician
To minister unto you: take his pills.

  Hor. They are somewhat bitter, sir, but very wholesome.
Take yet another; so: stand by, they'll work anon.

  Tib. Romans, return to your several seats: lictors, bring forward
the urn; and set the accused to the bar.

Tuc. Quickly, you whoreson egregious varlets; come forward. What! shall we sit all day upon you? You make no more haste now, than a beggar upon pattens; or a physician to a patient that has no money, you pilchers.

Tib. *Rufus Laberius Crispinus, and Demetrius Fannius, hold up your hands. You have, according to the Roman custom, put yourselves upon trial to the urn, for divers and sundry calumnies, whereof you have, before this time, been indicted, and are now presently arraigned: prepare yourselves to hearken to the verdict of your tryers. Caius Cilnius Mecænas pronounceth you, by this hand-writing, guilty. Cornelius Gallus, guilty. Pantilius Tucca—*

Tuc. Parcel-guilty, I.

Dem. He means himself; for it was he indeed, Suborn'd us to the calumny.

Tuc. I, you whoreson cantharides! was it I?

Dem. I appeal to your conscience, captain.

Tib. Then you confess it now?

Dem. I do, and crave the mercy of the court.

Tib. What saith Crispinus?

Cris. O, the captain, the captain—

Hor. My physic begins to work with my patient, I see.

Virg. Captain, stand forth and answer.

Tuc. Hold thy peace, poet prætor: I appeal from thee to Cæsar, I. Do me right, royal Cæsar.

Cæs. Marry, and I will, sir.—Lictors, gag him; do. And put a case of vizards o'er his head, That he may look bifronted, as he speaks.

Tuc. Gods and fiends! Cæsar! thou wilt not, Cæsar, wilt thou? Away, you whoreson vultures; away. You think I am a dead corps now, because Cæsar is disposed to jest with a man of mark, or so. Hold your hook'd talons out of my flesh, you inhuman harpies. Go to, do't. What! will the royal Augustus cast away a gentleman of worship, a captain and a commander, for a couple of condemn'd caitiff calumnious cargos?

Cæs. Dispatch, lictors.

Tuc. Cæsar!   [*The vizards are put upon him.*

Cæs. Forward, Tibullus.

Virg. Demand what cause they had to malign Horace.

Dem. In troth, no great cause, not I, I must confess; but that he kept better company, for the most part, than I; and that better men loved him than loved me; and that his writings thrived better than mine, and were better liked and graced: nothing else.

Virg. Thus envious souls repine at others' good.

Hor. If this be all, faith, I forgive thee freely. Envy me still, so long as Virgil loves me, Gallus, Tibullus, and the best-best Cæsar, My dear Mecænas; while these, with many more, Whose names I wisely slip, shall think me worthy Their honour'd and adored society,

And read and love, prove and applaud my poems;
I would not wish but such as you should spite them.

Cris. O—!

Tib. How now, Crispinus?

Cris. O, I am sick—!

Hor. A bason, a bason, quickly; our physic works. Faint not, man.

Cris. O———*retrograde*———*reciprocal*———*incubus.*

Cæs. What's that, Horace?

Hor. *Retrograde, reciprocal,* and *incubus,* are come up.

Gal. Thanks be to Jupiter!

Cris. O——*glibbery*——*lubrical*——*defunct*—O—!

Hor. Well said; here's some store.

Virg. What are they?

Hor. *Glibbery, lubrical,* and *defunct.*

Gal. O, they came up easy.

Cris. O——O—!

Tib. What's that?

Hor. Nothing yet.

Cris. *Magnificate*—

Mec. *Magnificate!* That came up somewhat hard.

Hor. Ay. What cheer, Crispinus?

Cris. O! I shall cast up my——*spurious*——*snotteries*—

Hor. Good. Again.

Cris. *Chilblain'd*——O——O——*clumsie*—

Hor. That *clumsie* stuck terribly.

Mec. What's all that, Horace?

Hor. *Spurious, snotteries, chilblain'd, clumsie.*

Tib. O Jupiter!

Gal. Who would have thought there should have been such a deal of filth in a poet?

Cris. O——*balmy froth*—

Cæs. What's that?

Cris. —*Puffie*——*inflate*——*turgidous*——*ventosity.*

Hor. *Barmy, froth, puffie, inflate, turgidous,* and *ventosity* are come up.

Tib. O terrible windy words.

Gal. A sign of a windy brain.

Cris. O——*oblatrant*——*furibund*——*fatuate*——*strenuous*—

Hor. Here's a deal; *oblatrant, furibund, fatuate, strenuous.*

Cæs. Now all's come up, I trow. What a tumult he had in his belly?

Hor. No, there's the often *conscious damp* behind still.

Cris. O——*conscious*——*damp.*

Hor. It is come up, thanks to Apollo and Æsculapius: yet there's another; you were best take a pill more.

Cris. O, no; O——O——O——O!

Hor. Force yourself then a little with your finger.

Cris. O——O——*prorumped.*

Tib. *Prorumped !* What a noise it made! as if his spirit would
have prorumpt with it.

Cris. O——O——O!

Virg. Help him, it sticks strangely, whatever it is.

Cris. O——*clutcht.*

Hor. Now it is come; *clutcht.*

Cæs. *Clutcht !* it is well that's come up; it had but a narrow
passage.

Cris. O—!

Virg. Again! hold him, hold his head there.

Cris. *Snarling gusts——quaking custard.*

Hor. How now, Crispinus?

Cris. O——*obstupefact.*

Tib. Nay, that are all we, I assure you.

Hor. How do you feel yourself?

Cris. Pretty and well, I thank you.

Virg. These pills can but restore him for a time,
Not cure him quite of such a malady,
Caught by so many surfeits, which have fill'd
His blood and brain thus full of crudities:
'Tis necessary therefore he observe
A strict and wholesome diet.   Look you take
Each morning of old Cato's principles
A good draught next your heart; that walk upon,
Till it be well digested: then come home,
And taste a piece of Terence, suck his phrase
Instead of liquorice; and, at any hand,
Shun Plautus and old Ennius: they are meats
Too harsh for a weak stomach.   Use to read
(But not without a tutor) the best Greeks,
As Orpheus, Musæus, Pindarus,
Hesiod, Callimachus, and Theocrite,
High Homer; but beware of Lycophron,
He is too dark and dangerous a dish.
You must not hunt for wild outlandish terms,
To stuff out a peculiar dialect;
But let your matter run before your words.
And if at any time you chance to meet
Some Gallo-Belgic phrase, you shall not straight
Rack your poor verse to give it entertainment,
But let it pass; and do not think yourself
Much damnified, if you do leave it out,
When nor your understanding, nor the sense
Could well receive it.   This fair abstinence,
In time, will render you more sound and clear:
And this have I prescribed to you, in place
Of a strict sentence; which till he perform,
Attire him in that robe.   And henceforth learn
To bear yourself more humbly; not to swell,

Or breathe your insolent and idle spite
On him whose laughter can your worst affright.

Tib. Take him away.

Cris. Jupiter guard Cæsar!

Virg. And for a week or two see him lock'd up
In some dark place, removed from company;
He will talk idly else after his physic.
Now to you, sir. [*to Demetrius.*] The extremity of law
Awards you to be branded in the front,
For this your calumny: but since it pleaseth
Horace, the party wrong'd, t' intreat of Cæsar
A mitigation of that juster doom,
With Cæsar's tongue thus we pronounce your sentence.
Demetrius Fannius, thou shalt here put on
That coat and cap, and henceforth think thyself
No other than they make thee; vow to wear them
In every fair and generous assembly,
Till the best sort of minds shall take to knowledge
As well thy satisfaction, as thy wrongs.

Hor. Only, grave prætor, here, in open court,
I crave the oath for good behaviour
May be administer'd unto them both.

Virg. Horace, it shall: Tibullus, give it them.

*Tib. Rufus Laberius Crispinus, and Demetrius Fannius, lay your
hands on your hearts. You shall here solemnly attest and swear, that
never, after this instant, either at booksellers' stalls, in taverns, two-
penny rooms, tyring-houses, noblemen's butteries, puisnés chambers,
(the best and farthest places where you are admitted to come,) you shall
once offer or dare (thereby to endear yourself the more to any player,
enghle, or guilty gull in your company) to malign, traduce, or detract
the person or writings of Quintus Horatius Flaccus, or any other
eminent men, transcending you in merit, whom your envy shall find
cause to work upon, either for that, or for keeping himself in better
acquaintance, or enjoying better friends: or if, transported by any
sudden and desperate resolution, you do, that then you shall not under
the batoon, or in the next presence, being an honourable assembly of
his favourers, be brought as voluntary gentlemen to undertake the for-
swearing of it. Neither shall you, at any time, ambitiously affecting
the title of the Untrussers or Whippers of the age, suffer the itch of
writing to over-run your performance in libel, upon pain of being
taken up for lepers in wit, and, losing both your time and your papers,
be irrecoverably forfeited to the hospital of fools. So help you our
Roman gods and the Genius of great Cæsar.*

Virg. So! now dissolve the court.

Hor. Tib. Gal. Mec. And thanks to Cæsar,
That thus hath exercised his patience.

Cæs. We have, indeed, you worthiest friends of Cæsar.
It is the bane and torment of our ears,
To hear the discords of those jangling rhymers,

That with their bad and scandalous practices
Bring all true arts and learning in contempt.
But let not your high thoughts descend so low
As these despised objects; let them fall,
With their flat grovelling souls: be you yourselves;
And as with our best favours you stand crown'd,
So let your mutual loves be still renown'd.
Envy will dwell where there is want of merit,
Though the deserving man should crack his spirit.

> Blush, folly, blush; here's none that fears
> The wagging of an ass's ears,
> Although a wolfish case he wears.
> Detraction is but baseness' varlet;
> And apes are apes, though clothed in scarlet.   [*Exeunt.*

Rumpatur, quisquis rumpitur invidiâ.

" Here, reader, in place of the epilogue, was meant to thee an apology
from the author, with his reasons for the publishing of this book: but,
since he is no less restrained, than thou deprived of it by authority, he
prays thee to think charitably of what thou hast read, till thou mayest
hear him speak what he hath written."

HORACE AND TREBATIUS.

A DIALOGUE.

Sat. 1. *Lib.* 2.

Hor. There are to whom I seem excessive sour,
And past a satire's law t' extend my power:
Others, that think whatever I have writ
Wants pith and matter to eternise it;
And that they could, in one day's light, disclose
A thousand verses, such as I compose.
What shall I do, Trebatius? say.
    Treb. Surcease.
    Hor. And shall my muse admit no more increase?
    Treb. So I advise.
    Hor. An ill death let me die,
If 'twere not best; but sleep avoids mine eye,
And I use these, lest nights should tedious seem.
    Treb. Rather, contend to sleep, and live like them,
That, holding golden sleep in special price,
Rubb'd with sweet oils, swim silver Tyber thrice,
And every even with neat wine steeped be:
Or, if such love of writing ravish thee,
Then dare to sing unconquer'd Cæsar's deeds;
Who cheers such actions with abundant meeds.
    Hor. That, father, I desire; but, when I try,

I feel defects in every faculty:
Nor is't a labour fit for every pen,
To paint the horrid troops of armed men,
The lances burst, in Gallia's slaughter'd forces;
Or wounded Parthians, tumbled from their horses:
Great Cæsar's wars cannot be fought with words.

    Treb. Yet, what his virtue in his peace affords,
His fortitude and justice thou canst shew
As wise Lucilius honour'd Scipio.

    Hor. Of that, my powers shall suffer no neglect,
When such slight labours may aspire respect:
But, if I watch not a most chosen time,
The humble words of Flaccus cannot climb
Th' attentive ear of Cæsar; nor must I
With less observance shun gross flattery:
For he, reposed safe in his own merit,
Spurns back the gloses of a fawning spirit.

    Treb. But how much better would such accents sound
Than with a sad and serious verse to wound
Pantolabus, railing in his saucy jests,
Or Nomentanus spent in riotous feasts?
In satires, each man, though untouch'd, complains
As he were hurt; and hates such biting strains.

    Hor. What shall I do? Milonius shakes his heels
In ceaseless dances, when his brain once feels
The stirring fervour of the wine ascend;
And that his eyes false numbers apprehend.
Castor his horse, Pollux loves handy-fights;
A thousand heads, a thousand choice delights.
My pleasure is in feet my words to close,
As, both our better, old Lucilius does:
He, as his trusty friends, his books did trust
With all his secrets; nor, in things unjust,
Or actions lawful, ran to other men:
So that the old man's life described, was seen
As in a votive table in his lines:
And to his steps my genius inclines;
Lucanian, or Apulian, I know not whether,
For the Venusian colony ploughs either;
Sent thither, when the Sabines were forced thence,
As old Fame sings, to give the place defence
'Gainst such as, seeing it empty, might make road
Upon the empire; or there fix abode:
Whether the Apulian borderer it were,
Or the Lucanian violence they fear.—
But this my style no living man shall touch,
If first I be not forced by base reproach;
But like a sheathed sword it shall defend
My innocent life; for why should I contend

To draw it out, when no malicious thief
Robs my good name, the treasure of my life?
O Jupiter, let it with rust be eaten,
Before it touch, or insolently threaten
The life of any with the least disease;
So much I love, and woo a general peace.
But, he that wrongs me, better, I proclaim,
He never had assay'd to touch my fame.
For he shall weep, and walk with every tongue
Throughout the city, infamously sung.
Servius the prætor threats the laws, and urn,
If any at his deeds repine or spurn;
The witch Canidia, that Albutius got,
Denounceth witchcraft, where she loveth not;
Thurius the judge, doth thunder worlds of ill,
To such as strive with his judicial will.
All men affright their foes in what they may,
Nature commands it, and men must obey.
   Observe with me: The wolf his tooth doth use,
The bull his horn; and who doth this infuse,
But nature? There's luxurious Scæva; trust
His long-lived mother with him; his so just
And scrupulous right-hand no mischief will;
No more than with his heel a wolf will kill,
Or ox with jaw: marry, let him alone
With temper'd poison to remove the croan.
But briefly, if to age I destined be,
Or that quick death's black wings environ me;
If rich, or poor; at Rome; or fate command
I shall be banished to some other land;
What hue soever my whole state shall bear,
I will write satires still, in spite of fear.
   Treb. Horace, I fear thou draw'st no lasting breath;
And that some great man's friend will be thy death.
   Hor. What! when the man that first did satirise
Durst pull the skin over the ears of vice,
And make who stood in outward fashion clear,
Give place, as foul within; shall I forbear?
Did Lælius, or the man so great with fame,
That from sack'd Carthage fetch'd his worthy name,
Storm that Lucilius did Metellus pierce,
Or bury Lupus quick in famous verse?
Rulers and subjects, by whole tribes he checkt,
But virtue and her friends did still protect:
And when from sight, or from the judgment-seat,
The virtuous Scipio and wise Lælius met,
Unbraced, with him in all light sports they shared,
Till their most frugal suppers were prepared.
Whate'er I am, though both for wealth and wit

Beneath Lucilius I am pleased to sit;
Yet Envy, spite of her empoison'd breast,
Shall say, I lived in grace here with the best;
And seeking in weak trash to make her wound,
Shall find me solid, and her teeth unsound:
'Less learn'd Trebatius' censure disagree.
 Treb. No, Horace, I of force must yield to thee:
Only take heed, as being advised by me,
Lest thou incur some danger: better pause,
Than rue thy ignorance of the sacred laws;
There's justice, and great action may be sued
'Gainst such as wrong men's fames with verses lewd.
 Hor. Ay, with lewd verses, such as libels be,
And aim'd at persons of good quality:
I reverence and adore that just decree.
But if they shall be sharp, yet modest rhymes,
That spare men's persons, and but tax their crimes,
Such shall in open court find current pass,
Were Cæsar judge, and with the maker's grace.
 Treb. Nay, I'll add more; if thou thyself, being clear,
Shall tax in person a man fit to bear
Shame and reproach, his suit shall quickly be
Dissolved in laughter, and thou thence set free.

TO THE READER

If, by looking on what is past, thou hast deserved that name, I am willing thou shouid'st yet know more, by that which follows, an APOLOGETICAL DIALOGUE; which was only once spoken upon the stage, and all the answer I ever gave to sundry impotent libels then cast out (and some yet remaining) against me, and this play. Wherein I take no pleasure to revive the times; but that posterity may make a difference between their manners that provoked me then, and mine that neglected them ever. For, in these strifes, and on such persons, were as wretched to affect a victory, as it is unhappy to be committed with them.

Non annorum canities est laudanda, sed morum.

SCENE, *The* Author's *Lodgings.*

Enter NASUTUS *and* POLYPOSUS.

 *Nas. I pray you, let's go see him, how he looks
After these libels.*
 Pol. O vex'd, vex'd, I warrant you.
 *Nas. Do you think so ? I should be sorry for him,
If I found that.*
 *Pol. O, they are such bitter things,
He cannot choose.*
 Nas. But, is he guilty of them ?
 Pol. Fuh ! that's no matter.
 Nas. No !
 Pol. No. Here's his lodging.

We'll steal upon him: or let's listen; stay.
He has a humour oft to talk t' himself.

    Nas. *They are your manners lead me, not mine own.*
      [They come forward; the scene opens, and discovers the
          Author in his study.

    Aut. *The fates have not spun him the coarsest thread,*
That (free from knots of perturbation)
Doth yet so live, although but to himself,
As he can safely scorn the tongues of slaves,
And neglect fortune, more than she can him.
It is the happiest thing this, not to be
Within the reach of malice; it provides
A man so well, to laugh off injuries;
And never sends him farther for his vengeance,
Than the vex'd bosom of his enemy.
I, now, but think how poor their spite sets off,
Who, after all their waste of sulphurous terms,
And burst-out thunder of their charged mouths,
Have nothing left but the unsavoury smoke
Of their black vomit, to upbraid themselves:
Whilst I, at whom they shot, sit here shot-free,
And as unhurt of envy, as unhit.
      [Pol. and Nas. discover themselves.

    Pol. *Ay, but the multitude they think not so, sir;*
They think you hit, and hurt: and dare give out,
Your silence argues it in not rejoining
To this or that late libel.

    Aut. *'Las, good rout!*
I can afford them leave to err so still;
And like the barking students of Bears-college,
To swallow up the garbage of the time
With greedy gullets, whilst myself sit by,
Pleased, and yet tortured, with their beastly feeding.
'Tis a sweet madness runs along with them,
To think, all that are aim'd at still are struck:
Then, where the shaft still lights, make that the mark:
And so each fear or fever-shaken fool
May challenge Teucer's hand in archery.
Good troth, if I knew any man so vile,
To act the crimes these Whippers reprehend,
Or what their servile apes gesticulate,
I should not then much muse their shreds were liked;
Since ill men have a lust t' hear others' sins,
All good men have a zeal to hear sin shamed.
But when it is all excrement they vent,
Base filth and offal; or thefts, notable
As ocean-piracies, or highway-stands;
And not a crime there tax'd, but is their own,
Or what their own foul thoughts suggested to them;

And that, in all their heat of taxing others,
Not one of them but lives himself, if known,
Improbior satiram scribente cinædo,
What should I say more, than turn stone with wonder !
    Nas. *I never saw this play bred all this tumult:*
What was there in it could so deeply offend,
And stir so many hornets ?
    Aut. *Shall I tell you ?*
    Nas. *Yes, and ingenuously.*
    Aut. *Then, by the hope*
Which I prefer unto all other objects,
I can profess, I never writ that piece
More innocent or empty of offence.
Some salt it had, but neither tooth nor gall,
Nor was there in it any circumstance
Which, in the setting down, I could suspect
Might be perverted by an enemy's tongue;
Only it had the fault to be call'd mine;
That was the crime.
    Pol. *No ! why, they say you tax'd*
The law and lawyers, captains and the players,
By their particular names.
    Aut. *It is not so.*
I used no name.   My books have still been taught
To spare the persons, and to speak the vices.
These are mere slanders, and enforced by such
As have no safer ways to men's disgraces.
But their own lies and loss of honesty:
Fellows of practised and most laxative tongues,
Whose empty and eager bellies, in the year,
Compel their brains to many desperate shifts,
(I spare to name them, for their wretchedness
Fury itself would pardon).   These, or such,
Whether of malice, or of ignorance,
Or itch t' have me their adversary, I know not,
Or all these mixt; but sure I am, three years
They did provoke me with their petulant styles
On every stage: and I at last unwilling,
But weary, I confess, of so much trouble,
Thought I would try if shame could win upon 'em;
And therefore chose Augustus Cæsar's times,
When wit and arts were at their height in Rome,
To shew that Virgil, Horace, and the rest
Of those great master-spirits, did not want
Detractors then, or practicers against them:
And by this line, although no parallel,
I hoped at last they would sit down and blush;
But nothing I could find more contrary.
And though the impudence of flies be great,

Yet this hath so provok'd the angry wasps,
Or, as you said, of the next nest, the hornets,
That they fly buzzing, mad, about my nostrils,
And, like so many screaming grasshoppers
Held by the wings, fill every ear with noise.
And what ? those former calumnies you mention'd.
First, of the law: indeed I brought in Ovid
Chid by his angry father for neglecting
The study of their laws for poetry:
And I am warranted by his own words:

Sæpe pater dixit, studium quid inutile tentas?
Mæonides nullas ipse reliquit opes.

And in far harsher terms elsewhere, as these:

Non me verbosas leges ediscere, non me
Ingrato voces prostituisse foro.

But how this should relate unto our laws,
Or the just ministers, with least abuse,
I reverence both too much to understand !
Then, for the captain, I will only speak
An epigram I here have made: it is
UNTO TRUE SOLDIERS. *That's the lemma: mark it.*
Strength of my country, whilst I bring to view
Such as are mis-call'd captains, and wrong you,
And your high names; I do desire, that thence,
Be nor put on you, nor you take offence:
I swear by your true friend, my muse, I love
Your great profession which I once did prove;
And did not shame it with my actions then,
No more than I dare now do with my pen.
He that not trusts me, having vow'd thus much,
But's angry for the captain, still: is such.
Now for the players, it is true, I tax'd them,
And yet but some; and those so sparingly,
As all the rest might have sat still unquestion'd,
Had they but had the wit or conscience
To think well of themselves. But impotent, they
Thought each man's vice belong'd to their whole tribe;
And much good do't them ! What they have done 'gainst me,
I am not moved with: if it gave them meat,
Or got them clothes, 'tis well; that was their end.
Only amongst them, I am sorry for
Some better natures, by the rest so drawn,
To run in that vile line.
　　Pol. *And is this all !*
Will you not answer then the libels ?
　　Aut. *No.*
　　Pol. *Nor the Untrussers ?*

Aut. *Neither.*

Pol. *Y'are undone then.*

Aut. *With whom?*

Pol. *The world.*

Aut. *The bawd!*

Pol. *It will be taken*
To be stupidity or tameness in you.

Aut. *But they that have incensed me, can in soul*
Acquit me of that guilt. They know I dare
To spurn or baffle them, or squirt their eyes
With ink or urine; or I could do worse,
Arm'd with Archilochus' fury, write Iambics,
Should make the desperate lashers hang themselves;
Rhime them to death, as they do Irish rats
In drumming tunes. Or, living, I could stamp
Their foreheads with those deep and public brands,
That the whole company of barber-surgeons
Should not take off with all their art and plasters.
And these my prints should last, still to be read
In their pale fronts; when, what they write 'gainst me
Shall, like a figure drawn in water, fleet,
And the poor wretched papers be employed
To clothe tobacco, or some cheaper drug:
This I could do, and make them infamous.
But, to what end? when their own deeds have mark'd 'em;
And that I know, within his guilty breast
Each slanderer bears a whip that shall torment him
Worse than a million of these temporal plagues:
Which to pursue, were but a feminine humour,
And far beneath the dignity of man.

Nas. *'Tis true; for to revenge their injuries,*
Were to confess you felt them. Let them go,
And use the treasure of the fool, their tongues,
Who makes his gain, by speaking worst of best.

Pol. *O, but they lay particular imputations—*

Aut. *As what?*

Pol. *That all your writing is mere railing.*

Aut. *Ha?*
If all the salt in the old comedy
Should be so censured, or the sharper wit
Of the bold satire termed scolding rage,
What age could then compare with those for buffoons?
What should be said of Aristophanes,
Persius, or Juvenal, whose names we now
So glorify in schools, at least pretend it?—
Have they no other?

Pol. *Yes; they say you are slow,*
And scarce bring forth a play a year.

Aut. *'Tis true.*

I would they could not say that I did that !
There's all the joy that I take in their trade,
Unless such scribes as these might be proscribed
Th' abused theatres.   They would think it strange, now,
A man should take but colts-foot for one day,
And, between whiles, spit out a better poem
Than e'er the master of art, or giver of wit,
Their belly, made.   Yet, this is possible,
If a free mind had but the patience,
To think so much together and so vile.
But that these base and beggarly conceits
Should carry it, by the multitude of voices,
Against the most abstracted work, opposed
To the stuff'd nostrils of the drunken rout !
O, this would make a learn'd and liberal soul
To rive his stained quill up to the back,
And damn his long-watch'd labours to the fire;
Things that were born when none but the still night
And his dumb candle, saw his pinching throes;
Were not his own free merit a more crown
Unto his travails than their reeling claps.
This 'tis that strikes me silent, seals my lips,
And apts me rather to sleep out my time,
Than I would waste it in contemned strifes
With these vile Ibides, these unclean birds,
That make their mouths their clysters, and still purge
From their hot entrails.   But I leave the monsters
To their own fate.   And, since the Comic Muse
Hath proved so ominous to me, I will try
If TRAGEDY *have a more kind aspect;*
Her favours in my next I will pursue,
Where, if I prove the pleasure but of one,
So he judicious be, he shall be alone
A theatre unto me; Once I'll say
To strike the ear of time in those fresh strains,
As shall, beside the cunning of their ground,
Give cause to some of wonder, some despite,
And more despair, to imitate their sound.
I, that spend half my nights, and all my days,
Here in a cell, to get a dark pale face,
To come forth worth the ivy or the bays,
And in this age can hope no other grace—
Leave me !   There's something come into my thought,
That must and shall be sung high and aloof,
Safe from the wolf's black jaw, and the dull ass's hoof.
     Nas. *I reverence these raptures, and obey them.*

[The scene closes.

SEJANUS: HIS FALL

TO THE NO LESS NOBLE BY VIRTUE THAN BLOOD

ESME LORD AUBIGNY

My Lord,—If ever any ruin were so great as to survive, I think this be one I send you, The Fall of Sejanus. It is a poem, that, if I well remember, in your lordship's sight, suffered no less violence from our people here, than the subject of it did from the rage of the people of Rome; but with a different fate, as, I hope, merit: for this hath outlived their malice, and begot itself a greater favour than he lost, the love of good men. Amongst whom, if I make your lordship the first it thanks, it is not without a just confession of the bond your benefits have, and ever shall hold upon me,

Your lordship's most faithful honourer. Ben Jonson.

TO THE READERS

The following and voluntary labours of my friends, prefixed to my book, have relieved me in much whereat, without them, I should necessarily have touched. Now I will only use three or four short and needful notes, and so rest.

First, if it be objected, that what I publish is no true poem, in the strict laws of time, I confess it: as also in the want of a proper chorus; whose habit and moods are such and so difficult, as not any, whom I have seen, since the ancients, no, not they who have most presently affected laws, have yet come in the way of. Nor is it needful, or almost possible in these our times, and to such auditors as commonly things are presented, to observe the old state and splendour of dramatic poems, with preservation of any popular delight. But of this I shall take more seasonable cause to speak, in my observations upon Horace his Art of Poetry, which, with the text translated, I intend shortly to publish. In the mean time, if in truth of argument, dignity of persons, gravity and height of elocution, fulness and frequency of sentence, I have discharged the other offices of a tragic writer, let not the absence of these forms be imputed to me, wherein I shall give you occasion hereafter, and without my boast, to think I could better prescribe, than omit the due use for want of a convenient knowledge.

The next is, lest in some nice nostril the quotations might savour affected, I do let you know, that I abhor nothing more; and I have only done it to shew my integrity in the story, and save myself in those common torturers that bring all wit to the rack; whose noses are ever like swine, spoiling and rooting up the Muses' gardens; and their whole bodies like moles, as blindly working under earth, to cast any, the least, hills upon virtue.

Whereas they are in Latin, and the work in English, it was presupposed none but the learned would take the pains to confer them: the authors themselves being all in the learned tongues, save one, with whose English side I have had little to do. To which it may be required, since I have quoted the page, to name what editions I followed: Tacit. Lips. in quarto, Antwerp, edit. 1600; Dio. folio, Hen. Steph. 1592. For the rest, as Sueton., Seneca, etc., the chapter doth sufficiently direct, or the edition is not varied.

Lastly, I would inform you, that this book, in all numbers, is not the same with that which was acted on the public stage; wherein a second pen had good share: in place of which, I have rather chosen to put weaker, and, no doubt, less pleasing, of mine own, than to defraud so happy a genius of his right by my loathed usurpation.

Fare you well, and if you read farther of me, and like, I shall not be afraid of it, though you praise me out.

Neque enim mihi cornea fibra est.

But that I should plant my felicity in your general saying, good, or well etc., were a weakness which the better sort of you might worthily contemn, if not absolutely hate me for. BEN JONSON;

and no such,

Quem
Palma negata macrum, donata reducit opimum.

THE ARGUMENT

ÆLIUS SEJANUS, son to Seius Strabo, a gentleman of Rome, and born at Vulsinium; after his long service in court, first under Augustus; afterward, Tiberius; grew into that favour with the latter, and won him by those arts, as there wanted nothing but the name to make him a co-partner of the empire. Which greatness of his, Drusus, the emperor's son, not brooking; after many smothered dislikes, it one day breaking out, the prince struck him publicly on the face. To revenge which disgrace, Livia, the wife of Drusus (being before corrupted by him to her dishonour, and the discovery of her husband's counsels) Sejanus practiseth with, together with her physician called Eudemus, and one Lygdus an eunuch, to poison Drusus. This their inhuman act having successful and unsuspected passage, it emboldeneth Sejanus to further and more insolent projects, even the ambition of the empire; where finding the lets he must encounter to be many and hard, in respect of the issue of Germanicus, who were next in hope for the succession, he deviseth to make Tiberius' self his means, and instils into his ears many doubts and suspicions, both against the princes, and their mother Agrippina; which Cæsar jealously hearkening to, as covetously consenteth to their ruin, and their friends. In this time, the better to mature and strengthen his design, Sejanus labours to marry Livia, and worketh with all his ingine, to remove Tiberius from the knowledge of public business, with allurements of a quiet and retired life; the latter of which, Tiberius, out of a proneness to lust, and a desire to hide those unnatural pleasures which he could not so publicly practise, embraceth: the former enkindleth his fears, and there gives him first cause of doubt or suspect towards Sejanus: against whom he raiseth in private a new instrument, one Sertorius Macro, and by him underworketh, discovers the other's counsels, his means, his ends, sounds the affections of the senators, divides, distracts them: at last, when Sejanus least looketh, and is most secure; with pretext of doing him an unwonted honour in the senate, he trains him from his guards, and with a long doubtful letter, in one day hath him suspected, accused, condemned, and torn in pieces by the rage of the people.

DRAMATIS PERSONÆ

TIBERIUS.	HATERIUS.
DRUSUS SENIOR.	SANQUINIUS.
NERO.	POMPONIUS.
DRUSUS JUNIOR.	JULIUS POSTHUMUS.
CALIGULA.	FULCINIUS TRIO.
LUCIUS ARRUNTIUS.	MINUTIUS.
CAIUS SILIUS.	SATRIUS SECUNDUS.
TITIUS SABINUS.	PINNARIUS NATTA.
MARCUS LEPIDUS.	OPSIUS.
CREMUTIUS CORDUS.	
ASINIUS GALLUS.	*Tribuni.*
REGULUS.	*Præcones.*
TERENTIUS.	*Flamen.*
GRACINUS LACO.	*Tubicines.*
EUDEMUS.	*Nuntius.*
RUFUS.	*Lictores.*
SEJANUS.	*Ministri.*
LATIARIS.	*Tibicines.*
VARRO.	*Servi, etc.*
SERTORIUS MACRO.	AGRIPPINA.
COTTA.	LIVIA.
DOMITIUS AFER.	SOSIA.

SCENE,—ROME

ACT I

SCENE I.—*A State Room in the Palace.*

Enter SABINUS *and* SILIUS, *followed by* LATIARIS.

Sab. Hail, Caius [1] Silius!
Sil. Titius Sabinus,[2] hail!
You're rarely met in court.
Sab. Therefore, well met.
Sil. 'Tis true: indeed, this place is not our sphere.
Sab. No, Silius, we are no good inginers.
We want their fine arts, and their thriving use
Should make us graced, or favour'd of the times:
We have no shift of faces, no cleft tongues,
No soft and glutinous bodies, that can stick,
Like snails on painted walls; or, on our breasts,
Creep up, to fall from that proud height, to which
We did by slavery,[3] not by service climb.
We are no guilty men, and then no great;
We have no place in court, office in state,
That we can say,[4] we owe unto our crimes:

---

[1] De Caio Silio, vid. Tacit. Lips. edit. quarto; Ann. Lib. i. p. 11, Lib ii. p. 28 et 33.
[2] De Titio Sabino, vid. Tacit. Lib. iv. p. 79.
[3] Tacit. Ann. Lib. i. p. 2.   [4] Juv. Sat. i. v. 75.

We burn with no black secrets,[1] which can make
Us dear to the pale authors; or live fear'd
Of their still waking jealousies, to raise
Ourselves a fortune, by subverting theirs.
We stand not in the lines, that do advance
To that so courted point.

Enter SATRIUS *and* NATTA, *at a distance.*

Sil. But yonder lean
A pair that do.
 Sab. [*salutes Latiaris.*] Good cousin Latiaris.— [2]
 Sil. Satrius Secundus,[3] and Pinnarius Natta,[4]
The great Sejanus' clients: there be two,
Know more than honest counsels; whose close breasts,
Were they ripp'd up to light, it would be found
A poor and idle sin, to which their trunks
Had not been made fit organs. These can lie,
Flatter, and swear, forswear, deprave,[5] inform,
Smile, and betray; make guilty men; then beg
The forfeit lives, to get their livings; cut
Men's throats with whisperings; sell to gaping suitors
The empty smoke, that flies about the palace;
Laugh when their patron laughs; sweat when he sweats;
Be hot and cold with him; change every mood,
Habit, and garb, as often as he varies;
Observe him, as his watch observes his clock;
And, true, as turquoise in the dear lord's ring,
Look well or ill with him: [6] ready to praise
His lordship, if he spit, or but p— fair,
Have an indifferent stool, or break wind well;
Nothing can 'scape their catch.
 Sab. Alas! these things
Deserve no note, conferr'd with other vile
And filthier flatteries,[7] that corrupt the times;
When, not alone our gentries chief are fain
To make their safety from such sordid acts;
But all our consuls,[8] and no little part
Of such as have been prætors, yea, the most
Of senators,[9] that else not use their voices,
Start up in public senate and there strive
Who shall propound most abject things, and base.

---

[1] Juv. Sat. iii. v. 49, etc.
[2] De Latiari, cons. Tacit. Ann. Lib. iv. p. 94, et Dion. Step. edit. fol. Lib. lviii. p. 711.
[3] De Satrio Secundo, et
[4] Pinnario Natta, leg. Tacit. Ann. Lib. iv. p. 83. Et de Satrio cons. Senec. Consol. ad Marciam.
[5] Vid. Sen. de Benef. Lib. iii. cap. 26.
[6] Juv. Sat. iii. ver. 105, etc.   [7] Vid. Tacit. Ann. Lib. i. p. 3.
[8] Tacit. Ann. Lib. iii. p. 69.   [9] Pedarii.

So much, as oft Tiberius hath been heard,
Leaving the court, to cry,[1] O race of men,
Prepared for servitude!—which shew'd that he,
Who least the public liberty could like,
As lothly brook'd their flat servility.

Sil. Well, all is worthy of us, were it more,
Who with our riots, pride, and civil hate,
Have so provok'd the justice of the gods:
We, that, within these fourscore years, were born
Free, equal lords of the triumphed world,
And knew no masters, but affections;
To which betraying first our liberties,
We since became the slaves to one man's lusts;
And now to many: [2] every minist'ring spy
That will accuse and swear, is lord of you,
Of me, of all our fortunes and our lives.
Our looks are call'd to question,[3] and our words,
How innocent soever, are made crimes;
We shall not shortly dare to tell our dreams,
Or think, but 'twill be treason.

Sab. Tyrants' arts
Are to give flatterers grace; accusers, power;
That those may seem to kill whom they devour.

Enter CORDUS *and* ARRUNTIUS.

Now, good Cremutius Cordus.[4]

Cor. [*salutes Sabinus*] Hail to your lordship!

Nat. [*whispers Latiaris.*] Who's that salutes your cousin?

Lat. 'Tis one Cordus,
A gentleman of Rome: one that has writ
Annals of late, they say, and very well.

Nat. Annals! of what times?

Lat. I think of Pompey's,[5]
And Caius Cæsar's; and so down to these.

Nat. How stands he affected to the present state?
Is he or Drusian,[6] or Germanican,
Or ours, or neutral?

Lat. I know him not so far.

Nat. Those times are somewhat queasy to be touch'd.
Have you or seen, or heard part of his work?

Lat. Not I; he means they shall be public shortly.

---

[1] Tacit. Ann. Lib. iii. p. 69.
[2] Lege Tacit. Ann. Lib. i. p. 24. de Romano, Hispano, et cæteris, ibid. et Lib. iii. Ann. p. 61 et 62.   Juv. Sat. x. v. 87.   Suet. Tib. cap. 61.
[3] Vid. Tacit. Ann. i. p. 4, et Lib. iii. p. 62.   Suet. Tib. cap. 61.   Senec. de Benef. Lib. iii. cap. 26.
[4] De Crem. Cordo, vid. Tacit. Ann. Lib. iv. p. 83, 84.   Senec. Cons. ad Marciam. Dio. Lib. lvii. p. 710.   Suet. Aug. c. 35.   Tib. c. 61.   Cal. c. 16.
[5] Suet. Aug. cap. 35.
[6] Vid. de faction. Tacit. Ann. Lib. ii. p. 39. et Lib. iv. p. 79.

Nat. O, Cordus do you call him?
Lat. Ay.   [*Exeunt Natta and Satrius.*
Sab. But these our times
Are not the same, Arruntius.[1]
      Arr. Times! the men,
The men are not the same: 'tis we are base,
Poor, and degenerate from the exalted strain
Of our great fathers.   Where is now the soul
Of god-like Cato? he, that durst be good,
When Cæsar durst be evil; and had power,
As not to live his slave, to die his master?
Or where's the constant Brutus, that being proof
Against all charm of benefits, did strike
So brave a blow into the monster's heart
That sought unkindly to captive his country?
O, they are fled the light! Those mighty spirits
Lie raked up with their ashes in their urns,
And not a spark of their eternal fire
Glows in a present bosom.   All's but blaze,
Flashes and smoke, wherewith we labour so,
There's nothing Roman in us; nothing good,
Gallant, or great: 'tis true that Cordus says,
" Brave Cassius was the last of all that race."

DRUSUS *passes over the stage, attended by* HATERIUS, *etc.*

Sab. Stand by! lord Drusus.[2]
Hat. The emperor's son! give place.
Sil. I like the prince well.
Arr. A riotous youth;[3]
There's little hope of him.
      Sab. That fault his age
Will, as it grows, correct.   Methinks he bears
Himself each day more nobly than other;
And wins no less on men's affections,
Than doth his father lose.   Believe me, I love him;
And chiefly for opposing to Sejanus.[4]
      Sil. And I, for gracing his young kinsmen so,[5]
The sons[6] of prince Germanicus:[7] it shews
A gallant clearness in him, a straight mind,
That envies not, in them, their father's name.

---

[1] De Lu. Arrun. isto vid. Tacit. Ann. Lib. i. p. 6. et Lib. iii. p. 60. et Dion. Rom. Hist. Lib. 58.
[2] Lege de Druso Tacit. Ann. Lib. i. p. 9.   Suet. Tib. c. 52. Dio. Rom. Hist. Lib. lvii. p. 699.
[3] Tacit. Ann. Lib. iii. p. 62.
[4] Vid. Tacit. Ann. Lib. iv. p. 74.   [5] Ann. Lib. iv. p. 75, 76.
[6] Nero, Drusus, Caius, qui in castris genitus, et Caligula nominatus. Tacit. Ann. Lib. 1.
[7] De Germanico Cons. Tacit. Ann. Lib. i. p. 14. et Dion. Rom. Hist. Lib. lvii. p. 694.

  Arr. His name was, while he lived, above all envy;
And, being dead, without it. O, that man!
If there were seeds of the old virtue left,
They lived in him.
  Sil. He had the fruits, Arruntius,
More than the seeds: [1] Sabinus, and myself
Had means to know him within; and can report him.
We were his followers, he would call us friends;
He was a man most like to virtue; in all,
And every action, nearer to the gods,
Than men, in nature; of a body as fair
As was his mind; and no less reverend
In face, than fame: [2] he could so use his state,
Tempering his greatness with his gravity,
As it avoided all self-love in him,
And spite in others. What his funerals lack'd
In images and pomp, they had supplied
With honourable sorrow, soldiers' sadness,
A kind of silent mourning, such, as men,
Who know no tears, but from their captives, use
To shew in so great losses.
  Cor. I thought once,
Considering their forms, age, manner of deaths,
The nearness of the places where they fell,
To have parallel'd him with great Alexander:
For both were of best feature, of high race,
Year'd but to thirty, and, in foreign lands,
By their own people alike made away.
  Sab. I know not, for his death, how you might wrest it:
But, for his life, it did as much disdain
Comparison, with that voluptuous, rash,
Giddy, and drunken Macedon's, as mine
Doth with my bondman's. All the good in him,
His valour and his fortune, he made his;
But he had other touches of late Romans,
That more did speak him: [3] Pompey's dignity,
The innocence of Cato, Cæsar's spirit,
Wise Brutus' temperance; and every virtue,
Which, parted unto others, gave them name,
Flow'd mix'd in him. He was the soul of goodness;
And all our praises of him are like streams
Drawn from a spring, that still rise full, and leave
The part remaining greatest.
  Arr. I am sure

---

[1] Vid. Tacit. Ann. Lib. iv. p. 79.
[2] Tacit. Ann. Lib. ii. p. 47, et Dion. Rom. Hist. Lib. lvii. p. 705.
[3] Vid. apud Vell. Paterc. Lips. 4to. p. 35-47, istorum hominum characteres.

He was too great for us,[1] and that they knew
Who did remove him hence.
   Sab. When men grow fast
Honour'd and loved, there is a trick in state,
Which jealous princes never fail to use,
How to decline that growth, with fair pretext,
And honourable colours of employment,
Either by embassy, the war, or such,
To shift them forth into another air,
Where they may purge and lessen; so was he: [2]
And had his seconds there, sent by Tiberius,
And his more subtile dam, to discontent him;
To breed and cherish mutinies; detract
His greatest actions; give audacious check
To his commands; and work to put him out
In open act of treason. All which snares
When his wise cares prevented,[3] a fine poison
Was thought on, to mature their practices.

Enter SEJANUS *talking to* TERENTIUS, *followed by* SATRIUS,
       NATTA, *etc.*

   Cor. Here comes Sejanus.[4]
   Sil. Now observe the stoops,
The bendings, and the falls.
   Arr. Most creeping base!
   Sej. [*to Natta.*] I note them well: no more.
Say you?
   Sat. My lord,
There is a gentleman of Rome would buy—
   Sej. How call you him you talk'd with?
   Sat. Please your lordship,
It is Eudemus,[5] the physician
To Livia, Drusus' wife.
   Sej. On with your suit.
Would buy, you said—
   Sat. A tribune's place, my lord.
   Sej. What will he give?
   Sat. Fifty sestertia.[6]
   Sej. Livia's physician, say you, is that fellow?
   Sat. It is, my lord: Your lordship's answer.

---

[1] Vid. Tacit. Lib. ii. Ann. p. 28 et p. 34. Dio Rom. Hist. Lib. lvii. p. 705.
[2] Con. Tacit. Ann. Lib. ii. p. 39. de occultis mandatis Pisoni, et postea p. 42, 43, 48. Orat. D. Celeris. Est Tibi Augustæ conscientia, est Cæsaris favor, sed in occulto, etc. Leg. Suet. Tib. c. 52. Dio. p. 706.
[3] Vid. Tacit. Ann. Lib. ii. p. 46, 47. Lib. iii. p. 54. et Suet. Cal. c. 1 et 2.
[4] De Sejano vid. Tacit. Ann. Lib. i. p. 9. Lib. iv. princip. et per tot. Suet. Tib. Dio. Lib. lvii. lviii. et Plin. et Senec.
[5] De Eudemo istó vid. Tacit. Ann. Lib. iv. p. 74.
[6] Monetæ nostræ 375 lib. vid. Budæum de asse, Lib. ii. p. 64.

Sej. To what?

Sat. The place, my lord. 'Tis for a gentleman
Your lordship will well like of, when you see him;
And one, that you may make yours, by the grant.

Sej. Well, let him bring his money, and his name.

Sat. 'Thank your lordship. He shall, my lord.

Sej. Come hither.
Know you this same Eudemus? is he learn'd?

Sat. Reputed so, my lord, and of deep practice.

Sej. Bring him in, to me, in the gallery;
And take you cause to leave us there together:
I would confer with him, about a grief—

On.   [*Exeunt Sejanus, Satrius, Terentius, etc.*

Arr. So! yet another? yet? O desperate state
Of grovelling honour! seest thou this, O sun,
And do we see thee after? Methinks, day
Should lose his light, when men do lose their shames,
And for the empty circumstance of life,
Betray their cause of living.

Sil. Nothing so.[1]
Sejanus can repair, if Jove should ruin.
He is now the court god; and well applied
With sacrifice of knees, of crooks, and cringes;
He will do more than all the house of heaven
Can, for a thousand hecatombs. 'Tis he
Makes us our day, or night; hell, and elysium
Are in his look: we talk of Rhadamanth,
Furies, and firebrands; but it is his frown
That is all these; where, on the adverse part,
His smile is more, than e'er yet poets feign'd
Of bliss, and shades, nectar—

Arr. A serving boy!
I knew him, at Caius' trencher,[2] when for hire
He prostituted his abused body
To that great gormond, fat Apicius;
And was the noted pathic of the time.

Sab. And, now,[3] the second face of the whole world!
The partner of the empire, hath his image
Rear'd equal with Tiberius, born in ensigns;
Commands, disposes every dignity,
Centurions, tribunes, heads of provinces,
Prætors and consuls; all that heretofore
Rome's general suffrage gave, is now his sale.
The gain, or rather spoil of all the earth,

---

[1] De ingenio, moribus, et potentia Sejani, leg. Tacit. Ann. Lib. iv. p. 74. Dio Rom. Hist. Lib. lvii. p. 708.

[2] Caius divi Augusti nepos. Cons. Tacit. Ann. Lib. iv. p. 74, et Dio. Lib. lvii. p. 706

[3] Juv. Sat. x. v. 63, etc. Tacit. ibid. Dion. ibid. et sic passim.

One, and his house, receives.

 Sil. He hath of late
Made him a strength too, strangely, by reducing
All the prætorian bands into one camp,
Which he commands: pretending that the soldiers,
By living loose and scatter'd, fell to riot;
And that if any sudden enterprise
Should be attempted, their united strength
Would be far more than sever'd; and their life
More strict, if from the city more removed.

 Sab. Where, now, he builds what kind of forts he please,
Is heard to court the soldier by his name,
Woos, feasts the chiefest men of action,
Whose wants, not loves, compel them to be his.
And though he ne'er were liberal by kind,
Yet to his own dark ends, he's most profuse,
Lavish, and letting fly, he cares not what
To his ambition.

 Arr. Yet, hath he ambition?
Is there that step in state can make him higher,
Or more, or anything he is, but less?

 Sil. Nothing but emperor.

 Arr. The name Tiberius,
I hope, will keep, howe'er he hath foregone
The dignity and power.

 Sil. Sure, while he lives.

 Arr. And dead, it comes to Drusus. Should he fail,
To the brave issue of Germanicus;
And they are three:[1] too many—ha? for him
To have a plot upon!

 Sab. I do not know
The heart of his designs; but, sure, their face
Looks farther than the present.

 Arr. By the gods,
If I could guess he had but such a thought,
My sword should cleave him down from head to heart,
But I would find it out: and with my hand
I'd hurl his panting brain about the air
In mites, as small as atomi, to undo
The knotted bed—

 Sab. You are observ'd, Arruntius.

 Arr. [*turns to Natta, Terentius, etc.*] Death! I dare tell him
  so; and all his spies:
You, sir, I would, do you look? and you.

 Sab. Forbear.

---

[1] Nero, Drusus, et Caligula.—Tacit. ibid.

SCENE II.

(*The former Scene continued.*)

A Gallery discovered opening into the State Room.

Enter SATRIUS *with* EUDEMUS.

Sat. Here he will instant be: let's walk a turn;
You're in a muse, Eudemus.
    Eud. Not I, sir.
I wonder he should mark me out so! well,
Jove and Apollo form it for the best.   [*Aside.*
    Sat. Your [1] fortune's made unto you now, Eudemus,
If you can but lay hold upon the means;
Do but observe his humour, and—believe it—
He is the noblest Roman, where he takes—

Enter SEJANUS.

Here comes his lordship.
    Sej. Now, good Satrius.
    Sat. This is the gentleman, my lord.
    Sej. Is this?
Give me your hand—we must be more acquainted.
Report, sir, hath spoke out your art and learning:
And I am glad I have so needful cause,
However in itself painful and hard,
To make me known to so great virtue.—Look,
Who is that, Satrius? [*Exit Sat.*]—I have a grief, sir,
That will desire your help.   Your name's Eudemus?
    Eud. Yes.
    Sej. Sir?
    Eud. It is, my lord.
    Sej. I hear you are
Physician to Livia,[2] the princess.
    Eud. I minister unto her, my good lord.
    Sej. You minister to a royal lady, then.
    Eud. She is, my, lord, and fair.
    Sej. That's understood
Of all her sex, who are or would be so;
And those that would be, physic soon can make them:
For those that are, their beauties fear no colours.
    Eud. Your lordship is conceited.
    Sej. Sir, you know it,
And can, if need be, read a learned lecture
On this, and other secrets. 'Pray you, tell me,
What more of ladies besides Livia,
Have you your patients?

[1] Lege Terentii defensionem Tacit. Ann. Lib. vi. p. 102.
[2] Germanici soror, uxor Drusi. Vid. Tacit. Ann. Lib. iv. p. 74.

Eud. Many, my good lord.
The great Augusta,[1] Urgulania,[2]
Mutilia Prisca,[3] and Plancina;[4] divers—
Sej. And all these tell you the particulars
Of every several grief? how first it grew,
And then increased; what action caused that;
What passion that: and answer to each point
That you will put them?
Eud. Else, my lord, we know not
How to prescribe the remedies.
Sej. Go to,
You are a subtile nation, you physicians!
And grown the only cabinets in court,[5]
To ladies' privacies. Faith, which of these
Is the most pleasant lady in her physic?
Come, you are modest now.
Eud. 'Tis fit, my lord.
Sej. Why, sir, I do not ask you of their urines,
Whose smell's most violet, or whose siege is best,
Or who makes hardest faces on her stool?
Which lady sleeps with her own face a nights?
Which puts her teeth off, with her clothes, in court?
Or, which her hair, which her complexion,
And, in which box she puts it; These were questions,
That might, perhaps, have put your gravity
To some defence of blush. But, I enquired,
Which was the wittiest, merriest, wantonnest?
Harmless intergatories, but conceits.—
Methinks Augusta should be most perverse,
And froward in her fit.
Eud. She's so, my lord.
Sej. I knew it: and Mutilia the most jocund.
Eud. 'Tis very true, my lord.
Sej. And why would you
Conceal this from me, now? Come, what is Livia?
I know she's quick and quaintly spirited,
And will have strange thoughts, when she is at leisure:
She tells them all to you.
Eud. My noblest lord,
He breathes not in the empire, or on earth,
Whom I would be ambitious to serve
In any act, that may preserve mine honour,
Before your lordship.

[1] Mater Tiberii. vid. Tacit. Ann. 1, 2, 3, 4, moritur 5. Suet. Tib. Dio. Rom. Hist. 57, 58.
[2] Delicium Augustæ. Tacit. Ann. Lib. ii. et iv.
[3] Adultera Julii Posthumi. Tacit. Ann. Lib. iv. p. 77.
[4] Pisonis uxor. Tacit. Ann. Lib. ii. iii. iv.
[5] Vid. Tacit. Ann. Lib. iv. p. 74. et Plin. Nat. Hist. Lib. xxix. c. 1.

Sej. Sir, you can lose no honour,
By trusting aught to me. The coarsest act
Done to my service, I can so requite,
As all the world shall style it honourable:
Your idle, virtuous definitions,
Keep honour poor, and are as scorn'd as vain:
Those deeds breathe honour that do suck in gain.

Eud. But, good my lord, if I should thus betray
The counsels of my patient, and a lady's
Of her high place and worth; what might your lordship,
Who presently are to trust me with your own,
Judge of my faith?

Sej. Only the best I swear.
Say now that I should utter you my grief,
And with it the true cause; that it were love,
And love to Livia; [1] you should tell her this:
Should she suspect your faith; I would you could
Tell me as much from her; see if my brain
Could be turn'd jealous.

Eud. Happily, my lord,
I could in time tell you as much and more;
So I might safely promise but the first
To her from you.

Sej. As safely, my Eudemus,
I now dare call thee so, as I have put
The secret into thee.

Eud. My lord—

Sej. Protest not,
Thy looks are vows to me; use only speed,
And but affect her with Sejanus' love, [2]
Thou art a man, made to make consuls. Go.

Eud. My lord, I'll promise you a private meeting
This day together.

Sej. Canst thou?

Eud. Yes.

Sej. The place?

Eud. My gardens, whither I shall fetch your lordship.

Sej. Let me adore my Æsculapius.
Why, this indeed is physic! and outspeaks
The knowledge of cheap drugs, or any use
Can be made out of it! more comforting
Than all your opiates, juleps, apozems,
Magistral syrups, or——Be gone, my friend,
Not barely styled, but created so;
Expect things greater than thy largest hopes,
To overtake thee: Fortune shall be taught
To know how ill she hath deserv'd thus long,
To come behind thy wishes. Go, and speed. [*Exit Eudemus.*

[1] Cons. Tacit. Ann. Lib. iv. p. 74.   [2] Tacet. ibid.

Ambition makes more trusty slaves than need.
These fellows,[1] by the favour of their art,
Have still the means to tempt; oft-times the power.
If Livia will be now corrupted, then
Thou hast the way, Sejanus, to work out
His secrets, who, thou know'st, endures thee not,
Her husband, Drusus: and to work against them.
Prosper it, Pallas, thou that better'st wit;
For Venus hath the smallest share in it.

Enter TIBERIUS [2] *and* DRUSUS, *attended.*

Tib. [*to Haterius, who kneels to him.*] We not endure these
       flatteries; let him stand;
Our empire, ensigns, axes, rods and state
Take not away our human nature from us:
Look up on us, and fall before the gods.
  Sej. How like a god speaks Cæsar!
  Arr. There, observe!
He can endure that second, that's no flattery.
O, what is it, proud slime will not believe
Of his own worth, to hear it equal praised
Thus with the gods!
  Cor. He did not hear it, sir.
  Arr. He did not! Tut, he must not, we think meanly.
'Tis your most courtly known confederacy,
To have your private parasite redeem
What he, in public, subtilely will lose,
To making him a name.
  Hat. Right mighty lord—   [*Gives him letters.*
  Tib. We must make up our ears 'gainst these assaults
Of charming tongues;[3] we pray you use no more
These contumelies to us; style not us
Or lord, or mighty, who profess ourself
The servant of the senate, and are proud
T' enjoy them our good, just, and favouring lords.
  Cor. Rarely [4] dissembled!
  Arr. Prince-like to the life.
  Sab. When power that may command, so much descends,
Their bondage, whom it stoops to, it intends.
  Tib. Whence are these letters?
  Hat. From the senate.
  Tib. So.   [*Lat. gives him letters.*
Whence these?

---

[1] Eud. specie artis frequens secretis. Tacit. ibid. Vid. Plin. Nat. Hist Lib. xxix. c. 1. in criminat. medicorum.
[2] De initio Tiberii principatus vid. Tacit. Ann. Lib. i. p. 23, Lib. iv. p. 75. et Suet. Tib. c. 27. De Haterio vid. Tacit. Ann. Lib. i. p. 6.
[3] Cons. Tacit. Ann. Lib. ii. p. 50. et Suet. Tib. c. 27 et 29.
[4] Nullam æque Tiberius ex virtutibus suis quam dissimulationem diligebat. Tacit. Ann. Lib. iv. p. 95.

Lat. From thence too.

Tib. Are they sitting now?

Lat. They stay thy answer, Cæsar.

Sil. If this man
Had but a mind allied unto his words,
How blest a fate were it to us, and Rome!
We could not think that state for which to change,
Although the aim were our old liberty:
The ghosts [1] of those that fell for that, would grieve
Their bodies lived not, now, again to serve.
Men are deceived, who think there can be thrall
Beneath a virtuous prince: Wish'd liberty
Ne'er lovelier looks, than under such a crown.
But, when his grace [2] is merely but lip-good,
And that, no longer than he airs himself
Abroad in public, there, to seem to shun
The strokes and stripes of flatterers, which within
Are lechery unto him, and so feed
His brutish sense with their afflicting sound,
As, dead to virtue, he permits himself
Be carried like a pitcher by the ears,
To every act of vice: this is the case
Deserves our fear, and doth presage the nigh
And close approach of blood and tyranny.
Flattery is midwife [3] unto prince's rage:
And nothing sooner doth help forth a tyrant,
Than that and whisperers' grace, who have the time,
The place, the power, to make all men offenders.

Arr. He should be told this; and be bid dissemble
With fools and blind men: we that know the evil,
Should hunt the palace-rats,[4] or give them bane;
Fright hence these worse than ravens, that devour
The quick, where they but prey upon the dead:
He shall be told it.

Sab. Stay, Arruntius,
We must abide our opportunity;
And practise what is fit, as what is needful.
It is not safe t' enforce a sovereign's ear:
Princes hear well, if they at all will hear.

Arr. Ha, say you so? well! In the mean time, Jove,
(Say not, but I do call upon thee now,)

[1] Bruti, Cassii, Catonis, etc.

[2] Vid. Dio. Hist. Lib. lvii. de moribus Tiberii.

[3] Tyrannis fere oritur ex nimia procerum adulatione in principem. Arist.
Pol. Lib. v. c. 10, 11. et delatorum auctoritate. Leg. Tacit. Dio. Suet.
Tib. per totum. Sub quo decreta accusatoribus præcipua præmia. Vid.
Suet. Tib. c. 61, et Sen. Benef. Lib. iii. c. 6.

[4] Tineas soricesque Palatii vocat istos Sex. Aurel. Vict. et Tacit. Hist.
Lib. i. p. 233, qui secretis criminat. infamant ignarum, et quo incautior
deciperetur, palam laudatum, etc.

Of all wild beasts preserve me from a tyrant:
And of all tame, a flatterer.

    Sil. 'Tis well pray'd.

    Tib. [*having read the letters.*] Return the lords this voice,
—We are their creature,
And it is fit a good and honest prince,
Whom they, out of their bounty, have instructed [1]
With so dilate and absolute a power,
Should owe the office of it to their service,
And good of all and every citizen.
Nor shall it e'er repent us to have wish'd
The senate just, and favouring lords unto us,
Since their free loves do yield no less defence
To a prince's state, than his own innocence.
Say then, there can be nothing in their thought
Shall want to please us, that hath pleased them;
Our suffrage rather shall prevent than stay
Behind their wills: 'tis empire to obey,
Where such, so great, so grave, so good determine.
Yet, for the suit of Spain,[2] to erect a temple
In honour of our mother and our self,
We must, with pardon of the senate, not
Assent thereto.   Their lordships may object
Our not denying the same late request
Unto the Asian cities: we desire
That our defence for suffering that be known
In these brief reasons, with our after purpose.
Since deified Augustus hindered not
A temple to be built at Pergamum,
In honour of himself and sacred Rome;
We, that have all his deeds [3] and words observed
Ever, in place of laws, the rather follow'd
That pleasing precedent, because with ours,
The senate's reverence, also, there was join'd.
But as, t' have once received it, may deserve
The gain of pardon; so, to be adored
With the continued style, and note of gods,
Through all the provinces, were wild ambition,
And no less pride: yea, even Augustus' name
Would early vanish, should it be profaned
With such promiscuous flatteries. For our part,
We here protest it, and are covetous
Posterity should know it, we are mortal;
And can but deeds of men: 'twere glory enough,
Could we be truly a prince.   And, they shall add
Abounding grace unto our memory,

---

[1] Vid. Suet. Tib. c. 20. et Dio. Hist. Lib. lvii. p. 696.
[2] Tacit. Ann. Lib. iv. p. 84 et 85.
[3] Cons. Strab. Lib. vi. de Tib.

That shall report us worthy our forefathers,
Careful of your affairs, constant in dangers,
And not afraid of any private frown
For public good.   These things shall be to us
Temples and statues, reared in your minds,
The fairest, and most during imagery:
For those of stone or brass, if they become
Odious in judgment of posterity,
Are more contemn'd as dying sepulchres,
Than ta'en for living monuments.   We then
Make here our suit, alike to gods and men;
The one, until the period of our race,
To inspire us with a free and quiet mind,
Discerning both divine and human laws;
The other, to vouchsafe us after death,
An honourable mention, and fair praise,
To accompany our actions and our name:
The rest of greatness princes may command,
And, therefore, may neglect; only, a long,
A lasting, high, and happy memory
They should, without being satisfied, pursue:
Contempt of fame begets contempt of virtue.

   Nat. Rare!
   Sat. Most divine!
   Sej. The oracles are ceased,
That only Cæsar, with their tongue, might speak.
   Arr. Let me be gone: most felt and open this!
   Cor. Stay.
   Arr. What! to hear more cunning and fine words,
With their sound flatter'd ere their sense be meant?
   Tib. Their choice of Antium,[1] there to place the gift
Vow'd to the goddess [2] for our mother's health,
We will the senate know, we fairly like:
As also of their grant [3] to Lepidus,
For his repairing the Æmilian place,
And restoration of those monuments:
Their grace [4] too in confining of Silanus
To the other isle Cithera, at the suit
Of his religious [5] sister, much commends
Their policy, so temper'd with their mercy.
But for the honours which they have decreed
To our Sejanus,[6] to advance his statue
In Pompey's theatre, (whose ruining fire
His vigilance and labour kept restrain'd

---

[1] Tacit. Lib. iii. p. 71.   [2] Fortuna equestris, ibid.
[3] Tacit. ibid.   [4] Tacit. Ann. Lib. iii. p. 170.
[5] Torquata virgo vestalis, cujas memoriam servat marmor Romæ. vid.
Lips. comment. in Tacit.
[6] Tacit. Ann. Lib. iii. p. 71.

In that one loss,) they have therein out-gone
Their own great wisdoms, by their skilful choice,
And placing of their bounties on a man,
Whose merit more adorns the dignity,
Than that can him; and gives a benefit,
In taking, greater than it can receive.
Blush not, Sejanus,[1] thou great aid of Rome,
Associate of our labours, our chief helper;
Let us not force thy simple modesty
With offering at thy praise, for more we cannot,
Since there's no voice can take it. No man here
Receive our speeches as hyperboles:
For we are far from flattering our friend,
Let envy know, as from the need to flatter.
Nor let them ask the causes of our praise:
Princes have still their grounds rear'd with themselves,
Above the poor low flats of common men;
And who will search the reasons of their acts,
Must stand on equal bases. Lead, away:
Our loves unto the senate.

        [Exeunt Tib., Sejan., Natta, Hat., Lat., Officers, etc

  Arr. Cæsar!

  Sab. Peace.

  Cor. Great Pompey's theatre [2] was never ruin'd
Till now, that proud Sejanus hath a statue
Rear'd on his ashes.

  Arr. Place the shame of soldiers,
Above the best of generals? crack the world,
And bruise the name of Romans into dust,
Ere we behold it!

  Sil. Check your passion;
Lord Drusus tarries.

  Dru. Is my father mad,[3]
Weary of life, and rule, lords? thus to heave
An idol up with praise! make him his mate,
His rival in the empire!

  Arr. O, good prince.

  Dru. Allow him statues,[4] titles, honours, such
As he himself refuseth!

  Arr. Brave, brave Drusus!

  Dru. The first ascents to sovereignty are hard;
But, entered once, there never wants or means,
Or ministers, to help the aspirer on.

  Arr. True, gallant Drusus.

  Dru. We must shortly pray
To Modesty, that he will rest contented—

  Arr. Ay, where he is, and not write emperor.

---

[1] Tacit. Ann. Lib. iv. p. 74-76.   [2] Vid. Sen. Cons. ad. Marc. c. 22.
[3] Tacit. Ann. Lib. iv. p. 76.   [4] Tacit. ibid.

Re-enter SEJANUS, SATRIUS, LATIARIS, Clients, *etc.*

Sej. There is your bill, and yours; bring you your man.
　　　　　　　　　　　　　　　　　　　　[To Satrius.

I have moved for you, too, Latiaris.
　　Dru. What!
Is your vast greatness grown so blindly bold,
That you will over us?
　　Sej. Why then give way.
　　Dru. Give way, Colossus! do you lift? advance you?
Take that![1]　　　　　　　　　　　　　　*[Strikes him.*
　　Arr. Good! brave! excellent, brave prince!
　　Dru. Nay, come, approach.　　　*[Draws his sword.*
　　　　　　　　　What, stand you off? at gaze?
It looks too full of death for thy cold spirits.
Avoid mine eye, dull camel, or my sword
Shall make thy bravery fitter for a grave,
Than for a triumph.　I'll advance a statue
O' your own bulk; but 't shall be on the cross;[2]
Where I will nail your pride at breadth and length,
And crack those sinews, which are yet but stretch'd
With your swoln fortune's rage.
　　Arr. A noble prince!
　　All. A Castor,[3] a Castor, a Castor, a Castor!
　　　　　　　　　　　　　[Exeunt all but Sejanus.
　　Sej. He that, with such wrong moved, can bear it through
With patience, and an even mind, knows how
To turn it back.　Wrath cover'd carries fate:
Revenge is lost, if I profess my hate.
What was my practice late, I'll now pursue,
As my fell justice: this hath styled it new.　　　　*[Exit.*

ACT II

SCENE I.—*The Garden of* EUDEMUS.

Enter SEJANUS, LIVIA, *and* EUDEMUS.

　　Sej. Physician, thou art worthy of a province,
For the great favours done unto our loves;
And, but that greatest Livia bears a part
In the requital of thy services,
I should alone despair of aught, like means,
To give them worthy satisfaction.
　　Liv. Eudemus, I will see it, shall receive

---

[1] Vid. Tacit. Ann. Lib. iv. p. 74-76.
[2] Tacit. ibidem.
[3] Tacit. sequimur Ann. Lib. iv. p. 74, quanquam apud Dionem et
Zonaram aliter legitur.

A fit and full reward for his large merit.—
But for this potion [1] we intend to Drusus,
No more our husband now, whom shall we choose
As the most apt and able instrument,
To minister it to him?

Eud. I say, Lygdus.[2]

Sej. Lygdus? what's he?

Liv. An eunuch Drusus loves.

Eud. Ay, and his cup-bearer.

Sej. Name not a second.
If Drusus love him, and he have that place,
We cannot think a fitter.

Eud. True, my lord.
For free access and trust are two main aids.

Sej. Skilful physician!

Liv. But he must be wrought
To the undertaking, with some labour'd art.

Sej. Is he ambitious?

Liv. No.

Sej. Or covetous?

Liv. Neither.

Eud. Yet, gold is a good general charm.

Sej. What is he, then?

Liv. Faith, only wanton, light.

Sej. How! is he young and fair?

Eud. A delicate youth.

Sej. Send him to me,[3] I'll work him.—Royal lady,
Though I have loved you long, and with that height
Of zeal and duty, like the fire, which more
It mounts it trembles, thinking nought could add
Unto the fervour which your eye had kindled;
Yet, now I see your wisdom, judgment, strength,
Quickness, and will, to apprehend the means
To your own good and greatness, I protest
Myself through rarified, and turn'd all flame
In your affection: such a spirit as yours,
Was not created for the idle second
To a poor flash, as Drusus; but to shine
Bright as the moon among the lesser lights,
And share the sov'reignty of all the world.
Then Livia triumphs in her proper sphere,
When she and her Sejanus shall divide
The name of Cæsar, and Augusta's star

[1] Servile, apud Romanos, et ignominiosissimum mortis genus erat
supplicium crucis, ut ex Liv. ipso. Tacit. Dio. et omnibus fere antiquis,
præsertim historicis constet. vid. Plaut. in. Mil. Amph. Aulii. Hor. Lib. i.
Ser 3. et Jev. Sat. vi. Pone crucem servo, etc.

[2] Sic Drusus ob violentiam cognominatus, vid. Dion. Rom. Hist. Lib.
lvii. p. 701.

[3] Spadonis animum stupro devinxit. Tacit. ibid.

Be dimm'd with glory of a brighter beam:
When Agrippina's [1] fires are quite extinct,
And the scarce-seen Tiberius borrows all
His little light from us, whose folded arms
Shall make one perfect orb. [*Knocking within.*] Who's that?
      Eudemus,
Look. [*Exit Eudemus.*] 'Tis not Drusus, lady, do not fear.
   Liv. Not I, my lord: my fear and love of him
Left me at once.
   Sej. Illustrious lady, stay—
   Eud. [*within.*] I'll tell his lordship.

Re-enter EUDEMUS.

   Sej. Who is it, Eudemus?
   Eud. One of your lordship's servants brings you word
The emperor hath sent for you.
   Sej. O! where is he?
With your fair leave, dear princess, I'll but ask
A question and return.   [*Exit.*
   Eud. Fortunate princess!
How are you blest in the fruition
Of this unequall'd man, the soul of Rome,
The empire's life, and voice of Cæsar's world!
   Liv. So blessed, my Eudemus, as to know
The bliss I have, with what I ought to owe
The means that wrought it. How do I look to-day?
   Eud. Excellent clear, believe it. This same fucus
Was well laid on.
   Liv. Methinks 'tis here not white.
   Eud. Lend me your scarlet, lady. 'Tis the sun,
Hath giv'n some little taint unto the ceruse; [2]
You should have used of the white oil I gave you.
Sejanus, for your love! his very name
Commandeth above Cupid or his shafts—   [*Paints her cheeks.*
   Liv. Nay, now you've made it worse.
   Eud. I'll help it straight—
And but pronounced, is a sufficient charm
Against all rumour; and of absolute power
To satisfy for any lady's honour.
   Liv. What do you now, Eudemus?
   Eud. Make a light fucus,
To touch you o'er withal.—Honour'd Sejanus!
What act, though ne'er so strange and insolent,
But that addition will at least bear out,

---

[1] Germanici vidua.
[2] Cerussa (apud Romanos) inter fictitiores colores erat et quæ solem ob
calorem timebat. vid. Mart. Lib. ii. Epig. 11.
                Quæ cretata timet Fabulla nimbum,
                Cerussata timet Sabella solem.

If't do not expiate?

　L v. Here, good physician.

　Eud. I like this study to preserve the love
Of such a man, that comes not every hour
To greet the world.—'Tis now well, lady, you should
Use of the dentifrice I prescribed you too,
To clear your teeth, and the prepared pomatum,
To smooth the skin:—A lady cannot be
Too curious of her form, that still would hold
The heart of such a person, made her captive,
As you have his: who, to endear him more
In your clear eye, hath put away his wife,[1]
The trouble of his bed, and your delights,
Fair Apicata, and made spacious room
To your new pleasures.

　Liv. Have not we return'd
That with our hate to Drusus, and discovery [2]
Of all his counsels?

　Eud. Yes, and wisely, lady.
The ages that succeed, and stand far off
To gaze at your high prudence, shall admire,
And reckon it an act without your sex:
It hath that rare appearance. Some will think
Your fortune could not yield a deeper sound,
Than mix'd with Drusus; but, when they shall hear
That, and the thunder of Sejanus meet,
Sejanus, whose high name doth strike the stars,
And rings about the concave; great Sejanus,
Whose glories, style, and titles are himself,
The often iterating of Sejanus:
They then will lose their thoughts, and be ashamed
To take acquaintance of them.

Re-enter SEJANUS.

　Sej. I must make
A rude departure, lady: Cæsar sends
With all his haste both of command and prayer.
Be resolute in our plot; you have my soul,
As certain yours as it is my body's.
And, wise physician,[3] so prepare the poison,
As you may lay the subtile operation
Upon some natural disease of his:
Your eunuch send to me. I kiss your hands,
Glory of ladies, and commend my love
To your best faith and memory.

[1] Ex qua tres liberos genuerat, ne pellici suspectaretur Tacit. Ann. Lib iv. p. 74.
[2] Leg. Tacit. Ann. Lib. iv. p. 76.
[3] Tacit. ibid. et Dion. Rom. Hist. Lib. lvii. p. 709.

Liv. My lord,
I shall but change your words.   Farewell.   Yet, this
Remember for your heed, he loves you not;
You know what I have told you: his designs
Are full of grudge and danger; we must use
More than a common speed.
    Sej. Excellent lady,
How you do fire my blood!
    Liv. Well, you must go?
The thoughts be best, are least set forth to shew.   [*Exit Sejanus.*
    Eud. When will you take some physic, lady?
    Liv. When
I shall, Eudemus: but let Drusus' drug
Be first prepared.
    Eud. Were Lygdus made, that's done;
I have it ready.   And to-morrow morning
I'll send you a perfume, first to resolve
And procure sweat, and then prepare a bath
To cleanse and clear the cutis; against when
I'll have an excellent new fucus made,
Resistive 'gainst the sun, the rain, or wind,
Which you shall lay on with a breath, or oil,
As you best like, and last some fourteen hours.
This change came timely, lady, for your health,
And the restoring your complexion,
Which Drusus' choler had almost burnt up!
Wherein your fortune hath prescribed you better
Than art could do.
    Liv. Thanks, good physician,
I'll use my fortune, you shall see, with reverence.
Is my coach ready?
    Eud. It attends your highness.   [*Exeunt.*

SCENE II.—*An Apartment in the Palace.*

Enter SEJANUS.

    Sej. If this be not revenge, when I have done
And made it perfect, let Egyptian slaves,[1]
Parthians, and bare-foot Hebrews brand my face,
And print my body full of injuries.
Thou lost thyself, child Drusus, when thou thoughtst
Thou couldst outskip my vengeance; or outstand
The power I had to crush thee into air.
Thy follies now shall taste what kind of man
They have provoked, and this thy father's house
Crack in the flame of my incensed rage,
Whose fury shall admit no shame or mean.—
Adultery! it is the lightest ill

    [1] Hi apud Romanos barbari et vilissimi æstimab. Juv. Mart. etc.

I will commit. A race of wicked acts
Shall flow out of my anger, and o'erspread
The world's wide face, which no posterity
Shall e'er approve, nor yet keep silent: things
That for their cunning, close, and cruel mark,
Thy father would wish his: and shall, perhaps,
Carry the empty name, but we the prize.
On, then, my soul, and start not in thy course;
Though heaven drop sulphur, and hell belch out fire,
Laugh at the idle terrors; tell proud Jove,
Between his power and thine there is no odds:
'Twas only fear first in the world made gods.[1]

Enter TIBERIUS, *attended.*

Tib. Is yet Sejanus come?
Sej. He's here, dread Cæsar.
Tib. Let all depart that chamber, and the next.

[*Exeunt Attendants.*

Sit down, my comfort.[2] When the master prince
Of all the world, Sejanus, saith he fears,
Is it not fatal?
Sej. Yes, to those are fear'd.
Tib. And not to him?
Sej. Not, if he wisely turn
That part of fate he holdeth, first on them.
Tib. That nature, blood, and laws of kind forbid.
Sej. Do policy and state forbid it?
Tib. No.
Sej. The rest of poor respects, then, let go by;
State is enough to make the act just, them guilty.
Tib. Long hate pursues such acts.
Sej. Whom hatred frights,
Let him not dream of sovereignty.
Tib. Are rites
Of faith, love, piety, to be trod down,
Forgotten, and made vain?
Sej. All for a crown.
The prince who shames a tyrant's name to bear,
Shall never dare do any thing, but fear;
All the command of sceptres quite doth perish,
If it begin religious thoughts to cherish:
Whole empires fall, sway'd by those nice respects;
It is the license of dark deeds protects
Ev'n states most hated, when no laws resist
The sword, but that it acteth what it list.
Tib. Yet so, we may do all things cruelly,
Not safely.

---

[1] Idem, et Petro. Arbiter, Sat. et Statius, Lib. iii.
[2] De hac consultatione, vid. Suet. Tib. c. 55.

Sej. Yes, and do them thoroughly.

Tib. Knows yet Sejanus whom we point at?

Sej. Ay,
Or else my thought, my sense, or both do err:
'Tis Agrippina.[1]

Tib. She, and her proud race.

Sej. Proud! dangerous,[2] Cæsar: for in them apace
The father's spirit shoots up. Germanicus[3]
Lives in their looks, their gait, their form, t' upbraid us
With his close death, if not revenge the same.

Tib. The act's not known.

Sej. Not proved: but whispering Fame
Knowledge and proof doth to the jealous give,
Who, than to fail, would their own thought believe.
It is not safe, the children draw long breath,
That are provoked by a parent's death.

Tib. It is as dangerous to make them hence,
If nothing but their birth be their offence.

Sej. Stay, till they strike at Cæsar; then their crime
Wil' be enough; but late and out of time
For him to punish.

Tib. Do they purpose it?

Sej. You know, sir, thunder speaks not till it hit.
Be not secure; none swiftlier are opprest,
Than they whom confidence betrays to rest.
Let not your daring make your danger such:
All power is to be fear'd, where 'tis too much.
The youths are of themselves hot, violent,
Full of great thought; and that male-spirited dame,[4]
Their mother, slacks no means to put them on,
By large allowance, popular presentings,
Increase of train and state, suing for titles;
Hath them commended with like prayers,[5] like vows,
To the same gods, with Cæsar: days and nights
She spends in banquets and ambitious feasts
For the nobility; where Caius Silius,
Titius Sabinus, old Arruntius,
Asinius Gallus, Furnius, Regulus,
And others of that discontented list,
Are the prime guests. There, and to these, she tells
Whose niece she was,[6] whose daughter, and whose wife.

---

[1] De Agrip. vid. Dio. Rom. Hist. Lib. lvii. p. 69.

[2] De Sejani consil. in Agrip. leg. Tacit. Ann. Lib. i. p. 23, et Lib. iv. p. 77-79. de Tib. susp. Lib. iii. p. 52.

[3] Gnaris omnibus lætam Tiberio Germanici mortem male dissimulari. Tacit. Lib. iii. ibid. Huc confer Tacit. narrat. de morte Pisonis. p. 55. et Lib. iv. p. 74. Germanici mortem inter prospera ducebat.

[4] De anim. virili Agrip. cons. Tacit. Ann. Lib. i. p. 12 et 22. Lib. ii. p. 47.

[5] Tacit. Ann. Lib. iv. p. 79.

[6] Erat enim neptis Augusti, Agrippæ et Juliæ filia, Germanici uxor. Suet. Aug. c. 64.

And then must they compare her with Augusta,
Ay, and prefer her too; commend her form,
Extol her [1] fruitfulness; at which a shower
Falls for the memory of Germanicus,
Which they blow over straight with windy praise,
And puffing hopes of her aspiring sons;
Who, with these hourly ticklings, grow so pleased,
And wantonly conceited of themselves,
As now, they stick not to believe they're such
As these do give them out; and wou d be thought
More than competitors, immediate heirs.
Whilst to their thirst of rule, they win the rout
(That's still the friend of novelty)[2] with hope
Of future freedom, which on every change
That greedily, though emptily expects.
Cæsar, 'tis age in all things breeds neglects,
And princes that will keep old dignity
Must not admit too youthful heirs stand by;
Not their own issue; but so darkly set
As shadows are in picture, to give height
And lustre to themselves.

    Tib. We will command [3]
Their rank thoughts down, and with a stricter hand
Than we have yet put forth; their trains must bate,
Their titles, feasts, and factions.

    Sej. Or your state.
But how, sir, will you work?

    Tib. Confine them.

    Sej. No.
They are too great, and that too faint a blow
To give them now; it would have serv'd at first,
When with the weakest touch their knot had burst.
But, now, your care must be, not to detect
The smallest cord, or line of your suspect;
For such, who know the weight of prince's fear,
Will, when they find themselves discover'd, rear
Their forces, like seen snakes, that else would lie
Roll'd in their circles, close: nought is more high,
Daring, or desperate, than offenders found;
Where guilt is, rage and courage both abound.
The course must be, to let them still swell up,
Riot, and surfeit on blind fortune's cup;
Give them more place, more dignities, more style,
Call them to court, to senate; in the while,

---

[1] De fœcund. ejus. vid. Tacit. Ann. Lib. ii. p. 39. et Lib. iv. p. 77.
[2] Displicere regnantibus civilia filiorum ingenia: neque ob aliud inter-
ceptos quam quia Pop. Rom. æquo jure complecti, reddita libertate,
agitaverint. Nat. Tacit. Lib. ii. Ann. p. 49.
[3] Vid. Suet. Tib. c. 54.

Take from their strength some one or twain, or more,
Of the main fautors, (it will fright the store,)
And, by some by-occasion. Thus, with slight
You shall disarm them first; and they, in night
Of their ambition, not perceive the train,
Till in the engine they are caught and slain.

   Tib. We would not kill, if we knew how to save;
Yet, than a throne, 'tis cheaper give a grave.
Is there no way to bind them by deserts?

   Sej. Sir, wolves do change their hair, but not their hearts.
While thus your thought unto a mean is tied,
You neither dare enough, nor do provide.
All modesty is fond: and chiefly where
The subject is no less compell'd to bear,
Than praise his sovereign's acts.

   Tib. We can no longer [1]
Keep on our mask to thee, our dear Sejanus;
Thy thoughts are ours, in all, and we but proved
Their voice, in our designs, which by assenting
Hath more confirm'd us, than if heart'ning Jove
Had, from his hundred statues, bid us strike,
And at the stroke click'd all his marble thumbs.[2]
But who shall first be struck?

   Sej. First Caius Silius;
He is the most of mark, and most of danger:
In power and reputation equal strong,
Having commanded [3] an imperial army
Seven years together, vanquish'd Sacrovir
In Germany, and thence obtain'd to wear
The ornaments triumphal. His steep fall,
By how much it doth give the weightier crack,
Will send more wounding terror to the rest,
Command them stand aloof, and give more way
To our surprising of the principal.

   Tib. But what,[4] Sabinus?

   Sej. Let him grow a while,
His fate is not yet ripe: we must not pluck
At all together, lest we catch ourselves.
And there's Arruntius too, he only talks.
But Sosia,[5] Silius' wife, would be wound in

---

[1] Tiberium variis artibus devinxit adeo Sejanus, ut obscurum adversum alios, sibi uni incautum, intectumque efficeret. Tacit. Ann. Lib. iv. p. 74. Vid. Dio. Hist. Rom. Lib. lvii. p. 707.

[2] Premere pollicem, apud Romanos, maximi favoris erat signum. Horat. Epist. ad Lollium. Fautor utroque horum laudabit pollice ludum. Et Plin. Nat. Hist. Lib. xxviii. cap. 2. Pollices, cum faveamus, premere etiam proverbio jubemur. De interp. loci, vid. Ang. Pol. Miscell. cap. xlii. et Turn. Adver. Lib. xi. cap. vi.

[3] Tacit. Ann. Lib. iii. p. 63. et Lib. iv. p. 79.

[4] Tacit. ibid.   [5] Tacit. ibid.

Now, for she hath a fury in her breast,
More than hell ever knew; and would be sent
Thither in time.   Then is there one Cremutius [1]
Cordus, a writing fellow, they have got
To gather notes of the precedent times,
And make them into Annals; a most tart
And bitter spirit, I hear; who, under colour
Of praising those, doth tax the present state,
Censures the men, the actions, leaves no trick,
No practice unexamined, parallels
The times, the governments; a profest champion
For the old liberty—
   Tib. A perishing wretch!
As if there were that chaos bred in things,
That laws and liberty would not rather choose
To be quite broken, and ta'en hence by us,
Than have the stain to be preserved by such.
Have we the means to make these guilty first?
   Sej. Trust that to me: let Cæsar, by his power
But cause a formal meeting of the senate,
I will have matter and accusers ready.
   Tib. But how? let us consult.
   Sej. We shall misspend
The time of action.   Counsels are unfit
In business, where all rest is more pernicious
Than rashness can be.   Acts of this close kind
Thrive more by execution than advice.
There is no lingering in that work begun,
Which cannot praised be, until through done.
   Tib. Our edicts shall forthwith command a court.[2]
While I can live, I will prevent earth's fury:
'Εμοῦ θανόντος γαῖα μιχθήτω πυρί.[3]

                                                    [*Exit.*

Enter JULIUS POSTHUMUS.

   Pos. My lord Sejanus—
   Sej. Julius [4] Posthumus!
Come with my wish!   What news from Agrippina's?
   Pos. Faith, none.   Thay all lock up themselves a'late,
Or talk in character; I have not seen
A company so changed.   Except they had
Intelligence by augury of our practice.—
   Sej. When were you there?

[1] Vid. Tacit. Ann. Lib. iv. p. 83.   Dio. Hist. Rom. Lib. lvii. p. 710. et Sen. Cons. ad Marc. cap. 1. et fusius, cap. 22.
[2] Edicto ut plurimum Senatores in curiam vocatos constat. Tacit. Ann. Lib. i. p. 3.
[3] Vulgaris quidam versus, quem sæpe Tiber. recitasse memoratur. Dion. Hist. Rom. Lib. lviii. p. 729.
[4] De Julio Postumo. vid. Tacit. Ann. Lib. iv. p. 77

Pos. Last night.

Sej. And what guests found you?

Pos. Sabinus, Silius, the old list, Arruntius,
Furnius, and Gallus.

Sej. Would not these talk?

Pos. Little:
And yet we offer'd choice of argument.
Satrius was with me.

Sej. Well; 'tis guilt enough
Their often meeting.   You forgot to extol [1]
The hospitable lady?

Pos. No; that trick
Was well put home, and had succeeded too,
But that Sabinus cough'd a caution out;
For she began to swell.

Sej. And may she burst!
Julius, I would have you go instantly
Unto the palace of the great Augusta,
And, by your [2] kindest friend, get swift access;
Acquaint her with these meetings: tell the words [3]
You brought me the other day, of Silius,
Add somewhat to them.   Make her understand
The danger of Sabinus, and the times,
Out of his closeness.   Give Arruntius' words
Of malice against Cæsar; so, to Gallus:
But, above all, to Agrippina.   Say,
As you may truly, that her infinite pride,[4]
Propt with the hopes of her too fruitful womb,
With popular studies gapes for sovereignty,
And threatens Cæsar.   Pray Augusta then,
That for her own, great Cæsar's, and the pub-
Lic safety, she be pleased to urge these dangers.
Cæsar is too secure, he must be told,
And best he'll take it from a mother's tongue.
Alas! what is't for us to sound, to explore,
To watch, oppose, plot, practise, or prevent,
If he, for whom it is so strongly labour'd,
Shall, out of greatness and free spirit, be
Supinely negligent? our city's now [5]
Divided as in time o' the civil war,
And men forbear not to declare themselves
Of Agrippina's party.   Every day
The faction multiplies; and will do more,
If not resisted: you can best enlarge it,

[1] Proximi Agrip. inliciebantur pravis sermonibus tumidos spiritus
perstimulare.   Tacit. Ann. Lib. iv. p. 77.

[2] Mutilia Prisca, quæ in animum Augustæ valida.   Tac. ibid.

[3] Verba Silii immodice jactata, vid. apud Tac. Ann. Lib. iv. p. 79.

[4] Tacit. Ann. Lib. iv. p. 77.

[5] Hæc apud Tacit. leg. Ann. Lib. iv. p 79.

As you find audience.   Noble Posthumus,
Commend me to your Prisca: and pray her,
She will solicit this great business,
To earnest and most present execution,
With all her utmost credit with Augusta.
    Pos. I shall not fail in my instructions.   [*Exit.*
    Sej. This second, from his mother, will well urge
Our late design, and spur on Cæsar's rage;
Which else might grow remiss.   The way to put
A prince in blood, is to present the shapes
Of dangers, greater than they are, like late,
Or early shadows; and, sometimes, to feign
Where there are none, only to make him fear?
His fear will make him cruel: and once enter'd,
He doth not easily learn to stop, or spare
Where he may doubt.   This have I made my rule,
To thrust Tiberius into tyranny,
And make him toil, to turn aside those blocks,
Which I alone could not remove with safety,
Drusus once gone, Germanicus' three sons [1]
Would clog my way; whose guards have too much faith
To be corrupted: and their mother known
Of too, too unreproved a chastity,
To be attempted, as light Livia was.
Work then, my art, on Cæsar's fears, as they
On those they fear 'till all my lets be clear'd,
And he in ruins of his house, and hate
Of all his subjects, bury his own state;
When with my peace and safety, I will rise,
By making him the public sacrifice.   [*Exit.*

    SCENE III.—*A Room in* AGRIPPINA'S *House.*
        Enter SATRIUS *and* NATTA.

    Sat. They're grown exceeding circumspect, and wary.
    Nat. They have us in the wind: and yet Arruntius
Cannot contain himself.
    Sat. Tut, he's not yet
Look'd after; there are others more desired [2]
That are more silent.
    Nat. Here he comes.   Away.   [*Exeunt.*

    Enter SABINUS, ARRUNTIUS, *and* CORDUS.

    Sab. How is it, that these beagles haunt the house
Of Agrippina?

---

[1] Quorum non dubia successio, neque spargi venenum in tres poterat
etc. Tacit. Ann. Lib. iv. p. 77.
[2] Silius, Sabinus, de quibus supra.

Arr. O, they hunt,[1] they hunt!
There is some game here lodged, which they must rouse,
To make the great ones sport.
    Cor. Did you observe
How they inveigh'd 'gainst Cæsar?
    Arr. Ay, baits, baits,
For us to bite at: would I have my flesh
Torn by the public hook, these qualified hangmen
Should be my company.
    Cor. Here comes another.   [*Dom. Afer passes over the stage.*
    Arr. Ay, there's a man,[2] Afer the orator!
One that hath phrases, figures, and fine flowers,
To strew his rhetoric with,[3] and doth make haste,
To get him note, or name, by any offer
Where blood or gain be objects; steeps his words,
When he would kill, in artificial tears:
The crocodile of Tyber! him I love,
That man is mine; he hath my heart and voice
When I would curse! he, he.
    Sab. Contemn the slaves,
Their present lives will be their future graves.   [*Exeunt.*

SCENE IV.—*Another Apartment in the same.*

Enter Silius, Agrippina, Nero, *and* Sosia.

    Sil. May't please your highness not forget yourself;
I dare not, with my manners, to attempt
Your trouble farther.
    Agr. Farewell, noble Silius!
    Sil. Most royal princess.
    Agr. Sosia stays with us?
    Sil. She is your servant, and doth owe your grace
An honest, but unprofitable love.
    Agr. How can that be, when there's no gain but virtue's?
    Sil. You take the moral, not the politic sense.
I meant, as she is bold, and free of speech,
Earnest [4] to utter what her zealous thought
Travails withal, in honour of your house;
Which act, as it is simply born in her,
Partakes of love and honesty; but may,
By the over-often, and unseason'd use,

---

[1] Tib. tempor. delatores genus hominum publico exitio repertum, et pœnis quidem nunquam satis coërcitum, per præmia eliciebantur. Tac. Ann. Lib. iv. p. 82.
[2] De Domit. Af. vid. Tac. Ann. Lib. iv. p. 89-93.
[3] Quoquo facinore properus clarescere. Tacit. ibid. Et infra. prosperiore eloquentiæ quam morum famâ fuit. Et p. 93. diu egens, et parto nuper præmio male usus, plura ad flagitia accingeretur.
[4] Vid. Tac. Ann. Lib. iv. p. 79.

Turn to your loss and danger:[1] for your state
Is waited on by envies, as by eyes;
And every second guest your tables take
Is a fee'd spy, to observe who goes, who comes;
What conference you have, with whom, where, when,
What the discourse is, what the looks, the thoughts
Of every person there, they do extract,
And make into a substance.

    Agr. Hear me, Silius.
Were all Tiberius' body stuck with eyes,
And every wall and hanging in my house
Transparent, as this lawn I wear, or air;
Yea, had Sejanus both his ears as long
As to my inmost closet, I would hate
To whisper any thought, or change an act,
To be made Juno's rival. Virtue's forces
Shew ever noblest in conspicuous courses.

    Sil. 'Tis great, and bravely spoken, like the spirit
Of Agrippina: yet, your highness knows,
There is nor loss nor shame in providence;
Few can, what all should do, beware enough.
You may perceive [2] with what officious face,
Satrius, and Natta, Afer, and the rest
Visit your house, of late, to enquire the secrets;
And with what bold and privileged art, they rail
Against Augusta, yea, and at Tiberius;
Tell tricks of Livia, and Sejanus; all
To excite, and call your indignation on,
That they might hear it at more liberty.

    Agr. You're too suspicious, Silius.
    Sil. Pray the gods,
I be so, Agrippina; but I fear
Some subtle practice.[3] They that durst to strike
At so exampless, and unblamed a life,
As that of the renowned Germanicus,
Will not sit down with that exploit alone:
He threatens many that hath injured one.

    Nero. 'Twere best rip forth their tongues, sear out their eyes,
When next they come.

    Sos. A fit reward for spies.

Enter DRUSUS, jun.

    Dru. jun. Hear you the rumour?
    Agr. What?
    Dru. jun. Drusus is dying.[4]
    Agr. Dying!

---

[1] Vid. Isc. Ann. Lib. iv. p. 77.   [2] Tacit. ibid. et pp. 90 et 92.
[3] Suet. Tib. c. 2. Dion. Rom. Hist. Lib. lvii. p. 705.
[4] Tac. Ann. Lib. iv. pp. 74, 75, 76, 77.

Nero. That's strange!

Agr. You were with him yesternight.

Dru. jun. One met Eudemus the physician,
Sent for, but now; who thinks he cannot live.

Sil. Thinks! if it be arrived at that, he knows,
Or none.

Agr. 'Tis quick! what should be his disease?

Sil. Poison, poison—

Agr. How, Silius!

Nero. What's that?

Sil. Nay, nothing.   There was late a certain blow
Giv n o' the face.

Nero. Ay, to Sejanus.

Sil. True.

Dru. jun. And what of that?

Sil. I'm glad I gave it not.

Nero. But there is somewhat else?

Sil. Yes, private meetings,
With a great lady [sir], at a physician's,
And a wife turn'd away.

Nero. Ha!

Sil. Toys, mere toys:
What wisdom's now in th' streets, in the common mouth?

Dru. jun. Fears, whisperings, tumults, noise, I know not what:
They say the Senate sit.[1]

Sil. I'll thither straight;
And see what's in the forge.

Agr. Good Silius do;
Sosia and I will in.

Sil. Haste you, my lords,
To visit the sick prince; tender your loves,
And sorrows to the people.   This Sejanus,
Trust my divining soul, hath plots on all:
No tree, that stops his prospect, but must fall.   [*Exeunt.*

ACT III

SCENE I.—*The Senate-House.*

Enter Præcones, Lictores, Sejanus, Varro, Latiaris, Cotta,
and Afer.

Sej. 'Tis only [2] you must urge against him, Varro;
Nor I nor Cæsar may appear therein,
Except in your defence, who are the consul;
And, under colour of late enmity
Between your father and his, may better do it,

[1] Vid. Tac. Ann. Lib. iv. p. 76.
[2] Tacit. Ann. Lib. iv. p. 79.

As free from all suspicion of a practice.
Here be your notes, what points to touch at; read:
Be cunning in them. Afer has them too.

  Var. But is he summon'd?

  Sej. No. It was debated
By Cæsar, and concluded as most fit
To take him unprepared.

  Afer. And prosecute
All under name of treason.[1]

  Var. I conceive.

Enter Sabinus, Gallus, Lepidus, *and* Arruntius.

  Sab. Drusus being dead, Cæsar will not be here.

  Gal. What should the business of this senate be?

  Arr. That can my subtle whisperers tell you: we
That are the good-dull-noble lookers on,
Are only call'd to keep the marble warm.
What should we do with those deep mysteries,
Proper to these fine heads? let them alone.
Our ignorance may, perchance, help us be saved
From whips and furies.

  Gall. See, see, see their action!

  Arr. Ay, now their heads do travail, now they work;
Their faces run like shittles; they are weaving
Some curious cobweb to catch flies.

  Sab. Observe,
They take their places.

  Arr. What,[2] so low!

  Gal. O yes,
They must be seen to flatter Cæsar's grief,
Though but in sitting.

  Var. Bid us silence.

  Præ. Silence!

  *Var. Fathers conscript,[3] may this our present meeting
Turn fair, and fortunate to the common-wealth !*

Enter Silius, *and other* Senators.

  Sej. See, Silius enters.

  Sil. Hail, grave fathers!

  Lic. Stand.
Silius, forbear thy place.

  Sen. How!

  Præ. Silius, stand forth,
The consul hath to charge thee.

  Lic. Room for Cæsar.

---

[1] Tacit. Ann. Lib. iv. p. 79. Sed cuncta quæstione majestatis exercita.
[2] Tacit. cod. Lib. iv. p. 76. Consulesque sede vulgari per speciem mæstitiæ sedentes.
[3] Præfatio solennis Consulum Rom. vid. Bar. Briss. de for. Lib. ii.

Arr. Is he come too! nay then expect a trick.
Sab. Silius accused! sure he will answer nobly.

Enter TIBERIUS, *attended.*

Tib. We stand amazed, fathers, to behold
This general dejection. Wherefore sit
Rome's consuls thus dissolved,[1] as they had lost
All the remembrance both of style and place?
It not becomes. No woes are of fit weight,
To make the honour of the empire stoop:
Though I, in my peculiar self, may meet
Just reprehension, that so suddenly,
And, in so fresh a grief, would greet the senate,
When private tongues, of kinsmen and allies,
Inspired with comforts, lothly are endured,
The face of men not seen, and scarce the day,
To thousands that communicate our loss.
Nor can I argue these of weakness; since
They take but natural ways; yet I must seek
For stronger aids, and those fair helps draw out
From warm embraces of the common-wealth.
Our mother, great Augusta, 's struck with time,
Our self imprest with aged characters,
Drusus is gone, his children young and babes;
Our aims must now reflect on those that may
Give timely succour to these present ills,
And are our only glad-surviving hopes,
The noble issue of Germanicus,
Nero and Drusus: might it please the consul
Honour them in, they both attend without.
I would present them to the senate's care,
And raise those suns of joy that should drink up
These floods of sorrow in your drowned eyes.
    Arr. By Jove, I am not Œdipus enough
To understand this Sphynx.
    Sab. The princes come.

Enter NERO, *and* DRUSUS, junior.

Tib. Approach you, noble Nero, noble Drusus.
These princes, fathers, when their parent died,
I gave unto their uncle, with this prayer,
That though he had proper issue of his own,
He would no less bring up, and foster these,
Than that self-blood; and by that act confirm
Their worths to him, and to posterity.
Drusus ta'en hence, I turn my prayers to you,
And 'fore our country, and our gods, beseech
You take, and rule Augustus' nephew's sons,

[1] Tacit. Ann. Lib. iv. p. 76.

Sprung of the noblest ancestors; and so
Accomplish both my duty, and your own.
Nero, and Drusus, these shall be to you
In place of parents, these your fathers, these;
And not unfitly: for you are so born,
As all your good, or ill's the common-wealth's.
Receive them, you strong guardians; and blest gods,
Make all their actions answer to their bloods:
Let their great titles find increase by them,
Not they by titles. Set them as in place,
So in example, above all the Romans:
And may they know no rivals but themselves.
Let Fortune give them nothing; but attend
Upon their virtue: and that still come forth
Greater than hope, and better than their fame.
Relieve me, fathers, with your general voice.

Senators. May all the gods consent to Cæsar's wish,
And add to any honours that may crown
The hopeful issue of Germanicus!

Tib. We thank you, reverend fathers, in their right.

Arr. If this were true now! but the space, the space
Between the breast and lips—Tiberius' heart
Lies a thought further than another man's.   *[Aside.*

Tib. My comforts are so flowing in my joys,
As, in them, all my streams of grief are lost,
No less than are land-waters in the sea,
Or showers in rivers; though their cause was such,
As might have sprinkled ev'n the gods with tears:
Yet, since the greater doth embrace the less,
We covetously obey.

Arr. Well acted, Cæsar.   *[Aside.*

Tib. And now I am the happy witness made
Of your so much desired affections
To this great issue, I could wish, the Fates
Would here set peaceful period to my days;
However to my labours, I entreat,
And beg it of this senate, some fit ease.

Arr. Laugh, fathers, laugh:[1] have you no spleens about you?   *[Aside.*

Tib. The burden is too heavy I sustain
On my unwilling shoulders; and I pray
It may be taken off, and reconferred
Upon the consuls, or some other Roman,
More able, and more worthy.

Arr. Laugh on still.   *[Aside.*

Sab. Why this doth render all the rest suspected!

Gal. It poisons all.

[1] Tacit. Lib. iv. p. 76. Ad vana et toties inrisa revolutus de reddenda Rep. utque consules, seu quis alius regimen susciperent.

Arr. O, do you taste it then?

Sab. It takes away my faith to any thing
He shall hereafter speak.

Arr. Ay, to pray that,
Which would be to his head as hot as thunder,
'Gainst which he wears that charm [1] should but the court
Receive him at his word.

Gal. Hear!

Tib. For myself
I know my weakness, and so little covet,
Like some gone past, the weight that will oppress me,
As my ambition is the counter-point.

Arr. Finely maintained; good still!

Sej. But Rome, whose blood,
Whose nerves, whose life, whose very frame relies
On Cæsar's strength, no less than heaven on Atlas,
Cannot admit it but with general ruin.

Arr. Ah! are you there to bring him off?   [*Aside.*

Sej. Let Cæsar
No more then urge a point so contrary
To Cæsar's greatness, the grieved senate's vows,
Or Rome's necessity.

\ *Gal.* He comes about—

Arr. More nimbly than Vertumnus.

Tib. For the publick,
I may be drawn to shew I can neglect
All private aims, though I affect my rest;
But if the senate still command me serve,
I must be glad to practise my obedience.[2]

Arr. You must and will, sir. We do know it.   [*Aside.*

Senators. *Cæsar,*
Live long and happy, great and royal Cæsar;
The gods preserve thee and thy modesty,
Thy wisdom and thy innocence!

Arr. Where is't?
The prayer is made before the subject.   [*Aside.*

Senators. *Guard*
His meekness, Jove; his piety, his care,
His bounty—

Arr. And his subtility, I'll put in:
Yet he'll keep that himself, without the gods.
All prayers are vain for him.   [*Aside.*

    Tib. We will not hold
Your patience, fathers, with long answer; but

---

[1] *'Gainst which he wears a charm.*] Tonitrua præter modum expavescebat; et turbatiore cœlo nunquam non coronam lauream capite gestavit, quod fulmine afflari negetur id genus frondis. Suet. Tib. c. 69. Plin. Nat. Hist. Lib. xv. c. 20.

[2] Semper perplexa et obscura orat. Tib. vid. Tacit. Ann. Lib. i. p. 5.

Shall still contend to be what you desire,
And work to satisfy so great a hope.
Proceed to your affairs.
    Arr. Now, Silius, guard thee;
The curtain's drawing. Afer advanceth.   [*Aside.*
    Prœ. Silence!
    Afer. Cite [1] Caius Silius.
    Prœ. Caius Silius!
    Sil. Here.
    Afer. The triumph that thou hadst in Germany
For thy late victory on Sacrovir,
Thou hast enjoy'd so freely, Caius Silius,
As no man it envied thee; nor would Cæsar,
Or Rome admit, that thou wert then defrauded
Of any honours thy deserts could claim,
In the fair service of the common-wealth:
But now, if, after all their loves and graces,
(Thy actions, and their courses being discover'd)
It shall appear to Cæsar and this senate,
Thou hast defiled those glories with thy crimes—
    Sil. Crimes!
    Afer. Patience, Silius.
    Sil. Tell thy mule of patience;
I am a Roman. What are my crimes? proclaim them.
Am I too rich, too honest for the times?
Have I or treasure, jewels, land, or houses
That some informer gapes for? is my strength
Too much to be admitted, or my knowledge?
These now are crimes.[2]
    Afer. Nay, Silius, if the name
Of crime so touch thee, with what impotence
Wilt thou endure the matter to be search'd?
    Sil. I tell thee, Afer, with more scorn than fear:
Employ your mercenary tongue and art.
Where's my accuser?
    Var. Here.
    Arr. Varro, the consul!
Is he thrust in?   [*Aside.*
    Var. 'Tis I accuse thee, Silius.
Against the majesty of Rome, and Cæsar,
I do pronounce thee here a guilty cause,
First of beginning [3] and occasioning,
    Next, drawing out the war in [4] Gallia,

---

[1] Citabatur reus e tribunali voce præconis. vid. Bar. Brisson. Lib. 5, de form.

[2] Vid. Suet. Tib. Tacit. Dio. Senec.

[3] Tacit. Lib. iv. p. 79. Conscientiâ belli, Sacrovir diu dissimulatus, victoria per avaritiam fœdata, et uxor Sosia arguebantur.

[4] Bellum Sacrovirianum in Gall. erat. Triumph. in Germ. vid. Tacit. Ann. Lib. iii. p. 63.

For which thou late triumph'st; dissembling long
That Sacrovir to be an enemy,
Only to make thy entertainment more.
Whilst thou, and thy wife Sosia, poll'd the province:
Wherein, with sordid, base desire of gain,
Thou hast discredited thy actions' worth,
And been a traitor to the state.

   Sil. Thou liest.

   Arr. I thank thee, Silius, speak so still and often.

   Var. If I not prove it, Cæsar,[1] but unjustly
Have call'd him into trial; here I bind
Myself to suffer, what I claim against him;
And yield to have what I have spoke, confirm'd
By judgment of the court, and all good men.

   Sil. Cæsar, I crave to have my cause deferr'd,
Till this man's consulship be out.

   Tib. We cannot,
Nor may we grant it.

   Sil. Why? shall he design
My day of trial?   Is he my accuser,
And must he be my judge?

   Tib. It hath been usual,
And is a right that custom hath allow'd
The magistrate,[2] to call forth private men;
And to appoint their day: which privilege
We may not in the consul see infringed,
By whose deep watches, and industrious care
It is so labour'd, as the common-wealth
Receive no loss, by any oblique course.

   Sil. Cæsar, thy fraud is worse than violence.

   Tib. Silius, mistake us not, we dare not use
The credit of the consul to thy wrong;
But only to preserve his place and power,
So far as it concerns the dignity
And honour of the state.

   Arr. Believe him, Silius.

   Cot. Why, so he may, Arruntius.

   Arr. I say so.
And he may choose too.

   Tib. By the Capitol,
And all our gods, but that the dear republic,
Our sacred laws, and just authority
Are interess'd therein, I should be silent.

   Afer. 'Please Cæsar to give way unto his trial,
He shall have justice.

   Sil. Nay, I shall have law;

[1] Vid. accusandi formulam apud Brisson. Lib. v. de form.

[2] Tacit. Ann. Lib. iv. p. 79. Adversatus est Cæsar, solirum quippe magistratibus diem privatis dicere, nec infringendum Consulis jus, cujus vigiliis, etc.

Shall I not, Afer? speak.

   Afer. Would you have more?

   Sil. No, my well-spoken man, I would no more;
Nor less: might I enjoy it natural,
Not taught to speak unto your present ends,
Free from thine, his, and all your unkind handling,
Furious enforcing, most unjust presuming,
Malicious, and manifold applying,
Foul wresting, and impossible construction.

   Afer. He raves, he raves.

   Sil. Thou durst not tell me so,
Hadst thou not Cæsar's warrant. I can see
Whose power condemns me.

   Var. This betrays his spirit:
This doth enough declare him what he is.

   Sil. What am I? speak.

   Var. An enemy to the state.

   Sil. Because I am an enemy to thee,
And such corrupted ministers o' the state,
That here art made a present instrument
To [1] gratify it with thine own disgrace.

   Sej. This, to the consul, is most insolent,
And impious!

   Sil. Ay, take part. Reveal yourselves,
Alas! I scent not your confederacies,
Your plots, and combinations! I not know
Minion Sejanus hates me: and that all,
This boast of law, and law, is but a form,
A net of Vulcan's filing, a mere ingine,
To take that life by a pretext of justice,
Which you pursue in malice! I want brain,
Or nostril to persuade me, that your ends,
And purposes are made to what they are,
Before my answer! O, you equal gods,
Whose justice not a world of wolf-turn'd men
Shall make me to accuse, howe'er provoked;
Have I for this so oft engaged myself?
Stood in the heat and fervour of a fight,
When Phœbus sooner hath forsook the day
Than I the field, against the blue-eyed Gauls,
And crisped Germans? when our Roman eagles
Have fann'd the fire, with their labouring wings,
And no blow dealt, that left not death behind it?
When I have charged, alone, into the troops
Of curl'd Sicambrians,[2] routed them, and came

[1] Tacit. Ann. Lib. iv. p. 79. Immissusque Varro consul qui paternas inimicitias obtendens, odiis Sejani per dedecus suum gratificabatur.

[2] Populi Germ. hodie Geldri in Belgica sunt inter Mosam et Rhenum, quos celebrat Mart. Spec. 3.
       Crinibus in nodum tortis venere Sicambri.

Not off, with backward ensigns of a slave;
But forward marks, wounds on my breast and face,
Were meant to thee, O Cæsar, and thy Rome?
And have I this return! did I, for this,
Perform so noble and so brave defeat
On Sacrovir! O Jove, let it become me
To boast my deeds, when he whom they concern,
Shall thus forget them.

    Afer. Silius, Silius,
These are the common customs of thy blood,
When it is high with wine, as now with rage:
This well agrees with that intemperate vaunt,
Thou lately mad'st [1] at Agrippina's table,
That, when all other of the troops were prone
To fall into rebellion, only thine
Remain'd in their obedience.   Thou wert he
That saved the empire, which had then been lost
Had but thy legions, there, rebell'd, or mutined;
Thy virtue met, and fronted every peril.
Thou gav'st to Cæsar, and to Rome their surety;
Their name, their strength, their spirit, and their state,
Their being was a donative from thee.

    Arr. Well worded, and most like an orator.

    Tib. Is this true, Silius?

    Sil. Save thy question, Cæsar;
Thy spy of famous credit hath affirm'd it.

    Arr. Excellent Roman!

    Sab. He doth answer stoutly.

    Sej. If this be so, there needs no farther cause
Of crime against him.

    Var. What can more impeach
The royal dignity and state of Cæsar,
Than to be urged with a benefit
He cannot pay?

    Cot. In this, all Cæsar's fortune
Is made unequal to the courtesy.

    Lat. His means are clean destroyed that should requite.

    Gal. Nothing is great enough for Silius' merit.

    Arr. Gallus on that side too!   [*Aside.*

    Sil. Come, do not hunt,
And labour so about for circumstance,
To make him guilty whom you have foredoom'd:
Take shorter ways, I'll meet your purposes.
The words were mine, and more I now will say:
Since I have done thee that great service, Cæsar,
Thou still hast fear'd me; and in place of grace,
Return'd me hatred: so soon all best turns,
With doubtful princes, turn deep injuries

             [1] Tacit. Ann. Lib. iv. p. 79.

In estimation, when they greater rise
Than can be answer'd. Benefits, with you,
Are of no longer pleasure, than you can
With ease restore them; that transcended once,
Your studies are not how to thank, but kill.
It is your nature, to have all men slaves
To you, but you acknowledging to none.
The means that make your greatness, must not come
In mention of it; if it do, it takes
So much away, you think: and that which help'd,
Shall soonest perish, if it stand in eye,
Where it may front, or but upbraid the high.

    Cot. Suffer him speak no more.

    Var. Note but his spirit.

    Afer. This shews him in the rest.

    Lat. Let him be censured.

    Sej. He hath spoke enough to prove him Cæsar's foe.

    Cot. His thoughts look through his words.

    Sej. A censure.

    Sil. Stay,
Stay, most officious senate, I shall straight
Delude thy fury. Silius hath not placed
His guards within him, against fortune's spite,
So weakly, but he can escape your gripe
That are but hands of fortune: she herself,
When virtue doth oppose, must lose her threats.
All that can happen in humanity,
The frown of Cæsar, proud Sejanus' hatred,
Base Varro's spleen, and Afer's bloodying tongue,
The senate's servile flattery, and these
Muster'd to kill, I'm fortified against;
And can look down upon: they are beneath me.
It is not life whereof I stand enamour'd;
Nor shall my end make me accuse my fate.
The coward and the valiant man must fall,
Only the cause and manner how, discerns them:
Which then are gladdest, when they cost us dearest.
Romans, if any here be in this senate,
Would know to mock Tiberius' tyranny,
Look upon Silius, and so learn to die.   [*Stabs himself.*

    Var. O desperate act!

    Arr. An honourable hand!

    Tib. Look, is he dead?

    Sab. 'Twas nobly struck, and home.

    Arr. My thought did prompt him to it. Farewell, Silius,
Be famous ever for thy great example.

    Tib. We are not pleased in this sad accident,
That thus hath stalled, and abused our mercy,
Intended to preserve thee, noble Roman,

And to prevent thy hopes.
    Arr. Excellent wolf!
Now he is full he howls.   [*Aside.*
    Sej. Cæsar doth wrong
His dignity and safety thus to mourn
The deserv'd end of so profest a traitor,
And doth, by this his lenity, instruct
Others as factious to the like offence.
    Tib. The confiscation merely of his state
Had been enough.
    Arr. O, that was gaped for then?   [*Aside.*
    Var. Remove the body.
    Sej. Let citation
Go out for Sosia.
    Gal. Let her be proscribed:
And for the goods, I think it fit that half
Go to the treasure, half unto the children.
    Lep. With leave of Cæsar, I would think that fourth,
The which the law doth cast on the informers,
Should be enough; the rest go to the children.
Wherein the prince shall shew humanity,
And bounty; not to force them by their want,
Which in their parents' trespass they deserv'd,
To take ill courses.
    Tib. It shall please us.
    Arr. Ay,
Out of necessity. This [1] Lepidus
Is grave and honest, and I have observed
A moderation still in all his censures.
    Sab. And bending to the better——Stay, who's this?

Enter SATRIUS *and* NATTA, *with* CREMUTIUS CORDUS *guarded.*

Cremutius Cordus! What! is he brought in?
    Arr. More blood into the banquet! Noble Cordus,[2]
I wish thee good: be as thy writings, free,
And honest.
    Tib. What is he?
    Sej. For the Annals, Cæsar.
    Præ. Cremutius Cordus!
    Cor. Here.
    Præ. Satrius Secundus,
Pinnarius Natta, you are his accusers.
    Arr. Two of Sejanus' blood-hounds, whom he breeds
With human flesh, to bay at citizens.
    Afer. Stand forth before the senate, and confront him.
    Sat. I do accuse thee here, Cremutius Cordus,
To be a man factious and dangerous,
A sower of sedition in the state,

A turbulent and discontented spirit,
Which I will prove from thine own writings, here,
The Annals thou hast publish'd: where thou bit'st
The present age, and with a viper's tooth,
Being a member of it, dar'st that ill
Which never yet degenerous bastard did
Upon his parent.

 Nat. To this, I subscribe;
And, forth a world of more particulars,
Instance in only one: comparing men,
And times, thou praisest Brutus, and affirm'st
That Cassius was the last of all the Romans.

 Cot. How! what are we then?

 Var. What is Cæsar? nothing?

 Afer. My lords, this strikes at every Roman's private,
In whom reigns gentry, and estate of spirit,
To have a Brutus brought in parallel,
A parricide, an enemy of his country,
Rank'd, and preferr'd to any real worth
That Rome now holds. This is most strangely invective,
Most full of spite, and insolent upbraiding.
Nor is't the time alone is here disprised,
But the whole man of time, yea, Cæsar's self
Brought in disvalue; and he aimed at most,
By oblique glance of his licentious pen.
Cæsar, if Cassius were the last of Romans,
Thou hast no name.

 Tib. Let's hear him answer. Silence!

 Cor. So innocent I am of fact, my lords,
As but my words are argued: yet those words
Not reaching either prince or prince's parent:
The which your law of treason comprehends. ¶
Brutus and Cassius I am charged to have praised;
Whose deeds, when many more, besides myself,
Have writ, not one hath mention'd without honour.
Great Titus Livius, great for eloquence,
And faith amongst us, in his history,
With so great praises Pompey did extol, ⌐
As oft Augustus call'd him a Pompeian:
Yet this not hurt their friendship. In his book
He often names Scipio, Afranius,
Yea, the same Cassius, and this Brutus too,
As worthiest men; not thieves and parricides,
Which notes upon their fames are now imposed.
Asinius Pollio's writings quite throughout
Give them a noble memory; so [1] Messala
Renown'd his general Cassius: yet both these
Lived with Augustus, full of wealth and honours.

     [1] Septem dec. lib. Hist. scripsit. vid. Suid. Suet.

To Cicero's book, where Cato was heav'd up
Equal with Heaven, what else did Cæsar answer,
Being then dictator, but with a penn'd oration,
As if before the judges? Do but see
Antonius' letters; read but Brutus' pleadings:
What vile reproach they hold against Augustus,
False, I confess, but with much bitterness.
The epigrams of Bibaculus and Catullus
Are read, full stuft with spite of both the Cæsars;
Yet deified Julius, and no less Augustus,
Both bore them, and contemn'd them: I not know,
Promptly to speak it, whether done with more
Temper, or wisdom; for such obloquies
If they despised be, they die supprest;
But if with rage acknowledg'd, they are confest.
The Greeks I slip, whose license not alone,
But also lust did scape unpunished:
Or where some one, by chance, exception took,
He words with words revenged. But, in my work,
What could be aim'd more free, or farther off
From the time's scandal, than to write of those,
Whom death from grace or hatred had exempted?
Did I, with Brutus and with Cassius,
Arm'd, and possess'd of the Philippi fields,
Incense the people in the civil cause,
With dangerous speeches? Or do they, being slain
Seventy years since, as by their images,
Which not the conqueror hath defaced, appears,
Retain that guilty memory with writers?
Posterity pays every man his honour;
Nor shall there want, though I condemned am,
That will not only Cassius well approve,
And of great Brutus' honour mindful be,
But that will also mention make of me.
   Arr. Freely and nobly spoken!
   Sab. With good temper;
I like him, that he is not moved with passion.
   Arr. He puts them to their whisper.
   Tib. Take him hence; [1]
We shall determine of him at next sitting.
                [Exeunt Officers with Cordus.
   Cot. Mean time, give order, that his books be burnt,
To the ædiles.
   Sej. You have well advised.
   Afer. It fits not such licentious things should live
T' upbraid the age.
   Arr. If the age were good, they might.

---

[1] Egressus dein senatu vitam abstinentiâ finivit. Tacit. ibid. Generosam jeus mortem vid. apud Sen. Cons. ad Marc. cap. 22.

Lat. Let them be burnt.

Gal. All sought, and burnt to-day.

Præ. The court is up; lictors, resume the fasces.

        [Exeunt all but Arruntius, Sabinus, and Lepidus.

Arr. Let them be burnt! O, how ridiculous
Appears the senate's brainless diligence,
Who think they can, with present power, extinguish
The memory of all succeeding times!

Sab. 'Tis true; when, contrary, the punishment
Of wit, doth make the authority increase.
Nor do they aught, that use this cruelty
Of interdiction, and this rage of burning,
But purchase to themselves rebuke and shame,
And to the writers [1] an eternal name.

Lep. It is an argument the times are sore,
When virtue cannot safely be advanced;
Nor vice reproved.

Arr. Ay, noble Lepidus;
Augustus well foresaw what we should suffer
Under Tiberius, when he did pronounce
The Roman race most wretched,[2] that should live
Between so slow jaws, and so long a bruising.   *[Exeunt.*

SCENE II.—*A Room in the Palace.*

Enter TIBERIUS *and* SEJANUS.

Tib. This business hath succeeded well, Sejanus,
And quite removed all jealousy of practice
'Gainst Agrippina, and our nephews. Now,
We must bethink us how to plant our ingine,
For th' other pair, Sabinus and Arruntius,
And Gallus [3] too: howe'er he flatter us,
His heart we know.

Sej. Give it some respite, Cæsar.
Time shall mature, and bring to perfect crown,
What we, with so good vultures have begun:
Sabinus shall be next.

Tib. Rather Arruntius.

Sej. By any means, preserve him. His frank tongue
Being let the reins, would take away all thought
Of malice, in your course against the rest:
We must keep him to stalk with.

Tib. Dearest head,
To thy most fortunate design I yield it.

---

[1] Manserunt ejus libri occultati et editi. Tacit. ibid. Scripserat his Cremut. bella civilia, et res Aug. extantque fragmenta in Suasoriâ sextâ Senec.

[2] Vid. Suet. Tib. c. 21.

[3] Vid. Tacit. Ann. Lib. i. p. 6. Lib. ii. p. 85.

Sej. Sir,[1]—I have been so long train'd up in grace,
First with your father, great Augustus; since,
With your most happy bounties so familiar
As I not sooner would commit my hopes
Or wishes to the gods, than to your ears.
Nor have I ever, yet, been covetous
Of over-bright and dazzling honours; rather
To watch and travail in great Cæsar's safety,
With the most common soldier.

    Tib. 'Tis confest.

    Sej. The only gain, and which I count most fair
Of all my fortunes, is, that mighty Cæsar
Has thought me worthy his alliance.[2]   Hence
Begin my hopes.

    Tib. Umph!

    Sej. I have heard, Augustus,
In the bestowing of his daughter, thought
But even of gentlemen of Rome: if so,—
I know not how to hope so great a favour—
But if a husband should be sought for Livia,
And I be had in mind, as Cæsar's friend,
I would but use the glory of the kindred:
It should not make me slothful, or less caring
For Cæsar's state: it were enough to me
It did confirm, and strengthen my weak house,
Against the now unequal opposition
Of Agrippina; and for dear regard
Unto my children, this I wish: myself
Have no ambition farther than to end
My days in service of so dear a master.

    Tib. We cannot but commend thy piety,
Most loved Sejanus, in acknowledging
Those bounties; which we, faintly, such remember—
But to thy suit. The rest of mortal men,
In all their drifts and counsels, pursue profit;
Princes alone are of a different sort,
Directing their main actions still to fame:
We therefore will take time to think and answer.
For Livia she can best, herself, resolve
If she will marry, after Drusus, or
Continue in the family; besides,
She hath a mother, and a grandam yet,
Whose nearer counsels she may guide her by:
But I will simply deal. That enmity
Thou fear'st in Agrippina, would burn more,
If Livia's marriage should, as 'twere in parts,
Divide the imperial house; an emulation

---

[1] Tacit. Ann. Lib. iv. p. 85.
[2] Filia ejus Claudii filio desponsa.

Between the women might break forth; and discord
Ruin the sons and nephews on both hands.
What if it cause some present difference?
Thou art not safe, Sejanus, if thou prove it.
Canst thou believe, that Livia, first the wife
To Caius Cæsar,[1] then my Drusus, now
Will be contented to grow old with thee,
Born but a private gentleman of Rome,
And raise thee with her loss, if not her shame?
Or say that I should wish it, canst thou think
The senate, or the people (who have seen
Her brother, father, and our ancestors,
In highest place of empire) will endure it?
The state thou hold'st already, is in talk;
Men murmur at thy greatness; and the nobles
Stick not, in public, to upbraid thy climbing
Above our father's favours, or thy scale:
And dare accuse me, from their hate to thee.
Be wise, dear friend. We would not hide these things,
For friendship's dear respect: Nor will we stand
Adverse to thine, or Livia's designments.
What we have purposed to thee, in our thought,
And with what near degrees of love to bind thee,
And make thee equal to us; for the present,
We will forbear to speak. Only thus much
Believe, our loved Sejanus, we not know
That height in blood or honour, which thy virtue
And mind to us, may not aspire with merit.
And this we'll publish on all watch'd occasion
The senate or the people shall present.

Sej. I am restored, and to my sense again,
Which I had lost in this so blinding suit.
Cæsar hath taught me better to refuse,
Than I knew how to ask. How pleaseth Cæsar[2]
T' embrace my late advice for leaving Rome?

Tib. We are resolved.

Sej. Here are some motives more,   *[Gives him a paper.*
Which I have thought on since, may more confirm.

Tib. Careful Sejanus! we will straight peruse them:
Go forward in our main design, and prosper.   *[Exit.*

Sej. If those but take, I shall. Dull, heavy Cæsar!
Wouldst thou tell me, thy favours were made crimes,
And that my fortunes were esteem'd thy faults,
That thou for me wert hated, and not think
I would with winged haste prevent that change,
When thou might'st win all to thyself again,
By forfeiture of me! Did those fond words

---

[1] August. nepoti et M. Vapsanii Agrippæ filio ex Julia.
[2] Tacit. Ann. Lib. iv. p. 85, Dio. Lib. lviii.

Fly swifter from thy lips, than this my brain,
This sparkling forge, created me an armour
T' encounter chance and thee? Well, read my charms,
And may they lay that hold upon thy senses,
As thou hadst snuft up hemlock, or ta'en down
The juice of poppy and of mandrakes. Sleep,
Voluptuous Cæsar, and security
Seize on thy stupid powers, and leave them dead
To public cares; awake but to thy lusts,
The strength of which makes thy libidinous soul
Itch to leave Rome! and I have thrust it on;
With blaming of the city business,
The multitude of suits, the confluence
Of suitors; then their importunacies,
The manifold distractions he must suffer,
Besides ill-rumours, envies, and reproaches,
All which a quiet and retired life,
Larded with ease and pleasure,[1] did avoid:
And yet for any weighty and great affair,
The fittest place to give the soundest counsels.
By this I shall remove him both from thought
And knowledge of his own most dear affairs;
Draw all dispatches through my private hands;
Know his designments, and pursue mine own;
Make mine own strengths by giving suits and places,
Conferring dignities and offices;
And these that hate me now, wanting access
To him, will make their envy none, or less:
For when they see me arbiter of all,
They must observe; or else, with Cæsar fall.   [*Exit.*

SCENE III.—*Another Room in the same.*

Enter TIBERIUS.

Tib. To marry Livia! will no less, Sejanus,
Content thy aim? no lower object? well!
Thou know'st how thou art wrought into our trust;
Woven in our design; and think'st we must
Now use thee, whatsoe'er thy projects are:
'Tis true. But yet with caution and fit care.
And, now we better think——who's there within?

Enter an Officer.

Off. Cæsar!
Tib. To leave our journey off, were sin
'Gainst our decreed delights; and would appear
Doubt; or, what less becomes a prince, low fear.
Yet doubt hath law, and fears have their excuse.

[1] Tacit. Ann. Lib. iv. p. 85.

Where princes' states plead necessary use;
As ours doth now: more in Sejanus' pride,
Than all fell Agrippina's hates beside.
Those are the dreadful enemies we raise
With favours, and make dangerous with praise;
The injured by us may have will alike,
But 'tis the favourite hath the power to strike;
And fury ever boils more high and strong,
Heat with ambition, than revenge of wrong.
'Tis then a part of supreme skill, to grace
No man too much; but hold a certain space
Between the ascender's rise, and thine own flat,
Lest, when all rounds be reach'd, his aim be that.
'Tis thought. [*Aside.*]—Is Macro [1] in the palace? see:
If not, go seek him, to come to us. [*Exit Offi.*]—He
Must be the organ we must work by now;
Though none less apt for trust: need doth allow
What choice would not. I have heard that aconite,
Being timely taken, hath a healing might
Against the scorpion's stroke: the proof we'll give:
That, while two poisons wrestle, we may live.
He hath a spirit too working to be used
But to the encounter of his like; excused
Are wiser sov'reigns then, that raise one ill
Against another, and both safely kill:
The prince that feeds great natures, they will sway him;
Who nourisheth a lion must obey him.—

Re-enter Officer, *with* MACRO.

Macro, we sent for you.
    Mac. I heard so, Cæsar.
    Tib. Leave us a while. [*Exit Officer.*]—When you shall know,
      good Macro,
The causes of our sending, and the ends,
You will then hearken nearer; and be pleas'd
You stand so high both in our choice and trust.
    Mac. The humblest place in Cæsar's choice or trust,
May make glad Macro proud; without ambition,
Save to do Cæsar service.
    Tib. Leave your courtings.
We are in purpose, Macro,[2] to depart
The city for a time, and see Campania;
Not for our pleasures, but to dedicate
A pair of temples, one to Jupiter
At Capua; th' other at [3] Nola, to Augustus:

---

[1] De Macrone isto, vid. Dio. Rom. Hist. Lib. lii. p. 718, et Tacit. Ann.
Lib. vi. p. 109, etc.
[2] Suet. Tib. c. 4. Dio. Rom. Hist. Lib. lviii. p. 711.
[3] Suet. Tib. c. 43. Tacit. Ann. Lib. iv. p. 91.

In which great work, perhaps our stay will be
Beyond our will produced.   Now since we are
Not ignorant what danger may be born
Out of our shortest absence in a state
So subject unto envy, and embroil'd
With hate and faction; we have thought on thee,
Amongst a field of Romans, worthiest Macro,
To be our eye and ear: to keep strict watch
On Agrippina, Nero, Drusus; ay,
And on Sejanus: not that we distrust
His loyalty, or do repent one grace
Of all that heap we have conferred on him;
For that were to disparage our election,
And call that judgment now in doubt, which then
Seem'd as unquestion'd as an oracle—
But, greatness hath his cankers.   Worms and moths
Breed out of too much humour, in the things
Which after they consume, transferring quite
The substance of their makers into themselves.
Macro is sharp, and apprehends: besides,
I know him subtle, close, wise, and well-read
In man, and his large nature; he hath studied
Affections, passions, knows their springs, their ends,
Which way, and whether they will work: 'tis proof
Enough of his great merit, that we trust him.
Then to a point, because our conference
Cannot be long without suspicion—
Here, Macro, we assign thee, both to spy,
Inform, and chastise; think, and use thy means,
Thy ministers, what, where, on whom thou wilt;
Explore, plot, practise: all thou dost in this
Shall be, as if the senate, or the laws
Had given it privilege, and thou thence styled
The saviour both of Cæsar and of Rome.
We will not take thy answer but in act:
Whereto, as thou proceed'st, we hope to hear
By trusted messengers.   If 't be inquired,
Wherefore we call'd you, say you have in charge
To see our chariots ready, and our horse.—
Be still our loved and, shortly, honour'd Macro.   [*Exit.*

   Mac. I will not ask, why Cæsar bids do this;
But joy that he bids me.[1]   It is the bliss
Of courts to be employ'd, no matter how;
A prince's power makes all his actions virtue.
We, whom he works by, are dumb instruments,
To do, but not inquire: his great intents
Are to be served, not search'd.   Yet, as that bow
Is most in hand, whose owner best doth know

[1] De Macrone et ingenio ejus, cons. Tacit. Ann. Lib. vi. pp. 114, 115.

To affect his aims; so let that statesman hope
Most use, most price, can hit his prince's scope.
Nor must he look at what, or whom to strike,
But loose at all; each mark be alike.
Were it to plot against the fame, the life
Of one, with whom I twinn'd; remove a wife
From my warm side, as loved as is the air;
Practise away each parent; draw mine heir
In compass, though but one; work all my kin
To swift perdition; leave no untrain'd engine,
For friendship, or for innocence; nay, make
The gods all guilty; I would undertake
This, being imposed me, both with gain and ease:
The way to rise is to obey and please.
He that will thrive in state, he must neglect
The trodden paths that truth and right respect;
And prove new, wilder ways: for virtue there
Is not that narrow thing, she is elsewhere;
Men's fortune there is virtue; reason their will;
Their license, law; and their observance, skill.
Occasion is their foil; conscience, their stain;
Profit their lustre; and what else is, vain.
If then it be the lust of Cæsar's power,[1]
To have raised Sejanus up, and in an hour
O'erturn him, tumbling down, from height of all;
We are his ready engine: and his fall
May be our rise.   It is no uncouth thing
To see fresh buildings from old ruins spring.   *[Exit.*

ACT IV

SCENE I.—*An Apartment in* AGRIPPINA'S *House.*

Enter GALLUS *and* AGRIPPINA.

Gal. You must have patience,[2] royal Agrippina.
Agr. I must have vengeance, first; and that were nectar
Unto my famish'd spirits.   O, my fortune,
Let it be sudden thou prepar'st against me;
Strike all my powers of understanding blind,
And ignorant of destiny to come!
Let me not fear that cannot hope.
Gal. Dear princess,
These tyrannies on yourself, are worse than Cæsar's.
Agr. Is this the happiness of being born great?
Still to be aim'd at? still to be suspected?

[1] Vide Dio. Rom. Hist. Lib. lvii. p. 718, etc.
[2] Agrippina semper atrox, tum et periculo propinquo accensa.   Tacit.
Ann. Lib. iv. p. 89.

To live the subject of all jealousies?
At least the colour made, if not the ground
To every painted danger? who would not
Choose once to fall, than thus to hang for ever?
   Gal. You might be safe if you would—
   Agr. What, my Gallus!
Be lewd Sejanus' strumpet, or the bawd
To Cæsar's lusts, he now is gone to practise?
Not these are safe, where nothing is. Yourself,
While thus you stand but by me, are not safe.
Was Silius safe? or the good Sosia safe?
Or was my niece, dear Claudia Pulchra,[1] safe,
Or innocent Furnius? they that latest have
(By being made guilty) added reputation [2]
To Afer's eloquence? O, foolish friends,
Could not so fresh example warn your loves,
But you must buy my favours with that loss
Unto yourselves; and when you might perceive
That Cæsar's cause of raging must forsake him,
Before his will! Away, good Gallus, leave me.
Here to be seen, is danger; to speak, treason:
To do me least observance, is call'd faction.
You are unhappy in me, and I in all.
Where are my sons, Nero and Drusus? We
Are they be shot at; let us fall apart;
Not in our ruins, sepulchre our friends.
Or shall we do some action like offence,
To mock their studies that would make us faulty,
And frustrate practice by preventing it?
The danger's like: for what they can contrive,
They will make good. No innocence is safe,
When power contests: nor can they trespass more,
Whose only being was all crime before.

     Enter NERO, DRUSUS, *and* CALIGULA.

   Ner. You hear Sejanus is come back from Cæsar?
   Gal. No. How? disgraced?
   Dru. More graced now than ever.
   Gal. By what mischance?
   Cal. A fortune like enough
Once to be bad.
   Dru. But turn'd too good to both.
   Gal. What was't?
   Ner. Tiberius [3] sitting at his meat,
In a farm-house they call Spelunca,[4] sited

---

[1] Pulchra et Furnius damnat. Tacit. Ann. Lib. iv. p. 89.
[2] Afer primoribus oratorum additus, divulgato ingenio, etc.   Tacit. Ann. Lib. iv. p. 89.
[3] Tacit. Ann. Lib. iv. p. 91.
[4] Prætorium Suet. appellat. Tib. c. 39.

By the sea-side, among the Fundane hills,
Within a natural cave; part of the grot,
About the entry, fell, and overwhelm'd
Some of the waiters; others ran away:
Only Sejanus with his knees, hands, face,
O'erhanging Cæsar, did oppose himself
To the remaining ruins, and was found
In that so labouring posture by the soldiers
That came to succour him.   With which adventure,
He hath so fix'd himself in Cæsar's trust,[1]
As thunder cannot move him, and is come
With all the height of Cæsar's praise to Rome.
   Agr. And power, to turn those ruins all on us;
And bury whole posterities beneath them.
Nero, and Drusus, and Caligula,
Your places are the next, and therefore most
In their offence.   Think on your birth and blood,
Awake your spirits, meet their violence;
'Tis princely when a tyrant doth oppose,
And is a fortune sent to exercise
Your virtue, as the wind doth try strong trees,
Who by vexation grow more sound and firm.
After your father's fall, and uncle's fate,
What can you hope, but all the change of stroke
That force or sleight can give? then stand upright;
And though you do not act, yet suffer nobly:
Be worthy of my womb, and take strong chear;
What we do know will come, we should not fear.   [*Exeunt.*

SCENE II.—*The Street.*

Enter MACRO.

   Mac. Return'd so soon! renew'd in trust and grace!
Is Cæsar then so weak, or hath the place
But wrought this alteration with the air;
And he, on next remove, will all repair?
Macro, thou art engaged: and what before
Was public; now, must be thy private, more.
The weal of Cæsar, fitness did imply;
But thine own fate confers necessity
On thy employment; and the thoughts born nearest
Unto ourselves, move swiftest still, and dearest.
If he recover, thou art lost; yea, all
The weight of preparation to his fall
Will turn on thee, and crush thee: therefore strike
Before he settle, to prevent the like
Upon thyself.   He doth his vantage know,
That makes it home, and gives the foremost blow.   [*Exit.*

---

[1] Præbuitque ipsi materiem cur amicitæ constantiæque Sejani magis fideret.   Tacit. Ann. Lib. iv. p. 91.

SCENE III.—*An upper Room of* AGRIPPINA'S *House.*

Enter LATIARIS, RUFUS, *and* OPSIUS.

Lat. It is a service [1] lord Sejanus will
See well requited, and accept of nobly.
Here place yourself between the roof and ceiling;
And when I bring him to his words of danger,
Reveal yourselves, and take him.

    Ruf. Is he come?

    Lat. I'll now go fetch him.   *[Exit.*

    Ops. With good speed.—I long
To merit from the state in such an action.

    Ruf. I hope, it will obtain the consulship
For one of us.

    Ops. We cannot think of less,
To bring in one so dangerous as Sabinus.

    Ruf. He was a follower of Germanicus,
And still is an observer of his wife
And children,[2] though they be declined in grace
A daily visitant, keeps them company
In private and in public, and is noted
To be the only client of the house:
Pray Jove, he will be free to Latiaris.

    Ops. He's allied to him, and doth trust him well.

    Ruf. And he'll requite his trust!

    Ops. To do an office
So grateful to the state, I know no man
But would strain nearer bands, than kindred—

    Ruf. List!
I hear them come.

    Ops. Shift to our holes [3] with silenc   *[They retire.*

Re-enter LATIARIS *and* SABINUS.

    Lat. It is a noble constancy you shew
To this afflicted house; that not like others,
The friends of season, you do follow fortune,
And, in the winter of their fate, forsake
The place whose glories warm'd you. You are just,
And worthy such a princely patron's love,
As was the world's renown'd Germanicus:
Whose ample merit when I call to thought,
And see his wife and issue, objects made
To so much envy, jealousy, and hate;

---

[1] Sabinum aggrediuntur cupidine consulatus, ad quem non nisi per Sejanum aditus, neque Sejani voluntas nisi scelere quærebatur. Tacit. Lib. iv. p. 94. Dio. Hist. Rom. Lib. lviii. p. 711.

[2] Eoque apud bonos laudatus, et gravis iniquis. Tacit. Lib. iv. p. 94.

[3] Haud minus turpi latebrâ quam detestandâ fraude, sese abstrudunt; foraminibus et rimis aurem admovent. Tacit. Ann. Lib. iv. c. 69.

It makes me ready to accuse the gods
Of negligence, as men of tyranny.
   Sab. They must be patient, so must we.
   Lat. O Jove,
What will become of us or of the times,
When, to be high or noble, are made crimes,
When land and treasure are most dangerous faults?
   Sab. Nay, when our table, yea our bed,[1] assaults
Our peace and safety? when our writings are,
By any envious instruments, that dare
Apply them to the guilty, made to speak
What they will have to fit their tyrannous wreak?
When ignorance is scarcely innocence;
And knowledge made a capital offence?
When not so much, but the bare empty shade
Of liberty is reft us; and we made
The prey to greedy vultures and vile spies,
That first transfix us with their murdering eyes.
   Lat. Methinks the genius of the Roman race
Should not be so extinct, but that bright flame
Of liberty might be revived again,
(Which no good man but with his life should lose)
And we not sit like spent and patient fools,
Still puffing in the dark at one poor coal,
Held on by hope till the last spark is out.
The cause is public, and the honour, name,
The immortality of every soul,
That is not bastard or a slave in Rome,
Therein concern'd: whereto, if men would change
The wearied arm, and for the weighty shield
So long sustain'd, employ the facile sword,
We might soon have assurance of our vows.
This ass's fortitude doth tire us all:
It must be active valour must redeem
Our loss, or none. The rock and our hard steel
Should meet to enforce those glorious fires again,
Whose splendour cheer'd the world, and heat gave life,
No less than doth the sun's.
   Sab. 'Twere better stay
In lasting darkness, and despair of day.
No ill should force the subject undertake
Against the sovereign, more than hell should make
The gods do wrong. A good man should and must
Sit rather down with loss, than rise unjust.
Though, when the Romans first did yield themselves
To one man's power, they did not mean their lives,
Their fortunes and their liberties, should be

---

[1] Ne nox quidem secura, cum uxor (Neronis) vigilias, somnos, suspiria matri Liviæ, atque illa Sejano patefaceret. Tacit. Ann. Lib. iv. p. 92.

His absolute spoil, as purchased by the sword.

Lat. Why we are worse, if to be slaves, and bond
To Cæsar's slave be such, the proud Sejanus!
He that is all, does all, gives Cæsar leave
To hide his ulcerous and anointed face,[1]
With his bald crown at Rhodes,[2] while he here stalks
Upon the heads of Romans, and their princes,
Familiarly to empire.

Sab. Now you touch
A point indeed, wherein he shews his art,
As well as power.

Lat. And villainy in both.
Do you observe where Livia lodges? how
Drusus came dead? what men have been cut off?

Sab. Yes, those are things removed: I nearer look'd
Into his later practice, where he stands
Declared a master in his mystery.
First, ere Tiberius went, he wrought his fear
To think that Agrippina sought his death.
Then put those doubts in her; sent her oft word,
Under the show of friendship, to beware
Of Cæsar, for he laid to poison[3] her:
Drave them to frowns, to mutual jealousies,
Which, now, in visible hatred are burst out.
Since, he hath had his hired instruments
To work[4] on Nero, and to heave him up;
To tell him Cæsar's old, that all the people,
Yea, all the army have their eyes on him;
That both do long to have him undertake
Something of worth, to give the world a hope;
Bids him to court their grace: the easy youth
Perhaps gives ear, which straight he writes to Cæsar;
And with this comment: *See yon dangerous boy;*
Note but the practice of the mother, there;
She's tying him for purposes at hand,
With men of sword. Here's Cæsar put in fright
'Gainst son and mother. Yet, he leaves not thus.
The second brother, Drusus, a fierce nature,
And fitter for his snares, because ambitious
And full of envy, him[5] he clasps and hugs,
Poisons with praise, tells him what hearts he wears,
How bright he stands in popular expectance;
That Rome doth suffer with him in the wrong
His mother does him, by preferring Nero:

[1] Facies ulcerosa ac plerumque medicaminibus interstincta. Tacit. Ann. Lib. iv. p. 91.
[2] Tacit. ibid. Et Rhodi secreto, vitare cœtus, recondere voluptates insuerat.
[3] Tacit. Ann. Lib. iv. p. 90.   [4] Tacit. Lib. eod. pp. 91, 92.
[5] Tacit. Ann. Lib. iv. pp. 91, 92.

Thus sets he them asunder, each 'gainst other,
Projects the course that serves him to condemn,
Keeps in opinion of a friend to all,
And all drives on to ruin.

    Lat. Cæsar sleeps,
And nods at this.

    Sab. Would he might ever sleep,
Bogg'd in his filthy lusts!   *[Opsius and Rufus rush in.*

    Ops. Treason to Cæsar!

    Ruf. Lay hands upon the traitor, Latiaris,
Or take the name thyself.

    Lat. I am for Cæsar.

    Sab. Am I then catch'd?

    Ruf. How think you, sir? you are.

    Sab. Spies of this head, so white, so full of years!
Well, my most reverend monsters, you may live
To see yourselves thus snared.

    Ops. Away with him!

    Lat. Hale him away.

    Ruf. To be a spy for traitors,
Is honourable vigilance.

    Sab. You do well,[1]
My most officious instruments of state;
Men of all uses: drag me hence, away.
The year is well begun, and I fall fit
To be an offering to Sejanus. Go!

    Ops. Cover him with his garments, hide his face.

    Sab. It shall not need. Forbear your rude assault.
The fault's not shameful, villainy makes a fault.   *[Exeunt.*

SCENE IV.—*The Street before* AGRIPPINA'S *House.*

Enter MACRO *and* CALIGULA.

    Mac. Sir, but observe how thick your dangers meet
In his clear drifts! your mother and your brothers,[2]
Now cited to the senate; their friend Gallus,[3]
Feasted to-day by Cæsar, since committed!
Sabinus here we met, hurried to fetters:
The senators all strook with fear and silence,
Save those whose hopes depend not on good means,
But force their private prey from public spoil.
And you must know, if here you stay, your state
Is sure to be the subject of his hate,
As now the object.

    Cal. What would you advise me?

    Mac. To go for Capreæ presently; and there

---

[1] Tacit. Ann. Lib. iv. pp. 94, 95.   [2] Tacit. Ann. Lib. v. p. 98.
[3] Asinium Gal. eodem die et convivam Tiberii fuisse et eo subornante damnatum narrat Dio. Lib. lviii. p. 713.

Give up yourself entirely to your uncle.
Tell Cæsar (since your [1] mother is accused
To fly for succours to Augustus' statue,
And to the army with your brethren) you
Have rather chose to place your aids in him,
Than live suspected; or in hourly fear
To be thrust out, by bold Sejanus' plots:
Which, you shall confidently urge to be
Most full of peril to the state, and Cæsar,
As being laid to his peculiar ends,
And not to be let run with common safety.
All which, upon the second, I'll make plain,
So both shall love and trust with Cæsar gain.
    Cal. Away then, let's prepare us for our journey.   [*Exeunt.*

SCENE V.—*Another part of the Street.*

Enter ARRUNTIUS.

    Arr. Still dost thou suffer, heaven! will no flame,
No heat of sin, make thy just wrath to boil
In thy distemper'd bosom, and o'erflow
The pitchy blazes of impiety,
Kindled beneath thy throne! Still canst thou sleep,
Patient, while vice doth make an antick face
At thy dread power, and blow dust and smoke
Into thy nostrils! Jove! will nothing wake thee?
Must vile Sejanus pull thee by the beard,
Ere thou wilt open thy black-lidded eye,
And look him dead? Well! snore on, dreaming gods,
And let this last of that proud giant-race
Heave mountain upon mountain, 'gainst your state—
Be good unto me, Fortune and you powers,
Whom I, expostulating, have profaned;
I see what's equal with a prodigy,
A great, a noble Roman, and an honest,
Live an old man!—

Enter LEPIDUS.

             O Marcus Lepidus,[2]
When is our turn to bleed? Thyself and I,
Without our boast, are almost all the few
Left to be honest in these impious times.
    Lep. What we are left to be, we will be, Lucius;
Though tyranny did stare as wide as death,

---

[1] Vid. Tacit. Lib. v. p. 94. Suet. Tib. c. 53.
    De Lepido isto vid. Tacit. Ann. Lib. i. p. 6. Lib. iii. pp. 60, 65, et Lib. iv. p. 81.

To fright us from it.

Arr. 'T hath so on Sabinus.

Lep. I saw him now drawn from the Gemonies,[1]
And, what increased the direness of the fact,
His faithful dog,[2] upbraiding all us Romans,
Never forsook the corps, but, seeing it thrown
Into the stream, leap'd in, and drown'd with it.

Arr. O act, to be envied him of us men!
We are the next the hook lays hold on, Marcus:
What are thy arts, good patriot, teach them me,
That have preserved thy hairs to this white dye,
And kept so reverend and so dear a head
Safe on his comely shoulders?

Lep. Arts, Arruntius!
None,[3] but the plain and passive fortitude,
To suffer and be silent; never stretch
These arms against the torrent; live at home,
With my own thoughts, and innocence about me,
Not tempting the wolves' jaws: these are my arts.

Arr. I would begin to study 'em, if I thought
They would secure me.   May I pray to Jove
In secret and be safe? ay, or aloud,
With open wishes, so I do not mention
Tiberius or Sejanus? yes, I must,
If I speak out. 'Tis hard that.   May I think,
And not be rack'd?   What danger is't to dream,
Talk in one's sleep, or cough?   Who knows the law?
May I shake my head without a comment?   say
It rains, or it holds up, and not be thrown
Upon the Gemonies?   These now are things,
Whereon men's fortune, yea, their faith depends.
Nothing hath privilege 'gainst the violent ear.
No place, no day, no hour, we see, is free,
Not our religious and most sacred times,
From some one kind of cruelty: all matter
Nay, all occasion pleaseth.   Madmen's rage,
The idleness of drunkards, women's nothing,
Jester's simplicity, all, all is good
That can be catcht at.   Nor is now the event
Of any person, or for any crime,
To be expected; for 'tis always one:
Death, with some little difference of place,
Or time——What's this?   Prince Nero, guarded!

[1] Scalæ Gemoniæ fuerunt in Aventino, prope templum Junonis reginæ a Camillo captis Veiis dicatum; a planctu et gemitu dictas vult Rhodig. In quas contumeliæ causâ cadavera projecta; aliquando a carnifice unco trahebantur.   Vid. Tac. Suet. Dio. Senec. Juvenal.

[2] Dio. Rom. Hist. Lib. lviii. p. 712.   Et Tacit. Ann. Lib. iv. p. 94.

[3] Tacit. Ann. Lib. iv. p. 80.

Enter LACO [1] *and* NERO, *with* Guards.

Lac. On, lictors, keep your way. My lords, forbear.
On pain of Cæsar's wrath, no man attempt
Speech with the prisoner.
   Nero. Noble friends, be safe;
To lose yourselves for words, were as vain hazard,
As unto me small comfort: fare you well.
Would all Rome's sufferings in my fate did dwell!
   Lac. Lictors, away.
   Lep. Where goes he, Laco?
   Lac. Sir,
He's banish'd into Pontia [2] by the senate.
   Arr. Do I see, hear, and feel? May I trust sense,
Or doth my phant'sie form it?
   Lep. Where's his brother?
   Lac. Drusus [3] is prisoner in the palace.
   Arr. Ha!
I smell it now: 'tis rank. Where's Agrippina?
   Lac. The princess is confined to Pandataria. [4]
   Arr. Bolts, Vulcan; bolts for Jove! Phœbus, thy bow;
Stern Mars, thy sword: and, blue-ey'd maid, thy spear;
Thy club, Alcides: all the armoury
Of heaven is too little!—Ha!—to guard
The gods, I meant. Fine, rare dispatch! this same
Was swiftly born! Confined, imprison'd, banish'd?
Most tripartite! the cause, sir?
   Lac. Treason.
   Arr. O!
The complement [5] of all accusings! that
Will hit, when all else fails.
   Lep. This turn is strange!
But yesterday the people would not hear,
Far less objected, but cried [6] Cæsar's letters
Were false and forged; that all these plots were malice;
And that the ruin of the prince's house
Was practised 'gainst his knowledge. Where are now
Their voices, now, that they behold his heirs
Lock'd up, disgraced, led into exile?
   Arr. Hush'd,
Drown'd in their bellies. Wild Sejanus' breath
Hath, like a whirlwind, scatter'd that poor dust,
With this rude blast.—We'll talk no treason, sir, [*Turns to Laco*
If that be it you stand for. Fare you well.   *and the rest.*
We have no need of horse-leeches. Good spy,
Now you are spied, be gone. [*Exeunt Laco, Nero, and Guards.*

---

[1] De Lacon. vid. Dio. Rom. Hist. Lib. lviii. p. 718.
[2] Suet. Tib. c. 54.   [3] Suet ibid.   [4] Suet. ibid.
[5] Tacit. Ann. Lib. iii. p. 62.   [6] Tacit. Lib. v. p. 98.

Lep. I fear you wrong him:
He has the voice to be an honest Roman.
    Arr. And trusted to this office! Lepidus,
I'd sooner trust Greek Sinon, than a man
Our state employs.   He's gone: and being gone,
I dare tell you, whom I dare better trust,
That our night-eyed Tiberius [1] doth not see
His minion's drifts; or, if he do, he's not
So arrant subtile, as we fools do take him;
To breed a mungrel up, in his own house,
With his own blood, and, if the good gods please,
At his own throat, flesh him, to take a leap.
I do not beg it, heaven; but if the fates
Grant it these eyes, they must not wink.
    Lep. They must
Not see it, Lucius.
    Arr. Who should let them?
    Lep. Zeal,
And duty: with the thought he is our prince.
    Arr. He is our monster: forfeited to vice
So far, as no rack'd virtue can redeem him.
His loathed person [2] fouler than all crimes:
An emperor, only in his lusts.   Retired,
From all regard of his own fame, or Rome's,
Into an obscure island; [3] where he lives
Acting his tragedies with a comic face,
Amidst his route of Chaldees: [4] spending hours,
Days, weeks, and months, in the unkind abuse
Of grave astrology, to the bane of men,
Casting the scope of men's nativities,
And having found aught worthy in their fortune,
Kill, or precipitate them in the sea,
And boast, he can mock fate.   Nay, muse not: these
Are far from ends of evil, scarce degrees.
He hath his slaughter-house at Capreæ;
Where he doth study murder, as an art;
And they are dearest in his grace, that can
Devise the deepest tortures.   Thither, too,
He hath his boys, and beauteous girls ta'en up
Out of our noblest houses, the best form'd,
Best nurtured, and most modest; what's their good,
Serves to provoke his bad.   Some are allured,[5]
Some threaten'd; others, by their friends detained,

---

[1] Tiberius in tenebris videret; testibus Dio. Hist. Rom. Lib. lvii. p. 691.
Et Plin. Nat. Hist. Lib. ii. c. 37.
[2] Cons. Tacit. Ann. Lib. iv. p. 91.   (Juv. Sat. 4.)
[3] Vid. Suet. Tib. de secessu Caprensi, c. 43.   Dio. p. 715.   Juv. Sat. 10.
[4] Tacit. Ann. Lib. vi. p. 106. Dio. Rom. Hist. Lib. lvii. p. 706.   Suet.
Tib. c. 62, etc., 44.
[5] Tacit. Ann. Lib. vi. p. 100.   Suet. Tib. c. 43.

Are ravish'd hence, like captives, and, in sight
Of their most grieved parents, dealt away
Unto his spintries, sellaries, and slaves,
Masters of strange and new commented lusts,
For which wise nature hath not left a name.
To this (what most strikes us, and bleeding Rome)
He is, with all his craft, become [1] the ward
To his own vassal, a stale catamite:
Whom he, upon our low and suffering necks,
Hath raised from excrement to side the gods,
And have his proper sacrifice in Rome:
Which Jove beholds, and yet will sooner rive
A senseless oak with thunder than his trunk!—

Re-enter LACO,[2] *with* POMPONIUS *and* MINUTIUS.

Lac. These letters [3] make men doubtful what t' expect,
Whether his coming, or his death.
    Pom. Troth, both:
And which comes soonest, thank the gods for.
    Arr. List!
Their talk is Cæsar; I would hear all voices.
                    [*Arrunt. and Lepidus stand aside.*
    Min. One day,[4] he's well; and will return to Rome;
The next day, sick; and knows not when to hope it.
    Lac. True; and to-day, one of Sejanus' friends
Honour'd by special writ; and on the morrow
Another punish'd—
    Pom. By more special writ.
    Min. This man [5] receives his praises of Sejanus,
A second but slight mention, a third none,
A fourth rebukes: and thus he leaves the senate
Divided and suspended, all uncertain.
    Lac. These forked tricks, I understand them not:
Would he would tell us whom he loves or hates,
That we might follow, without fear or doubt.
    Arr. Good Heliotrope! Is this your honest man?
Let him be yours so still; he is my knave.
    Pom. I cannot tell, Sejanus still goes on,
And mounts, we see; [6] new statues are advanced,
Fresh leaves of titles, large inscriptions read,
His fortune sworn by,[7] himself new gone out
Cæsar's [8] colleague in the fifth consulship;

---

[1] Leg. Dio. Rom. Hist. Lib. lviii. p. 714.
[2] De Pomponio et Minutio vid. Tacit. Ann. Lib. vi.
[3] Dio. Rom. Hist. Lib. lviii. p. 716.
[4] Dio. ibid.   [5] Dio. ibid.
[6] Leg. Tacit. Ann. Lib. iv. p. 96.
[7] Adulationis pleni omnes ejus Fortunam jurabant. Dio. Hist. Rom
Lib. lviii. p. 714.
[8] Dio. p. 714. Suet. Tib. c. 65.

More altars smoke to him than all the gods:
What would we more?
 Arr. That the dear smoke would choke him,
That would I more.
 Lep. Peace, good Arruntius.
 Lat. But there are letters [1] come, they say, ev'n now,
Which do forbid that last.
 Min. Do you hear so?
 Lac. Yes.
 Pom. By Castor, that's the worst.
 Arr. By Pollux, best.
 Min. I did not like the sign, when Regulus,[2]
Whom all we know no friend unto Sejanus,
Did, by Tiberius' so precise command,
Succeed a fellow in the consulship:
It boded somewhat.
 Pom. Not a mote.   His partner,[3]
Fulcinius Trio, is his own, and sure.—
Here comes Terentius.

    Enter TERENTIUS.

     He can give us more.
      [They whisper with Terentius.
 Lep. I'll ne'er believe, but Cæsar hath some scent
Of bold Sejanus' footing.[4]   These cross points
Of varying letters, and opposing consuls,
Mingling his honours and his punishments,
Feigning now ill, now well,[5] raising Sejanus,
And then depressing him, as now of late
In all reports we have it, cannot be
Empty of practice: 'tis Tiberius' art.
For having found his favourite grown too great,
And with his greatness [6] strong; that all the soldiers
Are, with their leaders, made a his devotion;
That almost all the senate are his creatures,
Or hold on him their main dependencies,
Either for benefit, or hope, or fear;
And that himself hath lost much of his own,
By parting unto him; and, by th' increase
Of his rank lusts and rages, quite disarm'd
Himself of love, or other public means,
To dare an open contestation;
His subtilty hath chose this doubling line,
To hold him even in: not so to fear him,
As wholly put him out, and yet give check
Unto his farther boldness.   In mean time,
By his employments, makes him odious

---

[1] Dio. Lib. lviii. p. 718. [2] De Regulo cons. Dio. ibid. [3] Dio. ibid.
[4] Suet. Tib. c. 65. [5] Dio. p. 726.   [6] Dio. p. 714.

Unto the staggering rout, whose aid, in fine,
He hopes to use, as sure, who, when they sway,
Bear down, o'erturn all objects in their way.

Arr. You may be a Lynceus, Lepidus: yet I
See no such cause, but that a politic tyrant,
Who can so well disguise it, should have ta'en
A nearer way: feign'd honest, and come home
To cut his throat, by law.

Lep. Ay, but his fear
Would ne'er be mask'd, allbe his vices were.

Pom. His lordship then is still in grace?

Ter. Assure you,
Never in more, either of grace or power.

Pom. The gods are wise and just.

Arr. The fiends they are,
To suffer thee belie 'em.

Ter. I have here
His last and present letters, where he writes him,
The partner of his cares, and *his Sejanus.*—

Lac. But is that true,[1] it is prohibited
To sacrifice unto him?

Ter. Some such thing
Cæsar makes scruple of, but forbids it not;
No more than to himself: says he could wish
It were forborn to all.

Lac. Is it no other?

Ter. No other, on my trust.   For your more surety,
Here is that letter too.

Arr. How easily
Do wretched men believe, what they would have!
Looks this like plot?

Lep. Noble Arruntius, stay.

Lac. He names him here [2] without his titles.

Lep. Note!

Arr. Yes, and come off your notable fool.   I will.

Lac. No other than Sejanus.

Pom. That's but haste
In him that writes: here he gives large amends.

Mar. And with his own hand written?

Pom. Yes.

Lac. Indeed?

Ter. Believe it, gentlemen, Sejanus' breast
Never received more full contentments in,
Than at this present.

Pom. Takes he well [3] the escape
Of young Caligula, with Macro?

Ter. Faith,
At the first air it somewhat troubled him.

---

[1] Dio. Hist. Rom. Lib. lviii. p. 718.   [2] Dio. ibid.   [3] Dio. p. 717.

Lep. Observe you?

Arr. Nothing; riddles. Till I see
Sejanus struck, no sound thereof strikes me.

                      [Exeunt Arrun. and Lepidus.

Pom. I like it not. I muse he would not attempt
Somewhat against him in the consulship,[1]
Seeing the people 'gin to favour him.

Ter. He doth repent it now; but he has employ'd
Pagonianus after him: [2] and he holds
That correspondence there, with all that are
Near about Cæsar, as no thought can pass
Without his knowledge, thence in act to front him.

Pom. I gratulate the news.

Lac. But how comes Macro
So in trust and favour with Caligula?

Pom. O, sir, he has a wife; [3] and the young prince
An appetite: he can look up, and spy
Flies in the roof, when there are fleas i' the bed;
And hath a learned nose to assure his sleeps.
Who to be favour'd of the rising sun,
Would not lend little of his waning moon?
It is the saf'st ambition. Noble Terentius!

Ter. The night grows fast upon us. At your service.   *[Exeunt.*

ACT V

SCENE I.—*An Apartment in* SEJANUS' *House.*

Enter SEJANUS.

  Sej. Swell, swell, my joys; and faint not to declare
Yourselves as ample as your causes are.
I did not live till now; this my first hour;
Wherein I see my thoughts reach'd by my power.
But this, and gripe my wishes.[4] Great and high,
The world knows only two, that's Rome and I.
My roof receives me not; 'tis air I tread;
And, at each step, I feel my advanced head
Knock out a star in heaven! rear'd to this height,
All my desires seem modest, poor, and slight,
That did before sound impudent: 'tis place,
Not blood, discerns the noble and the base.
Is there not something more than to be Cæsar?
Must we rest there? it irks t' have come so far,
To be so near a stay. Caligula,

---

[1] Dio. p. 717.

[2] De Pagoniano, vid. Tacit. Ann. Lib. vi. p. 101. alibi Paconiano.

[3] Tacit. cons. Ann. Lib. vi. p. 114.

[4] De fastu Sejani leg. Dio. Hist. Rom. Lib. lviii. p. 715, et Tacit. Ann.
Lib. iv. p. 96.

Would thou stood'st stiff, and many in our way!
Winds lose their strength, when they do empty fly,
Unmet of woods or buildings; great fires die,
That want their matter to withstand them: so,
It is our grief, and will be our loss, to know
Our power shall want opposites; unless
The gods, by mixing in the cause, would bless
Our fortune with their conquest. That were worth
Sejanus' strife; durst fates but bring it forth.

Enter TERENTIUS.

Ter. Safety to great Sejanus!
Sej. Now, Terentius?
Ter. Hears not my lord the wonder?
Sej. Speak it, no.
Ter. I meet it violent in the people's mouths,
Who run in routs to Pompey's theatre,
To view your statue,[1] which, they say, sends forth
A smoke, as from a furnace, black and dreadful.
Sej. Some traitor hath put fire in: you, go see,
And let the head be taken off, to look
What 'tis. [*Exit Terentius.*]—Some slave hath practised an imposture,
To stir the people.—How now! why return you?

Re-enter TERENTIUS, *with* SATRIUS *and* NATTA.

Sat. The head,[2] my lord, already is ta'en off,
I saw it; and, at opening, there leapt out
A great and monstrous serpent.
Sej. Monstrous! why?
Had it a beard, and horns? no heart? a tongue
Forked as flattery? look'd it of the hue,
To such as live in great men's bosoms? was
The spirit of it Macro's?
Nat. May it please
The most divine Sejanus, in my days,
(And by his sacred fortune, I affirm it,)
I have not seen a more extended, grown,
Foul, spotted, venomous, ugly—
Sej. O, the fates!
What a wild muster's here of attributes,
T' express a worm, a snake!
Ter. But how that should
Come there, my lord!
Sej. What, and you too, Terentius!
I think you mean to make 't a prodigy
In your reporting.
Ter. Can the wise Sejanus

[1] Dio. Hist. Rom. Lib. lviii. p. 717.   [2] Dio. ibid.

Think heaven hath meant it less?

   Sej. O, superstition!
Why, then the falling [1] of our bed, that brake
This morning, burden'd with the populous weight,
Of our expecting clients, to salute us;
Or running [2] of the cat betwixt our legs,
As we set forth unto the Capitol,
Were prodigies.

   Ter. I think them ominous;
And would they had not happened! As, to-day,
The fate of some [3] your servants: who, declining
Their way, not able, for the throng, to follow,
Slipt down the Gemonies, and brake their necks!
Besides, in taking your last augury,[4]
No prosperous bird appear'd; but croaking ravens
Flagg'd up and down, and from the sacrifice
Flew to the prison, where they sat all night,
Beating the air with their obstreperous beaks!
I dare not counsel, but I could entreat,
That great Sejanus would attempt the gods
Once more with sacrifice.

   Sej. What excellent fools
Religion makes of men! Believes Terentius,
If these were dangers, as I shame to think them,
The gods could change the certain course of fate?
Or, if they could they would, now in a moment,
For a beeve's fat, or less, be bribed to invert
Those long decrees? Then think the gods, like flies,
Are to be taken with the steam of flesh,
Or blood, diffused about their altars: think
Their power as cheap as I esteem it small.—
Of all the throng that fill th' Olympian hall,
And, without pity, lade poor Atlas' back,
I know not that one deity, but Fortune,
To whom I would throw up, in begging smoke,
One grain of incense; [5] or whose ear I'd buy
With thus much oil. Her I, indeed, adore;
And keep her grateful image [6] in my house,
Sometime belonging to a Roman king.
But now call'd mine, as by the better style:
To her I care not, if, for satisfying
Your scrupulous phant'sies, I go offer. Bid
Our priest prepare us honey, milk, and poppy,[7]

---

[1] Dio. Rom. Hist. Lib. lviii. p. 715.   [2] Dio. ibid. p. 716.
[3] Dio. ibid.   [4] Dio. ibid.
[5] Grani turis. Plaut. Pænu. A. I. Sc. 1. et Ovid. Fast. Lib. iv.
[6] Dio. Hist. Rom. Lib. lviii. p. 717.
[7] De sacris Fortunæ, vid. Lil. Gre. Gyr. Synt. 17. et Stuch. lib. de
Sacrif. Gent. p. 48.

His masculine odours, and night-vestments: say,
Our rites are instant; which perform'd, you'll see
How vain, and worthy laughter, your fears be.   [*Exeunt.*

SCENE II.—*Another Room in the same.*

Enter COTTA *and* POMPONIUS.

Cot. Pomponius, whither in such speed?

Pom. I go
To give my lord Sejanus notice—

Cot. What?

Pom. Of Macro.

Cot. Is he come?

Pom. Enter'd but now
The house of Regulus.[1]

Cot. The opposite consul!

Pom. Some half hour since.

Cot. And by night too! Stay, sir;
I'll bear you company.

Pom. Along then—   [*Exeunt.*

SCENE III.—*A Room in* REGULUS'S *House.*

Enter MACRO, REGULUS, *and* Attendant.

Mac. 'Tis Cæsar's will to have a frequent senate;
And therefore must your edict [2] lay deep mulct
On such as shall be absent.

Reg. So it doth.
Bear it my fellow consul to adscribe.

Mac. And tell him it must early be proclaim'd:
The place Apollo's temple.[3]   [*Exit Attendant.*

Reg. That's remember'd.

Mac. And at what hour?

Reg. Yes.

Mac. You do forget [4]
To send one for the provost of the watch.

Reg. I have not: here he comes.

Enter LACO.

Mac. Gracinus Laco,
You are a friend most welcome: by and by,
I'll speak with you.—You must procure this list
Of the prætorian cohorts, with the names
Of the centurions, and their tribunes.

Reg. Ay.

[1] Dio. Hist. Rom. Lib. lviii. p. 718.
[2] Edicto ut plurimum senatores in curiam vocatos constat, ex Tacit. Ann. Lib. i. et Liv. Lib. ii. Fest. Pon. Lib. xv. vid. Bar. Briss. de form. Lib. i. et Lips Sat. Menip.
[3] Dio. Rom. Hist. Lib. lvii. p. 718.   [4] Dio. ibid.

Mac. I bring you letters,[1] and a health from Cæsar—
Lac. Sir, both come well.
    Mac. And hear you? with your note,
Which are the eminent men, and most of action.
    Reg. That shall be done you too.
    Mac. Most worthy Laco,
Cæsar salutes you. [*Exit Regulus.*]—Consul! death and furies!
Gone now!—The argument will please you, sir.
Ho! Regulus! The anger of the gods
Follow your diligent legs, and overtake 'em,
In likeness of the gout!—

Re-enter REGULUS.

          O, my good lord,
We lack'd you present; I would pray you send
Another to Fulcinius Trio, straight,
To tell him you will come, and speak with him:
The matter we'll devise, to stay him there,
While I with Laco do survey the watch.   [*Exit Regulus.*
What are your strengths, Gracinus?
    Lac. Seven cohorts.[2]
    Mac. You see what Cæsar writes; and——Gone again!
H' has sure a vein of mercury in his feet.—
Know you what store of the prætorian soldiers
Sejanus holds about him, for his guard?
    Lac. I cannot the just number; but, I think,
Three centuries.
    Mac. Three! good.
    Lac. At most not four.
    Mac. And who be those centurions?
    Lac. That the consul
Can best deliver you.
    Mac. When he's away!
Spite on his nimble industry—Gracinus,
You find what place you hold, there, in the trust
Of royal Cæsar?
    Lac. Ay, and I am—
    Mac. Sir,
The honours there proposed are but beginnings
Of his great favours.
    Lac. They are more—
    Mac. I heard him
When he did study what to add.
    Lac. My life,
And all I hold—
    Mac. You were his own first choice:

---

[1] Dio. Rom. Hist. Lib. lviii. p. 718.
[2] De prefecto vigilum vid. Ros. Antiq. Rom. Lib. vii. et Dio. Rom. Hist.
1 ib. lv.

Which doth confirm as much as you can speak;
And will, if we succeed, make more——Your guards
Are seven cohorts, you say?
Lac. Yes.
Mac. Those we must
Hold still in readiness [1] and undischarged.
Lac. I understand so much. But how it can—
Mac. Be done without suspicion, you'll object?

Re-enter REGULUS.

Reg. What's that?
Lac. The keeping of the watch in arms,
When morning comes.
Mac. The senate shall be met, and set
So early in the temple, as all mark
Of that shall be avoided.
Reg. If we need,
We have commission to possess the palace,[2]
Enlarge prince Drusus, and make him our chief.
Mac. That secret would have burnt his reverend mouth,
Had he not spit it out now: by the gods,
You carry things too——Let me borrow a man
Or two, to bear these——That of freeing Drusus,
Cæsar projected as the last and utmost;
Not else to be remember'd.

Enter Servants.

Reg. Here are servants.
Mac. These to Arruntius, these to Lepidus;
This bear to Cotta, this to Latiaris.
If they demand you of me, say I have ta'en
Fresh horse, and am departed.   [*Exeunt Servants.*
                                   You, my lord,
To your colleague, and be you sure to hold him
With long narration of the new fresh favours,
Meant to Sejanus, his great patron; I,
With trusted Laco, here, are for the guards:
Then to divide. For, night hath many eyes,
Whereof, though most do sleep, yet some are spies.   [*Exeunt.*

SCENE IV.—*A Sacellum (or Chapel) in* SEJANUS'S *House.*

Enter Præcones,[3] Flamen,[4] Tubicines, Tibicines, Ministri,
SEJANUS, TERENTIUS, SATRIUS, NATTA, *etc.*

Præ. Be all profane far hence; [5] fly, fly far off:

[1] Dio. Rom. Hist. Lib. lviii. p. 718.
[2] Vid. Tacit. Ann. Lib. vi. p. 107. et Suet. Tib. c. 65.
[3] Præcones, Flamen, hi omnibus sacrificiis interesse solebant. Ros.
Ant. Rom. Lib. iii. Stuch. de Sac. p. 72.
[4] Ex iis, qui Flamines Curiales dicerentur, vid. Lil. Greg. Gyr. Synt.
17, et Onup. Panvin. Rep. Rom. Comment. 2.
[5] Moris antiqui erat, Præcones præcedere, et sacris arcere profanos. Cons.
Briss. Ross. Stuch. Lil. Gyr. etc.

Be absent far; far hence be all profane!
> [*Tub. and Tib. sound while the Flamen washeth.*[1]

Fla. We have been faulty, but repent us now,
And bring pure hands, pure vestments, and pure minds.[2]

1 *Min.* Pure vessels.

2 *Min.* And pure offerings.

3 *Min.* Garlands pure.

Fla. Bestow your garlands: [3] and, with reverence, place
The vervin on the altar.

Prœ. Favour your tongues.[4]

> [*While they sound again, the Flamen takes of the honey with his finger,*[5] *and tastes, then ministers to all the rest; so of the milk,*[6] *in an earthen vessel, he deals about; which done, he sprinkleth upon the altar, milk; then imposeth the honey, and kindleth his gums, and after censing about the altar, placeth his censer thereon, into which they put several branches of poppy,*[7] *and the music ceasing, proceeds.*

Fla. Great mother Fortune,[8] *queen of human state,*
Rectress of action, arbitress of fate,
To whom all sway, all power, all empire bows,
Be present, and propitious to our vows!

Prœ. Favour [9] it with your tongues.

Min. Be present and propitious to our vows!

Omnes. Accept our offering [10] and be pleased, great goddess.

Ter. See, see, the image stirs!

Sat. And turns away!

---

[1] Observatum antiquis invenimus, ut qui rem divinam facturus erat, lautus, ac mandus accederet, et ad suas levandas culpas, se imprimis reum dicere solitum, et noxæ pœnituisse. Lil. Gyr. Synt. 17.

[2] In sacris puras manus, puras vestes, pura vasa, etc., antiqui desiderabunt; ut ex Virg. Plaut. Tibul. Ovid, etc., pluribus locis constat.

[3] Alius ritus sertis aras coronare, et verbenas imponere.

[4] Hujusmodi verbis silentium imperatum fuisse constat. Vid. Sen. in lib. de beata vita. Serv. et Don. ad eum versum, Lib. v. Æneid.

> Ore favete omnes, et cingite tempora ramis.

[5] Vocabatur hic ritus Libatio. Lege Rosin. Ant. Lib. iii. Bas. Brisson. de form. Lib. i. Stuchium de Sacrif. et Lil. Synt. 17.

[6] In sacris Fortunæ lacte non vino libabant. iisdem test. Talia sacrificia ἀρίνα et νηφάλια dicta. Hoc est sobria, et vino carentia.

[7] Hoc reddere erat et litare, id est propitiare, et votum impetrare; secundum Nonium Marcellum. Litare enim Mac. Lib. iii. c. 5, explicat, sacrificio facto placare numen. In quo sens. leg. apud Plaut. Senec. Suet. etc.

[8] His solemnibus præfationibus in sacris utebantur.

[9] Quibus, in clausu, populus vel cætus a præconibus favere jubebatur; id est bona verba fari. Talis enim altera hujus formæ interpretatio apud Briss. Lib. i. extat. Ovid. Lib. i. Fast. Linguis animisque favete. Et Metam. Lib. xv.

> ———————— piumque
> Æneadæ præstant et mente, et voce favorem.

[10] Solemnis formula in Ionis cuivis nomini offerendis.

Nat. Fortune [1] averts her face.

Fla. Avert, you gods,
The prodigy.   Still! still, some pious rite
We have neglected.   Yet, heaven be appeased,
And be all tokens false and void, that speak
Thy present wrath!

Sej. Be thou dumb, scrupulous priest:
And gather up thyself, with these thy wares
Which I, in spite of thy blind mistress, or
Thy juggling mystery, religion, throw
Thus scorned on the earth.   [*Overturns the statue and the altar.*
                              Nay, hold thy look
Averted till I woo thee turn again;
And thou shalt stand to all posterity,
The eternal game and laughter, with thy neck
Writh'd to thy tail, like a ridiculous cat.
Avoid these fumes, these superstitious lights,
And all these cozening ceremonies: you,
Your pure and spiced conscience!
                [*Exeunt all but Sejanus, Terent., Satri., and Natta.*
                              I, the slave
And mock of fools, scorn on my worthy head!
That have been titled and adored a god,[2]
Yea,[3] sacrificed unto, myself, in Rome,
No less than Jove: and I be brought to do
A peevish giglot, rites! perhaps the thought
And shame of that, made fortune turn her face,
Knowing herself the lesser deity,
And but my servant.—Bashful queen, if so,
Sejanus thanks thy modesty.—Who's that?

Enter POMPONIUS *and* MINUTIUS.[4]

Pom. His fortune suffers, till he hears my news:
I have waited here too long.   Macro, my lord—

Sej. Speak lower and withdraw.   [*Takes him aside.*

Ter. Are these things true?

Min. Thousands are gazing at it in the streets.

Sej. What's that?

Ter. Minutius tells us here, my lord,
That a new head being set upon your statue,
A rope [5] is since found wreath'd about it! and,
But now [6] a fiery meteor in the form
Of a great ball was seen to roll along

---

[1] Leg. Dio. Rom. Hist. Lib. lviii. p. 717. de hoc sacrificio.
[2] Tacit. Ann. Lib. iv. p. 96.
[3] Dio. Lib. lviii. p. 716.
[4] De Minutio vid. Tacit. Ann. Lib. vi.
[5] Dio. Hist. Rom. Lib. lviii. p. 717.
[6] Vid. Senec. Nat. Quest. Lib. i. c. 1.

The troubled air, where yet it hangs unperfect,
The amazing wonder of the multitude!
Sej. No more. That Macro's come, is more than all!
Ter. Is Macro come?
Pom. I saw him.
Ter. Where? with whom?
Pom. With Regulus.
Sej. Terentius!
Ter. My lord.
Sej. Send for the tribunes,[1] we will straight have up
More of the soldiers for our guard. [*Exit Ter.*] Minutius,
We pray you go for Cotta, Latiaris,
Trio, the consul, or what senators
You know are sure, and ours. [*Exit Min.*] You, my good Natta,
For Laco, provost of the watch. [*Exit Nat.*] Now, Satrius,
The time of proof comes on; arm all our servants,
And without tumult. [*Exit Sat.*] You, Pomponius,
Hold some good correspondence with the consul:
Attempt him, noble friend. [*Exit Pomp.*] These things begin
To look like dangers, now, worthy my fates.
Fortune, I see thy worst: let doubtful states,
And things uncertain, hang upon thy will:
Me surest death shall render certain still.
Yet, why is now my thought turn'd toward death,
Whom fates have let go on, so far in breath,
Uncheck'd or unreproved? I,[2] that did help
To fell the lofty cedar of the world,
Germanicus; that at one stroke cut down [3]
Drusus, that upright elm; wither'd his vine;
Laid Silius [4] and Sabinus,[5] two strong oaks,
Flat on the earth; besides those other shrubs,
Cordus [6] and Sosia,[7] Claudia Pulchra,[8]
Furnius and Gallus,[9] which I have grubb'd up;
And since, have set my axe so strong and deep
Into the root of spreading Agrippina; [10]
Lopt off and scatter'd her proud branches, Nero,
Drusus; and Caius [11] too, although re-planted.
If you will, Destinies, that after all,

[1] Dio. Hist. Rom. Lib. lviii. p. 718.
[2] Vid. Tacit. Ann. Lib. i. p. 23.
[3] Tacit. Ann. Lib. iv. pp. 74, 75. et Dio. Lib. lvii. p. 709.
[4] Tacit. Lib. iv. p. 79.
[5] Ibid. p. 94.
[6] De Cremut. Cor. vid. Dio. Rom. Hist. Lib. lvii. p. 710. Tacit. Ann. Lib iv. p. 83.
[7] De Sosia. Tacit. Ann. Lib. iv. p. 94.
[8] De Clau. et Furnio. quære Tacit. Ann. Lib. iv. p. 89.
[9] De Gallo. Tacit. Lib. iv. p. 95. et Dio. Lib. lviii. p. 713.
[10] De Agr. Ner. et Dru. leg. Suet. Tib. cap. 53, 4.
[11] De Caio. cons. Dio. Lib. lviii. p. 727

I faint now ere I touch my period,
You are but cruel; and I already have done
Things great enough.   All Rome hath been my slave;
The senate sate an idle looker on,
And witness of my power; when I have blush'd
More to command than it to suffer: all
The fathers have sate ready and prepared,
To give me empire, temples, or their throats,
When I would ask 'em; and what crowns the top,
Rome, senate, people, all the world have seen
Jove, but my equal; Cæsar, but my second.
'Tis then your malice, Fates, who, but your own,
Envy and fear to have any power long known.   [*Exit.*

SCENE V.—*A Room in the same.*

Enter TERENTIUS *and* Tribunes.

Ter. Stay here: I'll give his lordship, you are come.

Enter MINUTIUS, *with* COTTA *and* LATIARIS.

Min. Marcus Terentius, 'pray you tell my lord
Here's Cotta, and Latiaris.
     Ter. Sir, I shall.   [*Exit.*
     Cot. My letter is the very same with yours;
Only requires me to be present there,
And give my voice to strengthen his design.
     Lat. Names he not what it is?
     Cot. No, nor to you.
     Lat. 'Tis strange and singular doubtful!
     Cot. So it is.
It may be all is left to lord Sejanus.

Enter NATTA *and* GRACINUS LACO.

Nat. Gentlemen, where's my lord?
Tri. We wait him here.
Cot. The provost Laco! what's the news?
Lat. My lord—

Enter SEJANUS.

Sej. Now, my right dear, noble, and trusted friends,
How much I am a captive to your kindness!
Most worthy Cotta, Latiaris, Laco,
Your valiant hand; and, gentlemen, your loves.
I wish I could divide myself unto you;
Or that it lay within our narrow powers,
To satisfy for so enlarged bounty.
Gracinus, we must pray you, hold your guards
Unquit when morning comes.   Saw you the consul?
     Min. Trio will presently be here, my lord.

Cot. They are but giving order for the edict,[1]
To warn the senate.

Sej. How! the senate?

Lac. Yes.
This morning in Apollo's temple.

Cot. We
Are charged by letter to be there, my lord.

Sej. By letter! pray you, let's see.

Lat. Knows not his lordship?

Cot. It seems so!

Sej. A senate warn'd! without my knowledge!
And on this sudden! Senators by letters
Required to be there! who brought these?

Cot. Macro.

Sej. Mine enemy![2] and when?

Cot. This midnight.

Sej. Time,
With every other circumstance, doth give
It hath some strain of engine in't!—How now?

Enter SATRIUS.

Sat. My lord, Sertorius Macro is without,
Alone, and prays t' have private conference
In business of high nature with your lordship,
He says to me, and which regards you much.

Sej. Let him come here.

Sat. Better, my lord, withdraw:
You will betray what store and strength of friends
Are now about you; which he comes to spy.

Sej. Is he not arm'd?

Sat. We'll search him.

Sej. No; but take,
And lead him to some room, where you conceal'd
May keep a guard upon us. *[Exit Sat.]* Noble Laco,
You are our trust; and till our own cohorts
Can be brought up, your strengths must be our guard.
Now, good Minutius, honour'd Latiaris,   *[He salutes them humbly.*
Most worthy and my most unwearied friends:
I return instantly.   *[Exit.*

Lat. Most worthy lord.

Cot. His lordship is turn'd instant kind, methinks;
I have not observed it in him, heretofore.

1 Tri. 'Tis true, and it becomes him nobly.

Min. I
Am wrapt withal.

2 Tri. By Mars, he has my lives,
Were they a million, for this only grace.

Lac. Ay, and to name a man!

---

[1] Vid. Dio. Rom. Hist. Lib. lviii. p. 718.   [2] Dio. Lib. lviii. p. 718.

Lat. As he did me!

Min. And me!

Lat. Who would not spend his life and fortunes,
To purchase but the look of such a lord?

Lac. He that would nor be lord's fool, nor the world's. [*Aside.*

SCENE VI.—*Another Room in the same.*

Enter SEJANUS, MACRO, *and* SATRIUS.

Sej. Macro![1] most welcome, a most coveted friend!
Let me enjoy my longings. When arrived you?

Mac. About the noon of night.[2]

Sej. Satrius, give leave. [*Exit Sat.*

Mac. I have been, since I came, with both the consuls,
On a particular design from Cæsar.

Sej. How fares it with our great and royal master?

Mac. Right plentifully well; as, with a prince,
That still holds out [3] the great proportion
Of his large favours, where his judgment hath
Made once divine election: like the god
That wants not, nor is wearied to bestow
Where merit meets his bounty, as it doth
In you, already the most happy, and ere
The sun shall climb the south, most high Sejanus.
Let not my lord be amused. For, to this end
Was I by Cæsar sent for to the isle,
With special caution to conceal my journey;
And, thence, had my dispatch as privately
Again to Rome; charged to come here by night;
And only to the consuls make narration
Of his great purpose; that the benefit
Might come more full, and striking, by how much
It was less look'd for, or aspired by you,
Or least informed to the common thought.

Sej. What may be this? part of myself, dear Macro,
If good, speak out; and share with your Sejanus.

Mac. If bad, I should for ever loath myself
To be the messenger to so good a lord.
I do exceed my instructions to acquaint
Your lordship with thus much; but 'tis my venture
On your retentive wisdom: and because
I would no jealous scruple should molest
Or rack your peace of thought. For I assure
My noble lord, no senator yet knows
The business meant: though all by several letters
Are warned to be there, and give their voices,

---

[1] Dio. Hist. Rom. Lib. lviii. p. 78.
[2] Meridies noctis, Varr. Marcipor. vid. Non. Mar. cap. vi.
[3] Dio. Lib. lviii. p. 78.

Only to add unto the state and grace
Of what is purposed.

    Sej. You take pleasure, Macro,
Like a coy wench, in torturing your lover.
What can be worth this suffering?

    Mac. That which follows,
The tribunitial dignity and power: [1]
Both which Sejanus is to have this day
Conferr'd upon him, and by public senate.

    Sej. Fortune be mine again! thou hast satisfied
For thy suspected loyalty.   [*Aside.*

    Mac. My lord,
I have no longer time, the day approacheth,
And I must back to Cæsar.

    Sej. Where's Caligula?

    Mac. That I forgot to tell your lordship. Why,
He lingers yonder about Capreæ,
Disgraced; Tiberius hath not seen him yet:
He needs would thrust himself to go with me,
Against my wish or will; but I have quitted
His forward trouble, with as tardy note
As my neglect or silence could afford him.
Your lordship cannot now command me aught,
Because I take no knowledge that I saw you;
But I shall boast to live to serve your lordship:
And so take leave.

    Sej. Honest and worthy Macro;
Your love and friendship.   [*Exit Macro.*] — Who's there?
    Satrius,
Attend my honourable friend forth.—O!
How vain and vile a passion is this fear,
What base uncomely things it makes men do!
Suspect their noblest friends, as I did this,
Flatter poor enemies, entreat their servants,
Stoop, court, and catch at the benevolence
Of creatures, unto whom, within this hour,
I would not have vouchsafed a quarter-look,
Or piece of face! By you that fools call gods,
Hang all the sky with your prodigious signs,
Fill earth with monsters, drop the scorpion down,
Out of the zodiac, or the fiercer lion,
Shake off the loosen'd globe from her long hinge,
Roll all the world in darkness, and let loose
The enraged winds to turn up groves and towns!
When I do fear again, let me be struck,
With forked fire, and unpitied die:
Who fears, is worthy of calamity.   [*Exit.*

[1] Dio. Lib. lviii. p. 78. vid. Suet. de oppress. Sejan. Tib. c. 65.

SCENE VII.—*Another Room in the same.*

Enter TERENTIUS, MINUTIUS, LACO, COTTA, LATIARIS, *and* POM-
　　PONIUS; REGULUS, TRIO, *and others, on different sides.*

Pom. Is not my lord here?
Ter. Sir, he will be straight.
Cot. What news, Fulcinius Trio?
Tri. Good, good tidings;
But keep it to yourself. My lord Sejanus
Is to receive this day in open senate
The tribunitial dignity.
Cot. Is't true?
Tri. No words, not to your thought: but, sir, believe it.
Lat. What says the consul?
Cot. Speak it not again:
He tells me, that to-day my lord Sejanus—
Tri. I must entreat you, Cotta, on your honour
Not to reveal it.
Cot. On my life, sir.
Lat. Say.
Cot. Is to receive the tribunitial power.
But, as you are an honourable man,
Let me conjure you not to utter it;
For it is trusted to me with that bond.
Lat. I am Harpocrates.
Ter. Can you assure it?
Pom. The consul told it me, but keep it close.
Min. Lord Latiaris, what's the news?
Lat. I'll tell you;
But you must swear to keep it secret.

Enter SEJANUS.

Sej. I knew the Fates had on their distaff left
More of our thread, than so.
Reg. Hail, great Sejanus!
Tri. Hail, the most honour'd![1]
Cot. Happy!
Lat. High Sejanus!
Sej. Do you bring prodigies too?
Tri. May all presage
Turn to those fair effects, whereof we bring
Your lordship news.
Reg. May't please my lord withdraw.
Sej. Yes:—I will speak with you anon. [*To some that stand by.*
Ter. My lord,
What is your pleasure for the tribunes?
Sej. Why,

---

[1] Dio. Rom. Hist. Lib. lviii. p. 718.

Let them be thank'd and sent away.
    Min. My lord—
    Lac. Will't please your lordship to command me—
    Sej. No:
You are troublesome.
    Min. The mood is changed.[1]
    Tri. Not speak,
Nor look!
    Lac. Ay, he is wise, will make him friends
Of such who never love, but for their ends.   [*Exeunt.*

SCENE VIII.—*A Space before the Temple of Apollo.*

Enter ARRUNTIUS *and* LEPIDUS, *divers* Senators *passing by them.*

    Arr. Ay, go, make haste; take heed you be not last
To tender your All Hail [2] in the wide hall
Of huge Sejanus: run a lictor's pace:
Stay not to put your robes on; but away,
With the pale troubled ensigns of great friendship
Stamp'd in your face! Now, Marcus Lepidus,
You still believe your former augury!
Sejanus must go downward! You perceive
His wane approaching fast!
    Lep. Believe me, Lucius,
I wonder at this rising.
    Arr. Ay, and that we
Must give our suffrage to it. You will say,
It is to make his fall more steep and grievous:
It may be so. But think it, they that can
With idle wishes 'say to bring back time:
In cases desperate, all hope is crime.
See, see! what troops of his officious friends
Flock to salute my lord, and start before
My great proud lord! to get a lord-like nod!
Attend my lord unto the senate-house!
Bring back my lord! like servile ushers, make
Way for my lord! proclaim his idol lordship,
More than ten criers, or six noise of trumpets!
Make legs, kiss hands, and take a scatter'd hair
From my lord's eminent shoulder!
              [*Sanquinius and Haterius pass over the stage.*
              See, Sanquinius [3]
With his slow belly, and his dropsy! look,
What toiling haste he makes! yet here's another
Retarded with the gout, will be afore him.

---

[1] Dio. Rom. Hist. Lib. lviii. p. 718.
[2] Ave, matutina vox salutanti propria, apud Romanos, vid. Briss. de form. Lib. viii.
[3] De Sanquinio vid. Tacit. Ann. Lib. vi. et de Haterio, ibid.

Get thee Liburnian [1] porters, thou gross fool,
To bear thy obsequious fatness, like thy peers.
They are met! the gout returns, and his great carriage.

    [*Lictors, Regulus, Trio, Sejanus, Satrius, and many other
       Senators, pass over the stage.*

  Lict. Give way, make place, room for the consul!
  San. Hail,
Hail, great Sejanus!
  Hat. Hail, my honour'd lord!
  Arr. We shall be mark'd anon, for our not Hail.
  Lep. That is already done.
  Arr. It is a note
Of upstart greatness, to observe and watch
For these poor trifles, which the noble mind
Neglects and scorns.
  Lep. Ay, and they think themselves
Deeply dishonour'd where they are omitted,
As if they were necessities that help'd
To the perfection of their dignities; [2]
And hate the men that but refrain them.
  Arr. O!
There is a farther cause of hate. Their breasts
Are guilty, that we know their obscure springs,
And base beginnings; thence the anger grows.
On. Follow.

SCENE IX.—*Another part of the same.*

Enter MACRO *and* LACO.

  Mac. When all are enter'd,[3] shut the temple doors;
And bring your guards up to the gate.
  Lac. I will.
  Mac. If you shall hear commotion in the senate,
Present yourself: and charge on any man
Shall offer to come forth.
  Lac. I am instructed.   [*Exeunt.*

SCENE X.—*The Temple of Apollo.*

Enter HATERIUS, TRIO, SANQUINIUS, COTTA, REGULUS, SEJANUS, POMPONIUS, LATIARIS, LEPIDUS, ARRUNTIUS, *and divers other* Senators; Præcones, *and* Lictors.

  Hat. How well his lordship looks to-day!
  Tri. As if
He had been born, or made for this hour's state.

---

[1] Ex Liburnia, magnæ et proceræ staturæ mittebantur, qui erant Rom. Lecticarii; test. Juv. Sat. iii. v. 240.
      ——————— Turba cedente vehetur
    Dives, et ingenti curret super ora Liburno.
[2] Dio. Rom. Hist. Lib. lviii.   [3] Dio. ibid. p. 718.

Cot. Your fellow consul's come about, methinks?

Tri. Ay, he is wise.

San. Sejanus trusts him well.

Tri. Sejanus is a noble, bounteous lord.[1]

Hat. He is so, and most valiant.

Lat. And most wise.

1 Sen. He's every thing.

Lat. Worthy of all, and more
Than bounty can bestow.

Tri. This dignity
Will make him worthy.

Pom. Above Cæsar.

San. Tut,
Cæsar is but the rector of an isle,[2]
He of the empire.

Tri. Now he will have power
More to reward than ever.

Cot. Let us look
We be not slack in giving him our voices.[3]

Lat. Not I.

San. Nor I.

Cot. The readier we seem
To propagate his honours, will more bind
His thoughts to ours.

Hat. I think right with your lordship;
It is the way to have us hold our places.

San. Ay, and get more.

Lat. More office and more titles.

Pom. I will not lose the part I hope to share
In these his fortunes, for my patrimony.

Lat. See, how Arruntius sits, and Lepidus!

Tri. Let them alone, they will be mark'd anon.

1 Sen. I'll do with others.

2 Sen. So will I.

3 Sen. And I.
Men grow not in the state, but as they are planted
Warm in his favours.

Cot. Noble Sejanus!

Hat. Honour'd Sejanus!

Lat. Worthy and great Sejanus!

Arr. Gods! how the sponges open and take in,
And shut again! look, look! is not he blest
That gets a seat in eye-reach of him? more,
That comes in ear, or tongue-reach? O but most,
Can claw his subtle elbow, or with a buz
Fly-blow his ears?

Præt. Proclaim the senate's peace,

---

[1] Vid. acclamation. Senat. Dio. Rom. Hist. Lib. lviii. p. 719.
[2] Dio. p. 715.   [3] Dio. p. 719.

And give last summons by the edict.

Prœ. Silence!

In name of Cæsar, and the senate, silence!

Memmius Regulus, and Fulcinius Trio,[1] *consuls, these present kalends of June, with the first light, shall hold a senate, in the temple of Apollo Palatine:*[2] *all that are fathers, and are registered fathers, that have right of entering the senate, we warn or command you be frequently present, take knowledge the business is the commonwealth's: whosoever is absent, his fine or mulct will be taken, his excuse will not be taken.*

Tri. Note who are absent, and record their names.

Reg. Fathers conscript,[3] may what I am to utter
Turn good and happy for the commonwealth!
And thou, Apollo, in whose holy house
We here have met, inspire us all with truth,
And liberty of censure to our thought!
The majesty of great Tiberius Cæsar
Propounds to this grave senate, the bestowing
Upon the man he loves, honour'd Sejanus,
The tribunitial dignity and power:[4]
Here are his letters, signed with his signet.
What pleaseth now the fathers to be done?[5]

Sen. Read, read them, open, publicly read them.

Cot. Cæsar hath honour'd his own greatness much
In thinking of this act.

Tri. It was a thought
Happy, and worthy Cæsar.

Lat. And the lord
As worthy it, on whom it is directed!

Hat. Most worthy!

San. Rome did never boast the virtue
That could give envy bounds, but his: Sejanus—

1 Sen. Honour'd and noble!

2 Sen. Good and great Sejanus!

Arr. O, most tame slavery, and fierce flattery!

Prœ. Silence!

TIBERIUS CÆSAR *to the* Senate, *greeting.*

If you, conscript fathers,[6] *with your children, be in health, it is abundantly well: we with our friends here are so. The care of the commonwealth, howsoever we are removed in person, cannot be absent to our thought; although, oftentimes, even to princes most present, the truth of their own affairs is hid; than which, nothing falls out more miserable*

[1] Vid. Brissonium de formul. Lib. ii. et Lipsium Sat. Menip.
[2] Palatinus, a monte Palatino dictus.
[3] Solemnis præfatio consulum in relationibus.   Dio. p. 718.
[4] Vid. Suet. Tib. cap. 65.
[5] Alia formula solemnis, vid. Briss. Lib. ii. et Dio. p. 719.
[6] Solenne exordium epistolar. apud Romanos. cons. Briss. de formul. Lib. viii.

*to a state, or makes the art of governing more difficult. But since it
hath been our easeful happiness to enjoy both the aids and industry
of so vigilant a senate, we profess to have been the more indulgent to
our pleasures, not as being careless of our office, but rather secure of
the necessity. Neither do these common rumours of many, and
infamous libels published against our retirement, at all afflict us;
being born more out of men's ignorance than their malice: and will,
neglected, find their own grave quickly; whereas, too sensibly acknowledged, it would make their obloquy ours. Nor do we desire their
authors, though found, be censured, since in a free state,[1] as ours, all
men ought to enjoy both their minds and tongues free.*

Arr. The lapwing, the lapwing!

*Yet in things which shall worthily and more near concern the majesty
of a prince, we shall fear to be so unnaturally cruel to our own fame,
as to neglect them. True it is, conscript fathers, that we have raised
Sejanus from obscure, and almost unknown gentry*

Sen. How, how!

*to the highest and most conspicuous point of greatness, and, we hope,
deservingly; yet not without danger: it being a most bold hazard in
that sovereign, who, by his particular love to one, dares adventure the
hatred of all his other subjects.*

Arr. This touches; the blood turns.

*But we affy in your loves and understandings, and do no way suspect
the merit of our Sejanus, to make our favours offensive to any.*

Sen. O! good, good.

*Though we could have wished his zeal had run a calmer course against
Agrippina and our nephews, howsoever the openness of their actions
declared them delinquents; and, that he would have remembered, no
innocence is so safe, but it rejoiceth to stand in the sight of mercy: the
use of which in us, he hath so quite taken away, towards them, by his
loyal fury, as now our clemency would be thought but wearied cruelty,
if we should offer to exercise it.*

Arr. I thank him; there I look'd for't. A good fox!

*Some there be that would interpret this his public severity to be par-
ticular ambition;[2] and that, under a pretext of service to us, he doth
but remove his own lets: alleging the strengths he hath made to himself,
by the prætorian soldiers, by his faction in court and senate, by the
offices he holds himself, and confers on others, his popularity and
dependents, his urging and almost driving us to this our unwilling
retirement, and, lastly, his aspiring to be our son-in-law.*

Sen. This is strange!

Arr. I shall anon believe your vultures, Marcus.

*Your wisdoms, conscript fathers, are able to examine, and censure
these suggestions. But, were they left to our absolving voice, we durst
pronounce them, as we think them, most malicious.*

Sen. O, he has restored all; list!

---

[1] Firmus et patiens subinde jactabat, in civitate libera, linguam men-
temque liberas esse debere. Suet. Tib. c. 28.

[2] De hac epist. vid. Dio. Rom. Hist. Lib. lviii. p. 719, et Juv. Sat. x.

Yet are they offered to be averred, and on the lives of the informers.
What we should say, or rather what we should not say, lords of the
senate, if this be true, our gods and goddesses confound us if we know !
Only we must think, we have placed our benefits ill; and conclude, that
in our choice, either we were wanting to the gods, or the gods to us.

       [The Senators shift their places.

 Arr. The place grows hot; they shift.
We have not been covetous, honourable fathers, to change; neither is
it now any new lust that alters our affection, or old lothing; but those
needful jealousies of state, that warn wiser princes hourly to provide
their safety; and do teach them how learned a thing it is to beware of
the humblest enemy; much more of those great ones, whom their own
employed favours have made fit for their fears.

 1 *Sen.* Away.
 2 *Sen.* Sit farther.
 Cot. Let's remove—
 Arr. Gods! how the leaves drop off, this little wind!
We therefore desire, that the offices he holds be first seized by the senate;
and himself suspended from all exercise of place or power—

 Sen. How!
 San. [*thrusting by.*] By your leave.
 Arr. Come, porpoise; where's Haterius?
His gout keeps him most miserably constant;
Your dancing shews a tempest.

 Sej. Read no more.
 Reg. Lords of the senate, hold your seats: read on.
 Sej. These letters they are forged.
 Reg. A guard! sit still.

    Enter LACO, *with the* Guards.

 Arr. Here's change!
 Reg. Bid silence, and read forward.
 Præ. Silence!——*and himself suspended from all exercise of place*
or power, but till due and mature trial be made of his innocency, which
yet we can faintly apprehend the necessity to doubt. If, conscript
fathers, to your more searching wisdoms, there shall appear farther
cause—or of farther proceeding, either to seizure of lands, goods, or
more—it is not our power that shall limit your authority, or our
favour that must corrupt your justice: either were dishonourable in
you, and both uncharitable to ourself. We would willingly [1] *be present*
with your counsels in this business; but the danger of so potent a
faction, if it should prove so, forbids our attempting it: except one of
the consuls would be entreated for our safety, to undertake the guard of
us home; then we should most readily adventure. In the mean time,
it shall not be fit for us to importune so judicious a senate, who know
how much they hurt the innocent, that spare the guilty; and how
grateful a sacrifice to the gods is the life of an ingrateful person. We
reflect not, in this, on Sejanus, (notwithstanding, if you keep an eye

    [1] Dio. Rom. Hist. Lib. lviii. p. 719, et Suet. Tib.

upon him—and there is Latiaris, a senator, and Pinnarius Natta,
two of his most trusted ministers, and so professed, whom we desire not
to have apprehended,) but as the necessity of the cause exacts it.

Reg. A guard on Latiaris!

Arr. O, the spy,
The reverend spy is caught! who pities him?
Reward, sir, for your service: now, you have done
Your property, you see what use is made!

                  [Exeunt Latiaris and Natta, guarded.

Hang up the instrument.

Sej. Give leave.

Lac. Stand, stand!
He comes upon his death, that doth advance
An inch toward my point.

Sej. Have we no friends here?

Arr. Hush'd!
Where now are all the hails and acclamations?

Enter MACRO.

Mac. Hail to the consuls, and this noble senate!

Sej. Is Macro here? O, thou art lost, Sejanus!   *[Aside.*

Mac. Sit still, and unaffrighted, reverend fathers:
Macro, by Cæsar's grace, the new-made provost,
And now possest of the prætorian bands,
An honour late belong'd to that proud man,
Bids you be safe: and to your constant doom
Of his deservings, offers you the surety
Of all the soldiers, tribunes, and centurions,
Received in our command.

Reg. Sejanus, Sejanus,
Stand forth, Sejanus!

Sej. Am I call'd?

Mac. Ay, thou,
Thou insolent monster, art bid stand.

Sej. Why, Macro,
It hath been otherwise between you and I;
This court, that knows us both, hath seen a difference,
And can, if it be pleased to speak, confirm
Whose insolence is most.

Mac. Come down, Typhœus.
If mine be most, lo! thus I make it more;
Kick up thy heels in air, tear off thy robe,
Play with thy beard and nostrils. Thus 'tis fit
(And no man take compassion of thy state)
To use th' ingrateful viper, tread his brains
Into the earth.

Reg. Forbear.

Mac. If I could lose
All my humanity now, 'twere well to torture

So meriting a traitor.—Wherefore, fathers,
Sit you amazed and silent; and not censure
This wretch, who, in the hour he first rebell'd
'Gainst Cæsar's bounty, did condemn himself?
Phlegra, the field where all the sons of earth
Muster'd against the gods, did ne'er acknowledge
So proud and huge a monster.
　　Reg. Take him hence;
And all the gods guard Cæsar!
　　Tri. Take him hence.
　　Hat. Hence.
　　Cot. To the dungeon with him.
　　San. He deserves it.
　　Sen. Crown all our doors [1] with bays.
　　San. And let an ox,
With gilded horns and garlands, straight be led
Unto the Capitol—
　　Hat. And sacrificed
To Jove, for Cæsar's safety.
　　Tri. All our gods
Be present still to Cæsar!
　　Cot. Phœbus.
　　San. Mars.
　　Hat. Diana.
　　San. Pallas.
　　Sen. Juno, Mercury,
All guard him!
　　Mac. Forth, thou prodigy of men!　　　　[*Exit Sejanus, guarded.*
　　Cot. Let all the traitor's titles be defaced.
　　Tri. His images and statues be pull'd down.
　　Hat. His chariot-wheels be broken.
　　Arr. And the legs
Of the poor horses, that deserved nought,
Let them be broken too!
　　　　[*Exeunt Lictors, Præcones, Macro, Regulus, Trio, Haterius, and
　　　　　　Sanquinius: manent Lepidus, Arruntius, and a few Senators.*
　　Lep. O violent change,
And whirl of men's affections!
　　Arr. Like, as both
Their bulks and souls were bound on Fortune's wheel,
And must act only with her motion.
　　Lep. Who would depend upon the popular air,
Or voice of men, that have to-day beheld
That which, if all the gods had fore-declared,
Would not have been believed, Sejanus' fall?
He, that this morn rose proudly, as the sun,
And, breaking through a mist of clients' breath,
Came on, as gazed at and admired as he,

　　　　　　　　　[1] Leg. Juv. Sat. **x.**

When superstitious Moors salute his light!
That had our servile nobles waiting him
As common grooms; and hanging on his look,
No less than human life on destiny!
That had men's knees as frequent as the gods;
And sacrifices [1] more than Rome had altars:
And this man fall! fall? ay, without a look
That durst appear his friend, or lend so much
Of vain relief, to his changed state, as pity!
 Arr. They that before, like gnats, play'd in his beams,
And throng'd to circumscribe him, now not seen
Nor deign to hold a common seat with him!
Others, that waited him unto the senate,
Now inhumanely ravish him to prison,
Whom, but this morn, they follow'd as their lord!
Guard through the streets, bound like a fugitive,
Instead of wreaths give fetters, strokes for stoops,
Blind shames for honours, and black taunts for titles!
Who would trust slippery chance?
 Lep. They that would make
Themselves her spoil; and foolishly forget,
When she doth flatter, that she comes to prey.
Fortune, thou hadst no deity, if men
Had wisdom: we have placed thee so high,
By fond belief in thy felicity.
 [*Shout within.*] The gods guard Cæsar! All the gods guard Cæsar!

Re-enter MACRO, REGULUS, *and divers* Senators.

 Mac. Now, great Sejanus,[2] you that awed the state,
And sought to bring the nobles to your whip;
That would be Cæsar's tutor, and dispose
Of dignities and offices! that had
The public head still bare to your designs,
And made the general voice to echo yours!
That look'd for salutations twelve score off,
And would have pyramids, yea temples, rear'd
To your huge greatness; now you lie as flat,
As was your pride advanced!
 Reg. Thanks to the gods!
 Sen. And praise to Macro, that hath saved Rome!
Liberty, liberty, liberty! Lead on,
And praise to Macro, that hath saved Rome!
     [*Exeunt all but Arruntius and Lepidus.*
 Arr. I prophesy, out of the senate's flattery,
That this new fellow, Macro, will become
A greater prodigy in Rome, than he
That now is fallen.

     [1] Dio. Rom. Hist. Lib. lviii. p. 719, etc.
     [2] Vid. Dio. Rom. Hist. Lib. lviii. p. 720, etc.

Enter TERENTIUS.

Ter. O you, whose minds are good,
And have not forced all mankind from your breasts;
That yet have so much stock of virtue left,
To pity guilty states, when they are wretched:
Lend your soft ears to hear, and eyes to weep,
Deeds done by men, beyond the acts of furies.
The eager multitude (who never yet
Knew why to love or hate, but only pleased
T' express their rage of power) no sooner heard
The murmur of Sejanus in decline,
But with that speed and heat of appetite,
With which they greedily devour the way
To some great sports, or a new theatre,
They fill'd the Capitol, and Pompey's Cirque,
Where, like so many mastiffs, biting stones,
As if his statues now were sensitive
Of their wild fury; first, they tear them down; [1]
Then fastening ropes, drag them along the streets,
Crying in scorn, This, this was that rich head
Was crown'd with garlands, and with odours, this
That was in Rome so reverenced!　Now
The furnace and the bellows shall to work,
The great Sejanus crack, and piece by piece
Drop in the founder's pit.
　　Lep. O popular rage!
　　Ter. The whilst the senate at the temple of Concord [2]
Make haste to meet again, and thronging cry,
Let us condemn him, tread him down in water,
While he doth lie upon the bank; away!
While some more tardy, cry unto their bearers,
He will be censured ere we come; run, knaves,
And use that furious diligence, for fear
Their bondmen should inform against their slackness,
And bring their quaking flesh unto the hook:
The rout they follow with confused voice,
Crying, they're glad, say, they could ne'er abide him,
Enquire what man he was, what kind of face,
What beard he had, what nose, what lips?　Protest
They ever did presage he'd come to this;
They never thought him wise, nor valiant; ask
After his garments, when he dies, what death;
And not a beast of all the herd demands,
What was his crime, or who were his accusers,
Under what proof or testimony he fell?
There came, says one, a huge long-worded letter
From Capreæ against him.　Did there so?

---

[1] Vid. Juv. Sat. x.　　　　　[2] Dio. Rom. Hist. Lib. lviii. p. 720.

O, they are satisfied; no more.

    Lep. Alas!

They follow Fortune,[1] and hate men condemn'd,
Guilty or not.

    Arr. But had Sejanus thrived
In his design, and prosperously opprest
The old Tiberius; then, in that same minute,
These very rascals, that now rage like furies,
Would have proclaim'd Sejanus emperor.

    Lep. But what hath follow'd?

    Ter. Sentence [2] by the senate,
To lose his head; which was no sooner off,
But that and the unfortunate trunk were seized
By the rude multitude; who not content
With what the forward justice of the state
Officiously had done, with violent rage
Have rent it limb from limb. A thousand heads,
A thousand hands, ten thousand tongues and voices,
Employ'd at once in several acts of malice!
Old men not staid with age, virgins with shame,
Late wives with loss of husbands, mothers of children,
Losing all grief in joy of his sad fall,
Run quite transported with their cruelty!
These mounting at his head, these at his face,
These digging out his eyes, those with his brains
Sprinkling themselves, their houses and their friends;
Others are met, have ravish'd thence an arm,
And deal small pieces of the flesh for favours;
These with a thigh, this hath cut off his hands,
And this his feet; these fingers and these toes;
That hath his liver, he his heart: there wants
Nothing but room for wrath, and place for hatred!
What cannot oft be done, is now o'erdone.
The whole, and all of what was great Sejanus,
And, next to Cæsar, did possess the world,
Now torn and scatter'd, as he needs no grave;
Each little dust covers a little part:
So lies he no where, and yet often buried!

Enter NUNTIUS.

    Arr. More of Sejanus?

    Nun. Yes.

    Lep. What can be added?
We know him dead.

    Nun. Then there begin your pity.
There is enough behind to melt ev'n Rome,

---

[1] Juv. Sat. **x.**

[2] Dio. Rom. Hist. Lib. lviii. p. 720. Senec. lib. de Tranq. Anim. **c. 11.**
Quo die illum senatus deduxerat, populus in frusta divisit, etc.

And Cæsar into tears; since never slave
Could yet so highly offend, but tyranny,
In torturing him, would make him worth lamenting.—
A son and daughter to the dead Sejanus,
(Of whom [1] there is not now so much remaining
As would give fast'ning to the hangman's hook,)
Have they drawn forth for farther sacrifice;
Whose tenderness of knowledge, unripe years,
And childish silly innocence was such,
As scarce would lend them feeling of their danger:
The girl [2] so simple, as she often ask'd
" Where they would lead her? for what cause they dragg'd her? "
Cried, " She would do no more: " that she could take
" Warning with beating."   And because our laws
Admit no virgin [3] immature to die,
The wittily and strangely cruel Macro
Deliver'd her to be deflower'd and spoil'd,
By the rude lust of the licentious hangman,
Then to be strangled with her harmless brother.
    Lep. O, act most worthy hell, and lasting night,
To hide it from the world!
    Nun. Their bodies thrown
Into the Gemonies, (I know not how,
Or by what accident return'd,) the mother,
The expulsed [4] Apicata, finds them there;
Whom when she saw lie spread on the degrees,[5]
After a world of fury on herself,
Tearing her hair, defacing of her face,
Beating her breasts and womb, kneeling amaz'd,
Crying to heaven, then to them; at last,
Her drowned voice gat up above her woes,
And with such black and bitter execrations,
As might affright the gods, and force the sun
Run backward to the east; nay, make the old
Deformed chaos rise again, to o'erwhelm
Them, us, and all the world, she fills the air,
Upbraids the heavens with their partial dooms,
Defies their tyrannous powers,[6] and demands,
What she, and those poor innocents have transgress'd,
That they must suffer such a share in vengeance,
Whilst Livia, Lygdus, and Eudemus live,
Who, as she says, and firmly vows to prove it
To Cæsar and the senate, poison'd Drusus?

[1] Vid. Senec. lib. de Tranq. Ani. c. xi.
[2] Tac. Ann. Lib. v. p. 99.   Et Dio. Lib. lviii. p. 720.
[3] Lex non tam virginitati ignotum cautumque voluit quam ætati.   Cons. Lips. comment. Tac.
[4] Dio. Lib. lviii. c. 720.
[5] Scalæ Gemoniæ in quas erant projecta damnator. corpora.
[6] Dio. Lib. lviii. p. 720.

Lep. Confederates with her husband!

Nun. Ay.

Lep. Strange act!

Arr. And strangely open'd: what says now my monster,
The multitude? they reel now, do they not?

Nun. Their gall is gone, and now they 'gin to weep
The mischief they have done.

Arr. I thank 'em, rogues.

Nun. Part are so stupid, or so flexible,
As they believe him innocent; all grieve:
And some whose hands yet reek with his warm blood,
And gripe the part which they did tear of him,
Wish him collected and created new.

Lep. How Fortune plies her sports, when she begins
To practise them! pursues, continues, adds,
Confounds with varying her impassion'd moods!

Arr. Dost thou hope, Fortune, to redeem thy crimes,
To make amend for thy ill-placed favours,
With these strange punishments? Forbear, you things
That stand upon the pinnacles of state,
To boast your slippery height; when you do fall,
You pash yourselves in pieces, ne'er to rise;
And he that lends you pity, is not wise.

Ter. Let this example move the insolent man,
Not to grow proud and careless of the gods.
It is an odious wisdom to blaspheme,
Much more to slighten, or deny their powers:
For, whom the morning saw so great and high,
Thus low and little, 'fore the even doth lie.   [*Exeunt.*

VOLPONE; OR, THE FOX

TO THE MOST NOBLE AND MOST EQUAL SISTERS,

THE TWO FAMOUS UNIVERSITIES,

FOR THEIR LOVE AND ACCEPTANCE SHEWN TO HIS POEM IN THE
PRESENTATION,

BEN JONSON,

THE GRATEFUL ACKNOWLEDGER,

DEDICATES BOTH IT AND HIMSELF.

NEVER, most equal Sisters, had any man a wit so presently excellent, as that it could raise itself; but there must come both matter, occasion, commenders, and favourers to it. If this be true, and that the fortune of all writers doth daily prove it, it behoves the careful to provide well towards these accidents; and, having acquired them, to preserve that part of reputation most tenderly, wherein the benefit of a friend is also defended. Hence is it, that I now render myself grateful, and am studious to justify the bounty of your act; to which, though your mere authority were satisfying, yet it being an age wherein poetry and the professors of it hear so ill on all sides, there will a reason be looked for in the subject. It is certain, nor can it with any forehead be opposed, that the too much license of poetasters in this time, hath much deformed their mistress; that, every day, their manifold and manifest ignorance doth stick unnatural reproaches upon her: but for their petulancy, it were an act of the greatest injustice, either to let the learned suffer, or so divine a skill (which indeed should not be attempted with unclean hands) to fall under the least contempt. For, if men will impartially, and not asquint, look toward the offices and function of a poet, they will easily conclude to themselves the impossibility of any man's being the good poet, without first being a good man. He that is said to be able to inform young men to all good disciplines, inflame grown men to all great virtues, keep old men in their best and supreme state, or, as they decline to childhood, recover them to their first strength; that comes forth the interpreter and arbiter of nature, a teacher of things divine no less than human, a master in manners; and can alone, or with a few, effect the business of mankind: this, I take him, is no subject for pride and ignorance to exercise their railing rhetoric upon. But it will here be hastily answered, that the writers of these days are other things; that not only their manners, but their natures, are inverted, and nothing remaining with them of the dignity of poet, but the abused name, which every scribe usurps; that now, especially in dramatic, or, as they term it, stage-poetry, nothing but ribaldry, profanation, blasphemy, all license of offence to God and man is practised. I dare not deny a great part of this, and am sorry I dare not, because in some men's abortive features (and would they had never boasted the light) it is over-true; but that all are embarked in this bold adventure for hell, is a most uncharitable thought, and, uttered, a more malicious slander. For my particular, I can, and from a most clear conscience, affirm, that I have ever trembled to think toward the least profaneness; have loathed the use of such foul and un-

washed bawdry, as is now made the food of the scene: and, howsoever
I cannot escape from some, the imputation of sharpness, but that they will
say, I have taken a pride, or lust, to be bitter, and not my youngest infant
but hath come into the world with all his teeth; I would ask of these
supercilious politics, what nation, society, or general order or state, I
have provoked? What public person? Whether I have not in all these
preserved their dignity, as mine own person, safe? My works are read,
allowed, (I speak of those that are intirely mine,) look into them, what
broad reproofs have I used? where have I been particular? where personal?
except to a mimic, cheater, bawd, or buffoon, creatures, for their insolencies,
worthy to be taxed? yet to which of these so pointingly, as he might not
either ingenuously have confest, or wisely dissembled his disease? But it
is not rumour can make men guilty, much less entitle me to other men's
crimes. I know, that nothing can be so innocently writ or carried, but
may be made obnoxious to construction; marry, whilst I bear mine
innocence about me, I fear it not. Application is now grown a trade with
many; and there are that profess to have a key for the decyphering of
every thing: but let wise and noble persons take heed how they be too
credulous, or give leave to these invading interpreters to be over-familiar
with their fames, who cunningly, and often, utter their own virulent malice,
under other men's simplest meanings. As for those that will (by faults
which charity hath raked up, or common honesty concealed) make themselves a name with the multitude, or, to draw their rude and beastly claps,
care not whose living faces they intrench with their petulant styles, may
they do it without a rival, for me! I choose rather to live graved in
obscurity, than share with them in so preposterous a fame. Nor can I
blame the wishes of those severe and wise patriots, who providing the hurts
these licentious spirits may do in a state, desire rather to see fools and
devils, and those antique relics of barbarism retrieved, with all other
ridiculous and exploded follies, than behold the wounds of private men,
of princes and nations: for, as Horace makes Trebatius speak among these,

" Sibi quisque timet, quanquam est intactus, et odit."

And men may justly impute such rages, if continued, to the writer, as his
sports. The increase of which lust in liberty, together with the present
trade of the stage, in all their miscelline interludes, what learned or liberal
soul doth not already abhor? where nothing but the filth of the time is
uttered, and with such impropriety of phrase, such plenty of solecisms,
such dearth of sense, so bold prolepses, so racked metaphors, with brothely,
able to violate the ear of a pagan, and blasphemy, to turn the blood of a
Christian to water. I cannot but be serious in a cause of this nature,
wherein my fame, and the reputation of divers honest and learned are the
question; when a name so full of authority, antiquity, and all great mark,
is, through their insolence, become the lowest scorn of the age; and those
men subject to the petulancy of every vernaculous orator, that were wont
to be the care of kings and happiest monarchs. This it is that hath not
only rapt me to present indignation, but made me studious heretofore,
and by all my actions, to stand off from them; which may most appear
in this my latest work, which you, most learned Arbitresses, have seen,
judged, and to my crown, approved; wherein I have laboured for their
instruction and amendment, to reduce not only the ancient forms, but
manners of the scene, the easiness, the propriety, the innocence, and last,
the doctrine, which is the principal end of poesie, to inform men in the best
reason of living. And though my catastrophe may, in the strict rigour of
comic law, meet with censure, as turning back to my promise; I desire the
learned and charitable critic, to have so much faith in me, to think it was
done of industry: for, with what ease I could have varied it nearer his
scale (but that I fear to boast my own faculty) I could here insert. But
my special aim being to put the snaffle in their mouths, that cry out, We

never punish vice in our interludes, etc., I took the more liberty; though not without some lines of example, drawn even in the ancients themselves, the goings out of whose comedies are not always joyful, but oft times the bawds, the servants, the rivals, yea, and the masters are mulcted; and fitly, it being the office of a comic poet to imitate justice, and instruct to life, as well as purity of language, or stir up gentle affections; to which I shall take the occasion elsewhere to speak.

For the present, most reverenced Sisters, as I have cared to be thankful for your affections past, and here made the understanding acquainted with some ground of your favours; let me not despair their continuance, to the maturing of some worthier fruits; wherein, if my muses be true to me, I shall raise the despised head of poetry again, and stripping her out of those rotten and base rags wherewith the times have adulterated her form, restore her to her primitive habit, feature, and majesty, and render her worthy to be embraced and kist of all the great and master-spirits of our world. As for the vile and slothful, who never affected an act worthy of celebration, or are so inward with their own vicious natures, as they worthily fear her, and think it an high point of policy to keep her in contempt, with their declamatory and windy invectives; she shall out of just rage incite her servants (who are *genus irritabile*) to spout ink in their faces, that shall eat farther than their marrow into their fames; and not Cinnamus the barber, with his art, shall be able to take out the brands; but they shall live, and be read, till the wretches die, as things worst deserving of themselves in chief, and then of all mankind.

From my House in the Black-Friars,
this 11th day of February, 1607.

<h2 style="text-align:center">DRAMATIS PERSONÆ</h2>

VOLPONE, *a Magnifico.*
MOSCA, *his Parasite.*
VOLTORE, *an Advocate.*
CORBACCIO, *an old Gentleman.*
CORVINO, *a Merchant.*
BONARIO, *son to Corbaccio.*
SIR POLITICK WOULD-BE, *a Knight.*
PEREGRINE, *a Gentleman Traveller.*
NANO, *a Dwarf.*
CASTRONE, *an Eunuch.*
ANDROGYNO, *an Hermaphrodite.*

GREGE (*or Mob*)

Commandadori, *Officers of Justice.*
Mercatori, *three Merchants.*
Avocatori, *four Magistrates.*
Notario, *the Register.*

LADY WOULD-BE, *Sir Politick's Wife.*
CELIA, *Corvino's Wife.*

Servitori, Servants, *two* Waiting-women, *etc.*

<h3 style="text-align:center">SCENE,—VENICE</h3>

THE ARGUMENT.

V *olpone, childless, rich, feigns sick, despairs,*
O *ffers his state to hopes of several heirs,*
L *ies languishing: his parasite receives*
P *resents of all, assures, deludes; then weaves*
O *ther cross plots, which ope themselves, are told.*
N *ew tricks for safety are sought; they thrive: when bold,* }
E *ach tempts the other again, and all are sold.* }

PROLOGUE.

Now, luck yet send us, and a little wit
  Will serve to make our play hit;
(According to the palates of the season)
  Here is rhime, not empty of reason.
This we were bid to credit from our poet,
  Whose true scope, if you would know it,
In all his poems still hath been this measure,
  To mix profit with your pleasure;
And not as some, whose throats their envy failing,
  Cry hoarsely, All he writes is railing:
And when his plays come forth, think they can flout them,
  With saying, he was a year about them.
To this there needs no lie, but this his creature,
  Which was two months since no feature;
And though he dares give them five lives to mend it,
  'Tis known, five weeks fully penn'd it,
From his own hand, without a co-adjutor,
  Novice, journey-man, or tutor.
Yet thus much I can give you as a token
  Of his play's worth, no eggs are broken,
Nor quaking custards with fierce teeth affrighted,
  Wherewith your rout are so delighted;
Nor hales he in a gull old ends reciting,
  To stop gaps in his loose writing;
With such a deal of monstrous and forced action,
  As might make Bethlem a faction:
Nor made he his play for jests stolen from each table,
  But makes jests to fit his fable;

And so presents quick comedy refined,
  As best critics have designed;
The laws of time, place, persons he observeth,
  From no needful rule he swerveth,
All gall and copperas from his ink he draineth,
  Only a little salt remaineth,
Wherewith he'll rub your cheeks, till red, with laughter,
  They shall look fresh a week after.

ACT I

SCENE I.—*A Room in* VOLPONE'S *House.*

Enter VOLPONE *and* MOSCA.

Volp. Good morning to the day; and next, my gold!—
Open the shrine, that I may see my saint.
  [*Mosca withdraws the curtain, and discovers piles of gold,*
    plate, jewels, etc.
Hail the world's soul, and mine! more glad than is
The teeming earth to see the long'd-for sun
Peep through the horns of the celestial Ram,
Am I, to view thy splendour darkening his;
That lying here, amongst my other hoards,
Shew'st like a flame by night, or like the day
Struck out of chaos, when all darkness fled
Unto the centre. O thou son of Sol,
But brighter than thy father, let me kiss,
With adoration, thee, and every relick
Of sacred treasure in this blessed room.
Well did wise poets, by thy glorious name,
Title that age which they would have the best;
Thou being the best of things, and far transcending
All style of joy, in children, parents, friends,
Or any other waking dream on earth:
Thy looks when they to Venus did ascribe,
They should have given her twenty thousand Cupids;
Such are thy beauties and our loves! Dear saint,
Riches, the dumb god, that giv'st all men tongues,
Thou canst do nought, and yet mak'st men do all things;
The price of souls; even hell, with thee to boot,
Is made worth heaven. Thou art virtue, fame,
Honour, and all things else. Who can get thee,

He shall be noble valiant, honest, wise—
   Mos. And what he will, sir.   Riches are in fortune
A greater good than wisdom is in nature.
   Volp. True, my beloved Mosca.   Yet I glory
More in the cunning purchase of my wealth,
Than in the glad possession, since I gain
No common way; I use no trade, no venture;
I wound no earth with plough-shares, fat no beasts,
To feed the shambles; have no mills for iron,
Oil, corn, or men, to grind them into powder:
I blow no subtle glass, expose no ships
To threat'nings of the furrow-faced sea;
I turn no monies in the public bank,
Nor usure private.
   Mos. No, sir, nor devour
Soft prodigals.   You shall have some will swallow
A melting heir as glibly as your Dutch
Will pills of butter, and ne'er purge for it;
Tear forth the fathers of poor families
Out of their beds, and coffin them alive
In some kind clasping prison, where their bones
May be forth-coming, when the flesh is rotten:
But your sweet nature doth abhor these courses;
You lothe the widow's or the orphan's tears
Should wash your pavements, or their piteous cries
Ring in your roofs, and beat the air for vengeance.
   Volp. Right, Mosca; I do lothe it.
   Mos. And besides, sir,
You are not like the thresher that doth stand
With a huge flail, watching a heap of corn,
And, hungry, dares not taste the smallest grain,
But feeds on mallows, and such bitter herbs;
Nor like the merchant, who hath fill'd his vaults
With Romagnia, and rich Candian wines,
Yet drinks the lees of Lombard's vinegar:
You will lie not in straw, whilst moths and worms
Feed on your sumptuous hangings and soft beds;
You know the use of riches, and dare give now
From that bright heap, to me, your poor observer,
Or to your dwarf, or your hermaphrodite,
Your eunuch, or what other household trifle
Your pleasure allows maintenance—
   Volp. Hold thee, Mosca,   *[Gives him money.*
Take of my hand; thou strik'st on truth in all,
And they are envious term thee parasite.
Call forth my dwarf, my eunuch, and my fool,
And let them make me sport. *[Exit Mos.]* What should I do,
But cocker up my genius, and live free
To all delights my fortune calls me to?

I have no wife, no parent, child, ally,
To give my substance to; but whom I make
Must be my heir: and this makes men observe me:
This draws new clients daily to my house,
Women and men of every sex and age,
That bring me presents, send me plate, coin, jewels,
With hope that when I die (which they expect
Each greedy minute) it shall then return
Ten-fold upon them; whilst some, covetous
Above the rest, seek to engross me whole,
And counter-work the one unto the other,
Contend in gifts, as they would seem in love:
All which I suffer, playing with their hopes,
And am content to coin them into profit,
And look upon their kindness, and take more,
And look on that; still bearing them in hand,
Letting the cherry knock against their lips,
And draw it by their mouths, and back again.—
How now!

Re-enter MOSCA *with* NANO, ANDROGYNO, *and* CASTRONE.

Nan. Now, room for fresh gamesters, who do will you to know,
  They do bring you neither play nor university show;
And therefore do entreat you, that whatsoever they rehearse,
  May not fare a whit the worse, for the false pace of the verse.
If you wonder at this, you will wonder more ere we pass,
  For know, here is inclosed the soul of Pythagoras,
That juggler divine, as hereafter shall follow;
  Which soul, fast and loose, sir, came first from Apollo,
And was breath'd into Æthalides, Mercurius his son,
  Where it had the gift to remember all that ever was done.
From thence it fled forth, and made quick transmigration
  To goldly-lock'd Euphorbus, who was killed in good fashion,
At the siege of old Troy, by the cuckold of Sparta.
  Hermotimus was next (I find it in my charta)
To whom it did pass, where no sooner it was missing
  But with one Pyrrhus of Delos it learn'd to go a fishing;
And thence did it enter the sophist of Greece.
  From Pythagore, she went into a beautiful piece,
Hight Aspasia, the meretrix; and the next toss of her
  Was again of a whore, she became a philosopher,
Crates the cynick, as it self doth relate it:
  Since kings, knights, and beggars, knaves, lords, and fools gat it,
Besides ox and ass, camel, mule, goat, and brock,
  In all which it hath spoke, as in the cobler's cock.
But I come not here to discourse of that matter,
  Or his one, two, or three, or his great oath, BY QUATER!
His musics, his trigon, his golden thigh,
  Or his telling how elements shift, but I

Would ask, how of late thou hast suffered translation,
And shifted thy coat in these days of reformation.
And. *Like one of the reformed, a fool, as you see,*
Counting all old doctrine heresie.
Nan. *But not on thine own forbid meats hast thou ventured ?*
And. *On fish, when first a Carthusian I enter'd.*
Nan. *Why, then thy dogmatical silence hath left thee ?*
And. *Of that an obstreperous lawyer bereft me.*
Nan. *O wonderful change, when sir lawyer forsook thee !*
For Pythagore's sake, what body then took thee ?
And. *A good dull mule.* Nan. *And how ! by that means*
Thou wert brought to allow of the eating of beans ?
And. *Yes.* Nan. *But from the mule into whom didst thou pass ?*
And. *Into a very strange beast, by some writers call'd an ass;*
By others, a precise, pure, illuminate brother,
Of those devour flesh, and sometimes one another;
And will drop you forth a libel, or a sanctified lie,
Betwixt every spoonful of a nativity-pie.
Nan. *Now quit thee, for heaven, of that profane nation,*
And gently report thy next transmigration.
And. *To the same that I am.* Nan. *A creature of delight,*
And, what is more than a fool, an hermaphrodite !
Now, prithee, sweet soul, in all thy variation,
Which body would'st thou choose, to keep up thy station ?
And. *Troth, this I am in: even here would I tarry.*
Nan. *'Cause here the delight of each sex thou canst vary ?*
And. *Alas, those pleasures be stale and forsaken;*
No, 'tis your fool wherewith I am so taken,
The only one creature that I can call blessed;
For all other forms I have proved most distressed.
Nan. *Spoke true, as thou wert in Pythagoras still,*
This learned opinion we celebrate will,
Fellow eunuch, as behoves us, with all our wit and art,
To dignify that whereof ourselves are so great and special a part.
Volp. Now, very, very pretty! Mosca, this
Was thy invention?
Mos. If it please my patron,
Not else.
Volp. It doth, good Mosca.
Mos. Then it was, sir.

NANO *and* CASTRONE *sing.*

Fools, they are the only nation
Worth men's envy or admiration:
Free from care or sorrow-taking:
Selves and others merry making:
All they speak or do is sterling.
Your fool he is your great man's darling,
And your ladies' sport and pleasure;

> Tongue and bauble are his treasure.
> E'en his face begetteth laughter,
> And he speaks truth free from slaughter;
> He's the grace of every feast,
> And sometimes the chiefest guest;
> Hath his trencher and his stool,
> When wit waits upon the fool.
>   O, who would not be
>   He, he, he?   [*Knocking without.*

Volp. Who's that? Away! [*Exeunt Nano and Castrone.*]
    Look, Mosca. Fool, begone!   [*Exit Androgyno.*
  Mos. 'Tis signior Voltore, the advocate;
I know him by his knock.
  Volp. Fetch me my gown,
My furs and night-caps; say, my couch is changing,
And let him entertain himself awhile
Without i' the gallery. [*Exit Mosca.*] Now, now, my clients
Begin their visitation! Vulture, kite,
Raven, and gorcrow, all my birds of prey,
That think me turning carcase, now they come;
I am not for them yet—

                Re-enter Mosca, *with the gown, etc.*

                      How now! the news?
  Mos. A piece of plate, sir.
  Volp. Of what bigness?
  Mos. Huge,
Massy, and antique, with your name inscribed,
And arms engraven.
  Volp. Good! and not a fox
Stretch'd on the earth, with fine delusive sleights.
Mocking a gaping crow? ha, Mosca!
  Mos. Sharp, sir.
  Volp. Give me my furs. [*Puts on his sick dress.*] Why dost
        thou laugh so, man?
  Mos. I cannot choose, sir, when I apprehend
What thoughts he has without now, as he walks:
That this might be the last gift he should give;
That this would fetch you; if you died to-day,
And gave him all, what he should be to-morrow;
What large return would come of all his ventures;
How he should worship'd be, and reverenced;
Ride with his furs, and foot-cloths; waited on
By herds of fools, and clients; have clear way
Made for his mule, as letter'd as himself;
Be call'd the great and learned advocate:
And then concludes, there's nought impossible.
  Volp. Yes, to be learned, Mosca.

Mos. O, no: rich
Implies it. Hood an ass with reverend purple,
So you can hide his two ambitious ears,
And he shall pass for a cathedral doctor.
   Volp. My caps, my caps, good Mosca. Fetch him in.
   Mos. Stay, sir; your ointment for your eyes.
   Volp. That's true;
Dispatch, dispatch: I long to have possession
Of my new present.
   Mos. That, and thousands more,
I hope to see you lord of.
   Volp. Thanks, kind Mosca.
   Mos. And that, when I am lost in blended dust,
And hundred such as I am, in succession—
   Volp. Nay, that were too much, Mosca.
   Mos. You shall live,
Still, to delude these harpies.
   Volp. Loving Mosca!
'Tis well: my pillow now, and let him enter.   [*Exit Mosca.*
Now, my feign'd cough, my phthisic, and my gout,
My apoplexy, palsy, and catarrhs,
Help, with your forced functions, this my posture,
Wherein, this three year, I have milk'd their hopes.
He comes; I hear him—Uh! [*coughing.*] uh! uh! uh! O—

Re-enter MOSCA, *introducing* VOLTORE, *with a piece of Plate.*

   Mos. You still are what you were, sir. Only you,
Of all the rest, are he commands his love,
And you do wisely to preserve it thus,
With early visitation, and kind notes
Of your good meaning to him, which, I know,
Cannot but come most grateful. Patron! sir!
Here's signior Voltore is come—
   Volp. [*faintly.*] What say you?
   Mos. Sir, signior Voltore is come this morning
To visit you.
   Volp. I thank him.
   Mos. And hath brought
A piece of antique plate, bought of St. Mark,
With which he here presents you.
   Volp. He is welcome.
Pray him to come more often.
   Mos. Yes.
   Volt. What says he?
   Mos. He thanks you, and desires you see him often.
   Volp. Mosca.
   Mos. My patron!
   Volp. Bring him near, where is he?
I long to feel his hand.

Mos. The plate is here, sir.

Volt. How fare you, sir?

Volp. I thank you, signior Voltore;
Where is the plate? mine eyes are bad.

Volt. [*putting it into his hands.*] I'm sorry,
To see you still thus weak.

Mos. That he's not weaker.   [*Aside.*

Volp. You are too munificent.

Volt. No, sir; would to heaven,
I could as well give health to you, as that plate!

Volp. You give, sir, what you can: I thank you. Your love
Hath taste in this, and shall not be unanswer'd:
I pray you see me often.

Volt. Yes, I shall, sir.

Volp. Be not far from me.

Mos. Do you observe that, sir?

Volp. Hearken unto me still; it will concern you.

Mos. You are a happy man, sir; know your good.

Volp. I cannot now last long—

Mos. You are his heir, sir.

Volt. Am I?

Volp. I feel me going; Uh! uh! uh! uh!
I'm sailing to my port, Uh! uh! uh! uh!
And I am glad I am so near my haven.

Mos. Alas, kind gentleman! Well, we must all go—

Volt. But, Mosca—

Mos. Age will conquer.

Volt. 'Pray thee, hear me:
Am I inscribed his heir for certain?

Mos. Are you!
I do beseech you, sir, you will vouchsafe
To write me in your family. All my hopes
Depend upon your worship: I am lost,
Except the rising sun do shine on me.

Volt. It shall both shine, and warm thee, Mosca.

Mos. Sir,
I am a man, that hath not done your love
All the worst offices: here I wear your keys,
See all your coffers and your caskets lock'd,
Keep the poor inventory of your jewels,
Your plate and monies; am your steward, sir,
Husband your goods here.

Volt. But am I sole heir?

Mos. Without a partner, sir; confirm'd this morning:
The wax is warm yet, and the ink scarce dry
Upon the parchment.

Volt. Happy, happy, me!
By what good chance, sweet Mosca?

Mos. Your desert, sir;

I know no second cause.
   Volt. Thy modesty
Is not to know it; well, we shall requite it.
   Mos. He ever liked your course, sir; that first took him.
I oft have heard him say, how he admired
Men of your large profession, that could speak
To every cause, and things mere contraries,
Till they were hoarse again, yet all be law;
That, with most quick agility, could turn,
And [re-] return; [could] make knots, and undo them;
Give forked counsel; take provoking gold
On either hand, and put it up: these men,
He knew, would thrive with their humility.
And, for his part, he thought he should be blest
To have his heir of such a suffering spirit,
So wise, so grave, of so perplex'd a tongue,
And loud withal, that would not wag, nor scarce
Lie still, without a fee; when every word
Your worship but lets fall, is a chequin!—   [*Knocking without.*
Who's that? one knocks; I would not have you seen, sir.
And yet—pretend you came, and went in haste:
I'll fashion an excuse——and, gentle sir,
When you do come to swim in golden lard,
Up to the arms in honey, that your chin
Is borne up stiff, with fatness of the flood,
Think on your vassal; but remember me:
I have not been your worst of clients.
   Volt. Mosca!—
   Mos. When will you have your inventory brought, sir?
Or see a copy of the will?—Anon!—
I'll bring them to you, sir. Away, be gone,
Put business in your face.   [*Exit Voltore.*
   Volp. [*springing up.*] Excellent Mosca!
Come hither, let me kiss thee.
   Mos. Keep you still, sir.
Here is Corbaccio.
   Volp. Set the plate away:
The vulture's gone, and the old raven's come!
   Mos. Betake you to your silence, and your sleep.
Stand there and multiply. [*Putting the plate to the rest.*] Now,
   shall we see
A wretch who is indeed more impotent
Than this can feign to be; yet hopes to hop
Over his grave—

         Enter CORBACCIO.

       Signior Corbaccio!
You're very welcome, sir.
   Corb. How does your patron?

Mos. Troth, as he did, sir; no amends.

Corb. What! mends he?

Mos. No, sir: he's rather worse.

Corb. That's well. Where is he?

Mos. Upon his couch, sir, newly fall'n asleep.

Corb. Does he sleep well?

Mos. No wink, sir, all this night.
Nor yesterday; but slumbers.

Corb. Good! he should take
Some counsel of physicians: I have brought him
An opiate here, from mine own doctor.

Mos. He will not hear of drugs.

Corb. Why? I myself
Stood by while it was made, saw all the ingredients:
And know, it cannot but most gently work:
My life for his, 'tis but to make him sleep.

Volp. Ay, his last sleep, if he would take it.   [*Aside.*

Mos. Sir,
He has no faith in physic.

Corb. Say you, say you?

Mos. He has no faith in physic: he does think
Most of your doctors are the greater danger,
And worse disease, to escape. I often have
Heard him protest, that your physician
Should never be his heir.

Corb. Not I his heir?

Mos. Not your physician, sir.

Corb. O, no, no, no,
I do not mean it.

Mos. No, sir, nor their fees
He cannot brook: he says, they flay a man,
Before they kill him.

Corb. Right, I do conceive you.

Mos. And then they do it by experiment;
For which the law not only doth absolve them,
But gives them great reward: and he is loth
To hire his death, so.

Corb. It is true, they kill
With as much license as a judge.

Mos. Nay, more;
For he but kills, sir, where the law condemns,
And these can kill him too.

Corb. Ay, or me;
Or any man. How does his apoplex?
Is that strong on him still?

Mos. Most violent.
His speech is broken, and his eyes are set,
His face drawn longer than 'twas wont—

Corb. How! how!

Stronger than he was wont?

Mos. No, sir: his face
Drawn longer than 'twas wont.

Corb. O, good!

Mos. His mouth
Is ever gaping, and his eyelids hang.

Corb. Good.

Mos. A freezing numbness stiffens all his joints,
And makes the colour of his flesh like lead.

Corb. 'Tis good.

Mos. His pulse beats slow, and dull.

Corb. Good symptoms still.

Mos. And from his brain—

Corb. I conceive you; good.

Mos. Flows a cold sweat, with a continual rheum,
Forth the resolved corners of his eyes.

Corb. Is't possible? Yet I am better, ha!
How does he, with the swimming of his head?

Mos. O, sir, 'tis past the scotomy; he now
Hath lost his feeling, and hath left to snort:
You hardly can perceive him, that he breathes.

Corb. Excellent, excellent! sure I shall outlast him:
This makes me young again, a score of years.

Mos. I was a coming for you, sir.

Corb. Has he made his will?
What has he given me?

Mos. No, sir.

Corb. Nothing! ha?

Mos. He has not made his will, sir.

Corb. Oh, oh, oh!
What then did Voltore, the lawyer, here?

Mos. He smelt a carcase, sir, when he but heard
My master was about his testament;
As I did urge him to it for your good—

Corb. He came unto him, did he? I thought so.

Mos. Yes, and presented him this piece of plate.

Corb. To be his heir?

Mos. I do not know, sir.

Corb. True:
I know it too.

Mos. By your own scale, sir.   [*Aside.*

Corb. Well,
I shall prevent him, yet. See, Mosca, look,
Here, I have brought a bag of bright chequines,
Will quite weigh down his plate.

Mos. [*taking the bag.*] Yea, marry, sir.
This is true physic, this your sacred medicine;
No talk of opiates, to this great elixir!

Corb. 'Tis aurum palpabile, if not potabile.

Mos. It shall be minister'd to him, in his bowl.

Corb. Ay, do, do, do.

Mos. Most blessed cordial!

This will recover him.

Corb. Yes, do, do, do.

Mos. I think it were not best, sir.

Corb. What?

Mos. To recover him.

Corb. O, no, no, no; by no means.

Mos. Why, sir, this

Will work some strange effect, if he but feel it.

Corb. 'Tis true, therefore forbear; I'll take my venture:

Give me it again.

Mos. At no hand; pardon me:

You shall not do yourself that wrong, sir.   I

Will so advise you, you shall have it all.

Corb. How?

Mos. All, sir; 'tis your right, your own: no man

Can claim a part: 'tis yours, without a rival,

Decreed by destiny.

Corb. How, how, good Mosca?

Mos. I'll tell you, sir.   This fit he shall recover.

Corb. I do conceive you.

Mos. And, on first advantage

Of his gain'd sense, will I re-importune him

Unto the making of his testament:

And shew him this.   [*Pointing to the money.*

Corb. Good, good.

Mos. 'Tis better yet,

If you will hear, sir.

Corb. Yes, with all my heart.

Mos. Now, would I counsel you, make home with speed;

There, frame a will; whereto you shall inscribe

My master your sole heir.

Corb. And disinherit

My son!

Mos. O, sir, the better: for that colour

Shall make it much more taking.

Corb. O, but colour?

Mos. This will, sir, you shall send it unto me.

Now, when I come to inforce, as I will do,

Your cares, your watchings, and your many prayers,

Your more than many gifts, your this day's present,

And last, produce your will; where, without thought,

Or least regard, unto your proper issue,

A son so brave, and highly meriting,

The stream of your diverted love hath thrown you

Upon my master, and made him your heir:

He cannot be so stupid, or stone-dead,

But out of conscience, and mere gratitude—
 Corb. He must pronounce me his?
 Mos. 'Tis true.
 Corb. This plot
Did I think on before.
 Mos. I do believe it.
 Corb. Do you not believe it?
 Mos. Yes, sir.
 Corb. Mine own project.
 Mos. Which, when he hath done, sir—
 Corb. Publish'd me his heir?
 Mos. And you so certain to survive him—
 Corb. Ay.
 Mos. Being so lusty a man—
 Corb. 'Tis true.
 Mos. Yes, sir—
 Corb. I thought on that too. See, how he should be
The very organ to express my thoughts!
 Mos. You have not only done yourself a good—
 Corb. But multiplied it on my son.
 Mos. 'Tis right, sir.
 Corb. Still, my invention.
 Mos. 'Las, sir! heaven knows,
It hath been all my study, all my care,
(I e'en grow gray withal,) how to work things—
 Corb. I do conceive, sweet Mosca.
 Mos. You are he,
For whom I labour here.
 Corb. Ay, do, do, do:
I'll straight about it.   *[Going.*
 Mos. Rook go with you, raven!
 Corb. I know thee honest.
 Mos. You do lie, sir!   *[Aside.*
 Corb. And—
 Mos. Your knowledge is no better than your ears, sir.
 Corb. I do not doubt, to be a father to thee.
 Mos. Nor I to gull my brother of his blessing.
 Corb. I may have my youth restored to me, why not?
 Mos. Your worship is a precious ass!
 Corb. What say'st thou?
 Mos. I do desire your worship to make haste, sir.
 Corb. 'Tis done, 'tis done; I go.   *[Exit.*
 Volp. [*leaping from his couch.*] O, I shall burst!
Let out my sides, let out my sides—
 Mos. Contain
Your flux of laughter, sir: you know this hope
Is such a bait, it covers any hook.
 Volp. O, but thy working, and thy placing it!
I cannot hold; good rascal, let me kiss thee:

I never knew thee in so rare a humour.

Mos. Alas, sir, I but do as I am taught;
Follow your grave instructions; give them words;
Pour oil into their ears, and send them hence.

Volp. 'Tis true, 'tis true.   What a rare punishment
Is avarice to itself!

Mos. Ay, with our help, sir.

Volp. So many cares, so many maladies,
So many fears attending on old age,
Yea, death so often call'd on, as no wish
Can be more frequent with them, their limbs faint,
Their senses dull, their seeing, hearing, going,
All dead before them; yea, their very teeth,
Their instruments of eating, failing them:
Yet this is reckon'd life! nay, here was one,
Is now gone home, that wishes to live longer!
Feels not his gout, nor palsy; feigns himself
Younger by scores of years, flatters his age
With confident belying it, hopes he may,
With charms, like Æson, have his youth restored:
And with these thoughts so battens, as if fate
Would be as easily cheated on, as he,
And all turns air! [*Knocking within.*]   Who's that there, now?
    a third!

Mos. Close, to your couch again; I hear his voice:
It is Corvino, our spruce merchant.

Volp. [*lies down as before.*] Dead.

Mos. Another bout, sir, with your eyes.   [*Anointing them.*]
    —Who's there?

Enter CORVINO.

Signior Corvino! come most wish'd for!   O,
How happy were you, if you knew it, now!

Corv. Why? what? wherein?

Mos. The tardy hour is come, sir.

Corv. He is not dead?

Mos. Not dead, sir, but as good;
He knows no man.

Corv. How shall I do then?

Mos. Why, sir?

Corv. I have brought him here a pearl.

Mos. Perhaps he has
So much remembrance left, as to know you, sir:
He still calls on you; nothing but your name
Is in his mouth.   Is your pearl orient, sir?

Corv. Venice was never owner of the like.

Volp. [*faintly.*] Signior Corvino!

Mos. Hark.

Volp. Signior Corvino!

Mos. He calls you; step and give it him.—He's here, sir,
And he has brought you a rich pearl.

Corv. How do you, sir?
Tell him, it doubles the twelfth caract.

Mos. Sir,
He cannot understand, his hearing's gone;
And yet it comforts him to see you—

Corv. Say,
I have a diamond for him, too.

Mos. Best shew it, sir;
Put it into his hand; 'tis only there
He apprehends: he has his feeling, yet.
See how he grasps it!

Corv. 'Las, good gentleman!
How pitiful the sight is!

Mos. Tut! forget, sir.
The weeping of an heir should still be laughter
Under a visor.

Corv. Why, am I his heir?

Mos. Sir, I am sworn, I may not shew the will
Till he be dead; but here has been Corbaccio,
Here has been Voltore, here were others too,
I cannot number 'em, they were so many;
All gaping here for legacies: but I,
Taking the vantage of his naming you,
Signior Corvino, Signior Corvino, took
Paper, and pen, and ink, and there I asked him,
Whom he would have his heir? *Corvino.* Who
Should be executor? *Corvino.* And,
To any question he was silent to,
I still interpreted the nods he made,
Through weakness, for consent: and sent home th' others,
Nothing bequeath'd them, but to cry and curse.

Corv. O, my dear Mosca! [*They embrace.*] Does he not perceive
us?

Mos. No more than a blind harper. He knows no man,
No face of friend, nor name of any servant,
Who 'twas that fed him last, or gave him drink:
Not those he hath begotten, or brought up,
Can he remember.

Corv. Has he children?

Mos. Bastards,
Some dozen, or more, that he begot on beggars,
Gypsies, and Jews, and black-moors, when he was drunk.
Knew you not that, sir? 'tis the common fable.
The dwarf, the fool, the eunuch, are all his;
He's the true father of his family,
In all, save me:—but he has given them nothing.

Corv. That's well, that's well! Art sure he does not hear us?

Mos. Sure, sir! why, look you, credit your own sense.

[*Shouts in Vol.'s ear.*

The pox approach, and add to your diseases,
If it would send you hence the sooner, sir,
For your incontinence, it hath deserv'd it
Thoroughly, and thoroughly, and the plague to boot!—
You may come near, sir.—Would you would once close
Those filthy eyes of yours, that flow with slime,
Like two frog-pits; and those same hanging cheeks,
Cover'd with hide instead of skin—Nay, help, sir—
That look like frozen dish-clouts set on end!

Corv. [*aloud.*] Or like an old smoked wall, on which the rain
Ran down in streaks!

Mos. Excellent, sir! speak out:
You may be louder yet; a culverin
Discharged in his ear would hardly bore it.

Corv. His nose is like a common sewer, still running.

Mos. 'Tis good! And what his mouth?

Corv. A very draught.

Mos. O, stop it up—

Corv. By no means.

Mos. 'Pray you, let me:
Faith I could stifle him rarely with a pillow,
As well as any woman that should keep him.

Corv. Do as you will; but I'll begone.

Mos. Be so:
It is your presence makes him last so long.

Corv. I pray you, use no violence.

Mos. No, sir! why?
Why should you be thus scrupulous, pray you, sir?

Corv. Nay, at your discretion.

Mos. Well, good sir, begone.

Corv. I will not trouble him now, to take my pearl.

Mos. Puh! nor your diamond. What a needless care
Is this afflicts you? Is not all here yours?
Am not I here, whom you have made your creature?
That owe my being to you?

Corv. Grateful Mosca!
Thou art my friend, my fellow, my companion,
My partner, and shalt share in all my fortunes.

Mos. Excepting one.

Corv. What's that?

Mos. Your gallant wife, sir,—　　　　　　　　　[*Exit Corv.*
Now is he gone: we had no other means
To shoot him hence, but this.

Volp. My divine Mosca!
Thou hast to-day outgone thyself. [*Knocking within.*]—Who's there?
I will be troubled with no more. Prepare
Me music, dances, banquets, all delights;

The Turk is not more sensual in his pleasures,
Than will Volpone. [*Exit Mos.*] Let me see; a pearl!
A diamond! plate! chequines! Good morning's purchase.
Why, this is better than rob churches, yet;
Or fat, by eating, once a month, a man—

Re-enter MOSCA.

Who is't?
    Mos. The beauteous lady Would-be, sir,
Wife to the English knight, sir Politick Would-be,
(This is the style, sir, is directed me,)
Hath sent to know how you have slept to-night,
And if you would be visited?
    Volp. Not now:
Some three hours hence—
    Mos. I told the squire so much.
    Volp. When I am high with mirth and wine; then, then:
'Fore heaven, I wonder at the desperate valour
Of the bold English, that they dare let loose
Their wives to all encounters!
    Mos. Sir, this knight
Had not his name for nothing, he is *politick*,
And knows, howe'er his wife affect strange airs,
She hath not yet the face to be dishonest:
But had she signior Corvino's wife's face—
    Volp. Has she so rare a face?
    Mos. O, sir, the wonder,
The blazing star of Italy! a wench
Of the first year! a beauty ripe as harvest!
Whose skin is whiter than a swan all over,
Than silver, snow, or lilies! a soft lip,
Would tempt you to eternity of kissing!
And flesh that melteth in the touch to blood!
Bright as your gold, and lovely as your gold!
    Volp. Why had not I known this before?
    Mos. Alas, sir,
Myself but yesterday discover'd it.
    Volp. How might I see her?
    Mos. O, not possible;
She's kept as warily as is your gold;
Never does come abroad, never takes air,
But at a window. All her looks are sweet,
As the first grapes or cherries, and are watch'd
As near as they are.
    Volp. I must see her.
    Mos. Sir,
There is a guard of spies ten thick upon her,
All his whole household; each of which is set
Upon his fellow, and have all their charge,

When he goes out, when he comes in, examined.
   Volp. I will go see her, though but at her window.
   Mos. In some disguise, then.
   Volp. That is true; I must
Maintain mine own shape still the same: we'll think.   [*Exeunt.*

ACT II

SCENE I.—St. Mark's Place; *a retired corner before*
Corvino's *House.*

Enter Sir Politick Would-be, *and* Peregrine.

   Sir P. Sir, to a wise man, all the world's his soil:
It is not Italy, nor France, nor Europe,
That must bound me, if my fates call me forth.
Yet, I protest, it is no salt desire
Of seeing countries, shifting a religion,
Nor any disaffection to the state
Where I was bred, and unto which I owe
My dearest plots, hath brought me out; much less,
That idle, antique, stale, gray-headed project
Of knowing men's minds and manners, with Ulysses!
But a peculiar humour of my wife's
Laid for this height of Venice, to observe,
To quote, to learn the language, and so forth—
I hope you travel, sir, with license?
   Per. Yes.
   Sir P. I dare the safelier converse——How long, sir,
Since you left England?
   Per. Seven weeks.
   Sir P. So lately!
You have not been with my lord ambassador?
   Per. Not yet, sir.
   Sir P. Pray you, what news, sir, vents our climate?
I heard last night a most strange thing reported
By some of my lord's followers, and I long
To hear how 'twill be seconded.
   Per. What was't, sir?
   Sir P. Marry, sir, of a raven that should build
In a ship royal of the king's.
   Per. This fellow,
Does he gull me, trow? or is gull'd? [*Aside.*] Your name, sir.
   Sir P. My name is Politick Would-be.
   Per. O, that speaks him.—[*Aside.*]
A knight, sir?
   Sir P. A poor knight, sir.
   Per. Your lady
Lies here in Venice, for intelligence

Of tires, and fashions, and behaviour,
Among the courtezans? the fine lady Would-be?

Sir P. Yes, sir; the spider and the bee, ofttimes,
Suck from one flower.

Per. Good sir Politick,
I cry you mercy; I have heard much of you:
'Tis true, sir, of your raven.

Sir P. On your knowledge?

Per. Yes, and your lion's whelping in the Tower.

Sir P. Another whelp!

Per. Another, sir.

Sir P. Now heaven!
What prodigies be these? The fires at Berwick!
And the new star! these things concurring, strange,
And full of omen! Saw you those meteors?

Per. I did, sir.

Sir P. Fearful! Pray you, sir, confirm me,
Were there three porpoises seen above the bridge,
As they give out?

Per. Six, and a sturgeon, sir.

Sir P. I am astonish'd.

Per. Nay, sir, be not so;
I'll tell you a greater prodigy than these.

Sir P. What should these things portend?

Per. The very day
(Let me be sure) that I put forth from London,
There was a whale discover'd in the river,
As high as Woolwich, that had waited there,
Few know how many months, for the subversion
Of the Stode fleet.

Sir P. Is't possible? believe it,
'Twas either sent from Spain, or the archdukes:
Spinola's whale, upon my life, my credit!
Will they not leave these projects? Worthy sir,
Some other news.

Per. Faith, Stone the fool is dead,
And they do lack a tavern fool extremely.

Sir P. Is Mass Stone dead?

Per. He's dead, sir; why, I hope
You thought him not immortal?—O, this knight,
Were he well known, would be a precious thing
To fit our English stage: he that should write
But such a fellow, should be thought to feign
Extremely, if not maliciously.   [*Aside.*

Sir P. Stone dead!

Per. Dead.—Lord! how deeply, sir, you apprehend it?
He was no kinsman to you?

Sir P. That I know of.
Well! that same fellow was an unknown fool.

Per. And yet you knew him, it seems?

Sir P. I did so.   Sir,
I knew him one of the most dangerous heads
Living within the state, and so I held him.

Per. Indeed, sir?

Sir P. While he lived, in action.
He has received weekly intelligence,
Upon my knowledge, out of the Low Countries,
For all parts of the world, in cabbages;
And those dispensed again to ambassadors,
In oranges, musk-melons, apricocks,
Lemons, pome-citrons, and such-like; sometimes
In Colchester oysters, and your Selsey cockles.

Per. You make me wonder.

Sir P. Sir, upon my knowledge.
Nay, I've observed him, at your public ordinary,
Take his advertisement from a traveller,
A conceal'd statesman, in a trencher of meat;
And instantly, before the meal was done,
Convey an answer in a tooth-pick.

Per. Strange!
How could this be, sir?

Sir P. Why, the meat was cut
So like his character, and so laid, as he
Must easily read the cipher.

Per. I have heard,
He could not read, sir.

Sir P. So 'twas given out,
In policy, by those that did employ him:
But he could read, and had your languages,
And to't, as sound a noddle—

Per. I have heard, sir,
That your baboons were spies, and that they were
A kind of subtle nation near to China.

Sir P. Ay, ay, your Mamaluchi.   Faith, they had
Their hand in a French plot or two; but they
Were so extremely given to women, as
They made discovery of all: yet I
Had my advices here, on Wednesday last.
From one of their own coat, they were return'd,
Made their relations, as the fashion is,
And now stand fair for fresh employment.

Per. 'Heart!
This sir Pol will be ignorant of nothing.   [*Aside.*
It seems, sir, you know all.

Sir P. Not all, sir, but
I have some general notions.   I do love
To note and to observe: though I live out,
Free from the active torrent, yet I'd mark

The currents and the passages of things,
For mine own private use; and know the ebbs
And flows of state.
    Per. Believe it, sir, I hold
Myself in no small tie unto my fortunes,
For casting me thus luckily upon you,
Whose knowledge, if your bounty equal it,
May do me great assistance, in instruction
For my behaviour, and my bearing, which
Is yet so rude and raw.
    Sir P. Why, came you forth
Empty of rules for travel?
    Per. Faith, I had
Some common ones, from out that vulgar grammar,
Which he that cried Italian to me, taught me.
    Sir P. Why this it is that spoils all our brave bloods,
Trusting our hopeful gentry unto pedants,
Fellows of outside, and mere bark. You seem
To be a gentleman, of ingenuous race:—
I not profess it, but my fate hath been
To be, where I have been consulted with,
In this high kind, touching some great men's sons,
Persons of blood and honour.—

Enter Mosca *and* Nano *disguised, followed by persons with
materials for erecting a Stage.*

    Per. Who be these, sir?
    Mos. Under that window, there 't must be. The same.
    Sir P. Fellows, to mount a bank. Did your instructor
In the dear tongues, never discourse to you
Of the Italian mountebanks?
    Per. Yes, sir.
    Sir P. Why,
Here you shall see one.
    Per. They are quacksalvers;
Fellows, that live by venting oils and drugs.
    Sir P. Was that the character he gave you of them?
    Per. As I remember.
    Sir P. Pity his ignorance.
They are the only knowing men of Europe!
Great general scholars, excellent physicians,
Most admired statesmen, profest favourites,
And cabinet counsellors to the greatest princes;
The only languaged men of all the world!
    Per. And, I have heard, they are most lewd impostors;
Made all of terms and shreds; no less beliers
Of great men's favours, than their own vile med'cines;
Which they will utter upon monstrous oaths:
Selling that drug for two-pence, ere they part,

Which they have valued at twelve crowns before.

Sir P. Sir, calumnies are answer'd best with silence.

Yourself shall judge.—Who is it mounts, my friends?

Mos. Scoto of Mantua, sir.

Sir P. Is't he? Nay, then
I'll proudly promise, sir, you shall behold
Another man than has been phant'sied to you.
I wonder yet, that he should mount his bank,
Here in this nook, that has been wont t'appear
In face of the Piazza!—Here he comes.

Enter VOLPONE, *disguised as a mountebank Doctor, and followed
by a crowd of people.*

Volp. Mount, zany. [*to Nano.*]

Mob. Follow, follow, follow, follow!

Sir P. See how the people follow him! he's a man
May write ten thousand crowns in bank here. Note,
[*Volpone mounts the Stage.*
Mark but his gesture:—I do use to observe
The state he keeps in getting up.

Per. 'Tis worth it, sir.

*Volp. Most noble gentlemen, and my worthy patrons! It may
seem strange, that I, your Scoto Mantuano, who was ever wont to fix my
bank in face of the public Piazza, near the shelter of the Portico to the
Procuratia, should now, after eight months' absence from this illustrious
city of Venice, humbly retire myself into an obscure nook of the Piazza.*

Sir P. Did not I now object the same?

Per. Peace, sir.

*Volp. Let me tell you: I am not, as your Lombard proverb saith,
cold on my feet; or content to part with my commodities at a cheaper
rate, than I accustomed: look not for it. Nor that the calumnious
reports of that impudent detractor, and shame to our profession,
(Alessandro Buttone, I mean,) who gave out, in public, I was condemned
a sforzato to the galleys, for poisoning the cardinal Bembo's —— cook,
hath at all attached, much less dejected me. No, no, worthy gentlemen;
to tell you true, I cannot endure to see the rabble of these ground ciar-
litani, that spread their cloaks on the pavement, as if they meant to
do feats of activity, and then come in lamely, with their mouldy tales out
of Boccacio, like stale Tabarine, the fabulist: some of them discoursing
their travels, and of their tedious captivity in the Turks' gallies, when,
indeed, were the truth known, they were the Christians' gallies, where
very temperately they eat bread, and drunk water, as a wholesome
penance, enjoined them by their confessors, for base pilferies.*

Sir P. Note but his bearing, and contempt of these.

*Volp. These turdy-facy-nasty-paty-lousy-fartical rogues, with one
poor groat's-worth of unprepared antimony, finely wrapt up in several
scartoccios, are able, very well, to kill their twenty a week, and play;
yet, these meagre, starved spirits, who have half stopt the organs of
their minds with earthy oppilations, want not their favourers among*

*your shrivell'd sallad-eating artizans, who are overjoyed that they may
have their half-pe'rth of physic; though it purge them into another
world, it makes no matter.*

Sir P. Excellent! have you heard better language, sir?

*Volp. Well, let them go. And, gentlemen, honourable gentlemen,
know, that for this time, our bank, being thus removed from the clamours
of the canaglia, shall be the scene of pleasure and delight; for I have
nothing to sell, little or nothing to sell.*

Sir P. I told you, sir, his end.

Per. You did so, sir.

*Volp. I protest, I, and my six servants, are not able to make of this
precious liquor, so fast as it is fetch'd away from my lodging by gentlemen of your city; strangers of the Terra-firma; worshipful merchants;
ay, and senators too: who, ever since my arrival, have detained me to
their uses, by their splendidous liberalities. And worthily; for, what
avails your rich man to have his magazines stuft with moscadelli, or of
the purest grape, when his physicians prescribe him, on pain of death,
to drink nothing but water cocted with aniseeds? O, health! health!
the blessing of the rich! the riches of the poor! who can buy thee at
too dear a rate, since there is no enjoying this world without thee?
Be not then so sparing of your purses, honourable gentlemen, as to
abridge the natural course of life—*

Per. You see his end.

Sir P. Ay, is't not good?

*Volp. For, when a humid flux, or catarrh, by the mutability of air,
falls from your head into an arm or shoulder, or any other part; take
you a ducket, or your chequin of gold, and apply to the place affected:
see what good effect it can work. No, no, 'tis this blessed unguento,
this rare extraction, that hath only power to disperse all malignant
humours, that proceed either of hot, cold, moist, or windy causes—*

Per. I would he had put in dry too.

Sir P. 'Pray you, observe.

*Volp. To fortify the most indigest and crude stomach, ay, were it
of one that, through extreme weakness, vomited blood, applying only a
warm napkin to the place, after the unction and fricace;—for the
vertigine in the head, putting but a drop into your nostrils, likewise
behind the ears; a most sovereign and approved remedy: the mal caduco,
cramps, convulsions, paralysies, epilepsies, tremor-cordia, retired
nerves, ill vapours of the spleen, stopping of the liver, the stone, the
strangury, hernia ventosa, iliaca passio; stops a dysenteria immediately; easeth the torsion of the small guts; and cures melancholia
hypondriaca, being taken and applied according to my printed receipt.*
[Pointing to his bill and his vial.] *For, this is the physician, this the
medicine; this counsels, this cures; this gives the direction, this works
the effect; and, in sum, both together may be termed an abstract of the
theorick and practick in the Æsculapian art. 'Twill cost you eight
crowns. And,—Zan Fritada, prithee sing a verse extempore in
honour of it.*

Sir P. How do you like him, sir?

Per. Most strangely, I!

Sir P. Is not his language rare?

Per. But alchemy,
I never heard the like; or Broughton's books.

NANO *sings.*

> Had old Hippocrates, or Galen,
> That to their books put med'cines all in,
> But known this secret, they had never
> (Of which they will be guilty ever)
> Been murderers of so much paper,
> Or wasted many a hurtless taper;
> No Indian drug had e'er been famed,
> Tobacco, sassafras not named;
> Ne yet, of guacum one small stick, sir,
> Nor Raymund Lully's great elixir.
> Ne had been known the Danish Gonswart,
> Or Paracelsus, with his long sword.

Per. All this, yet, will not do; eight crowns is high.

Volp. No more.—*Gentlemen, if I had but time to discourse to you the miraculous effects of this my oil, surnamed Oglio del Scoto; with the countless catalogue of those I have cured of the aforesaid, and many more diseases; the patents and privileges of all the princes and commonwealths of Christendom; or but the depositions of those that appeared on my part, before the signiory of the Sanità and most learned College of Physicians; where I was authorised, upon notice taken of the admirable virtues of my medicaments, and mine own excellency in matter of rare and unknown secrets, not only to disperse them publicly in this famous city, but in all the territories, that happily joy under the government of the most pious and magnificent states of Italy. But may some other gallant fellow say, O, there be divers that make profession to have as good, and as experimented receipts as yours: indeed, very many have assayed, like apes, in imitation of that, which is really and essentially in me, to make of this oil; bestowed great cost in furnaces, stills, alembecks, continual fires, and preparation of the ingredients, (as indeed there goes to it six hundred several simples, besides some quantity of human fat, for the conglutination, which we buy of the anatomists,) but, when these practitioners come to the last decoction, blow, blow, puff, puff, and all flies in fumo: ha, ha, ha! Poor wretches! I rather pity their folly and indiscretion, than their loss of time and money; for these may be recovered by industry: but to be a fool born, is a disease incurable.*

For myself, I always from my youth have endeavoured to get the rarest secrets, and book them, either in exchange, or for money: I spared nor cost nor labour, where any thing was worthy to be learned. And, gentlemen, honourable gentlemen, I will undertake, by virtue of chemical art, out of the honourable hat that covers your head, to extract the four elements; that is to say, the fire, air, water, and earth, and return you your felt without burn or stain. For, whilst others have been at the Balloo, I have been at my book; and am now past the craggy paths of study, and come to the flowery plains of honour and reputation.

Sir P. I do assure you, sir, that is his aim.

Volp. *But to our price—*

Per. And that withal, sir Pol.

Volp. *You all know, honourable gentlemen, I never valued this ampulla, or vial, at less than eight crowns; but for this time, I am content to be deprived of it for six: six crowns is the price, and less in courtesy I know you cannot offer me; take it or leave it, howsoever, both it and I am at your service. I ask you not as the value of the thing, for then I should demand of you a thousand crowns, so the cardinals Montalto, Fernese, the great Duke of Tuscany, my gossip, with divers other princes, have given me; but I despise money. Only to shew my affection to you, honourable gentlemen, and your illustrious State here, I have neglected the messages of these princes, mine own offices, framed my journey hither, only to present you with the fruits of my travels.—Tune your voices once more to the touch of your instruments, and give the honourable assembly some delightful recreation.*

Per. What monstrous and most painful circumstance
Is here, to get some three or four gazettes,
Some three-pence in the whole! for that 'twill come to.

NANO *sings.*

You that would last long, list to my song,
Make no more coil, but buy of this oil.
Would you be ever fair and young?
Stout of teeth, and strong of tongue?
Tart of palate? quick of ear?
Sharp of sight? of nostril clear?
Moist of hand? and light of foot?
Or, I will come nearer to't,
Would you live free from all diseases?
Do the act your mistress pleases,
Yet fright all aches from your bones?
Here's a medicine for the nones.

Volp. *Well, I am in a humour at this time to make a present of the small quantity my coffer contains; to the rich in courtesy, and to the poor for God's sake. Wherefore now mark: I ask'd you six crowns; and six crowns, at other times, you have paid me; you shall not give me six crowns, nor five, nor four, nor three, nor two, nor one; nor half a ducat; no, nor a moccinigo. Sixpence it will cost you, or six hundred pound—expect no lower price, for, by the banner of my front, I will not bate a bagatine,—that I will have, only, a pledge of your loves, to carry something from amongst you, to shew I am not contemn'd by you. Therefore, now, toss your handkerchiefs, cheerfully, cheerfully; and be advertised, that the first heroic spirit that deigns to grace me with a handkerchief, I will give it a little remembrance of something, beside, shall please it better, than if I had presented it with a double pistolet.*

Per. Will you be that *heroic spark*, sir Pol?

       [*Celia at a window above, throws down her handkerchief.*
O, see! the window has prevented you.

Volp. Lady, I kiss your bounty; and for this timely grace you have done your poor Scoto of Mantua, I will return you, over and above my oil, a secret of that high and inestimable nature, shall make you for ever enamour'd on that minute, wherein your eye first descended on so mean, yet not altogether to be despised, an object. Here is a powder conceal'd in this paper, of which, if I should speak to the worth, nine thousand volumes were but as one page, that page as a line, that line as a word; so short is this pilgrimage of man (which some call life) to the expressing of it. Would I reflect on the price? why, the whole world is but as an empire, that empire as a province, that province as a bank, that bank as a private purse to the purchase of it. I will only tell you; it is the powder that made Venus a goddess (given her by Apollo,) that kept her perpetually young, clear'd her wrinkles, firm'd her gums, fill'd her skin, colour'd her hair; from her derived to Helen, and at the sack of Troy unfortunately lost: till now, in this our age, it was as happily recovered, by a studious antiquary, out of some ruins of Asia, who sent a moiety of it to the court of France, (but much sophisticated,) wherewith the ladies there, now, colour their hair. The rest, at this present, remains with me; extracted to a quintessence: so that, wherever it but touches, in youth it perpetually preserves, in age restores the complexion; seats your teeth, did they dance like virginal jacks, firm as a wall; makes them white as ivory, that were black as—

Enter CORVINO.

      Cor. Spight o' the devil, and my shame! come down here;
Come down;—No house but mine to make your scene?
Signior Flaminio, will you down, sir? down?
What, is my wife your Franciscina, sir?
No windows on the whole Piazza, here, here,
To make your properties, but mine? but mine?

          [*Beats away Volpone, Nano, etc.*
Heart! ere to-morrow I shall be new-christen'd,
And call'd the Pantalone di Besogniosi,
About the town.

      Per. What should this mean, sir Pol?

      Sir P. Some trick of state, believe it; I will home.

      Per. It may be some design on you.

      Sir P. I know not,
I'll stand upon my guard.

      Per. It is your best, sir.

      Sir P. This three weeks, all my advices, all my letters,
They have been intercepted.

Per. Indeed, sir!
Best have a care.
    Sir P. Nay, so I will.
    Per. This knight,
I may not lose him, for my mirth, till night.   [*Exeunt.*

SCENE II.—*A Room in* VOLPONE'S *House.*

Enter VOLPONE *and* MOSCA.

Volp. O, I am wounded!
    Mos. Where, sir?
    Volp. Not without;
Those blows were nothing: I could bear them ever.
But angry Cupid, bolting from her eyes,
Hath shot himself into me like a flame;
Where, now, he flings about his burning heat,
As in a furnace an ambitious fire,
Whose vent is stopt. The fight is all within me.
I cannot live, except thou help me, Mosca;
My liver melts, and I, without the hope
Of some soft air, from her refreshing breath,
Am but a heap of cinders.
    Mos. 'Las, good sir,
Would you had never seen her!
    Volp. Nay, would thou
Had'st never told me of her!
    Mos. Sir, 'tis true;
I do confess I was unfortunate,
And you unhappy: but I'm bound in conscience,
No less than duty, to effect my best
To your release of torment, and I will, sir.
    Volp. Dear Mosca, shall I hope?
    Mos. Sir, more than dear,
I will not bid you to despair of aught
Within a human compass.
    Volp. O, there spoke
My better angel. Mosca, take my keys,
Gold, plate, and jewels, all's at thy devotion;
Employ them how thou wilt; nay, coin me too:
So thou, in this, but crown my longings, Mosca.
    Mos. Use but your patience.
    Volp. So I have.
    Mos. I doubt not
To bring success to your desires.
    Volp. Nay, then,
I not repent me of my late disguise.
    Mos. If you can horn him, sir, you need not.
    Volp. True:
Besides, I never meant him for my heir.—

Is not the colour of my beard and eyebrows
To make me known?
   Mos. No jot.
   Volp. I did it well.
   Mos. So well, would I could follow you in mine,
With half the happiness!—and yet I would
Escape your epilogue.   [*Aside.*
   Volp. But were they gull'd
With a belief that I was Scoto?
   Mos. Sir,
Scoto himself could hardly have distinguish'd!
I have not time to flatter you now; we'll part;
And as I prosper, so applaud my art.   [*Exeunt.*

SCENE III.—*A Room in* CORVINO'S *House.*

Enter CORVINO, *with his sword in his hand, dragging in* CELIA.

   Corv. Death of mine honour, with the city's fool!
A juggling, tooth-drawing, prating mountebank!
And at a public window! where, whilst he,
With his strain'd action, and his dole of faces,
To his drug-lecture draws your itching ears,
A crew of old, unmarried, noted letchers,
Stood leering up like satyrs; and you smile
Most graciously, and fan your favours forth,
To give your hot spectators satisfaction!
What, was your mountebank their call? their whistle?
Or were you enamour'd on his copper rings,
His saffron jewel, with the toad-stone in't,
Or his embroider'd suit, with the cope-stitch,
Made of a herse cloth? or his old tilt-feather?
Or his starch'd beard? Well, you shall have him, yes!
He shall come home, and minister unto you
The fricace for the mother. Or, let me see,
I think you'd rather mount; would you not mount?
Why, if you'll mount, you may; yes, truly, you may:
And so you may be seen, down to the foot.
Get you a cittern, lady Vanity,
And be a dealer with the virtuous man;
Make one: I'll but protest myself a cuckold,
And save your dowry. I'm a Dutchman, I!
For, if you thought me an Italian,
You would be damn'd, ere you did this, you whore!
Thou'dst tremble, to imagine, that the murder
Of father, mother, brother, all thy race,
Should follow, as the subject of my justice.
   Cel. Good sir, have patience.
   Corv. What couldst thou propose
Less to thyself, than in this heat of wrath.

And stung with my dishonour, I should strike
This steel into thee, with as many stabs,
As thou wert gaz'd upon with goatish eyes?
  Cel. Alas, sir, be appeased! I could not think
My being at the window should more now
Move your impatience, than at other times.
  Corv. No! not to seek and entertain a parley
With a known knave, before a multitude!
You were an actor with your handkerchief,
Which he most sweetly kist in the receipt,
And might, no doubt, return it with a letter,
And point the place where you might meet; your sister's,
Your mother's, or your aunt's might serve the turn.
  Cel. Why, dear sir, when do I make these excuses,
Or ever stir abroad, but to the church?
And that so seldom—
  Corv. Well, it shall be less;
And thy restraint before was liberty,
To what I now decree: and therefore mark me.
First, I will have this bawdy light damm'd up;
And till't be done, some two or three yards off,
I'll chalk a line: o'er which if thou but chance
To set thy desperate foot, more hell, more horror,
More wild remorseless rage shall seize on thee,
Than on a conjuror, that had heedless left
His circle's safety ere his devil was laid.
Then here's a lock which I will hang upon thee,
And, now I think on't, I will keep thee backwards;
Thy lodging shall be backwards; thy walks backwards;
Thy prospect, all be backwards; and no pleasure,
That thou shalt know but backwards: nay, since you force
My honest nature, know, it is your own,
Being too open, makes me use you thus:
Since you will not contain your subtle nostrils
In a sweet room, but they must snuff the air
Of rank and sweaty passengers. [*Knocking within.*]—One knocks.
Away, and be not seen, pain of thy life;
Nor look toward the window: if thou dost—
Nay, stay, hear this—let me not prosper, whore,
But I will make thee an anatomy,
Dissect thee mine own self, and read a lecture
Upon thee to the city, and in public.
Away!—   [*Exit Celia.*
          Enter Servant.
      Who's there?
  Serv. 'Tis signior Mosca, sir.
  Corv. Let him come in. [*Exit Serv.*] His master's dead: there's
    yet
Some good to help the bad.—

Enter MOSCA.

My Mosca, welcome!

I guess your news.

    Mos. I fear you cannot, sir.

    Corv. Is't not his death?

    Mos. Rather the contrary.

    Corv. Not his recovery?

    Mos. Yes, sir.

    Corv. I am curs'd,

I am bewitch'd, my crosses meet to vex me.

How? how? how? how?

    Mos. Why, sir, with Scoto's oil;

Corbaccio and Voltore brought of it,

Whilst I was busy in an inner room—

    Corv. Death! that damn'd mountebank; but for the law

Now, I could kill the rascal: it cannot be,

His oil should have that virtue.   Have not I

Known him a common rogue, come fidling in

To the osteria, with a tumbling whore,

And, when he has done all his forced tricks, been glad

Of a poor spoonful of dead wine, with flies in't?

It cannot be.   All his ingredients

Are a sheep's gall, a roasted bitch's marrow,

Some few sod earwigs, pounded caterpillars,

A little capon's grease, and fasting spittle:

I know them to a dram.

    Mos. I know not, sir;

But some on't, there, they pour'd into his ears,

Some in his nostrils, and recover'd him;

Applying but the fricace.

    Corv. Pox o' that fricace!

    Mos. And since, to seem the more officious

And flatt'ring of his health, there, they have had,

At extreme fees, the college of physicians

Consulting on him, how they might restore him;

Where one would have a cataplasm of spices,

Another a flay'd ape clapp'd to his breast,

A third would have it a dog, a fourth an oil,

With wild cats' skins: at last, they all resolved

That, to preserve him, was no other means,

But some young woman must be straight sought out,

Lusty, and full of juice, to sleep by him;

And to this service, most unhappily,

And most unwillingly, am I now employ'd,

Which here I thought to pre-acquaint you with,

For your advice, since it concerns you most;

Because, I would not do that thing might cross

Your ends, on whom I have my whole dependance, sir:

Yet, if I do it not, they may delate
My slackness to my patron, work me out
Of his opinion; and there all your hopes,
Ventures, or whatsoever, are all frustrate!
I do but tell you, sir. Besides, they are all
Now striving, who shall first present him; therefore—
I could entreat you, briefly conclude somewhat;
Prevent them if you can.

   Corv. Death to my hopes,
This is my villainous fortune! Best to hire
Some common courtezan.

   Mos. Ay, I thought on that, sir;
But they are all so subtle, full of art—
And age again doting and flexible,
So as—I cannot tell—we may, perchance,
Light on a quean may cheat us all.

   Corv. 'Tis true.

   Mos. No, no: it must be one that has no tricks, sir,
Some simple thing, a creature made unto it;
Some wench you may command. Have you no kinswoman?
Odso—Think, think, think, think, think, think, think, sir.
One o' the doctors offer'd there his daughter.

   Corv. How!

   Mos. Yes, signior Lupo, the physician.

   Corv. His daughter!

   Mos. And a virgin, sir. Why, alas,
He knows the state of's body, what it is;
That nought can warm his blood, sir, but a fever;
Nor any incantation raise his spirit:
A long forgetfulness hath seized that part.
Besides sir, who shall know it? some one or two—

   Corv. I pray thee give me leave. [*Walks aside.*] If any man
But I had had this luck—The thing in't self,
I know, is nothing—Wherefore should not I
As well command my blood and my affections,
As this dull doctor? In the point of honour,
The cases are all one of wife and daughter.

   Mos. I hear him coming.   [*Aside.*

   Corv. She shall do't: 'tis done.
Slight! if this doctor, who is not engaged,
Unless 't be for his counsel, which is nothing,
Offer his daughter, what should I, that am
So deeply in? I will prevent him: Wretch!
Covetous wretch!—Mosca, I have determined.

   Mos. How, sir?

   Corv. We'll make all sure. The party you wot of
Shall be mine own wife, Mosca.

   Mos. Sir, the thing,
But that I would not seem to counsel you,

I should have motion'd to you, at the first:
And make your count, you have cut all their throats.
Why, 'tis directly taking a possession!
And in his next fit, we may let him go.
'Tis but to pull the pillow from his head,
And he is throttled: it had been done before,
But for your scrupulous doubts.
   Corv. Ay, a plague on't,
My conscience fools my wit! Well, I'll be brief,
And so be thou, lest they should be before us:
Go home, prepare him, tell him with what zeal
And willingness I do it; swear it was
On the first hearing, as thou may'st do, truly,
Mine own free motion.
   Mos. Sir, I warrant you,
I'll so possess him with it, that the rest
Of his starv'd clients shall be banish'd all;
And only you received. But come not, sir,
Until I send, for I have something else
To ripen for your good, you must not know't.
   Corv. But do not you forget to send now.
   Mos. Fear not.   *[Exit.*
   Corv. Where are you, wife? my Celia! wife!

Re-enter CELIA.

                              —What, blubbering?
Come, dry those tears. I think thou thought'st me in earnest;
Ha! by this light I talk'd so but to try thee:
Methinks the lightness of the occasion
Should have confirm'd thee. Come, I am not jealous.
   Cel. No!
   Corv. Faith I am not, I, nor never was;
It is a poor unprofitable humour.
Do not I know, if women have a will,
They'll do 'gainst all the watches of the world,
And that the fiercest spies are tamed with gold?
Tut, I am confident in thee, thou shalt see't;
And see I'll give thee cause too, to believe it.
Come kiss me. Go, and make thee ready, straight,
In all thy best attire, thy choicest jewels,
Put them all on, and, with them, thy best looks:
We are invited to a solemn feast,
At old Volpone's, where it shall appear
How far I am free from jealousy or fear.   *[Exeunt.*

ACT III

SCENE I.—*A Street.*

Enter MOSCA.

Mos. I fear, I shall begin to grow in love
With my dear self, and my most prosperous parts,
They do so spring and burgeon; I can feel
A whimsy in my blood: I know not how,
Success hath made me wanton. I could skip
Out of my skin, now, like a subtle snake,
I am so limber. O! your parasite
Is a most precious thing, dropt from above,
Not bred 'mongst clods and clodpoles, here on earth.
I muse, the mystery was not made a science,
It is so liberally profest! almost
All the wise world is little else, in nature,
But parasites or sub-parasites.—And yet,
I mean not those that have your bare town-art,
To know who's fit to feed them; have no house,
No family, no care, and therefore mould
Tales for men's ears, to bait that sense; or get
Kitchen-invention, and some stale receipts
To please the belly, and the groin; nor those,
With their court dog-tricks, that can fawn and fleer,
Make their revenue out of legs and faces,
Echo my lord, and lick away a moth:
But your fine elegant rascal, that can rise,
And stoop, almost together, like an arrow;
Shoot through the air as nimbly as a star;
Turn short as doth a swallow; and be here,
And there, and here, and yonder, all at once;
Present to any humour, all occasion;
And change a visor, swifter than a thought!
This is the creature had the art born with him;
Toils not to learn it, but doth practise it
Out of most excellent nature: and such sparks
Are the true parasites, others but their zanis.

Enter BONARIO.

Who's this? Bonario, old Corbaccio's son?
The person I was bound to seek.—Fair sir,
You are happily met.
    Bon. That cannot be by thee.
    Mos. Why, sir?
    Bon. Nay, pray thee, know thy way, and leave me:
I would be loth to interchange discourse
With such a mate as thou art.

Mos. Courteous sir,
Scorn not my poverty.

Bon. Not I, by heaven;
But thou shalt give me leave to hate thy baseness.

Mos. Baseness!

Bon. Ay; answer me, is not thy sloth
Sufficient argument? thy flattery?
Thy means of feeding?

Mos. Heaven be good to me!
These imputations are too common, sir,
And easily stuck on virtue when she's poor.
You are unequal to me, and however
Your sentence may be righteous, yet you are not
That, ere you know me, thus proceed in censure:
St. Mark bear witness 'gainst you, 'tis inhuman.   [*Weeps.*

Bon. What! does he weep? the sign is soft and good:
I do repent me that I was so harsh.   [*Aside.*

Mos. 'Tis true, that, sway'd by strong necessity,
I am enforced to eat my careful bread
With too much obsequy; 'tis true, beside,
That I am fain to spin mine own poor raiment
Out of my mere observance, being not born
To a free fortune: but that I have done
Base offices, in rending friends asunder,
Dividing families, betraying counsels,
Whispering false lies, or mining men with praises,
Train'd their credulity with perjuries,
Corrupted chastity, or am in love
With mine own tender ease, but would not rather
Prove the most rugged, and laborious course,
That might redeem my present estimation,
Let me here perish, in all hope of goodness.

Bon. This cannot be a personated passion.—   [*Aside.*
I was to blame, so to mistake thy nature;
Prithee, forgive me: and speak out thy business.

Mos. Sir, it concerns you; and though I may seem,
At first to make a main offence in manners,
And in my gratitude unto my master;
Yet, for the pure love, which I bear all right,
And hatred of the wrong, I must reveal it.
This very hour your father is in purpose
To disinherit you

Bon. How!

Mos. And thrust you forth,
As a mere stranger to his blood; 'tis true, sir,
The work no way engageth me, but, as
I claim an interest in the general state
Of goodness and true virtue, which I hear
To abound in you: and, for which mere respect,

Without a second aim, sir, I have done it.

    Bon. This tale hath lost thee much of the late trust
Thou hadst with me; it is impossible:
I know not how to lend it any thought,
My father should be so unnatural.

    Mos. It is a confidence that well becomes,
Your piety; and form'd, no doubt, it is
From your own simple innocence: which makes
Your wrong more monstrous and abhorr'd. But, sir,
I now will tell you more. This very minute,
It is, or will be doing; and, if you
Shall be but pleased to go with me, I'll bring you,
I dare not say where you shall see, but where
Your ear shall be a witness of the deed;
Hear yourself written bastard, and profest
The common issue of the earth.

    Bon. I am amazed!

    Mos. Sir, if I do it not, draw your just sword,
And score your vengeance on my front and face:
Mark me your villain: you have too much wrong,
And I do suffer for you, sir. My heart
Weeps blood in anguish—

    Bon. Lead; I follow thee.   [*Exeunt.*

SCENE II.—*A Room in* VOLPONE's *House.*

Enter VOLPONE.

    Volp. Mosca stays long, methinks.—Bring forth your sports,
And help to make the wretched time more sweet.

Enter NANO, ANDROGYNO, *and* CASTRONE.

    Nan. Dwarf, fool, and eunuch, well met here we be.
A question it were now, whether of us three,
Being all the known delicates of a rich man,
In pleasing him, claim the precedency can?

    Cas. I claim for myself.

    And. And so doth the fool.

    Nan. 'Tis foolish indeed: let me set you both to school.
First for your dwarf, he's little and witty,
And every thing, as it is little, is pretty;
Else why do men say to a creature of my shape,
So soon as they see him, It's a pretty little ape?
And why a pretty ape, but for pleasing imitation
Of greater men's actions, in a ridiculous fashion?
Beside, this feat body of mine doth not crave
Half the meat, drink, and cloth, one of your bulks will have.
Admit your fool's face be the mother of laughter,
Yet, for his brain, it must always come after:
And though that do feed him, it's a pitiful case,
His body is beholding to such a bad face.   [*Knocking within.*

Volp. Who's there? my couch; away! look! Nano, see:

                                [*Exe. And. and Cas.*

Give me my caps, first——go, enquire. [*Exit Nano.*]—Now, Cupid
Send it be Mosca, and with fair return!

    Nan. [*within.*] It is the beauteous madam—

    Volp. Would-be—is it?

    Nan. The same.

    Volp. Now torment on me! Squire her in;
For she will enter, or dwell here for ever:
Nay, quickly. [*Retires to his couch.*]—That my fit were past! I fear
A second hell too, that my lothing this
Will quite expel my appetite to the other:
Would she were taking now her tedious leave.
Lord, how it threats me what I am to suffer!

Re-enter NANO, *with* Lady POLITICK WOULD-BE.

    Lady P. I thank you, good sir. 'Pray you signify
Unto your patron, I am here.—This band
Shews not my neck enough.—I trouble you, sir;
Let me request you, bid one of my women
Come hither to me.—In good faith, I am drest
Most favourably to-day! It is no matter:
'Tis well enough.—

Enter 1 Waiting-woman.

                   Look, see, these petulant things,
How they have done this!

    Volp. I do feel the fever
Entering in at mine ears; O, for a charm,
To fright it hence!   [*Aside.*

    Lady P. Come nearer: is this curl
In his right place, or this? Why is this higher
Than all the rest? You have not wash'd your eyes, yet!
Or do they not stand even in your head?
Where is your fellow? call her.   [*Exit* 1 *Woman.*

    Nan. Now, St. Mark
Deliver us! anon, she'll beat her women,
Because her nose is red.

Re-enter 1 *with* 2 Woman.

    Lady P. I pray you, view
This tire, forsooth: are all things apt, or no?

    1 *Wom.* One hair a little, here, sticks out, forsooth.

    Lady P. Does't so, forsooth! and where was your dear sight,
When it did so, forsooth! What now! bird-eyed?
And you, too? 'Pray you, both approach and mend it.
Now, by that light, I muse you are not ashamed!
I, that have preach'd these things so oft unto you,
Read you the principles, argued all the grounds,

Disputed every fitness, every grace,
Call'd you to counsel of so frequent dressings—
 Nan. More carefully than of your fame or honour.   *[Aside.*
 Lady P. Made you acquainted, what an ample dowry
The knowledge of these things would be unto you,
Able, alone, to get you noble husbands
At your return: and you thus to neglect it!
Besides you seeing what a curious nation
The Italians are, what will they say of me?
The English lady cannot dress herself.
Here's a fine imputation to our country!
Well, go your ways, and stay in the next room.
This fucus was too coarse too; it's no matter.—
Good sir, you'll give them entertainment?
        [Exeunt Nano and Waiting-women.
 Volp. The storm comes toward me.
 Lady P. [*goes to the couch.*] How does my Volpone?
 Volp. Troubled with noise, I cannot sleep; I dreamt
That a strange fury enter'd, now, my house,
And, with the dreadful tempest of her breath,
Did cleave my roof asunder.
 Lady P. Believe me, and I
Had the most fearful dream, could I remember't—
 Volp. Out on my fate! I have given her the occasion
How to torment me: she will tell me her's.   *[Aside.*
 Lady P. Me thought, the golden mediocrity,
Polite and delicate—
 Volp. O, if you do love me,
No more: I sweat, and suffer, at the mention
Of any dream; feel how I tremble yet.
 Lady P. Alas, good soul! the passion of the heart.
Seed-pearl were good now, boil'd with syrup of apples,
Tincture of gold, and coral, citron-pills,
Your elicampane root, myrobalanes—
 Volp. Ah me, I have ta'en a grass-hopper by the wing! *[Aside.*
 Lady P. Burnt silk, and amber: You have muscadel
Good in the house—
 Volp. You will not drink, and part?
 Lady P. No, fear not that. I doubt, we shall not get
Some English saffron, half a dram would serve;
Your sixteen cloves, a little musk, dried mints,
Bugloss, and barley-meal—
 Volp. She's in again!
Before I feign'd diseases, now I have one.   *[Aside.*
 Lady P. And these applied with a right scarlet cloth.
 Volp. Another flood of words! a very torrent!   *[Aside.*
 Lady P. Shall I, sir, make you a poultice?
 Volp. No, no, no,
I'm very well, you need prescribe no more.

Lady P. I have a little studied physic; but now,
I'm all for music, save, in the forenoons,
An hour or two for painting. I would have
A lady, indeed, to have all, letters and arts,
Be able to discourse, to write, to paint,
But principal, as Plato holds, your music,
And so does wise Pythagoras, I take it,
Is your true rapture: when there is concent
In face, in voice, and clothes: and is, indeed,
Our sex's chiefest ornament.
　　Volp. The poet
As old in time as Plato, and as knowing,
Says, that your highest female grace is silence.
　　Lady P. Which of your poets? Petrarch, or Tasso, or Dante?
Guarini? Ariosto? Aretine?
Cieco di Hadria? I have read them all.
　　Volp. Is every thing a cause to my destruction? 　　[*Aside.*
　　Lady P. I think I have two or three of them about me.
　　Volp. The sun, the sea, will sooner both stand still
Than her eternal tongue! nothing can 'scape it. 　　[*Aside.*
　　Lady P. Here's Pastor Fido—
　　Volp. Profess obstinate silence;
That's now my safest. 　　[*Aside.*
　　Lady P. All our English writers,
I mean such as are happy in the Italian,
Will deign to steal out of this author, mainly:
Almost as much as from Montagnié:
He has so modern and facile a vein,
Fitting the time, and catching the court-ear!
Your Petrarch is more passionate, yet he,
In days of sonnetting, trusted them with much:
Dante is hard, and few can understand him.
But, for a desperate wit, there's Aretine;
Only, his pictures are a little obscene—
You mark me not.
　　Volp. Alas, my mind's perturb'd.
　　Lady P. Why, in such cases, we must cure ourselves,
Make use of our philosophy—
　　Volp. Oh me!
　　Lady P. And as we find our passions do rebel,
Encounter them with reason, or divert them,
By giving scope unto some other humour
Of lesser danger: as, in politic bodies,
There's nothing more doth overwhelm the judgment,
And cloud the understanding, than too much
Settling and fixing, and, as 'twere, subsiding
Upon one object. For the incorporating
Of these same outward things, into that part,
Which we call mental, leaves some certain faeces

That stop the organs, and as Plato says,
Assassinate our knowledge.
 Volp. Now, the spirit
Of patience help me!   [*Aside.*
 Lady P. Come, in faith, I must
Visit you more a days; and make you well:
Laugh and be lusty.
 Volp. My good angel save me!   [*Aside.*
 Lady P. There was but one sole man in all the world,
With whom I e'er could sympathise; and he
Would lie you, often, three, four hours together
To hear me speak; and be sometimes so rapt,
As he would answer me quite from the purpose,
Like you, and you are like him, just. I'll discourse,
An't be but only, sir, to bring you asleep,
How we did spend our time and loves together,
For some six years.
 Volp. Oh, oh, oh, oh, oh, oh!
 Lady P. For we were coætanei, and brought up—
 Volp. Some power, some fate, some fortune rescue me!

Enter MOSCA.

 Mos. God save you, madam!
 Lady P. Good sir.
 Volp. Mosca! welcome,
Welcome to my redemption.
 Mos. Why, sir?
 Volp. Oh,
Rid me of this my torture, quickly, there;
My madam, with the everlasting voice:
The bells, in time of pestilence, ne'er made
Like noise, or were in that perpetual motion!
The Cock-pit comes not near it. All my house,
But now, steam'd like a bath with her thick breath,
A lawyer could not have been heard; nor scarce
Another woman, such a hail of words
She has let fall. For hell's sake, rid her hence.
 Mos. Has she presented?
 Volp. O, I do not care;
I'll take her absence, upon any price,
With any loss.
 Mos. Madam—
 Lady P. I have brought your patron
A toy, a cap here, of mine own work.
 Mos. 'Tis well.
I had forgot to tell you, I saw your knight,
Where you would little think it.—
 Lady P. Where?
 Mos. Marry,

Where yet, if you make haste, you may apprehend
Rowing upon the water in a gondole
With the most cunning courtezan of Venice.

Lady P. Is't true?

Mos. Pursue them, and believe your eyes:
Leave me, to make your gift. [*Exit Lady P. hastily.*]—I knew
     'twould take:
For, lightly, they that use themselves most license,
Are still most jealous.

Volp. Mosca, hearty thanks,
For thy quick fiction, and delivery of me.
Now to my hopes, what say'st thou?

Re-enter Lady P. Would-be.

Lady P. But do you hear, sir?—

Volp. Again! I fear a paroxysm.

Lady P. Which way
Row'd they together?

Mos. Toward the Rialto.

Lady P. I pray you lend me your dwarf.

Mos. I pray you take him.—   [*Exit Lady P.*
Your hopes, sir, are like happy blossoms, fair,
And promise timely fruit, if you will stay
But the maturing; keep you at your couch,
Corbaccio will arrive straight, with the Will;
When he is gone, I'll tell you more.   [*Exit.*

Volp. My blood,
My spirits are return'd; I am alive:
And, like your wanton gamester at primero,
Whose thought had whisper'd to him, not go less,
Methinks I lie, and draw—for an encounter.

[The scene closes upon Volpone.

SCENE II.—The Passage leading to VOLPONE'S Chamber.

Enter MOSCA and BONARIO.

Mos. Sir, here conceal'd, [*shews him a closet.*] you may hear all·
     But, pray you,
Have patience, sir; [*knocking within.*]—the same's your father
     knocks:
I am compell'd to leave you.   [*Exit.*

Bon. Do so.—Yet
Cannot my thought imagine this a truth.   [*Goes into the closet.*

SCENE III.—Another Part of the same.

Enter MOSCA and CORVINO, CELIA following.

Mos. Death on me! you are come too soon, what meant you?
Did not I say, I would send?

Corv. Yes, but I fear'd

You might forget it, and then they prevent us.
   Mos. Prevent! did e'er man haste so, for his horns?
A courtier would not ply it so, for a place.   [*Aside.*
Well, now there is no helping it, stay here;
I'll presently return.   [*Exit.*
   Corv. Where are you, Celia?
You know not wherefore I have brought you hither?
   Cel. Not well, except you told me.
   Corv. Now, I will:
Hark hither.   [*Exeunt.*

SCENE IV.—*A Closet opening into a Gallery.*

Enter MOSCA *and* BONARIO.

   Mos. Sir, your father hath sent word,
It will be half an hour ere he come;
And therefore, if you please to walk the while
Into that gallery—at the upper end,
There are some books to entertain the time:
And I'll take care no man shall come unto you, sir.
   Bon. Yes, I will stay there.—I do doubt this fellow.
     [*Aside, and exit.*
   Mos. [*looking after him.*] There; he is far enough; he can
    hear nothing:
And, for his father, I can keep him off.   [*Exit.*

SCENE V.—VOLPONE'S *Chamber.*—VOLPONE *on his couch.*
MOSCA *sitting by him.*

Enter CORVINO, *forcing in* CELIA.

   Corv. Nay, now, there is no starting back, and therefore,
Resolve upon it: I have so decreed.
It must be done. Nor would I move't afore,
Because I would avoid all shifts and tricks,
That might deny me.
   Cel. Sir, let me beseech you,
Affect not these strange trials; if you doubt
My chastity, why, lock me up for ever;
Make me the heir of darkness. Let me live,
Where I may please your fears, if not your trust.
   Corv. Believe it, I have no such humour, I.
All that I speak I mean; yet I'm not mad;
Nor horn-mad, see you? Go to, shew yourself
Obedient, and a wife.
   Cel. O heaven!
   Corv. I say it,
Do so.
   Cel. Was this the train?
   Corv. I've told you reasons;

What the physicians have set down: how much
It may concern me; what my engagements are;
My means; and the necessity of those means,
For my recovery: wherefore, if you be
Loyal, and mine, be won, respect my venture.

   Cel. Before your honour?

   Corv. Honour! tut, a breath:
There's no such thing in nature: a mere term
Invented to awe fools. What is my gold
The worse for touching, clothes for being look'd on?
Why, this is no more. An old decrepit wretch,
That has no sense, no sinew; takes his meat
With others' fingers; only knows to gape,
When you do scald his gums; a voice, a shadow;
And, what can this man hurt you?

   Cel. Lord! what spirit
Is this hath enter'd him?   [*Aside.*

   Corv. And for your fame,
That's such a jig; as if I would go tell it,
Cry it on the Piazza! who shall know it,
But he that cannot speak it, and this fellow,
Whose lips are in my pocket? save yourself,
(If you'll proclaim't, you may,) I know no other
Shall come to know it.

   Cel. Are heaven and saints then nothing?
Will they be blind or stupid?

   Corv. How!

   Cel. Good sir,
Be jealous still, emulate them; and think
What hate they burn with toward every sin.

   Corv. I grant you: if I thought it were a sin,
I would not urge you. Should I offer this
To some young Frenchman, or hot Tuscan blood
That had read Aretine, conn'd all his prints,
Knew every quirk within lust's labyrinth,
And were professed critic in lechery;
And I would look upon him, and applaud him,
This were a sin: but here, 'tis contrary,
A pious work, mere charity for physic,
And honest polity, to assure mine own.

   Cel. O heaven! canst thou suffer such a change?

   Volp. Thou art mine honour, Mosca, and my pride,
My joy, my tickling, my delight! Go bring them.

   Mos. [*advancing.*] Please you draw near, sir.

   Corv. Come on, what—
You will not be rebellious? by that light—

   Mos. Sir,
Signior Corvino, here, is come to see you.

   Volp. Oh!

Mos. And hearing of the consultation had,
So lately, for your health, is come to offer,
Or rather, sir, to prostitute—
    Corv. Thanks, sweet Mosca.
    Mos. Freely, unask'd, or unintreated—
    Corv. Well.
    Mos. As the true fervent instance of his love,
His own most fair and proper wife; the beauty,
Only of price in Venice—
    Corv. 'Tis well urged.
    Mos. To be your comfortress, and to preserve you.
    Volp. Alas, I am past, already! Pray you, thank him
For his good care and promptness; but for that,
'Tis a vain labour e'en to fight 'gainst heaven;
Applying fire to stone—uh, uh, uh, uh! [*coughing.*]
Making a dead leaf grow again. I take
His wishes gently, though; and you may tell him,
What I have done for him: marry, my state is hopeless.
Will him to pray for me; and to use his fortune
With reverence, when he comes to't.
    Mos. Do you hear, sir?
Go to him with your wife.
    Corv. Heart of my father!
Wilt thou persist thus? come, I pray thee, come.
Thou seest 'tis nothing, Celia. By this hand,
I shall grow violent. Come, do't, I say.
    Cel. Sir, kill me, rather: I will take down poison,
Eat burning coals, do any thing.—
    Corv. Be damn'd!
Heart, I will drag thee hence, home, by the hair;
Cry thee a strumpet through the streets; rip up
Thy mouth unto thine ears; and slit thy nose,
Like a raw rochet!—Do not tempt me; come,
Yield, I am loth—Death! I will buy some slave
Whom I will kill, and bind thee to him, alive;
And at my window hang you forth, devising
Some monstrous crime, which I, in capital letters,
Will eat into thy flesh with aquafortis,
And burning corsives, on this stubborn breast.
Now, by the blood thou hast incensed, I'll do it!
    Cel. Sir, what you please, you may, I am your martyr.
    Corv. Be not thus obstinate, I have not deserved it:
Think who it is intreats you. 'Prithee, sweet;—
Good faith, thou shalt have jewels, gowns, attires,
What thou wilt think, and ask. Do but go kiss him.
Or touch him, but. For my sake.—At my suit.—
This once.—No! not! I shall remember this.
Will you disgrace me thus? Do you thirst my undoing?
    Mos. Nay, gentle lady, be advised.

Corv. No, no.
She has watch'd her time.   Ods precious, this is scurvy,
'Tis very scurvy; and you are—
　　Mos. Nay, good sir.
　　Corv. An arrant locust, by heaven, a locust!
Whore, crocodile, that hast thy tears prepared,
Expecting how thou'lt bid them flow—
　　Mos. Nay, 'pray you, sir!
She will consider.
　　Cel. Would my life would serve
To satisfy—
　　Corv. S'death! if she would but speak to him,
And save my reputation, it were somewhat;
But spightfully to affect my utter ruin!
　　Mos. Ay, now you have put your fortune in her hands.
Why i'faith, it is her modesty, I must quit her.
If you were absent, she would be more coming;
I know it: and dare undertake for her.
What woman can before her husband? 'pray you,
Let us depart, and leave her here.
　　Corv. Sweet Celia,
Thou may'st redeem all, yet; I'll say no more:
If not, esteem yourself as lost.   Nay, stay there.
　　　　　　　[*Shuts the door, and exit with Mosca.*
　　Cel. O God, and his good angels! whither, whither,
Is shame fled human breasts? that with such ease,
Men dare put off your honours, and their own?
Is that, which ever was a cause of life,
Now placed beneath the basest circumstance,
And modesty an exile made, for money?
　　Volp. Ay, in Corvino, and such earth-fed minds,
　　　　　　　　　　　[*Leaping from his couch.*
That never tasted the true heaven of love.
Assure thee, Celia, he that would sell thee,
Only for hope of gain, and that uncertain,
He would have sold his part of Paradise
For ready money, had he met a cope-man.
Why art thou mazed to see me thus revived?
Rather applaud thy beauty's miracle;
'Tis thy great work: that hath, not now alone,
But sundry times raised me, in several shapes,
And, but this morning, like a mountebank,
To see thee at thy window: ay, before
I would have left my practice, for thy love,
In varying figures, I would have contended
With the blue Proteus, or the horned flood.
Now art thou welcome.
　　Cel. Sir!
　　Volp. Nay, fly me not.

Nor let thy false imagination
That I was bed-rid, make thee think I am so:
Thou shalt not find it.   I am, now, as fresh,
As hot, as high, and in as jovial plight,
As when, in that so celebrated scene,
At recitation of our comedy,
For entertainment of the great Valois,
I acted your g Antinous; and attracted
The eyes and ears of all the ladies present,
To admire each graceful gesture, note, and footing.   [*Sings.*

> Come, my Celia, let us prove,
> While we can, the sports of love,
> Time will not be ours for ever,
> He, at length, our good will sever;
> Spend not then his gifts in vain;
> Suns, that set, may rise again;
> But if once we lose this light,
> 'Tis with us perpetual night.
> Why should we defer our joys?
> Fame and rumour are but toys.
> Cannot we delude the eyes
> Of a few poor household spies?
> Or his easier ears beguile,
> Thus removed by our wile?—
> 'Tis no sin love's fruits to steal:
> But the sweet thefts to reveal;
> To be taken, to be seen,
> These have crimes accounted been.

Cel. Some serene blast me, or dire lightning strike
This my offending face!
Volp. Why droops my Celia?
Thou hast, in place of a base husband, found
A worthy lover: use thy fortune well,
With secrecy and pleasure.   See, behold,
What thou art queen of; not in expectation,
As I feed others: but possess'd and crown'd.
See, here, a rope of pearl; and each, more orient
Than that the brave Ægyptian queen caroused:
Dissolve and drink them.   See, a carbuncle,
May put out both the eyes of our St. Mark;
A diamond, would have bought Lollia Paulina,
When she came in like star-light, hid with jewels,
That were the spoils of provinces; take these,
And wear, and lose them: yet remains an ear-ring
To purchase them again, and this whole state.
A gem but worth a private patrimony,
Is nothing: we will eat such at a meal.
The heads of parrots, tongues of nightingales,

The brains of peacocks, and of estriches,
Shall be our food: and, could we get the phœnix,
Though nature lost her kind, she were our dish.
   Cel. Good sir, these things might move a mind affected
With such delights; but I, whose innocence
Is all I can think wealthy, or worth th' enjoying,
And which, once lost, I have nought to lose beyond it,
Cannot be taken with these sensual baits:
If you have conscience—
   Volp. 'Tis the beggar's virtue;
If thou hast wisdom, hear me, Celia.
Thy baths shall be the juice of July-flowers,
Spirit of roses, and of violets,
The milk of unicorns, and panthers' breath
Gather'd in bags, and mixt with Cretan wines.
Our drink shall be prepared gold and amber;
Which we will take, until my roof whirl round
With the vertigo: and my dwarf shall dance,
My eunuch sing, my fool make up the antic,
Whilst we, in changed shapes, act Ovid's tales,
Thou, like Europa now, and I like Jove,
Then I like Mars, and thou like Erycine:
So, of the rest, till we have quite run through,
And wearied all the fables of the gods.
Then will I have thee in more modern forms,
Attired like some sprightly dame of France,
Brave Tuscan lady, or proud Spanish beauty;
Sometimes, unto the Persian sophy's wife;
Or the grand signior's mistress; and, for change,
To one of our most artful courtezans,
Or some quick Negro, or cold Russian;
And I will meet thee in as many shapes:
Where we may so transfuse our wandering souls
Out at our lips, and score up sums of pleasures,   *[Sings.*

      That the curious shall not know
      How to tell them as they flow;
      And the envious, when they find
      What their number is, be pined.

   Cel. If you have ears that will be pierced—or eyes
That can be open'd—a heart that may be touch'd—
Or any part that yet sounds man about you—
If you have touch of holy saints—or heaven—
Do me the grace to let me 'scape—if not,
Be bountiful and kill me. You do know,
I am a creature, hither ill betray'd,
By one, whose shame I would forget it were:
If you will deign me neither of these graces,
Yet feed your wrath, sir, rather than your lust,

(It is a vice comes nearer manliness,)
And punish that unhappy crime of nature,
Which you miscall my beauty: flay my face,
Or poison it with ointments, for seducing
Your blood to this rebellion. Rub these hands,
With what may cause an eating leprosy,
E'en to my bones and marrow: any thing,
That may disfavour me, save in my honour—
And I will kneel to you, pray for you, pay down
A thousand hourly vows, sir, for your health;
Report, and think you virtuous—

  Volp. Think me cold,
Frozen and impotent, and so report me?
That I had Nestor's hernia, thou wouldst think.
I do degenerate, and abuse my nation,
To play with opportunity thus long;
I should have done the act, and then have parley'd.
Yield, or I'll force thee.   *[Seizes her.*

  Cel. O! just God!

  Volp. In vain—

  Bon. [*rushing in.*] Forbear, foul ravisher, libidinous swine!
Free the forced lady, or thou diest, impostor.
But that I'm loth to snatch thy punishment
Out of the hand of justice, thou shouldst, yet,
Be made the timely sacrifice of vengeance,
Before this altar, and this dross, thy idol.—
Lady, let's quit the place, it is the den
Of villainy; fear nought, you have a guard:
And he, ere long, shall meet his just reward.

                        [Exeunt Bon. and Cel.

  Volp. Fall on me, roof, and bury me in ruin!
Become my grave, that wert my shelter! O!
I am unmask'd, unspirited, undone,
Betray'd to beggary, to infamy—

      Enter MOSCA, *wounded and bleeding.*

  Mos. Where shall I run, most wretched shame of men,
To beat out my unlucky brains?

  Volp. Here, here.
What! dost thou bleed?

  Mos. O that his well-driv'n sword
Had been so courteous to have cleft me down
Unto the navel, ere I lived to see
My life, my hopes, my spirits, my patron, all
Thus desperately engaged, by my error!

  Volp. Woe on thy fortune!

  Mos. And my follies, sir.

  Volp. Thou hast made me miserable.

  Mos. And myself, sir.

Who would have thought he would have hearken'd so?
   Volp. What shall we do?
   Mos. I know not; if my heart
Could expiate the mischance, I'd pluck it out.
Will you be pleased to hang me, or cut my throat?
And I'll requite you, sir. Let's die like Romans,
Since we have lived like Grecians.   [*Knocking within.*
   Volp. Hark! who's there?
I hear some footing; officers, the saffi,
Come to apprehend us! I do feel the brand
Hissing already at my forehead; now,
Mine ears are boring.
   Mos. To your couch, sir, you,
Make that place good, however.   [*Volpone lies down, as before.*]
   —Guilty men
Suspect what they deserve still.

Enter CORBACCIO.

Signior Corbaccio!
   Corb. Why, how now, Mosca?
   Mos. O, undone, amazed, sir.
Your son, I know not by what accident,
Acquainted with your purpose to my patron,
Touching your Will, and making him your heir,
Enter'd our house with violence, his sword drawn
Sought for you, call'd you wretch, unnatural,
Vow'd he would kill you.
   Corb. Me!
   Mos. Yes, and my patron.
   Corb. This act shall disinherit him indeed;
Here is the Will.
   Mos. 'Tis well, sir.
   Corb. Right and well:
Be you as careful now for me.

Enter VOLTORE, *behind.*

   Mos. My life, sir,
Is not more tender'd; I am only yours.
   Corb. How does he? will he die shortly, think'st thou?
   Mos. I fear
He'll outlast May.
   Corb. To-day?
   Mos. No, last out May, sir.
   Corb. Could'st thou not give him a dram?
   Mos. O, by no means, sir.
   Corb. Nay, I'll not bid you.
   Volt. [*coming forward.*] This is a knave, I see.
   Mos. [*seeing Voltore.*] How! signior Voltore! did he hear me?
                            [*Aside.*

Volt. Parasite!

Mos. Who's that?—O, sir, most timely welcome—

Volt. Scarce,

To the discovery of your tricks, I fear.
You are his, *only ?* and mine also, are you not?

    Mos. Who? I, sir?

    Volt. You, sir. What device is this
About a Will?

    Mos. A plot for you, sir.

    Volt. Come,

Put not your foists upon me; I shall scent them.

    Mos. Did you not hear it?

    Volt. Yes, I hear Corbaccio
Hath made your patron there his heir.

    Mos. 'Tis true,
By my device, drawn to it by my plot,
With hope—

    Volt. Your patron should reciprocate?
And you have promised?

    Mos. For your good, I did, sir.
Nay, more, I told his son, brought, hid him here,
Where he might hear his father pass the deed:
Being persuaded to it by this thought, sir,
That the unnaturalness, first, of the act,
And then his father's oft disclaiming in him,
(Which I did mean t'help on,) would sure enrage him
To do some violence upon his parent,
On which the law should take sufficient hold,
And you be stated in a double hope:
Truth be my comfort, and my conscience,
My only aim was to dig you a fortune
Out of these two old rotten sepulchres—

    Volt. I cry thee mercy, Mosca.

    Mos. Worth your patience,
And your great merit, sir. And see the change!

    Volt. Why, what success?

    Mos. Most hapless! you must help, sir.
Whilst we expected the old raven, in comes
Corvino's wife, sent hither by her husband—

    Volt. What, with a present?

    Mos. No, sir, on visitation;
(I'll tell you how anon;) and staying long,
The youth he grows impatient, rushes forth,
Seizeth the lady, wounds me, makes her swear
(Or he would murder her, that was his vow)
To affirm my patron to have done her rape:
Which how unlike it is, you see! and hence,
With that pretext he's gone, to accuse his father,
Defame my patron, defeat you—

Volt. Where is her husband?
Let him be sent for straight.
    Mos. Sir, I'll go fetch him.
    Volt. Bring him to the Scrutineo.
    Mos. Sir, I will.
    Volt. This must be stopt.
    Mos. O you do nobly, sir.
Alas, 'twas labour'd all, sir, for your good;
Nor was there want of counsel in the plot:
But fortune can, at any time, o'erthrow
The projects of a hundred learned clerks, sir.
    Corb. [*listening.*] What's that?
    Volt. Will't please you, sir, to go along?
                   [*Exit Corbaccio, followed by Voltore.*
    Mos. Patron, go in, and pray for our success.
    Volp. [*rising from his couch.*] Need makes devotion: heaven
      your labour bless!   [*Exeunt.*

ACT IV

SCENE I.—*A Street.*

Enter Sir Politick Would-be *and* Peregrine.

    Sir P. I told you, sir, it was a plot; you see
What observation is! You mention'd me
For some instructions: I will tell you, sir,
(Since we are met here in this height of Venice,)
Some few particulars I have set down,
Only for this meridian, fit to be known
Of your crude traveller; and they are these.
I will not touch, sir, at your phrase, or clothes,
For they are old.
    Per. Sir, I have better.
    Sir P. Pardon,
I meant, as they are themes.
    Per. O, sir, proceed:
I'll slander you no more of wit, good sir.
    Sir P. First, for your garb, it must be grave and serious,
Very reserv'd and lock'd; not tell a secret
On any terms, not to your father; scarce
A fable, but with caution: make sure choice
Both of your company, and discourse; beware
You never speak a truth—
    Per. How!
    Sir P. Not to strangers,
For those be they you must converse with most;
Others I would not know, sir, but at distance,
So as I still might be a saver in them:

You shall have tricks else past upon you hourly.
And then, for your religion, profess none,
But wonder at the diversity, of all:
And, for your part, protest, were there no other
But simply the laws o' the land, you could content you,
Nic. Machiavel, and Monsieur Bodin, both
Were of this mind.   Then must you learn the use
And handling of your silver fork at meals,
The metal of your glass; (these are main matters
With your Italian;) and to know the hour
When you must eat your melons, and your figs.
   Per. Is that a point of state too?
   Sir P. Here it is:
For your Venetian, if he see a man
Preposterous in the least, he has him straight;
He has; he strips him.   I'll acquaint you, sir,
I now have lived here, 'tis some fourteen months
Within the first week of my landing here,
All took me for a citizen of Venice,
I knew the forms so well—
   Per. And nothing else.   *[Aside.*
   Sir P. I had read Contarene, took me a house,
Dealt with my Jews to furnish it with moveables—
Well, if I could but find one man, one man
To mine own heart, whom I durst trust, I would—
   Per. What, what, sir?
   Sir P. Make him rich; make him a fortune:
He should not think again.   I would command it.
   Per. As how?
   Sir P. With certain projects that I have;
Which I may not discover.
   Per. If I had
But one to wager with, I would lay odds now,
He tells me instantly.   *[Aside.*
   Sir P. One is, and that
I care not greatly who knows, to serve the state
Of Venice with red herrings for three years,
And at a certain rate, from Rotterdam,
Where I have correspondence.   There's a letter,
Sent me from one o' the states, and to that purpose:
He cannot write his name, but that's his mark.
   Per. He is a chandler?
   Sir P. No, a cheesemonger.
There are some others too with whom I treat
About the same negociation;
And I will undertake it: for, 'tis thus.
I'll do't with ease, I have cast it all: Your hoy
Carries but three men in her, and a boy;
And she shall make me three returns a year:

So, if there come but one of three, I save;
If two, I can defalk:—but this is now,
If my main project fail.
 Per. Then you have others?
 Sir P. I should be loth to draw the subtle air
Of such a place, without my thousand aims.
I'll not dissemble, sir: where'er I come,
I love to be considerative; and 'tis true,
I have at my free hours thought upon
Some certain goods unto the state of Venice,
Which I do call *my Cautions;* and, sir, which
I mean, in hope of pension, to propound
To the Great Council, then unto the Forty,
So to the Ten. My means are made already—
 Per. By whom?
 Sir P. Sir, one that, though his place be obscure,
Yet he can sway, and they will hear him. He's
A commandador.
 Per. What! a common serjeant?
 Sir P. Sir, such as they are, put it in their mouths,
What they should say, sometimes,; as well as greater:
I think I have my notes to shew you— [*Searching his pockets.*
 Per. Good sir.
 Sir P. But you shall swear unto me, on your gentry,
Not to anticipate—
 Per. I, sir!
 Sir P. Nor reveal
A circumstance——My paper is not with me.
 Per. O, but you can remember, sir.
 Sir P. My first is
Concerning tinder-boxes. You must know,
No family is here without its box.
Now, sir, it being so portable a thing,
Put case, that you or I were ill affected
Unto the state, sir; with it in our pockets,
Might not I go into the Arsenal,
Or you, come out again, and none the wiser?
 Per. Except yourself, sir.
 Sir P. Go to, then. I therefore
Advertise to the state, how fit it were,
That none but such as were known patriots,
Sound lovers of their country, should be suffer'd
To enjoy them in their houses; and even those
Seal'd at some office, and at such a bigness
As might not lurk in pockets.
 Per. Admirable!
 Sir P. My next is, how to enquire, and be resolv'd,
By present demonstration, whether a ship,
Newly arrived from Soria, or from

Any suspected part of all the Levant,
Be guilty of the plague: and where they use
To lie out forty, fifty days, sometimes,
About the Lazaretto, for their trial;
I'll save that charge and loss unto the merchant,
And in an hour clear the doubt.

    Per. Indeed, sir!

    Sir P. Or—I will lose my labour.

    Per. 'My faith, that's much.

    Sir P. Nay, sir, conceive me. It will cost me in onions,
Some thirty livres—

    Per. Which is one pound sterling.

    Sir P. Beside my water-works: for this I do, sir
First, I bring in your ship 'twixt two brick walls;
But those the state shall venture: On the one
I strain me a fair tarpauling, and in that
I stick my onions, cut in halves: the other
Is full of loop-holes, out at which I thrust
The noses of my bellows; and those bellows
I keep, with water-works, in perpetual motion,
Which is the easiest matter of a hundred.
Now, sir, your onion, which doth naturally
Attract the infection, and your bellows blowing
The air upon him, will show, instantly,
By his changed colour, if there be contagion;
Or else remain as fair as at the first.
—Now it is known, 'tis nothing.

    Per. You are right, sir.

    Sir P. I would I had my note.

    Per. 'Faith, so would I:
But you have done well for once, sir.

    Sir P. Were I false,
Or would be made so, I could shew you reasons
How I could sell this state now to the Turk,
Spite of their gallies, or their—   [*Examining his papers.*

    Per. Pray you, sir Pol.

    Sir P. I have them not about me.

    Per. That I fear'd:
They are there, sir.

    Sir P. No, this is my diary,
Wherein I note my actions of the day.

    Per. Pray you, let's see, sir. What is here? *Notandum,* [*Reads.*
A rat had gnawn my spur-leathers; notwithstanding,
I put on new, and did go forth: but first
I threw three beans over the threshold. Item,
I went and bought two tooth-picks, whereof one
I burst immediately, in a discourse
With a Dutch merchant, 'bout ragion del stato.
From him I went and paid a moccinigo

For piecing my silk stockings; by the way
I cheapen'd sprats; and at St. Mark's I urined.
'Faith these are politic notes!
　　Sir P. Sir, I do slip
No action of my life, but thus I quote it.
　　Per. Believe me, it is wise!
　　Sir P. Nay, sir, read forth.

Enter, at a distance, Lady POLITICK WOULD-BE, NANO, *and*
　　　　　　　two Waiting-women.

　　Lady P. Where should this loose knight be, trow? sure he's
　　　　housed.
　　Nan. Why, then he's fast.
　　Lady P. Ay, he plays both with me.
I pray you stay.　This heat will do more harm
To my complexion, than his heart is worth.
(I do not care to hinder, but to take him.)
How it comes off!　　　　　　　　　　[*Rubbing her cheeks.*
　　1 *Wom.* My master's yonder.
　　Lady P. Where?
　　2 *Wom.* With a young gentleman.
　　Lady P. That same's the party;
In man's apparel! 'Pray you, sir, jog my knight:
I will be tender to his reputation,
However he demerit.
　　Sir P. [*seeing her.*] My lady!
　　Per. Where?
　　Sir P. 'Tis she indeed, sir; you shall know her.　She is,
Were she not mine, a lady of that merit,
For fashion and behaviour; and for beauty
I durst compare—
　　Per. It seems you are not jealous,
That dare commend her.
　　Sir P. Nay, and for discourse—
　　Per. Being your wife, she cannot miss that.
　　Sir P. [*introducing Per.*] Madam,
Here is a gentleman, pray you, use him fairly;
He seems a youth, but he is—
　　Lady P. None.
　　Sir P. Yes, one
Has put his face as soon into the world—
　　Lady P. You mean, as early? but to-day?
　　Sir P. How's this?
　　Lady P. Why, in this habit, sir; you apprehend me:—
Well, master Would-be, this doth not become you;
I had thought the odour, sir, of your good name
Had been more precious to you; that you would not
Have done this dire massacre on your honour;
One of your gravity and rank besides!

But knights, I see, care little for the oath
They make to ladies; chiefly, their own ladies.
   Sir P. Now, by my spurs, the symbol of my knighthood,—
   Per. Lord, how his brain is humbled for an oath!   [*Aside.*
   Sir P. I reach you not.
   Lady P. Right, sir, your policy
May bear it through thus.—Sir, a word with you.   [*To Per.*
I would be loth to contest publicly
With any gentlewoman, or to seem
Froward, or violent, as the courtier says;
It comes too near rusticity in a lady,
Which I would shun by all means: and however
I may deserve from master Would-be, yet
T'have one fair gentlewoman thus be made
The unkind instrument to wrong another,
And one she knows not, ay, and to persévér;
In my poor judgment, is not warranted
From being a solecism in our sex,
If not in manners.
   Per. How is this!
   Sir P. Sweet madam,
Come nearer to your aim.
   Lady P. Marry, and will, sir.
Since you provoke me with your impudence,
And laughter of your light land-syren here,
Your Sporus, your hermaphrodite—
   Per. What's here?
Poetic fury, and historic storms!
   Sir P. The gentleman, believe it, is of worth,
And of our nation.
   Lady P. Ay, your White-friars nation.
Come, I blush for you, master Would-be, I;
And am asham'd you should have no more forehead,
Than thus to be the patron, or St. George,
To a lewd harlot, a base fricatrice,
A female devil, in a male outside.
   Sir P. Nay,
An you be such a one, I must bid adieu
To your delights. The case appears too liquid.   [*Exit.*
   Lady P. Ay, you may carry't clear, with your state-face!—
But for your carnival concupiscence,
Who here is fled for liberty of conscience,
From furious persecution of the marshal,
Her will I dis'ple.
   Per. This is fine, i'faith!
And do you use this often? Is this part
Of your wit's exercise, 'gainst you have occasion?
Madam—
   Lady P. Go to, sir.

Per. Do you hear me, lady?
Why, if your knight have set you to beg shirts,
Or to invite me home, you might have done it
A nearer way, by far.
Lady P. This cannot work you
Out of my snare.
Per. Why, am I in it, then?
Indeed your husband told me you were fair.
And so you are; only your nose inclines,
That side that's next the sun, to the queen-apple.
Lady P. This cannot be endur'd by any patience.

Enter MOSCA.

Mos. What is the matter, madam?
Lady P. If the senate
Right not my quest in this, I will protest them
To all the world, no aristocracy.
Mos. What is the injury, lady?
Lady P. Why, the callet
You told me of, here I have ta'en disguised.
Mos. Who? this! what means your ladyship? the creature
I mention'd to you is apprehended now,
Before the senate; you shall see her—
Lady P. Where?
Mos. I'll bring you to her. This young gentleman,
I saw him land this morning at the port.
Lady P. Is't possible! how has my judgment wander'd?
Sir, I must, blushing, say to you, I have err'd;
And plead your pardon.
Per. What, more changes yet!
Lady P. I hope you have not the malice to remember
A gentlewoman's passion. If you stay
In Venice here, please you to use me, sir—
Mos. Will you go, madam?
Lady P. 'Pray you, sir, use me; in faith,
The more you see me, the more I shall conceive
You have forgot our quarrel.
[*Exeunt Lady Would-be, Mosca, Nano, and Waiting-women.*
Per. This is rare!
Sir Politick Would-be? no; sir Politick Bawd,
To bring me thus acquainted with his wife!
Well, wise sir Pol, since you have practised thus
Upon my freshman-ship, I'll try your salt-head,
What proof it is against a counter-plot. [*Exit.*

SCENE II.—*The Scrutineo, or Senate-House.*

Enter VOLTORE, CORBACCIO, CORVINO, *and* MOSCA.

Volt. Well, now you know the carriage of the business,
Your constancy is all that is required

Unto the safety of it.
   Mos. Is the lie
Safely convey'd amongst us? is that sure?
Knows every man his burden?
   Corv. Yes.
   Mos. Then shrink not.
   Corv. But knows the advocate the truth?
   Mos. O, sir,
By no means; I devised a formal tale,
That salv'd your reputation. But be valiant, sir.
   Corv. I fear no one but him, that this his pleading
Should make him stand for a co-heir—
   Mos. Co-halter!
Hang him; we will but use his tongue, his noise,
As we do croakers here.
   Corv. Ay, what shall he do?
   Mos. When we have done, you mean?
   Corv. Yes.
   Mos. Why, we'll think:
Sell him for mummia; he's half dust already.
Do you not smile, [*to Voltore.*] to see this buffalo,
How he doth sport it with his head?—I should,
If all were well and past. [*Aside.*]—Sir, [*to Corbaccio.*] only you
Are he that shall enjoy the crop of all,
And these not know for whom they toil.
   Corb. Ay, peace.
   Mos. [*turning to Corvino.*] But you shall eat it. Much! [*Aside.*]
   —Worshipful sir, [*to Voltore.*]
Mercury sit upon your thundering tongue,
Or the French Hercules, and make your language
As conquering as his club, to beat along,
As with a tempest, flat, our adversaries;
But much more yours, sir.
   Volt. Here they come, have done.
   Mos. I have another witness, if you need, sir,
I can produce.
   Volt. Who is it?
   Mos. Sir, I have her.

Enter Avocatori *and take their seats,* BONARIO, CELIA, Notario,
   Commandadori, Saffi, *and other* Officers *of justice.*

   1 *Avoc.* The like of this the senate never heard of.
   2 *Avoc.* 'Twill come most strange to them when we report it.
   4 *Avoc.* The gentlewoman has been ever held
Of unreproved name.
   3 *Avoc.* So has the youth.
   4 *Avoc.* The more unnatural part that of his father.
   2 *Avoc.* More of the husband.
   1 *Avoc.* I not know to give

His act a name, it is so monstrous!

4 *Avoc.* But the impostor, he's a thing created
To exceed example!

1 *Avoc.* And all after-times!

2 *Avoc.* I never heard a true voluptuary
Described, but him.

3 *Avoc.* Appear yet those were cited?

Not. All but the old magnifico, Volpone.

1 *Avoc.* Why is not he here?

Mos. Please your fatherhoods,
Here is his advocate: himself's so weak,
So feeble—

4 *Avoc.* What are you?

Bon. His parasite,
His knave, his pandar: I beseech the court,
He may be forced to come, that your grave eyes
May bear strong witness of his strange impostures.

Volt. Upon my faith and credit with your virtues,
He is not able to endure the air.

2 *Avoc.* Bring him, however.

3 *Avoc.* We will see him.

4 *Avoc.* Fetch him.

Volt. Your fatherhoods' fit pleasures be obey'd;

[*Exeunt Officers.*

But sure, the sight will rather move your pities,
Than indignation. May it please the court,
In the mean time, he may be heard in me;
I know this place most void of prejudice,
And therefore crave it, since we have no reason
To fear our truth should hurt our cause.

3 *Avoc.* Speak free.

Volt. Then know, most honour'd fathers, I must now
Discover to your strangely abused ears,
The most prodigious and most frontless piece
Of solid impudence, and treachery,
That ever vicious nature yet brought forth
To shame the state of Venice. This lewd woman,
That wants no artificial looks or tears
To help the vizor she has now put on,
Hath long been known a close adulteress
To that lascivious youth there; not suspected,
I say, but known, and taken in the act
With him; and by this man, the easy husband,
Pardon'd; whose timeless bounty makes him now
Stand here, the most unhappy, innocent person,
That ever man's own goodness made accused.
For these not knowing how to owe a gift
Of that dear grace, but with their shame; being placed
So above all powers of their gratitude,

Began to hate the benefit; and, in place
Of thanks, devise to extirpe the memory
Of such an act: wherein I pray your fatherhoods
To observe the malice, yea, the rage of creatures
Discover'd in their evils; and what heart
Such take, even from their crimes:—but that anon
Will more appear.—This gentleman, the father,
Hearing of this foul fact, with many others,
Which daily struck at his too tender ears,
And grieved in nothing more than that he could not
Preserve himself a parent, (his son's ills
Growing to that strange flood,) at last decreed
To disinherit him.

   1 *Avoc.* These be strange turns!
   2 *Avoc.* The young man's fame was ever fair and honest.
   Volt. So much more full of danger is his vice,
That can beguile so under shade of virtue.
But, as I said, my honour'd sires, his father
Having this settled purpose, by what means
To him betray'd, we know not, and this day
Appointed for the deed; that parricide,
I cannot style him better, by confederacy
Preparing this his paramour to be there,
Enter'd Volpone's house, (who was the man,
Your fatherhoods must understand, design'd
For the inheritance,) there sought his father:—
But with what purpose sought he him, my lords?
I tremble to pronounce it, that a son
Unto a father, and to such a father,
Should have so foul, felonious intent!
It was to murder him: when being prevented
By his more happy absence, what then did he?
Not check his wicked thoughts; no, now new deeds,
(Mischief doth never end where it begins)
An act of horror, fathers! he dragg'd forth
The aged gentleman that had there lain bed-rid
Three years and more, out of his innocent couch,
Naked upon the floor, there left him; wounded
His servant in the face: and, with this strumpet
The stale to his forged practice, who was glad
To be so active,—(I shall here desire
Your fatherhoods to note but my collections,
As most remarkable,—) thought at once to stop
His father's ends, discredit his free choice
In the old gentleman, redeem themselves,
By laying infamy upon this man,
To whom, with blushing, they should owe their lives.

   1 *Avoc.* What proofs have you of this?
   Bon. Most honoured fathers,

I humbly crave there be no credit given
To this man's mercenary tongue.

2 Avoc. Forbear.

Bon. His soul moves in his fee.

3 Avoc. O, sir.

Bon. This fellow,

For six sols more, would plead against his Maker.

1 Avoc. You do forget yourself.

Volt. Nay, nay, grave fathers,
Let him have scope: can any man imagine
That he will spare his accuser, that would not
Have spared his parent?

1 Avoc. Well, produce your proofs.

Cel. I would I could forget I were a creature.

Volt. Signior Corbaccio!   [*Corbaccio comes forward.*

4 Avoc. What is he?

Volt. The father.

2 Avoc. Has he had an oath?

Not. Yes.

Corb. What must I do now?

Not. Your testimony's craved.

Corb. Speak to the knave?
I'll have my mouth first stopt with earth; my heart
Abhors his knowledge: I disclaim in him.

1 Avoc. But for what cause?

Corb. The mere portent of nature!
He is an utter stranger to my loins.

Bon. Have they made you to this?

Corb. I will not hear thee,
Monster of men, swine, goat, wolf, parricide!
Speak not, thou viper.

Bon. Sir, I will sit down,
And rather wish my innocence should suffer,
Than I resist the authority of a father.

Volt. Signior Corvino!   [*Corvino comes forward.*

2 Avoc. This is strange.

1 Avoc. Who's this?

Not. The husband.

4 Avoc. Is he sworn?

Not. He is.

3 Avoc. Speak, then

Corv. This woman, please your fatherhoods, is a whore,
Of most hot exercise, more than a partrich,
Upon record—

1 Avoc. No more.

Corv. Neighs like a jennet,

Not. Preserve the honour of the court.

Corv. I shall,
And modesty of your most reverend ears.

And yet I hope that I may say, these eyes
Have seen her glued unto that piece of cedar,
That fine well-timber'd gallant; and that here
The letters may be read, thorough the horn,
That make the story perfect.

   Mos. Excellent! sir.

   Corv. There is no shame in this now, is there? [*Aside to Mosca.*

   Mos. None.

   Corv. Or if I said, I hoped that she were onward
To her damnation, if there be a hell
Greater than whore and woman; a good catholic
May make the doubt.

   3 Avoc. His grief hath made him frantic.

   1 Avoc. Remove him hence.

   2 Avoc. Look to the woman.   [*Celia swoons.*

   Corv. Rare!
Prettily feign'd, again!

   4 Avoc. Stand from about her.

   1 Avoc. Give her the air.

   3 Avoc. What can you say?   [*To Mosca.*

   Mos. My wound,
May it please your wisdoms, speaks for me, received
In aid of my good patron, when he mist
His sought-for father, when that well-taught dame
Had her cue given her, to cry out, A rape!

   Bon. O most laid impudence! Fathers—

   3 Avoc. Sir, be silent;
You had your hearing free, so must they theirs.

   2 Avoc. I do begin to doubt the imposture here.

   4 Avoc. This woman has too many moods.

   Volt. Grave fathers,
She is a creature of a most profest
And prostituted lewdness.

   Corv. Most impetuous,
Unsatisfied, grave fathers!

   Volt. May her feignings
Not take your wisdoms: but this day she baited
A stranger, a grave knight, with her loose eyes,
And more lascivious kisses. This man saw them
Together on the water, in a gondola.

   Mos. Here is the lady herself, that saw them too;
Without; who then had in the open streets
Pursued them, but for saving her knight's honour.

   1 Avoc. Produce that lady.

   2 Avoc. Let her come.

   4 Avoc. These things,   [*Exit Mosca.*
They strike with wonder.

   3 Avoc. I am turn'd a stone.

Re-enter Mosca *with* Lady Would-be.

Mos. Be resolute, madam.
   Lady P. Ay, this same is she.   [*Pointing to Celia*
Out, thou camelion harlot! now thine eyes
Vie tears with the hyæna. Dar'st thou look
Upon my wronged face?—I cry your pardons,
I fear I have forgettingly transgrest
Against the dignity of the court—
   2 Avoc. No, madam.
   Lady P. And been exorbitant—
   2 Avoc. You have not, lady.
   4 Avoc. These proofs are strong.
   Lady P. Surely, I had no purpose
To scandalise your honours, or my sex's.
   3 Avoc. We do believe it.
   Lady P. Surely, you may believe it.
   2 Avoc. Madam, we do.
   Lady P. Indeed you may; my breeding
Is not so coarse—
   4 Avoc. We know it.
   Lady P. To offend
With pertinacy—
   3 Avoc. Lady—
   Lady P. Such a presence!
No surely.
   1 Avoc. We well think it.
   Lady P. You may think it.
   1 Avoc. Let her o'ercome. What witnesses have you
To make good your report?
   Bon. Our consciences.
   Cel. And heaven, that never fails the innocent.
   4 Avoc. These are no testimonies.
   Bon. Not in your courts,
Where multitude, and clamour overcomes.
   1 Avoc. Nay, then you do wax insolent.

Re-enter Officers, *bearing* Volpone *on a couch.*

   Volt. Here, here,
The testimony comes, that will convince,
And put to utter dumbness their bold tongues:
See here, grave fathers, here's the ravisher,
The rider on men's wives, the great impostor,
The grand voluptuary! Do you not think
These limbs should affect venery? or these eyes
Covet a concubine? pray you mark these hands;
Are they not fit to stroke a lady's breasts?—
Perhaps he doth dissemble!

Bon. So he does.

Volt. Would you have him tortured?

Bon. I would have him proved.

Volt. Best try him then with goads, or burning irons;
Put him to the strappado: I have heard
The rack hath cured the gout; 'faith, give it him,
And help him of a malady; be courteous.
I'll undertake, before these honour'd fathers,
He shall have yet as many left diseases,
As she has known adulterers, or thou strumpets.—
O, my most equal hearers, if these deeds,
Acts of this bold and most exorbitant strain,
May pass with sufferance, what one citizen
But owes the forfeit of his life, yea, fame,
To him that dares traduce him? which of you
Are safe, my honour'd fathers? I would ask,
With leave of your grave fatherhoods, if their plot
Have any face or colour like to truth?
Or if, unto the dullest nostril here,
It smell not rank, and most abhorred slander?
I crave your care of this good gentleman,
Whose life is much endanger'd by their fable;
And as for them, I will conclude with this,
That vicious persons, when they're hot and flesh'd
In impious acts, their constancy abounds:
Damn'd deeds are done with greatest confidence.

    1 Avoc. Take them to custody, and sever them.

    2 Avoc. 'Tis pity two such prodigies should live.

    1 Avoc. Let the old gentleman be return'd with care.

                    [Exeunt Officers with Volpone.
I'm sorry our credulity hath wrong'd him.

    4 Avoc. These are two creatures!

    3 Avoc. I've an earthquake in me.

    2 Avoc. Their shame, even in their cradles, fled their faces.

    4 Avoc. You have done a worthy service to the state, sir,
In their discovery.   *[To Volt.*

    1 Avoc. You shall hear, ere night,
What punishment the court decrees upon them.

    [Exeunt Avocat., Not., and Officers with Bonario and Celia.

Volt. We thank your fatherhoods.—How like you it?

    Mos. Rare.
I'd have your tongue, sir, tipt with gold for this;
I'd have you be the heir to the whole city;
The earth I'd have want men, ere you want living:
They're bound to erect your statue in St. Mark's.
Signior Corvino, I would have you go
And shew yourself, that you have conquer'd.

    Corv. Yes.

    Mos. It was much better that you should profess

Yourself a cuckold thus, than that the other
Should have been proved.

Corv. Nay, I consider'd that:
Now it is her fault.

    Mos. Then it had been yours.

    Corv. True; I do doubt this advocate still.

    Mos. I'faith
You need not, I dare ease you of that care.

    Corv. I trust thee, Mosca.   *[Exit.*

    Mos. As your own soul, sir.

    Corb. Mosca!

    Mos. Now for your business, sir.

    Corb. How! have you business?

    Mos. Yes, your's, sir.

    Corb. O, none else?

    Mos. None else, not I.

    Corb. Be careful, then.

    Mos. Rest you with both your eyes, sir.

    Corb. Dispatch it.

    Mos. Instantly.

    Corb. And look that all,
Whatever, be put in, jewels, plate, moneys,
Household stuff, bedding, curtains.

    Mos. Curtain-rings, sir:
Only the advocate's fee must be deducted.

    Corb. I'll pay him now; you'll be too prodigal.

    Mos. Sir, I must tender it.

    Corb. Two chequines is well.

    Mos. No, six, sir.

    Corb. 'Tis too much.

    Mos. He talk'd a great while;
You must consider that, sir.

    Corb. Well, there's three—

    Mos. I'll give it him.

    Corb. Do so, and there's for thee.   *[Exit.*

    Mos. Bountiful bones! What horrid strange offence
Did he commit 'gainst nature, in his youth,
Worthy this age? *[Aside.]*—You see, sir, *[to Volt.]* how I work
Unto your ends: take you no notice.

    Volt. No,
I'll leave you.   *[Exit.*

    Mos. All is yours, the devil and all:
Good advocate!—Madam, I'll bring you home.

    Lady P. No, I'll go see your patron.

    Mos. That you shall not:
I'll tell you why. My purpose is to urge
My patron to reform his Will; and for
The zeal you have shewn to-day, whereas before
You were but third or fourth, you shall be now

Put in the first: which would appear as begg'd,
If you were present. Therefore—
   Lady P. You shall sway me.   *[Exeunt.*

ACT V

SCENE I.—*A Room in* VOLPONE'S *House.*

Enter VOLPONE.

   Volp. Well, I am here, and all this brunt is past.
I ne'er was in dislike with my disguise
Till this fled moment: here 'twas good, in private;
But in your public,—*cave* whilst I breathe.
'Fore God, my left leg 'gan to have the cramp,
And I apprehended straight some power had struck me
With a dead palsy: Well! I must be merry,
And shake it off. A many of these fears
Would put me into some villainous disease,
Should they come thick upon me: I'll prevent 'em.
Give me a bowl of lusty wine, to fright
This humour from my heart. *[Drinks.]*—Hum, hum, hum!
'Tis almost gone already; I shall conquer.
Any device, now, of rare ingenious knavery,
That would possess me with a violent laughter,
Would make me up again. *[Drinks again.]*—So, so, so, so!
This heat is life; 'tis blood by this time:—Mosca!

Enter MOSCA.

   Mos. How now, sir? does the day look clear again?
Are we recover'd, and wrought out of error,
Into our way, to see our path before us?
Is our trade free once more?
   Volp. Exquisite Mosca!
   Mos. Was it not carried learnedly?
   Volp. And stoutly:
Good wits are greatest in extremities.
   Mos. It were a folly beyond thought, to trust
Any grand act unto a cowardly spirit:
You are not taken with it enough, methinks.
   Volp. O, more than if I had enjoy'd the wench:
The pleasure of all woman-kind's not like it.
   Mos. Why now you speak, sir. We must here be fix'd;
Here we must rest; this is our master-piece;
We cannot think to go beyond this.
   Volp. True,
Thou hast play'd thy prize, my precious Mosca.
   Mos. Nay, sir,
To gull the court—

Volp. And quite divert the torrent
Upon the innocent.
 Mos. Yes, and to make
So rare a music out of discords—
 Volp. Right.
That yet to me's the strangest, how thou hast borne it!
That these, being so divided 'mongst themselves,
Should not scent somewhat, or in me or thee,
Or doubt their own side.
 Mos. True, they will not see't.
Too much light blinds them, I think. Each of them
Is so possest and stuft with his own hopes,
That any thing unto the contrary,
Never so true, or never so apparent,
Never so palpable, they will resist it—
 Volp. Like a temptation of the devil.
 Mos. Right, sir.
Merchants may talk of trade, and your great signiors
Of land that yields well; but if Italy
Have any glebe more fruitful than these fellows,
I am deceiv'd. Did not your advocate rare?
 Volp. O—*My most honour'd fathers, my grave fathers,*
Under correction of your fatherhoods,
What face of truth is here? If these strange deeds
May pass, most honour'd fathers—I had much ado
To forbear laughing.
 Mos. It seem'd to me, you sweat, sir.
 Volp. In troth, I did a little.
 Mos. But confess, sir,
Were you not daunted?
 Volp. In good faith, I was
A little in a mist, but not dejected;
Never, but still my self.
 Mos. I think it, sir.
Now, so truth help me, I must needs say this, sir,
And out of conscience for your advocate,
He has taken pains, in faith, sir, and deserv'd,
In my poor judgment, I speak it under favour,
Not to contrary you, sir, very richly—
Well—to be cozen'd.
 Volp. Troth, and I think so too,
By that I heard him, in the latter end.
 Mos. O, but before, sir: had you heard him first
Draw it to certain heads, then aggravate,
Then use his vehement figures—I look'd still
When he would shift a shirt: and, doing this
Out of pure love, no hope of gain—
 Volp. 'Tis right.
I cannot answer him, Mosca, as I would,

Not yet; but for thy sake, at thy entreaty,
I will begin, even now—to vex them all,
This very instant.

 Mos. Good sir.

 Volp. Call the dwarf
And eunuch forth.

 Mos. Castrone, Nano!

    Enter CASTRONE *and* NANO.

 Nano. Here.

 Volp. Shall we have a jig now?

 Mos. What you please, sir.

 Volp. Go,
Straight give out about the streets, you two,
That I am dead; do it with constancy,
Sadly, do you hear? impute it to the grief
Of this late slander.   [*Exeunt Cast. and Nano.*

 Mos. What do you mean, sir?

 Volp. O,
I shall have instantly my Vulture, Crow,
Raven, come flying hither, on the news,
To peck for carrion, my she-wolf, and all,
Greedy, and full of expectation—

 Mos. And then to have it ravish'd from their mouths!

 Volp. 'Tis true. I will have thee put on a gown,
And take upon thee, as thou wert mine heir:
Shew them a will: Open that chest, and reach
Forth one of those that has the blanks; I'll straight
Put in thy name.

 Mos. It will be rare, sir.   [*Gives him a paper.*

 Volp. Ay,
When they ev'n gape, and find themselves deluded—

 Mos. Yes.

 Volp. And thou use them scurvily!
Dispatch, get on thy gown.

 Mos. [*putting on a gown.*] But what, sir, if they ask
After the body?

 Volp. Say, it was corrupted.

 Mos. I'll say, it stunk, sir; and was fain to have it
Coffin'd up instantly, and sent away.

 Volp. Any thing; what thou wilt. Hold, here's my will.
Get thee a cap, a count-book, pen and ink,
Papers afore thee; sit as thou wert taking
An inventory of parcels: I'll get up
Behind the curtain, on a stool, and hearken;
Sometime peep over, see how they do look,
With what degrees their blood doth leave their faces,
O, 'twill afford me a rare meal of laughter!

Mos. [*putting on a cap, and setting out the table, etc.*] Your
    advocate will turn stark dull upon it.

Volp. It will take off his oratory's edge.

Mos. But your clarissimo, old round-back, he
Will crump you like a hog-louse, with the touch.

Volp. And what Corvino?

Mos. O, sir, look for him,
To-morrow morning, with a rope and dagger,
To visit all the streets; he must run mad.
My lady too, that came into the court,
To bear false witness for your worship—

Volp. Yes,
And kiss'd me 'fore the fathers, when my face
Flow'd all with oils.

Mos. And sweat, sir. Why, your gold
Is such another med'cine, it dries up
All those offensive savours: it transforms
The most deformed, and restores them lovely,
As 'twere the strange poetical girdle. Jove
Could not invent t' himself a shroud more subtle
To pass Acrisius' guards. It is the thing
Makes all the world her grace, her youth, her beauty.

Volp. I think she loves me.

Mos. Who? the lady, sir?
She's jealous of you.

Volp. Dost thou say so?   [*Knocking within.*

Mos. Hark,
There's some already.

Volp. Look.

Mos. It is the Vulture;
He has the quickest scent.

Volp. I'll to my place,
Thou to thy posture.   [*Goes behind the curtain.*

Mos. I am set.

Volp. But, Mosca,
Play the artificer now, torture them rarely.

Enter VOLTORE.

Volt. How now, my Mosca?

Mos. [*writing.*] *Turkey carpets, nine*—

Volt. Taking an inventory! that is well.

Mos. *Two suits of bedding, tissue*—

Volt. Where's the Will?
Let me read that the while

Enter Servants, *with* CORBACCIO *in a chair.*

Corb. So, set me down,
And get you home.   [*Exeunt Servants.*

Volt. Is he come now, to trouble us!

Mos. *Of cloth of gold, two more—*
Corb. Is it done, Mosca?
Mos. *Of several velvets eight—*
Volt. I like his care.
Corb. Dost thou not hear?

Enter CORVINO.

Corb. Ha! is the hour come, Mosca?
Volp. [*peeping over the curtain.*] Ay, now they muster.
Corv. What does the advocate here,
Or this Corbaccio?
Corb. What do these here?

Enter Lady POL. WOULD-BE.

Lady P. Mosca!
Is his thread spun?
Mos. *Eight chests of linen—*
Volp. O,
My fine dame Would-be, too!
Corv. Mosca, the Will,
That I may shew it these, and rid them hence.
Mos. *Six chests of diaper, four of damask.*—There.
[*Gives them the Will carelessly, over his shoulder.*
Corb. Is that the Will?
Mos. *Down-beds and bolsters—*
Volp. Rare!
Be busy still. Now they begin to flutter:
They never think of me. Look, see, see, see!
How their swift eyes run over the long deed,
Unto the name, and to the legacies,
What is bequeathed them there—
Mos. *Ten suits of hangings—*
Volp. Ay, in their garters, Mosca. Now their hopes
Are at the gasp.
Volt. Mosca the heir!
Corb. What's that?
Volp. My advocate is dumb; look to my merchant,
He has heard of some strange storm, a ship is lost,
He faints; my lady will swoon. Old glazen eyes,
He hath not reach'd his despair yet.
Corb. All these
Are out of hope; I am, sure, the man. [*Takes the Will.*
Corv. But, Mosca—
Mos. *Two cabinets.*
Corv. Is this in earnest?
Mos. *One
Of ebony—*
Corv. Or do you but delude me?
Mos. *The other, mother of pearl*—I am very busy.

Good faith, it is a fortune thrown upon me—
Item, one salt of agate—not my seeking.
   Lady P. Do you hear, sir?
   Mos. *A perfumed box*—'Pray you forbear,
You see I'm troubled—*made of an onyx*—
   Lady P. How!
   Mos. To-morrow or next day, I shall be at leisure
To talk with you all.
   Corv. Is this my large hope's issue?
   Lady P. Sir, I must have a fairer answer.
   Mos. Madam!
Marry, and shall: 'pray you, fairly quit my house.
Nay, raise no tempest with your looks; but hark you,
Remember what your ladyship offer'd me
To put you in an heir; go to, think on it:
And what you said e'en your best madams did
For maintenance; and why not you? Enough.
Go home, and use the poor sir Pol, your knight, well,
For fear I tell some riddles; go, be melancholy.
                               [Exit Lady Would-be.

   Volp. O, my fine devil!
   Corv. Mosca, 'pray you a word.
   Mos. Lord! will you not take your dispatch hence yet?
Methinks, of all, you should have been the example.
Why should you stay here? with what thought, what promise?
Hear you; do you not know, I know you an ass,
And that you would most fain have been a wittol,
If fortune would have let you? that you are
A declared cuckold, on good terms? This pearl,
You'll say, was yours? right: this diamond?
I'll not deny't, but thank you. Much here else?
It may be so. Why, think that these good works
May help to hide your bad. I'll not betray you;
Although you be but extraordinary,
And have it only in title, it sufficeth:
Go home, be melancholy too, or mad.   *[Exit Corvino.*
   Volp. Rare Mosca! how his villainy becomes him!
   Volt. Certain he doth delude all these for me.
   Corb. Mosca the heir!
   Volp. O, his four eyes have found it.
   Corb. I am cozen'd, cheated, by a parasite slave;
Harlot, thou hast gull'd me.
   Mos. Yes, sir. Stop your mouth,
Or I shall draw the only tooth is left.
Are not you he, that filthy covetous wretch,
With the three legs, that here, in hope of prey,
Have, any time this three years, snuff'd about,
With your most grovelling nose, and would have hired
Me to the poisoning of my patron, sir?

Are not you he that have to-day in court
Profess'd the disinheriting of your son?
Perjured yourself?   Go home, and die, and stink.
If you but croak a syllable, all comes out:
Away, and call your porters! [*Exit Corbaccio.*]   Go, go, stink.
   Volp. Excellent varlet!
   Volt. Now, my faithful Mosca,
I find thy constancy.
   Mos. Sir!
   Volt. Sincere.
   Mos. [*writing.*] *A table
Of porphyry*—I marle you'll be thus troublesome.
   Volt. Nay, leave off now, they are gone.
   Mos. Why, who are you?
What! who did send for you?   O, cry you mercy,
Reverend sir!   Good faith, I am grieved for you,
That any chance of mine should thus defeat
Your (I must needs say) most deserving travails:
But I protest, sir, it was cast upon me,
And I could almost wish to be without it,
But that the will o' the dead must be observ'd.
Marry, my joy is that you need it not;
You have a gift, sir, (thank your education,)
Will never let you want, while there are men,
And malice, to breed causes. Would I had
But half the like, for all my fortune, sir!
If I have any suits, as I do hope,
Things being so easy and direct, I shall not,
I will make bold with your obstreperous aid,
Conceive me,—for your fee, sir. In mean time,
You that have so much law, I know have the conscience
Not to be covetous of what is mine.
Good sir, I thank you for my plate; 'twill help
To set up a young man. Good faith, you look
As you were costive; best go home and purge, sir. [*Exit Voltore.*
   Volp. [*comes from behind the curtain.*] Bid him eat lettuce well.
     My witty mischief,
Let me embrace thee. O that I could now
Transform thee to a Venus!—Mosca, go,
Straight take my habit of clarissimo,
And walk the streets; be seen, torment them more:
We must pursue, as well as plot. Who would
Have lost this feast?
   Mos. I doubt it will lose them.
   Volp. O, my recovery shall recover all.
That I could now but think on some disguise
To meet them in, and ask them questions:
How I would vex them still at every turn!
   Mos. Sir, I can fit you.

Volp. Canst thou?

Mos. Yes, I know
One o' the commandadori, sir, so like you;
Him will I straight make drunk, and bring you his habit.

Volp. A rare disguise, and answering thy brain!
O, I will be a sharp disease unto them.

Mos. Sir, you must look for curses—

Volp. Till they burst;
The Fox fares ever best when he is curst.   [*Exeunt.*

SCENE II.—*A Hall in* Sir POLITICK's *House.*

Enter PEREGRINE *disguised, and three* Merchants.

Per. Am I enough disguised?

1 Mer. I warrant you.

Per. All my ambition is to fright him only.

2 Mer. If you could ship him away, 'twere excellent.

3 Mer. To Zant, or to Aleppo?

Per. Yes, and have his
Adventures put i' the Book of Voyages,
And his gull'd story register'd for truth.
Well, gentlemen, when I am in a while,
And that you think us warm in our discourse,
Know your approaches.

1 Mer. Trust it to our care.   [*Exeunt Merchants.*

Enter Waiting-woman.

Per. Save you, fair lady! Is sir Pol within?

Wom. I do not know, sir.

Per. Pray you say unto him,
Here is a merchant, upon earnest business,
Desires to speak with him.

Wom. I will see, sir.   [*Exit.*

Per. Pray you.—
I see the family is all female here.

Re-enter Waiting-woman.

Wom. He says, sir, he has weighty affairs of state,
That now require him whole; some other time
You may possess him.

Per. Pray you say again.
If those require him whole, these will exact him,
Whereof I bring him tidings.   [*Exit Woman.*]—What might be
His grave affair of state now! how to make
Bolognian sausages here in Venice, sparing
One o' the ingredients?

Re-enter Waiting-woman.

Wom. Sir, he says, he knows
By your word *tidings*, that you are no statesman,

And therefore wills you stay.

Per. Sweet, pray you return him;
I have not read so many proclamations,
And studied them for words, as he has done—
But—here he deigns to come.   [*Exit Woman*

Enter Sir POLITICK.

Sir P. Sir, I must crave
Your courteous pardon. There hath chanced to-day,
Unkind disaster 'twixt my lady and me;
And I was penning my apology,
To give her satisfaction, as you came now.

Per. Sir, I am grieved I bring you worse disaster:
The gentleman you met at the port to-day,
That told you, he was newly arrived—

Sir P. Ay, was
A fugitive punk?

Per. No, sir, a spy set on you;
And he has made relation to the senate,
That you profest to him to have a plot
To sell the State of Venice to the Turk.

Sir P. O me!

Per. For which, warrants are sign'd by this time,
To apprehend you, and to search your study
For papers—

Sir P. Alas, sir, I have none, but notes
Drawn out of play-books—

Per. All the better, sir.

Sir P. And some essays. What shall I do?

Per. Sir, best
Convey yourself into a sugar-chest;
Or, if you could lie round, a frail were rare,
And I could send you aboard.

Sir P. Sir, I but talk'd so,
For discourse sake merely.   [*Knocking within.*

Per. Hark! they are there.

Sir P. I am a wretch, a wretch!

Per. What will you do, sir?
Have you ne'er a currant-butt to leap into?
They'll put you to the rack; you must be sudden.

Sir P. Sir, I have an ingine—

3 Mer. [*within.*] Sir Politick Would-be!

2 Mer. [*within.*] Where is he?

Sir P. That I have thought upon before time.

Per. What is it?

Sir P. I shall ne'er endure the torture.
Marry, it is, sir, of a tortoise-shell,
Fitted for these extremities: pray you, sir, help me.
Here I've a place, sir, to put back my legs,

Please you to lay it on, sir, [*lies down while Peregrine places
    the shell upon him.*]—with this cap,
And my black gloves. I'll lie, sir, like a tortoise,
'Till they are gone.
    Per. And call you this an ingine?
    Sir P. Mine own device——Good sir, bid my wife's women
To burn my papers.   [*Exit Peregrine.*

           The three Merchants *rush in.*

    1 *Mer.* Where is he hid?
    3 *Mer.* We must,
And will sure find him.
    2 *Mer.* Which is his study?

            Re-enter PEREGRINE.

    1 *Mer.* What
Are you, sir?
    Per. I am a merchant, that came here
To look upon this tortoise.
    3 *Mer.* How!
    1 *Mer.* St. Mark!
What beast is this!
    Per. It is a fish.
    2 *Mer.* Come out here!
    Per. Nay, you may strike him, sir, and tread upon him;
He'll bear a cart.
    1 *Mer.* What, to run over him?
    Per. Yes, sir.
    3 *Mer.* Let's jump upon him.
    2 *Mer.* Can he not go?
    Per. He creeps, sir.
    1 *Mer.* Let's see him creep.
    Per. No, good sir, you will hurt him.
    2 *Mer.* Heart, I will see him creep, or prick his guts.
    3 *Mer.* Come out here!
    Per. Pray you, sir!—Creep a little.   [*Aside to Sir Politick.*
    1 *Mer.* Forth.
    2 *Mer.* Yet farther.
    Per. Good sir!—Creep.
    2 *Mer.* We'll see his legs.
              [*They pull off the shell and discover him.*
    3 *Mer.* Ods so, he has garters!
    1 *Mer.* Ay, and gloves!
    2 *Mer.* Is this
Your fearful tortoise?
    Per. [*discovering himself.*] Now, sir Pol, we are even;
For your next project I shall be prepared:
I am sorry for the funeral of your notes, sir.
    1 *Mer.* 'Twere a rare motion to be seen in Fleet-street.

2 *Mer.* Ay, in the Term.
1 *Mer.* Or Smithfield, in the fair.
3 *Mer.* Methinks 'tis but a melancholy sight.
Per. Farewell, most politic tortoise!

[*Exeunt Per. and Merchants.*

Re-enter Waiting-woman.

Sir P. Where's my lady?
Knows she of this?
Wom. I know not, sir.
Sir P. Enquire.—
O, I shall be the fable of all feasts,
The freight of the gazetti, ship-boy's tale;
And, which is worst, even talk for ordinaries.
Wom. My lady's come most melancholy home,
And says, sir, she will straight to sea, for physic.
Sir P. And I to shun this place and clime for ever,
Creeping with house on back, and think it well
To shrink my poor head in my politic shell.   [*Exeunt.*

SCENE III.—*A Room in* VOLPONE'S *House.*

Enter MOSCA *in the habit of a Clarissimo, and* VOLPONE *in
that of a Commandadore.*

Volp. Am I then like him?
Mos. O, sir, you are he;
No man can sever you.
Volp. Good.
Mos. But what am I?
Volp. 'Fore heaven, a brave clarissimo; thou becom'st it!
Pity thou wert not born one.
Mos. If I hold
My made one, 'twill be well.   [*Aside.*
Volp. I'll go and see
What news first at the court.   [*Exit.*
Mos. Do so.   My Fox
Is out of his hole, and ere he shall re-enter,
I'll make him languish in his borrow'd case,
Except he come to composition with me.—
Androgyno, Castrone, Nano!

Enter ANDROGYNO, CASTRONE, *and* NANO.

All. Here.
Mos. Go, recreate yourselves abroad; go sport.—   [*Exeunt.*
So, now I have the keys, and am possest.
Since he will needs be dead afore his time,
I'll bury him, or gain by him: I am his heir,
And so will keep me, till he share at least.
To cozen him of all, were but a cheat

Well placed; no man would construe it a sin:
Let his sport pay for't. This is call'd the Fox-trap.   [*Exit.*

SCENE IV.—*A Street.*

Enter CORBACCIO *and* CORVINO.

Corb. They say, the court is set.

Corv. We must maintain
Our first tale good, for both our reputations.

Corb. Why, mine's no tale: my son would there have kill'd me.

Corv. That's true, I had forgot:—mine is, I'm sure.   [*Aside.*
But for your Will, sir.

Corb. Ay, I'll come upon him
For that hereafter, now his patron's dead.

Enter VOLPONE.

Volp. Signior Corvino! and Corbaccio! sir,
Much joy unto you.

Corv. Of what?

Volp. The sudden good
Dropt down upon you—

Corb. Where?

Volp. And none knows how,
From old Volpone, sir.

Corb. Out, arrant knave!

Volp. Let not your too much wealth, sir, make you furious.

Corb. Away, thou varlet!

Volp. Why, sir?

Corb. Dost thou mock me?

Volp. You mock the world, sir; did you not change Wills?

Corb. Out, harlot!

Volp. O! belike you are the man,
Signior Corvino? 'faith, you carry it well;
You grow not mad withal; I love your spirit:
You are not over-leaven'd with your fortune.
You should have some would swell now, like a wine-fat,
With such an autumn——Did he give you all, sir?

Corv. Avoid, you rascal!

Volp. Troth, your wife has shewn
Herself a very woman; but you are well,
You need not care, you have a good estate,
To bear it out, sir, better by this chance:
Except Corbaccio have a share.

Corb. Hence, varlet.

Volp. You will not be acknown, sir; why, 'tis wise.
Thus do all gamesters, at all games, dissemble:
No man will seem to win. [*Exeunt Corvino and Corbaccio.*]—Here
     comes my vulture,
Heaving his beak up in the air, and snuffing.

Enter VOLTORE.

Volt. Outstript thus, by a parasite! a slave,
Would run on errands, and make legs for crumbs!
Well, what I'll do—

Volp. The court stays for your worship.
I e'en rejoice, sir, at your worship's happiness,
And that it fell into so learned hands,
That understand the fingering—

Volt. What do you mean?

Volp. I mean to be a suitor to your worship,
For the small tenement, out of reparations,
That, to the end of your long row of houses,
By the Piscaria: it was, in Volpone's time,
Your predecessor, ere he grew diseased,
A handsome, pretty, custom'd bawdy-house
As any was in Venice, none dispraised;
But fell with him: his body and that house
Decay'd together.

Volt. Come, sir, leave your prating.

Volp. Why, if your worship give me but your hand,
That I may have the refusal, I have done.
'Tis a mere toy to you, sir; candle-rents;
As your learn'd worship knows—

Volt. What do I know?

Volp. Marry, no end of your wealth, sir; God decrease it!

Volt. Mistaking knave! what, mock'st thou my misfortune?
                                                    [*Exit.*

Volp. His blessing on your heart, sir; would 'twere more!—
Now to my first again, at the next corner.   [*Exit.*

SCENE V.—*Another part of the Street.*

Enter CORBACCIO *and* CORVINO;—MOSCA *passes over the
Stage, before them.*

Corb. See, in our habit! see the impudent varlet!

Corv. That I could shoot mine eyes at him like gun-stones!

Enter VOLPONE.

Volp. But is this true, sir, of the parasite?

Corb. Again, to afflict us! monster!

Volp. In good faith, sir,
I'm heartily grieved, a beard of your grave length
Should be so over-reach'd. I never brook'd
That parasite's hair; methought his nose should cozen:
There still was somewhat in his look, did promise
The bane of a clarissimo.

Corb. Knave—

Volp. Methinks

Yet you, that are so traded in the world,
A witty merchant, the fine bird, Corvino,
That have such moral emblems on your name,
Should not have sung your shame, and dropt your cheese,
To let the Fox laugh at your emptiness.

    Corv. Sirrah, you think the privilege of the place,
And your red saucy cap, that seems to me
Nail'd to your jolt-head with those two chequines,
Can warrant your abuses; come you hither:
You shall perceive, sir, I dare beat you; approach.

    Volp. No haste, sir, I do know your valour well,
Since you durst publish what you are, sir.

    Corv. Tarry,
I'd speak with you.

    Volp. Sir, sir, another time—

    Corv. Nay, now.

    Volp. O lord, sir! I were a wise man,
Would stand the fury of a distracted cuckold.

                            [As he is running off, re-enter Mosca.

    Corb. What, come again!

    Volp. Upon 'em, Mosca; save me.

    Corb. The air's infected where he breathes.

    Corv. Let's fly him   *[Exeunt Corv. and Corb.*

    Volp. Excellent basilisk! turn upon the vulture.

Enter VOLTORE.

    Volt. Well, flesh-fly, it is summer with you now;
Your winter will come on.

    Mos. Good advocate,
Prithee not rail, nor threaten out of place thus;
Thou'lt make a solecism, as madam says.
Get you a biggin more, your brain breaks loose.   *[Exit.*

    Volt. Well, sir.

    Volp. Would you have me beat the insolent slave,
Throw dirt upon his first good clothes?

    Volt. This same
Is doubtless some familiar.

    Volp. Sir, the court,
In troth, stays for you. I am mad, a mule
That never read Justinian, should get up,
And ride an advocate. Had you no quirk
To avoid gullage, sir, by such a creature?
I hope you do but jest; he has not done it,
'Tis but confederacy, to blind the rest.
You are the heir.

    Volt. A strange, officious,
Troublesome knave! thou dost torment me.

    Volp. I know—
It cannot be, sir, that you should be cozen'd;

'Tis not within the wit of man to do it;
You are so wise, so prudent; and 'tis fit
That wealth and wisdom still should go together.   *[Exeunt.*

SCENE VI.—*The Scrutineo or Senate-House.*

Enter Avocatori, Notario, BONARIO, CELIA, CORBACCIO,
CORVINO, Commandadori, Saffi, *etc.*

1 Avoc. Are all the parties here?
Not. All but the advocate.
2 Avoc. And here he comes.

Enter VOLTORE *and* VOLPONE.

1 Avoc. Then bring them forth to sentence.
  Volt. O, my most honour'd fathers, let your mercy
Once win upon your justice, to forgive—
I am distracted—
    Volp. What will he do now?   *[Aside.*
    Volt. O,
I know not which to address myself to first;
Whether your fatherhoods, or these innocents—
    Corv. Will he betray himself?   *[Aside.*
    Volt. Whom equally
I have abused, out of most covetous ends—
    Corv. The man is mad!
    Corb. What's that?
    Corv. He is possest.
  Volt. For which, now struck in conscience, here, I prostrate
Myself at your offended feet, for pardon.
    1, 2 Avoc. Arise.
    Cel. O heaven, how just thou art!
    Volp. I am caught
In mine own noose—   *[Aside.*
    Corv. [*to Corbaccio.*] Be constant, sir: nought now
Can help, but impudence.
    1 Avoc. Speak forward.
    Com. Silence!
  Volt. It is not passion in me, reverend fathers,
But only conscience, conscience, my good sires,
That makes me now tell truth. That parasite,
That knave, hath been the instrument of all.
    1 Avoc. Where is that knave? fetch him.
    Volp. I go.   *[Exit.*
    Corv. Grave fathers,
This man's distracted; he confest it now:
For, hoping to be old Volpone's heir,
Who now is dead—
    3 Avoc. How!
    2 Avoc. Is Volpone dead?

Corv. Dead since, grave fathers.

Bon. O sure vengeance!

1 *Avoc.* Stay,
Then he was no deceiver.

Volt. O no, none:
The parasite, grave fathers.

Corv. He does speak
Out of mere envy, 'cause the servant's made
The thing he gaped for: please your fatherhoods,
This is the truth, though I'll not justify
The other, but he may be some-deal faulty.

Volt. Ay, to your hopes, as well as mine, Corvino:
But I'll use modesty. Pleaseth your wisdoms,
To view these certain notes, and but confer them;
As I hope favour, they shall speak clear truth.

Corv. The devil has enter'd him!

Bon. Or bides in you.

4 *Avoc.* We have done ill, by a public officer
To send for him, if he be heir.

2 *Avoc.* For whom?

4 *Avoc.* Him that they call the parasite.

3 *Avoc.* 'Tis true,
He is a man of great estate, now left.

4 *Avoc.* Go you, and learn his name, and say, the court
Entreats his presence here, but to the clearing
Of some few doubts.   [*Exit Notary.*

2 *Avoc.* This same's a labyrinth!

1 *Avoc.* Stand you unto your first report?

Corv. My state,
My life, my fame—

Bon. Where is it?

Corv. Are at the stake.

1 *Avoc.* Is yours so too?

Corb. The advocate's a knave,
And has a forked tongue—

2 *Avoc.* Speak to the point.

Corb. So is the parasite too.

1 *Avoc.* This is confusion.

Volt. I do beseech your fatherhoods, read but those—
                          [*Giving them papers.*

Corv. And credit nothing the false spirit hath writ:
It cannot be, but he's possest, grave fathers.   [*The scene closes.*

SCENE VII.—*A Street.*

Enter VOLPONE.

Volp. To make a snare for mine own neck! and run
My head into it, wilfully! with laughter!
When I had newly 'scaped, was free, and clear,

Out of mere wantonness! O, the dull devil
Was in this brain of mine, when I devised it,
And Mosca gave it second; he must now
Help to sear up this vein, or we bleed dead.—

    Enter NANO, ANDROGYNO, *and* CASTRONE.

How now! who let you loose? whither go you now?
What, to buy gingerbread, or to drown kitlings?
  Nan. Sir, master Mosca call'd us out of doors,
And bid us all go play, and took the keys.
  And. Yes.
  Volp. Did master Mosca take the keys? why so!
I'm farther in. These are my fine conceits!
I must be merry, with a mischief to me!
What a vile wretch was I, that could not bear
My fortune soberly? I must have my crotchets,
And my conundrums! Well, go you, and seek him:
His meaning may be truer than my fear.
Bid him, he straight come to me to the court;
Thither will I, and, if't be possible,
Unscrew my advocate, upon new hopes:
When I provoked him, then I lost myself.   [*Exeunt.*

    SCENE VIII.—*The Scrutineo, or Senate-House.*

\vocatori, BONARIO, CELIA, CORBACCIO, CORVINO, Comman-
    dadori, Saffi, *etc., as before.*

  1 *Avoc.* These things can ne'er be reconciled. He, here,
                      [*Shewing the papers.*
Professeth, that the gentleman was wrong'd,
And that the gentlewoman was brought thither,
Forced by her husband, and there left.
  Volt. Most true.
  Cel. How ready is heaven to those that pray!
  1 *Avoc.* But that
Volpone would have ravish'd her, he holds
Utterly false, knowing his impotence.
  Corv. Grave fathers, he's possest; again, I say,
Possest: nay, if there be possession, and
Obsession, he has both.
  3 *Avoc.* Here comes our officer.

    Enter VOLPONE.

  Volp. The parasite will straight be here, grave fathers.
  4 *Avoc.* You might invent some other name, sir varlet.
  3 *Avoc.* Did not the notary meet him?
  Volp. Not that I know.
  4 *Avoc.* His coming will clear all.
  2 *Avoc.* Yet, it is misty.

Volt. May't please your fatherhoods—

Volp. [*whispers Volt.*] Sir, the parasite
Will'd me to tell you, that his master lives;
That you are still the man; your hopes the same;
And this was only a jest—

Volt. How?

Volp. Sir, to try
If you were firm, and how you stood affected.

Volt. Art sure he lives?

Volp. Do I live, sir?

Volt. O me!
I was too violent.

Volp. Sir, you may redeem it.
They said, you were possest; fall down, and seem so:
I'll help to make it good. [*Voltore falls.*]—God bless the man!—
Stop your wind hard, and swell—See, see, see, see!
He vomits crooked pins! his eyes are set,
Like a dead hare's hung in a poulter's shop!
His mouth's running away! Do you see, signior?
Now it is in his belly.

Corv. Ay, the devil!

Volp. Now in his throat.

Corv. Ay, I perceive it plain.

Volp. 'Twill out, 'twill out! stand clear. See where it flies,
In shape of a blue toad, with a bat's wings!
Do you not see it, sir?

Corb. What? I think I do.

Corv. 'Tis too manifest.

Volp. Look! he comes to himself!

Volt. Where am I?

Volp. Take good heart, the worst is past, sir.
You are dispossest.

1 Avoc. What accident is this!

2 Avoc. Sudden, and full of wonder!

3 Avoc. If he were
Possest, as it appears, all this is nothing.

Corv. He has been often subject to these fits.

1 Avoc. Shew him that writing:—do you know it, sir?

Volp. [*whispers Volt.*] Deny it, sir, forswear it; know it not.

Volt. Yes, I do know it well, it is my hand;
But all that it contains is false.

Bon. O practice!

2 Avoc. What maze is this!

1 Avoc. Is he not guilty then,
Whom you there name the parasite?

Volt. Grave fathers,
No more than his good patron, old Volpone.

4 Avoc. Why, he is dead.

Volt. O no, my honour'd fathers,

He lives—
  1 *Avoc.* How! lives?
  Volt. Lives.
  2 *Avoc.* This is subtler yet!
  3 *Avoc.* You said he was dead.
  Volt. Never.
  3 *Avoc.* You said so.
  Corv. I heard so.
  4 *Avoc.* Here comes the gentleman; make him way.

Enter MOSCA.

  3 *Avoc.* A stool.
  4 *Avoc.* A proper man; and, were Volpone dead,
A fit match for my daughter.   [*Aside.*
  3 *Avoc.* Give him way.
  Volp. Mosca, I was almost lost; the advocate
Had betrayed all; but now it is recovered;
All's on the hinge again——Say, I am living.   [*Aside to Mos.*
  Mos. What busy knave is this!—Most reverend fathers,
I sooner had attended your grave pleasures,
But that my order for the funeral
Of my dear patron, did require me—
  Volp. Mosca!   [*Aside.*
  Mos. Whom I intend to bury like a gentleman.
  Volp. Ay, quick, and cozen me of all.   [*Aside.*
  2 *Avoc.* Still stranger!
More intricate!
  1 *Avoc.* And come about again!
  4 *Avoc.* It is a match, my daughter is bestow'd.   [*Aside.*
  Mos. Will you give me half?   [*Aside to Volp.*
  Volp. First, I'll be hang'd.
  Mos. I know
Your voice is good, cry not so loud.
  1 *Avoc.* Demand
The advocate.—Sir, did you not affirm
Volpone was alive?
  Volp. Yes, and he is;
This gentleman told me so.—Thou shalt have half.—
                          [*Aside to Mos.*
  Mos. Whose drunkard is this same? speak, some that know him:
I never saw his face.—I cannot now
Afford it you so cheap.   [*Aside to Volp.*
  Volp. No!
  1 *Avoc.* What say you?
  Volt. The officer told me.
  Volp. I did, grave fathers,
And will maintain he lives, with mine own life,
And that this creature [*points to Mosca.*] told me.—I was born
With all good stars my enemies.   [*Aside.*

Mos. Most grave fathers,
If such an insolence as this must pass
Upon me, I am silent: 'twas not this
For which you sent, I hope.

    2 Avoc. Take him away.

    Volp. Mosca!

    3 Avoc. Let him be whipt.

    Volp. Wilt thou betray me?
Cozen me?

    3 Avoc. And taught to bear himself
Toward a person of his rank.

    4 Avoc. Away.   [*The Officers seize Volpone.*

    Mos. I humbly thank your fatherhoods.

    Volp. Soft, soft: Whipt!
And lose all that I have! If I confess,
It cannot be much more.   [*Aside.*

    4 Avoc. Sir, are you married?

    Volp. They'll be allied anon; I must be resolute:
The Fox shall here uncase.   [*Throws off his disguise.*

    Mos. Patron!

    Volp. Nay, now
My ruins shall not come alone: your match
I'll hinder sure: my substance shall not glue you,
Nor screw you into a family.

    Mos. Why, patron!

    Volp. I am Volpone, and this is my knave;   [*Pointing to Mosca.*
This, [*to Volt.*] his own knave; this, [*to Corb.*] avarice's fool;
This, [*to Corv.*] a chimera of wittol, fool, and knave:
And, reverend fathers, since we all can hope
Nought but a sentence, let's not now despair it.
You hear me brief.

    Corv. May it please your fatherhoods—

    Com. Silence.

    1 Avoc. The knot is now undone by miracle.

    2 Avoc. Nothing can be more clear.

    3 Avoc. Or can more prove
These innocent.

    1 Avoc. Give them their liberty.

    Bon. Heaven could not long let such gross crimes be hid.

    2 Avoc. If this be held the high-way to get riches,
May I be poor!

    3 Avoc. This is not the gain, but torment.

    1 Avoc. These possess wealth, as sick men possess fevers,
Which trulier may be said to possess them.

    2 Avoc. Disrobe that parasite.

    Corv. Mos. Most honour'd fathers!—

    1 Avoc. Can you plead aught to stay the course of justice?
If you can, speak.

    Corv. Volt. We beg favour.

Cel. And mercy.

1 *Avoc.* You hurt your innocence, suing for the guilty.
Stand forth; and first the parasite: You appear
T'have been the chiefest minister, if not plotter,
In all these lewd impostures; and now, lastly,
Have with your impudence abused the court,
And habit of a gentleman of Venice,
Being a fellow of no birth or blood:
For which our sentence is, first, thou be whipt;
Then live perpetual prisoner in our gallies.

Volp. I thank you for him.

Mos. Bane to thy wolvish nature!

1 *Avoc.* Deliver him to the saffi.   [*Mosca is carried out.*]—
Thou, Volpone,
By blood and rank a gentleman, canst not fall
Under like censure; but our judgment on thee
Is, that thy substance all be straight confiscate
To the hospital of the Incurabili:
And, since the most was gotten by imposture,
By feigning lame, gout, palsy, and such diseases,
Thou art to lie in prison, cramp'd with irons,
Till thou be'st sick and lame indeed.—Remove him.
    [*He is taken from the Bar.*

Volp. This is call'd mortifying of a Fox.

1 *Avoc.* Thou, Voltore, to take away the scandal
Thou hast given all worthy men of thy profession,
Art banish'd from their fellowship, and our state.
Corbaccio!—bring him near—We here possess
Thy son of all thy state, and confine thee
To the monastery of San Spirito;
Where, since thou knewest not how to live well here,
Thou shalt be learn'd to die well.

Corb. Ah! what said he?

Com. You shall know anon, sir.

1 *Avoc.* Thou, Corvino, shalt
Be straight embark'd from thine own house, and row'd
Round about Venice, through the grand canale,
Wearing a cap, with fair long ass's ears,
Instead of horns; and so to mount, a paper
Pinn'd on thy breast, to the Berlina—

Corv. Yes,
And have mine eyes beat out with stinking fish,
Bruised fruit, and rotten eggs—'Tis well. I am glad
I shall not see my shame yet.

1 *Avoc.* And to expiate
Thy wrongs done to thy wife, thou art to send her
Home to her father, with her dowry trebled:
And these are all your judgments.

All. Honour'd fathers.—

1 *Avoc.* Which may not be revoked.   Now you begin,
When crimes are done, and past, and to be punish'd,
To think what your crimes are: away with them.
Let all that see these vices thus rewarded,
Take heart and love to study 'em!   Mischiefs feed
Like beasts, till they be fat, and then they bleed.   [*Exeunt.*

VOLPONE *comes forward.*

The seasoning of a play, is the applause.
Now, though the Fox be punish'd by the laws,
He yet doth hope, there is no suffering due,
For any fact which he hath done 'gainst you;
If there be, censure him; here he doubtful stands:
If not, fare jovially, and clap your hands.   [*Exit.*

EPICŒNE; OR, THE SILENT WOMAN

TO THE TRULY NOBLE BY ALL TITLES
SIR FRANCIS STUART

SIR,—My hope is not so nourished by example, as it will conclude, this dumb piece should please you, because it hath pleased others before; but by trust , that when you have read it, you will find it worthy to have displeased none.   This makes that I now number you, not only in the names o f favour, but the names of justice to what I write; and do presently call you to the exercise of that noblest, and manliest virtue; as coveting rather to be freed in my fame, by the authority of a judge, than the credit of an undertaker.   Read, therefore, I pray you, and censure.   There is not a line, or syllable in it, changed from the simplicity of the first copy. And, when you shall consider, through the certain hatred o f some, how much a man's innocency may be endangered by an uncertain accusation; you will, I doubt not, so begin to hate the iniquity of such natures, as I shall love the contumely done me, whose end was so honourable as to be wiped off by your sentence.   Your unprofitable, but true Lover .

BEN JONSON.

DRAMATIS PERSONÆ

MOROSE, *a Gentleman that loves no noise.*
SIR DAUPHINE EUGENIE, *a Knight, his Nephew.*
NED CLERIMONT, *a Gentleman, his Friend.*
TRUEWIT, *another Friend.*
SIR JOHN DAW, *a Knight.*
SIR AMOROUS LA-FOOLE, *a Knight also.*
THOMAS OTTER, *a Land and Sea Captain.*
CUTBEARD, *a Barber.*
MUTE, *one of* MOROSE'S *Servants.*
Parson.

Page *to* CLERIMONT.

EPICŒNE, *supposed the* Silent Woman.
LADY HAUGHTY,
LADY CENTAURE,   *Ladies Colle-*
MISTRESS DOL.   *giates.*
MAVIS,
MISTRESS OTTER, *the Captain's Wife,*
MISTRESS TRUSTY,   *Pretenders.*
LADY HAUGHTY'S Woman,

Pages, Servants, *etc.*

SCENE,—LONDON

PROLOGUE.

Truth says, of old the art of making plays
Was to content the people; and their praise
Was to the poet money, wine, and bays.

But in this age, a sect of writers are,
That, only, for particular likings care,
And will taste nothing that is popular.

With such we mingle neither brains nor breasts;
Our wishes, like to those make public feasts,
Are not to please the cook's taste but the guests'.

Yet, if those cunning palates hither come,
They shall find guests' entreaty, and good room;
And though all relish not, sure there will be some,

That, when they leave their seats, shall make them say,
Who wrote that piece, could so have wrote a play,
But that he knew this was the better way.

For, to present all custard, or all tart,
And have no other meats to bear a part,
Or to want bread, and salt, were but coarse art.

The poet prays you then, with better thought
To sit; and, when his cates are all in brought,
Though there be none far-fet, there will dear-bought,

Be fit for ladies: some for lords, knights, 'squires;
Some for your waiting-wench, and city-wires;
Some for your men, and daughters of Whitefriars.

Nor is it, only, while you keep your seat
Here, that his feast will last; but you shall eat
A week at ord'naries, on his broken meat:
      If his muse be true,
      Who commends her to you.

ANOTHER.

The ends of all, who for the scene do write,
Are, or should be, to profit and delight.
And still't hath been the praise of all best times,
So persons were not touch'd, to tax the crimes.
Then, in this play, which we present to-night,
And make the object of your ear and sight,
On forfeit of yourselves, think nothing true:

Lest so you make the maker to judge you.
For he knows, poet never credit gain'd
By writing truths, but things, like truths, well feign'd.
If any yet will, with particular sleight
Of application, wrest what he doth write;
And that he meant, or him, or her, will say:
They make a libel, which he made a play.

ACT I

SCENE I.—*A Room in* CLERIMONT'S *House.*

Enter CLERIMONT, *making himself ready, followed by his* Page.

Cler. Have you got the song yet perfect, I gave you, boy?

Page. Yes, sir.

Cler. Let me hear it.

Page. You shall, sir; but i'faith let nobody else.

Cler. Why, I pray?

Page. It will get you the dangerous name of a poet in town, sir; besides me a perfect deal of ill-will at the mansion you wot of, whose lady is the argument of it; where now I am the welcomest thing under a man that comes there.

Cler. I think; and above a man too, if the truth were rack'd out of you.

Page. No, faith, I'll confess before, sir. The gentlewomen play with me, and throw me on the bed, and carry me in to my lady: and she kisses me with her oil'd face, and puts a peruke on my head; and asks me an I will wear her gown? and I say no: and then she hits me a blow o' the ear, and calls me Innocent! and lets me go.

Cler. No marvel if the door be kept shut against your master, when the entrance is so easy to you——well, sir, you shall go there no more, lest I be fain to seek your voice in my lady's rushes, a fortnight hence. Sing, sir. [*Page sings.*

Still to be neat, still to be drest—

Enter TRUEWIT.

True. Why, here's the man that can melt away his time and never feels it! What between his mistress abroad and his ingle at home, high fare, soft lodging, fine clothes, and his fiddle; he thinks the hours have no wings, or the day no post-horse. Well, sir gallant, were you struck with the plague this minute, or condemn'd to any capital punishment to-morrow, you would begin then to think, and value every article of your time, esteem it at the true rate, and give all for it.

Cler. Why what should a man do?

True. Why, nothing; or that which, when 'tis done, is as idle.

Hearken after the next horse-race, or hunting-match, lay wagers, praise Puppy, or Peppercorn, White-foot, Franklin; swear upon Whitemane's party; speak aloud, that my lords may hear you; visit my ladies at night, and be able to give them the character of every bowler or better on the green. These be the things wherein your fashionable men exercise themselves, and I for company.

Cler. Nay, if I have thy authority, I'll not leave yet. Come, the other are considerations, when we come to have gray heads and weak hams, moist eyes and shrunk members. We'll think on 'em then; and we'll pray and fast.

True. Ay, and destine only that time of age to goodness, which our want of ability will not let us employ in evil!

Cler. Why, then 'tis time enough.

True. Yes; as if a man should sleep all the term, and think to effect his business the last day. O, Clerimont, this time, because it is an incorporeal thing, and not subject to sense, we mock ourselves the fineliest out of it, with vanity and misery indeed! not seeking an end of wretchedness, but only changing the matter still.

Cler. Nay, thou'lt not leave now—

True. See but our common disease! with what justice can we complain, that great men will not look upon us, nor be at leisure to give our affairs such dispatch as we expect, when we will never do it to ourselves? nor hear, nor regard ourselves?

Cler. Foh! thou hast read Plutarch's morals, now, or some such tedious fellow; and it shews so vilely with thee! 'fore God, 'twill spoil thy wit utterly. Talk to me of pins, and feathers, and ladies, and rushes, and such things: and leave this Stoicity alone, till thou mak'st sermons.

True. Well, sir; if it will not take, I have learn'd to lose as little of my kindness as I can; I'll do good to no man against his will, certainly. When were you at the college?

Cler. What college?

True. As if you knew not!

Cler. No, faith, I came but from court yesterday.

True. Why, is it not arrived there yet, the news? A new foundation, sir, here in the town, of ladies, that call themselves the collegiates, an order between courtiers and country-madams, that live from their husbands; and give entertainment to all the wits, and braveries of the time, as they call them: cry down, or up, what they like or dislike in a brain or a fashion, with most masculine, or rather hermaphroditical authority; and every day gain to their college some new probationer.

Cler. Who is the president?

True. The grave and youthful matron, the lady Haughty.

Cler. A pox of her autumnal face, her pieced beauty! there's no man can be admitted till she be ready, now-a-days, till she has painted, and perfumed, and wash'd, and scour'd, but the boy, here; and him she wipes her oil'd lips upon, like a sponge. I have made a song (I pray thee hear it) on the subject. [*Page sings.*

> Still to be neat, still to be drest,
> As you were going to a feast;
> Still to be powder'd, still perfum'd;
> Lady, it is to be presumed,
> Though art's hid causes are not found,
> All is not sweet, all is not sound.
>
> Give me a look, give me a face,
> That makes simplicity a grace;
> Robes loosely flowing, hair as free:
> Such sweet neglect more taketh me,
> Than all the adulteries of art;
> They strike mine eyes, but not my heart.

True. And I am clearly on the other side: I love a good dressing before any beauty o' the world. O, a woman is then like a delicate garden; nor is there one kind of it; she may vary every hour; take often counsel of her glass, and choose the best. If she have good ears, shew them; good hair, lay it out; good legs, wear short clothes; a good hand, discover it often: practise any art to mend breath, cleanse teeth, repair eye-brows; paint, and profess it.

Cler. How! publicly?

True. The doing of it, not the manner: that must be private. Many things that seem foul in the doing, do please done. A lady should, indeed, study her face, when we think she sleeps; nor, when the doors are shut, should men be enquiring; all is sacred within, then. Is it for us to see their perukes put on, their false teeth, their complexion, their eye-brows, their nails? You see gilders will not work, but inclosed. They must not discover how little serves, with the help of art, to adorn a great deal. How long did the canvas hang afore Aldgate? Were the people suffered to see the city's Love and Charity, while they were rude stone, before they were painted and burnish'd? No; no more should servants approach their mistresses, but when they are complete and finish'd.

Cler. Well said, my Truewit.

True. And a wise lady will keep a guard always upon the place, that she may do things securely. I once followed a rude fellow into a chamber, where the poor madam, for haste, and troubled, snatch'd at her peruke to cover her baldness; and put it on the wrong way.

Cler. O prodigy!

True. And the unconscionable knave held her in compliment an hour with that reverst face, when I still look'd when she should talk from the t'other side.

Cler. Why, thou shouldst have relieved her.

True. No, faith, I let her alone, as we'll let this argument, if you please, and pass to another. When saw you Dauphine Eugenie?

Cler. Not these three days. Shall we go to him this morning? he is very melancholy, I hear.

True. Sick of the uncle, is he? I met that stiff piece of formality, his uncle, yesterday, with a huge turban of night-caps on his head, buckled over his ears.

Cler. O, that's his custom when he walks abroad. He can endure no noise, man.

True. So I have heard. But is the disease so ridiculous in him as it is made? They say he has been upon divers treaties with the fish-wives and orange-women; and articles propounded between them: marry, the chimney-sweepers will not be drawn in.

Cler. No, nor the broom-men: they stand out stiffly. He cannot endure a costard-monger, he swoons if he hear one.

True. Methinks a smith should be ominous.

Cler. Or any hammer-man. A brasier is not suffer'd to dwell in the parish, nor an armourer. He would have hang'd a pewterer's prentice once upon a Shrove-tuesday's riot, for being of that trade, when the rest were quit.

True. A trumpet should fright him terribly, or the hautboys.

Cler. Out of his senses. The waights of the city have a pension of him not to come near that ward. This youth practised on him one night like the bell-man; and never left till he had brought him down to the door with a long sword; and there left him flourishing with the air.

Page. Why, sir, he hath chosen a street to lie in so narrow at both ends, that it will receive no coaches, nor carts, nor any of these common noises: and therefore we that love him, devise to bring him in such as we may, now and then, for his exercise, to breathe him. He would grow resty else in his ease: his virtue would rust without action. I entreated a bearward, one day, to come down with the dogs of some four parishes that way, and I thank him he did; and cried his games under master Morose's window: till he was sent crying away, with his head made a most bleeding spectacle to the multitude. And, another time, a fencer marching to his prize, had his drum most tragically run through, for taking that street in his way at my request.

True. A good wag! How does he for the bells?

Cler. O, in the Queen's time, he was wont to go out of town every Saturday at ten o'clock, or on holy day eves. But now, by reason of the sickness, the perpetuity of ringing has made him devise a room, with double walls and treble ceilings; the windows close shut and caulk'd: and there he lives by candle-light. He turn'd away a man, last week, for having a pair of new shoes that creak'd. And this fellow waits on him now in tennis-court socks, or slippers soled with wool: and they talk each to other in a trunk. See, who comes here!

Enter Sir DAUPHINE EUGENIE.

Daup. How now! what ail you, sirs? dumb?

True. Struck into stone, almost, I am here, with tales o' thine uncle. There was never such a prodigy heard of.

Daup. I would you would once lose this subject, my masters, for my sake. They are such as you are, that have brought me into that predicament I am with him.

True. How is that?

Daup. Marry, that he will disinherit me; no more. He thinks, I and my company are authors of all the ridiculous Acts and Monuments are told of him.

True. 'Slid, I would be the author of more to vex him; that purpose deserves it: it gives thee law of plaguing him. I'll tell thee what I would do. I would make a false almanack, get it printed; and then have him drawn out on a coronation day to the Tower-wharf, and kill him with the noise of the ordnance. Disinherit thee! he cannot, man. Art not thou next of blood, and his sister's son?

Daup. Ay, but he will thrust me out of it, he vows, and marry.

True. How! that's a more portent. Can he endure no noise, and will venture on a wife?

Cler. Yes: why thou art a stranger, it seems, to his best trick, yet. He has employed a fellow this half year all over England to hearken him out a dumb woman; be she of any form, or any quality, so she be able to bear children: her silence is dowry enough, he says.

True. But I trust to God he has found none.

Cler. No; but he has heard of one that's lodged in the next street to him, who is exceedingly soft-spoken; thrifty of her speech; that spends but six words a day. And her he's about now, and shall have her.

True. Is't possible! who is his agent in the business?

Cler. Marry, a barber, one Cutbeard; an honest fellow, one that tells Dauphine all here.

True. Why you oppress me with wonder: a woman, and a barber, and love no noise!

Cler. Yes, faith. The fellow trims him silently, and has not the knack with his sheers or his fingers: and that continence in a barber he thinks so eminent a virtue, as it has made him chief of his counsel.

True. Is the barber to be seen, or the wench?

Cler. Yes, that they are.

True. I prithee, Dauphine, let's go thither.

Daup. I have some business now: I cannot, i'faith.

True. You shall have no business shall make you neglect this, sir: we'll make her talk, believe it; or, if she will not, we can give out at least so much as shall interrupt the treaty; we will break it. Thou art bound in conscience, when he suspects thee without cause, to torment him.

Daup. Not I, by any means. I'll give no suffrage to't. He shall never have that plea against me, that I opposed the least phant'sy of his. Let it lie upon my stars to be guilty, I'll be innocent.

True. Yes, and be poor, and beg; do, innocent: when some groom of his has got him an heir, or this barber, if he himself cannot·

Innocent!—I prithee, Ned, where lies she? let him be innocent still.

Cler. Why, right over against the barber's; in the house where sir John Daw lies.

True. You do not mean to confound me!

Cler. Why?

True. Does he that would marry her know so much?

Cler. I cannot tell.

True. 'Twere enough of imputation to her with him.

Cler. Why?

True. The only talking sir in the town! Jack Daw! and he teach her not to speak!—God be wi' you. I have some business too.

Cler. Will you not go thither, then?

True. Not with the danger to meet Daw, for mine ears.

Cler. Why, I thought you two had been upon very good terms.

True. Yes, of keeping distance.

Cler. They say, he is a very good scholar.

True. Ay, and he says it first. A pox on him, a fellow that pretends only to learning, buys titles, and nothing else of books in him!

Cler. The world reports him to be very learned.

True. I am sorry the world should so conspire to belie him.

Cler. Good faith, I have heard very good things come from him.

True. You may; there's none so desperately ignorant to deny that: would they were his own! God be wi' you, gentlemen.

[*Exit hastily.*

Cler. This is very abrupt!

Daup. Come, you are a strange open man, to tell every thing thus.

Cler. Why, believe it, Dauphine, Truewit's a very honest fellow.

Daup. I think no other: but this frank nature of his is not for secrets.

Cler. Nay, then, you are mistaken, Dauphine: I know where he has been well trusted, and discharged the trust very truly, and heartily.

Daup. I contend not, Ned; but with the fewer a business is carried, it is ever the safer. Now we are alone, if you'll go thither, I am for you.

Cler. When were you there?

Daup. Last night: and such a Decameron of sport fallen out! Boccace never thought of the like. Daw does nothing but court her; and the wrong way. He would lie with her, and praises her modesty; desires that she would talk and be free, and commends her silence in verses; which he reads, and swears are the best that ever man made. Then rails at his fortunes, stamps, and mutines, why he is not made a counsellor, and call'd to affairs of state.

Cler. I prithee let's go. I would fain partake this.—Some water, boy.   [*Exit Page.*

Daup. We are invited to dinner together, he and I, by one that came thither to him, sir La-Foole.

Cler. O, that's a precious mannikin!

Daup. Do you know him?

Cler. Ay, and he will know you too, if e'er he saw you but once, though you should meet him at church in the midst of prayers. He is one of the braveries, though he be none of the wits. He will salute a judge upon the bench, and a bishop in the pulpit, a lawyer when he is pleading at the bar, and a lady when she is dancing in a masque, and put her out. He does give plays, and suppers, and invites his guests to them, aloud, out of his window, as they ride by in coaches. He has a lodging in the Strand for the purpose: or to watch when ladies are gone to the china-houses, or the Exchange, that he may meet them by chance, and give them presents, some two or three hundred pounds' worth of toys, to be laugh'd at. He is never without a spare banquet, or sweet-meats in his chamber, for their women to alight at, and come up to for a bait.

Daup. Excellent! he was a fine youth last night; but now he is much finer! what is his Christian name? I have forgot.

Re-enter Page.

Cler. Sir Amorous La-Foole.

Page. The gentleman is here below that owns that name.

Cler. 'Heart, he's come to invite me to dinner, I hold my life.

Daup. Like enough: prithee, let's have him up.

Cler. Boy, marshal him.

Page. With a truncheon, sir?

Cler. Away, I beseech you. [*Exit Page.*]—I'll make him tell us his pedigree now; and what meat he has to dinner; and who are his guests; and the whole course of his fortunes; with a breath.

Enter Sir AMOROUS LA-FOOLE.

La-F. 'Save, dear sir Dauphine! honoured master Clerimont!

Cler. Sir Amorous! you have very much honested my lodging with your presence.

La-F. Good faith, it is a fine lodging: almost as delicate a lodging as mine.

Cler. Not so, sir.

La-F. Excuse me, sir, if it were in the Strand, I assure you. I am come, master Clerimont, to entreat you to wait upon two or three ladies, to dinner, to-day.

Cler. How, sir! wait upon them? did you ever see me carry dishes?

La-F. No, sir, dispense with me; I meant, to bear them company.

Cler. O, that I will, sir: the doubtfulness of your phrase, believe it, sir, would breed you a quarrel once an hour, with the terrible boys, if you should but keep them fellowship a day.

La-F. It should be extremely against my will, sir, if I contested with any man.

Cler. I believe it, sir: Where old you your feast?

La-F. At Tom Otter's, sir.

Daup. Tom Otter! what's he?

La-F. Captain Otter, sir; he is a kind of gamester, but he has had command both by sea and by land.

Daup. O, then he is *animal amphibium?*

La-F. Ay, sir: his wife was the rich china-woman, that the courtiers visited so often; that gave the rare entertainment. She commands all at home.

Cler. Then she is captain Otter.

La-F. You say very well, sir; she is my kinswoman, a La-Foole by the mother-side, and will invite any great ladies for my sake.

Daup. Not of the La-Fooles of Essex?

La-F. No, sir, the La-Fooles of London.

Cler. Now, he's in.   [*Aside.*

La-F. They all come out of our house, the La-Fooles of the north, the La-Fooles of the west, the La-Fooles of the east and south—we are as ancient a family as any is in Europe—but I myself am descended lineally of the French La-Fooles—and, we do bear for our coat yellow, or *or*, checker'd *azure*, and *gules*, and some three or four colours more, which is a very noted coat, and has, sometimes, been solemnly worn by divers nobility of our house—but let that go, antiquity is not respected now.—I had a brace of fat does sent me, gentlemen, and half a dozen of pheasants, a dozen or two of godwits, and some other fowl, which I would have eaten, while they are good, and in good company:—there will be a great lady or two, my lady Haughty, my lady Centaure, mistress Dol Mavis—and they come o' purpose to see the silent gentlewoman, mistress Epicœne, that honest sir John Daw has promised to bring thither—and then, mistress Trusty, my lady's woman, will be there too, and this honourable knight, sir Dauphine, with yourself, master Clerimont—and we'll be very merry, and have fidlers, and dance.—I have been a mad wag in my time, and have spent some crowns since I was a page in court, to my lord Lofty, and after, my lady's gentleman-usher, who got me knighted in Ireland, since it pleased my elder brother to die.—I had as fair a gold jerkin on that day, as any worn in the island voyage, or at Cadiz, none dispraised; and I came over in it hither, shew'd myself to my friends in court, and after went down to my tenants in the country, and surveyed my lands, let new leases, took their money, spent it in the eye o' the land here, upon ladies:—and now I can take up at my pleasure.

Daup. Can you take up ladies, sir?

Cler. O, let him breathe, he has not recover'd.

Daup. Would I were your half in that commodity!

La-F. No, sir, excuse me: I meant money, which can take up any thing. I have another guest or two, to invite, and say as much to, gentlemen. I'll take my leave abruptly, in hope you will not fail——Your servant.   [*Exit.*

Daup. We will not fail you, sir precious La-Foole; but she shall, that your ladies come to see, if I have credit afore sir Daw.

Cler. Did you ever hear such a wind-sucker, as this?

Daup. Or such a rook as the other, that will betray his mistress to be seen! Come, 'tis time we prevented it.

Cler. Go.   [*Exeunt.*

ACT II

SCENE I.—*A Room in* MOROSE'S *House.*

Enter MOROSE, *with a tube in his hand, followed by* MUTE.

Mor. Cannot I, yet, find out a more compendious method, than by this trunk, to save my servants the labour of speech, and mine ears the discords of sounds? Let me see: all discourses but my own afflict me; they seem harsh, impertinent, and irksome. Is it not possible, that thou shouldst answer me by signs, and I apprehend thee, fellow? Speak not, though I question you. You have taken the ring off from the street door, as I bade you? answer me not by speech, but by silence; unless it be otherwise [*Mute makes a leg.*]—very good. And you have fastened on a thick quilt, or flock-bed, on the outside of the door; that if they knock with their daggers, or with brick-bats, they can make no noise?—But with your leg, your answer, unless it be otherwise. [*makes a leg.*]—Very good. This is not only fit modesty in a servant, but good state and discretion in a master. And you have been with Cutbeard the barber, to have him come to me? [*makes a leg.*]—Good. And, he will come presently? Answer me not but with your leg, unless it be otherwise; if it be otherwise, shake your head, or shrug. [*makes a leg.*]—So! Your Italian and Spaniard are wise in these: and it is a frugal and comely gravity. How long will it be ere Cutbeard come? Stay; if an hour, hold up your whole hand, if half an hour, two fingers; if a quarter, one; [*holds up a finger bent.*]—Good: half a quarter? 'tis well. And have you given him a key, to come in without knocking? [*makes a leg.*]—good. And is the lock oil'd, and the hinges, to-day? [*makes a leg.*]—good. And the quilting of the stairs no where worn out and bare? [*makes a leg.*]—Very good. I see, by much doctrine, and impulsion, it may be effected; stand by. The Turk, in this divine discipline, is admirable, exceeding all the potentates of the earth; still waited on by mutes; and all his commands so executed; yea, even in the war, as I have heard, and in his marches, most of his charges and directions given by signs, and with silence: an exquisite art! and I am heartily ashamed, and angry oftentimes, that the princes of Christendom should suffer a barbarian to transcend them in so high a point of felicity. I will practise it hereafter. [*A horn winded within.*]—How now? oh! oh! what villain, what prodigy of mankind is that? look. [*Exit Mute.*] —[*Horn again.*]—Oh! cut his throat, cut his throat! what murderer, hell-hound, devil can this be?

Re-enter MUTE.

Mute. It is a post from the court—

Mor. Out, rogue! and must thou blow thy horn too?

Mute. Alas, it is a post from the court, sir, that says, he must speak with you, pain of death—

Mor. Pain of thy life, be silent!

Enter TRUEWIT *with a post-horn, and a halter in his hand.*

True. By your leave, sir;—I am a stranger here:—Is your name master Morose? is your name master Morose? Fishes! Pythagoreans all! This is strange. What say you, sir? nothing! Has Harpocrates been here with his club, among you? Well, sir, I will believe you to be the man at this time: I will venture upon you, sir. Your friends at court commend them to you, sir—

Mor. O men! O manners! was there ever such an impudence?

True. And are extremely solicitous for you, sir.

Mor. Whose knave are you?

True. Mine own knave, and your compeer, sir.

Mor. Fetch me my sword—

True. You shall taste the one half of my dagger, if you do, groom; and you the other, if you stir, sir: Be patient, I charge you, in the king's name, and hear me without insurrection. They say, you are to marry; to marry! do you mark, sir?

Mor. How then, rude companion!

True. Marry, your friends do wonder, sir, the Thames being so near, wherein you may drown, so handsomely; or London-bridge, at a low fall, with a fine leap, to hurry you down the stream; or, such a delicate steeple in the town, as Bow, to vault from; or, a braver height, as Paul's: Or, if you affected to do it nearer home, and a shorter way, an excellent garret-window into the street; or, a beam in the said garret, with this halter [*shews him the halter.*]— which they have sent, and desire, that you would sooner commit your grave head to this knot, than to the wedlock noose; or, take a little sublimate, and go out of the world like a rat; or a fly, as one said, with a straw in your arse: any way, rather than follow this goblin Matrimony. Alas, sir, do you ever think to find a chaste wife in these times? now? when there are so many masques, plays, Puritan preachings, mad folks, and other strange sights to be seen daily, private and public? If you had lived in king Etheldred's time, sir, or Edward the Confessor, you might, perhaps, have found one in some cold country hamlet, then, a dull frosty wench, would have been contented with one man: now, they will as soon be pleased with one leg, or one eye. I'll tell you, sir, the monstrous hazards you shall run with a wife.

Mor. Good sir, have I ever cozen'd any friends of yours of their land? bought their possessions? taken forfeit of their mortgage? begg'd a reversion from them? bastarded their issue? What have I done, that may deserve this?

True. Nothing, sir, that I know, but your itch of marriage.

Mor. Why, if I had made an assassinate upon your father, vitiated your mother, ravished your sisters—

True. I would kill you, sir, I would kill you, if you had.

Mor. Why, you do more in this, sir: it were a vengeance centuple, for all facinorous acts that could be named, to do that you do.

True. Alas, sir, I am but a messenger: I but tell you, what you must hear. It seems your friends are careful after your soul's health, sir, and would have you know the danger: (but you may do your pleasure for all them, I persuade not, sir.) If, after you are married, your wife do run away with a vaulter, or the Frenchman that walks upon ropes, or him that dances the jig, or a fencer for his skill at his weapon; why it is not their fault, they have discharged their consciences; when you know what may happen. Nay, suffer valiantly, sir, for I must tell you all the perils that you are obnoxious to. If she be fair, young and vegetous, no sweet-meats ever drew more flies; all the yellow doublets and great roses in the town will be there. If foul and crooked, she'll be with them, and buy those doublets and roses, sir. If rich, and that you marry her dowry, not her, she'll reign in your house as imperious as a widow. If noble, all her kindred will be your tyrants. If fruitful, as proud as May, and humorous as April; she must have her doctors, her midwives, her nurses, her longings every hour; though it be for the dearest morsel of man. If learned, there was never such a parrot; all your patrimony will be too little for the guests that must be invited to hear her speak Latin and Greek; and you must lie with her in those languages too, if you will please her. If precise, you must feast all the silenced brethren, once in three days; salute the sisters; entertain the whole family, or wood of them; and hear long-winded exercises, singings and catechisings, which you are not given to, and yet must give for; to please the zealous matron your wife, who for the holy cause, will cozen you over and above. You begin to sweat, sir! but this is not half, i'faith: you may do your pleasure, notwithstanding, as I said before: I come not to persuade you. [*Mute is stealing away.*]—Upon my faith, master serving-man, if you do stir, I will beat you.

Mor. O, what is my sin! what is my sin!

True. Then, if you love your wife, or rather dote on her, sir; O, how she'll torture you, and take pleasure in your torments! you shall lie with her but when she lists; she will not hurt her beauty, her complexion; or it must be for that jewel, or that pearl, when she does: every half hour's pleasure must be bought anew, and with the same pain and charge you woo'd her at first. Then you must keep what servants she please; what company she will; that friend must not visit you without her license; and him she loves most, she will seem to hate eagerliest, to decline your jealousy; or, feign to be jealous of you first; and for that cause go live with her she-friend, or cousin at the college, that can instruct her in all the mysteries of writing letters, corrupting servants, taming spies; where she must have that rich gown for such a great day; a new one for the next; a richer for the third; be served in silver; have the chamber fill'd with a succession of grooms, footmen, ushers, and other messengers; besides embroiderers, jewellers, tire-women, sempsters, feathermen, perfumers; whilst she feels not how the land drops away, nor the acres melt; nor foresees the change, when the mercer has your woods for her velvets; never weighs what her pride costs, sir; so she may kiss a page, or a smooth chin, that has the despair of a beard: be a stateswoman, know all the news, what was done at Salisbury, what at the Bath, what at court, what in progress; or, so she may censure poets, and authors, and styles, and compare them; Daniel with Spenser, Jonson with the t'other youth, and so forth: or be thought cunning in controversies, or the very knots of divinity; and have often in her mouth the state of the question; and then skip to the mathematics, and demonstration: and answer in religion to one, in state to another, in bawdry to a third.

Mor. O, O!

True. All this is very true, sir. And then her going in disguise to that conjurer, and this cunning woman: where the first question is, how soon you shall die? next, if her present servant love her? next, if she shall have a new servant? and how many? which of her family would make the best bawd, male or female? what precedence she shall have by her next match? and sets down the answers, and believes them above the scriptures. Nay, perhaps she'll study the art.

Mor. Gentle sir, have you done? have you had your pleasure of me? I'll think of these things.

True. Yes, sir: and then comes reeking home of vapour and sweat, with going a foot, and lies in a month of a new face, all oil and birdlime; and rises in asses' milk, and is cleansed with a new fucus: God be wi' you, sir. One thing more, which I had almost forgot. This too, with whom you are to marry, may have made a conveyance of her virginity afore hand, as your wise widows do of their states, before they marry, in trust to some friend, sir: Who can tell? Or if she have not done it yet, she may do, upon the wedding-day, or the night before, and antedate you cuckold. The like has been heard of in nature. 'Tis no devised, impossible thing, sir. God be wi' you: I'll be bold to leave this rope with you, sir, for a remembrance.—Farewell, Mute!   [*Exit.*

Mor. Come, have me to my chamber: but first shut the door. [*Truewit winds the horn without.*] O, shut the door, shut the door! is he come again?

Enter CUTBEARD.

Cut. 'Tis I, sir, your barber.

Mor. O, Cutbeard, Cutbeard, Cutbeard! here has been a cut-throat with me: help me in to my bed, and give me physic with thy counsel.   [*Exeunt.*

SCENE II.—*A Room in* Sir John Daw's *House.*

Enter Daw, Clerimont, Dauphine, *and* Epicœne.

Daw. Nay, an she will, let her refuse at her own charges; 'tis nothing to me, gentlemen: but she will not be invited to the like feasts or guests every day.

Cler. O, by no means, she may not refuse—to stay at home, if you love your reputation: 'Slight, you are invited thither o' purpose to be seen, and laughed at by the lady of the college, and her shadows. This trumpeter hath proclaim'd you. [*Aside to Epi.*

Daup. You shall not go; let him be laugh'd at in your stead, for not bringing you: and put him to his extemporal faculty of fooling and talking loud, to satisfy the company. [*Aside to Epi.*

Cler. He will suspect us; talk aloud.—'Pray, mistress Epicœne, let's see your verses; we have sir John Daw's leave; do not conceal your servant's merit, and your own glories.

Epi. They'll prove my servant's glories, if you have his leave so soon.

Daup. His vain-glories, lady!

Daw. Shew them, shew them, mistress; I dare own them.

Epi. Judge you, what glories.

Daw. Nay, I'll read them myself too: an author must recite his own works. It is a madrigal of Modesty.

> *Modest and fair, for fair and good are near*
> > *Neighbours, howe'er.—*

Daup. Very good.

Cler. Ay, is't not?

Daw. *No noble virtue ever was alone,*
> > *But two in one.*

Daup. Excellent!

Cler. That again, I pray, sir John.

Daup. It has something in't like rare wit and sense.

Cler. Peace.

Daw. *No noble virtue ever was alone,*
> > *But two in one.*
> *Then, when I praise sweet modesty, I praise*
> > *Bright beauty's rays:*
> *And having praised both beauty and modesty,*
> > *I have praised thee.*

Daup. Admirable!

Cler. How it chimes, and cries tink in the close, divinely!

Daup. Ay, 'tis Seneca.

Cler. No, I think 'tis Plutarch.

Daw. The dor on Plutarch and Seneca! I hate it: they are mine own imaginations, by that light. I wonder those fellows have such credit with gentlemen.

Cler. They are very grave authors.

Daw. Grave asses! mere essayists: a few loose sentences, and that's all. A man would talk so, his whole age: I do utter as good things every hour, if they were collected and observed, as either of them.

Daup. Indeed, sir John!

Cler. He must needs; living among the wits and braveries too.

Daup. Ay, and being president of them, as he is.

Daw. There's Aristotle, a mere common-place fellow; Plato, a discourser; Thucydides and Livy, tedious and dry; Tacitus, an entire knot; sometimes worth the untying, very seldom.

Cler. What do you think of the poets, sir John?

Daw. Not worthy to be named for authors. Homer, an old tedious, prolix ass, talks of curriers, and chines of beef; Virgil of dunging of land, and bees; Horace, of I know not what.

Cler. I think so.

Daw. And so, Pindarus, Lycophron, Anacreon, Catullus, Seneca the tragedian, Lucan, Propertius, Tibullus, Martial, Juvenal, Ausonius, Statius, Politian, Valerius Flaccus, and the rest—

Cler. What a sack full of their names he has got!

Daup. And how he pours them out! Politian with Valerius Flaccus!

Cler. Was not the character right of him?

Daup. As could be made, i'faith.

Daw. And Persius, a crabbed coxcomb, not to be endured.

Daup. Why, whom do you account for authors, sir John Daw?

Daw. Syntagma juris civilis; Corpus juris civilis; Corpus juris canonici; the king of Spain's bible—

Daup. Is the king of Spain's bible an author?

Cler. Yes, and Syntagma.

Daup. What was that Syntagma, sir?

Daw. A civil lawyer, a Spaniard.

Daup. Sure, Corpus was a Dutchman.

Cler. Ay, both the Corpuses, I knew 'em: they were very corpulent authors.

Daw. And then there's Vatablus, Pomponatius, Symancha: the other are not to be received, within the thought of a scholar.

Daup. 'Fore God, you have a simple learned servant, lady,—in titles.   [*Aside.*

Cler. I wonder that he is not called to the helm, and made a counsellor.

Daup. He is one extraordinary.

Cler. Nay, but in ordinary: to say truth, the state wants such.

Daup. Why that will follow.

Cler. I muse a mistress can be so silent to the dotes of such a servant.

Daw. 'Tis her virtue, sir. I have written somewhat of her silence too.

Daup. In verse, sir John?

Cler. What else?

Daup. Why, how can you justify your own being of a poet, that so slight all the old poets?

Daw. Why, every man that writes in verse is not a poet; you have of the wits that write verses, and yet are no poets: they are poets that live by it, the poor fellows that live by it.

Daup. Why, would not you live by your verses, sir John?

Cler. No, 'twere pity he should. A knight live by his verses! he did not make them to that end, I hope.

Daup. And yet the noble Sidney lives by his, and the noble family not ashamed.

Cler. Ay, he profest himself; but sir John Daw has more caution: he'll not hinder his own rising in the state so much. Do you think he will? Your verses, good sir John, and no poems.

Daw. *Silence in woman, is like speech in man;*
　　　　Deny't who can.

Daup. Not I, believe it: your reason, sir.

Daw. 　　*Nor is't a tale,*
　　That female vice should be a virtue male,
　　Or masculine vice a female virtue be:
　　　　　You shall it see
　　　　　Prov'd with increase;
　　I know to speak, and she to hold her peace.

Do you conceive me, gentlemen?

Daup. No, faith; how mean you *with increase*, sir John?

Daw. Why, with increase is, when I court her for the common cause of mankind, and she says nothing, but *consentire videtur;* and in time is *gravida.*

Daup. Then this is a ballad of procreation?

Cler. A madrigal of procreation; you mistake.

Epi. 'Pray give me my verses again, servant.

Daw. If you'll ask them aloud, you shall.

　　　　　　　　　　　　[Walks aside with the papers.

Enter TRUEWIT *with his horn.*

Cler. See, here's Truewit again!—Where hast thou been, in the name of madness, thus accoutred with thy horn?

True. Where the sound of it might have pierced your sense with gladness, had you been in ear-reach of it. Dauphine, fall down and worship me; I have forbid the bans, lad: I have been with thy virtuous uncle, and have broke the match.

Daup. You have not, I hope.

True. Yes, faith; and thou shouldst hope otherwise, I should repent me: this horn got me entrance; kiss it. I had no other way to get in, but by feigning to be a post; but when I got in once, I proved none, but rather the contrary, turn'd him into a post, or a stone, or what is stiffer, with thundering into him the incommodities of a wife, and the miseries of marriage. If ever Gorgon were seen in the shape of a woman, he hath seen her in my description: I have put him off o' that scent for ever.—Why do you not applaud and adore me, sirs? why stand you mute? are you stupid? You are not worthy of the benefit.

Daup. Did not I tell you? Mischief!—

Cler. I would you had placed this benefit somewhere else.

True. Why so?

Cler. 'Slight, you have done the most inconsiderate, rash, weak thing, that ever man did to his friend.

Daup. Friend! if the most malicious enemy I have, had studied to inflict an injury upon me, it could not be a greater.

True. Wherein, for God's sake? Gentlemen, come to yourselves again.

Daup. But I presaged thus much afore to you.

Cler. Would my lips had been solder'd when I spake on't! Slight, what moved you to be thus impertinent?

True. My masters, do not put on this strange face to pay my courtesy; off with this vizor. Have good turns done you, and thank 'em this way!

Daup. 'Fore heaven, you have undone me. That which I have plotted for, and been maturing now these four months, you have blasted in a minute: Now I am lost, I may speak. This gentle-woman was lodged here by me o' purpose, and, to be put upon my uncle, hath profest this obstinate silence for my sake; being my entire friend, and one that for the requital of such a fortune as to marry him, would have made me very ample conditions; where now, all my hopes are utterly miscarried by this unlucky accident.

Cler. Thus 'tis when a man will be ignorantly officious, do services, and not know his why; I wonder what courteous itch possest you. You never did absurder part in your life, nor a greater trespass to friendship or humanity.

Daup. Faith, you may forgive it best; 'twas your cause principally.

Cler. I know it; would it had not.

Enter CUTBEARD.

Daup. How now, Cutbeard! what news?

Cut. The best, the happiest that ever was, sir. There has been a mad gentleman with your uncle this morning, [*seeing Truewit.*]—I think this be the gentleman—that has almost talk'd him out of his wits, with threatening him from marriage—

Daup. On, I prithee.

Cut. And your uncle, sir, he thinks 'twas done by your procurement; therefore he will see the party you wot of presently; and if he like her, he says, and that she be so inclining to dumb as I have told him, he swears he will marry her to-day, instantly, and not defer it a minute longer.

Daup. Excellent! beyond our expectation!

True. Beyond our expectation! By this light, I knew it would be thus.

Daup. Nay, sweet Truewit, forgive me.

True. No, I was *ignorantly officious, impertinent;* this was the *absurd, weak part.*

Cler. Wilt thou ascribe that to merit now, was mere fortune!

True. Fortune! mere providence. Fortune had not a finger in't. I saw it must necessarily in nature fall out so: my genius is never false to me in these things. Shew me how it could be otherwise.

Daup. Nay, gentlemen, contend not; 'tis well now.

True. Alas, I let him go on with *inconsiderate*, and *rash*, and what he pleased.

Cler. Away, thou strange justifier of thyself, to be wiser than thou wert, by the event!

True. Event! by this light, thou shalt never persuade me, but I foresaw it as well as the stars themselves.

Daup. Nay, gentlemen, 'tis well now. Do you two entertain sir John Daw with discourse, while I send her away with instructions.

True. I'll be acquainted with her first, by your favour.

Cler. Master Truewit, lady, a friend of ours.

True. I am sorry I have not known you sooner, lady, to celebrate this rare virtue of your silence. [*Exeunt Daup., Epi., and Cutbeard.*

Cler. Faith, an you had come sooner, you should have seen and heard her well celebrated in sir John Daw's madrigals.

True. [*advances to Daw.*] Jack Daw, God save you! when saw you La-Foole?

Daw. Not since last night, master Truewit.

True. That's a miracle! I thought you two had been inseparable.

Daw. He's gone to invite his guests.

True. 'Odso! 'tis true! What a false memory have I towards that man! I am one: I met him even now, upon that he calls his delicate fine black horse, rid into foam, with posting from place to place, and person to person, to give them the cue—

Cler. Lest they should forget?

True. Yes: There was never poor captain took more pains at a muster to shew men, than he, at this meal, to shew friends.

Daw. It is his quarter-feast, sir.

Cler. What! do you say so, sir John?

True. Nay, Jack Daw will not be out, at the best friends he has, to the talent of his wit: Where's his mistress, to hear and applaud him? is she gone?

Daw. Is mistress Epicœne gone?

Cler. Gone afore, with sir Dauphine, I warrant, to the place.

True. Gone afore! that were a manifest injury, a disgrace and a half; to refuse him at such a festival-time as this, being a bravery, and a wit too!

Cler. Tut, he'll swallow it like cream: he's better read in Jure civili, than to esteem any thing a disgrace, is offer'd him from a mistress.

Daw. Nay, let her e'en go; she shall sit alone, and be dumb in her chamber a week together, for John Daw, I warrant her. Does she refuse me?

Cler. No, sir, do not take it so to heart; she does not refuse you, but a little neglects you. Good faith, Truewit, you were to blame, to put it into his head, that she does refuse him.

True. Sir, she does refuse him palpably, however you mince it. An I were as he, I would swear to speak ne'er a word to her to-day for't.

Daw. By this light, no more I will not.

True. Nor to any body else, sir.

Daw. Nay, I will not say so, gentlemen.

Cler. It had been an excellent happy condition for the company, if you could have drawn him to it. [*Aside.*

Daw. I'll be very melancholy, i'faith.

Cler. As a dog, if I were as you, sir John.

True. Or a snail, or a hog-louse: I would roll myself up for this day; in troth, they should not unwind me.

Daw. By this pick-tooth, so I will.

Cler. 'Tis well done: He begins already to be angry with his teeth.

Daw. Will you go, gentlemen?

Cler. Nay, you must walk alone, if you be right melancholy, sir John.

True. Yes, sir, we'll dog you, we'll follow you afar off. [*Exit Daw.*

Cler. Was there ever such a two yards of knighthood measured out by time, to be sold to laughter?

True. A mere talking mole, hang him! no mushroom was ever so fresh. A fellow so utterly nothing, as he knows not what he would be.

Cler. Let's follow him: but first let's go to Dauphine, he's hovering about the house to hear what news.

True. Content. [*Exeunt.*

SCENE III.—*A Room in* MOROSE'S *House.*

Enter MOROSE *and* MUTE, *followed by* CUTBEARD *with* EPICŒNE.

Mor. Welcome, Cutbeard! draw near with your fair charge: and in her ear softly entreat her to unmask. [*Epi. takes off her mask.*]—So! Is the door shut? [*Mute makes a leg.*]—Enough. Now, Cutbeard, with the same discipline I use to my family, I will question you. As I conceive, Cutbeard, this gentlewoman is she you have provided, and brought, in hope she will fit me in the place and person of a wife? Answer me not but with your leg, unless it be otherwise: [*Cut. makes a leg.*]—Very well done, Cutbeard. I conceive, besides, Cutbeard, you have been pre-acquainted with her birth, education, and qualities, or else you would not prefer her to my acceptance, in the weighty consequence of marriage. [*makes a leg.*]—This I conceive, Cutbeard. Answer me not but with your leg, unless it be otherwise. [*bows again.*]—Very well done, Cutbeard. Give aside now a little, and leave me to examine her condition, and aptitude to my affection. [*goes about her and views her.*]—She is exceeding fair, and of a special good favour; a sweet composition or harmony of limbs; her temper of beauty has the true height of my blood. The knave hath exceedingly well fitted me without: I will now try her within.—Come near, fair gentlewoman; let not my behaviour seem rude, though unto you, being rare, it may haply appear strange. [*Epicœne curtsies.*] Nay, lady, you may speak, though Cutbeard and my man might not; for of all sounds, only the sweet voice of a fair lady has the just length of mine ears. I beseech you, say, lady; out of the first fire of meeting eyes, they say, love is stricken: do you feel any such motion suddenly shot into you, from any part you see in me? ha, lady? [*Epi. curtsies.*]—Alas, lady, these answers by silent curtsies from you are too courtless and simple. I have ever had my breeding in court; and she that shall be my wife, must be accomplished with courtly and audacious ornaments. Can you speak, lady?

Epi. [*softly.*] Judge you, forsooth.

Mor. What say you, lady? Speak out, I beseech you.

Epi. Judge you, forsooth.

Mor. On my judgment, a divine softness! But can you naturally, lady, as I enjoin these by doctrine and industry, refer yourself to the search of my judgment, and, not taking pleasure in your tongue, which is a woman's chiefest pleasure, think it plausible to answer me by silent gestures, so long as my speeches jump right with what you conceive? [*Epi. curtsies.*]—Excellent! divine! if it were possible she should hold out thus!—Peace, Cutbeard, thou art made for ever, as thou hast made me, if this felicity have lasting: but I will try her further. Dear lady, I am courtly, I tell you, and I must have mine ears banqueted with pleasant and witty conferences, pretty girls, scoffs, and dalliance in her that I mean to choose for my bed-phere. The ladies in court think it a most desperate impair to their quickness of wit, and good carriage, if they cannot give occasion for a man to court 'em; and when an amorous discourse is set on foot, minister as good matter to continue it, as himself: And do you alone so much differ from all them, that what they, with so much circumstance, affect and toil for, to seem learn'd, to seem judicious, to seem sharp and conceited, you can bury in yourself with silence, and rather trust your graces to the fair conscience of virtue, than to the world's or your own proclamation?

Epi. [*softly.*] I should be sorry else.

Mor. What say you, lady? good lady, speak out.

Epi. I should be sorry else.

Mor. That sorrow doth fill me with gladness. O Morose, thou art happy above mankind! pray that thou mayest contain thyself. I will only put her to it once more, and it shall be with the utmost touch and test of their sex. But hear me, fair lady; I do also love to see her whom I shall choose for my heifer, to be the first and principal in all fashions, precede all the dames at court by a fortnight, have council of tailors, lineners, lace-women, embroiderers:

and sit with them sometimes twice a day upon French intelligences, and then come forth varied like nature, or oftener than she, and better by the help of art, her emulous servant. This do I affect: and how will you be able, lady, with this frugality of speech, to give the manifold but necessary instructions, for that bodice, these sleeves, those skirts, this cut, that stitch, this embroidery, that lace, this wire, those knots, that ruff, those roses, this girdle, that fan, the t'other scarf, these gloves? Ha! what say you, lady?

Epi. [*softly.*] I'll leave it to you, sir.

Mor. How, lady? pray you rise a note.

Epi. I leave it to wisdom and you, sir.

Mor. Admirable creature! I will trouble you no more: I will not sin against so sweet a simplicity. Let me now be bold to print on those divine lips the seal of being mine.—Cutbeard, I give thee the lease of thy house free; thank me not but with thy leg. [*Cutbeard shakes his head.*]—I know what thou wouldst say, she's poor, and her friends deceased. She has brought a wealthy dowry in her silence, Cutbeard; and in respect of her poverty, Cutbeard, I shall have her more loving and obedient, Cutbeard. Go thy ways, and get me a minister presently, with a soft low voice, to marry us; and pray him he will not be impertinent, but brief as he can; away: softly, Cutbeard. [*Exit Cut.*]—Sirrah, conduct your mistress into the dining-room, your now mistress. [*Exit Mute, followed by Epi.*]— O my felicity! how shall I be revenged on mine insolent kinsman, and his plots to fright me from marrying! This night I will get an heir, and thrust him out of my blood, like a stranger. He would be knighted, forsooth, and thought by that means to reign over me; his title must do it: No, kinsman, I will now make you bring me the tenth lord's and the sixteenth lady's letter, kinsman; and it shall do you no good, kinsman. Your knighthood itself shall come on its knees, and it shall be rejected; it shall be sued for its fees to execution, and not be redeem'd; it shall cheat at the twelve-penny ordinary, it knighthood, for its diet, all the term-time, and tell tales for it in the vacation to the hostess; or it knighthood shall do worse, take sanctuary in Cole-harbour, and fast. It shall fright all it friends with borrowing letters; and when one of the fourscore hath brought it knighthood ten shillings, it knighthood shall go to the Cranes, or the Bear at the Bridge-foot, and be drunk in fear; it shall not have money to discharge one tavern-reckoning, to invite the old creditors to forbear it knighthood, or the new, that should be, to trust it knighthood. It shall be the tenth name in the bond to take up the commodity of pipkins and stone-jugs: and the part thereof shall not furnish it knighthood forth for the attempting of a baker's widow, a brown baker's widow. It shall give it knighthood's name for a stallion, to all gamesome citizens' wives, and be refused, when the master of a dancing-school, or how do you call him, the worst reveller in the town is taken: it shall want clothes, and by reason of that, wit, to fool to lawyers. It shall not have hope to repair itself by Constantinople, Ireland, or Virginia;

but the best and last fortune to it knighthood shall be to make Dol Tear-sheet, or Kate Common a lady, and so it knighthood may eat.

[*Exit.*

SCENE IV.—*A Lane, near* Morose's *House.*

Enter Truewit, Dauphine, *and* Clerimont.

True. Are you sure he is not gone by?

Daup. No, I staid in the shop ever since.

Cler. But he may take the other end of the lane.

Daup. No, I told him I would be here at this end: I appointed him hither.

True. What a barbarian it is to stay then!

Daup. Yonder he comes.

Cler. And his charge left behind him, which is a very good sign, Dauphine.

Enter Cutbeard.

Daup. How now, Cutbeard! succeeds it, or no?

Cut. Past imagination, sir, *omnia secunda;* you could not have pray'd to have had it so well. *Saltat senex,* as it is in the proverb; he does triumph in his felicity, admires the party! he has given me the lease of my house too! and I am now going for a silent minister to marry them, and away.

True. 'Slight! get one of the silenced ministers; a zealous brother would torment him purely.

Cut. Cum privilegio, sir.

Daup. O, by no means; let's do nothing to hinder it now: when 'tis done and finished, I am for you, for any device of vexation.

Cut. And that shall be within this half hour, upon my dexterity, gentlemen.   Contrive what you can in the mean time, *bonis avibus.*

[*Exit.*

Cler. How the slave doth Latin it!

True. It would be made a jest to posterity, sirs, this day's mirth, if ye will.

Cler. Beshrew his heart that will not, I pronounce.

Daup. And for my part.   What is it?

True. To translate all La-Foole's company, and his feast thither, to-day, to celebrate this bride-ale.

Daup. Ay, marry; but how will't be done?

True. I'll undertake the directing of all the lady-guests thither, and then the meat must follow.

Cler. For God's sake, let's effect it; it will be an excellent comedy of affliction, so many several noises.

Daup. But are they not at the other place, already, think you?

True. I'll warrant you for the college-honours: one of their faces has not the priming colour laid on yet, nor the other her smock sleek'd.

Cler. O, but they'll rise earlier than ordinary to a feast.

True. Best go see, and assure ourselves.

Cler. Who knows the house?

True. I'll lead you: Were you never there yet?

Daup. Not I.

Cler. Nor I.

True. Where have you lived then? not know Tom Otter!

Cler. No: for God's sake, what is he?

True. An excellent animal, equal with your Daw or La-Foole, if not transcendant; and does Latin it as much as your barber: He is his wife's subject; he calls her princess, and at such times as these follows her up and down the house like a page, with his hat off, partly for heat, partly for reverence. At this instant he is marshalling of his bull, bear, and horse.

Daup. What be those, in the name of Sphynx?

True. Why, sir, he has been a great man at the Bear-garden in his time; and from that subtle sport has ta'en the witty denomination of his chief carousing cups. One he calls his bull, another his bear, another his horse. And then he has his lesser glasses, that he calls his deer and his ape; and several degrees of them too; and never is well, nor thinks any entertainment perfect, till these be brought out, and set on the cupboard.

Cler. For God's love!—we should miss this, if we should not go.

True. Nay, he has a thousand things as good, that will speak him all day. He will rail on his wife, with certain common places, behind her back; and to her face—

Daup. No more of him. Let's go see him, I petition you.

[*Exeunt.*

ACT III

SCENE I.—*A Room in* OTTER'S *House.*

Enter Captain OTTER *with his cups, and* Mistress OTTER.

Ott. Nay, good princess, hear me *pauca verba.*

Mrs. Ott. By that light, I'll have you chain'd up, with your bull-dogs and bear-dogs, if you be not civil the sooner. I'll send you to kennel, i'faith. You were best bait me with your bull, bear, and horse. Never a time that the courtiers or collegiates come to the house, but you make it a Shrove-tuesday! I would have you get your Whitsuntide velvet cap, and your staff in your hand, to entertain them: yes, in troth, do.

Ott. Not so, princess, neither; but under correction, sweet princess, give me leave.—These things I am known to the courtiers by: It is reported to them for my humour, and they receive it so, and do expect it. Tom Otter's bull, bear, and horse is known all over England, *in rerum natura.*

Mrs. Ott. 'Fore me, I will *na-ture* them over to Paris-garden, and *na-ture* you thither too, if you pronounce them again. Is a bear a fit beast, or a bull, to mix in society with great ladies? think in your discretion, in any good policy.

Ott. The horse then, good princess.

Mrs. Ott. Well, I am contented for the horse; they love to be well horsed, I know: I love it myself.

Ott. And it is a delicate fine horse this: *Poetarum Pegasus.* Under correction, princess, Jupiter did turn himself into a—*taurus,* or bull, under correction, good princess.

Enter TRUEWIT, CLERIMONT, *and* DAUPHINE, *behind.*

Mrs. Ott. By my integrity, I'll send you over to the Bank-side; I'll commit you to the master of the Garden, if I hear but a syllable more. Must my house or my roof be polluted with the scent of bears and bulls, when it is perfumed for great ladies? Is this according to the instrument, when I married you? that I would be princess, and reign in mine own house; and you would be my subject, and obey me? What did you bring me, should make you thus peremptory? do I allow you your half-crown a day, to spend where you will, among your gamesters, to vex and torment me at such times as these? Who gives you your maintenance, I pray you? who allows you your horse-meat and man's meat? your three suits of apparel a year? your four pair of stockings, one silk, three worsted? your clean linen, your bands and cuffs, when I can get you to wear them?—'tis marle you have them on now.—Who graces you with courtiers or great personages, to speak to you out of their coaches, and come home to your house? Were you ever so much as look'd upon by a lord or a lady, before I married you, but on the Easter or Whitsun-holidays? and then out at the banqueting-house window, when Ned Whiting or George Stone were at the stake?

True. For God's sake, let's go stave her off him.

Mrs. Ott. Answer me to that. And did not I take you up from thence, in an old greasy buff-doublet, with points, and green velvet sleeves, out at the elbows? you forget this.

True. She'll worry him, if we help not in time.

[*They come forward.*

Mrs. Ott. O, here are some of the gallants! Go to, behave yourself distinctly, and with good morality; or, I protest, I'll take away your exhibition.

True. By your leave, fair mistress Otter, I'll be bold to enter these gentlemen in your acquaintance.

Mrs. Ott. It shall not be obnoxious, or difficil, sir.

True. How does my noble captain? is the bull, bear, and horse in *rerum natura* still?

Ott. Sir, *sic visum superis.*

Mrs. Ott. I would you would but intimate them, do. Go your ways in, and get toasts and butter made for the woodcocks: that's a fit province for you. [*Drives him off.*

Cler. Alas, what a tyranny is this poor fellow married to!

True. O, but the sport will be anon, when we get him loose.

Daup. Dares he ever speak?

True. No Anabaptist ever rail'd with the like license: but mark her language in the mean time, I beseech you.

Mrs. Ott. Gentlemen, you are very aptly come. My cousin, sir Amorous, will be here briefly.

True. In good time, lady. Was not sir John Daw here, to ask for him, and the company?

Mrs. Ott. I cannot assure you, master Truewit. Here was a very melancholy knight in a ruff, that demanded my subject for somebody, a gentleman, I think.

Cler. Ay, that was he, lady.

Mrs. Ott. But he departed straight, I can resolve you.

Daup. What an excellent choice phrase this lady expresses in.

True. O, sir, she is the only authentical courtier, that is not naturally bred one, in the city.

Mrs. Ott. You have taken that report upon trust, gentlemen.

True. No, I assure you, the court governs it so, lady, in your behalf.

Mrs. Ott. I am the servant of the court and courtiers, sir.

True. They are rather your idolaters.

Mrs. Ott. Not so, sir.

Enter CUTBEARD.

Daup. How now, Cutbeard! any cross?

Cut. O no, sir, *omnia bene.* 'Twas never better on the hinges; all's sure. I have so pleased him with a curate, that he's gone to't almost with the delight he hopes for soon.

Daup. What is he for a vicar?

Cut. One that has catch'd a cold, sir, and can scarce be heard six inches off; as if he spoke out of a bulrush that were not pick'd, or his throat were full of pith: a fine quick fellow, and an excellent barber of prayers. I came to tell you, sir, that you might *omnem movere lapidem,* as they say, be ready with your vexation.

Daup. Gramercy, honest Cutbeard! be thereabouts with thy key, to let us in.

Cut. I will not fail you, sir; *ad manum.*   [*Exit.*

True. Well, I'll go watch my coaches.

Cler. Do; and we'll send Daw to you, if you meet him not.
                                                    [*Exit Truewit.*

Mrs. Ott. Is master Truewit gone?

Daup. Yes, lady, there is some unfortunate business fallen out.

Mrs. Ott. So I adjudged by the physiognomy of the fellow that came in; and I had a dream last night too of the new pageant, and my lady mayoress, which is always very ominous to me. I told it my lady Haughty t'other day, when her honour came hither to see some China stuffs; and she expounded it out of Artemidorus, and I have found it since very true. It has done me many affronts.

Cler. Your dream, lady?

Mrs. Ott. Yes, sir, any thing I do but dream of the city. It stain'd me a damask table-cloth, cost me eighteen pound, at one time; and burnt me a black satin gown, as I stood by the fire, at my lady Centaure's chamber in the college, another time. A third time, at the lords' masque, it dropt all my wire and my ruff with wax candle, that I could not go up to the banquet. A fourth time, as I was taking coach to go to Ware, to meet a friend, it dash'd me a new suit all over (a crimson satin doublet, and black velvet skirts) with a brewer's horse, that I was fain to go in and shift me, and kept my chamber a leash of days for the anguish of it.

Daup. These were dire mischances, lady.

Cler. I would not dwell in the city, an 'twere so fatal to me.

Mrs. Ott. Yes, sir; but I do take advice of my doctor to dream of it as little as I can.

Damp. You do well, mistress Otter.

Enter Sir JOHN DAW, *and is taken aside by* CLERIMONT.

Mrs. Ott. Will it please you to enter the house farther, gentlemen?

Daup. And your favour, lady: but we stay to speak with a knight, sir John Daw, who is here come. We shall follow you, lady.

Mrs. Ott. At your own time, sir. It is my cousin sir Amorous his feast—

Daup. I know it, lady.

Mrs. Ott. And mine together. But it is for his honour, and therefore I take no name of it, more than of the place.

Daup. You are a bounteous kinswoman.

Mrs. Ott. Your servant, sir.   [*Exit.*

Cler. [*coming forward with Daw.*] Why, do not you know it, sir John Daw?

Daw. No, I am a rook if I do.

Cler. I'll tell you, then; she's married by this time. And, whereas you were put in the head, that she was gone with sir Dauphine, I assure you, sir Dauphine has been the noblest, honestest friend to you, that ever gentleman of your quality could boast of. He has discover'd the whole plot, and made your mistress so acknowledging, and indeed so ashamed of her injury to you, that she desires you to forgive her, and but grace her wedding with your presence to-day— She is to be married to a very good fortune, she says, his uncle, old Morose; and she will'd me in private to tell you, that she shall be able to do you more favours, and with more security now than before.

Daw. Did she say so, i'faith?

Cler. Why, what do you think of me, sir John? ask sir Dauphine.

Daw. Nay, I believe you.—Good sir Dauphine, did she desire me to forgive her?

Daup. I assure you, sir John, she did.

Daw. Nay, then, I do with all my heart, and I'll be jovial.

Cler. Yes, for look you, sir, this was the injury to you. La-Foole intended this feast to honour her bridal day, and made you the property to invite the college ladies, and promise to bring her; and then at the time she would have appear'd, as his friend, to have given you the dor. Whereas now, sir Dauphine has brought her to a feeling of it, with this kind of satisfaction, that you shall bring all the ladies to the place where she is, and be very jovial; and there, she will have a dinner, which shall be in your name: and so disappoint La-Foole, to make you good again, and, as it were, a saver in the main.

Daw. As I am a knight, I honour her; and forgive her heartily.

Cler. About it then presently. Truewit is gone before to confront the coaches, and to acquaint you with so much, if he meet you. Join with him, and 'tis well.—

Enter Sir AMOROUS LA-FOOLE.

See; here comes your antagonist; but take you no notice, but be very jovial.

La-F. Are the ladies come, sir John Daw, and your mistress? [*Exit Daw.*]—Sir Dauphine! you are exceeding welcome, and honest master Clerimont. Where's my cousin? did you see no collegiates, gentlemen?

Daup. Collegiates! do you not hear, sir Amorous, how you are abused?

La-F. How, sir!

Cler. Will you speak so kindly to sir John Daw, that has done you such an affront?

La-F. Wherein, gentlemen? let me be a suitor to you to know, I beseech you.

Cler. Why, sir, his mistress is married to-day to sir Dauphine's uncle, your cousin's neighbour, and he has diverted all the ladies, and all your company thither, to frustrate your provision, and stick a disgrace upon you. He was here now to have enticed us away from you too: but we told him his own, I think.

La-F. Has sir John Daw wrong'd me so inhumanly?

Daup. He has done it, sir Amorous, most maliciously and treacherously: but, if you'll be ruled by us, you shall quit him, i'faith.

La-F. Good gentlemen, I'll make one, believe it. How, I pray?

Daup. Marry, sir, get me your pheasants, and your godwits, and your best meat, and dish it in silver dishes of your cousin's presently; and say nothing, but clap me a clean towel about you, like a sewer; and, bare-headed, march afore it with a good confidence, ('tis but over the way, hard by,) and we'll second you, where you shall set it on the board, and bid them welcome to't, which shall shew 'tis yours, and disgrace his preparation utterly: and for your cousin, whereas she should be troubled here at home with care of making and giving welcome, she shall transfer all that labour thither, and be a principal guest herself; sit rank'd with the college-honours, and be honour'd, and have her health drunk as often, as bare and as loud as the best of them.

La-F. I'll go tell her presently. It shall be done, that's resolved.
                                                                    [*Exit.*

Cler. I thought he would not hear it out, but 'twould take him.

Daup. Well, there be guests and meat now; how shall we do for music?

Cler. The smell of the venison, going through the street, will invite one noise of fiddlers or other.

Daup. I would it would call the trumpeters hither!

Cler. Faith, there is hope: they have intelligence of all feasts. There's good correspondence betwixt them and the London cooks: 'tis twenty to one but we have them.

Daup. 'Twill be a most solemn day for my uncle, and an excellent fit of mirth for us.

Cler. Ay, if we can hold up the emulation betwixt Foole and Daw, and never bring them to expostulate.

Daup. Tut, flatter them both, as Truewit says, and you may take their understandings in a purse-net. They'll believe themselves to be just such men as we make them, neither more nor less. They have nothing, not the use of their senses, but by tradition.

Re-enter LA-FOOLE, *like a Sewer.*

Cler. See! sir Amorous has his towel on already. Have you persuaded your cousin?

La-F. Yes, 'tis very feasible: she'll do any thing, she says, rather than the La-Fooles shall be disgraced.

Daup. She is a noble kinswoman. It will be such a pestling device, sir Amorous; it will pound all your enemy's practices to powder, and blow him up with his own mine, his own train.

La-F. Nay, we'll give fire, I warrant you.

Cler. But you must carry it privately, without any noise, and take no notice by any means—

Re-enter Captain OTTER.

Ott. Gentlemen, my princess says you shall have all her silver dishes, *festinate:* and she's gone to alter her tire a little, and go with you—

Cler. And yourself too, captain Otter?

Daup. By any means, sir.

Ott. Yes, sir, I do mean it: but I would entreat my cousin sir Amorous, and you, gentlemen, to be suitors to my princess, that I may carry my bull and my bear, as well as my horse.

Cler. That you shall do, captain Otter.

La-F. My cousin will never consent, gentlemen.

Daup. She must consent, sir Amorous, to reason.

La-F. Why, she says they are no decorum among ladies.

Ott. But they are *decora*, and that's better, sir.

Cler. Ay, she must hear argument. Did not Pasiphaë, who was a queen, love a bull? and was not Calisto, the mother of Arcas, turn'd into a bear, and made a star, mistress Ursula, in the heavens?

Ott. O lord! that I could have said as much! I will have these stories painted in the Bear-garden, *ex Ovidii metamorphosi.*

Daup. Where is your princess, captain? pray, be our leader.

Ott. That I shall, sir.

Cler. Make haste, good sir Amorous. [*Exeunt.*

SCENE II.—*A Room in* MOROSE'S *House.*

Enter MOROSE, EPICŒNE, Parson, *and* CUTBEARD.

Mor. Sir, there's an angel for yourself, and a brace of angels for your cold. Muse not at this manage of my bounty. It is fit we should thank fortune, double to nature, for any benefit she confers upon us; besides, it is your imperfection, but my solace.

Par. [*speaks as having a cold.*] I thank your worship; so it is mine, now.

Mor. What says he, Cutbeard?

Cut. He says, *præsto*, sir, whensoever your worship needs him, he can be ready with the like. He got this cold with sitting up late, and singing catches with cloth-workers.

Mor. No more. I thank him.

Par. God keep your worship, and give you much joy with your fair spouse!—uh! uh! uh!

Mor. O, O! stay, Cutbeard! let him give me five shillings of my money back. As it is bounty to reward benefits, so it is equity to mulct injuries. I will have it. What says he?

Cler. He cannot change it, sir.

Mor. It must be changed.

Cut. Cough again. [*Aside to Parson.*

Mor. What says he?

Cut. He will cough out the rest, sir.

Par. Uh, uh, uh!

Mor. Away, away with him! stop his mouth! away! I forgive it.— [*Exit Cut. thrusting out the Par.*

Epi. Fie, master Morose, that you will use this violence to a man of the church.

Mor. How!

Epi. It does not become your gravity, or breeding, as you pretend, in court, to have offer'd this outrage on a waterman, or any more boisterous creature, much less on a man of his civil coat.

Mor. You can speak then!

Epi. Yes, sir.

Mor. Speak out, I mean.

Epi. Ay, sir. Why, did you think you had married a statue, or a motion only? one of the French puppets, with the eyes turn'd with a wire? or some innocent out of the hospital, that would stand with her hands thus, and a plaise mouth, and look upon you?

Mor. O immodesty! a manifest woman! What, Cutbeard!

Epi. Nay, never quarrel with Cutbeard, sir; it is too late now. I confess it doth bate somewhat of the modesty I had, when I writ simply maid: but I hope I shall make it a stock still competent to the estate and dignity of your wife.

Mor. She can talk!

Epi. Yes, indeed, sir.

Enter MUTE.

Mor. What sirrah! None of my knaves there? where is this impostor Cutbeard?   [*Mute makes signs.*

Epi. Speak to him, fellow, speak to him! I'll have none of his coacted, unnatural dumbness in my house, in a family where I govern.   [*Exit Mute.*

Mor. She is my regent already! I have married a Penthesilea, a Semiramis; sold my liberty to a distaff.

Enter TRUEWIT.

True. Where's master Morose?

Mor. Is he come again! Lord have mercy upon me!

True. I wish you all joy, mistress Epicœne, with your grave and honourable match.

Epi. I return you the thanks, master Truewit, so friendly a wish deserves.

Mor. She has acquaintance, too!

True. God save you, sir, and give you all contentment in your fair choice, here! Before, I was the bird of night to you, the owl; but now I am the messenger of peace, a dove, and bring you the glad wishes of many friends to the celebration of this good hour.

Mor. What hour, sir?

True. Your marriage hour, sir. I commend your resolution, that, notwithstanding all the dangers I laid afore you, in the voice of a night-crow, would yet go on, and be yourself. It shews you are a man constant to your own ends, and upright to your purposes, that would not be put off with left-handed cries.

Mor. How should you arrive at the knowledge of so much?

True. Why, did you ever hope, sir, committing the secrecy of it to a barber, that less than the whole town should know it? you might as well have told it the conduit, or the bake-house, or the infantry that follow the court, and with more security. Could your gravity forget so old and noted a remnant, as, *lippis et tonsoribus notum?* Well, sir, forgive it yourself now, the fault, and be communicable with your friends. Here will be three or four fashionable ladies from the college to visit you presently, and their train of minions and followers.

Mor. Bar my doors! bar my doors! Where are all my eaters? my mouths, now?—

Enter Servants.

Bar up my doors, you varlets!

Epi. He is a varlet that stirs to such an office. Let them stand open. I would see him that dares move his eyes toward it. Shall I have a barricado made against my friends, to be barr'd of any pleasure they can bring in to me with their honourable visitation?   [*Exeunt Ser.*

Mor. O Amazonian impudence!

True. Nay, faith, in this, sir, she speaks but reason; and, me-thinks, is more continent than you. Would you go to bed so presently, sir, afore noon? a man of your head and hair should owe more to that reverend ceremony, and not mount the marriage-bed like a town-bull, or a mountain-goat; but stay the due season; and ascend it then with religion and fear. Those delights are to be steeped in the humour and silence of the night; and give the day to other open pleasures, and jollities of feasting, of music, of revels, of discourse: we'll have all, sir, that may make your Hymen high and happy.

Mor. O my torment, my torment!

True. Nay, if you endure the first half hour, sir, so tediously, and with this irksomeness; what comfort or hope can this fair gentle-woman make to herself hereafter, in the consideration of so many years as are to come —

Mor. Of my affliction. Good sir, depart, and let her do it alone.

True. I have done, sir.

Mor. That cursed barber.

True. Yes, faith, a cursed wretch indeed, sir.

Mor. I have married his cittern, that's common to all men. Some plague above the plague—

True. All Egypt's ten plagues.

Mor. Revenge me on him!

True. 'Tis very well, sir. If you laid on a curse or two more, I'll assure you he'll bear them. As, that he may get the pox with seeking to cure it, sir; or, that while he is curling another man's hair, his own may drop off; or, for burning some male-bawd's lock, he may have his brain beat out with the curling iron.

Mor. No, let the wretch live wretched. May he get the itch, and his shop so lousy, as no man dare come at him, nor he come at no man!

True. Ay, and if he would swallow all his balls for pills, let not them purge him.

Mor. Let his warming-pan be ever cold.

True. A perpetual frost underneath it, sir.

Mor. Let him never hope to see fire again.

True. But in hell, sir.

Mor. His chairs be always empty, his scissars rust, and his combs mould in their cases.

True. Very dreadful that! And may he lose the invention, sir, of carving lanterns in paper.

Mor. Let there be no bawd carted that year, to employ a bason of his: but let him be glad to eat his sponge for bread.

True. And drink lotium to it, and much good do him.

Mor. Or, for want of bread

True. Eat ear-wax, sir. I'll help you. Or, draw his own teeth, and add them to the lute-string.

Mor. No, beat the old ones to powder, and make bread of them.

True. Yes, make meal of the mill-stones.

Mor. May all the botches and burns that he has cured on others break out upon him.

True. And he now forget the cure of them in himself, sir; or, if he do remember it, let him have scraped all his linen into lint for't, and have not a rag left him for to set up with.

Mor. Let him never set up again, but have the gout in his hands for ever!—Now, no more, sir.

True. O, that last was too high set; you might go less with him, i'faith, and be revenged enough: as, that he be never able to new-paint his pole—

Mor. Good sir, no more, I forgot myself.

True. Or, want credit to take up with a comb-maker—

Mor. No more, sir.

True. Or, having broken his glass in a former despair, fall now into a much greater, of ever getting another—

Mor. I beseech you, no more.

True. Or, that he never be trusted with trimming of any but chimney-sweepers—

Mor. Sir—

True. Or, may he cut a collier's throat with his razor, by chance medley, and yet be hang'd for't.

Mor. I will forgive him, rather than hear any more. I beseech you, sir.

Enter DAW, *introducing* Lady HAUGHTY, CENTAURE, MAVIS, *and* TRUSTY.

Daw. This way, madam.

Mor. O, the sea breaks in upon me! another flood! an inundation! I shall be overwhelmed with noise. It beats already at my shores. I feel an earthquake in my self for't.

Daw. 'Give you joy, mistress.

Mor. Has she servants too!

Daw. I have brought some ladies here to see and know you. My lady Haughty—[*as he presents them severally, Epi. kisses them.*] this my lady Centaure—mistress Dol Mavis—mistress Trusty, my lady Haughty's woman. Where's your husband? let's see him: can he endure no noise? let me come to him.

Mor. What nomenclator is this!

True. Sir John Daw, sir, your wife's servant, this.

Mor. A Daw, and her servant! O, 'tis decreed, 'tis decreed of me, an she have such servants. [*Going.*

True. Nay, sir, you must kiss the ladies; you must not go away, now: they come toward you to seek you out.

Hau. I'faith, master Morose, would you steal a marriage thus, in the midst of so many friends, and not acquaint us? Well, I'll kiss you, notwithstanding the justice of my quarrel: you shall give me leave, mistress, to use a becoming familiarity with your husband.

Epi. Your ladyship does me an honour in it, to let me know he is so worthy your favour: as you have done both him and me grace to visit so unprepared a pair to entertain you.

Mor. Compliment! compliment!

Epi. But I must lay the burden of that upon my servant here.

Hau. It shall not need, mistress Morose; we will all bear, rather than one shall be opprest.

Mor. I know it: and you will teach her the faculty, if she be to learn it.   [*Walks aside while the rest talk apart.*

Hau. Is this the silent woman?

Cen. Nay, she has found her tongue since she was married, Master Truewit says.

Hau. O, master Truewit! 'save you. What kind of creature is your bride here? she speaks, methinks!

True. Yes, madam, believe it, she is a gentlewoman of very absolute behaviour, and of a good race.

Hau. And Jack Daw told us she could not speak!

True. So it was carried in plot, madam, to put her upon this old fellow, by sir Dauphine, his nephew, and one or two more of us: but she is a woman of an excellent assurance, and an extraordinary happy wit and tongue. You shall see her make rare sport with Daw ere night.

Hau. And he brought us to laugh at her!

True. That falls out often, madam, that he that thinks himself the master-wit, is the master-fool. I assure your ladyship, ye cannot laugh at her.

Hau. No, we'll have her to the college: An she have wit, she shall be one of us, shall she not, Centaure? we'll make her a collegiate.

Cen. Yes, faith, madam, and Mavis and she will set up a side.

True. Believe it, madam, and mistress Mavis she will sustain her part.

Mav. I'll tell you that, when I have talk'd with her, and tried her.

Hau. Use her very civilly, Mavis.

Mav. So I will, madam.   [*Whispers her.*

Mor. Blessed minute! that they would whisper thus ever!
                                                  [*Aside.*

True. In the mean time, madam, would but your ladyship help to vex him a little: you know his disease, talk to him about the wedding ceremonies, or call for your gloves, or—

Hau. Let me alone. Centaure, help me.—Master bridegroom, where are you?

Mor. O, it was too miraculously good to last!   [*Aside.*

Hau. We see no ensigns of a wedding here; no character of a bride-ale: where be our scarves and our gloves? I pray you, give them us. Let us know your bride's colours, and yours at least.

Cen. Alas, madam, he has provided none.

Mor. Had I known your ladyship's painter, I would.

Hau. He has given it you, Centaure, i'faith. But do you hear, master Morose? a jest will not absolve you in this manner. You that have suck'd the milk of the court, and from thence have been brought up to the very strong meats and wine of it; been a courtier from the biggen to the night-cap, as we may say, and you to offend in such a high point of ceremony as this, and let your nuptials want all marks of solemnity! How much plate have you lost to-day, (if you had but regarded your profit,) what gifts, what friends, through your mere rusticity!

Mor. Madam—

Hau. Pardon me, sir, I must insinuate your errors to you; no gloves? no garters? no scarves? no epithalamium? no masque?

Daw. Yes, madam, I'll make an epithalamium, I promise my mistress; I have begun it already: will your ladyship hear it?

Hau. Ay, good Jack Daw.

Mor. Will it please your ladyship command a chamber, and be private with your friend? you shall have your choice of rooms to retire to after: my whole house is yours. I know it hath been your ladyship's errand into the city at other times, however now you have been unhappily diverted upon me; but I shall be loth to break any honourable custom of your ladyship's. And therefore, good madam—

Epi. Come, you are a rude bridegroom, to entertain ladies of honour in this fashion.

Cen. He is a rude groom indeed.

True. By that light you deserve to be grafted, and have your horns reach from one side of the island to the other.—Do not mistake me, sir; I but speak this to give the ladies some heart again, not for any malice to you.

Mor. Is this your bravo, ladies?

True. As God [shall] help me, if you utter such another word, I'll take mistress bride in, and begin to you in a very sad cup; do you see? Go to, know your friends, and such as love you.

Enter CLERIMONT, *followed by a number of* Musicians.

Cler. By your leave, ladies. Do you want any music? I have brought you variety of noises. Play, sirs, all of you.

[*Aside to the Musicians, who strike up all together.*

Mor. O, a plot, a plot, a plot, a plot, upon me! this day I shall be their anvil to work on, they will grate me asunder. 'Tis worse than the noise of a saw.

Cler. No, they are hair, rosin, and guts: I can give you the receipt.

True. Peace, boys!

Cler. Play! I say.

True. Peace, rascals! You see who's your friend now, sir: take courage, put on a martyr's resolution. Mock down all their attemptings with patience: 'tis but a day, and I would suffer heroically. Should an ass exceed me in fortitude? no. You betray your infirmity with your hanging dull ears, and make them insult: bear up bravely, and constantly. [*La-Foole passes over the stage as a Sewer, followed by Servants carrying dishes, and Mistress Otter.*]—Look you here, sir, what honour is done you unexpected,

by your nephew; a wedding-dinner come, and a knight-sewer before
it, for the more reputation: and fine mistress Otter, your neighbour,
in the rump or tail of it.

Mor. Is that Gorgon, that Medusa come! hide me, hide me.

True. I warrant you, sir, she will not transform you. Look upon
her with a good courage. Pray you entertain her, and conduct
your guests in. No!—Mistress bride, will you entreat in the ladies?
your bridegroom is so shame-faced, here.

Epi. Will it please your ladyship, madam?

Hau. With the benefit of your company, mistress.

Epi. Servant, pray you perform your duties.

Daw. And glad to be commanded, mistress.

Cen. How like you her wit, Mavis?

Mav. Very prettily, absolutely well.

Mrs. Ott. 'Tis my place.

Mav. You shall pardon me, mistress Otter.

Mrs. Ott. Why, I am a collegiate.

Mav. But not in ordinary.

Mrs. Ott. But I am.

Mav. We'll dispute that within.   [*Exeunt Ladies.*

Cler. Would this had lasted a little longer.

True. And that they had sent for the heralds.

Enter Captain OTTER.

—Captain Otter! what news?

Ott. I have brought my bull, bear, and horse, in private, and
yonder are the trumpeters without, and the drum, gentlemen.

              [*The drum and trumpets sound within.*

Mor. O, O, O!

Ott. And we will have a rouse in each of them, anon, for bold
Britons, i'faith.   [*They sound again.*

Mor. O, O, O!   [*Exit hastily.*

Omnes. Follow, follow, follow!   [*Exeunt.*

ACT IV

SCENE I.—*A Room in* MOROSE'S *House.*

Enter TRUEWIT *and* CLERIMONT.

True. Was there ever poor bridegroom so tormented? or man,
indeed?

Cler. I have not read of the like in the chronicles of the land.

True. Sure, he cannot but go to a place of rest, after all this
purgatory.

Cler. He may presume it, I think.

True. The spitting, the coughing, the laughter, the neezing, the
farting, dancing, noise of the music, and her masculine and loud

commanding, and urging the whole family, makes him think he has married a fury.

Cler. And she carries it up bravely.

True. Ay, she takes any occasion to speak: that's the height on't.

Cler. And how soberly Dauphine labours to satisfy him, that it was none of his plot!

True. And has almost brought him to the faith, in the article. Here he comes.—

Enter Sir DAUPHINE.

Where is he now? what's become of him, Dauphine?

Daup. O, hold me up a little, I shall go away in the jest else. He has got on his whole nest of night-caps, and lock'd himself up in the top of the house, as high as ever he can climb from the noise. I peep'd in at a cranny, and saw him sitting over a cross-beam of the roof, like him on the saddler's horse in Fleet-street, upright: and he will sleep there.

Cler. But where are your collegiates?

Daup. Withdrawn with the bride in private.

True. O, they are instructing her in the college-grammar. If she have grace with them, she knows all their secrets instantly.

Cler. Methinks the lady Haughty looks well to-day, for all my dispraise of her in the morning. I think, I shall come about to thee again, Truewit.

True. Believe it, I told you right. Women ought to repair the losses time and years have made in their features, with dressings. And an intelligent woman, if she know by herself the least defect, will be most curious to hide it: and it becomes her. If she be short, let her sit much, lest, when she stands, she be thought to sit. If she have an ill foot, let her wear her gown the longer, and her shoe the thinner. If a fat hand, and scald nails, let her carve the less, and act in gloves. If a sour breath, let her never discourse fasting, and always talk at her distance. If she have black and rugged teeth, let her offer the less at laughter, especially if she laugh wide and open.

Cler. O, you shall have some women, when they laugh, you would think they brayed, it is so rude and—

True. Ay, and others, that will stalk in their gait like an estrich, and take huge strides. I cannot endure such a sight. I love measure in the feet, and number in the voice: they are gentlenesses, that oftentimes draw no less than the face.

Daup. How camest thou to study these creatures so exactly? I would thou wouldst make me a proficient.

True. Yes, but you must leave to live in your chamber, then, a month together upon Amadis de Gaul, or Don Quixote, as you are wont; and come abroad where the matter is frequent, to court, to tiltings, public shows and feasts, to plays, and church sometimes: thither they come to shew their new tires too, to see, and to be seen. In these places a man shall find whom to love, whom to play with, whom to touch once, whom to hold ever. The variety arrests his judgment. A wench to please a man comes not down dropping from the ceiling, as he lies on his back droning a tobacco-pipe. He must go where she is.

Daup. Yes, and be never the nearer.

True. Out, heretic! That diffidence makes thee worthy it should be so.

Cler. He says true to you, Dauphine.

Daup. Why?

True. A man should not doubt to overcome any woman. Think he can vanquish them, and he shall: for though they deny, their desire is to be tempted. Penelope herself cannot hold out long. Ostend, you saw, was taken at last. You must persévér, and hold to your purpose. They would solicit us, but that they are afraid. Howsoever, they wish in their hearts we should solicit them. Praise them, flatter them, you shall never want eloquence or trust: even the chastest delight to feel themselves that way rubb'd. With praises you must mix kisses too: if they take them, they'll take more—though they strive, they would be overcome.

Cler. O, but a man must beware of force.

True. It is to them an acceptable violence, and has oft-times the place of the greatest courtesy. She that might have been forced, and you let her go free without touching, though then she seem to thank you, will ever hate you after; and glad in the face, is assuredly sad at the heart.

Cler. But all women are not to be taken all ways.

True. 'Tis true; no more than all birds, or all fishes. If you appear learned to an ignorant wench, or jocund to a sad, or witty to a foolish, why she presently begins to mistrust herself. You must approach them in their own height, their own line; for the contrary makes many, that fear to commit themselves to noble and worthy fellows, run into the embraces of a rascal. If she love wit, give verses, though you borrow them of a friend, or buy them, to have good. If valour, talk of your sword, and be frequent in the mention of quarrels, though you be staunch in fighting. If activity, be seen on your barbary often, or leaping over stools, for the credit of your back. If she love good clothes or dressing, have your learned council about you every morning, your French tailor, barber, linener, etc. Let your powder, your glass, and your comb be your dearest acquaintance. Take more care for the ornament of your head, than the safety; and wish the commonwealth rather troubled, than a hair about you. That will take her. Then, if she be covetous and craving, do you promise any thing, and perform sparingly; so shall you keep her in appetite still. Seem as you would give, but be like a barren field, that yields little; or unlucky dice to foolish and hoping gamesters. Let your gifts be slight and dainty, rather than precious. Let cunning be above cost. Give cherries at time of year, or apricots; and say, they were sent you out of the country, though you bought them in Cheapside. Admire her tires: like her in all fashions; compare her in every habit to some deity; invent excellent dreams to flatter her, and riddles; or, if she be a great one, perform always the second parts to her: like what she likes, praise whom she praises, and fail not to make the household and servants yours, yea the whole family, and salute them by their names, ('tis but light cost, if you can purchase them so,) and make her physician your pensioner, and her chief woman. Nor will it be out of your gain to make love to her too, so she follow, not usher her lady's pleasure. All blabbing is taken away, when she comes to be a part of the crime.

Daup. On what courtly lap hast thou late slept, to come forth so sudden and absolute a courtling?

True. Good faith, I should rather question you, that are so hearkening after these mysteries. I begin to suspect your diligence, Dauphine. Speak, art thou in love in earnest?

Daup. Yes, by my troth, am I; 'twere ill dissembling before thee.

True. With which of them, I prithee?

Daup. With all the collegiates.

Cler. Out on thee! We'll keep you at home, believe it, in the stable, an you be such a stallion.

True. No; I like him well. Men should love wisely, and all women; some one for the face, and let her please the eye; another for the skin, and let her please the touch; a third for the voice, and let her please the ear; and where the objects mix, let the senses so too. Thou would'st think it strange, if I should make them all in love with thee afore night!

Daup. I would say, thou hadst the best philtre in the world, and couldst do more than madam Medea, or doctor Foreman.

True. If I do not, let me play the mountebank for my meat, while I live, and the bawd for my drink.

Daup. So be it, I say.

Enter OTTER, *with his three Cups,* DAW, *and* LA-FOOLE.

Ott. O lord, gentlemen, how my knights and I have mist you here!

Cler. Why, captain, what service, what service?

Ott. To see me bring up my bull, bear, and horse to fight.

Daw. Yes, faith, the captain says we shall be his dogs to bait them.

Daup. A good employment.

True. Come on, let's see your course, then.

La-F. I am afraid my cousin will be offended, if she come.

Ott. Be afraid of nothing.—Gentlemen, I have placed the drum and the trumpets, and one to give them the sign when you are ready. Here's my bull for myself, and my bear for sir John Daw, and my horse for sir Amorous. Now set your foot to mine, and yours to his, and—

La-F. Pray God my cousin come not.

Ott. St. George, and St. Andrew, fear no cousins. Come, sound, sound! [*Drum and trumpets sound.*] *Et rauco strepuerunt cornua cantu.* [*They drink.*

True. Well said, captain, i'faith; well fought at the bull.

Cler. Well held at the bear.

True. Low, low! captain.

Daup. O, the horse has kick'd off his dog already.

La-F. I cannot drink it, as I am a knight.

True. Ods so! off with his spurs, somebody.

La-F. It goes against my conscience. My cousin will be angry with it.

Daw. I have done mine.

True. You fought high and fair, sir John.

Cler. At the head.

Daup. Like an excellent bear-dog.

Cler. You take no notice of the business, I hope?

Daw. Not a word, sir; you see we are jovial.

Ott. Sir Amorous, you must not equivocate. It must be pull'd down, for all my cousin.

Cler. 'Sfoot, if you take not your drink, they'll think you are discontented with something; you'll betray all, if you take the least notice.

La-F. Not I; I'll both drink and talk then.

Ott. You must pull the horse on his knees, sir Amorous; fear no cousins. *Jacta est alea.*

True. O, now he's in his vein, and bold. The least hint given him of his wife now, will make him rail desperately.

Cler. Speak to him of her.

True. Do you, and I'll fetch her to the hearing of it. [*Exit.*

Daup. Captain He - Otter, your She - Otter is coming, your wife.

Ott. Wife! buz? *titivilitium!* There's no such thing in nature. I confess, gentlemen, I have a cook, a laundress, a house-drudge, that serves my necessary turns, and goes under that title; but he's an ass that will be so uxorious to tie his affections to one circle. Come, the name dulls appetite. Here, replenish again; another bout. [*Fills the cups again.*] Wives are nasty, sluttish animals.

Daup. O, captain.

Ott. As ever the earth bare, *tribus verbis.*—Where's master Truewit?

Daw. He's slipt aside, sir.

Cler. But you must drink and be jovial.

Daw. Yes, give it me.

La-F. And me too.

Daw. Let's be jovial.

La-F. As jovial as you will.

Ott. Agreed. Now you shall have the bear, cousin, and sir John Daw the horse, and I'll have the bull still. Sound, Tritons of the Thames! [*Drum and trumpets sound again.*] *Nunc est bibendum, nunc pede libero—*

Mor. [*above.*] Villains, murderers, sons of the earth, and traitors, what do you there?

Cler. O, now the trumpets have waked him, we shall have his company.

Ott. A wife is a scurvy clogdogdo, an unlucky thing, a very foresaid bear-whelp, without any good fashion or breeding, *mala bestia.*

Re-enter TRUEWIT *behind, with* Mistress OTTER.

Daup. Why did you marry one then, captain?

Ott. A pox!—I married with six thousand pound, I. I was in love with that. I have not kissed my Fury these forty weeks.

Cler. The more to blame you, captain.

True. Nay, mistress Otter, hear him a little first.

Ott. She has a breath worse than my grandmother's, *profecto.*

Mrs. Ott. O treacherous liar! kiss me, sweet master Truewit, and prove him a slandering knave.

True. I'll rather believe you, lady.

Ott. And she has a peruke that's like a pound of hemp, made up in shoe-threads.

Mrs. Ott. O viper, mandrake!

Ott. O most vile face! and yet she spends me forty pound a year in mercury and hogs-bones. All her teeth were made in the Black-friars, both her eyebrows in the Strand, and her hair in Silver-street. Every part of the town owns a piece of her.

Mrs. Ott. [*comes forward.*] I cannot hold.

Ott. She takes herself asunder still when she goes to bed, into some twenty boxes; and about next day noon is put together again, like a great German clock: and so comes forth, and rings a tedious larum to the whole house, and then is quiet again for an hour, but for her quarters—Have you done me right, gentlemen?

Mrs. Ott. [*falls upon him, and beats him.*] No, sir, I'll do you right with my quarters, with my quarters.

Ott. O, hold, good princess.

True. Sound, sound!   [*Drum and trumpets sound.*

Cler. A battle, a battle!

Mrs. Ott. You notorious stinkardly bearward, does my breath smell?

Ott. Under correction, dear princess.—Look to my bear and my horse, gentlemen.

Mrs. Ott. Do I want teeth, and eyebrows, thou bull-dog?

True. Sound, sound still.   [*They sound again.*

Ott. No, I protest, under correction—

Mrs. Ott. Ay, now you are under correction, you protest: but you did not protest before correction, sir. Thou Judas, to offer to betray thy princess! I'll make thee an example—   [*Beats him.*

Enter MOROSE *with his long sword.*

Mor. I will have no such examples in my house, lady Otter.

Mrs. Ott. Ah!—   [*Mrs. Otter, Daw, and La-Foole, run off.*

Mor. Mistress Mary Ambree, your examples are dangerous.—

Rogues, hell-hounds, Stentors! out of my doors, you sons of noise
and tumult, begot on an ill May-day, or when the galley-foist is
afloat to Westminster! [*Drives out the musicians.*] A trumpeter
could not be conceived but then.

Daup. What ails you, sir?

Mor. They have rent my roof, walls, and all my windows asunder,
with their brazen throats.   [*Exit.*

True. Best follow him, Dauphine.

Daup. So I will.   [*Exit.*

Cler. Where's Daw and La-Foole?

Ott. They are both run away, sir. Good gentlemen, help to
pacify my princess, and speak to the great ladies for me. Now
must I go lie with the bears this fortnight, and keep out of the way,
till my peace be made, for this scandal she has taken. Did you not
see my bull-head, gentlemen?

Cler. Is't not on, captain?

True. No; but he may make a new one, by that is on.

Ott. O, here it is. An you come over, gentlemen, and ask for
Tom Otter, we'll go down to Ratcliff, and have a course i'faith, for
all these disasters. There is *bona spes* left.

True. Away, captain, get off while you are well.   [*Exit Otter.*

Cler. I am glad we are rid of him.

True. You had never been, unless we had put his wife upon him.
His humour is as tedious at last, as it was ridiculous at first.

                                                           [*Exeunt.*

SCENE II.—*A long open Gallery in the same.*

Enter Lady HAUGHTY, Mistress OTTER, MAVIS, DAW, LA-FOOLE,
                    CENTAURE, *and* EPICŒNE.

Hau. We wonder'd why you shriek'd so, mistress Otter.

Mrs. Ott. O lord, madam, he came down with a huge long naked
weapon in both his hands, and look'd so dreadfully! sure he's beside
himself.

Mav. Why, what made you there, mistress Otter?

Mrs. Ott. Alas, mistress Mavis, I was chastising my subject, and
thought nothing of him.

Daw. Faith, mistress, you must do so too: learn to chastise.
Mistress Otter corrects her husband so, he dares not speak but
under correction.

La-F. And with his hat off to her: 'twould do you good to see.

Hau. In sadness, 'tis good and mature counsel; practise it,
Morose. I'll call you Morose still now, as I call Centaure and
Mavis; we four will be all one.

Cen. And you'll come to the college, and live with us?

Hau. Make him give milk and honey.

Mav. Look how you manage him at first, you shall have him
ever after.

Cen. Let him allow you your coach, and four horses, your woman, your chamber-maid, your page, your gentleman-usher, your French cook, and four grooms.

Hau. And go with us to Bedlam, to the china-houses, and to the Exchange.

Cen. It will open the gate to your fame.

Hau. Here's Centaure has immortalised herself, with taming of her wild male.

Mav. Ay, she has done the miracle of the kingdom.

Enter CLERIMONT *and* TRUEWIT.

Epi. But, ladies, do you count it lawful to have such plurality of servants, and do them all graces?

Hau. Why not? why should women deny their favours to men? are they the poorer or the worse?

Daw. Is the Thames the less for the dyers' water, mistress?

La-F. Or a torch for lighting many torches?

True. Well said, La-Foole; what a new one he has got!

Cen. They are empty losses women fear in this kind.

Hau. Besides, ladies should be mindful of the approach of age, and let no time want his due use. The best of our days pass first.

Mav. We are rivers, that cannot be call'd back, madam: she that now excludes her lovers, may live to lie a forsaken beldame, in a frozen bed.

Cen. 'Tis true, Mavis: and who will wait on us to coach then? or write, or tell us the news then, make anagrams of our names, and invite us to the Cockpit, and kiss our hands all the play-time, and draw their weapons for our honours?

Hau. Not one.

Daw. Nay, my mistress is not altogether unintelligent of these things; here be in presence have tasted of her favours.

Cler. What a neighing hobby-horse is this!

Epi. But not with intent to boast them again, servant.—And have you those excellent receipts, madam, to keep yourselves from bearing of children?

Hau. O yes, Morose: how should we maintain our youth and beauty else? Many births of a woman make her old, as many crops make the earth barren.

Enter MOROSE *and* DAUPHINE.

Mor. O my cursed angel, that instructed me to this fate!

Daup. Why, sir?

Mor. That I should be seduced by so foolish a devil as a barber will make!

Daup. I would I had been worthy, sir, to have partaken your counsel; you should never have trusted it to such a minister.

Mor. Would I could redeem it with the loss of an eye, nephew, a hand, or any other member.

Daup. Marry, God forbid, sir, that you should geld yourself, to anger your wife.

Mor. So it would rid me of her!—and, that I did supererogatory penance in a belfry, at Westminster-hall, in the Cockpit, at the fall of a stag, the Tower-wharf—what place is there else?—London-bridge, Paris-garden, Billinsgate, when the noises are at their height, and loudest. Nay, I would sit out a play, that were nothing but fights at sea, drum, trumpet, and target.

Daup. I hope there shall be no such need, sir. Take patience, good uncle. This is but a day, and 'tis well worn too now.

Mor. O, 'twill be so for ever, nephew, I foresee it, for ever. Strife and tumult are the dowry that comes with a wife.

True. I told you so, sir, and you would not believe me.

Mor. Alas, do not rub those wounds, master Truewit, to blood again: 'twas my negligence. Add not affliction to affliction. I have perceived the effect of it, too late, in madam Otter.

Epi. How do you, sir?

Mor. Did you ever hear a more unnecessary question? as if she did not see! Why, I do as you see, empress, empress.

Epi. You are not well, sir; you look very ill: something has distemper'd you.

Mor. O horrible, monstrous impertinencies! would not one of these have served, do you think, sir? would not one of these have served?

True. Yes, sir; but these are but notes of female kindness, sir; certain tokens that she has a voice, sir.

Mor. O, is it so! Come, an't be no otherwise——What say you?

Epi. How do you feel yourself, sir?

Mor. Again that!

True. Nay, look you, sir, you would be friends with your wife upon unconscionable terms; her silence.

Epi. They say you are run mad, sir.

Mor. Not for love, I assure you, of you; do you see?

Epi. O lord, gentlemen! lay hold on him, for God's sake. What shall I do? who's his physician, can you tell, that knows the state of his body best, that I might send for him? Good sir, speak; I'll send for one of my doctors else.

Mor. What, to poison me, that I might die intestate, and leave you possest of all!

Epi. Lord, how idly he talks, and how his eyes sparkle! he looks green about the temples! do you see what blue spots he has!

Cler. Ay, 'tis melancholy.

Epi. Gentlemen, for Heaven's sake, counsel me. Ladies;—servant, you have read Pliny and Paracelsus; ne'er a word now to comfort a poor gentlewoman? Ay me, what fortune had I, to marry a distracted man!

Daw. I'll tell you, mistress—

True. How rarely she holds it up!   [*Aside to Cler.*

Mor. What mean you, gentlemen?

Epi. What will you tell me, servant?

Daw. The disease in Greek is called μανία, in Latin *insania, furor, vel ecstasis melancholica*, that is, *egressio*, when a man *ex melancholico evadit fanaticus.*

Mor. Shall I have a lecture read upon me alive?

Daw. But he may be but *phreneticus* yet, mistress; and *phrenetis* it only *delirium*, or so.

Epi. Ay, that is for the disease, servant; but what is this to the cure? We are sure enough of the disease.

Mor. Let me go.

True. Why, we'll entreat her to hold her peace, sir.

Mor. O no, labour not to stop her. She is like a conduit-pipe, that will gush out with more force when she opens again.

Hau. I'll tell you, Morose, you must talk divinity to him altogether, or moral philosophy.

La-F. Ay, and there's an excellent book of moral philosophy, madam, of Reynard the Fox, and all the beasts, called Doni's Philosophy.

Cen. There is indeed, sir Amorous La-Foole.

Mor. O misery!

La-F. I have read it, my lady Centaure, all over, to my cousin here.

Mrs. Ott. Ay, and 'tis a very good book as any is, of the moderns.

Daw. Tut, he must have Seneca read to him, and Plutarch, and the ancients; the moderns are not for this disease.

Cler. Why, you discommended them too, to-day, sir John.

Daw. Ay, in some cases: but in these they are best, and Aristotle's ethics.

Mav. Say you so, sir John? I think you are deceived; you took it upon trust.

Hau. Where's Trusty, my woman? I'll end this difference. I prithee, Otter, call her. Her father and mother were both mad, when they put her to me.

Mor. I think so.—Nay, gentlemen, I am tame. This is but an exercise, I know, a marriage ceremony, which I must endure.

Hau. And one of them, I know not which, was cured with the Sick Man's Salve, and the other with Green's Groat's-worth of Wit.

True. A very cheap cure, madam.

Enter TRUSTY.

Hau. Ay, 'tis very feasible.

Mrs. Ott. My lady call'd for you, mistress Trusty: you must decide a controversy.

Hau. O, Trusty, which was it you said, your father, or your mother, that was cured with the Sick Man's Salve?

Trus. My mother, madam, with the Salve.

True. Then it was the sick woman's salve?

Trus. And my father with the Groat's-worth of Wit. But there was other means used: we had a preacher that would preach folk asleep still; and so they were prescribed to go to church, by an old woman that was their physician, thrice a week—

Epi. To sleep?

Trus. Yes, forsooth: and every night they read themselves asleep on those books.

Epi. Good faith, it stands with great reason. I would I knew where to procure those books.

Mor. Oh!

La-F. I can help you with one of them, mistress Morose, the Groat's-worth of Wit.

Epi. But I shall disfurnish you, sir Amorous: can you spare it?

La-F. O yes, for a week, or so; I'll read it myself to him.

Epi. No, I must do that, sir; that must be my office.

Mor. Oh, oh!

Epi. Sure he would do well enough, if he could sleep.

Mor. No, I should do well enough, if you could sleep. Have I no friend that will make her drunk, or give her a little laudanum, or opium?

True. Why, sir, she talks ten times worse in her sleep.

Mor. How!

Cler. Do you not know that, sir? never ceases all night.

True. And snores like a porpoise.

Mor. O redeem me, fate; redeem me, fate! For how many causes may a man be divorced, nephew?

Daup. I know not, truly, sir.

True. Some divine must resolve you in that, sir, or canon-lawyer.

Mor. I will not rest, I will not think of any other hope or comfort, till I know.   [*Exit with Dauphine.*

Cler. Alas, poor man!

True. You'll make him mad indeed, ladies, if you pursue this.

Hau. No, we'll let him breathe now, a quarter of an hour or so.

Cler. By my faith, a large truce!

Hau. Is that his keeper, that is gone with him?

Daw. It is his nephew, madam.

La-F. Sir Dauphine Eugenie.

Cen. He looks like a very pitiful knight—

Daw. As can be. This marriage has put him out of all.

La-F. He has not a penny in his purse, madam.

Daw. He is ready to cry all this day.

La-F. A very shark; he set me in the nick t'other night at Primero.

True. How these swabbers talk!

Cler. Ay, Otter's wine has swell'd their humours above a spring-tide.

Hau. Good Morose, let's go in again. I like your couches exceeding well; we'll go lie and talk there.

[*Exeunt Hau., Cen., Mav., Trus., La-Foole, and Daw.*

Epi. [*following them.*] I wait on you, madam.

True. [*stopping her.*] 'Slight, I will have them as silent as signs, and their post too, ere I have done. Do you hear, lady-bride? I pray thee now, as thou art a noble wench, continue this discourse of Dauphine within; but praise him exceedingly: magnify him with all the height of affection thou canst;—I have some purpose in't: and but beat off these two rooks, Jack Daw and his fellow, with any discontentment, hither, and I'll honour thee for ever.

Epi. I was about it here. It angered me to the soul, to hear them begin to talk so malépert.

True. Pray thee perform it, and thou winn'st me an idolater to thee everlasting.

Epi. Will you go in and hear me do't?

True. No, I'll stay here. Drive them out of your company, 'tis all I ask; which cannot be any way better done, than by extolling Dauphine, whom they have so slighted.

Epi. I warrant you; you shall expect one of them presently.

[*Exit.*

Cler. What a cast of kestrils are these, to hawk after ladies, thus!

True. Ay, and strike at such an eagle as Dauphine.

Cler. He will be mad when we tell him. Here he comes.

Re-enter DAUPHINE.

Cler. O sir, you are welcome.

True. Where's thine uncle?

Daup. Run out of doors in his night-caps, to talk with a casuist about his divorce. It works admirably.

True. Thou wouldst have said so, an thou hadst been here! The ladies have laugh'd at thee most comically, since thou went'st, Dauphine.

Cler. And ask'd, if thou wert thine uncle's keeper.

True. And the brace of baboons answer'd, Yes; and said thou wert a pitiful poor fellow, and didst live upon posts, and hadst nothing but three suits of apparel, and some few benevolences that the lords gave thee to fool to them, and swagger.

Daup. Let me not live, I'll beat them: I'll bind them both to grand-madam's bed-posts, and have them baited with monkies.

True. Thou shalt not need, they shall be beaten to thy hand, Dauphine. I have an execution to serve upon them, I warrant thee, shall serve; trust my plot.

Daup. Ay, you have many plots! so you had one to make all the wenches in love with me.

True. Why, if I do it not yet afore night, as near as 'tis, and that they do not every one invite thee, and be ready to scratch for thee, take the mortgage of my wit.

Cler. 'Fore God, I'll be his witness thou shalt have it, Dauphine: thou shalt be his fool for ever, if thou dost not.

True. Agreed. Perhaps 'twill be the better estate. Do you observe this gallery, or rather lobby, indeed? Here are a couple of studies, at each end one: here will I act such a tragi-comedy between the Guelphs and the Ghibellines, Daw and La-Foole— which of them comes out first, will I seize on;—you two shall be the chorus behind the arras, and whip out between the acts and speak

—If I do not make them keep the peace for this remnant of the day, if not of the year, I have failed once——I hear Daw coming: hide, [*they withdraw*] and do not laugh, for God's sake.

Re-enter DAW.

Daw. Which is the way into the garden, trow?

True. O, Jack Daw! I am glad I have met with you. In good faith, I must have this matter go no further between you: I must have it taken up.

Daw. What matter, sir? between whom?

True. Come, you disguise it: sir Amorous and you. If you love me, Jack, you shall make use of your philosophy now, for this once, and deliver me your sword. This is not the wedding the Centaurs were at, though there be a she one here. [*Takes his sword.*] The bride has entreated me I will see no blood shed at her bridal: you saw her whisper me erewhile.

Daw. As I hope to finish Tacitus, I intend no murder.

True. Do you not wait for sir Amorous?

Daw. Not I, by my knighthood.

True. And your scholarship too?

Daw. And my scholarship too.

True. Go to, then I return you your sword, and ask you mercy; but put it not up, for you will be assaulted. I understood that you had apprehended it, and walked here to brave him; and that you had held your life contemptible, in regard of your honour.

Daw. No, no; no such thing, I assure you. He and I parted now, as good friends as could be.

True. Trust not you to that visor. I saw him since dinner with another face: I have known many men in my time vex'd with losses, with deaths, and with abuses; but so offended a wight as sir Amorous, did I never see or read of. For taking away his guests, sir, to-day, that's the cause; and he declares it behind your back with such threatenings and contempts——He said to Dauphine, you were the arrant'st ass—

Daw. Ay, he may say his pleasure.

True. And swears you are so protested a coward, that he knows you will never do him any manly or single right; and therefore he will take his course.

Daw. I'll give him any satisfaction, sir—but fighting.

True. Ay, sir: but who knows what satisfaction he'll take: blood he thirsts for, and blood he will have; and whereabouts on you he will have it, who knows but himself?

Daw. I pray you, master Truewit, be you a mediator.

True. Well, sir, conceal yourself then in this study till I return. [*Puts him into the study.*] Nay, you must be content to be lock'd in; for, for mine own reputation, I would not have you seen to receive a public disgrace, while I have the matter in managing. Ods so, here he comes; keep your breath close, that he do not hear you sigh.—In good faith, sir Amorous, he is not this way; I pray you be merciful, do not murder him; he is a Christian, as good as you: you are arm'd as if you sought revenge on all his race. Good Dauphine, get him away from this place. I never knew a man's choler so high, but he would speak to his friends, he would hear reason.—Jack Daw, Jack! asleep!

Daw. [*within.*] Is he gone, master Truewit?

True. Ay; did you hear him?

Daw. O lord! yes.

True. What a quick ear fear has!

Daw. [*comes out of the closest.*] But is he so arm'd, as you say?

True. Arm'd! did you ever see a fellow set out to take possession?

Daw. Ay, sir.

True. That may give you some light to conceive of him; but 'tis nothing to the principal. Some false brother in the house has furnish'd him strangely; or, if it were out of the house, it was Tom Otter.

Daw. Indeed he's a captain, and his wife is his kinswoman.

True. He has got some body's old two-hand sword, to mow you off at the knees; and that sword hath spawn'd such a dagger!—But then he is so hung with pikes, halberds, petronels, calivers and muskets, that he looks like a justice of peace's hall; a man of two thousand a-year is not cess'd at so many weapons as he has on. There was never fencer challenged at so many several foils. You would think he meant to murder all St. Pulchre parish. If he could but victual himself for half a-year in his breeches, he is sufficiently arm'd to over-run a country.

Daw. Good lord! what means he, sir? I pray you, master Truewit, be you a mediator.

True. Well, I'll try if he will be appeased with a leg or an arm; if not you must die once.

Daw. I would be loth to lose my right arm, for writing madrigals.

True. Why, if he will be satisfied with a thumb or a little finger, all's one to me. You must think, I'll do my best.

[*Shuts him up again.*

Daw. Good sir, do.   [*Clerimont and Dauphine come forward.*

Cler. What hast thou done?

True. He will let me do nothing, he does all afore; he offers his left arm.

Cler. His left wing for a Jack Daw.

Daup. Take it by all means.

True. How! maim a man for ever, for a jest? What a conscience hast thou!

Daup. 'Tis no loss to him; he has no employment for his arms, but to eat spoon-meat. Beside, as good maim his body as his reputation.

True. He is a scholar and a wit, and yet he does not think so. But he loses no reputation with us; for we all resolved him an ass before. To your places again.

Cler. I pray thee, let be me in at the other a little.

True. Look, you'll spoil all; these be ever your tricks.

Cler. No, but I could hit of some things that thou wilt miss, and thou wilt say are good ones.

True. I warrant you. I pray forbear, I'll leave it off, else.

Daup. Come away, Clerimont.

[*Daup. and Cler. withdraw as before.*

Enter LA-FOOLE.

True. Sir Amorous!

La-F. Master Truewit.

True. Whither were you going?

La-F. Down into the court to make water.

True. By no means, sir; you shall rather tempt your breeches.

La-F. Why, sir?

True. Enter here, if you love your life.

[*Opening the door of the other study.*

La-F. Why? why?

True. Question till your throat be cut, do: dally till the enraged soul find you.

La-F. Who is that?

True. Daw it is: will you in?

La-F. Ay, ay, I'll in: what's the matter?

True. Nay, if he had been cool enough to tell us that, there had been some hope to atone you; but he seems so implacably enraged!

La-F. 'Slight, let him rage! I'll hide myself.

True. Do, good sir. But what have you done to him within, that should provoke him thus? You have broke some jest upon him afore the ladies.

La-F. Not I, never in my life, broke jest upon any man. The bride was praising sir Dauphine, and he went away in snuff, and I followed him; unless he took offence at me in his drink erewhile, that I would not pledge all the horse full.

True. By my faith, and that may be; you remember well: but he walks the round up and down, through every room o' the house, with a towel in his hand, crying, *Where's La-Foole? Who saw La-Foole?* And when Dauphine and I demanded the cause, we can force no answer from him, but—*O revenge, how sweet art thou! I will strangle him in this towel*—which leads us to conjecture that the main cause of his fury is, for bringing your meat to-day, with a towel about you, to his discredit.

La-F. Like enough. Why, an he be angry for that, I'll stay here till his anger be blown over.

True. A good becoming resolution, sir; if you can put it on o' the sudden.

La-F. Yes, I can put it on: or, I'll away into the country presently.

True. How will you go out of the house, sir? he knows you are in the house, and he'll watch this se'ennight, but he'll have you: he'll outwait a serjeant for you.

La-F. Why, then I'll stay here.

True. You must think how to victual yourself in time then.

La-F. Why, sweet master Truewit, will you entreat my cousin Otter to send me a cold venison pasty, a bottle or two of wine, and a chamber-pot?

True. A stool were better, sir, of sir Ajax his invention.

La-F. Ay, that will be better, indeed; and a pallat to lie on.

True. O, I would not advise you to sleep by any means.

La-F. Would you not, sir? Why, then I will not.

True. Yet, there's another fear—

La-F. Is there! what is't?

True. No, he cannot break open this door with his foot, sure.

La-F. I'll set my back against it, sir. I have a good back.

True. But then if he should batter.

La-F. Batter! if he dare, I'll have an action of battery against him.

True. Cast you the worst. He has sent for powder already, and what he will do with it, no man knows: perhaps blow up the corner of the house where he suspects you are. Here he comes; in quickly. [*Thrusts in La-Foole and shuts the door.*]—I protest, sir John Daw, he is not this way: what will you do? Before God, you shall hang no petard here: I'll die rather. Will you not take my word? I never knew one but would be satisfied.—Sir Amorous, [*speaks through the key-hole,*] there's no standing out: he has made a petard of an old brass pot, to force your door. Think upon some satisfaction, or terms to offer him.

La-F. [*within.*] Sir, I'll give him any satisfaction: I dare give any terms.

True. You'll leave it to me then?

La-F. Ay, sir: I'll stand to any conditions.

True. [*beckoning forward Cler. and Daup.*] How now, what think you, sirs? were't not a difficult thing to determine which of these two fear'd most?

Cler. Yes, but this fears the bravest: the other a whiniling dastard, Jack Daw! But La-Foole, a brave heroic coward! and is afraid in a great look and a stout accent; I like him rarely.

True. Had it not been pity these two should have been concealed?

Cler. Shall I make a motion?

True. Briefly: for I must strike while 'tis hot.

Cler. Shall I go fetch the ladies to the catastrophe?

True. Umph! ay, by my troth.

Daup. By no mortal means. Let them continue in the state of ignorance, and err still; think them wits and fine fellows, as they have done. 'Twere sin to reform them.

True. Well, I will have them fetch'd, now I think on't, for a private purpose of mine: do, Clerimont, fetch them, and discourse to them all that's past, and bring them into the gallery here.

Daup. This is thy extreme vanity, now: thou think'st thou wert undone, if every jest thou mak'st were not published.

True. Thou shalt see how unjust thou art presently. Clerimont, say it was Dauphine's plot. [*Exit Clerimont.*] Trust me not, if the whole drift be not for thy good. There is a carpet in the next room, put it on, with this scarf over thy face, and a cushion on thy head, and be ready when I call Amorous. Away! [*Exit Daup.*] John Daw! [*Goes to Daw's closet and brings him out.*

Daw. What good news, sir?

True. Faith, I have followed and argued with him hard for you. I told him you were a knight, and a scholar, and that you knew fortitude did consist *magis patiendo quam faciendo, magis ferendo quam feriendo.*

Daw. It doth so indeed, sir.

True. And that you would suffer, I told him: so at first he demanded by my troth, in my conceit, too much.

Daw. What was it, sir?

True. Your upper lip, and six of your fore-teeth.

Daw. 'Twas unreasonable.

True. Nay, I told him plainly, you could not spare them all. So after long argument *pro et con.* as you know, I brought him down to your two butter-teeth, and them he would have.

Daw. O, did you so? Why, he shall have them.

True. But he shall not, sir, by your leave. The conclusion is this, sir: because you shall be very good friends hereafter, and this never to be remembered or upbraided; besides, that he may not boast he has done any such thing to you in his own person; he is to come here in disguise, give you five kicks in private, sir, take your sword from you, and lock you up in that study during pleasure: which will be but a little while, we'll get it released presently.

Daw. Five kicks! he shall have six, sir, to be friends.

True. Believe me, you shall not over-shoot yourself, to send him that word by me.

Daw. Deliver it, sir; he shall have it with all my heart, to be friends.

True. Friends! Nay, an he should not be so, and heartily too, upon these terms, he shall have me to enemy while I live. Come, sir, bear it bravely.

Daw. O lord, sir, 'tis nothing.

True. True: what's six kicks to a man that reads Seneca?

Daw. I have had a hundred, sir.

True. Sir Amorous!

Re-enter DAUPHINE, *disguised.*

No speaking one to another, or rehearsing old matters.

Daw. [*as Daup. kicks him.*] One, two, three, four, five. I protest, sir Amorous, you shall have six.

True. Nay, I told you, you should not talk. Come give him six, an he will needs. [*Dauphine kicks him again.*]—Your sword. [*Takes his sword.*] Now return to your safe custody; you shall presently meet afore the ladies, and be the dearest friends one to another.

[*Puts Daw into the study.*]—Give me the scarf now, thou shalt beat the other bare-faced. Stand by: [*Dauphine retires, and Truewit goes to the other closet, and releases La-Foole.*]—Sir Amorous!

La-F. What's here! A sword?

True. I cannot help it, without I should take the quarrel upon myself. Here he has sent you his sword—

La-F. I'll receive none on't.

True. And he wills you to fasten it against a wall, and break your head in some few several places against the hilts.

La-F. I will not: tell him roundly. I cannot endure to shed my own blood.

True. Will you not?

La-F. No. I'll beat it against a fair flat wall, if that will satisfy him: if not, he shall beat it himself, for Amorous.

True. Why, this is strange starting off, when a man undertakes for you! I offer'd him another condition; will you stand to that?

La-F. Ay, what is't?

True. That you will be beaten in private.

La-F. Yes, I am content, at the blunt.

Enter, above, HAUGHTY, CENTAURE, MAVIS, Mistress OTTER,
EPICŒNE, *and* TRUSTY.

True. Then you must submit yourself to be hoodwinked in this scarf, and be led to him, where he will take your sword from you, and make you bear a blow over the mouth, gules, and tweaks by the nose *sans nombre.*

La-F. I am content. But why must I be blinded?

True. That's for your good, sir; because, if he should grow insolent upon this, and publish it hereafter to your disgrace, (which I hope he will not do,) you might swear safely, and protest, he never beat you, to your knowledge.

La-F. O, I conceive.

True. I do not doubt but you'll be perfect good friends upon't, and not dare to utter an ill thought one of another in future.

La-F. Not I, as God help me, of him.

True. Nor he of you, sir. If he should, [*binds his eyes.*]—Come, sir. [*leads him forward.*]—*All hid*, sir John!

Enter DAUPHINE, *and tweaks him by the nose.*

La-F. O, sir John, sir John! Oh, o-o-o-o-o-Oh—

True. Good sir John, leave tweaking, you'll blow his nose off.—
'Tis sir John's pleasure, you should retire into the study. [*Puts him up again.*]—Why, now you are friends. All bitterness between you, I hope, is buried; you shall come forth by and by, Damon and Pythias upon't, and embrace with all the rankness of friendship that can be.—I trust, we shall have them tamer in their language hereafter. Dauphine, I worship thee.—God's will, the ladies have surprised us!

Enter HAUGHTY, CENTAURE, MAVIS, Mistress OTTER, EPICŒNE, *and* TRUSTY, *behind.*

Hau. Centaure, how our judgments were imposed on by these adulterate knights!

Cen. Nay, madam, Mavis was more deceived than we; 'twas her commendation utter'd them in the college.

Mav. I commended but their wits, madam, and their braveries. I never look'd toward their valours.

Hau. Sir Dauphine is valiant, and a wit too, it seems.

Mav. And a bravery too.

Hau. Was this his project?

Mrs. Ott. So master Clerimont intimates, madam.

Hau. Good Morose, when you come to the college, will you bring him with you? he seems a very perfect gentleman.

Epi. He is so, madam, believe it.

Cen. But when will you come, Morose?

Epi. Three or four days hence, madam, when I have got me a coach and horses.

Hau. No, to-morrow, good Morose; Centaure shall send you her coach.

Mav. Yes faith, do, and bring sir Dauphine with you.

Hau. She has promised that, Mavis.

Mav. He is a very worthy gentleman in his exteriors, madam.

Hau. Ay, he shews he is judicial in his clothes.

Cen. And yet not so superlatively neat as some, madam, that have their faces set in a brake.

Hau. Ay, and have every hair in form.

Mav. That wear purer linen than ourselves, and profess more neatness than the French hermaphrodite!

Epi. Ay, ladies, they, what they tell one of us, have told a thousand; and are the only thieves of our fame, but think to take us with that perfume, or with that lace, and laugh at us unconscionably when they have done.

Hau. But sir Dauphine's carelessness becomes him.

Cen. I could love a man for such a nose.

Mav. Or such a leg.

Cen. He has an exceeding good eye, madam.

Mav. And a very good lock.

Cen. Good Morose, bring him to my chamber first.

Mrs. Ott. Please your honours to meet at my house, madam.

True. See how they eye thee, man! they are taken, I warrant thee.　　　　　　　　　　　　　　　[*Haughty comes forward.*

Hau. You have unbraced our brace of knights here, master Truewit.

True. Not I, madam; it was sir Dauphine's ingine: who, if he have disfurnish'd your ladyship of ny guard or service by it, is able to make the place good again in himself.

Hau. There is no suspicion of that, sir.

Cen. God so, Mavis, Haughty is kissing.

Mav. Let us go too, and take part.   [*They come forward.*

Hau. But I am glad of the fortune (beside the discovery of two such empty caskets) to gain the knowledge of so rich a mine of virtue as sir Dauphine.

Cen. We would be all glad to style him of our friendship, and see him at the college.

Mav. He cannot mix with a sweeter society, I'll prophesy; and I hope he himself will think so.

Daup. I should be rude to imagine otherwise, lady.

True. Did not I tell thee, Dauphine! Why, all their actions are governed by crude opinion, without reason or cause; they know not why they do any thing; but, as they are inform'd, believe, judge, praise, condemn, love, hate, and in emulation one of another, do all these things alike. Only they have a natural inclination sways them generally to the worst, when they are left to themselves. But pursue it, now thou hast them.

Hau. Shall we go in again, Morose?

Epi. Yes, madam.

Cen. We'll entreat sir Dauphine's company.

True. Stay, good madam, the interview of the two friends, Pylades and Orestes: I'll fetch them out to you straight.

Hau. Will you, master Truewit?

Daup. Ay, but noble ladies, do not confess in your countenance, or outward bearing to them, any discovery of their follies, that we may see how they will bear up again, with what assurance and erection.

Hau. We will not, sir Dauphine.

Cen. Mav. Upon our honours, sir Dauphine.

True. [*goes to the first closet.*] Sir Amorous, sir Amorous! The ladies are here.

La-F. [*within.*] Are they?

True. Yes; but slip out by and by, as their backs are turn'd, and meet sir John here, as by chance, when I call you. [*Goes to the other.*]—Jack Daw.

Daw. [*within.*] What say you, sir?

True. Whip out behind me suddenly, and no anger in your looks to your adversary. Now, now!

     [*La-Foole and Daw slip out of their respective closets, and salute each other.*

La-F. Noble sir John Daw, where have you been?

Daw. To seek you, sir Amorous.

La-F. Me! I honour you.

Daw. I prevent you, sir.

Cler. They have forgot their rapiers.

True. O, they meet in peace, man.

Daup. Where's your sword, sir John?

Cler. And yours, sir Amorous?

Daw. Mine! my boy had it forth to mend the handle, e'en now.

La-F. And my gold handle was broke too, and my boy had it forth.

Daup. Indeed, sir!—How their excuses meet!

Cler. What a consent there is in the handles!

True. Nay, there is so in the points too, I warrant you.

Enter MOROSE, *with the two swords, drawn in his hands.*

Mrs. Ott. O me! madam, he comes again, the madman! Away!
[*Ladies, Daw, and La-Foole, run off.*

Mor. What make these naked weapons here, gentlemen?

True. O sir! here hath like to have been murder since you went; a couple of knights fallen out about the bride's favours! We were fain to take away their weapons; your house had been begg'd by this time else.

Mor. For what?

Cler. For manslaughter, sir, as being accessary.

Mor. And for her favours?

True. Ay, sir, heretofore, not present—Clerimont, carry them their swords now. They have done all the hurt they will do.
[*Exit Cler. with the two swords.*

Daup. Have you spoke with the lawyer, sir?

Mor. O no! there is such a noise in the court, that they have frighted me home with more violence than I went! such speaking and counter-speaking, with their several voices of citations, appellations, allegations, certificates, attachments, intergatories, references, convictions, and afflictions indeed, among the doctors and proctors, that the noise here is silence to't, a kind of calm midnight!

True. Why, sir, if you would be resolved indeed, I can bring you hither a very sufficient lawyer, and a learned divine, that shall enquire into every least scruple for you.

Mor. Can you, master Truewit?

True. Yes, and are very sober, grave persons, that will dispatch it in a chamber, with a whisper or two.

Mor. Good sir, shall I hope this benefit from you, and trust myself into your hands?

True. Alas, sir! your nephew and I have been ashamed and oft-times mad, since you went, to think how you are abused. Go in, good sir, and lock yourself up till we call you; we'll tell you more anon, sir.

Mor. Do your pleasure with me gentlemen; I believe in you, and that deserves no delusion. [*Exit.*

True. You shall find none, sir;—but heap'd, heap'd plenty of vexation.

Daup. What wilt thou do now, Wit?

True. Recover me hither Otter and the barber, if you can, by any means, presently.

Daup. Why? to what purpose?

True. O, I'll make the deepest divine, and gravest lawyer, out of them two for him—

The Silent Woman

Daup. Thou canst not, man; these are waking dreams.

True. Do not fear me. Clap but a civil gown with a welt on the one, and a canonical cloke with sleeves on the other, and give them a few terms in their mouths, if there come not forth as able a doctor and complete a parson, for this turn, as may be wish'd, trust not my election: and I hope, without wronging the dignity of either profession, since they are but persons put on, and for mirth's sake, to torment him. The barber smatters Latin, I remember.

Daup. Yes, and Otter too.

True. Well then, if I make them not wrangle out this case to his no comfort, let me be thought a Jack Daw or La-Foole or anything worse. Go you to your ladies, but first send for them.

Daup. I will.   *[Exeunt.*

ACT V

SCENE I.—*A Room in* MOROSE's *House.*

Enter LA-FOOLE, CLERIMONT, *and* DAW.

La-F. Where had you our swords, master Clerimont?

Cler. Why, Dauphine took them from the madman.

La-F. And he took them from our boys, I warrant you.

Cler. Very like, sir.

La-F. Thank you, good master Clerimont. Sir John Daw and I are both beholden to you.

Cler. Would I knew how to make you so, gentlemen!

Daw. Sir Amorous and I are your servants, sir.

Enter MAVIS.

Mav. Gentlemen, have any of you a pen and ink? I would fain write out a riddle in Italian, for sir Dauphine to translate.

Cler. Not I, in troth, lady; I am no scrivener.

Daw. I can furnish you, I think, lady. *[Exeunt Daw and Mavis.*

Cler. He has it in the haft of a knife, I believe.

La-F. No, he has his box of instruments.

Cler. Like a surgeon!

La-F. For the mathematics: his square, his compasses, his brass pens, and black-lead, to draw maps of every place and person where he comes.

Cler. How, maps of persons!

La-F. Yes, sir, of Nomentack when he was here, and of the prince of Moldavia, and of his mistress, mistress Epicœne.

Re-enter DAW.

Cler. Away! he hath not found out her latitude, I hope.

La-F. You are a pleasant gentleman, sir.

Cler. Faith, now we are in private, let's wanton it a little, and talk waggishly.—Sir John, I am telling sir Amorous here, that you two govern the ladies wherever you come; you carry the feminine gender afore you.

Daw. They shall rather carry us afore them, if they will, sir.

Cler. Nay, I believe that they do, withal—but that you are the prime men in their affections, and direct all their actions—

Daw. Not I; sir Amorous is.

La-F. I protest, sir John is.

Daw. As I hope to rise in the state, sir Amorous, you have the person.

La-F. Sir John, you have the person, and the discourse too.

Daw. Not I, sir. I have no discourse—and then you have activity beside.

La-F. I protest, sir John, you come as high from Tripoly as I do, every whit: and lift as many join'd stools, and leap over them, if you would use it.

Cler. Well, agree on't together, knights; for between you, you divide the kingdom or commonwealth of ladies' affections: I see it, and can perceive a little how they observe you, and fear you, indeed. You could tell strange stories, my masters, if you would, I know.

Daw. Faith, we have seen somewhat, sir.

La-F. That we have—velvet petticoats, and wrought smocks, or so.

Daw. Ay, and—

Cler. Nay, out with it, sir John; do not envy your friend the pleasure of hearing, when you have had the delight of tasting.

Daw. Why—a——Do you speak, sir Amorous.

La-F. No, do you, sir John Daw.

Daw. I'faith, you shall.

La-F. I'faith, you shall.

Daw. Why, we have been—

La-F. In the great bed at Ware together in our time. On, sir John.

Daw. Nay, do you, sir Amorous.

Cler. And these ladies with you, knights?

La-F. No, excuse us, sir.

Daw. We must not wound reputation.

La-F. No matter—they were these, or others. Our bath cost us fifteen pound when we came home.

Cler. Do you hear, sir John? You shall tell me but one thing truly, as you love me.

Daw. If I can, I will, sir.

Cler. You lay in the same house with the bride here?

Daw. Yes, and conversed with her hourly, sir.

Cler. And what humour is she of? Is she coming and open, free?

Daw. O, exceeding open, sir. I was her servant, and sir Amorous was to be.

Cler. Come, you have both had favours from her: I know, and have heard so much.

Daw. O no, sir.

La-F. You shall excuse us, sir; we must not wound reputation.

Cler. Tut, she is married now, and you cannot hurt her with any report; and therefore speak plainly: how many times, i'faith? which of you led first? ha!

La-F. Sir John had her maidenhead, indeed.

Daw. O, it pleases him to say so, sir; but sir Amorous knows what's what, as well.

Cler. Dost thou, i'faith, Amorous?

La-F. In a manner, sir.

Cler. Why, I commend you, lads. Little knows don Bridegroom of this; nor shall he, for me.

Daw. Hang him, mad ox!

Cler. Speak softly; here comes his nephew, with the lady Haughty: he'll get the ladies from you, sirs, if you look not to him in time.

La-F. Why, if he do, we'll fetch them home again, I warrant you.

[*Exit with Daw. Cler. walks aside.*

Enter DAUPHINE and HAUGHTY.

Hau. I assure you, sir Dauphine, it is the price and estimation of your virtue only, that hath embark'd me to this adventure; and I could not but make out to tell you so: nor can I repent me of the act, since it is always an argument of some virtue in our selves, that we love and affect it so in others.

Daup. Your ladyship sets too high a price on my weakness.

Hau. Sir, I can distinguish gems from pebbles—

Daup. Are you so skilful in stones?   [*Aside.*

Hau. And howsoever I may suffer in such a judgment as yours, by admitting equality of rank or society with Centaure or Mavis—

Daup. You do not, madam; I perceive they are your mere foils.

Hau. Then, are you a friend to truth, sir; it makes me love you the more. It is not the outward, but the inward man that I affect. They are not apprehensive of an eminent perfection, but love flat and dully.

Cen. [*within.*] Where are you, my lady Haughty?

Hau. I come presently, Centaure.—My chamber, sir, my page shall shew you; and Trusty, my woman, shall be ever awake for you: you need not fear to communicate any thing with her, for she is a Fidelia. I pray you wear this jewel for my sake, sir Dauphine—

Enter CENTAURE.

Where's Mavis, Centaure?

Cen. Within, madam, a writing. I'll follow you presently: [*Exit Hau.*] I'll but speak a word with sir Dauphine.

Daup. With me, madam?

Cen. Good sir Dauphine, do not trust Haughty, nor make any credit to her whatever you do besides. Sir Dauphine, I give you this caution, she is a perfect courtier, and loves nobody but for her uses; and for her uses she loves all. Besides, her physicians give her out to be none o' the clearest, whether she pay them or no, heaven knows; and she's above fifty too, and pargets! See her in a forenoon. Here comes Mavis, a worse face than she! you would not like this by candle-light.

Re-enter MAVIS.

If you'll come to my chamber one o' these mornings early, or late in an evening, I'll tell you more. Where's Haughty, Mavis?

Mav. Within, Centaure.

Cen. What have you there?

Mav. An Italian riddle for sir Dauphine,—you shall not see it, i'faith, Centaure.—[*Exit Cen.*] Good sir Dauphine, solve it for me: I'll call for it anon. [*Exit.*

Cler. [*coming forward.*] How now, Dauphine! how dost thou quit thyself of these females?

Daup. 'Slight, they haunt me like fairies, and give me jewels here; I cannot be rid of them.

Cler. O, you must not tell though.

Daup. Mass, I forgot that: I was never so assaulted. One loves for virtue, and bribes me with this; [*shews the jewel.*]—another loves me with caution, and so would possess me; a third brings me a riddle here: and all are jealous, and rail each at other.

Cler. A riddle! pray let me see it. [*Reads.*

Sir Dauphine, I chose this way of intimation for privacy. The ladies here, I know, have both hope and purpose to make a collegiate and servant of you. If I might be so honoured, as to appear at any end of so noble a work, I would enter into a fame of taking physic to-morrow, and continue it four or five days, or longer, for your visitation. MAVIS.

By my faith, a subtle one! Call you this a riddle? what's their plain-dealing, trow?

Daup. We lack Truewit to tell us that.

Cler. We lack him for somewhat else too: his knights reformadoes are wound up as high and insolent as ever they were.

Daup. You jest.

Cler. No drunkards, either with wine or vanity, ever confess'd such stories of themselves. I would not give a fly's leg in balance against all the women's reputations here, if they could be but thought to speak truth: and for the bride, they have made their affidavit against her directly—

Daup. What, that they have lain with her?

Cler. Yes; and tell times and circumstances, with the cause why, and the place where. I had almost brought them to affirm that they had done it to-day.

Daup. Not both of them?

Cler. Yes, faith; with a sooth or two more I had effected it. They would have set it down under their hands.

Daup. Why, they will be our sport, I see, still, whether we will or no.

Enter TRUEWIT.

True. O, are you here? Come, Dauphine; go call your uncle presently: I have fitted my divine and my canonist, dyed their beards and all. The knaves do not know themselves, they are so exalted and altered. Preferment changes any man. Thou shalt keep one door and I another, and then Clerimont in the midst, that he may have no means of escape from their cavilling, when they grow hot once again. And then the women, as I have given the bride her instructions, to break in upon him in the l'envoy. O, 'twill be full and twanging! Away! fetch him.   [*Exit Dauphine.*

Enter OTTER *disguised as a divine, and* CUTBEARD *as a canon lawyer.*

Come, master doctor, and master parson, look to your parts now, and discharge them bravely; you are well set forth, perform it as well. If you chance to be out, do not confess it with standing still, or humming, or gaping one at another; but go on, and talk aloud and eagerly; use vehement action, and only remember your terms, and you are safe. Let the matter go where it will: you have many will do so. But at first be very solemn and grave, like your garments, though you loose your selves after, and skip out like a brace of jugglers on a table. Here he comes: set your faces, and look superciliously, while I present you.

Re-enter DAUPHINE *with* MOROSE.

Mor. Are these the two learned men?

True. Yes, sir; please you salute them.

Mor. Salute them! I had rather do any thing, than wear out time so unfruitfully, sir. I wonder how these common forms, as *God save you,* and *You are welcome,* are come to be a habit in our lives: or, *I am glad to see you!* when I cannot see what the profit can be of these words, so long as it is no whit better with him whose affairs are sad and grievous, that he hears this salutation.

True. 'Tis true, sir; we'll go to the matter then.—Gentlemen, master doctor, and master parson, I have acquainted you sufficiently with the business for which you are come hither; and you are not now to inform yourselves in the state of the question, I know. This is the gentleman who expects your resolution, and therefore, when you please, begin.

Ott. Please you, master doctor.

Cut. Please you, good master parson.

Ott. I would hear the canon-law speak first.

Cut. It must give place to positive divinity, sir.

Mor. Nay, good gentlemen, do not throw me into circumstances. Let your comforts arrive quickly at me, those that are. Be swift in affording me my peace, if so I shall hope any. I love not your disputations, or your court-tumults. And that it be not strange to you, I will tell you: My father, in my education, was wont to advise me, that I should always collect and contain my mind, not suffering it to flow loosely; that I should look to what things were necessary to the carriage of my life, and what not; embracing the one and eschewing the other: in short, that I should endear myself to rest, and avoid turmoil; which now is grown to be another nature to me. So that I come not to your public pleadings, or your places of noise; not that I neglect those things that make for the dignity of the commonwealth; but for the mere avoiding of clamours and impertinences of orators, that know not how to be silent. And for the cause of noise, am I now a suitor to you. You do not know in what a misery I have been exercised this day, what a torrent of evil! my very house turns round with the tumult! I dwell in a windmill: the perpetual motion is here, and not at Eltham.

True. Well, good master doctor, will you break the ice? master parson will wade after.

Cut. Sir, though unworthy, and the weaker, I will presume.

Ott. 'Tis no presumption, *domine* doctor.

Mor. Yet again!

Cut. Your question is, For how many causes a man may have *divortium legitimum*, a lawful divorce? First, you must understand the nature of the word, divorce, *à divertendo*—

Mor. No excursions upon words, good doctor; to the question briefly.

Cut. I answer then, the canon law affords divorce but in few cases; and the principal is in the common case, the adulterous case: But there are *duodecim impedimenta*, twelve impediments, as we call them, all which do not *dirimere contractum*, but *irritum reddere matrimonium*, as we say in the canon law, *not take away the bond, but cause a nullity therein.*

Mor. I understood you before: good sir, avoid your impertinency of translation.

Ott. He cannot open this too much, sir, by your favour.

Mor. Yet more!

True. O, you must give the learned men leave, sir.—To your impediments, master doctor.

Cut. The first is *impedimentum erroris*.

Ott. Of which there are several species.

Cut. Ay, as *error personæ.*

Ott. If you contract yourself to one person, thinking her another.

Cut. Then, *error fortunæ.*

Ott. If she be a beggar, and you thought her rich.

Cut. Then, *error qualitatis.*

Ott. If she prove stubborn or head-strong, that you thought obedient.

Mor. How! is that, sir, a lawful impediment? One at once, I pray you, gentlemen.

Ott. Ay, *ante copulam*, but not *post copulam*, sir.

Cut. Master parson says right. *Nec post nuptiarum benedictionem.*

It doth indeed but *irrita reddere sponsalia*, annul the contract; after marriage it is of no obstancy.

True. Alas, sir, what a hope are we fallen from by this time!

Cut. The next is *conditio:* if you thought her free born, and she prove a bond-woman, there is impediment of estate and condition.

Ott. Ay, but, master doctor, those servitudes are *sublatæ* now, among us Christians.

Cut. By your favour, master parson—

Ott. You shall give me leave, master doctor.

Mor. Nay, gentlemen, quarrel not in that question; it concerns not my case: pass to the third.

Cut. Well then, the third is *votum:* if either party have made a vow of chastity. But that practice, as master parson said of the other, is taken away among us, thanks be to discipline. The fourth is *cognatio;* if the persons be of kin within the degrees.

Ott. Ay: do you know what the degrees are, sir?

Mor. No, nor I care not, sir; they offer me no comfort in the question, I am sure.

Cut. But there is a branch of this impediment may, which is *cognatio spiritualis:* if you were her godfather, sir, then the marriage is incestuous.

Ott. That comment is absurd and superstitious, master doctor: I cannot endure it. Are we not all brothers and sisters, and as much akin in that, as godfathers and god-daughters?

Mor. O me! to end the controversy, I never was a godfather, I never was a godfather in my life, sir. Pass to the next.

Cut. The fifth is *crimen adulterii;* the known case. The sixth, *cultus disparitas*, difference of religion: Have you ever examined her, what religion she is of?

Mor. No, I would rather she were of none, than be put to the trouble of it.

Ott. You may have it done for you, sir.

Mor. By no means, good sir; on to the rest: shall you ever come to an end, think you?

True. Yes, he has done half, sir. On to the rest.—Be patient, and expect, sir.

Cut. The seventh is, *vis:* if it were upon compulsion or force.

Mor. O no, it was too voluntary, mine; too voluntary.

Cut. The eighth is, *ordo;* if ever she have taken holy orders.

Ott. That's superstitious too.

Mor. No matter, master parson; Would she would go into a nunnery yet.

Cut. The ninth is, *ligamen;* if you were bound, sir, to any other before.

Mor. I thrust myself too soon into these fetters.

Cut. The tenth is, *publica honestas;* which is *inchoata quædam affinitas.*

Ott. Ay, or *affinitas orta ex sponsalibus;* and is but *leve impedimentum.*

Mor. I feel no air of comfort blowing to me, in all this.

Cut. The eleventh is, *affinitas ex fornicatione.*

Ott. Which is no less *vera affinitas,* than the other, master doctor.

Cut. True, *quæ oritur ex legitimo matrimonio.*

Ott. You say right, venerable doctor: and, *nascitur ex eo, quod per conjugium duæ personæ efficiuntur una caro—*

True. Hey-day, now they begin!

Cut. I conceive you, master parson: *ita per fornicationem æque est verus pater, qui sic generat—*

Ott. Et vere filius qui sic generatur—

Mor. What's all this to me?

Cler. Now it grows warm.

Cut. The twelfth and last is, *si forte coire nequibis.*

Ott. Ay, that is *impedimentum gravissimum:* it doth utterly annul, and annihilate, that. If you have *manifestam frigiditatem,* you are well, sir.

True. Why, there is comfort come at length, sir. Confess yourself but a man unable, and she will sue to be divorced first.

Ott. Ay, or if there be *morbus perpetuus, et insanabilis;* as *paralysis, elephantiasis,* or so—

Daup. O, but *frigiditas* is the fairer way, gentlemen.

Ott. You say troth, sir, and as it is in the canon, master doctor—

Cut. I conceive you, sir.

Cler. Before he speaks!

Ott. That a boy, or child, under years, is not fit for marriage, because he cannot *reddere debitum.* So your *omnipotentes—*

True. Your *impotentes,* you whoreson lobster!   [*Aside to Ott.*

Ott. Your *impotentes,* I should say, are *minime apti ad contrahenda matrimonium.*

True. Matrimonium! we shall have most unmatrimonial Latin with you: *matrimonia,* and be hang'd.

Daup. You put them out, man.

Cut. But then there will arise a doubt, master parson, in our case, *post matrimonium:* that *frigiditate præditus*—do you conceive me, sir?

Ott. Very well, sir.

Cut. Who cannot *uti uxore pro uxore,* may *habere eam pro sorore.*

Ott. Absurd, absurd, absurd, and merely apostatical!

Cut. You shall pardon me, master parson, I can prove it.

Ott. You can prove a will, master doctor; you can prove nothing else. Does not the verse of your own canon say,

Hæc socianda vetant connubia, facta retractant ?

Cut. I grant you; but how do they *retractare,* master parson?

Mor. O, this was it I feared.

Ott. In æternum, sir.

Cut. That's false in divinity, by your favour.

Ott. 'Tis false in humanity to say so. Is he not *prorsus inutilis ad thorum ?* Can he *præstare fidem datam ?* I would fain know.

Cut. Yes; how if he do *convalere ?*

Ott. He cannot *convalere*, it is impossible.

True. Nay, good sir, attend the learned men; they'll think you neglect them else.

Cut. Or, if he do *simulare* himself *frigidum, odio uxoris,* or so?

Ott. I say, he is *adulter manifestus* then.

Daup. They dispute it very learnedly, i'faith.

Ott. And *prostitutor uxoris;* and this is positive.

Mor. Good sir, let me escape.

True. You will not do me that wrong, sir?

Ott. And, therefore, if he be *manifeste frigidus*, sir—

Cut. Ay, if he be *manifeste frigidus*, I grant you—

Ott. Why, that was my conclusion.

Cut. And mine too.

True. Nay, hear the conclusion, sir.

Ott. Then, *frigiditatis causa*—

Cut. Yes, *causa frigiditatis*—

Mor. O, mine ears!

Ott. She may have *libellum divortii* against you.

Cut. Ay, *divortii libellum* she will sure have.

Mor. Good echoes, forbear.

Ott. If you confess it.—

Cut. Which I would do, sir—

Mor. I will do any thing.

Ott. And clear myself *in foro conscientiæ*—

Cut. Because you want indeed—

Mor. Yet more!

Ott. *Exercendi potestate.*

EPICŒNE *rushes in, followed by* HAUGHTY, CENTAURE, MAVIS, Mistress OTTER, DAW, *and* LA-FOOLE.

Epi. I will not endure it any longer. Ladies, I beseech you, help me. This is such a wrong as never was offered to poor bride before: upon her marriage-day to have her husband conspire against her, and a couple of mercenary companions to be brought in for form's sake, to persuade a separation! If you had blood or virtue in you, gentlemen, you would not suffer such earwigs about a husband, or scorpions to creep between man and wife.

Mor. O the variety and changes of my torment!

Hau. Let them be cudgell'd out of doors by our grooms.

Cen. I'll lend you my footman.

Mav. We'll have our men blanket them in the hall.

Mrs. Ott. As there was one at our house, madam, for peeping in at the door.

Daw. Content, i'faith.

True. Stay, ladies and gentlemen; you'll hear before you proceed?

Mav. I'd have the bridegroom blanketted too.

Cen. Begin with him first.

Hau. Yes, by my troth.

Mor. O mankind generation!

Daup. Ladies, for my sake forbear.

Hau. Yes, for sir Dauphine's sake.

Cen. He shall command us.

La-F. He is as fine a gentleman of his inches, madam, as any is about the town, and wears as good colours when he lists.

True. Be brief, sir, and confess your infirmity; she'll be a-fire to be quit of you, if she but hear that named once, you shall not entreat her to stay: she'll fly you like one that had the marks upon him.

Mor. Ladies, I must crave all your pardons—

True. Silence, ladies.

Mor. For a wrong I have done to your whole sex, in marrying this fair and virtuous gentlewoman—

Cler. Hear him, good ladies.

Mor. Being guilty of an infirmity, which, before I conferred with these learned men, I thought I might have concealed—

True. But now being better informed in his conscience by them, he is to declare it, and give satisfaction, by asking your public forgiveness.

Mor. I am no man, ladies.

All. How!

Mor. Utterly unabled in nature, by reason of frigidity, to perform the duties, or any the least office of a husband.

Mav. Now out upon him, prodigious creature!

Cen. Bridegroom uncarnate!

Hau. And would you offer it to a young gentlewoman?

Mrs. Ott. A lady of her longings?

Epi. Tut, a device, a device, this! it smells rankly, ladies. A mere comment of his own.

True. Why, if you suspect that, ladies, you may have him search'd—

Daw. As the custom is, by a jury of physicians.

La-F. Yes, faith, 'twill be brave.

Mor. O me, must I undergo that?

Mrs. Ott. No, let women search him, madam; we can do it ourselves.

Mor. Out on me! worse.

Epi. No, ladies, you shall not need, I'll take him with all his faults.

Mor. Worst of all!

Cler. Why then, 'tis no divorce, doctor, if she consent not?

Cut. No, if the man be *frigidus*, it is *de parte uxoris*, that we grant *libellum divortii*, in the law.

Ott. Ay, it is the same in theology.

Mor. Worse, worse than worst!

True. Nay, sir, be not utterly disheartened; we have yet a small relic of hope left, as near as our comfort is blown out. Clerimont, produce your brace of knights. What was that, master parson, you told me *in errore qualitatis*, e'en now?—Dauphine, whisper the bride, that she carry it as if she were guilty, and ashamed. [*Aside.*

Ott. Marry, sir, *in errore qualitatis*, (which master doctor did forbear to urge,) if she be found *corrupta*, that is, vitiated or broken up, that was *pro virgine desponsa*, espoused for a maid—

Mor. What then, sir?

Ott. It doth *dirimere contractum*, and *irritum reddere* too.

True. If this be true, we are happy again, sir, once more. Here are an honourable brace of knights, that shall affirm so much.

Daw. Pardon us, good master Clerimont.

La-F. You shall excuse us, master Clerimont.

Cler. Nay, you must make it good now, knights, there is no remedy; I'll eat no words for you, nor no men: you know you spoke it to me.

Daw. Is this gentleman-like, sir?

True. Jack Daw, he's worse than sir Amorous; fiercer a great deal. [*Aside to Daw.*]—Sir Amorous, beware, there be ten Daws in this Clerimont. [*Aside to La-Foole.*

La-F. I'll confess it, sir.

Daw. Will you, sir Amorous, will you wound reputation?

La-F. I am resolved.

True. So should you be too, Jack Daw: what should keep you off? she's but a woman, and in disgrace: he'll be glad on't.

Daw. Will he? I thought he would have been angry.

Cler. You will dispatch, knights; it must be done, i'faith.

True. Why, an it must, it shall, sir, they say: they'll ne'er go back.—Do not tempt his patience. [*Aside to them.*

Daw. Is it true indeed, sir?

La-F. Yes, I assure you, sir.

Mor. What is true, gentlemen? what do you assure me?

Daw. That we have known your bride, sir—

La-F. In good fashion. She was our mistress, or so—

Cler. Nay, you must be plain, knights, as you were to me.

Ott. Ay, the question is, if you have *carnaliter*, or no?

La-F. Carnaliter! what else, sir?

Ott. It is enough; a plain nullity.

Epi. I am undone, I am undone!

Mor. O let me worship and adore you, gentlemen!

Epi. I am undone. [*Weeps.*

Mor. Yes, to my hand, I thank these knights. Master parson, let me thank you otherwise. [*Gives him money.*

Cen. And have they confess'd?

Mav. Now out upon them, informers!

True. You see what creatures you may bestow your favours on, madams.

Hau. I would except against them as beaten knights, wench, and not good witnesses in law.

Mrs. Ott. Poor gentlewoman, how she takes it!

Hau. Be comforted, Morose, I love you the better for't.

Cen. So do I, I protest.

Cut. But, gentlemen, you have not known her since *matrimonium?*

Daw. Not to-day, master doctor.

La-F. No, sir, not to-day.

Cut. Why, then I say, for any act before, the *matrimonium* is good and perfect; unless the worshipful bridegroom did precisely, before witness, demand, if she were *virgo ante nuptias.*

Epi. No, that he did not, I assure you, master doctor.

Cut. If he cannot prove that, it is *ratum conjugium,* notwithstanding the premisses; and they do no way *impedire.* And this is my sentence, this I pronounce.

Ott. I am of master doctor's resolution too, sir; if you made not that demand *ante nuptias.*

Mor. O my heart! wilt thou break? wilt thou break? this is worst of all worst worsts that hell could have devised! Marry a whore, and so much noise!

Daup. Come, I see now plain confederacy in this doctor and this parson, to abuse a gentleman. You study his affliction. I pray be gone, companions.—And, gentlemen, I begin to suspect you for having parts with them.—Sir, will it please you hear me?

Mor. O do not talk to me; take not from me the pleasure of dying in silence, nephew.

Daup. Sir, I must speak to you. I have been long your poor despised kinsman, and many a hard thought has strengthened you against me: but now it shall appear if either I love you or your peace, and prefer them to all the world beside. I will not be long or grievous to you, sir. If I free you of this unhappy match absolutely, and instantly, after all this trouble, and almost in your despair, now—

Mor. It cannot be.

Daup. Sir, that you be never troubled with a murmur of it more, what shall I hope for, or deserve of you?

Mor. O, what thou wilt, nephew! thou shalt deserve me, and have me.

Daup. Shall I have your favour perfect to me, and love hereafter?

Mor. That, and any thing beside. Make thine own conditions. My whole estate is thine; manage it, I will become thy ward.

Daup. Nay, sir, I will not be so unreasonable.

Epi. Will sir Dauphine be mine enemy too?

Daup. You know I have been long a suitor to you, uncle, that out of your estate, which is fifteen hundred a-year, you would allow me but five hundred during life, and assure the rest upon me after; to which I have often, by myself and friends, tendered you a writing to sign, which you would never consent or incline to. If you please but to effect it now—

Mor. Thou shalt have it, nephew: I will do it, and more.

Daup. If I quit you not presently, and for ever, of this cumber, you shall have power instantly, afore all these, to revoke your act, and I will become whose slave you will give me to, for ever.

Mor. Where is the writing? I will seal to it, that, or to a blank, and write thine own conditions.

Epi. O me, most unfortunate, wretched gentlewoman!

Hau. Will sir Dauphine do this?

Epi. Good sir, have some compassion on me.

Mor. O, my nephew knows you, belike; away, crocodile!

Cen. He does it not sure without good ground.

Daup. Here, sir.   *[Gives him the parchments.*

Mor. Come, nephew, give me the pen; I will subscribe to any thing, and seal to what thou wilt, for my deliverance. Thou art my restorer. Here, I deliver it thee as my deed. If there be a word in it lacking, or writ with false orthography, I protest before [heaven] I will not take the advantage.   *[Returns the writings.*

Daup. Then here is your release, sir. *[takes off Epicœne's peruke and other disguises.]* You have married a boy, a gentleman's son, that I have brought up this half year at my great charges, and for this composition, which I have now made with you.—What say you, master doctor? This is *justum impedimentum*, I hope, *error personæ?*

Ott. Yes, sir, *in primo gradu.*

Cut. In primo gradu.

Daup. I thank you, good doctor Cutbeard, and parson Otter. *[pulls their false beards and gowns off.]* You are beholden to them, sir, that have taken this pains for you; and my friend, master Truewit, who enabled them for the business. Now you may go in and rest; be as private as you will, sir. *[Exit Morose.]* I'll not trouble you, till you trouble me with your funeral, which I care not how soon it come.—Cutbeard, I'll make your lease good. *Thank me not, but with your leg, Cutbeard.* And Tom Otter, your princess shall be reconciled to you.—How now, gentlemen, do you look at me?

Cler. A boy!

Daup. Yes, mistress Epicœne.

True. Well, Dauphine, you have lurch'd your friends of the better half of the garland, by concealing this part of the plot: but much good do it thee, thou deserv'st it, lad. And, Clerimont, for thy unexpected bringing these two to confession, wear my part of it freely. Nay, sir Daw and sir La-Foole, you see the gentlewoman that has done you the favours! we are all thankful to you, and so should the woman-kind here, specially for lying on her, though not with her! you meant so, I am sure. But that we have stuck it upon you to-day, in your own imagined persons, and so lately, this Amazon, the champion of the sex, should beat you now thriftily, for the common slanders which ladies receive from such cuckoos as you are. You are they that, when no merit or fortune can make you hope to enjoy their bodies, will yet lie with their reputations, and make their fame suffer. Away, you common moths of these, and all ladies' honours. Go, travel to make legs and faces, and come home with some new matter to be laugh'd at; you deserve to live in an air as corrupted as that wherewith you feed rumour.

[*Exeunt Daw and La-Foole.*]—Madams, you are mute, upon this new metamorphosis! But here stands she that has vindicated your fames. Take heed of such insectæ hereafter. And let it not trouble you, that you have discovered any mysteries to this young gentleman: he is almost of years, and will make a good visitant within this twelvemonth. In the mean time, we'll all undertake for his secrecy, that can speak so well of his silence. [*Coming forward.*]—*Spectators, if you like this comedy, rise cheerfully, and now Morose is gone in, clap your hands. It may be, that noise will cure him, at least please him.* [Exeunt.

EVERY MAN IN HIS HUMOUR

TO THE MOST LEARNED, AND MY HONOURED FRIEND

MASTER CAMDEN

CLARENCIEUX

Sir,—There are, no doubt, a supercilious race in the world, who will esteem all office, done you in this kind, an injury; so solemn a vice it is with them to use the authority of their ignorance, to the crying down of Poetry, or the professors: but my gratitude must not leave to correct their error; since I am none of those that can suffer the benefits conferred upon my youth to perish with my age. It is a frail memory that remembers but present things: and, had the favour of the times so conspired with my disposition, as it could have brought forth other, or better, you had had the same proportion, and number of the fruits, the first. Now I pray you to accept this; such wherein neither the confession of my manners shall make you blush; nor of my studies, repent you to have been the instructer: and for the profession of my thankfulness, I am sure it will, with good men, find either praise or excuse. Your true lover,

Ben Jonson.

DRAMATIS PERSONÆ

Knowell, *an old Gentleman.*
Edward Knowell, *his Son.*
Brainworm, *the Father's Man.*
George Downright, *a plain Squire.*
Wellbred, *his Half-Brother.*
Kitely, *a Merchant.*
Captain Bobadill, *a Paul's Man.*
Master Stephen, *a Country Gull.*
Master Mathew, *the Town Gull.*
Thomas Cash, *Kitely's Cashier.*

Oliver Cob, *a Water-bearer.*
Justice Clement, *an old merry Magistrate.*
Roger Formal, *his Clerk.*
Wellbred's Servant

Dame Kitely, *Kitely's Wife.*
Mrs. Bridget, *his Sister.*
Tib, *Cob's Wife*

Servants, *etc.*

SCENE,—London

PROLOGUE.

*Though need make many poets, and some such
As art and nature have not better'd much;
Yet ours for want hath not so loved the stage,
As he dare serve the ill customs of the age,
Or purchase your delight at such a rate,
As, for it, he himself must justly hate:
To make a child now swaddled, to proceed
Man, and then shoot up, in one beard and weed,
Past threescore years; or, with three rusty swords,*

And help of some few foot and half-foot words,
Fight over York and Lancaster's long jars,
And in the tyring-house bring wounds to scars.
He rather prays you will be pleas'd to see
One such to-day, as other plays should be;
Where neither chorus wafts you o'er the seas,
Nor creaking throne comes down the boys to please;
Nor nimble squib is seen to make afeard
The gentlewomen; nor roll'd bullet heard
To say, it thunders; nor tempestuous drum
Rumbles, to tell you when the storm doth come;
But deeds, and language, such as men do use,
And persons, such as comedy would choose,
When she would shew an image of the times,
And sport with human follies, not with crimes.
Except we make them such, by loving still
Our popular errors, when we know they're ill.
I mean such errors as you'll all confess,
By laughing at them, they deserve no less:
Which when you heartily do, there's hope left then,
You, that have so grac'd monsters, may like men.

ACT I

SCENE I.—*A Street.*

Enter KNOWELL, *at the door of his house.*

Know. A goodly day toward, and a fresh morning.—Brainworm!

Enter BRAINWORM.

Call up your young master: bid him rise, sir.
Tell him, I have some business to employ him.
    Brai. I will, sir, presently.
    Know.   But hear you, sirrah,
If he be at his book, disturb him not.
    Brai. Very good, sir.   [*Exit.*
    Know. How happy yet should I esteem myself,
Could I, by any practice, wean the boy
From one vain course of study he affects.
He is a scholar, if a man may trust
The liberal voice of fame in her report,
Of good account in both our Universities,
Either of which hath favoured him with graces:
But their indulgence must not spring in me
A fond opinion that he cannot err.
Myself was once a student, and indeed,
Fed with the self-same humour he is now,
Dreaming on nought but idle poetry,

That fruitless and unprofitable art,
Good unto none, but least to the professors;
Which then I thought the mistress of all knowledge:
But since, time and the truth have waked my judgment,
And reason taught me better to distinguish
The vain from the useful learnings.

Enter Master STEPHEN.

                         Cousin Stephen,
What news with you, that you are here so early?
   Step. Nothing, but e'en come to see how you do, uncle.
   Know. That's kindly done; you are welcome, coz.
   Step. Ay, I know that, sir; I would not have come else.
How does my cousin Edward, uncle?
   Know. O, well, coz; go in and see; I doubt he be scarce stirring yet.
   Step. Uncle, afore I go in, can you tell me, an he have e'er a
book of the science of hawking and hunting; I would fain borrow it.
   Know. Why, I hope you will not a hawking now, will you?
   Step. No, wusse; but I'll practise against next year, uncle. I
have bought me a hawk, and a hood, and bells, and all; I lack
nothing but a book to keep it by.
   Know. Oh, most ridiculous!
   Step. Nay, look you now, you are angry, uncle:—Why, you know
an a man have not skill in the hawking and hunting languages
now-a-days, I'll not give a rush for him: they are more studied
than the Greek, or the Latin. He is for no gallant's company without them; and by gadslid I scorn it, I, so I do, to be a consort for
every humdrum: hang them, scroyles! there's nothing in them i'
the world. What do you talk on it? Because I dwell at Hogsden,
I shall keep company with none but the archers of Finsbury, or
the citizens that come a ducking to Islington ponds! A fine jest,
i' faith! 'Slid, a gentleman mun shew himself like a gentleman.
Uncle, I pray you be not angry; I know what I have to do, I trow,
I am no novice.
   Know. You are a prodigal, absurd coxcomb, go to!
Nay, never look at me, 'tis I that speak;
Take't as you will, sir, I'll not flatter you.
Have you not yet found means enow to waste
That which your friends have left you, but you must
Go cast away your money on a buzzard,
And know not how to keep it, when you have done?
O, it is comely! this will make you a gentleman!
Well, cousin, well, I see you are e'en past hope
Of all reclaim:—ay, so; now you are told on't,
You look another way.
   Step.   What would you ha' me do?
   Know. What would I have you do? I'll tell you, kinsman;
Learn to be wise, and practise how to thrive;
That would I have you do: and not to spend

Your coin on every bauble that you fancy,
Or every foolish brain that humours you.
I would not have you to invade each place,
Nor thrust yourself on all societies,
Till men's affections, or your own desert,
Should worthily invite you to your rank.
He that is so respectless in his courses,
Oft sells his reputation at cheap market.
Nor would I, you should melt away yourself
In flashing bravery, lest, while you affect
To make a blaze of gentry to the world,
A little puff of scorn extinguish it;
And you be left like an unsavoury snuff,
Whose property is only to offend.
I'd have you sober, and contain yourself,
Not that your sail be bigger than your boat;
But moderate your expenses now, at first,
As you may keep the same proportion still:
Nor stand so much on your gentility,
Which is an airy and mere borrow'd thing,
From dead men's dust and bones; and none of yours,
Except you make, or hold it.

Enter a Servant.

Who comes here?

Serv. Save you, gentlemen!

Step. Nay, we do not stand much on our gentility, friend; yet you are welcome: and I assure you mine uncle here is a man of a thousand a year, Middlesex land. He has but one son in all the world, I am his next heir, at the common law, master Stephen, as simple as I stand here, if my cousin die, as there's hope he will: I have a pretty living o' mine own too, beside, hard by here.

Serv. In good time, sir.

Step. In good time, sir! why, and in very good time, sir! You do not flout, friend, do you?

Serv. Not I, sir.

Step. Not you, sir! you were best not, sir; an you should, here be them can perceive it, and that quickly too; go to: and they can give it again soundly too, an need be.

Serv. Why, sir, let this satisfy you; good faith, I had no such intent.

Step. Sir, an I thought you had, I would talk with you, and that presently.

Serv. Good master Stephen, so you may, sir, at your pleasure.

Step. And so I would, sir, good my saucy companion! an you were out o' mine uncle's ground, I can tell you; though I do not stand upon my gentility neither, in't.

Know. Cousin, cousin, will this ne'er be left?

Step. Whoreson, base fellow! a mechanical serving-man! By this cudgel, an 'twere not for shame, I would—

Know. What would you do, you peremptory gull?
If you cannot be quiet, get you hence.
You see the honest man demeans himself
Modestly tow'rds you, giving no reply
To your unseason'd, quarrelling, rude fashion;
And still you huff it, with a kind of carriage
As void of wit, as of humanity.
Go, get you in; 'fore heaven, I am ashamed
Thou hast a kinsman's interest in me.   [*Exit Master Stephen.*

Serv. I pray, sir, is this master Knowell's house?

Know. Yes, marry is it, sir.

Serv. I should inquire for a gentleman here, one master Edward Knowell; do you know any such, sir, I pray you?

Know. I should forget myself else, sir.

Serv. Are you the gentleman? cry you mercy, sir: I was required by a gentleman in the city, as I rode out at this end o' the town, to deliver you this letter, sir.

Know. To me, sir! What do you mean? pray you remember your court'sy. [*Reads.*] *To his most selected friend, master Edward Knowell.* What might the gentleman's name be, sir, that sent it? Nay, pray you be covered.

Serv. One master Wellbred, sir.

Know. Master Wellbred! a young gentleman, is he not?

Serv. The same, sir; master Kitely married his sister; the rich merchant in the Old Jewry.

Know. You say very true.—Brainworm!

Enter BRAINWORM.

Brai. Sir.

Know. Make this honest friend drink here: pray you, go in.
    [*Exeunt Brainworm and Servant.*

This letter is directed to my son;
Yet I am Edward Knowell too, and may,
With the safe conscience of good manners, use
The fellow's error to my satisfaction.
Well, I will break it ope (old men are curious),
Be it but for the style's sake and the phrase;
To see if both do answer my son's praises,
Who is almost grown the idolater
Of this young Wellbred. What have we here? What's this?

[*Reads*] Why, Ned, I beseech thee, hast thou forsworn all thy friends in the Old Jewry? or dost thou think us all Jews that inhabit there? yet, if thou dost, come over, and but see our frippery; change an old shirt for a whole smock with us: do not conceive that antipathy between us and Hogsden, as was between Jews and hogs-flesh. Leave thy vigilant father alone, to number over his green apricots, evening and morning, on the north-west wall: an I had been his son, I had saved him the labour long since, if taking in all the young wenches that pass by at the back-door, and codling every kernel of the fruit for them, would have served. But, pr'ythee, come over to me quickly this morning; I have such a present for thee!—our Turkey company never sent the like to the Grand

Signior. One is a rhymer, sir, of your own batch, your own leaven; but doth think himself poet-major of the town, willing to be shewn, and worthy to be seen. The other—I will not venture his description with you, till you come, because I would have you make hither with an appetite. If the worst of 'em be not worth your journey, draw your bill of charges, as unconscionable as any Guildhall verdict will give it you, and you shall be allowed your viaticum.   *From the Windmill.*

From the Bordello it might come as well,
The Spittle, or Pict-hatch. Is this the man
My son hath sung so, for the happiest wit,
The choicest brain, the times have sent us forth!
I know not what he may be in the arts,
Nor what in schools; but, surely, for his manners,
I judge him a profane and dissolute wretch;
Worse by possession of such great good gifts,
Being the master of so loose a spirit.
Why, what unhallowed ruffian would have writ
In such a scurrilous manner to a friend!
Why should he think I tell my apricots,
Or play the Hesperian dragon with my fruit,
To watch it? Well, my son, I had thought you
Had had more judgment to have made election
Of your companions, than t' have ta'en on trust
Such petulant, jeering gamesters, that can spare
No argument or subject from their jest.
But I perceive affection makes a fool
Of any man too much the father.—Brainworm!

Enter BRAINWORM.

Brai. Sir.
Know. Is the fellow gone that brought this letter?
Brai. Yes, sir, a pretty while since.
Know. And where is your young master?
Brai. In his chamber, sir.
Know. He spake not with the fellow, did he?
Brai. No, sir, he saw him not.
Know. Take you this letter, and deliver it my son; but with no notice that I have opened it, on your life.
Brai. O Lord, sir! that were a jest indeed.   [*Exit.*
Know. I am resolved I will not stop his journey,
Nor practise any violent means to stay
The unbridled course of youth in him; for that
Restrain'd, grows more impatient; and in kind
Like to the eager, but the generous greyhound,
Who ne'er so little from his game withheld,
Turns head, and leaps up at his holder's throat.
There is a way of winning more by love,
And urging of the modesty, than fear:
Force works on servile natures, not the free.
He that's compell'd to goodness, may be good,

But 'tis but for that fit; where others, drawn
By softness and example, get a habit.
Then, if they stray, but warn them, and the same
They should for virtue have done, they'll do for shame.   [*Exit.*

SCENE II.—*A Room in* KNOWELL'S *House.*

Enter E. KNOWELL, *with a letter in his hand, followed by*
BRAINWORM.

E. Know. Did he open it, say'st thou?

Brai. Yes, o' my word, sir, and read the contents.

E. Know. That scarce contents me.   What countenance, prithee,
made he in the reading of it? was he angry, or pleased?

Brai. Nay, sir, I saw him not read it, nor open it, I assure your
worship.

E. Know. No! how know'st thou then that he did either?

Brai. Marry, sir, because he charged me, on my life, to tell
nobody that he open'd it; which, unless he had done, he would
never fear to have it revealed.

E. Know. That's true: well, I thank thee, Brainworm.

Enter STEPHEN.

Step. O, Brainworm, didst thou not see a fellow here in what-
sha-call-him doublet? he brought mine uncle a letter e'en now.

Brai. Yes, master Stephen; what of him?

Step. O, I have such a mind to beat him——where is he, canst
thou tell?

Brai. Faith, he is not of that mind: he is gone, master Stephen.

Step. Gone! which way? when went he? how long since?

Brai. He is rid hence; he took horse at the street-door.

Step. And I staid in the fields! Whoreson scanderbag rogue!
O that I had but a horse to fetch him back again!

Brai. Why, you may have my master's gelding, to save your
longing, sir.

Step. But I have no boots, that's the spite on't.

Brai. Why, a fine wisp of hay, roll'd hard, master Stephen.

Step. No, faith, it's no boot to follow him now: let him e'en go
and hang.   Prithee, help to truss me a little: he does so vex me—

Brai. You'll be worse vexed when you are trussed, master
Stephen.   Best keep unbraced, and walk yourself till you be cold;
your choler may founder you else.

Step. By my faith, and so I will, now thou tell'st me on't: how
dost thou like my leg, Brainworm?

Brai. A very good leg, master Stephen; but the woollen stocking
does not commend it so well.

Step. Foh! the stockings be good enough, now summer is coming
on, for the dust: I'll have a pair of silk against winter, that I go
to dwell in the town.   I think my leg would shew in a silk hose—

Brai. Believe me, master Stephen, rarely well.

Step. In sadness, I think it would: I have a reasonable good leg.

Brai. You have an excellent good leg, master Stephen; but I cannot stay to praise it longer now, and I am very sorry for it. [*Exit.*

Step. Another time will serve, Brainworm. Gramercy for this.

E. Know. Ha, ha, ha!

Step. 'Slid, I hope he laughs not at me; an he do—

E. Know. Here was a letter indeed, to be intercepted by a man's father, and do him good with him! He cannot but think most virtuously, both of me, and the sender, sure, that make the careful costermonger of him in our familiar epistles. Well, if he read this with patience I'll be gelt, and troll ballads for master John Trundle yonder, the rest of my mortality. It is true, and likely, my father may have as much patience as another man, for he takes much physic; and oft taking physic makes a man very patient. But would your packet, master Wellbred, had arrived at him in such a minute of his patience! then we had known the end of it, which now is doubtful, and threatens——[*Sees Master Stephen.*] What, my wise cousin! nay, then I'll furnish our feast with one gull more toward the mess. He writes to me of a brace, and here's one, that's three: oh, for a fourth, Fortune, if ever thou'lt use thine eyes, I entreat thee—

Step. Oh, now I see who he laughed at: he laughed at somebody in that letter. By this good light, an he had laughed at me—

E. Know. How now, cousin Stephen, melancholy?

Step. Yes, a little: I thought you had laughed at me, cousin.

E. Know. Why, what an I had, coz? what would you have done?

Step. By this light, I would have told mine uncle.

E. Know. Nay, if you would have told your uncle, I did laugh at you, coz.

Step. Did you, indeed?

E. Know. Yes, indeed.

Step. Why then—

E. Know. What then?

Step. I am satisfied; it is sufficient.

E. Know. Why, be so, gentle coz: and, I pray you, let me entreat a courtesy of you. I am sent for this morning by a friend in the Old Jewry, to come to him; it is but crossing over the fields to Moorgate: Will you bear me company? I protest it is not to draw you into bond or any plot against the state, coz.

Step. Sir, that's all one an it were; you shall command me twice so far as Moorgate, to do you good in such a matter. Do you think I would leave you? I protest—

E. Know. No, no, you shall not protest, coz.

Step. By my fackings, but I will, by your leave:—I'll protest more to my friend, than I'll speak of at this time.

E. Know. You speak very well, coz.

Step. Nay, not so neither, you shall pardon me: but I speak to serve my turn.

E. Know. Your turn, coz! do you know what you say? A

gentleman of your sorts, parts, carriage, and estimation, to talk of your turn in this company, and to me alone, like a tankard-bearer at a conduit! fie! A wight that, hitherto, his every step hath left the stamp of a great foot behind him, as every word the savour of a strong spirit, and he! this man! so graced, gilded, or, to use a more fit metaphor, so tinfoiled by nature, as not ten housewives' pewter, again a good time, shews more bright to the world than he! and he! (as I said last, so I say again, and still shall say it) this man! to conceal such real ornaments as these, and shadow their glory, as a milliner's wife does her wrought stomacher, with a smoaky lawn, or a black cyprus! O, coz! it cannot be answered; go not about it: Drake's old ship at Deptford may sooner circle the world again. Come, wrong not the quality of your desert, with looking downward, coz; but hold up your head, so: and let the idea of what you are be portrayed in your face, that men may read in your physnomy, *here within this place is to be seen the true, rare, and accomplished monster, or miracle of nature,* which is all one. What think you of this, coz?

Step. Why, I do think of it: and I will be more proud, and melancholy, and gentlemanlike, than I have been, I'll insure you.

E. Know. Why, that's resolute, master Stephen!—Now, if I can but hold him up to his height, as it is happily begun, it will do well for a suburb humour: we may hap have a match with the city, and play him for forty pound.—Come, coz.

Step. I'll follow you.

E. Know. Follow me! you must go before.

Step. Nay, an I must, I will. Pray you shew me, good cousin.

[*Exeunt.*

SCENE III.—*The Lane before* COB'S *House.*

Enter Master MATHEW.

Mat. I think this be the house: what ho!

Enter COB.

Cob. Who's there? O, master Mathew! give your worship good morrow.

Mat. What, Cob! how dost thou, good Cob? dost thou inhabit here, Cob?

Cob. Ay, sir, I and my lineage have kept a poor house here, in our days.

Mat. Thy lineage, monsieur Cob! what lineage, what lineage?

Cob. Why, sir, an ancient lineage, and a princely. Mine ance'try came from a king's belly, no worse man; and yet no man either, by your worship's leave, I did lie in that, but herring, the king of fish (from his belly I proceed), one of the monarchs of the world, I assure you. The first red herring that was broiled in Adam and Eve's kitchen, do I fetch my pedigree from, by the harrot's book. His cob was my great, great, mighty great grandfather.

Mat. Why mighty, why mighty, I pray thee?

Cob. O, it was a mighty while ago, sir, and a mighty great cob.

Mat. How know'st thou that?

Cob. How know I! why, I smell his ghost ever and anon.

Mat. Smell a ghost! O unsavoury jest! and the ghost of a herring cob?

Cob. Ay, sir: With favour of your worship's nose, master Mathew, why not the ghost of a herring cob, as well as the ghost of Rasher Bacon?

Mat. Roger Bacon, thou would'st say.

Cob. I say Rasher Bacon. They were both broiled on the coals; and a man may smell broiled meat, I hope! you are a scholar, upsolve me that now.

Mat. O raw ignorance!—Cob, canst thou shew me of a gentleman, one captain Bobadill, where his lodging is?

Cob. O, my guest, sir, you mean.

Mat. Thy guest! alas, ha, ha, ha!

Cob. Why do you laugh, sir? do you not mean captain Bobadill?

Mat. Cob, pray thee advise thyself well; do not wrong the gentleman, and thyself too. I dare be sworn, he scorns thy house; he! he lodge in such a base obscure place as thy house! Tut, I know his disposition so well, he would not lie in thy bed if thou'dst give it him.

Cob. I will not give it him though, sir. Mass, I thought somewhat was in it, we could not get him to bed all night: Well, sir, though he lie not on my bed, he lies on my bench: an't please you to go up, sir, you shall find him with two cushions under his head, and his cloak wrapped about him, as though he had neither won nor lost, and yet, I warrant, he ne'er cast better in his life, than he has done to-night.

Mat. Why, was he drunk?

Cob. Drunk, sir! you hear not me say so: perhaps he swallowed a tavern-token, or some such device, sir, I have nothing to do withal. I deal with water and not with wine—Give me my tankard there, ho!—God be wi' you, sir. It's six o'clock: I should have carried two turns by this. What ho! my stopple! come.

Enter Tib *with a water-tankard.*

Mat. Lie in a water-bearer's house! a gentleman of his havings! Well, I'll tell him my mind.

Cob. What, Tib; shew this gentleman up to the captain. [*Exit Tib with Master Mathew.*] Oh, an my house were the Brazen-head now! faith it would e'en speak *Moe fools yet.* You should have some now would take this master Mathew to be a gentleman, at the least. His father's an honest man, a worshipful fishmonger, and so forth; and now does he creep and wriggle into acquaintance with all the brave gallants about the town, such as my guest is (O, my guest is a fine man!), and they flout him invincibly. He useth every day to a merchant's house where I serve water, one master Kitely's, in the Old Jewry; and here's the jest, he is in love with

my master's sister, Mrs. Bridget, and calls her mistress; and there
he will sit you a whole afternoon sometimes, reading of these same
abominable, vile (a pox on 'em! I cannot abide them), rascally
verses, poetrie, poetrie, and speaking of interludes; 'twill make a
man burst to hear him.   And the wenches, they do so jeer, and
ti-he at him—Well, should they do so much to me, I'd forswear
them all, by the foot of Pharaoh! There's an oath! How many
water-bearers shall you hear swear such an oath? O, I have a
guest—he teaches me—he does swear the legiblest of any man
christened: *By St. George! the foot of Pharaoh! the body of me! as
I am a gentleman and a soldier!* such dainty oaths! and withal he
does take this same filthy roguish tobacco, the finest and cleanliest! it would do a man good to see the fumes come forth at's
tonnels.—Well, he owes me forty shillings, my wife lent him out of
her purse, by sixpence at a time, besides his lodging: I would I
had it! I shall have it, he says, the next action.   Helter skelter,
hang sorrow, care'll kill a cat, up-tails all, and a louse for the
hangman.   [*Exit.*

SCENE IV.—*A Room in* Cob's *House.*   Bobadill *discovered
lying on a bench.*

   Bob. Hostess, hostess!

Enter Tib.

   Tib. What say you, sir?
   Bob. A cup of thy small beer, sweet hostess.
   Tib. Sir, there's a gentleman below would speak with you.
   Bob. A gentleman! 'odso, I am not within.
   Tib. My husband told him you were, sir.
   Bob. What a plague—what meant he?
   Mat. [*below.*] Captain Bobadill!
   Bob. Who's there!—Take away the bason, good hostess;—Come
up, sir.
   Tib. He would desire you to come up, sir.   You come into a
cleanly house, here!

Enter Mathew.

   Mat. Save you, sir; save you, captain!
   Bob. Gentle master Mathew! Is it you, sir? please you to sit
down.
   Mat. Thank you, good captain; you may see I am somewhat
audacious.
   Bob. Not so, sir.   I was requested to supper last night by a sort
of gallants, where you were wished for, and drunk to, I assure you.
   Mat. Vouchsafe me, by whom, good captain?
   Bob. Marry, by young Wellbred, and others.—Why, hostess, a
stool here for this gentleman.
   Mat. No haste, sir, 'tis very well.

Bob. Body o' me! it was so late ere we parted last night, I can scarce open my eyes yet; I was but new risen, as you came; how passes the day abroad, sir? you can tell.

Mat. Faith, some half hour to seven; Now, trust me, you have an exceeding fine lodging here, very neat, and private.

Bob. Ay, sir: sit down, I pray you. Master Mathew, in any case possess no gentlemen of our acquaintance with notice of my lodging.

Mat. Who? I, sir; no.

Bob. Not that I need to care who know it, for the cabin is convenient; but in regard I would not be too popular, and generally visited, as some are.

Mat. True, captain, I conceive you.

Bob. For, do you see, sir, by the heart of valour in me, except it be to some peculiar and choice spirits, to whom I am extraordinarily engaged, as yourself, or so, I could not extend thus far.

Mat. O Lord, sir! I resolve so.

Bob. I confess I love a cleanly and quiet privacy, above all the tumult and roar of fortune. What new book have you there? What! Go by, Hieronymo?

Mat. Ay: did you ever see it acted? Is't not well penned?

Bob. Well penned! I would fain see all the poets of these times pen such another play as that was: they'll prate and swagger, and keep a stir of art and devices, when, as I am a gentleman, read 'em, they are the most shallow, pitiful, barren fellows, that live upon the face of the earth again.

[*While Master Mathew reads, Bobadill makes himself ready.*

Mat. Indeed here are a number of fine speeches in this book. *O eyes, no eyes, but fountains fraught with tears!* there's a conceit! *fountains fraught with tears! O life, no life, but lively form of death!* another. *O world, no world, but mass of public wrongs!* a third. *Confused and fill'd with murder and misdeeds!* a fourth. O, the muses! Is't not excellent? Is't not simply the best that ever you heard, captain? Ha! how do you like it?

Bob. 'Tis good.

Mat. *To thee, the purest object to my sense,*
    The most refined essence heaven covers,
    Send I these lines, wherein I do commence
    The happy state of turtle-billing lovers.
    If they prove rough, unpolish'd, harsh, and rude,
    Haste made the waste: thus mildly I conclude.

Bob. Nay, proceed, proceed. Where's this?

Mat. This, sir! a toy of mine own, in my non-age; the infancy of my muses. But when will you come and see my study? good faith, I can shew you some very good things I have done of late.— That boot becomes your leg passing well, captain, methinks.

Bob. So, so; it's the fashion gentlemen now use.

Mat. Troth, captain, and now you speak of the fashion, master Wellbred's elder brother and I are fallen out exceedingly: This other day, I happened to enter into some discourse of a hanger, which, I assure you, both for fashion and workmanship, was most peremptory beautiful and gentlemanlike: yet he condemned, and cried it down for the most pied and ridiculous that ever he saw.

Bob. Squire Downright, the half-brother, was't not?

Mat. Ay, sir, he.

Bob. Hang him, rook! he! why he has no more judgment than a malt-horse: By St. George, I wonder you'd lose a thought upon such an animal; the most peremptory absurd clown of Christendom, this day, he is holden. I protest to you, as I am a gentleman and a soldier, I ne'er changed with his like. By his discourse, he should eat nothing but hay; he was born for the manger, pannier, or pack-saddle. He has not so much as a good phrase in his belly, but all old iron and rusty proverbs: a good commodity for some smith to make hob-nails of.

Mat. Ay, and he thinks to carry it away with his manhood still, where he comes: he brags he will give me the bastinado, as I hear.

Bob. How! he the bastinado! how came he by that word, trow?

Mat. Nay, indeed, he said cudgel me; I termed it so, for my more grace.

Bob. That may be: for I was sure it was none of his word; but when, when said he so?

Mat. Faith, yesterday, they say; a young gallant, a friend of mine, told me so.

Bob. By the foot of Pharaoh, an 'twere my case now, I should send him a chartel presently. The bastinado! a most proper and sufficient dependence, warranted by the great Caranza. Come hither, you shall chartel him; I'll shew you a trick or two you shall kill him with at pleasure; the first stoccata, if you will, by this air.

Mat. Indeed, you have absolute knowledge in the mystery, I have heard, sir.

Bob. Of whom, of whom, have you heard it, I beseech you?

Mat. Troth, I have heard it spoken of divers, that you have very rare, and un-in-one-breath-utterable skill, sir.

Bob. By heaven, no, not I; no skill in the earth; some small rudiments in the science, as to know my time, distance, or so. I have professed it more for noblemen and gentlemen's use, than mine own practice, I assure you.—Hostess, accommodate us with another bed-staff here quickly. Lend us another bed-staff—the woman does not understand the words of action.—Look you, sir: exalt not your point above this state, at any hand, and let your poniard maintain your defence, thus:—give it the gentleman, and leave us. [*Exit Tib.*] So, sir. Come on: O, twine your body more about, that you may fall to a more sweet, comely, gentlemanlike guard; so! indifferent: hollow your body more, sir, thus: now, stand fast o' your left leg, note your distance, keep your due pro-portion of time—oh, you disorder your point most irregularly.

Mat. How is the bearing of it now, sir?

Bob. O, out of measure ill: a well-experienced hand would pass upon you at pleasure.

Mat. How mean you, sir, pass upon me?

Bob. Why, thus, sir,—make a thrust at me—[*Master Mathew pushes at Bobadill*] come in upon the answer, control your point, and make a full career at the body: The best-practised gallants of the time name it the passado; a most desperate thrust, believe it.

Mat. Well, come, sir.

Bob. Why, you do not manage your weapon with any facility or grace to invite me. I have no spirit to play with you; your dearth of judgment renders you tedious.

Mat. But one venue, sir.

Bob. Venue! fie; the most gross denomination as ever I heard: O, the stoccata, while you live, sir; note that.—Come, put on your cloke, and we'll go to some private place where you are acquainted; some tavern, or so—and have a bit. I'll send for one of these fencers, and he shall breathe you, by my direction; and then I will teach you your trick: you shall kill him with it at the first, if you please. Why, I will learn you, by the true judgment of the eye, hand, and foot, to control any enemy's point in the world. Should your adversary confront you with a pistol, 'twere nothing, by this hand! you should, by the same rule, control his bullet, in a line, except it were hail shot, and spread. What money have you about you, master Mathew?

Mat. Faith, I have not past a two shilling or so.

Bob. 'Tis somewhat with the least; but come; we will have a bunch of radish and salt to taste our wine, and a pipe of tobacco to close the orifice of the stomach: and then we'll call upon young Wellbred: perhaps we shall meet the Corydon his brother there, and put him to the question.

ACT II

SCENE I.—*The Old Jewry. A Hall in* KITELY'S *House.*

Enter KITELY, CASH, *and* DOWNRIGHT.

Kit. Thomas, come hither.
There lies a note within upon my desk;
Here take my key: it is no matter neither.—
Where is the boy?

    Cash.   Within, sir, in the warehouse.

Kit. Let him tell over straight that Spanish gold,
And weigh it, with the pieces of eight. Do you
See the delivery of those silver stuffs
To Master Lucar: tell him, if he will,
He shall have the grograns, at the rate I told him,
And I will meet him on the Exchange anon.

    Cash. Good, sir.   [*Exit.*

Kit. Do you see that fellow, brother Downright?
Dow. Ay, what of him?
Kit. He is a jewel, brother.
I took him of a child up at my door,
And christen'd him, gave him mine own name, Thomas:
Since bred him at the Hospital; where proving
A toward imp, I call'd him home, and taught him
So much, as I have made him my cashier,
And giv'n him, who had none, a surname, Cash:
And find him in his place so full of faith,
That I durst trust my life into his hands.
    Dow. So would not I in any bastard's, brother,
As it is like he is, although I knew
Myself his father.   But you said you had somewhat
To tell me, gentle brother: what is't, what is't?
    Kit. Faith, I am very loath to utter it,
As fearing it may hurt your patience:
But that I know your judgment is of strength,
Against the nearness of affection—
    Dow. What need this circumstance? pray you, be direct.
    Kit. I will not say how much I do ascribe
Unto your friendship, nor in what regard
I hold your love; but let my past behaviour,
And usage of your sister, [both] confirm
How well I have been affected to your—
    Dow. You are too tedious; come to the matter, the matter.
    Kit. Then, without further ceremony, thus.
My brother Wellbred, sir, I know not how,
Of late is much declined in what he was,
And greatly alter'd in his disposition.
When he came first to lodge here in my house,
Ne'er trust me if I were not proud of him:
Methought he bare himself in such a fashion,
So full of man, and sweetness in his carriage,
And what was chief, it shew'd not borrow'd in him,
But all he did became him as his own,
And seem'd as perfect, proper, and possest,
As breath with life, or colour with the blood.
But now, his course is so irregular,
So loose, affected, and deprived of grace,
And he himself withal so far fallen off
From that first place, as scarce no note remains,
To tell men's judgments where he lately stood.
He's grown a stranger to all due respect,
Forgetful of his friends; and not content
To stale himself in all societies,
He makes my house here common as a mart,
A theatre, a public receptacle
For giddy humour, and deceased riot;

And here, as in a tavern or a stews,
He and his wild associates spend their hours,
In repetition of lascivious jests,
Swear, leap, drink, dance, and revel night by night,
Control my servants; and, indeed, what not?

Dow. 'Sdeins, I know not what I should say to him, in the whole world! He values me at a crack'd three-farthings, for aught I see. It will never out of the flesh that's bred in the bone. I have told him enough, one would think, if that would serve; but counsel to him is as good as a shoulder of mutton to a sick horse. Well! he knows what to trust to, for George: let him spend, and spend, and domineer, till his heart ake; an he think to be relieved by me, when he is got into one o' your city pounds, the counters, he has the wrong sow by the ear, i'faith; and claps his dish at the wrong man's door: I'll lay my hand on my halfpenny, ere I part with it to fetch him out, I'll assure him.

Kit. Nay, good brother, let it not trouble you thus.

Dow. 'Sdeath! he mads me; I could eat my very spur-leathers for anger! But, why are you so tame? why do you not speak to him, and tell him how he disquiets your house?

Kit. O, there are divers reasons to dissuade me.
But, would yourself vouchsafe to travail in it
(Though but with plain and easy circumstance),
It would both come much better to his sense,
And savour less of stomach, or of passion.
You are his elder brother, and that title
Both gives and warrants your authority,
Which, by your presence seconded, must breed
A kind of duty in him, and regard:
Whereas, if I should intimate the least,
It would but add contempt to his neglect,
Heap worse on ill, make up a pile of hatred,
That in the rearing would come tottering down,
And in the ruin bury all our love.
Nay, more than this, brother; if I should speak,
He would be ready, from his heat of humour,
And overflowing of the vapour in him,
To blow the ears of his familiars
With the false breath of telling what disgraces,
And low disparagements, I had put upon him.
Whilst they, sir, to relieve him in the fable,
Make their loose comments upon every word,
Gesture, or look, I use; mock me all over,
From my flat cap unto my shining shoes;
And, out of their impetuous rioting phant'sies,
Beget some slander that shall dwell with me.
And what would that be, think you? marry, this:
They would give out, because my wife is fair,
Myself but lately married, and my sister

Here sojourning a virgin in my house,
That I were jealous!—nay, as sure as death,
That they would say: and, how that I had quarrell'd
My brother purposely, thereby to find
An apt pretext to banish them my house.

Dow. Mass, perhaps so; they're like enough to do it.

Kit. Brother, they would, believe it; so should I,
Like one of these penurious quack-salvers,
But set the bills up to mine own disgrace,
And try experiments upon myself;
Lend scorn and envy opportunity
To stab my reputation and good name—

Enter Master MATHEW *struggling with* BOBADILL.

Mat. I will speak to him.

Bob. Speak to him! away! By the foot of Pharaoh, you shall not! you shall not do him that grace.—The time of day to you, gentleman o' the house. Is master Wellbred stirring?

Dow. How then? what should he do?

Bob. Gentleman of the house, it is to you: is he within, sir?

Kit. He came not to his lodging to-night, sir, I assure you.

Dow. Why, do you hear? you!

Bob. The gentleman citizen hath satisfied me; I'll talk to no scavenger.   *[Exeunt Bob. and Mat.*

Dow. How! scavenger! stay, sir, stay!

Kit. Nay, brother Downright.

Dow. 'Heart! stand you away, an you love me.

Kit. You shall not follow him now, I pray you, brother, good faith you shall not; I will overrule you.

Dow. Ha! scavenger! well, go to, I say little: but, by this good day (God forgive me I should swear), if I put it up so, say I am the rankest cow that ever pist. 'Sdeins, an I swallow this, I'll ne'er draw my sword in the sight of Fleet-street again while I live; I'll sit in a barn with madge-howlet, and catch mice first. Scavenger! heart!—and I'll go near to fill that huge tumbrel-slop of yours with somewhat, an I have good luck: your Garagantua breech cannot carry it away so.

Kit. Oh, do not fret yourself thus: never think on't.

Dow. These are my brother's consorts, these! these are his camerades, his walking mates! he's a gallant, a cavaliero too, right hangman cut! Let me not live, an I could not find in my heart to swinge the whole gang of 'em, one after another, and begin with him first. I am grieved it should be said he is my brother, and take these courses: Well, as he brews, so shall he drink, for George, again. Yet he shall hear on't, and that tightly too, an I live, i'faith.

Kit. But, brother, let your reprehension, then,
Run in an easy current, not o'er high
Carried with rashness, or devouring choler;
But rather use the soft persuading way,

Whose powers will work more gently, and compose
The imperfect thoughts you labour to reclaim;
More winning, than enforcing the consent.

Dow. Ay, ay, let me alone for that, I warrant you.

Kit. How now! [*Bell rings.*] Oh, the bell rings to breakfast.
Brother, I pray you go in, and bear my wife company till I come;
I'll but give order for some despatch of business to my servants.

[*Exit Downright.*

Enter COB, *with his tankard.*

Kit. What, Cob! our maids will have you by the back, i'faith,
for coming so late this morning.

Cob. Perhaps so, sir; take heed somebody have not them by the
belly, for walking so late in the evening.   [*Exit.*

Kit. Well; yet my troubled spirit's somewhat eased,
Though not reposed in that security
As I could wish: but I must be content,
Howe'er I set a face on't to the world.
Would I had lost this finger at a venture,
So Wellbred had ne'er lodged within my house.
Why't cannot be, where there is such resort
Of wanton gallants, and young revellers,
That any woman should be honest long.
Is't like, that factious beauty will preserve
The public weal of chastity unshaken,
When such strong motives muster, and make head
Against her single peace? No, no: beware.
When mutual appetite doth meet to treat,
And spirits of one kind and quality
Come once to parley in the pride of blood,
It is no slow conspiracy that follows.
Well, to be plain, if I but thought the time
Had answer'd their affections, all the world
Should not persuade me but I were a cuckold.
Marry, I hope they have not got that start;
For opportunity hath balk'd them yet,
And shall do still, while I have eyes and ears
To attend the impositions of my heart.
My presence shall be as an iron bar,
'Twixt the conspiring motions of desire:
Yea, every look or glance mine eye ejects
Shall check occasion, as one doth his slave,
When he forgets the limits of prescription.

Enter Dame KITELY *and* BRIDGET.

Dame K. Sister Bridget, pray you fetch down the rose-water,
above in the closet.   [*Exit Bridget.*
—Sweet-heart, will you come in to breakfast?

Kit. An she have overheard me now!—

Dame K. I pray thee, good muss, we stay for you.

Kit. By heaven, I would not for a thousand angels.

Dame K. What ail you, sweet-heart? are you not well? speak, good muss.

Kit. Troth my head akes extremely on a sudden.

Dame K. [*putting her hand to his forehead.*] O, the Lord!

Kit. How now! What?

Dame K. Alas, how it burns! Muss, keep you warm; good truth it is this new disease, there's a number are troubled withal. For love's sake, sweet-heart, come in, out of the air.

Kit. How simple, and how subtle are her answers!
A new disease, and many troubled with it?
Why true; she heard me, all the world to nothing.

Dame K. I pray thee, good sweet-heart, come in; the air will do you harm, in troth.

Kit. The air! she has me in the wind.—Sweet-heart, I'll come to you presently; 'twill away, I hope.

Dame K. Pray Heaven it do. [*Exit.*

Kit. A new disease! I know not, new or old,
But it may well be call'd poor mortals' plague;
For, like a pestilence, it doth infect
The houses of the brain. First it begins
Solely to work upon the phantasy,
Filling her seat with such pestiferous air,
As soon corrupts the judgment; and from thence
Sends like contagion to the memory:
Still each to other giving the infection.
Which as a subtle vapour spreads itself
Confusedly through every sensive part,
Till not a thought or motion in the mind
Be free from the black poison of suspect.
Ah! but what misery is it to know this?
Or, knowing it, to want the mind's erection
In such extremes? Well, I will once more strive,
In spite of this black cloud, myself to be,
And shake the fever off that thus shakes me. [*Exit.*

SCENE II.—*Moorfields.*

Enter BRAINWORM *disguised like a maimed Soldier.*

Brai. 'Slid, I cannot choose but laugh to see myself translated thus, from a poor creature to a creator; for now must I create an intolerable sort of lies, or my present profession loses the grace: and yet the lie, to a man of my coat, is as ominous a fruit as the fico. O, sir, it holds for good polity ever, to have that outwardly in vilest estimation, that inwardly is most dear to us: so much for my borrowed shape. Well, the troth is, my old master intends to follow my young master, dry-foot, over Moorfields to London, this morning; now, I knowing of this hunting-match, or rather conspiracy, and to insinuate with my young master (for so must we that are blue waiters, and men of hope and service do, or perhaps we may wear motley at the year's end, and who wears motley, you know), have got me afore in this disguise, determining here to lie in ambuscado, and intercept him in the mid-way. If I can but get his cloke, his purse, and his hat, nay, any thing to cut him off, that is, to stay his journey, *Veni, vidi, vici,* I may say with captain Cæsar, I am made for ever, i'faith. Well, now I must practise to get the true garb of one of these lance-knights, my arm here, and my——Odso! my young master, and his cousin, master Stephen, as I am true counterfeit man of war, and no soldier!

Enter E. KNOWELL *and* STEPHEN.

E. Know. So, sir! and how then, coz?

Step. 'Sfoot! I have lost my purse, I think.

E. Know. How! lost your purse? where? when had you it?

Step. I cannot tell; stay.

Brai. 'Slid, I am afraid they will know me: would I could get by them!

E. Know. What, have you it?

Step. No; I think I was bewitched, I——   [*Cries.*

E. Know. Nay, do not weep the loss: hang it, let it go.

Step. Oh, it's here: No, an it had been lost, I had not cared, but for a jet ring mistress Mary sent me.

E. Know. A jet ring! O the poesie, the poesie?

Step. Fine, i'faith.——

Though Fancy sleep,
My love is deep.

Meaning, that though I did not fancy her, yet she loved me dearly.

E. Know. Most excellent!

Step. And then I sent her another, and my poesie was,

The deeper the sweeter,
I'll be judg'd by St. Peter.

E. Know. How, by St. Peter? I do not conceive that.

Step. Marry, St. Peter, to make up the metre.

E. Know. Well, there the saint was your good patron, he help'd you at your need; thank him, thank him.

Brai. I cannot take leave on 'em so; I will venture, come what will. [*Comes forward.*] Gentlemen, please you change a few crowns for a very excellent blade here? I am a poor gentleman, a soldier, one that, in the better state of my fortunes, scorned so mean a refuge; but now it is the humour of necessity to have it so. You seem to be gentlemen well affected to martial men, else I should rather die with silence, than live with shame: however, vouchsafe to remember it is my want speaks, not myself; this condition agrees not with my spirit——

E. Know. Where hast thou served?

Brai. May it please you, sir, in all the late wars of Bohemia. Hungary, Dalmatia, Poland, where not, sir? I have been a poor servitor by sea and land any time this fourteen years, and followed the fortunes of the best commanders in Christendom. I was twice shot at the taking of Aleppo, once at the relief of Vienna; I have been at Marseilles, Naples, and the Adriatic gulf, a gentleman-slave in the gallies, thrice; where I was most dangerously shot in the head, through both the thighs; and yet, being thus maimed, I am void of maintenance, nothing left me but my scars, the noted marks of my resolution.

Step. How will you sell this rapier, friend?

Brai. Generous sir, I refer it to your own judgment; you are a gentleman, give me what you please.

Step. True, I am a gentleman, I know that, friend; but what though! I pray you say, what would you ask?

Brai. I assure you, the blade may become the side or thigh of the best prince in Europe.

E. Know. Ay, with a velvet scabbard, I think.

Step. Nay, an't be mine, it shall have a velvet scabbard, coz. that's flat; I'd not wear it, as it is, an you would give me an angel.

Brai. At your worship's pleasure, sir; nay, 'tis a most pure Toledo.

Step. I had rather it were a Spaniard. But tell me, what shall I give you for it? An it had a silver hilt—

E. Know. Come, come, you shall not buy it: hold, there's a shilling, fellow; take thy rapier.

Step. Why, but I will buy it now, because you say so; and there's another shilling, fellow; I scorn to be out-bidden. What, shall I walk with a cudgel, like Higginbottom, and may have a rapier for money!

E. Know. You may buy one in the city.

Step. Tut! I'll buy this i' the field, so I will: I have a mind to't, because 'tis a field rapier. Tell me your lowest price.

E. Know. You shall not buy it, I say.

Step. By this money, but I will, though I give more than 'tis worth.

E. Know. Come away, you are a fool.

Step. Friend, I am a fool, that's granted; but I'll have it, for that word's sake. Follow me for your money.

Brai. At your service, sir. [*Exeunt.*

SCENE III.—*Another Part of Moorfields.*

Enter KNOWELL.

Know. I cannot lose the thought yet of this letter,
Sent to my son; nor leave t' admire the change
Of manners, and the breeding of our youth
Within the kingdom, since myself was one.—
When I was young, he lived not in the stews

Durst have conceived a scorn, and utter'd it,
On a gray head; age was authority
Against a buffoon, and a man had then
A certain reverence paid unto his years,
That had none due unto his life: so much
The sanctity of some prevail'd for others.
But now we all are fallen; youth, from their fear,
And age, from that which bred it, good example.
Nay, would ourselves were not the first, even parents,
That did destroy the hopes in our own children;
Or they not learn'd our vices in their cradles,
And suck'd in our ill customs with their milk;
Ere all their teeth be born, or they can speak,
We make their palates cunning; the first words
We form their tongues with, are licentious jests:
Can it call whore? cry bastard? O, then, kiss it!
A witty child! can't swear? the father's darling!
Give it two plums. Nay, rather than't shall learn
No bawdy song, the mother herself will teach it!—
But this is in the infancy, the days
Of the long coat; when it puts on the breeches,
It will put off all this: Ay, it is like,
When it is gone into the bone already!
No, no; this dye goes deeper than the coat,
Or shirt, or skin; it stains into the liver,
And heart, in some: and, rather than it should not,
Note what we fathers do! look how we live!
What mistresses we keep! at what expense,
In our sons' eyes! where they may handle our gifts,
Hear our lascivious courtships, see our dalliance,
Taste of the same provoking meats with us,
To ruin of our states! Nay, when our own
Portion is fled, to prey on the remainder,
We call them into fellowship of vice;
Bait 'em with the young chamber-maid, to seal,
And teach 'em all bad ways to buy affliction.
This is one path: but there are millions more,
In which we spoil our own, with leading them.
Well, I thank heaven, I never yet was he
That travell'd with my son, before sixteen,
To shew him the Venetian courtezans;
Nor read the grammar of cheating I had made,
To my sharp boy, at twelve; repeating still
The rule, *Get money; still, get money, boy;*
No matter by what means; money will do
More, boy, than my lord's letter. Neither have I
Drest snails or mushrooms curiously before him,
Perfumed my sauces, and taught him how to make them;
Preceding still, with my gray gluttony,

At all the ord'naries, and only fear'd
His palate should degenerate, not his manners.
These are the trade of fathers now; however,
My son, I hope, hath met within my threshold
None of these household precedents, which are strong,
And swift, to rape youth to their precipice.
But let the house at home be ne'er so clean
Swept, or kept sweet from filth, nay dust and cobwebs,
If he will live abroad with his companions,
In dung and leystals, it is worth a fear;
Nor is the danger of conversing less
Than all that I have mention'd of example.

Enter BRAINWORM, *disguised as before.*

Brai. My master! nay, faith, have at you; I am flesh'd now, I have sped so well. [*Aside.*] Worshipful sir, I beseech you, respect the estate of a poor soldier; I am ashamed of this base course of life,— God's my comfort—but extremity provokes me to't: what remedy?

Know. I have not for you, now.

Brai. By the faith I bear unto truth, gentleman, it is no ordinary custom in me, but only to preserve manhood. I protest to you, a man I have been: a man I may be, by your sweet bounty.

Know. Pray thee, good friend, be satisfied.

Brai. Good sir, by that hand, you may do the part of a kind gentleman, in lending a poor soldier the price of two cans of beer, a matter of small value: the king of heaven shall pay you, and I shall rest thankful: Sweet worship—

Know. Nay, an you be so importunate—

Brai. Oh, tender sir! need will have its course: I was not made to this vile use. Well, the edge of the enemy could not have abated me so much: it's hard when a man hath served in his prince's cause, and be thus. [*Weeps.*] Honourable worship, let me derive a small piece of silver from you, it shall not be given in the course of time. By this good ground, I was fain to pawn my rapier last night for a poor supper; I had suck'd the hilts long before, I am a pagan else: Sweet honour—

Know. Believe me, I am taken with some wonder,
To think a fellow of thy outward presence,
Should, in the frame and fashion of his mind,
Be so degenerate, and sordid-base.
Art thou a man? and sham'st thou not to beg,
To practise such a servile kind of life?
Why, were thy education ne'er so mean,
Having thy limbs, a thousand fairer courses
Offer themselves to thy election.
Either the wars might still supply thy wants,
Or service of some virtuous gentleman,
Or honest labour; nay, what can I name,
But would become thee better than to beg:

But men of thy condition feed on sloth,
As doth the beetle on the dung she breeds in;
Nor caring how the metal of your minds
Is eaten with the rust of idleness.
Now, afore me, whate'er he be, that should
Relieve a person of thy quality,
While thou insist'st in this loose desperate course,
I would esteem the sin not thine, but his.

Brai. Faith, sir, I would gladly find some other course, if so—

Know. Ay,
You'd gladly find it, but you will not seek it.

Brai. Alas, sir, where should a man seek? in the wars, there's no ascent by desert in these days; but——and for service, would it were as soon purchased, as wished for! the air's my comfort.—[*Sighs.*]—I know what I would say.

Know. What's thy name?

Brai.   Please you, Fitz-Sword, sir.

Know.   Fitz-Sword!
Say that a man should entertain thee now,
Wouldst thou be honest, humble, just, and true?

Brai. Sir, by the place and honour of a soldier—

Know. Nay, nay, I like not these affected oaths; speak plainly, man, what think'st thou of my words?

Brai. Nothing, sir, but wish my fortunes were as happy as my service should be honest.

Know. Well, follow me; I'll prove thee, if thy deeds
Will carry a proportion to thy words.   [*Exit.*

Brai. Yes, sir, straight; I'll but garter my hose. Oh that my belly were hoop'd now, for I am ready to burst with laughing! never was bottle or bagpipe fuller. 'Slid, was there ever seen a fox in years to betray himself thus! now shall I be possest of all his counsels; and, by that conduit, my young master. Well, he is resolved to prove my honesty; faith, and I'm resolved to prove his patience: Oh, I shall abuse him intolerably. This small piece of service will bring him clean out of love with the soldier for ever. He will never come within the sign of it, the sight of a cassock, or a musket-rest again. He will hate the musters at Mile-end for it, to his dying day. It's no matter, let the world think me a bad counterfeit, if I cannot give him the slip at an instant: why, this is better than to have staid his journey: well, I'll follow him. Oh, how I long to be employed!   [*Exit.*

ACT III

SCENE I.—*The Old Jewry. A Room in the Windmill Tavern.*

Enter Master MATHEW, WELLBRED, *and* BOBADILL.

Mat. Yes, faith, sir, we were at your lodging to seek you too.

Wel. Oh, I came not there to-night.

Bob. Your brother delivered us as much.

Wel. Who, my brother Downright?

Bob. He. Mr. Wellbred, I know not in what kind you hold me; but let me say to you this: as sure as honour, I esteem it so much out of the sunshine of reputation, to throw the least beam of regard upon such a—

Wel. Sir, I must hear no ill words of my brother.

Bob. I protest to you, as I have a thing to be saved about me, I never saw any gentlemanlike part—

Wel. Good captain, faces about to some other discourse.

Bob. With your leave, sir, an there were no more men living upon the face of the earth, I should not fancy him, by St. George!

Mat. Troth, nor I; he is of a rustical cut, I know not how: he doth not carry himself like a gentleman of fashion.

Wel. Oh, master Mathew, that's a grace peculiar but to a few, *quos æquus amavit Jupiter.*

Mat. I understand you, sir.

Wel. No question, you do,—or do you not, sir.

Enter E. KNOWELL *and* Master STEPHEN.

Ned Knowell! by my soul, welcome: how dost thou, sweet spirit, my genius? 'Slid, I shall love Apollo and the mad Thespian girls the better, while I live, for this, my dear Fury; now, I see there's some love in thee. Sirrah, these be the two I writ to thee of: nay, what a drowsy humour is this now! why dost thou not speak?

E. Know. Oh, you are a fine gallant; you sent me a rare letter.

Wel. Why, was't not rare?

E. Know. Yes, I'll be sworn, I was ne'er guilty of reading the like; match it in all Pliny, or Symmachus's epistles, and I'll have my judgment burn'd in the ear for a rogue: make much of thy vein, for it is inimitable. But I marle what camel it was, that had the carriage of it; for, doubtless, he was no ordinary beast that brought it.

Wel. Why?

E. Know. Why, say'st thou! why, dost thou think that any reasonable creature, especially in the morning, the sober time of the day too, could have mistaken my father for me?

Wel. 'Slid, you jest, I hope.

E. Know. Indeed, the best use we can turn it to, is to make a jest on't, now: but I'll assure you, my father had the full view of your flourishing style some hour before I saw it.

Wel. What a dull slave was this! but, sirrah, what said he to it, i'faith?

E. Know. Nay, I know not what he said; but I have a shrewd guess what he thought.

Wel. What, what?

E. Know. Marry, that thou art some strange, dissolute young fellow, and I—a grain or two better, for keeping thee company.

Wel. Tut! that thought is like the moon in her last quarter, 'twill change shortly: but, sirrah, I pray thee be acquainted with my two hang-by's here; thou wilt take exceeding pleasure in them if thou hear'st 'em once go; my wind-instruments; I'll wind them up——But what strange piece of silence is this, the sign of the Dumb Man?

E. Know. Oh, sir, a kinsman of mine, one that may make your music the fuller, an he please; he has his humour, sir.

Wel. Oh, what is't, what is't?

E. Know. Nay, I'll neither do your judgment nor his folly that wrong, as to prepare your apprehension: I'll leave him to the mercy of your search; if you can take him, so!

Wel. Well, captain Bobadill, master Mathew, pray you know this gentleman here; he is a friend of mine, and one that will deserve your affection. I know not your name, sir, [*to Stephen.*] but I shall be glad of any occasion to render me more familiar to you.

Step. My name is master Stephen, sir; I am this gentleman's own cousin, sir; his father is mine uncle, sir: I am somewhat melancholy, but you shall command me, sir, in whatsoever is incident to a gentleman.

Bob. Sir, I must tell you this, I am no general man; but for master Wellbred's sake, (you may embrace it at what height of favour you please,) I do communicate with you, and conceive you to be a gentleman of some parts; I love few words.

E. Know. And I fewer, sir; I have scarce enough to thank you.

Mat. But are you, indeed, sir, so given to it?

Step. Ay, truly, sir, I am mightily given to melancholy.

Mat. Oh, it's your only fine humour, sir: your true melancholy breeds your perfect fine wit, sir. I am melancholy myself, diver times, sir, and then do I no more but take pen and paper, presently, and overflow you half a score, or a dozen of sonnets at a sitting.

E. Know. Sure he utters them then by the gross.   [*Aside.*

Step. Truly, sir, and I love such things out of measure.

E. Know. I'faith, better than in measure, I'll undertake.

Mat. Why, I pray you, sir, make use of my study, it's at your service.

Step. I thank you, sir, I shall be bold I warrant you; have you a stool there to be melancholy upon?

Mat. That I have, sir, and some papers there of mine own doing, at idle hours, that you'll say there's some sparks of wit in 'em, when you see them.

Wel. Would the sparks would kindle once, and become a fire amongst them! I might see self-love burnt for her heresy. [*Aside.*

Step. Cousin, is it well? am I melancholy enough?

E. Know. Oh ay, excellent.

Wel. Captain Bobadill, why muse you so?

E. Know. He is melancholy too.

Bob. Faith, sir, I was thinking of a most honourable piece of service, was performed to-morrow, being St. Mark's day, shall be some ten years now.

E. Know. In what place, captain?

Bob. Why, at the beleaguering of Strigonium, where, in less than two hours, seven hundred resolute gentlemen, as any were in Europe, lost their lives upon the breach. I'll tell you, gentlemen, it was the first, but the best leaguer that ever I beheld with these eyes, except the taking in of—what do you call it? last year, by the Genoways; but that, of all other, was the most fatal and dangerous exploit that ever I was ranged in, since I first bore arms before the face of the enemy, as I am a gentleman and a soldier!

Step. So! I had as lief as an angel I could swear as well as that gentleman.

E. Know. Then, you were a servitor at both, it seems; at Strigonium, and what do you call't?

Bob. O lord, sir! By St. George, I was the first man that entered the breach; and had I not effected it with resolution, I had been slain if I had had a million of lives.

E. Know. 'Twas pity you had not ten; a cat's and your own, i'faith. But, was it possible?

Mat. Pray you mark this discourse, sir.

Step. So I do.

Bob. I assure you, upon my reputation, 'tis true, and yourself shall confess.

E. Know. You must bring me to the rack, first. [*Aside.*

Bob. Observe me judicially, sweet sir; they had planted me three demi-culverins just in the mouth of the breach; now, sir, as we were to give on, their master-gunner (a man of no mean skill and mark, you must think,) confronts me with his linstock, ready to give fire; I, spying his intendment, discharged my petronel in his bosom, and with these single arms, my poor rapier, ran violently upon the Moors that guarded the ordnance, and put them pell-mell to the sword.

Wel. To the sword! To the rapier, captain.

E. Know. Oh, it was a good figure observed, sir: but did you all this, captain, without hurting your blade?

Bob. Without any impeach o' the earth: you shall perceive, sir. [*Shews his rapier.*] It is the most fortunate weapon that ever rid on poor gentleman's thigh. Shall I tell you, sir? You talk of Morglay, Excalibur, Durindana, or so; tut! I lend no credit to that is fabled of 'em: I know the virtue of mine own, and therefore I dare the boldlier maintain it.

Step. I marle whether it be a Toledo or no.

Bob. A most perfect Toledo, I assure you, sir.

Step. I have a countryman of his here.

Mat. Pray you, let's see, sir; yes, faith, it is.

Bob. This a Toledo! Pish!

Step. Why do you pish, captain?

Bob. A Fleming, by heaven! I'll buy them for a guilder a-piece, an I would have a thousand of them.

E. Know. How say you, cousin? I told you thus much.

Wel. Where bought you it, master Stephen?

Step. Of a scurvy rogue soldier: a hundred of lice go with him! He swore it was a Toledo.

Bob. A poor provant rapier, no better.

Mat. Mass, I think it be indeed, now I look on't better.

E. Know. Nay, the longer you look on't, the worse. Put it up, put it up.

Step. Well, I will put it up; but by—I have forgot the captain's oath, I thought to have sworn by it—an e'er I meet him—

Wel. O, it is past help now, sir; you must have patience.

Step. Whoreson, coney-hatching rascal! I could eat the very hilts for anger.

E. Know. A sign of good digestion; you have an ostrich stomach, cousin.

Step. A stomach! would I had him here, you should see an I had a stomach.

Wel. It's better as it is.—Come, gentlemen, shall we go?

Enter BRAINWORM, *disguised as before.*

E. Know. A miracle, cousin; look here, look here!

Step. Oh—'Od's lid. By your leave, do you know me, sir?

Brai. Ay, sir, I know you by sight.

Step. You sold me a rapier, did you not?

Brai. Yes, marry did I, sir.

Step. You said it was a Toledo, ha?

Brai. True, I did so.

Step. But it is none.

Brai. No, sir, I confess it; it is none.

Step. Do you confess it? Gentlemen, bear witness, he has confest it:—'Od's will, an you had not confest it—

E. Know. Oh, cousin, forbear, forbear!

Step. Nay, I have done, cousin.

Wel. Why, you have done like a gentleman; he has confest it, what would you more?

Step. Yet, by his leave, he is a rascal, under his favour, do you see.

E. Know. Ay, by his leave, he is, and under favour: a pretty piece of civility! Sirrah, how dost thou like him?

Wel. Oh, it's a most precious fool, make much on him: I can compare him to nothing more happily than a drum; for every one may play upon him.

E. Know. No, no, a child's whistle were far the fitter.

Brai. Shall I intreat a word with you?

E. Know. With me, sir? you have not another Toledo to sell, have you?

Brai. You are conceited, sir: Your name is Master Knowell, as I take it?

E. Know. You are in the right; you mean not to proceed in the catechism, do you?

Brai. No, sir; I am none of that coat.

E. Know. Of as bare a coat, though: well, say, sir.

Brai. [*taking E. Know. aside.*] Faith, sir, I am but servant to the drum extraordinary, and indeed, this smoky varnish being washed off, and three or four patches removed, I appear your worship's in reversion, after the decease of your good father, Brainworm.

E. Know. Brainworm! 'Slight, what breath of a conjurer hath blown thee hither in this shape?

Brai. The breath of your letter, sir, this morning; the same that blew you to the Windmill, and your father after you.

E. Know. My father!

Brai. Nay, never start, 'tis true; he has followed you over the fields by the foot, as you would do a hare in the snow.

E. Know. Sirrah Wellbred, what shall we do, sirrah? my father is come over after me.

Wel. Thy father! Where is he?

Brai. At justice Clement's house, in Coleman-street, where he but stays my return; and then—

Wel. Who's this? Brainworm!

Brai. The same, sir.

Wel. Why how, in the name of wit, com'st thou transmuted thus?

Brai. Faith, a device, a device; nay, for the love of reason, gentlemen, and avoiding the danger, stand not here; withdraw, and I'll tell you all.

Wel. But art thou sure he will stay thy return?

Brai. Do I live, sir? what a question is that!

Wel. We'll prorogue his expectation, then, a little: Brainworm, thou shalt go with us.—Come on, gentlemen.—Nay, I pray thee, sweet Ned, droop not; 'heart, an our wits be so wretchedly dull, that one old plodding brain can outstrip us all, would we were e'en prest to make porters of, and serve out the remnant of our days in Thames-street, or at Custom-house key, in a civil war against the carmen!

Brai. Amen, amen, amen, say I. [*Exeunt.*

SCENE II.—*The Old Jewry.* KITELY's *Warehouse.*

Enter KITELY *and* CASH.

Kit. What says he, Thomas? did you speak with him?

Cash. He will expect you, sir, within this half hour.

Kit. Has he the money ready, can you tell?

Cash. Yes, sir, the money was brought in last night.

Kit. O, that is well; fetch me my cloak, my cloak!—

                                          [Exit Cash.

Stay, let me see, an hour to go and come;
Ay, that will be the least; and then 'twill bo
An hour before I can dispatch with him,
Or very near; well, I will say two hours.
Two hours! ha! things never dreamt of yet,
May be contrived, ay, and effected too,
In two hours' absence; well, I will not go.
Two hours! No, fleering Opportunity,
I will not give your subtilty that scope.
Who will not judge him worthy to be robb'd,
That sets his doors wide open to a thief,
And shews the felon where his treasure lies?
Again, what earthly spirit but will attempt
To taste the fruit of beauty's golden tree,
When leaden sleep seals up the dragon's eyes?
I will not go. Business, *go by* for once.
No, beauty, no; you are of too good caract,
To be left so, without a guard, or open.
Your lustre, too, 'll inflame at any distance,
Draw courtship to you, as a jet doth straws;
Put motion in a stone, strike fire from ice,
Nay, make a porter leap you with his burden.
You must be then kept up, close, and well watch'd,
For, give you opportunity, no quick-sand
Devours or swallows swifter! He that lends
His wife, if she be fair, or time or place,
Compels her to be false. I will not go!
The dangers are too many;—and then the dressing
Is a most main attractive! Our great heads
Within this city never were in safety
Since our wives wore these little caps: I'll change 'em;
I'll change 'em straight in mine: mine shall no more
Wear three-piled acorns, to make my horns ake.
Nor will I go; I am resolved for that.

Re-enter CASH *with a cloak.*

Carry in my cloak again. Yet stay. Yet do, too:
1 will defer going, on all occasions.

    Cash. Sir, Snare, your scrivener, will be there with the bonds.

    Kit. That's true: fool on me! I had clean forgot it;
I must go. What's a clock?

    Cash.   Exchange-time, sir.

    Kit. 'Heart, then will Wellbred presently be here too,
With one or other of his loose consorts.
I am a knave, if I know what to say,
What course to take, or which way to resolve.

My brain, methinks, is like an hour-glass,
Wherein my imaginations run like sands,
Filling up time; but then are turn'd and turn'd:
So that I know not what to stay upon,
And less, to put in act.—It shall be so.
Nay, I dare build upon his secrecy,
He knows not to deceive me.—Thomas!

  Cash.   Sir.
  Kit. Yet now I have bethought me too, I will not.—
Thomas, is Cob within?
  Cash.   I think he be, sir.
  Kit. But he'll prate too, there is no speech of him.
No, there were no man on the earth to Thomas,
If I durst trust him; there is all the doubt.
But should he have a clink in him, I were gone.
Lost in my fame for ever, talk for th' Exchange!
The manner he hath stood with, till this present,
Doth promise no such change: what should I fear then?
Well, come what will, I'll tempt my fortune once.
Thomas—you may deceive me, but, I hope—
Your love to me is more—
  Cash.   Sir, if a servant's
Duty, with faith, may be call'd love, you are
More than in hope, you are possess'd of it.
  Kit. I thank you heartily, Thomas: give me your hand:
With all my heart, good Thomas. I have, Thomas,
A secret to impart unto you—but,
When once you have it, I must seal your lips up;
So far I tell you, Thomas.
  Cash.   Sir, for that—
  Kit. Nay, hear me out. Think I esteem you, Thomas,
When I will let you in thus to my private.
It is a thing sits nearer to my crest,
Than thou art 'ware of, Thomas; if thou should'st
Reveal it, but—
  Cash.   How, I reveal it?
  Kit.   Nay,
I do not think thou would'st; but if thou should'st,
'Twere a great weakness.
  Cash.   A great treachery:
Give it no other name.
  Kit.   Thou wilt not do't, then?
  Cash. Sir, if I do, mankind disclaim me ever!
  Kit. He will not swear, he has some reservation,
Some conceal'd purpose, and close meaning sure;
Else, being urg'd so much, how should he choose
But lend an oath to all this protestation?
He's no precisian, that I'm certain of,
Nor rigid Roman Catholic: he'll play

At fayles, and tick-tack; I have heard him swear.
What should I think of it? urge him again,
And by some other way! I will do so.
Well, Thomas, thou hast sworn not to disclose:—
Yes, you did swear?

    Cash.   Not yet, sir, but I will,
Please you—

    Kit.   No, Thomas, I dare take thy word,
But, if thou wilt swear, do as thou think'st good;
I am resolv'd without it; at thy pleasure.

    Cash. By my soul's safety then, sir, I protest,
My tongue shall ne'er take knowledge of a word
Deliver'd me in nature of your trust.

    Kit. It is too much; these ceremonies need not:
I know thy faith to be as firm as rock.
Thomas, come hither, near; we cannot be
Too private in this business. So it is,—
Now he has sworn, I dare the safelier venture.   *[Aside.*
I have of late, by divers observations—
But whether his oath can bind him, yea, or no,
Being not taken lawfully? ha! say you?
I will ask council ere I do proceed:—   *[Aside.*
Thomas, it will be now too long to stay,
I'll spy some fitter time soon, or to-morrow.

    Cash. Sir, at your pleasure.

    Kit.   I will think:—and, Thomas,
I pray you search the books 'gainst my return,
For the receipts 'twixt me and Traps.

    Cash.   I will, sir.

    Kit. And hear you, if your mistress's brother, Wellbred,
Chance to bring hither any gentleman,
Ere I come back, let one straight bring me word.

    Cash. Very well, sir.

    Kit.   To the Exchange, do you hear?
Or here in Coleman-street, to justice Clement's.
Forget it not, nor be not out of the way.

    Cash. I will not, sir.

    Kit.   I pray you have a care on't.
Or, whether he come or no, if any other,
Stranger, or else; fail not to send me word.

    Cash. I shall not, sir.

    Kit.   Be it your special business
Now to remember it.

    Cash.   Sir, I warrant you.

    Kit. But, Thomas, this is not the secret, Thomas,
I told you of.

    Cash.   No, sir; I do suppose it.

    Kit. Believe me, it is not.

    Cash.   Sir, I do believe you.

Kit. By heaven it is not, that's enough: but, Thomas,
I would not you should utter it, do you see,
To any creature living; yet I care not.
Well, I must hence. Thomas, conceive thus much;
It was a trial of you, when I meant
So deep a secret to you, I mean not this,
But that I have to tell you; this is nothing, this.
But, Thomas, keep this from my wife, I charge you,
Lock'd up in silence, midnight, buried here.—
No greater hell than to be slave to fear.   [*Exit.*

   Cash. Lock'd up in silence, midnight, buried here!
Whence should this flood of passion, trow, take head? ha!
Best dream no longer of this running humour,
For fear I sink; the violence of the stream
Already hath transported me so far,
That I can feel no ground at all: but soft—
Oh, 'tis our water-bearer: somewhat has crost him now.

Enter COB, *hastily.*

   Cob. Fasting-days! what tell you me of fasting-days? 'Slid,
would they were all on a light fire for me! they say the whole world
shall be consumed with fire one day, but would I had these Ember-
weeks and villanous Fridays burnt in the mean time, and then—

   Cash. Why, how now, Cob? what moves thee to this choler, ha?

   Cob. Collar, master Thomas! I scorn your collar, I, sir; I am
none o' your cart-horse, though I carry and draw water. An you
offer to ride me with your collar or halter either, I may hap shew you
a jade's trick, sir.

   Cash. O, you'll slip your head out of the collar? why, goodman
Cob, you mistake me.

   Cob. Nay, I have my rheum, and I can be angry as well as
another, sir.

   Cash. Thy rheum, Cob! thy humour, thy humour—thou mis-
tak'st.

   Cob. Humour! mack, I think it be so indeed; what is that
humour? some rare thing, I warrant.

   Cash. Marry I'll tell thee, Cob: it is a gentlemanlike monster,
bred in the special gallantry of our time, by affectation; and fed
by folly.

   Cob. How! must it be fed?

   Cash. Oh ay, humour is nothing if it be not fed: didst thou never
hear that? it's a common phrase, *feed my humour.*

   Cob. I'll none on it: humour, avaunt! I know you not, be gone!
let who will make hungry meals for your monstership, it shall not
be I. Feed you, quoth he! 'slid, I have much ado to feed myself;
especially on these lean rascally days too; an't had been any
other day but a fasting-day—a plague on them all for me! By this
light, one might have done the commonwealth good service, and
have drown'd them all in the flood, two or three hundred thousand

years ago. O, I do stomach them hugely. I have a maw now, and 'twere for sir Bevis his horse, against them.

Cash. I pray thee, good Cob, what makes thee so out of love with fasting days?

Cob. Marry, that which will make any man out of love with 'em, I think; their bad conditions, an you will needs know. First, they are of a Flemish breed, I am sure on't, for they raven up more butter than all the days of the week beside; next, they stink of fish and leek-porridge miserably; thirdly, they'll keep a man devoutly hungry all day, and at night send him supperless to bed.

Cash. Indeed, these are faults, Cob.

Cob. Nay, an this were all, 'twere something; but they are the only known enemies to my generation. A fasting-day no sooner comes, but my lineage goes to wrack; poor cobs! they smoak for it, they are made martyrs o' the gridiron, they melt in passion: and your maids to know this, and yet would have me turn Hannibal, and eat my own flesh and blood. My princely coz, [*pulls out a red herring.*] fear nothing; I have not the heart to devour you, an I might be made as rich as king Cophetua. O that I had room for my tears, I could weep salt-water enough now to preserve the lives of ten thousand thousand of my kin! But I may curse none but these filthy almanacks; for an't were not for them, these days of persecution would never be known. I'll be hang'd an some fishmonger's son do not make of 'em, and puts in more fasting-days than he should do, because he would utter his father's dried stockfish and stinking conger.

Cash. 'Slight peace! thou'lt be beaten like a stock-fish else: here's master Mathew.

Enter WELLBRED, E. KNOWELL, BRAINWORM, MATHEW, BOBADILL, *and* STEPHEN.

Now must I look out for a messenger to my master. [*Exit with Cob.*

Wel. Beshrew me, but it was an absolute good jest, and exceedingly well carried!

E. Know. Ay, and our ignorance maintain'd it as well, did it not?

Wel. Yes, faith; but was it possible thou shouldst not know him? I forgive master Stephen, for he is stupidity itself.

E. Know. 'Fore God, not I, an I might have been join'd patten with one of the seven wise masters for knowing him. He had so writhen himself into the habit of one of your poor infantry, your decayed, ruinous, worm-eaten gentlemen of the round; such as have vowed to sit on the skirts of the city, let your provost and his half-dozen of halberdiers do what they can; and have translated begging out of the old hackney-pace to a fine easy amble, and made it run as smooth off the tongue as a shove-groat shilling. Into the likeness of one of these reformados had he moulded himself so perfectly, observing every trick of their action, as, varying the accent, swearing with an emphasis, indeed, all with so special and exquisite a grace, that, hadst thou seen him, thou wouldst have sworn he might have been sergeant-major, if not lieutenant-colonel to the regiment.

Wel. Why, Brainworm, who would have thought thou hadst been such an artificer?

E. Know. An artificer! an architect. Except a man had studied begging all his life time, and been a weaver of language from his infancy for the cloathing of it, I never saw his rival.

Wel. Where got'st thou this coat, I marle?

Brai. Of a Hounsditch man, sir, one of the devil's near kinsmen, a broker.

Wel. That cannot be, if the proverb hold; for *A crafty knave needs no broker.*

Brai. True, sir; but I did *need a broker, ergo—*

Wel. Well put off:—*no crafty knave*, you'll say.

E. Know. Tut, he has more of these shifts.

Brai. And yet, where I have one the broker has ten, sir.

Re-enter CASH.

Cash. Francis! Martin! ne'er a one to be found now? what a spite's this!

Wel. How now, Thomas? Is my brother Kitely within?

Cash. No, sir, my master went forth e'en now; but master Downright is within.—Cob! what, Cob! Is he gone too?

Wel. Whither went your master, Thomas, canst thou tell?

Cash. I know not: to justice Clement's, I think, sir—Cob!

[*Exit.*

E. Know. Justice Clement! what's he?

Wel. Why, dost thou not know him? He is a city-magistrate, a justice here, an excellent good lawyer, and a great scholar; but the only mad, merry old fellow in Europe. I shewed him you the other day.

E. Know. Oh, is that he? I remember him now. Good faith, and he is a very strange presence methinks; it shews as if he stood out of the rank from other men: I have heard many of his jests in the University. They say he will commit a man for taking the wall of his horse.

Wel. Ay, or wearing his cloak on one shoulder, or serving of God; any thing, indeed, if it come in the way of his humour.

Re-enter CASH.

Cash. Gasper! Martin! Cob! 'Heart, where should they be, trow?

Bob. Master Kitely's man, pray thee vouchsafe us the lighting of this match.

Cash. Fire on your match! no time but now to *vouchsafe?*— Francis! Cob!

[*Exit.*

Bob. Body o' me! here's the remainder of seven pound since yesterday was seven-night. 'Tis your right Trinidado: did you never take any, master Stephen?

Step. No, truly, sir; but I'll learn to take it now, since you commend it so.

Bob. Sir, believe me, upon my relation for what I tell you, the world shall not reprove. I have been in the Indies, where this herb grows, where neither myself, nor a dozen gentlemen more of my knowledge, have received the taste of any other nutriment in the world, for the space of one and twenty weeks, but the fume of this simple only: therefore, it cannot be, but 'tis most divine. Further, take it in the nature, in the true kind; so, it makes an antidote, that, had you taken the most deadly poisonous plant in all Italy, it should expel it, and clarify you, with as much ease as I speak. And for your green wound,—your Balsamum and your St. John's wort, are all mere gulleries and trash to it, especially your Trinidado: your Nicotian is good too. I could say what I know of the virtue of it, for the expulsion of rheums, raw humours, crudities, obstructions, with a thousand of this kind; but I profess myself no quacksalver. Only thus much; by Hercules, I do hold it, and will affirm it before any prince in Europe, to be the most sovereign and precious weed that ever the earth tendered to the use of man.

E. Know. This speech would have done decently in a tobacco-trader's mouth.

Re-enter CASH with COB.

Cash. At justice Clement's he is, in the middle of Coleman-street.

Cob. Oh, oh!

Bob. Where's the match I gave thee, master Kitely's man?

Cash. Would his match and he, and pipe and all, were at Sancto Domingo! I had forgot it.   [*Exit.*

Cob. 'Od's me, I marle what pleasure or felicity they have in taking this roguish tobacco. It's good for nothing but to choke a man, and fill him full of smoke and embers: there were four died out of one house last week with taking of it, and two more the bell went for yesternight; one of them, they say, will never scape it; he voided a bushel of soot yesterday, upward and downward. By the stocks, an there were no wiser men than I, I'd have it present whipping, man or woman, that should but deal with a tobacco pipe: why, it will stifle them all in the end, as many as use it; it's little better than ratsbane or rosaker.   [*Bobadill beats him.*

All. Oh, good captain, hold, hold!

Bob. You base cullion, you!

Re-enter CASH.

Cash. Sir, here's your match. Come, thou must needs be talking too, thou'rt well enough served.

Cob. Nay, he will not meddle with his match, I warrant you: well, it shall be a dear beating, an I live.

Bob. Do you prate, do you murmur?

E. Know. Nay, good captain, will you regard the humour of a fool? Away, knave.

Wel. Thomas, get him away. *[Exit Cash with Cob.*

Bob. A whoreson filthy slave, a dung-worm, an excrement! Body o' Cæsar, but that I scorn to let forth so mean a spirit, I'd have stabb'd him to the earth.

Wel. Marry, the law forbid, sir!

Bob. By Pharaoh's foot, I would have done it.

Step. Oh, he swears most admirably! By Pharaoh's foot! Body o' Cæsar!—I shall never do it, sure. Upon mine honour, and by St. George!—No, I have not the right grace.

Mat. Master Stephen, will you any? By this air, the most divine tobacco that ever I drunk.

Step. None, I thank you, sir. O, this gentleman does it rarely too: but nothing like the other. By this air! *[Practises at the post.]* As I am a gentleman! By— *[Exeunt Bob. and Mat.*

Brai. *[pointing to Master Stephen.]* Master, glance, glance! master Wellbred!

Step. As I have somewhat to be saved, I protest—

Wel. You are a fool; it needs no affidavit.

E. Know. Cousin, will you any tobacco?

Step. I, sir! Upon my reputation—

E. Know. How now, cousin!

Step. I protest, as I am a gentleman, but no soldier, indeed—

Wel. No, master Stephen! As I remember, your name is entered in the artillery-garden.

Step. Ay, sir, that's true. Cousin, may I swear, as I am a soldier, by that?

E. Know. O yes, that you may; it is all you have for your money.

Step. Then, as I am a gentleman, and a soldier, it is " divine tobacco! "

Wel. But soft, where's master Mathew? Gone?

Brai. No, sir; they went in here.

Wel. O let's follow them: master Mathew is gone to salute his mistress in verse; we shall have the happiness to hear some of his poetry now; he never comes unfinished.—Brainworm!

Step. Brainworm! Where? Is this Brainworm?

E. Know. Ay, cousin; no words of it, upon your gentility.

Step. Not I, body of me! By this air! St. George! and the foot of Pharaoh!

Wel. Rare! Your cousin's discourse is simply drawn out with oaths.

E. Know. 'Tis larded with them; a kind of French dressing, if you love it. *[Exeunt.*

SCENE III.—*Coleman-Street. A Room in* JUSTICE
CLEMENT'S *House.*

Enter KITELY *and* COB.

Kit. Ha! how many are there, say'st thou?

Cob. Marry, sir, your brother, master Wellbred—

Kit. Tut, beside him: what strangers are there, man?

Cob. Strangers? let me see, one, two; mass, I know not well, there are so many.

Kit. How! so many?

Cob. Ay, there's some five or six of them at the most.

Kit. A swarm, a swarm!
Spite of the devil, how they sting my head
With forked stings, thus wide and large! But, Cob,
How long hast thou been coming hither, Cob?

Cob. A little while, sir.

Kit.   Didst thou come running?

Cob. No, sir.

Kit. Nay, then I am familiar with thy haste.
Bane to my fortunes! what meant I to marry?
I, that before was rank'd in such content,
My mind at rest too, in so soft a peace,
Being free master of mine own free thoughts,
And now become a slave? What! never sigh;
Be of good cheer, man; for thou art a cuckold:
'Tis done, 'tis done! Nay, when such flowing-store,
Plenty itself, falls into my wife's lap,
The cornucopiæ will be mine, I know.—
But, Cob,
What entertainment had they? I am sure
My sister and my wife would bid them welcome: ha?

Cob. Like enough, sir; yet I heard not a word of it.

Kit. No;
Their lips were seal'd with kisses, and the voice,
Drown'd in a flood of joy at their arrival,
Had lost her motion, state and faculty.—
Cob,
Which of them was it that first kiss'd my wife,
My sister, I should say?—My wife, alas!
I fear not her: ha! who was it say'st thou?

Cob. By my troth, sir, will you have the truth of it?

Kit. Oh, ay, good Cob, I pray thee heartily.

Cob. Then I am a vagabond, and fitter for Bridewell than your worship's company, if I saw any body to be kiss'd, unless they would have kiss'd the post in the middle of the warehouse; for there I left them all at their tobacco, with a pox!

Kit. How! were they not gone in then ere thou cam'st?

Cob. O no, sir.

Kit. Spite of the devil! what do I stay here then? Cob, follow me.   [*Exit.*

Cob. Nay, soft and fair; I have eggs on the spit; I cannot go yet, sir. Now am I, for some five and fifty reasons, hammering, hammering revenge: oh for three or four gallons of vinegar, to sharpen my wits! Revenge, vinegar revenge, vinegar and mustard revenge! Nay, an he had not lien in my house, 'twould never have grieved me; but being my guest, one that, I'll be sworn, my wife has lent him her smock off her back, while his own shirt has been at washing; pawned her neck-kerchers for clean bands for him; sold almost all my platters, to buy him tobacco; and he to turn monster of ingratitude, and strike his lawful host! Well, I hope to raise up an host of fury for't: here comes justice Clement.

Enter Justice CLEMENT, KNOWELL, *and* FORMAL.

Clem. What's master Kitely gone, Roger?

Form. Ay, sir.

Clem. 'Heart o' me! what made him leave us so abruptly?—How now, sirrah! what make you here? what would you have, ha?

Cob. An't please your worship, I am a poor neighbour of your worship's—

Clem. A poor neighbour of mine! Why, speak, poor neighbour.

Cob. I dwell, sir, at the sign of the Water-tankard, hard by the Green Lattice: I have paid scot and lot there any time this eighteen years.

Clem. To the Green Lattice?

Cob. No, sir, to the parish: Marry, I have seldom scaped scot-free at the Lattice.

Clem. O, well; what business has my poor neighbour with me?

Cob. An't like your worship, I am come to crave the peace of your worship.

Clem. Of me, knave! Peace of me, knave! Did I ever hurt thee, or threaten thee, or wrong thee, ha?

Cob. No, sir; but your worship's warrant for one that has wrong'd me, sir: his arms are at too much liberty, I would fain have them bound to a treaty of peace, an my credit could compass it with your worship.

Clem. Thou goest far enough about for't, I am sure.

Kno. Why, dost thou go in danger of thy life for him, friend?

Cob. No, sir; but I go in danger of my death every hour, by his means; an I die within a twelve-month and a day, I may swear by the law of the land that he killed me.

Clem. How, how, knave, swear he killed thee, and by the law? What pretence, what colour hast thou for that?

Cob. Marry, an't please your worship, both black and blue; colour enough, I warrant you. I have it here to shew your worship.

Clem. What is he that gave you this, sirrah?

Cob. A gentleman and a soldier, he says, he is, of the city here.

Clem. A soldier of the city! What call you him?

Cob. Captain Bobadill.

Clem. Bobadill! and why did he bob and beat you, sirrah? How began the quarrel betwixt you, ha? speak truly, knave, I advise you.

Cob. Marry, indeed, an't please your worship, only because I spake against their vagrant tobacco, as I came by them when they were taking on't; for nothing else.

Clem. Ha! you speak against tobacco? Formal, his name.

Form. What's your name, sirrah?

Cob. Oliver, sir, Oliver Cob, sir.

Clem. Tell Oliver Cob he shall go to the jail, Formal.

Form. Oliver Cob, my master, justice Clement, says you shall go to the jail.

Cob. O, I beseech your worship, for God's sake, dear master justice!

Clem. 'Sprecious! an such drunkards and tankards as you are, come to dispute of tobacco once, I have done: away with him!

Cob. O, good master justice! Sweet old gentleman!

                                                            [To Knowell.

Know. "Sweet Oliver," would I could do thee any good!—justice Clement, let me intreat you, sir.

Clem. What! a thread-bare rascal, a beggar, a slave that never drunk out of better than piss-pot metal in his life! and he to deprave and abuse the virtue of an herb so generally received in the courts of princes, the chambers of nobles, the bowers of sweet ladies, the cabins of soldiers!—Roger, away with him! 'Od's precious——I say, go to.

Cob. Dear master justice, let me be beaten again, I have deserved it: but not the prison, I beseech you.

Know. Alas, poor Oliver!

Clem. Roger, make him a warrant:—he shall not go. I but fear the knave.

Form. Do not stink, sweet Oliver, you shall not go; my master will give you a warrant.

Cob. O, the Lord maintain his worship, his worthy worship!

Clem. Away, dispatch him. [*Exeunt Formal and Cob.*] How now, master Knowell, in dumps, in dumps! Come, this becomes not.

Know. Sir, would I could not feel my cares.

Clem. Your cares are nothing: they are like my cap, soon put on, and as soon put off. What! your son is old enough to govern himself: let him run his course, it's the only way to make him a staid man. If he were an unthrift, a ruffian, a drunkard, or a licentious liver, then you had reason; you had reason to take care: but, being none of these, mirth's my witness, an I had twice so many cares as you have, I'd drown them all in a cup of sack. Come, come, let's try it: I muse your parcel of a soldier returns not all this while.   [*Exeunt.*

ACT IV

SCENE I.—*A Room in* KITELY'S *House.*

Enter DOWNRIGHT *and* Dame KITELY.

Dow. Well, sister, I tell you true; and you'll find it so in the end.

Dame K. Alas, brother, what would you have me to do? I cannot help it; you see my brother brings them in here; they are his friends.

Dow. His friends! his fiends. 'Slud! they do nothing but haunt him up and down like a sort of unlucky spirits, and tempt him to all manner of villainy that can be thought of. Well, by this light, a little thing would make me play the devil with some of them: an 'twere not more for your husband's sake than any thing else, I'd make the house too hot for the best on 'em; they should say, and swear, hell were broken loose, ere they went hence. But, by God's will, 'tis nobody's fault but yours; for an you had done as you might have done, they should have been parboiled, and baked too, every mother's son, ere they should have come in, e'er a one of them.

Dame K. God's my life! did you ever hear the like? what a strange man is this! Could I keep out all them, think you? I should put myself against half a dozen men, should I? Good faith, you'd mad the patien'st body in the world, to hear you talk so, without any sense or reason.

Enter Mistress BRIDGET, Master MATHEW, *and* BOBADILL; *followed, at a distance, by* WELLBRED, E. KNOWELL, STEPHEN, *and* BRAINWORM.

Brid. Servant, in troth you are too prodigal
Of your wit's treasure, thus to pour it forth
Upon so mean a subject as my worth.

Mat. You say well, mistress, and I mean as well.

Dow. Hoy-day, here is stuff!

Wel. O, now stand close; pray Heaven, she can get him to read! he should do it of his own natural impudency.

Brid. Servant, what is this same, I pray you?

Mat. Marry, an elegy, an elegy, an odd toy—

Dow. To mock an ape withal! O, I could sew up his mouth, now.

Dame K. Sister, I pray you let's hear it.

Dow. Are you rhyme-given too?

Mat. Mistress, I'll read it if you please.

Brid. Pray you do, servant.

Dow. O, here's no foppery! Death! I can endure the stocks better.   [*Exit.*

E. Know. What ails thy brother? can he not hold his water at reading of a ballad?

Wel. O, no; a rhyme to him is worse than cheese, or a bag-pipe; but mark; you lose the protestation.

Mat. Faith, I did it in a humour; I know not how it is; but please you come near, sir. This gentleman has judgment, he knows how to censure of a——pray you, sir, you can judge?

Step. Not I, sir; upon my reputation, and by the foot of Pharaoh!

Wel. O, chide your cousin for swearing.

E. Know. Not I, so long as he does not forswear himself.

Bob. Master Mathew, you abuse the expectation of your dear mistress, and her fair sister: fie! while you live avoid this prolixity.

Mat. I shall, sir, well; *incipere dulce.*

E. Know. How, *insipere dulce !* a sweet thing to be a fool, indeed!

Wel. What, do you take *incipere* in that sense?

E. Know. You do not, you! This was your villainy, to gull him with a motte.

Wel. O, the benchers' phrase: *pauca verba, pauca verba !*

Mat. *Rare creature, let me speak without offence,*
> *Would God my rude words had the influence*
> *To rule thy thoughts, as thy fair looks do mine,*
> *Then shouldst thou be his prisoner, who is thine.*

E. Know. This is Hero and Leander.

Wel. O, ay: peace, we shall have more of this.

Mat. *Be not unkind and fair: misshapen stuff*
> *Is of behaviour boisterous and rough.*

Wel. How like you that, sir? [*Master Stephen shakes his head.*

E. Know. 'Slight, he shakes his head like a bottle, to feel an there be any brain in it.

Mat. But observe the catastrophe, now:
> *And I in duty will exceed all other,*
> *As you in beauty do excel Love's mother.*

E. Know. Well, I'll have him free of the wit-brokers, for he utters nothing but stolen remnants.

Wel. O, forgive it him.

E. Know. A filching rogue, hang him!—and from the dead! it's worse than sacrilege.

WELLBRED, E. KNOWELL, *and* Master STEPHEN, *come forward.*

Wel. Sister, what have you here, verses? pray you let's see: who made these verses? they are excellent good.

Mat. O, Master Wellbred, 'tis your disposition to say so, sir. They were good in the morning: I made them *ex tempore* this morning.

Wel. How! *ex tempore?*

Mat. Ay, would I might be hanged else; ask Captain Bobadill: he saw me write them, at the—pox on it!—the Star, yonder.

Brai. Can he find in his heart to curse the stars so?

E. Know. Faith, his are even with him; they have curst him enough already.

Step. Cousin, how do you like this gentleman's verses?

E. Know. O, admirable! the best that ever I heard, coz.

Step. Body o' Cæsar, they are admirable! the best that I ever heard, as I am a soldier!

Re-enter DOWNRIGHT.

Dow. I am˜vext, I can hold ne'er a bone of me still: 'Heart, I think they mean to build and breed here.

Wel. Sister, you have a simple servant here, that crowns your beauty with such encomiums and devices; you may see what it is to be the mistress of a wit, that can make your perfections so transparent, that every blear eye may look through them, and see him drowned over head and ears in the deep well of desire: Sister Kitely, I marvel you get you not a servant that can rhyme, and do tricks too.

Dow. O monster! impudence itself! tricks!

Dame K. Tricks, brother! what tricks?

Brid. Nay, speak, I pray you what tricks?

Dame K. Ay, never spare any body here; but say, what tricks.

Brid. Passion of my heart, do tricks!

Wel. 'Slight, here's a trick vied and revied! Why, you monkeys, you, what a cater-wauling do you keep! has he not given you rhymes and verses and tricks?

Dow. O, the fiend!

Wel. Nay, you lamp of virginity, that take it in snuff so, come, and cherish this tame poetical fury in your servant; you'll be begg'd else shortly for a concealment: go to, reward his muse. You cannot give him less than a shilling in conscience, for the book he had it out of cost him a teston at least. How now, gallants! Master Mathew! Captain! what, all sons of silence, no spirit?

Dow. Come, you might practise your ruffian tricks somewhere else, and not here, I wuss; this is no tavern or drinking-school, to vent your exploits in.

Wel. How now; whose cow has calved?

Dow. Marry, that has mine, sir. Nay, boy, never look askance at me for the matter; I'll tell you of it, I, sir; you and your companions mend yourselves when I have done.

Wel. My companions!

Dow. Yes, sir, your companions, so I say; I am not afraid of you, nor them neither; your hang - byes here. You must have your poets and your potlings, your soldados and foolados to follow you up and down the city; and here they must come to domineer and swagger. Sirrah, you ballad-singer, and slops your fellow there, get you out, get you home; or by this steel, I'll cut off your ears, and that presently.

Wel. 'Slight, stay, let's see what he dare do; cut off his ears! cut a whetstone. You are an ass, do you see; touch any man here, and by this hand I'll run my rapier to the hilts in you.

Dow. Yea, that would I fain see, boy.   [*They all draw.*

Dame K. O Jesu! murder! Thomas! Gasper!

Brid. Help, help! Thomas!

Enter CASH *and some of the house to part them.*

E. Know. Gentlemen, forbear, I pray you.

Bob. Well, sirrah, you Holofernes; by my hand, I will pink your flesh full of holes with my rapier for this; I will, by this good heaven! nay, let him come, let him come, gentlemen; by the body of St. George, I'll not kill him. [*Offer to fight again, and are parted.*

Cash. Hold, hold, good gentlemen.

Dow. You whoreson, bragging coystril!

Enter KITELY.

Kit. Why, how now! what's the matter, what's the stir here? Whence springs the quarrel? Thomas! where is he?
Put up your weapons, and put off this rage:
My wife and sister, they are the cause of this.
What, Thomas! where is the knave?

Cash. Here, sir.

Wel. Come, let's go: this is one of my brother's ancient humours, this.

Step. I am glad nobody was hurt by his ancient humour.

[*Exeunt Wellbred, Stephen, E. Knowell, Bobadill, and Brainworm.*

Kit. Why, how now, brother, who enforced this brawl?

Dow. A sort of lewd rake-hells, that care neither for God nor the devil. And they must come here to read ballads, and roguery, and trash! I'll mar the knot of 'em ere I sleep, perhaps; especially Bob there, he that's all manner of shapes: and songs and sonnets, his fellow.

Brid. Brother, indeed you are too violent,
Too sudden in your humour: and you know
My brother Wellbred's temper will not bear
Any reproof, chiefly in such a presence,
Where every slight disgrace he should receive
Might wound him in opinion and respect.

Dow. Respect! what talk you of respect among such, as have no spark of manhood, nor good manners? 'Sdeins, I am ashamed to hear you! respect! [*Exit.*

Brid. Yes, there was one a civil gentleman,
And very worthily demeaned himself.

Kit. O, that was some love of yours, sister.

Brid. A love of mine! I would it were no worse, brother;
You'd pay my portion sooner than you think for.

Dame K. Indeed he seem'd to be a gentleman of a very exceeding fair disposition, and of excellent good parts.

[*Exeunt Dame Kitely and Bridget.*

Kit. Her love, by heaven! my wife's minion.
Fair disposition! excellent good parts!
Death! these phrases are intolerable.
Good parts! how should she know his parts?
His parts! Well, well, well, well, well, well;

It is too plain, too clear: Thomas, come hither.
What, are they gone?
Cash.   Ay, sir, they went in.
My mistress and your sister—
  Kit. Are any of the gallants within?
  Cash. No, sir, they are all gone.
  Kit.   Art thou sure of it?
  Cash. I can assure you, sir.
  Kit. What gentleman was that they praised so, Thomas?
  Cash. One, they call him Master Knowell, a handsome young
gentleman, sir.
  Kit. Ay, I thought so; my mind gave me as much:
I'll die, but they have hid him in the house,
Somewhere, I'll go and search; go with me, Thomas:
Be true to me, and thou shalt find me a master.   [*Exeunt.*

SCENE II.—*The Lane before* Cob's *House.*

Enter Cob.

Cob. [*knocks at the door.*] What, Tib! Tib, I say!
Tib. [*within.*] How now, what cuckold is that knocks so hard?

Enter Tib.

O, husband! is it you? What's the news?
  Cob. Nay, you have stunn'd me, i'faith; you have given me a
knock o' the forehead will stick by me. Cuckold! 'Slid, cuckold!
  Tib. Away, you fool! did I know it was you that knocked?
Come, come, you may call me as bad when you list.
  Cob. May I? Tib, you are a whore.
  Tib. You lie in your throat, husband.
  Cob. How, the lie! and in my throat too! do you long to be
stabb'd, ha?
  Tib. Why, you are no soldier, I hope.
  Cob. O, must you be stabbed by a soldier? Mass, that's true!
when was Bobadill here, your captain? that rogue, that foist, that
fencing Burgullion? I'll tickle him, i'faith.
  Tib. Why, what's the matter, trow?
  Cob. O, he has basted me rarely, sumptuously! but I have it
here in black and white, [*pulls out the warrant.*] for his black and
blue shall pay him. O, the justice, the honestest old brave Trojan
in London; I do honour the very flea of his dog. A plague on him,
though, he put me once in a villanous filthy fear; marry, it vanished
away like the smoke of tobacco; but I was smoked soundly first.
I thank the devil, and his good angel, my guest. Well, wife, or
Tib, which you will, get you in, and lock the door; I charge you
let nobody in to you, wife; nobody in to you; those are my words:
not Captain Bob himself, nor the fiend in his likeness. You are a
woman, you have flesh and blood enough in you to be tempted;
therefore keep the door shut upon all comers.

Tib. I warrant you, there shall nobody enter here without my consent.

Cob. Nor with your consent, sweet Tib; and so I leave you.

Tib. It's more than you know, whether you leave me so.

Cob. How?

Tib. Why, *sweet.*

Cob. Tut, sweet or sour, thou art a flower.
Keep close thy door, I ask no more.   [*Exeunt.*

SCENE III.—*A Room in the Windmill Tavern.*

Enter E. KNOWELL, WELLBRED, STEPHEN, *and* BRAINWORM,
disguised as before.

E. Know. Well, Brainworm, perform this business happily, and thou makest a purchase of my love for ever.

Wel. I'faith, now let thy spirits use their best faculties: but, at any hand, remember the message to my brother; for there's no other means to start him.

Brai. I warrant you, sir; fear nothing; I have a nimble soul has waked all forces of my phant'sie by this time, and put them in true motion. What you have possest me withal, I'll discharge it amply, sir; make it no question.   [*Exit.*

Wel. Forth, and prosper, Brainworm. Faith, Ned, how dost thou approve of my abilities in this device?

E. Know. Troth, well, howsoever; but it will come excellent if it take.

Wel. Take, man! why it cannot choose but take, if the circumstances miscarry not: but, tell me ingenuously, dost thou affect my sister Bridget as thou pretend'st?

E. Know. Friend, am I worth belief?

Wel. Come, do not protest. In faith, she is a maid of good ornament, and much modesty; and, except I conceived very worthily of her, thou should'st not have her.

E. Know. Nay, that I am afraid, will be a question yet, whether I shall have her, or no.

Wel. 'Slid, thou shalt have her; by this light thou shalt.

E. Know. Nay, do not swear.

Wel. By this hand thou shalt have her; I'll go fetch her presently. 'Point but where to meet, and as I am an honest man I'll bring her.

E. Know. Hold, hold, be temperate.

Wel. Why, by——what shall I swear by? thou shalt have her, as I am—

E. Know. Praythee, be at peace, I am satisfied; and do believe thou wilt omit no offered occasion to make my desires complete.

Wel. Thou shalt see, and know, I will not.   [*Exeunt.*

SCENE IV.—*The Old Jewry.*

Enter FORMAL *and* KNOWELL.

Form. Was your man a soldier, sir?
Know.   Ay, a knave
I took him begging o' the way, this morning,
As I came over Moorfields.

Enter BRAINWORM, *disguised as before.*

O, here he is!—you've made fair speed, believe me,
Where, in the name of sloth, could you be thus?
Brai. Marry, peace be my comfort, where I thought I should have
had little comfort of your worship's service.
Know. How so?
Brai. O, sir, your coming to the city, your entertainment of me,
and your sending me to watch—indeed all the circumstances either
of your charge, or my employment, are as open to your son, as to
yourself.
Know. How should that be, unless that villain, Brainworm,
Have told him of the letter, and discover'd
All that I strictly charg'd him to conceal?
'Tis so.
Brai. I am partly o' the faith, 'tis so, indeed.
Know. But, how should he know thee to be my man?
Brai. Nay, sir, I cannot tell; unless it be by the black art. Is
not your son a scholar, sir?
Know. Yes, but I hope his soul is not allied
Unto such hellish practice: if it were,
I had just cause to weep my part in him,
And curse the time of his creation.
But, where didst thou find them, Fitz-Sword?
Brai. You should rather ask where they found me, sir; for I'll
be sworn, I was going along in the street, thinking nothing, when,
of a sudden, a voice calls, *Mr. Knowell's man!* another cries,
Soldier! and thus half a dozen of them, till they had call'd me
within a house, where I no sooner came, but they seem'd men, and
out flew all their rapiers at my bosom, with some three or four score
oaths to accompany them; and all to tell me, I was but a dead man,
if I did not confess where you were, and how I was employed, and
about what; which when they could not get out of me, (as, I protest,
they must have dissected, and made an anatomy of me first, and so
I told them,) they lock'd me up into a room in the top of a high
house, whence by great miracle (having a light heart) I slid down
by a bottom of packthread into the street, and so 'scaped. But,
sir, thus much I can assure you, for I heard it while I was lock'd up,
there were a great many rich merchants and brave citizens' wives
with them at a feast; and your son, master Edward, withdrew with
one of them, and has 'pointed to meet her anon at one Cob's house

a water-bearer that dwells by the Wall. Now, there your worship shall be sure to take him, for there he preys, and fail he will not.

Know. Nor will I fail to break his match, I doubt not.
Go thou along with justice Clement's man,
And stay there for me. At one Cob's house, say'st thou?

Brai. Ay, sir, there you shall have him. [*Exit Knowell.*] Yes—invisible! Much wench, or much son! 'Slight, when he has staid there three or four hours, travailing with the expectation of wonders, and at length be deliver'd of air! O the sport that I should then take to look on him, if I durst! But now, I mean to appear no more afore him in this shape: I have another trick to act yet. O that I were so happy as to light on a nupson now of this justice's novice!—Sir, I make you stay somewhat long.

Form. Not a whit, sir. Pray you what do you mean, sir?

Brai. I was putting up some papers.

Form. You have been lately in the wars, sir, it seems.

Brai. Marry have I, sir, to my loss, and expense of all, almost.

Form. Troth, sir, I would be glad to bestow a bottle of wine on you, if it please you to accept it—

Brai. O, sir—

Form. But to hear the manner of your services, and your devices in the wars; they say they be very strange, and not like those a man reads in the Roman histories, or sees at Mile-end.

Brai. No, I assure you, sir; why at any time when it please you, I shall be ready to discourse to you all I know;—and more too somewhat. [*Aside.*

Form. No better time than now, sir; we'll go to the Windmill: there we shall have a cup of neat grist, we call it. I pray you, sir, let me request you to the Windmill.

Brai. I'll follow you, sir;—and make grist of you, if I have good luck. [*Aside.*] [*Exeunt.*

SCENE V.—*Moorfields.*

Enter MATHEW, E. KNOWELL, BOBADILL, *and* STEPHEN.

Mat. Sir, did your eyes ever taste the like clown of him where we were to-day, Mr. Wellbred's half-brother? I think the whole earth cannot shew his parallel, by this daylight.

E. Know. We were now speaking of him: captain Bobadill tells me he is fallen foul of you too.

Mat. O, ay, sir, he threatened me with the bastinado.

Bob. Ay, but I think, I taught you prevention this morning, for that: You shall kill him beyond question; if you be so generously minded.

Mat. Indeed, it is a most excellent trick. [*Fences.*

Bob. O, you do not give spirit enough to your motion, you are too tardy, too heavy! O, it must be done like lightning, hay! [*Practises at a post with his cudgel.*

Mat. Rare, captain!

Bob. Tut! 'tis nothing, an't be not done in a—punto.

E. Know. Captain, did you ever prove yourself upon any of our masters of defence here?

Mat. O good sir! yes, I hope he has.

Bob. I will tell you, sir. Upon my first coming to the city, after my long travel for knowledge, in that mystery only, there came three or four of them to me, at a gentleman's house, where it was my chance to be resident at that time, to intreat my presence at their schools: and withal so much importuned me, that I protest to you, as I am a gentleman, I was ashamed of their rude demeanour out of all measure: Well, I told them that to come to a public school, they should pardon me, it was opposite, in diameter, to my humour; but if so be they would give their attendance at my lodging, I protested to do them what right or favour I could, as I was a gentleman, and so forth.

E. Know. So, sir! then you tried their skill?

Bob. Alas, soon tried: you shall hear, sir. Within two or three days after, they came; and, by honesty, fair sir, believe me, I graced them exceedingly, shewed them some two or three tricks of prevention have purchased them since a credit to admiration: they cannot deny this; and yet now they hate me, and why? because I am excellent; and for no other vile reason on the earth.

E. Know. This is strange and barbarous, as ever I heard.

Bob. Nay, for a more instance of their preposterous natures; but note, sir. They have assaulted me some three, four, five, six of them together, as I have walked alone in divers skirts i' the town, as Turnbull, Whitechapel, Shoreditch, which were then my quarters; and since, upon the Exchange, at my lodging, and at my ordinary: where I have driven them afore me the whole length of a street, in the open view of all our gallants, pitying to hurt them, believe me. Yet all this lenity will not overcome their spleen; they will be doing with the pismire, raising a hill a man may spurn abroad with his foot at pleasure. By myself, I could have slain them all, but I delight not in murder. I am loth to bear any other than this bastinado for them: yet I hold it good polity not to go disarmed, for though I be skilful, I may be oppressed with multitudes.

E. Know. Ay, believe me, may you, sir: and in my conceit, our whole nation should sustain the loss by it, if it were so.

Bob. Alas, no? what's a peculiar man to a nation? not seen.

E. Know. O, but your skill, sir.

Bob. Indeed, that might be some loss; but who respects it? I will tell you, sir, by the way of private, and under seal; I am a gentleman, and live here obscure, and to myself; but were I known to her majesty and the lords,—observe me,—I would undertake, upon this poor head and life, for the public benefit of the state, not only to spare the entire lives of her subjects in general; but to save the one half, nay, three parts of her yearly charge in holding war, and against what enemy soever. And how would I do it, think you?

E. Know. Nay, I know not, nor can I conceive.

Bob. Why thus, sir. I would select nineteen more, to myself, throughout the land; gentlemen they should be of good spirit, strong and able constitution; I would choose them by an instinct, a character that I have: and I would teach these nineteen the special rules, as your punto, your reverso, your stoccata, your imbroccato, your passada, your montanto; till they could all play very near, or altogether as well as myself. This done, say the enemy were forty thousand strong, we twenty would come into the field the tenth of March, or thereabouts; and we would challenge twenty of the enemy; they could not in their honour refuse us: Well, we would kill them; challenge twenty more, kill them; twenty more, kill them; twenty more, kill them too; and thus would we kill every man his twenty a day, that's twenty score; twenty score that's two hundred; two hundred a day, five days a thousand: forty thousand; forty times five, five times forty, two hundred days kills them all up by computation. And this will I venture my poor gentlemanlike carcase to perform, provided there be no treason practised upon us, by fair and discreet manhood; that is, civilly by the sword.

E. Know. Why, are you so sure of your hand, captain, at all times?

Bob. Tut! never miss thrust, upon my reputation with you.

E. Know. I would not stand in Downright's state then, an you meet him, for the wealth of any one street in London.

Bob. Why, sir, you mistake me: if he were now, by this welkin, I would not draw my weapon on him. Let this gentleman do his mind: but I will bastinado him, by the bright sun, wherever I meet him.

Mat. Faith, and I'll have a fling at him, at my distance.

E. Know. 'Od's, so, look where he is! yonder he goes.

[*Downright crosses the stage.*

Dow. What peevish luck have I, I cannot meet with these bragging rascals?

Bob. It is not he, is it?

E. Know. Yes, faith, it is he.

Mat. I'll be hang'd then if that were he.

E. Know. Sir, keep your hanging good for some greater matter, for I assure you that were he.

Step. Upon my reputation, it was he.

Bob. Had I thought it had been he, he must not have gone so: but I can hardly be induced to believe it was he yet.

E. Know. That I think, sir.

Re-enter DOWNRIGHT.

But see, he is come again.

Dow. O, Pharaoh's foot, have I found you? Come, draw to your tools; draw, gipsy, or I'll thrash you.

Bob. Gentleman of valour, I do believe in thee; hear me——

Dow. Draw your weapon then.

Bob. Tall man, I never thought on it till now——Body of me, I

had a warrant of the peace served on me, even now as I came along,
by a water-bearer; this gentleman saw it, Master Mathew.

Dow. 'Sdeath! you will not draw then?

               [Disarms and beats him.   Mathew runs away.

Bob. Hold, hold! under thy favour forbear!

Dow. Prate again, as you like this, you whoreson foist you!
You'll control the point, you! Your consort is gone; had he staid
he had shared with you, sir.   *[Exit.*

Bob. Well, gentlemen, bear witness, I was bound to the peace,
by this good day.

E. Know. No, faith, it's an ill day, captain, never reckon it other:
but, say you were bound to the peace, the law allows you to defend
yourself: that will prove but a poor excuse.

Bob. I cannot tell, sir; I desire good construction in fair sort.   I
never sustain'd the like disgrace, by heaven! sure I was struck
with a planet thence, for I had no power to touch my weapon.

E. Know. Ay, like enough; I have heard of many that have been
beaten under a planet: go, get you to a surgeon. 'Slid! an these be
your tricks, your passadoes, and your montantos, I'll none of them.
[Exit Bobadill.] O, manners! that this age should bring forth such
creatures! that nature should be at leisure to make them! Come,
coz.

Step. Mass, I'll have this cloak.

E. Know. 'Od's will, 'tis Downright's.

Step. Nay, it's mine now, another might have ta'en it up as well
as I: I'll wear it, so I will.

E. Know. How an he see it? he'll challenge it, assure yourself.

Step. Ay, but he shall not have it: I'll say I bought it.

E. Know. Take heed you buy it not too dear, coz.   *[Exeunt.*

SCENE IV.—*A Room in* KITELY'S *House.*

Enter KITELY, WELLBRED, Dame KITELY, *and* BRIDGET.

Kit. Now, trust me, brother, you were much to blame,
T" incense his anger, and disturb the peace
Of my poor house, where there are sentinels
That every minute watch to give alarms
Of civil war, without adjection
Of your assistance or occasion.

Wel. No harm done, brother, I warrant you: since there is no
harm done, anger costs a man nothing; and a tall man is never his
own man till he be angry. To keep his valour in obscurity, is to
keep himself as it were in a cloak-bag. What's a musician, unless
he play? What's a tall man unless he fight? For, indeed, all this
my wise brother stands upon absolutely; and that made me fall in
with him so resolutely.

Dame K. Ay, but what harm might have come of it, brother?

Wel. Might, sister? so might the good warm clothes your husband

wears be poisoned, for any thing he knows: or the wholesome wine
he drank, even now at the table.

Kit. Now, God forbid! O me! now I remember
My wife drank to me last, and changed the cup,
And bade me wear this cursed suit to-day.
See, if Heaven suffer murder undiscover'd!
I feel me ill; give me some mithridate,
Some mithridate and oil, good sister, fetch me:
O, I am sick at heart, I burn, I burn.
If you will save my life, go fetch it me.

Wel. O strange humour! my very breath has poison'd him.

Brid. Good brother, be content, what do you mean?
The strength of these extreme conceits will kill you.

Dame K. Beshrew your heart-blood, brother Wellbred, now,
For putting such a toy into his head!

Wel. Is a fit simile a toy? will he be poison'd with a simile?
Brother Kitely, what a strange and idle imagination is this! For
shame, be wiser. O' my soul there's no such matter.

Kit. Am I not sick? how am I then not poison'd? Am I not
poison'd? how am I then so sick?

Dame K. If you be sick, your own thoughts make you sick.

Wel. His jealousy is the poison he has taken.

Enter BRAINWORM, *disguised in* FORMAL's *clothes.*

Brai. Master Kitely, my master, justice Clement, salutes you;
and desires to speak with you with all possible speed.

Kit. No time but now, when I think I am sick, very sick! well,
I will wait upon his worship. Thomas! Cob! I must seek them
out, and set them sentinels till I return. Thomas! Cob! Thomas!
[*Exit.*

Wel. This is perfectly rare, Brainworm; [*takes him aside.*] but
how got'st thou this apparel of the justice's man?

Brai. Marry, sir, my proper fine pen-man would needs bestow
the grist on me, at the Windmill, to hear some martial discourse;
where I so marshall'd him, that I made him drunk with admiration:
and, because too much heat was the cause of his distemper, I stript
him stark naked as he lay along asleep, and borrowed his suit to
deliver this counterfeit message in, leaving a rusty armour, and an
old brown bill to watch him till my return; which shall be, when I
have pawn'd his apparel, and spent the better part o' the money,
perhaps.

Wel. Well, thou art a successful merry knave, Brainworm: his
absence will be a good subject for more mirth. I pray thee return
to thy young master, and will him to meet me and my sister Bridget
at the Tower instantly; for, here, tell him the house is so stored with
jealousy, there is no room for love to stand upright in. We must
get our fortunes committed to some larger prison, say; and than
the Tower, I know no better air, nor where the liberty of the house
may do us more present service. Away.   [*Exit Brai.*

Re-enter KITELY, *talking aside to* CASH.

Kit. Come hither, Thomas. Now my secret's ripe,
And thou shalt have it: lay to both thine ears.
Hark what I say to thee. I must go forth, Thomas;
Be careful of thy promise, keep good watch,
Note every gallant, and observe him well,
That enters in my absence to thy mistress:
If she would shew him rooms, the jest is stale,
Follow them, Thomas, or else hang on him,
And let him not go after; mark their looks;
Note if she offer but to see his band,
Or any other amorous toy about him;
But praise his leg, or foot: or if she say
The day is hot, and bid him feel her hand,
How hot it is; O, that's a monstrous thing!
Note me all this, good Thomas, mark their sighs,
And if they do but whisper, break 'em off:
I'll bear thee out in it. Wilt thou do this?
Wilt thou be true, my Thomas?
  Cash.   As truth's self, sir.
  Kit. Why, I believe thee: Where is Cob, now? Cob! [*Exit.*
  Dame K. He's ever calling for Cob: I wonder how he employs
Cob so.
  Wel. Indeed, sister, to ask how he employs Cob, is a necessary
question for you that are his wife, and a thing not very easy for you
to be satisfied in; but this I'll assure you, Cob's wife is an excellent
bawd, sister, and oftentimes your husband haunts her house; marry,
to what end? I cannot altogether accuse him; imagine you what
you think convenient: but I have known fair hides have foul hearts
ere now, sister.
  Dame K. Never said you truer than that, brother, so much I can
tell you for your learning. Thomas, fetch your cloak and go with
me. [*Exit Cash.*] I'll after him presently: I would to fortune I
could take him there, i'faith, I'd return him his own, I warrant
him!   [*Exit.*
  Wel. So, let 'em go; this may make sport anon. Now, my fair
sister-in-law, that you knew but how happy a thing it were to be
fair and beautiful.
  Brid. That touches not me, brother.
  Wel. That's true; that's even the fault of it; for indeed, beauty
stands a woman in no stead, unless it procure her touching.—But,
sister, whether it touch you or no, it touches your beauties; and I
am sure they will abide the touch; an they do not, a plague of all
ceruse, say I! and it touches me too in part, though not in the——
Well, there's a dear and respected friend of mine, sister, stands very
strongly and worthily affected toward you, and hath vowed to
inflame whole bonfires of zeal at his heart, in honour of your perfections. I have already engaged my promise to bring you where

you shall hear him confirm much more. Ned Knowell is the man, sister: there's no exception against the party. You are ripe for a husband; and a minute's loss to such an occasion, is a great trespass in a wise beauty. What say you, sister? On my soul he loves you; will you give him the meeting?

Brid. Faith, I had very little confidence in mine own constancy, brother, if I durst not meet a man: but this motion of yours savours of an old knight adventurer's servant a little too much, methinks.

Wel. What's that, sister?

Brid. Marry, of the squire.

Wel. No matter if it did, I would be such an one for my friend. But see, who is return'd to hinder us!

Re-enter KITELY.

Kit. What villainy is this? call'd out on a false message! This was some plot; I was not sent for.—Bridget, Where is your sister?

Brid.   I think she be gone forth, sir.

Kit. How! is my wife gone forth? whither, for God's sake?

Brid. She's gone abroad with Thomas.

Kit. Abroad with Thomas! oh, that villain dors me: Beast that I was, to trust him! whither, I pray you, Went she?

Brid.   I know not, sir.

Wel.   I'll tell you, brother, Whither I suspect she's gone.

Kit.   Whither, good brother?

Wel. To Cob's house, I believe: but, keep my counsel.

Kit. I will, I will: to Cob's house! doth she haunt Cob's? She's gone a purpose now to cuckold me, With that lewd rascal, who, to win her favour, Hath told her all.   [*Exit.*

Wel.   Come, he is once more gone, Sister, let's lose no time; the affair is worth it.   [*Exeunt.*

SCENE VII.—*A Street.*

Enter MATHEW *and* BOBADILL.

Mat. I wonder, captain, what they will say of my going away, ha?

Bob. Why, what should they say, but as of a discreet gentleman; quick, wary, respectful of nature's fair lineaments? and that's all.

Mat. Why so! but what can they say of your beating?

Bob. A rude part, a touch with soft wood, a kind of gross battery used, laid on strongly, borne most patiently; and that's all.

Mat. Ay, but would any man have offered it in Venice, as you say?

Bob. Tut! I assure you, no: you shall have there your nobilis, your gentilezza, come in bravely upon your reverse, stand you close, stand you firm, stand you fair, save your retricato with his left leg, come to the assalto with the right, thrust with brave steel, defy

your base wood! But wherefore do I awake this remembrance?
I was fascinated, by Jupiter; fascinated, but I will be unwitch'd
and revenged by law.

Mat. Do you hear? is it not best to get a warrant, and have him
arrested and brought before justice Clement?

Bob. It were not amiss; would we had it!

Enter BRAINWORM *disguised as* FORMAL.

Mat. Why, here comes his man; let's speak to him.

Bob. Agreed, do you speak.

Mat. Save you, sir.

Brai. With all my heart, sir.

Mat. Sir, there is one Downright hath abused this gentleman and
myself, and we determine to make our amends by law: now, if you
would do us the favour to procure a warrant to bring him afore your
master, you shall be well considered, I assure you, sir.

Brai. Sir, you know my service is my living; such favours as
these gotten of my master is his only preferment, and therefore you
must consider me as I may make benefit of my place.

Mat. How is that, sir?

Brai. Faith, sir, the thing is extraordinary, and the gentleman
may be of great account ; yet, be he what he will, if you will lay
me down a brace of angels in my hand you shall have it, otherwise
not.

Mat. How shall we do, captain? he asks a brace of angels, you
have no money?

Bob. Not a cross, by fortune.

Mat. Nor I, as I am a gentleman, but twopence left of my two
shillings in the morning for wine and radish: let's find him some
pawn.

Bob. Pawn! we have none to the value of his demand.

Mat. O, yes; I'll pawn this jewel in my ear, and you may pawn
your silk stockings, and pull up your boots, they will ne'er be mist:
it must be done now.

Bob. Well, an there be no remedy, I'll step aside and pull them off.
         [*Withdraws.*

Mat. Do you hear, sir? we have no store of money at this time,
but you shall have good pawns; look you, sir, this jewel, and that
gentleman's silk stockings; because we would have it dispatch'd
ere we went to our chambers.

Brai. I am content, sir; I will get you the warrant presently.
What's his name, say you? Downright?

Mat. Ay, ay, George Downright.

Brai. What manner of man is he?

Mat. A tall big man, sir; he goes in a cloak most commonly of
silk-russet, laid about with russet lace.

Brai. 'Tis very good, sir.

Mat. Here, sir, here's my jewel.

Bob. [*returning.*] And here are my stockings.

Brai. Well, gentlemen, I'll procure you this warrant presently; but who will you have to serve it?

Mat. That's true, captain: that must be considered.

Bob. Body o' me, I know not; 'tis service of danger.

Brai. Why, you were best get one o' the varlets of the city, a serjeant: I'll appoint you one, if you please.

Mat. Will you, sir? why, we can wish no better.

Bob. We'll leave it to you, sir.   [*Exeunt Bob. and Mat.*

Brai. This is rare! Now will I go and pawn this cloak of the justice's man's at the broker's, for a varlet's suit, and be the varlet myself; and get either more pawns, or more money of Downright, for the arrest.   [*Exit.*

SCENE VIII.—*The Lane before* COB's *House.*

Enter KNOWELL.

Know. Oh, here it is; I am glad I have found it now;
Ho! who is within here?

Tib. [*within.*] I am within, sir; what's your pleasure?

Know. To know who is within beside yourself.

Tib. Why, sir, you are no constable, I hope?

Know. O, fear you the constable? then I doubt not,
You have some guests within deserve that fear;
I'll fetch him straight.

Enter TIB.

Tib.   O' God's name, sir!

Know. Go to: come tell me, is not young Knowell here?

Tib. Young Knowell! I know none such, sir, o' mine honesty.

Know. Your honesty, dame! it flies too lightly from you.
There is no way but fetch the constable.

Tib. The constable! the man is mad, I think.

          [*Exit, and claps to the door.*

Enter Dame KITELY *and* CASH.

Cash. Ho! who keeps house here?

Know. O, this is the female copesmate of my son:
Now shall I meet him straight.

Dame K.   Knock, Thomas, hard.

Cash. Ho, goodwife!

Re-enter TIB.

Tib.   Why, what's the matter with you?

Dame K. Why, woman, grieves it you to ope your door?
Belike you get something to keep it shut.

Tib. What mean these questions, pray ye?

Dame K. So strange you make it! is not my husband here?

Know. Her husband!
Dame K. My tried husband, master Kitely?
Tib. I hope he needs not to be tried here.
Dame K. No, dame, he does it not for need, but pleasure.
Tib. Neither for need nor pleasure is he here.
Know. This is but a device to balk me withal:

Enter KITELY, *muffled in his cloak.*

Soft, who is this? 'tis not my son disguised?
    Dame K. [*spies her husband, and runs to him.*] O, sir, have I fore-
        stall'd your honest market,
Found your close walks? You stand amazed now, do you?
I'faith, I am glad I have smok'd you yet at last.
What is your jewel, trow? In, come, let's see her;
Fetch forth your housewife, dame; if she be fairer,
In any honest judgment, than myself,
I'll be content with it: but she is change,
She feeds you fat, she soothes your appetite,
And you are well! Your wife, an honest woman,
Is meat twice sod to you, sir! O, you treachour!
    Know. She cannot counterfeit thus palpably.
    Kit. Out on thy more than strumpet impudence!
Steal'st thou thus to thy haunts? and have I taken
Thy bawd and thee, and thy companion,
This hoary-headed letcher, this old goat,
Close at your villainy, and would'st thou 'scuse it
With this stale harlot's jest, accusing me?
O, old incontinent, [*to Knowell.*] dost thou not shame,
When all thy powers in chastity are spent,
To have a mind so hot? and to entice,
And feed the enticements of a lustful woman?
    Dame K. Out, I defy thee, I, dissembling wretch!
    Kit. Defy me, strumpet! Ask thy pander here,
Can he deny it; or that wicked elder?
    Know. Why, hear you, sir.
    Kit. Tut, tut, tut; never speak:
Thy guilty conscience will discover thee.
    Know. What lunacy is this, that haunts this man?
    Kit. Well, good wife bawd, Cob's wife, and you,
That make your husband such a hoddy-doddy;
And you, young apple-squire, and old cuckold-maker;
I'll have you every one before a justice:
Nay, you shall answer it, I charge you go.
    Know. Marry, with all my heart, sir, I go willingly;
Though I do taste this as a trick put on me,
To punish my impertinent search, and justly,
And half forgive my son for the device.
    Kit. Come, will you go?
    Dame K. Go! to thy shame believe it.

Enter COB.

Cob. Why, what's the matter here, what's here to do?

Kit. O, Cob, art thou come? I have been abused,
And in thy house; was never man so wrong'd!

Cob. 'Slid, in my house, my master Kitely! who wrongs you in my house?

Kit. Marry, young lust in old, and old in young here:
Thy wife's their bawd, here have I taken them.

Cob. How, bawd! is my house come to that? Am I preferr'd thither? Did I not charge you to keep your doors shut, Isbel? and—you let them lie open for all comers!   [*Beats his wife.*

Know. Friend, know some cause, before thou beat'st thy wife.
This is madness in thee.

Cob.   Why, is there no cause?

Kit. Yes, I'll shew cause before the justice, Cob:
Come, let her go with me.

Cob.   Nay, she shall go.

Tib. Nay, I will go. I'll see an you may be allowed to make a bundle of hemp of your right and lawful wife thus, at every cuckoldy knave's pleasure. Why do you not go?

Kit. A bitter quean! Come, we will have you tamed.   [*Exeunt.*

SCENE IX.—*A Street.*

Enter BRAINWORM, *disguised as a City Serjeant.*

Brai. Well, of all my disguises yet, now am I most like myself, being in this serjeant's gown. A man of my present profession never counterfeits, till he lays hold upon a debtor, and says, he rests him; for then he brings him to all manner of unrest. A kind of little kings we are, bearing the diminutive of a mace, made like a young artichoke, that always carries pepper and salt in itself. Well, I know not what danger I undergo by this exploit; pray Heaven I come well off!

Enter MATHEW *and* BOBADILL.

Mat. See, I think, yonder is the varlet, by his gown.

Bob. Let's go in quest of him.

Mat. 'Save you, friend! are not you here by appointment of justice Clement's man?

Brai. Yes, an't please you, sir; he told me, two gentlemen had will'd him to procure a warrant from his master, which I have about me, to be served on one Downright.

Mat. It is honestly done of you both; and see where the party comes you must arrest; serve it upon him quickly, afore he be aware.

Bob. Bear back, master Mathew.

Enter STEPHEN *in* DOWNRIGHT'S *cloak.*

Brai. Master Downright, I arrest you in the queen's name, and must carry you afore a justice by virtue of this warrant.

Step. Me, friend! I am no Downright, I; I am master Stephen: You do not well to arrest me, I tell you, truly; I am in nobody's bonds nor books, I would you should know it. A plague on you heartily, for making me thus afraid afore my time!

Brai. Why, now you are deceived, gentlemen.

Bob. He wears such a cloak, and that deceived us: but see, here a' comes indeed; this is he, officer.

Enter DOWNRIGHT.

Dow. Why how now, signior gull! are you turn'd filcher of late! Come, deliver my cloak.

Step. Your cloak, sir! I bought it even now, in open market.

Brai. Master Downright, I have a warrant I must serve upon you, procured by these two gentlemen.

Dow. These gentlemen! these rascals!   [*Offers to beat them.*

Brai. Keep the peace, I charge you in her majesty's name.

Dow. I obey thee. What must I do, officer?

Brai. Go before master justice Clement, to answer that they can object against you, sir: I will use you kindly, sir.

Mat. Come, let's before, and make the justice, captain.

Bob. The varlet's a tall man, afore heaven! [*Exeunt Bob. and Mat.*

Dow. Gull, you'll give me my cloak.

Step. Sir, I bought it, and I'll keep it.

Dow. You will?

Step. Ay, that I will.

Dow. Officer, there's thy fee, arrest him.

Brai. Master Stephen, I must arrest you.

Step. Arrest me! I scorn it. There, take your cloak, I'll none on't.

Dow. Nay, that shall not serve your turn now, sir. Officer, I'll go with thee to the justice's; bring him along.

Step. Why, is not here your cloak? what would you have?

Dow. I'll have you answer it, sir.

Brai. Sir, I'll take your word, and this gentleman's too, for his appearance.

Dow. I'll have no words taken: bring him along.

Brai. Sir, I may choose to do that, I may take bail.

Dow. 'Tis true, you may take bail, and choose at another time; but you shall not now, varlet: bring him along, or I'll swinge you.

Brai. Sir, I pity the gentleman's case: here's your money again.

Dow. 'Sdeins, tell not me of my money; bring him away, I say.

Brai. I warrant you he will go with you of himself, sir.

Dow. Yet more ado?

Brai. I have made a fair mash on't.   [*Aside.*

Step. Must I go?

Brai. I know no remedy, master Stephen.

Dow. Come along afore me here; I do not love your hanging look behind.

Step. Why, sir, I hope you cannot hang me for it: can he, fellow?

Brai. I think not, sir; it is but a whipping matter, sure.

Step. Why then let him do his worst, I am resolute.   [*Exeunt.*

ACT V

SCENE I.—*Coleman Street. A Hall in* Justice CLEMENT'S *House.*

Enter CLEMENT, KNOWELL, KITELY, Dame K., TIB, CASH, COB, *and* Servants.

Clem. Nay, but stay, stay, give me leave: my chair, sirrah. You, master Knowell, say you went thither to meet your son?

Know. Ay, sir.

Clem. But who directed you thither?

Know. That did mine own man, sir.

Clem. Where is he?

Know. Nay, I know not now; I left him with your clerk, and appointed him to stay here for me.

Clem. My clerk! about what time was this?

Know. Marry, between one and two, as I take it.

Clem. And what time came my man with the false message to you, master Kitely?

Kit. After two, sir.

Clem. Very good: but, mistress Kitely, how chance that you were at Cob's, ha?

Dame K. An't please you, sir, I'll tell you: my brother Wellbred told me, that Cob's house was a suspected place—

Clem. So it appears, methinks: but on.

Dame K. And that my husband used thither daily.

Clem. No matter, so he used himself well, mistress.

Dame K. True, sir: but you know what grows by such haunts oftentimes.

Clem. I see rank fruits of a jealous brain, mistress Kitely: but id you find your husband there, in that case as you suspected?

Kit. I found her there, sir.

Clem. Did you, so! that alters the case. Who gave you knowledge of your wife's being there?

Kit. Marry, that did my brother Wellbred.

Clem. How, Wellbred first tell her; then tell you after! Where Wellbred?

Kit. Gone with my sister, sir, I know not whither.

Clem. Why this is a mere trick, a device; you are gull'd in this most grossly all. Alas, poor wench! wert thou beaten for this?

Tib. Yes, most pitifully, an't please you.

Cob. And worthily, I hope, if it shall prove so.

Clem. Ay, that's like, and a piece of a sentence.—

Enter a Servant.

How now, sir! what's the matter?

Serv. Sir, there's a gentleman in the court without, desires to speak with your worship.

Clem. A gentleman! what is he?

Serv. A soldier, sir, he says.

Clem. A soldier! take down my armour, my sword quickly. A soldier speak with me! Why, when, knaves? Come on, come on; [*arms himself.*] hold my cap there, so; give me my gorget, my sword: stand by, I will end your matters anon.—Let the soldier enter.   [*Exit Servant.*

Enter BOBADILL, *followed by* MATHEW.

Now, sir, what have you to say to me?

Bob. By your worship's favour—

Clem. Nay, keep out, sir; I know not your pretence. You send me word, sir, you are a soldier: why, sir, you shall be answer'd here: here be them that have been amongst soldiers. Sir, your pleasure.

Bob. Faith, sir, so it is, this gentleman and myself have been most uncivilly wrong'd and beaten by one Downright, a coarse fellow, about the town here; and for mine own part, I protest, being a man in no sort given to this filthy humour of quarrelling, he hath assaulted me in the way of my peace, despoiled me of mine honour, disarmed me of my weapons, and rudely laid me along in the open streets, when I not so much as once offered to resist him.

Clem. O, God's precious! is this the soldier? Here, take my armour off quickly, 'twill make him swoon, I fear; he is not fit to look on't, that will put up a blow.

Mat. An't please your worship, he was bound to the peace.

Clem. Why, an he were, sir, his hands were not bound, were they?

Re-enter Servant.

Serv. There's one of the varlets of the city, sir, has brought two gentlemen here; one, upon your worship's warrant.

Clem. My warrant!

Serv. Yes, sir; the officer says, procured by these two.

Clem. Bid him come in. [*Exit Servant.*] Set by this picture.

Enter DOWNRIGHT, STEPHEN, *and* BRAINWORM, *disguised as before.*

What, Master Downright! are you brought in at Mr. Freshwater's suit here?

Dow. I'faith, sir, and here's another brought at my suit.

Clem. What are you, sir?

Step. A gentleman, sir. O, uncle!

Clem. Uncle! who, Master Knowell?

Know. Ay, sir; this is a wise kinsman of mine.

Step. God's my witness, uncle, I am wrong'd here monstrously, he charges me with stealing of his cloak, and would I might never stir, if I did not find it in the street by chance.

Dow. O, did you find it now? You said you bought it ere-while.

Step. And you said, I stole it: nay, now my uncle is here, I'll do well enough with you.

Clem. Well, let this breathe awhile. You that have cause to complain there, stand forth: Had you my warrant for this gentleman's apprehension?

Bob. Ay, an't please your worship.

Clem. Nay, do not speak in passion so: where had you it?

Bob. Of your clerk, sir.

Clem. That's well! an my clerk can make warrants, and my hand not at them! Where is the warrant—officer, have you it?

Brai. No, sir; your worship's man, Master Formal, bid me do it for these gentlemen, and he would be my discharge.

Clem. Why, Master Downright, are you such a novice, to be served and never see the warrant?

Dow. Sir, he did not serve it on me.

Clem. No! how then?

Dow. Marry, sir, he came to me, and said he must serve it, and he would use me kindly, and so—

Clem. O, God's pity, was it so, sir? *He must serve it!* Give me my long sword there, and help me off. So, come on, sir varlet, I *must* cut off your legs, sirrah; [*Brainworm kneels.*] nay, stand up, *I'll use you kindly;* I *must* cut off your legs, I say.

                             [*Flourishes over him with his long sword.*

Brai. O, good sir, I beseech you; nay, good master justice!

Clem. I must do it, there is no remedy; I *must* cut off your legs, sirrah, I *must* cut off your ears, you rascal, I must do it: I *must* cut off your nose, I *must* cut off your head.

Brai. O, good your worship!

Clem. Well, rise; how dost thou do now? dost thou feel thyself well? hast thou no harm?

Brai. No, I thank your good worship, sir.

Clem. Why so! I said I must cut off thy legs, and I must cut off thy arms, and I must cut off thy head; but I did not do it: so you said you must serve this gentleman with my warrant, but you did not serve him. You knave, you slave, you rogue, do you say you *must*, sirrah! away with him to the jail; I'll teach you a trick for your *must*, sir.

Brai. Good sir, I beseech you, be good to me.

Clem. Tell him he shall to the jail; away with him, I say.

Brai. Nay, sir, if you will commit me, it shall be for committing more than this: I will not lose by my travail any grain of my fame, certain.   [*Throws off his serjeant's gown.*

Clem. How is this?

Know. My man Brainworm!

Step. O, yes, uncle; Brainworm has been with my cousin Edward and I all this day.

Clem. I told you all there was some device.

Brai. Nay, excellent justice, since I have laid myself thus open to you, now stand strong for me; both with your sword and your balance.

Clem. Body o' me, a merry knave! give me a bowl of sack: if he belong to you, Master Knowell, I bespeak your patience.

Brai. That is it I have most need of; Sir, if you'll pardon me, only, I'll glory in all the rest of my exploits.

Know. Sir, you know I love not to have my favours come hard from me. You have your pardon, though I suspect you shrewdly for being of counsel with my son against me.

Brai. Yes, faith, I have, sir, though you retain'd me doubly this morning for yourself: first as Brainworm; after, as Fitz-Sword. I was your reform'd soldier, sir. 'Twas I sent you to Cob's upon the errand without end.

Know. Is it possible? or that thou should'st disguise thy language so as I should not know thee?

Brai. O, sir, this has been the day of my metamorphosis. It is not that shape alone that I have run through to-day. I brought this gentleman, master Kitely, a message too, in the form of master Justice's man here, to draw him out o' the way, as well as your worship, while master Wellbred might make a conveyance of mistress Bridget to my young master.

Kit. How! my sister stolen away?

Know. My son is not married, I hope.

Brai. Faith, sir, they are both as sure as love, a priest, and three thousand pound, which is her portion, can make them; and by this time are ready to bespeak their wedding-supper at the Windmill, except some friend here prevent them, and invite them home.

Clem. Marry, that will I; I thank thee for putting me in mind on't. Sirrah, go you and fetch them hither upon my warrant. [*Exit Servant.*] Neither's friends have cause to be sorry, if I know the young couple aright. Here, I drink to thee for thy good news. But I pray thee, what hast thou done with my man, Formal?

Brai. Faith, sir, after some ceremony past, as making him drunk, first with story, and then with wine, (but all in kindness,) and stripping him to his shirt, I left him in that cool vein; departed, sold your worship's warrant to these two, pawn'd his livery for that varlet's gown, to serve it in; and thus have brought myself by my activity to your worship's consideration.

Clem. And I will consider thee in another cup of sack. Here's to thee, which having drunk off this my sentence: Pledge me. Thou hast done, or assisted to nothing, in my judgment, but deserves to be pardon'd for the wit of the offence. If thy master, or any man here, be angry with thee, I shall suspect his ingine, while I know him, for't. How now, what noise is that?

Enter Servant.

Serv. Sir, it is Roger is come home.
Clem. Bring him in, bring him in.

Enter FORMAL *in a suit of armour.*

What! drunk? in arms against me? your reason, your reason for this?

Form. I beseech your worship to pardon me; I happened into ill company by chance, that cast me into a sleep, and stript me of all my clothes.

Clem. Well, tell him I am Justice Clement, and do pardon him: but what is this to your armour? what may that signify?

Form. An't please you, sir, it hung up in the room where I was stript; and I borrow'd it of one of the drawers to come home in, because I was loth to do penance through the street in my shirt.

Clem. Well, stand by a while.

Enter E. KNOWELL, WELLBRED, *and* BRIDGET.

Who be these? O, the young company; welcome, welcome! Give you joy. Nay, mistress Bridget, blush not; you are not so fresh a bride, but the news of it is come hither afore you. Master bridegroom, I have made your peace, give me your hand: so will I for all the rest ere you forsake my roof.

E. Know. We are the more bound to your humanity, sir.

Clem. Only these two have so little of man in them, they are no part of my care.

Wel. Yes, sir, let me pray you for this gentleman, he belongs to my sister the bride.

Clem. In what place, sir?

Wel. Of her delight, sir, below the stairs, and in public: her poet, sir.

Clem. A poet! I will challenge him myself presently at extempore,

> *Mount up thy Phlegon, Muse, and testify,*
> *How Saturn, sitting in an ebon cloud,*
> *Disrobed his podex, white as ivory,*
> *And through the welkin thunder'd all aloud.*

Wel. He is not for extempore, sir: he is all for the pocket muse; please you command a sight of it.

Clem. Yes, yes, search him for a taste of his vein.

[They search Mathew's pockets.

Wel. You must not deny the queen's justice, sir, under a writ of rebellion.

Clem. What! all this verse? body o' me, he carries a whole realm, a commonwealth of paper in his hose: let us see some of his subjects.　　　　　　　　　　　　　　　　　　*[Reads.*

Unto the boundless ocean of thy face,
Runs this poor river, charg'd with streams of eyes.

How! this is stolen.

E. Know. A parody! a parody! with a kind of miraculous gift, to make it absurder than it was.

Clem. Is all the rest of this batch? bring me a torch; lay it together, and give fire. Cleanse the air. [*Sets the papers on fire.*] Here was enough to have infected the whole city, if it had not been taken in time. See, see, how our poet's glory shines! brighter and brighter! still it increases! O, now it is at the highest; and now it declines as fast. You may see, *sic transit gloria mundi!*

Know. There's an emblem for you, son, and your studies.

Clem. Nay, no speech or act of mine be drawn against such as profess it worthily. They are not born every year, as an alderman. There goes more to the making of a good poet, than a sheriff. Master Kitely, you look upon me!—though I live in the city here, amongst you, I will do more reverence to him, when I meet him, than I will to the mayor out of his year. But these paper-pedlars! these ink-dabblers! they cannot expect reprehension or reproach; they have it with the fact.

E. Know. Sir, you have saved me the labour of a defence.

Clem. It shall be discourse for supper between your father and me, if he dare undertake me. But to dispatch away these, you sign o' the soldier, and picture of the poet, (but both so false, I will not have you hanged out at my door till midnight,) while we are at supper, you two shall penitently fast it out in my court without; and, if you will, you may pray there that we may be so merry within as to forgive or forget you when we come out. Here's a third, because we tender your safety, shall watch you, he is provided for the purpose. Look to your charge, sir.

Step. And what shall I do?

Clem. O! I had lost a sheep an he had not bleated: why, sir, you shall give master Downright his cloak; and I will intreat him to take it. A trencher and a napkin you shall have in the buttery, and keep Cob and his wife company here; whom I will intreat first to be reconciled; and you to endeavour with your wit to keep them so.

Step. I'll do my best.

Cob. Why, now I see thou art honest, Tib, I receive thee as my dear and mortal wife again.

Tib. And I you, as my loving and obedient husband.

Clem. Good compliment! It will be their bridal night too. They are married anew. Come, I conjure the rest to put off all discontent. You, master Downright, your anger; you, master Knowell, your cares; Master Kitely and his wife, their jealousy. For, I must tell you both, while that is fed,
Horns in the mind are worse than on the head.

Kit. Sir, thus they go from me; kiss me, sweetheart.

See what a drove of horns fly in the air,
Wing'd with my cleansed and my credulous breath !
Watch 'em suspicious eyes, watch where they fall.
See, see ! on heads that think they have none at all !
O, what a plenteous world of this will come !
When air rains horns, all may be sure of some.

I have learn'd so much verse out of a jealous man's part in a play.

    Clem. 'Tis well, 'tis well! This night we'll dedicate to friendship, love, and laughter. Master bridegroom, take your bride and lead; every one a fellow. Here is my mistress, Brainworm! to whom all my addresses of courtship shall have their reference: whose adventures this day, when our grandchildren shall hear to be made a fable, I doubt not but it shall find both spectators and applause.

                                                     [Exeunt.

GLOSSARY

ABATE, cast down, subdue
ABHORRING, repugnant (to), at variance
ABJECT, base, degraded thing, outcast
ABRASE, smooth, blank
ABSOLUTE(LY), faultless(ly)
ABSTRACTED, abstract, abstruse
ABUSE, deceive, insult, dishonour, make ill use of
ACATER, caterer
ACATES, cates
ACCEPTIVE, willing, ready to accept, receive
ACCOMMODATE, fit, befitting. (The word was a fashionable one and used on all occasions. *See* "Henry IV.," pt. 2, iii. 4)
ACCOST, draw near, approach
ACKNOWN, confessedly acquainted with
ACME, full maturity
ADALANTADO, lord deputy or governor of a Spanish province
ADJECTION, addition
ADMIRATION, astonishment
ADMIRE, wonder, wonder at
ADROP, philosopher's stone, or substance from which obtained
ADSCRIBE, subscribe
ADULTERATE, spurious, counterfeit
ADVANCE, lift
ADVERTISE, inform, give intelligence
ADVERTISED, "be —," be it known to you
ADVERTISEMENT, intelligence
ADVISE, consider, bethink oneself, deliberate
ADVISED, informed, aware; "are you —? " have you found that out?
AFFECT, love, like; aim at; move
AFFECTED, disposed; beloved
AFFECTIONATE, obstinate; prejudiced
AFFECTS, affections
AFFRONT, "give the —," face
AFFY, have confidence in; betroth
AFTER, after the manner of
AGAIN, AGAINST, in anticipation of
AGGRAVATE, increase, magnify, enlarge upon
AGNOMINATION. *See* Paranomasie
AIERY, nest, brood
AIM, guess
ALL HID, children's cry at hide-and-seek
ALL-TO, completely, entirely (" all-to-beladen ")
ALLOWANCE, approbation, recognition
ALMA-CANTARAS (astron.), parallels of altitude
ALMAIN, name of a dance
ALMUTEN, planet of chief influence in the horoscope
ALONE, unequalled, without peer
ALUDELS, subliming pots
AMAZED, confused, perplexed
AMBER, AMBRE, ambergris
AMBREE, MARY, a woman noted for her valour at the siege of Ghent, 1458

AMES-ACE, lowest throw at dice
AMPHIBOLIES, ambiguities
AMUSED, bewildered, amazed
AN, if
ANATOMY, skeleton, or dissected body
ANDIRONS, fire-dogs
ANGEL, gold coin worth 10s., stamped with the figure of the archangel Michael
ANNESH CLEARE, spring known as Agnes le Clare
ANSWER, return hit in fencing
ANTIC, ANTIQUE, clown, buffoon
ANTIC, like a buffoon
ANTIPERISTASIS, an opposition which enhances the quality it opposes
APOZEM, decoction
APPERIL, peril
APPLE-JOHN, APPLE-SQUIRE, pimp, pander
APPLY, attach
APPREHEND, take into custody
APPREHENSIVE, quick of perception; able to perceive and appreciate
APPROVE, prove, confirm
APT, suit, adapt; train, prepare; dispose, incline
APT(LY), suitable(y), opportune(ly)
APTITUDE, suitableness
ARBOR, "make the —," cut up the game (Gifford)
ARCHES, Court of Arches
ARCHIE, Archibald Armstrong, jester to James I. and Charles I.
ARGAILE, argol, crust or sediment in wine casks
ARGENT-VIVE, quicksilver
ARGUMENT, plot of a drama; theme, subject; matter in question; token, proof
ARRIDE, please
ARSEDINE, mixture of copper and zinc, used as an imitation of gold-leaf
ARTHUR, PRINCE, reference to an archery show by a society who assumed arms, etc., of Arthur's knights
ARTICLE, item
ARTIFICIALLY, artfully
ASCENSION, evaporation, distillation
ASPIRE, try to reach, obtain, long for
ASSALTO (Ital.), assault
ASSAY, draw a knife along the belly of the deer, a ceremony of the hunting-field
ASSOIL, solve
ASSURE, secure possession or reversion of
ATHANOR, a digesting furnace, calculated to keep up a constant heat
ATONE, reconcile
ATTACH, attack, seize
AUDACIOUS, having spirit and confidence
AUTHENTIC(AL), of authority, authorised, trustworthy, genuine
AVISEMENT, reflection, consideration

AVOID, begone! get rid of

AWAY WITH, endure

AZOCH, Mercurius Philosophorum

BABION, baboon

BABY, doll

BACK-SIDE, back premises

BAFFLE, treat with contempt

BAGATINE, Italian coin, worth about the third of a farthing

BAIARD, horse of magic powers known to old romance

BALDRICK, belt worn across the breast to support bugle, etc.

BALE (of dice), pair

BALK, overlook, pass by, avoid

BALLACE, ballast

BALLOO, game at ball

BALNEUM (BAIN MARIE), a vessel for holding hot water in which other vessels are stood for heating

BANBURY, "brother of —," Puritan

BANDOG, dog tied or chained up

BANE, woe, ruin

BANQUET, a light repast; dessert

BARB, to clip gold

BARBEL, fresh-water fish

BARE, meer; bareheaded; it was "a particular mark of state and grandeur for the coachman to be uncovered" (Gifford)

BARLEY-BREAK, game somewhat similar to base

BASE, game of prisoner's base

BASES, richly embroidered skirt reaching to the knees, or lower

BASILISK, fabulous reptile, believed to slay with its eye

BASKET, used for the broken provision collected for prisoners

BASON, basons, etc., were beaten by the attendant mob when bad characters were "carted"

BATE, be reduced; abate, reduce

BATOON, baton, stick

BATTEN, feed, grow fat

BAWSON, badger

BEADSMAN, prayer-man, one engaged to pray for another

BEAGLE, small hound; fig. spy

BEAR IN HAND, keep in suspense, deceive with false hopes

BEARWARD, bear leader

BEDPHERE. See Phere

BEDSTAFF, (?) wooden pin in the side of the bedstead for supporting the bedclothes (Johnson); one of the sticks or "laths"; a stick used in making a bed

BEETLE, heavy mallet

BEG, "I'd — him," the custody of minors and idiots was begged for; likewise property fallen forfeit to the Crown ("your house had been begged")

BELL-MAN, night watchman

BENJAMIN, an aromatic gum

BERLINA, pillory

BESCUMBER, defile

BESLAVE, beslabber

BESOGNO, beggar

BESPAWLE, bespatter

BETHLEM GABOR, Transylvanian hero, proclaimed King of Hungary

BEVER, drinking

BEVIS, SIR, knight of romance whose horse was equally celebrated

BEWRAY, reveal, make known

BEZANT, heraldic term: small gold circle

BEZOAR'S STONE, a remedy known by this name was a supposed antidote to poison

BID-STAND, highwayman

BIGGIN, cap, similar to that worn by the Beguines; nightcap

BILIVE (belive), with haste

BILK, nothing, empty talk

BILL, kind of pike

BILLET, wood cut for fuel, stick

BIRDING, thieving

BLACK SANCTUS, burlesque hymn, any unholy riot

BLANK, originally a small French coin

BLANK, white

BLANKET, toss in a blanket

BLAZE, outburst of violence

BLAZE, (her.) blazon; publish abroad

BLAZON, armorial bearings; fig. all that pertains to good birth and breeding

BLIN, "withouten —," without ceasing

BLOW, puff up

BLUE, colour of servants' livery, hence "— order," "— waiters"

BLUSHET, blushing one

BOB, jest, taunt

BOB, beat, thump

BODGE, measure

BODKIN, dagger, or other short, pointed weapon; long pin with which the women fastened up their hair

BOLT, roll (of material)

BOLT, dislodge, rout out; sift (boulting-tub)

BOLT'S-HEAD, long, straight-necked vessel for distillation

BOMBARD SLOPS, padded, puffed-out breeches

BONA ROBA, "good, wholesome, plum-cheeked wench" (Johnson)—not always used in compliment

BONNY-CLABBER, sour butter-milk

BOOKHOLDER, prompter

BOOT, "to —," into the bargain; "no —," of no avail

BORACHIO, bottle made of skin

BORDELLO, brothel

BORNE IT, conducted, carried it through

BOTTLE (of hay), bundle, truss

BOTTOM, skein or ball of thread; vessel

BOURD, jest

BOVOLI, snails or cockles dressed in the Italian manner (Gifford)

BOW-POT, flower vase or pot

BOYS, "terrible —," "angry —," roystering young bucks. (See Nares)

BRABBLES (BRABBLESH), brawls

BRACH, bitch

BRADAMANTE, a heroine in *Orlando Furioso*

BRADLEY, ARTHUR OF, a lively character commemorated in ballads

BRAKE, frame for confining a horse's feet

while being shod, or strong curb or bridle; trap

BRANCHED, with "detached sleeve ornaments, projecting from the shoulders of the gown" (Gifford)

BRANDISH, flourish of weapon

BRASH, brace

BRAVE, bravado, braggart speech

BRAVE (adv.), gaily, finely (apparelled)

BRAVERIES, gallants

BRAVERY, extravagant gaiety of apparel

BRAVO, bravado, swaggerer

BRAZEN-HEAD, speaking head made by Roger Bacon

BREATHE, pause for relaxation; exercise

BREATHE UPON, speak dispraisingly of

BREND, burn

BRIDE-ALE, wedding feast

BRIEF, abstract; (mus.) breve

BRISK, smartly dressed

BRIZE, breese, gadfly

BROAD-SEAL, state seal

BROCK, badger (term of contempt)

BROKE, transact business as a broker

BROOK, endure, put up with

BROUGHTON, HUGH, an English divine and Hebrew scholar

BRUIT, rumour

BUCK, wash

BUCKLE, bend

BUFF, leather made of buffalo skin, used for military and serjeants' coats, etc.

BUFO, black tincture

BUGLE, long-shaped bead

BULLED, (?) bolled, swelled

BULLIONS, trunk hose

BULLY, term of familiar endearment

BUNGY, Friar Bungay, who had a familiar in the shape of a dog

BURDEN, refrain, chorus

BURGONET, closely-fitting helmet with visor

BURGULLION, braggadocio

BURN, mark wooden measures ("—ing of cans ")

BURROUGH, pledge, security

BUSKIN, half-boot, foot gear reaching high up the leg

BUTT-SHAFT, barbless arrow for shooting at butts

BUTTER, NATHANIEL (" Staple of News "), a compiler of general news. (See Cunningham)

BUTTERY-HATCH, half-door shutting off the buttery, where provisions and liquors were stored

BUY, " he bought me," formerly the guardianship of wards could be bought

BUZ, exclamation to enjoin silence

BUZZARD, simpleton

BY AND BY, at once

BY(E), " on the —," incidentally, as of minor or secondary importance; at the side

BY-CHOP, by-blow, bastard

CADUCEUS, Mercury's wand

CALIVER, light kind of musket

CALLET, woman of ill repute

CALLOT, coif worn on the wigs of our judges or serjeants-at-law (Gifford)

CALVERED, crimped, or sliced and pickled. (See Nares)

CAMOUCCIO, wretch, knave

CAMUSED, flat

CAN, knows

CANDLE-RENT, rent from house property

CANDLE-WASTER, one who studies late

CANTER, sturdy beggar

CAP OF MAINTENCE, an insignia of dignity, a cap of state borne before kings at their coronation; also an heraldic term

CAPABLE, able to comprehend, fit to receive instruction, impression

CAPANEUS, one of the " Seven against Thebes "

CARACT, carat, unit of weight for precious stones, etc.; value, worth

CARANZA, Spanish author of a book on duelling

CARCANET, jewelled ornament for the neck

CARE, take care; object

CAROCH, coach, carriage

CARPET, table-cover

CARRIAGE, bearing, behaviour

CARWHITCHET, quip, pun

CASAMATE, casemate, fortress

CASE, a pair

CASE, " in —," in condition

CASSOCK, soldier's loose overcoat

CAST, flight of hawks, couple

CAST, throw dice; vomit; forecast, calculate

CAST, cashiered

CASTING-GLASS, bottle for sprinkling perfume

CASTRIL, kestrel, falcon

CAT, structure used in sieges

CATAMITE, old form of " ganymede "

CATASTROPHE, conclusion

CATCHPOLE, sheriff's officer

CATES, dainties, provisions

CATSO, rogue, cheat

CAUTELOUS, crafty, artful

CENSURE, criticism; sentence

CENSURE, criticise; pass sentence, doom

CERUSE, cosmetic containing white lead

CESS, assess

CHANGE, " hunt —," follow a fresh scent

CHAPMAN, retail dealer

CHARACTER, handwriting

CHARGE, expense

CHARM, subdue with magic, lay a spell on, silence

CHARMING, exercising magic power

CHARTEL, challenge

CHEAP, bargain, market

CHEAR, CHEER, comfort, encouragement; food, entertainment

CHECK AT, aim reproof at

CHEQUIN, gold Italian coin

CHEVRIL, from kidskin, which is elastic and pliable

CHIAUS, Turkish envoy; used for a cheat, swindler

CHILDERMASS DAY, Innocents' Day

CHOKE-BAIL, action which does not allow of bail

CHRYSOPŒIA, alchemy

CHRYSOSPERM, ways of producing gold

CIBATION, adding fresh substances to supply the waste of evaporation

CIMICI, bugs

CINOPER, cinnabar

CIOPPINI, chopine, lady's high shoe

CIRCLING BOY, "a species of roarer; one who in some way drew a man into a snare, to cheat or rob him" (Nares)

CIRCUMSTANCE, circumlocution, beating about the bush; ceremony, everything pertaining to a certain condition; detail, particular

CITRONISE, turn citron colour

CITTERN, kind of guitar

CITY-WIRES, woman of fashion, who made use of wires for hair and dress

CIVIL, legal

CLAP, clack, chatter

CLAPPER-DUDGEON, downright beggar

CLAPS HIS DISH, a clap, or clack, dish (dish with a movable lid) was carried by beggars and lepers to show that the vessel was empty, and to give sound of their approach

CLARIDIANA, heroine of an old romance

CLARISSIMO, Venetian noble

CLEM, starve

CLICKET, latch

CLIM O' THE CLOUGHS, etc., wordy heroes of romance

CLIMATE, country

CLOSE, secret, private; secretive

CLOSENESS, secrecy

CLOTH, arras, hangings

CLOUT, mark shot at, bull's-eye

CLOWN, countryman, clodhopper

COACH-LEAVES, folding blinds

COALS, "bear no —," submit to no affront

COAT-ARMOUR, coat of arms

COAT-CARD, court-card

COB-HERRING, HERRING-COB, a young herring

COB-SWAN, male swan

COCK-A-HOOP, denoting unstinted jollity; thought to be derived from turning on the tap that all might drink to the full of the flowing liquor

COCKATRICE, reptile supposed to be produced from a cock's egg and to kill by its eye—used as a term of reproach for a woman

COCK-BRAINED, giddy, wild

COCKER, pamper

COCKSCOMB, fool's cap

COCKSTONE, stone said to be found in a cock's gizzard, and to possess particular virtues

CODLING, softening by boiling

COFFIN, raised crust of a pie

COG, cheat, wheedle

COIL, turmoil, confusion, ado

COKELY, master of a puppet-show (Whalley)

COKES, fool, gull

COLD-CONCEITED, having cold opinion of, coldly affected towards

COLE-HARBOUR, a retreat for people of all sorts

COLLECTION, composure; deduction

COLLOP, small slice, piece of flesh

COLLY, blacken

COLOUR, pretext

COLOURS, "fear no —," no enemy (quibble)

COLSTAFF, cowlstaff, pole for carrying a cowl=tub

COME ABOUT, charge, turn round

COMFORTABLE BREAD, spiced gingerbread

COMING, forward, ready to respond, com plaisant

COMMENT, commentary; "sometime it is taken for a lie or fayned tale" (Bullokar, 1616)

COMMODITY, "current for —," allusion to practice of money-lenders, who forced the borrower to take part of the loan in the shape of worthless goods on which the latter had to make money if he could

COMMUNICATE, share

COMPASS, "in —," within the range, sphere

COMPLEMENT, completion, completement; anything required for the perfecting or carrying out of a person or affair; accomplishment

COMPLEXION, natural disposition, constitution

COMPLIMENT. See Complement

COMPLIMENTARIES, masters of accomplishments

COMPOSITION, constitution; agreement, contract

COMPOSURE, composition

COMPTER, COUNTER, debtors' prison

CONCEALMENT, a certain amount of church property had been retained at the dissolution of the monasteries; Elizabeth sent commissioners to search it out, and the courtiers begged for it

CONCEIT, idea, fancy, witty invention, conception, opinion

CONCEIT, apprehend

CONCEITED, fancifully, ingeniously devised or conceived; possessed of intelligence, witty, ingenious (hence well conceited, etc.); disposed to joke; of opinion, possessed of an idea

CONCEIVE, understand

CONCENT, harmony, agreement

CONCLUDE, infer, prove

CONCOCT, assimilate, digest

CONDEN'T, probably conducted

CONDUCT, escort, conductor

CONEY-CATCH, cheat

CONFECT, sweetmeat

CONFER, compare

CONGIES, bows

CONNIVE, give a look, wink, of secret intelligence

CONSORT, company, concert

CONSTANCY, fidelity, ardour, persistence

CONSTANT, confirmed, persistent, faithful

CONSTANTLY, firmly, persistently

CONTEND, strive

CONTINENT, holding together

CONTROL (the point), bear or beat down

CONVENT, assembly, meeting

CONVERT, turn (oneself)

CONVEY, transmit from one to another

CONVINCE, evince, prove; overcome, overpower; convict

COP, head, top; tuft on head of birds; " a cop " may have reference to one or other meaning; Gifford and others interpret as " conical, terminating in a point "

COPE-MAN, chapman

COPESMATE, companion

COPY (Lat. *copia*), abundance, copiousness

CORN (" powder — "), grain

COROLLARY, finishing part or touch

CORSIVE, corrosive

CORTINE, curtain, (arch.) wall between two towers, etc.

CORYAT, famous for his travels, published as *Coryat's Crudities*

COSSET, pet lamb, pet

COSTARD, head

COSTARD - MONGER, apple - seller, coster-monger

COSTS, ribs

COTE, hut

COTHURNAL, from " cothurnus," a particular boot worn by actors in Greek tragedy

COTQUEAN, hussy

COUNSEL, secret

COUNTENANCE, means necessary for support; credit, standing

COUNTER. *See* Compter

COUNTER, pieces of metal or ivory for calculating at play

COUNTER, " hunt —," follow scent in reverse direction

COUNTERFEIT, false coin

COUNTERPANE, one part or counterpart of a deed or indenture

COUNTERPOINT, opposite, contrary point

COURT-DISH, a kind of drinking-cup (Halliwell); N.E.D. quotes from Bp. Goodman's *Court of James I.:* " The king . . . caused his carver to cut him out a court-dish, that is, something of every dish, which he sent him as part of his reversion," but this does not sound like short allowance or small receptacle

COURT-DOR, fool

COURTEAU, curtal, small horse with docked tail

COURTSHIP, courtliness

COVETISE, avarice

COWSHARD, cow dung

COXCOMB, fool's cap, fool

COY, shrink; disdain

COYSTREL, low varlet

COZEN, cheat

CRACK, lively young rogue, wag

CRACK, crack up, boast; come to grief

CRAMBE, game of crambo, in which the players find rhymes for a given word

CRANCH, craunch

CRANION, spider-like; also fairy appellation for a fly (Gifford, who refers to lines in Drayton's " Nimphidia ")

CRIMP, game at cards

CRINCLE, draw back, turn aside

CRISPED, with curled or waved hair

CROP, gather, reap

CROPSHIRE, a kind of herring. (*See* N.E.D.)

CROSS, any piece of money, many coins being stamped with a cross

CROSS AND PILE, heads and tails

CROSSLET, crucible

CROWD, fiddle

CRUDITIES, undigested matter

CRUMP, curl up

CRUSADO, Portuguese gold coin, marked with a cross

CRY (" he that cried Italian "), " speak in a musical cadence," intone, or declaim (?); cry up

CUCKING-STOOL, used for the ducking of scolds, etc.

CUCURBITE, a gourd-shaped vessel used for distillation

CUERPO, " in —," in undress

CULLICE, broth

CULLION, base fellow, coward

CULLISEN, badge worn on their arm by servants

CULVERIN, kind of cannon

CUNNING, skill

CUNNING, skilful

CUNNING-MAN, fortune-teller

CURE, care for

CURIOUS(LY), scrupulous, particular; elaborate, elegant(ly), dainty(ly) (hence " in curious ")

CURST, shrewish, mischievous

CURTAL, dog with docked tail, of inferior sort

CUSTARD, " quaking —," " — politic," reference to a large custard which formed part of a city feast and afforded huge entertainment, for the fool jumped into it, and other like tricks were played. (*See* " All's Well, etc." ii. 5, 40)

CUTWORK, embroidery, open-work

CYPRES (CYPRUS) (quibble), cypress (or cyprus) being a transparent material, and when black used for mourning

DAGGER (" — frumety "), name of tavern

DARGISON, apparently some person known in ballad or tale

DAUPHIN MY BOY, refrain of old comic song

DAW, daunt

DEAD LIFT, desperate emergency

DEAR, applied to that which in any way touches us nearly

DECLINE, turn off from; turn away, aside

DEFALK, deduct, abate

DEFEND, forbid

DEGENEROUS, degenerate

DEGREES, steps

DELATE, accuse

DEMI-CULVERIN, cannon carrying a ball of about ten pounds

DENIER, the smallest possible coin, being the twelfth part of a sou

DEPART, part with

DEPENDANCE, ground of quarrel in duello language

DESERT, reward

DESIGNMENT, design

DESPERATE, rash, reckless

DETECT, allow to be detected, betray, inform against

DETERMINE, terminate

DETRACT, draw back, refuse

630   Ben Jonson's Plays

DEVICE, masque, show; a thing moved by wires, etc., puppet

DEVISE, exact in every particular

DEVISED, invented

DIAPASM, powdered aromatic herbs, made into balls of perfumed paste. (*See* Pomander)

DIBBLE, (?) moustache (N.E.D.); (?) dagger (Cunningham)

DIFFUSED, disordered, scattered, irregular

DIGHT, dressed

DILDO, refrain of popular songs; vague term of low meaning

DIMBLE, dingle, ravine

DIMENSUM, stated allowance

DISBASE, debase

DISCERN, distinguish, show a difference between

DISCHARGE, settle for

DISCIPLINE, reformation; ecclesiastical system

DISCLAIM, renounce all part in

DISCOURSE, process of reasoning, reasoning faculty

DISCOURTSHIP, discourtesy

DISCOVER, betray, reveal; display

DISFAVOUR, disfigure

DISPARAGEMENT, legal term applied to the unfitness in any way of a marriage arranged for in the case of wards

DISPENSE WITH, grant dispensation for

DISPLAY, extend

DIS'PLE, discipline, teach by the whip

DISPOSED, inclined to merriment

DISPOSURE, disposal

DISPRISE, depreciate

DISPUNCT, not punctilious

DISQUISITION, search

DISSOLVED, enervated by grief

DISTANCE, (?) proper measure

DISTASTE, offence, cause of offence

DISTASTE, render distasteful

DISTEMPERED, upset, out of humour

DIVISION (mus.), variation, modulation

DOG-BOLT, term of contempt

DOLE, given in dole, charity

DOLE OF FACES, distribution of grimaces

DOOM, verdict, sentence

DOP, dip, low bow

DOR, beetle, buzzing insect, drone, idler

DOR, (?) buzz; "give the —," make a fool of

DOSSER, pannier, basket

DOTES, endowments, qualities

DOTTEREL, plover; gull, fool

DOUBLE, behave deceitfully

DOXY, wench, mistress

DRACHM, Greek silver coin

DRESS, groom, curry

DRESSING, coiffure

DRIFT, intention

DRYFOOT, track by mere scent of foot

DUCKING, punishment for minor offences

DUILL, grieve

DUMPS, melancholy, originally a mournful melody

DURINDANA, Orlando's sword

DWINDLE, shrink away, be overawed

EAN, yean, bring forth young

EASINESS, readiness

EBOLITION, ebullition

EDGE, sword

EECH, eke

EGREGIOUS, eminently excellent

EKE, also, moreover

E-LA, highest note in the scale

EGGS ON THE SPIT, important business on hand

ELF-LOCK, tangled hair, supposed to be the work of elves

EMMET, ant

ENGAGE, involve

ENGHLE. *See* Ingle

ENGHLE, cajole; fondle

ENGIN(E), device, contrivance; agent; in genuity, wit

ENGINER, engineer, deviser, plotter

ENGINOUS, crafty, full of devices; witty, ingenious

ENGROSS, monopolise

ENS, an existing thing, a substance

ENSIGNS, tokens, wounds

ENSURE, assure

ENTERTAIN, take into service

ENTREAT, plead

ENTREATY, entertainment

ENTRY, place where a deer has lately passed

ENVOY, dénouement, conclusion

ENVY, spite, calumny, dislike, odium

EPHEMERIDES, calendars

EQUAL, just, impartial

ERECTION, elevation in esteem

ERINGO, candied root of the sea-holly, formerly used as a sweetmeat and aphro-disiac

ERRANT, arrant

ESSENTIATE, become assimilated

ESTIMATION, esteem

ESTRICH, ostrich

ETHNIC, heathen

EURIPUS, flux and reflux

EVEN, just, equable

EVENT, fate, issue

EVENT(ED), issue(d)

EVERT, overturn

EXACUATE, sharpen

EXAMPLESS, without example or parallel

EXCALIBUR, King Arthur's sword

EXEMPLIFY, make an example of

EXEMPT, separate, exclude

EXEQUIES, obsequies

EXHALE, drag out

EXHIBITION, allowance for keep, pocket-money

EXORBITANT, exceeding limits of propriety or law, inordinate

EXORNATION, ornament

EXPECT, wait

EXPIATE, terminate

EXPLICATE, explain, unfold

EXTEMPORAL, extempore, unpremeditated

EXTRACTION, essence

EXTRAORDINARY, employed for a special or temporary purpose

EXTRUDE, expel

EYE, " in —," in view

EYEBRIGHT, (?) a malt liquor in which the

herb of this name was infused, or a person who sold the same (Gifford)

EYE-TINGE, least shade or gleam

FACE, appearance

FACES ABOUT, military word of command

FACINOROUS, extremely wicked

FACKINGS, faith

FACT, deed, act, crime

FACTIOUS, seditious, belonging to a party, given to party feeling

FAECES, dregs

FAGIOLI, French beans

FAIN, forced, necessitated

FAITHFUL, believing

FALL, ruff or band turned back on the shoulders; or, veil

FALSIFY, feign (fencing term)

FAME, report

FAMILIAR, attendant spirit

FANTASTICAL, capricious, whimsical

FARCE, stuff

FAR-FET. See Fet

FARTHINGAL, hooped petticoat

FAUCET, tapster

FAULT, lack; loss, break in line of scent; " for —," in default of

FAUTOR, partisan

FAYLES, old table game similar to backgammon

FEAR(ED), affright(ed)

FEAT, activity, operation; deed, action

FEAT, elegant, trim

FEE, " in — " by feudal obligation

FEIZE, beat, belabour

FELLOW, term of contempt

FENNEL, emblem of flattery

FERE, companion, fellow

FERN-SEED, supposed to have power of rendering invisible

FET, fetched

FETCH, trick

FEUTERER (Fr. vautrier), dog-keeper

FEWMETS, dung

FICO, fig

FIGGUM, (?) jugglery

FIGMENT, fiction, invention

FIRK, frisk, move suddenly, or in jerks; " — up," stir up, rouse; " firks mad," suddenly behaves like a madman

FIT, pay one out, punish

FITNESS, readiness

FITTON (FITTEN), lie, invention

FIVE-AND-FIFTY, " highest number to stand on at primero " (Gifford)

FLAG, to fly low and waveringly

FLAGON CHAIN, for hanging a smelling-bottle (Fr. flacon) round the neck (?). (See N.E.D.)

FLAP-DRAGON, game similar to snap-dragon

FLASKET, some kind of basket

FLAW, sudden gust or squall of wind

FLAWN, custard

FLEA, catch fleas

FLEER, sneer, laugh derisively

FLESH, feed a hawk or dog with flesh to incite it to the chase; initiate in bloodshed; satiate

FLICKER-MOUSE, bat

FLIGHT, light arrow

FLITTER-MOUSE, bat

FLOUT, mock, speak and act contemptuously

FLOWERS, pulverised substance

FLY, familiar spirit

FOIL, weapon used in fencing; that which sets anything off to advantage

FOIST, cut-purse, sharper

FOND(LY), foolish(ly)

FOOT-CLOTH, housings of ornamental cloth which hung down on either side a horse to the ground

FOOTING, foothold; footstep; dancing

FOPPERY, foolery

FOR, " — failing," for fear of failing

FORBEAR, bear with; abstain from

FORCE, " hunt at —," run the game down with dogs

FOREHEAD, modesty; face, assurance, effrontery

FORESLOW, delay

FORESPEAK, bewitch; foretell

FORETOP, front lock of hair which fashion required to be worn upright

FORGED, fabricated

FORM, state formally

FORMAL, shapely; normal; conventional

FORTHCOMING, produced when required

FOUNDER, disable with over-riding

FOURM, form, lair

FOX, sword

FRAIL, rush basket in which figs or raisins were packed

FRAMPULL, peevish, sour-tempered

FRAPLER, blusterer, wrangler

FRAYING, " a stag is said to fray his head when he rubs it against a tree to . . . cause the outward coat of the new horns to fall off " (Gifford)

FREIGHT (of the gazetti), burden (of the newspapers)

FREQUENT, full

FRICACE, rubbing

FRICATRICE, woman of low character

FRIPPERY, old clothes shop

FROCK, smock-frock

FROLICS, (?) humorous verses circulated at a feast (N.E.D.); couplets wrapped round sweetmeats (Cunningham)

FRONTLESS, shameless

FROTED, rubbed

FRUMETY, hulled wheat boiled in milk and spiced

FRUMP, flout, sneer

FUCUS, dye

FUGEAND, (?) figent: fidgety, restless (N.E.D.)

FULLAM, false dice

FULMART, polecat

FULSOME, foul, offensive

FURIBUND, raging, furious

GALLEY-FOIST, city-barge, used on Lord Mayor's Day, when he was sworn into his office at Westminster (Whalley)

GALLIARD, lively dance in triple time

GAPE, be eager after

GARAGANTUA, Rabelais' giant

GARB, sheaf (Fr. *gerbe*); manner, fashion, behaviour

GARD, guard, trimming, gold or silver lace, or other ornament

GARDED, faced or trimmed

GARNISH, fee

GAVEL-KIND, name of a land-tenure existing chiefly in Kent; from 16th century often used to denote custom of dividing a deceased man's property equally among his sons (N.E.D.)

GAZETTE, small Venetian coin worth about three-farthings

GEANCE, jaunt, errand

GEAR (GEER), stuff, matter, affair

GELID, frozen

GEMONIES, steps from which the bodies of criminals were thrown into the river

GENERAL, free, affable

GENIUS, attendant spirit

GENTRY, gentlemen; manners characteristic of gentry, good breeding

GIB-CAT, tom-cat

GIGANTOMACHIZE, start a giants' war

GIGLOT, wanton

GIMBLET, gimlet

GING, gang

GLASS (" taking in of shadows, etc."), crystal or beryl

GLEEK, card game played by three; party of three, trio; side glance

GLICK (GLEEK), jest, gibe

GLIDDER, glaze

GLORIOUSLY, of vain glory

GODWIT, bird of the snipe family

GOLD-END-MAN, a buyer of broken gold and silver

GOLL, hand

GONFALIONIER, standard - bearer, chief magistrate, etc.

GOOD, sound in credit

GOOD-YEAR, good luck

GOOSE-TURD, colour of. (*See* Turd)

GORCROW, carrion crow

GORGET, neck armour

GOSSIP, godfather

GOWKED, from "gowk," to stand staring and gaping like a fool

GRANNAM, grandam

GRASS, (?) grease, fat

GRATEFUL, agreeable, welcome

GRATIFY, give thanks to

GRATITUDE, gratuity

GRATULATE, welcome, congratulate

GRAVITY, dignity

GRAY, badger

GRICE, cub

GRIEF, grievance

GRIPE, vulture, griffin

GRIPE'S EGG, vessel in shape of

GROAT, fourpence

GROGRAN, coarse stuff made of silk and mohair, or of coarse silk

GROOM-PORTER, officer in the royal household

GROPE, handle, probe

GROUND, pit (hence "grounded judgments ")

GUARD, caution, heed

GUARDANT, heraldic term: turning the head only

GUILDER, Dutch coin worth about 4*d*.

GULES, gullet, throat; heraldic term for red

GULL, simpleton, dupe

GUST, taste

HAB NAB, by, on, chance

HABERGEON, coat of mail

HAGGARD, wild female hawk; hence coy, wild

HALBERD, combination of lance and battle-axe

HALL, " a —! " a cry to clear the room for the dancers

HANDSEL, first money taken

HANGER, loop or strap on a sword-belt from which the sword was suspended

HAP, fortune, luck

HAPPILY, haply

HAPPINESS, appropriateness, fitness

HAPPY, rich

HARBOUR, track, trace (an animal) to its shelter

HARD-FAVOURED, harsh-featured

HARPOCRATES, Horus the child, son of Osiris, figured with a finger pointing to his mouth, indicative of silence

HARRINGTON, a patent was granted to Lord H. for the coinage of tokens (*q.v.*)

HARROT, herald

HARRY NICHOLAS, founder of a community called the " Family of Love "

HAY, net for catching rabbits, etc.

HAY! (Ital. *hai!*), you have it (a fencing term)

HAY IN HIS HORN, ill-tempered person

HAZARD, game at dice; that which is staked

HEAD, " first —," young deer with antlers first sprouting; fig. a newly-ennobled man

HEADBOROUGH, constable

HEARKEN AFTER, inquire; " hearken out," find, search out

HEARTEN, encourage

HEAVEN AND HELL (" Alchemist "), names of taverns

HECTIC, fever

HEDGE IN, include

HELM, upper part of a retort

HER'NSEW, hernshaw, heron

HIERONIMO (JERONIMO), hero of Kyd's " Spanish Tragedy "

HOBBY, nag

HOBBY-HORSE, imitation horse of some light material, fastened round the waist of the morrice-dancer, who imitated the movements of a skittish horse

HODDY-DODDY, fool

HOIDEN, hoyden, formerly applied to both sexes (ancient term for leveret? Gifford)

HOLLAND, name of two famous chemists

HONE AND HONERO, wailing expressions of lament or discontent

HOOD-WINK'D, blindfolded

HORARY, hourly

HORN-MAD, stark mad (quibble)

HORN-THUMB, cut-purses were in the habit of wearing a horn shield on the thumb

HORSE-BREAD-EATING, horses were often fed on coarse bread
HORSE-COURSER, horse-dealer
HOSPITAL, Christ's Hospital
HOWLEGLAS, Eulenspiegel, the hero of a popular German tale which relates his buffooneries and knavish tricks
HUFF, hectoring, arrogance
HUFF IT, swagger
HUISHER (Fr. *huissier*), usher
HUM, beer and spirits mixed together
HUMANITIAN, humanist, scholar
HUMOROUS, capricious, moody, out of humour; moist
HUMOUR, a word used in and out of season in the time of Shakespeare and Ben Jonson, and ridiculed by both
HUMOURS, manners
HUMPHREY, DUKE, those who were dinnerless spent the dinner-hour in a part of St. Paul's where stood a monument, said to be that of the duke's; hence "dine with Duke Humphrey," to go hungry
HURTLESS, harmless

IDLE, useless, unprofitable
ILL-AFFECTED, ill-disposed
ILL-HABITED, unhealthy
ILLUSTRATE, illuminate
IMBIBITION, saturation, steeping
IMBROCATA, fencing term: a thrust in tierce
IMPAIR, impairment
IMPART, give money
IMPARTER, any one ready to be cheated and to part with his money
IMPEACH, damage
IMPERTINENCIES, irrelevancies
IMPERTINENT(LY), irrelevant(ly), without reason or purpose
IMPOSITION, duty imposed by
IMPOTENTLY, beyond power of control
IMPRESS, money in advance
IMPULSION, incitement
IN AND IN, a game played by two or three persons with four dice
INCENSE, incite, stir up
INCERATION, act of covering with wax; or reducing a substance to softness of wax
INCH, "to their —es," according to their stature, capabilities
INCH-PIN, sweet-bread
INCONVENIENCE, inconsistency, absurdity
INCONY, delicate, rare (used as a term of affection)
INCUBEE, incubus
INCUBUS, evil spirit that oppresses us in sleep, nightmare
INCURIOUS, unfastidious, uncritical
INDENT, enter into engagement
INDIFFERENT, tolerable, passable
INDIGESTED, shapeless, chaotic
INDUCE, introduce
INDUE, supply
INEXORABLE, relentless
INFANTED, born, produced
INFLAME, augment charge
INGENIOUS, used indiscriminately for ingenuous; intelligent, talented
INGENUITY, ingenuousness

INGENUOUS, generous
INGINE. *See* Engin
INGINER, engineer. (*See* Enginer)
INGLE, OR ENGHLE, bosom friend, intimate, minion
INHABITABLE, uninhabitable
INJURY, insult, affront
IN-MATE, resident, indwelling
INNATE, natural
INNOCENT, simpleton
INQUEST, jury, or other official body of inquiry
INQUISITION, inquiry
INSTANT, immediate
INSTRUMENT, legal document
INSURE, assure
INTEGRATE, complete, perfect
INTELLIGENCE, secret information, news
INTEND, note carefully, attend, give ear to, be occupied with
INTENDMENT, intention
INTENT, intention, wish
INTENTION, concentration of attention or gaze
INTENTIVE, attentive
INTERESSED, implicated
INTRUDE, bring in forcibly or without leave
INVINCIBLY, invisibly
INWARD, intimate
IRPE (uncertain), "a fantastic grimace, or contortion of the body" (Gifford)

JACK, Jack o' the clock, automaton figure that strikes the hour; Jack-a-lent, puppet thrown at in Lent
JACK, key of a virginal
JACOB'S STAFF, an instrument for taking altitudes and distances
JADE, befool
JEALOUSY, JEALOUS, suspicion, suspicious
JERKING, lashing
JEW'S TRUMP, Jew's harp
JIG, merry ballad or tune; a fanciful dialogue or light comic act introduced at the end or during an interlude of a play
JOINED (JOINT)-STOOL, folding stool
JOLL, jowl
JOLTHEAD, blockhead
JUMP, agree, tally
JUST YEAR, no one was capable of the consulship until he was forty-three

KELL, cocoon
KELLY, an alchemist
KEMB, comb
KEMIA, vessel for distillation
KIBE, chap, sore
KILDERKIN, small barrel
KILL, kiln
KIND, nature; species; "do one's —," act according to one's nature
KIRTLE, woman's gown of jacket and petticoat
KISS OR DRINK AFORE ME, "this is a familiar expression, employed when what the speaker is just about to say is anticipated by another" (Gifford)
KIT, fiddle

KNACK, snap, click

KNIPPER-DOLING, a well-known Anabaptist

KNITTING CUP, marriage cup

KNOCKING, striking, weighty

KNOT, company, band; a sandpiper, or robin snipe (*Tringa canutus*); flower-bed laid out in fanciful design

KURSINED, KYRSIN, christened

LABOURED, wrought with labour and care

LADE, load(ed)

LADING, load

LAID, plotted

LANCE-KNIGHT (*Lanzknecht*), a German mercenary foot-soldier

LAP, fold

LAR, household god

LARD, garnish

LARGE, abundant

LARUM, alarum, call to arms

LATTICE, tavern windows were furnished with lattices of various colours

LAUNDER, to wash gold in *aqua regia*, so as imperceptibly to extract some of it

LAVE, ladle, bale

LAW, " give —," give a start (term of chase)

LAXATIVE, loose

LAY ABOARD, run alongside generally with intent to board

LEAGUER, siege, or camp of besieging army

LEASING, lying

LEAVE, leave off, desist

LEER, leering, or " empty, hence, perhaps, leer horse, a horse without a rider; leer is an adjective meaning uncontrolled, hence ' leer drunkards' " (Halliwell); according to Nares, a leer (empty) horse meant also a led horse; leeward, left

LEESE, lose

LEGS, " make —," do obeisance

LEIGER, resident representative

LEIGERITY, legerdemain

LEMMA, subject proposed, or title of the epigram

LENTER, slower

LET, hinder

LET, hindrance

LEVEL COIL, a rough game . . . in which one hunted another from his seat. Hence used for any noisy riot (Halliwell)

LEWD, ignorant

LEYSTALLS, receptacles of filth

LIBERAL, ample

LIEGER, ledger, register

LIFT(ING), steal(ing); theft

LIGHT, alight

LIGHTLY, commonly, usually, often

LIKE, please

LIKELY, agreeable, pleasing

LIME-HOUND, leash-, blood-hound

LIMMER, vile, worthless

LIN, leave off

LINE, " by —," by rule

LINSTOCK, staff to stick in the ground, with forked head to hold a lighted match for firing cannon

LIQUID, clear

LIST, listen, hark; like, please

LIVERY, legal term, delivery of the possession, etc.

LOGGET, small log, stick

LOOSE, solution; upshot, issue; release of an arrow

LOSE, give over, desist from; waste

LOUTING, bowing, cringing

LUCULENT, bright of beauty

LUDGATHIANS, dealers on Ludgate Hill

LURCH, rob, cheat

LUTE, to close a vessel with some kind of cement

MACK, unmeaning expletive

MADGE-HOWLET or OWL, barn-owl

MAIM, hurt, injury

MAIN, chief concern (used as a quibble on heraldic term for " hand ")

MAINPRISE, becoming surety for a prisoner so as to procure his release

MAINTENANCE, giving aid, or abetting

MAKE, mate

MAKE, MADE, acquaint with business, prepare(d), instruct(ed)

MALLANDERS, disease of horses

MALT HORSE, dray horse

MAMMET, puppet

MAMMOTHREPT, spoiled child

MANAGE, control (term used for breaking-in horses); handling, administration

MANGO, slave-dealer

MANGONISE, polish up for sale

MANIPLES, bundles, handfuls

MANKIND, masculine, like a virago

MANKIND, humanity

MAPLE FACE, spotted face (N.E.D.)

MARCHPANE, a confection of almonds, sugar, etc.

MARK, " fly to the —," " generally said of a goshawk when, having ' put in ' a covey of partridges, she takes stand, marking the spot where they disappeared from view until the falconer arrives to put them out to her " (Harting, Bibl. Accip, Gloss. 226)

MARLE, marvel

MARROW-BONE MAN, one often on his knees for prayer

MARRY! exclamation derived from the Virgin's name

MARRY GIP, " probably originated from By Mary Gipcy = St. Mary of Egypt' (N.E.D.)

MARTAGAN, Turk's cap lily

MARYHINCHCO, stringhalt

MASORETH, Masora, correct form of the scriptural text according to Hebrew tradition

MASS, abb. for master

MAUND, beg

MAUTHER, girl, maid

MEAN, moderation

MEASURE, dance, more especially a stately one

MEAT, " carry — in one's mouth," be a source of money or entertainment

MEATH, metheglin

MECHANICAL, belonging to mechanics; mean, vulgar

MEDITERRANEO, middle aisle of St. Paul's, a general resort for business and amusement

MEET WITH, even with

MELICOTTON, a late kind of peach

MENSTRUE, solvent

MERCAT, market

MERD, excrement

MERE, undiluted; absolute, unmitigated

MESS, party of four

METHEGLIN, fermented liquor, of which one ingredient was honey

METOPOSCOPY, study of physiognomy

MIDDLING GOSSIP, go-between

MIGNIARD, dainty, delicate

MILE-END, training-ground of the city

MINE-MEN, sappers

MINION, form of cannon

MINSITIVE, (?) mincing, affected (N.E.D.)

MISCELLANY MADAM, "a female trader in miscellaneous articles; a dealer in trinkets or ornaments of various kinds, such as kept shops in the New Exchange" (Nares)

MISCELLINE, mixed grain; medley

MISCONCEIT, misconception

MISPRISE, MISPRISION, mistake, misunderstanding

MISTAKE AWAY, carry away as if by mistake

MITHRIDATE, an antidote against poison

MOCCINIGO, small Venetian coin, worth about ninepence

MODERN, in the mode; ordinary, commonplace

MOMENT, force or influence of value

MONTANTO, upward stroke

MONTH'S MIND, violent desire

MOORISH, like a moor or waste

MORGLAY, sword of Bevis of Southampton

MORRICE-DANCE, dances on May Day, etc., in which certain personages were represented

MORTALITY, death

MORT-MAL, old sore, gangrene

MOSCADINO, confection flavoured with musk

MOTHER, *Hysterica passio*

MOTION, proposal, request; puppet, puppet-show; "one of the small figures on the face of a large clock which was moved by the vibration of the pendulum" (Whalley)

MOTION, suggest, propose

MOTLEY, parti-coloured dress of a fool; hence used to signify pertaining to, or like, a fool

MOTTE, motto

MOURNIVAL, set of four aces or court cards in a hand; a quartette

Mow, setord hay or sheaves of grain

MUCH! expressive of irony and incredulity

MUCKINDER, handkerchief

MULE, "born to ride on —," judges or serjeants-at-law formerly rode on mules when going in state to Westminster (Whalley)

MULLETS, small pincers

MUM-CHANCE, game of chance, played in silence

MUN, must

MUREY, dark crimson red

MUSCOVY-GLASS, mica

MUSE, wonder

MUSICAL, in harmony

MUSS, mouse; scramble

MYROBOLANE, foreign conserve, "a dried plum, brought from the Indies"

MYSTERY, art, trade, profession

NAIL, "to the — " (*ad unguem*), to perfection, to the very utmost

NATIVE, natural

NEAT, cattle

NEAT, smartly apparelled; unmixed; dainty

NEATLY, neatly finished

NEATNESS, elegance

NEIS, nose, scent

NEUF (NEAF, NEIF), fist

NEUFT, newt

NIAISE, foolish, inexperienced person

NICE, fastidious, trivial, finical, scrupulous

NICENESS, fastidiousness

NICK, exact amount; right moment; "set in the —," meaning uncertain

NICK, suit, fit; hit, seize the right moment, etc., exactly hit on, hit off

NOBLE, gold coin worth 6s. 8d.

NOCENT, harmful

NIL, not will

NOISE, company of musicians

NOMENTACK, an Indian chief from Virginia

NONES, nonce

NOTABLE, egregious

NOTE, sign, token

NOUGHT, "be —," go to the devil, be hanged, etc.

NOWT-HEAD, blockhead

NUMBER, rhythm

NUPSON, oaf, simpleton

OADE, woad

OBARNI, preparation of mead

OBJECT, oppose; expose; interpose

OBLATRANT, barking, railing

OBNOXIOUS, liable, exposed; offensive

OBSERVANCE, homage, devoted service

OBSERVANT, attentive, obsequious

OBSERVE, show deference, respect

OBSERVER, one who shows deference, or waits upon another

OBSTANCY, legal phrase, "juridical opposition"

OBSTREPEROUS, clamorous, vociferous

OBSTUPEFACT, stupefied

ODLING, (?) "must have some relation to tricking and cheating" (Nares)

OMINOUS, deadly, fatal

ONCE, at once; for good and all; used also for additional emphasis

ONLY, pre-eminent, special

OPEN, make public; expound

OPPILATION, obstruction

OPPONE, oppose

OPPOSITE, antagonist

OPPRESS, suppress

ORIGINOUS, native

ORT, remnant, scrap

Out, "to be —," to have forgotten one's part; not at one with each other

Outcry, sale by auction

Outrecuidance, arrogance, presumption

Outspeak, speak more than

Overparted, given too difficult a part to play

Owlspiegel. See Howleglass

Oyez! (O yes!), hear ye! call of the public crier when about to make a proclamation

Packing penny, "give a —," dismiss, send packing

Pad, highway

Pad-horse, road-horse

Pained (Paned) slops, full breeches made of strips of different colour and material

Painful, diligent, painstaking

Paint, blush

Palinode, ode of recantation

Pall, weaken, dim, make stale

Palm, triumph

Pan, skirt of dress or coat

Pannel, pad, or rough kind of saddle

Pannier-ally, inhabited by tripe-sellers

Pannier-man, hawker; a man employed about the inns of court to bring in provisions, set the table, etc.

Pantofle, indoor shoe, slipper

Paramentos, fine trappings

Paranomasie, a play upon words

Parantory, (?) peremptory

Parcel, particle, fragment (used contemptuously); article

Parcel, part, partly

Parcel-poet, poetaster

Parerga, subordinate matters

Parget, to paint or plaster the face

Parle, parley

Parlous, clever, shrewd

Part, apportion

Partake, participate in

Parted, endowed, talented

Particular, individual person

Partizan, kind of halberd

Partrich, partridge

Parts, qualities, endowments

Pash, dash, smash

Pass, care, trouble oneself

Passado, fencing term: a thrust

Passage, game at dice

Passingly, exceedingly

Passion, effect caused by external agency

Passion, "in —," in so melancholy a tone, so pathetically

Patoun, (?) Fr. *pâton*, pellet of dough; perhaps the "moulding of the tobacco . . . for the pipe" (Gifford); (?) variant of Petun, South American name of tobacco

Patrico, the recorder, priest, orator of strolling beggars or gipsies

Patten, shoe with wooden sole; "go —," keep step with, accompany

Pauca verba, few words

Pavin, a stately dance

Peace, "with my master's —," by leave, favour

Peculiar, individual, single

Pedant, teacher of the languages

Peel, baker's shovel

Peep, speak in a small or shrill voice

Peevish(ly), foolish(ly), capricious(ly); childish(ly)

Pelican, a retort fitted with tube or tubes, for continuous distillation

Pencil, small tuft of hair

Perdue, soldier accustomed to hazardous service

Peremptory, resolute, bold; imperious; thorough, utter, absolute(ly)

Perimeter, circumference of a figure

Period, limit, end

Perk, perk up

Perpetuana, "this seems to be that glossy kind of stuff now called *everlasting*, and anciently worn by serjeants and other city officers" (Gifford)

Perspective, a view, scene or scenery; an optical device which gave a distortion to the picture unless seen from a particular point; a relief, modelled to produce an optical illusion

Perspicil, optic glass

Perstringe, criticise, censure

Persuade, inculcate, commend

Persway, mitigate

Pertinacy, pertinacity

Pestling, pounding, pulverising, like a pestle

Petasus, broad-brimmed hat or winged cap worn by Mercury

Petitionary, supplicatory

Petronel, a kind of carbine or light gun carried by horsemen

Petulant, pert, insolent

Phere. See Fere

Phlegma, watery distilled liquor (old chem. "water")

Phrenetic, madman

Picardil, stiff upright collar fastened on to the coat (Whalley)

Pickt-hatch, disreputable quarter of London

Piece, person, used for woman or girl; a gold coin worth in Jonson's time 20s. or 22s.

Pieces of eight, Spanish coin: piastre equal to eight reals

Pied, variegated

Pie-poudres (Fr. *pied-poudreux*, dusty-foot), court held at fairs to administer justice to itinerant vendors and buyers

Pilcher, term of contempt; one who wore a buff or leather jerkin, as did the serjeants of the counter; a pilferer

Piled, pilled, peeled, bald

Pill'd, polled, fleeced

Pimlico, "sometimes spoken of as a person —perhaps master of a house famous for a particular ale" (Gifford)

Pine, afflict, distress

Pink, stab with a weapon; pierce or cut in scallops for ornament

Pinnace, a go-between in infamous sense

Pismire, ant

Pistolet, gold coin, worth about 6s.

Pitch, height of a bird of prey's flight

Plague, punishment, torment

PLAIN, lament

PLAIN SONG, simple melody

PLAISE, plaice

PLANET, " struck with a —," planets were supposed to have powers of blasting or exercising secret influences

PLAUSIBLE, pleasing

PLAUSIBLY, approvingly

PLOT, plan

PLY, apply oneself to

POESIE, posy, motto inside a ring

POINT IN HIS DEVICE, exact in every particular

POINTS, tagged laces or cords for fastening the breeches to the doublet

POINT-TRUSSER, one who trussed (tied) his master's points (q.v.)

POISE, weigh, balance

POKING-STICK, stick used for setting the plaits of ruffs

POLITIC, politician

POLITIC, judicious, prudent, political

POLITICIAN, plotter, intriguer

POLL, strip, plunder, gain by extortion

POMANDER, ball of perfume, worn or hung about the person to prevent infection, or for foppery

POMMADO, vaulting on a horse without the aid of stirrups

PONTIC, sour

POPULAR, vulgar, of the populace

POPULOUS, numerous

PORT, gate; print of a deer's foot

PORT, transport

PORTAGUE, Portuguese gold coin, worth over £3 or £4

PORTCULLIS, " — of coin," some old coins have a portcullis stamped on their reverse (Whalley)

PORTENT, marvel, prodigy; sinister omen

PORTENTOUS, prophesying evil, threatening

PORTER, references appear " to allude to Parsons, the king's porter, who was . . . near seven feet high " (Whalley)

POSSESS, inform, acquaint

POST AND PAIR, a game at cards

POSY, motto. (See Poesie)

POTCH, poach

POULT-FOOT, club-foot

POUNCE, claw, talon

PRACTICE, intrigue, concerted plot

PRACTISE, plot, conspire

PRAGMATIC, an expert, agent

PRAGMATIC, officious, conceited, meddling

PRECEDENT, record of proceedings

PRECEPT, warrant, summons

PRECISIAN(ISM), Puritan(ism), preciseness

PREFER, recommend

PRESENCE, presence chamber

PRESENT(LY), immediate(ly), without delay; at the present time; actually

PRESS, force into service

PREST, ready

PRETEND, assert, allege

PREVENT, anticipate

PRICE, worth, excellence

PRICK, point, dot used in the writing of Hebrew and other languages

PRICK, prick out, mark off; select; trace. track; " — away," make off with speed

PRIMERO, game of cards

PRINCOX, pert boy

PRINT, " in —," to the letter, exactly

PRISTINATE, former

PRIVATE, private interests

PRIVATE, privy, intimate

PROCLIVE, prone to

PRODIGIOUS, monstrous, unnatural

PRODIGY, monster

PRODUCED, prolonged

PROFESS, pretend

PROJECTION, the throwing of the " powder of projection " into the crucible to turn the melted metal into gold or silver

PROLATE, pronounce drawlingly

PROPER, of good appearance, handsome; own, particular

PROPERTIES, stage necessaries

PROPERTY, duty; tool

PRORUMPED, burst out

PROTEST, vow, proclaim (an affected word of that time); formally declare non-payment, etc., of bill of exchange; fig. failure of personal credit, etc.

PROVANT, soldier's allowance — hence, of common make

PROVIDE, foresee

PROVIDENCE, foresight, prudence

PUBLICATION, making a thing public or common property (N.E.D.)

PUCKFIST, puff-ball; insipid, insignificant, boasting fellow

PUFF-WING, shoulder puff

PUISNE, judge of inferior rank, a junior

PULCHRITUDE, beauty

PUMP, shoe

PUNGENT, piercing

PUNTO, point, hit

PURCEPT, precept, warrant

PURE, fine, capital, excellent

PURELY, perfectly, utterly

PURL, pleat or fold of a ruff

PURSE-NET, net of which the mouth is drawn together with a string

PURSUIVANT, state messenger who summoned the persecuted seminaries; warrant officer

PURSY, PURSINESS, shortwinded(ness)

PUT, make a push, exert yourself (N.E.D.)

PUT OFF, excuse, shift

PUT ON, incite, encourage; proceed with, take in hand, try

QUACKSALVER, quack

QUAINT, elegant, elaborated, ingenious, clever

QUAR, quarry

QUARRIED, seized, or fed upon, as prey

QUEAN, hussy, jade

QUEASY, hazardous, delicate

QUELL, kill, destroy

QUEST, request; inquiry

QUESTION, decision by force of arms

QUESTMAN, one appointed to make official inquiry

QUIB, QUIBLIN, quibble, quip

QUICK, the living

QUIDDIT, quiddity, legal subtlety
QUIRK, clever turn or trick
QUIT, requite, repay; acquit, absolve; rid; forsake, leave
QUITTER-BONE, disease of horses
QUODLING, codling
QUOIT, throw like a quoit, chuck
QUOTE, take note, observe, write down

RACK, neck of mutton or pork (Halliwell)
RAKE UP, cover over
RAMP, rear, as a lion, etc.
RAPT, carry away
RAPT, enraptured
RASCAL, young or inferior deer
RASH, strike with a glancing oblique blow, as a boar with its tusk
RATSEY, GOMALIEL, a famous highwayman
RAVEN, devour
REACH, understand
REAL, regal
REBATU, ruff, turned-down collar
RECTOR, RECTRESS, director, governor
REDARGUE, confute
REDUCE, bring back
REED, rede, counsel, advice
REEL, run riot
REFEL, refute
REFORMADOES, disgraced or disbanded soldiers
REGIMENT, government
REGRESSION, return
REGULAR ("Tale of a Tub"), regular noun (quibble) (N.E.D.)
RELIGION, "make — of," make a point of, scruple of
RELISH, savour
REMNANT, scrap of quotation
REMORA, species of fish
RENDER, depict, exhibit, show
REPAIR, reinstate
REPETITION, recital, narration
REREMOUSE, bat
RESIANT, resident
RESIDENCE, sediment
RESOLUTION, judgment, decision
RESOLVE, inform; assure; prepare, make up one's mind; dissolve; come to a decision, be convinced; relax, set at ease
RESPECTIVE, worthy of respect; regardful, discriminative
RESPECTIVELY, with reverence
RESPECTLESS, regardless
RESPIRE, exhale; inhale
RESPONSIBLE, correspondent
REST, musket-rest
REST, "set up one's —," venture one's all, one's last stake (from game of primero)
REST, arrest
RESTIVE, RESTY, dull, inactive
RETCHLESS(NESS), reckless(ness)
RETIRE, cause to retire
RETRICATO, fencing term
RETRIEVE, rediscovery of game once sprung
RETURNS, ventures sent abroad, for the safe return of which so much money is received
REVERBERATE, dissolve or blend by reflected heat

REVERSE, REVERSO, back-handed thrust, etc., in fencing
REVISE, reconsider a sentence
RHEUM, spleen, caprice
RIBIBE, abusive term for an old woman
RID, destroy, do away with
RIFLING, raffling, dicing
RING, "cracked within the —," coins so cracked were unfit for currency
RISSE, risen, rose
RIVELLED, wrinkled
ROARER, swaggerer
ROCHET, fish of the gurnet kind
ROCK, distaff
RODOMONTADO, braggadocio
ROGUE, vagrant, vagabond
RONDEL, "a round mark in the score of a public-house" (Nares); roundel
ROOK, sharper; fool, dupe
ROSAKER, similar to ratsbane
ROSA-SOLIS, a spiced spirituous liquor
ROSES, rosettes
ROUND, "gentlemen of the —," officers of inferior rank
ROUND TRUNKS, trunk hose, short loose breeches reaching almost or quite to the knees
ROUSE, carouse, bumper
ROVER, arrow used for shooting at a random mark at uncertain distance
ROWLY-POWLY, roly-poly
RUDE, RUDENESS, unpolished, rough(ness), coarse(ness)
RUFFLE, flaunt, swagger
RUG, coarse frieze
RUG-GOWNS, gown made of rug
RUSH, reference to rushes with which the floors were then strewn
RUSHER, one who strewed the floor with rushes
RUSSET, homespun cloth of neutral or reddish-brown colour

SACK, loose, flowing gown
SADLY, seriously, with gravity
SAD(NESS), sober, serious(ness)
SAFFI, bailiffs
ST. THOMAS À WATERINGS, place in Surrey where criminals were executed
SAKER, small piece of ordnance
SALT, leap
SALT, lascivious
SAMPSUCHINE, sweet marjoram
SARABAND, a slow dance
SATURNALS, began December 17
SAUCINESS, presumption, insolence
SAUCY, bold, impudent, wanton
SAUNA (Lat.), a gesture of contempt
SAVOUR, perceive; gratify, please; to partake of the nature
SAY, sample
SAY, assay, try
SCALD, word of contempt, implying dirt and disease
SCALLION, shalot, small onion
SCANDERBAG, "name which the Turks (in allusion to Alexander the Great) gave to the brave Castriot, chief of Albania, with whom they had continual wars. His

romantic life had just been translated "
(Gifford)

SCAPE, escape

SCARAB, beetle

SCARTOCCIO, fold of paper, cover, cartouch, cartridge

SCONCE, head

SCOPE, aim

SCOT AND LOT, tax, contribution (formerly a parish assessment)

SCOTOMY, dizziness in the head

SCOUR, purge

SCOURSE, deal, swap

SCRATCHES, disease of horses

SCROYLE, mean, rascally fellow

SCRUPLE, doubt

SEAL, put hand to the giving up of property or rights

SEALED, stamped as genuine

SEAM-RENT, ragged

SEAMING LACES, insertion or edging

SEAR UP, close by searing, burning

SEARCED, sifted

SECRETARY, able to keep a secret

SECULAR, worldly, ordinary, commonplace

SECURE, confident

SEELIE, happy, blest

SEISIN, legal term: possession

SELLARY, lewd person

SEMBLABLY, similarly

SEMINARY, a Romish priest educated in a foreign seminary

SENSELESS, insensible, without sense or feeling

SENSIBLY, perceptibly

SENSIVE, sensitive

SENSUAL, pertaining to the physical or material

SERENE, harmful dew of evening

SERICON, red tincture

SERVANT, lover

SERVICES, doughty deeds of arms

SESTERCE, Roman copper coin

SET, stake, wager

SET UP, drill

SETS, deep plaits of the ruff

SEWER, officer who served up the feast, and brought water for the hands of the guests

SHAPE, a suit by way of disguise

SHIFT, fraud, dodge

SHIFTER, cheat

SHITTLE, shuttle; "shittle-cock," shuttlecock

SHOT, tavern reckoning

SHOT-CLOG, one only tolerated because he paid the shot (reckoning) for the rest

SHOT-FREE, scot-free, not having to pay

SHOVE-GROAT, low kind of gambling amusement, perhaps somewhat of the nature of pitch and toss

SHOT-SHARKS, drawers

SHREWD, mischievous, malicious, curst

SHREWDLY, keenly, in a high degree

SHRIVE, sheriff; posts were set up before his door for proclamations, or to indicate his residence

SHROVING, Shrovetide, season of merriment

SIGILLA, seal, mark

SILENCED BRETHREN, MINISTERS, those of the Church or Nonconformists who had been silenced, deprived, etc.

SILLY, simple, harmless

SIMPLE, silly, witless; plain, true

SIMPLES, herbs

SINGLE, term of chase, signifying when the hunted stag is separated from the herd, or forced to break covert

SINGLE, weak, silly

SINGLE-MONEY, small change

SINGULAR, unique, supreme

SI-QUIS, bill, advertisement

SKELDRING, getting money under false pretences; swindling

SKILL, "it —s not," matters not

SKINK(ER), pour, draw(er), tapster

SKIRT, tail

SLEEK, smooth

SLICE, fire shovel or pan (dial.)

SLICK, sleek, smooth

'SLID, 'SLIGHT, 'SPRECIOUS, irreverent oaths

SLIGHT, sleight, cunning, cleverness; trick

SLIP, counterfeit coin, bastard

SLIPPERY, polished and shining

SLOPS, large loose breeches

SLOT, print of a stag's foot

SLUR, put a slur on; cheat (by sliding a die in some way)

SMELT, gull, simpleton

SNORLE, "perhaps snarl, as Puppy is addressed" (Cunningham)

SNOTTERIE, filth

SNUFF, anger, resentment; "take in —," take offence at

SNUFFERS, small open silver dishes for holding snuff, or receptacle for placing snuffers in (Halliwell)

SOCK, shoe worn by comic actors

SOD, seethe

SOGGY, soaked, sodden

SOIL, "take —," said of a hunted stag when he takes to the water for safety

SOL, sou

SOLDADOES, soldiers

SOLICIT, rouse, excite to action

SOOTH, flattery, cajolery

SOOTHE, flatter, humour

SOPHISTICATE, adulterate

SORT, company, party; rank, degree

SORT, suit, fit; select

SOUSE, ear

SOUSED ("Devil is an Ass"), fol. read "sou't," which Dyce interprets as "a variety of the spelling of shu'd : to shu is to scare a bird away." (See his Webster, p. 350)

SOWTER, cobbler

SPAGYRICA, chemistry according to the teachings of Paracelsus

SPAR, bar

SPEAK, make known, proclaim

SPECULATION, power of sight

SPED, to have fared well, prospered

SPEECE, species

SPIGHT, anger, rancour

SPINNER, spider

SPINSTRY, lewd person

SPITTLE, hospital, lazar-house

SPLEEN, considered the seat of the emotions
SPLEEN, caprice, humour, mood
SPRUNT, spruce
SPURGE, foam
SPUR-RYAL, gold coin worth 15s.
SQUIRE, square, measure; " by the —," exactly
STAGGERING, wavering, hesitating
STAIN, disparagement, disgrace
STALE, decoy, or cover, stalking-horse
STALE, make cheap, common
STALK, approach stealthily or under cover
STALL, forestall
STANDARD, suit
STAPLE, market, emporium
STARK, downright
STARTING-HOLES, loopholes of escape
STATE, dignity; canopied chair of state; estate
STATUMINATE, support vines by poles or stakes; used by Pliny (Gifford)
STAY, gag
STAY, await; detain
STICKLER, second or umpire
STIGMATISE, mark, brand
STILL, continual(ly), constant(ly)
STINKARD, stinking fellow
STINT, stop
STIPTIC, astringent
STOCCATA, thrust in fencing
STOCK-FISH, salted and dried fish
STOMACH, pride, valour
STOMACH, resent
STOOP, swoop down as a hawk
STOP, fill, stuff
STOPPLE, stopper
STOTE, stoat, weasel
STOUP, stoop, swoop=bow
STRAIGHT, straightway
STRAMAZOUN (Ital. *stramazzone*), a down blow, as opposed to the thrust
STRANGE, like a stranger, unfamiliar
STRANGENESS, distance of behaviour
STREIGHTS, OR BERMUDAS, labyrinth of alleys and courts in the Strand
STRIGONIUM, Grau in Hungary, taken from the Turks in 1597
STRIKE, balance (accounts)
STRINGHALT, disease of horses
STROKER, smoother, flatterer
STROOK, p.p. of " strike "
STRUMMEL-PATCHED, strummel is glossed in dialect dicts. as "a long, loose and dishevelled head of hair"
STUDIES, studious efforts
STYLE, title; pointed instrument used for writing on wax tablets
SUBTLE, fine, delicate, thin; smooth, soft
SUBTLETY (SUBTILITY), subtle device
SUBURB, connected with loose living
SUCCUBÆ, demons in form of women
SUCK, extract money from
SUFFERANCE, suffering
SUMMED, term of falconry: with full-grown plumage
SUPER-NEGULUM, topers turned the cup bottom up when it was empty
SUPERSTITIOUS, over-scrupulous
SUPPLE, to make pliant

SURBATE, make sore with walking
SURCEASE, cease
SUR-REVERENCE, save your reverence
SURVISE, peruse
SUSCITABILITY, excitability
SUSPECT, suspicion
SUSPEND, suspect
SUSPENDED, held over for the present
SUTLER, victualler
SWAD, clown, boor
SWATH BANDS, swaddling clothes
SWINGE, beat

TABERD, emblazoned mantle or tunic worn by knights and heralds
TABLE(S), " pair of —," tablets, note-book
TABOR, small drum
TABRET, tabor
TAFFETA, silk; "tuft-taffeta," a more costly silken fabric
TAINT, " — a staff," break a lance at tilting in an unscientific or dishonourable manner
TAKE IN, capture, subdue
TAKE ME WITH YOU, let me understand you
TAKE UP, obtain on credit, borrow
TALENT, sum or weight of Greek currency
TALL, stout, brave
TANKARD-BEARERS, men employed to fetch water from the conduits
TARLETON, celebrated comedian and jester
TARTAROUS, like a Tartar
TAVERN-TOKEN, " to swallow a —," get drunk
TELL, count
TELL-TROTH, truth-teller
TEMPER, modify, soften
TENDER, show regard, care for cherish; manifest
TENT, " take —," take heed
TERSE, swept and polished
TERTIA, " that portion of an army levied out of one particular district or division of a country " (Gifford)
TESTON, tester, coin worth 6d.
THIRDBOROUGH, constable
THREAD, quality
THREAVES, droves
THREE-FARTHINGS, piece of silver current under Elizabeth
THREE-PILED, of finest quality, exaggerated
THRIFTILY, carefully
THRUMS, ends of the weaver's warp; coarse yarn made from
THUMB-RING, familiar spirits were supposed capable of being carried about in various ornaments or parts of dress
TIBICINE, player on the tibia, or pipe
TICK-TACK, game similar to backgammon
TIGHTLY, promptly
TIM, (?) expressive of a climax of nonentity
TIMELESS, untimely, unseasonable
TINCTURE, an essential or spiritual principle supposed by alchemists to be transfusible into material things; an imparted characteristic or tendency
TINK, tinkle

Glossary

TIPPET, "turn —," change behaviour or way of life

TIPSTAFF, staff tipped with metal

TIRE, head-dress

TIRE, feed ravenously, like a bird of prey

TITILLATION, that which tickles the senses, as a perfume

TOD, fox

TOILED, worn out, harassed

TOKEN, piece of base metal used in place of very small coin, when this was scarce

TONNELS, nostrils

TOP, "parish —," large top kept in villages for amusement and exercise in frosty weather when people were out of work

TOTER, tooter, player on a wind instrument

TOUSE, pull, rend

TOWARD, docile, apt; on the way to; as regards; present, at hand

TOY, whim; trick; term of contempt

TRACT, attraction

TRAIN, allure, entice

TRANSITORY, transmittable

TRANSLATE, transform

TRAY-TRIP, game at dice (success depended on throwing a three) (Nares)

TREACHOUR (TRECHER), traitor

TREEN, wooden

TRENCHER, serving-man who carved or served food

TRENDLE-TAIL, trundle-tail, curly-tailed

TRICK (TRICKING), term of heraldry: to draw outline of coat of arms, etc., without blazoning

TRIG, a spruce, dandified man

TRILL, trickle

TRILLIBUB, tripe, any worthless, trifling thing

TRIPOLY, "come from —," able to perform feats of agility, a "jest nominal," depending on the first part of the word (Gifford)

TRITE, worn, shabby

TRIVIA, three-faced goddess (Hecate)

TROJAN, familiar term for an equal or inferior; thief

TROLL, sing loudly

TROMP, trump, deceive

TROPE, figure of speech

TROW, think, believe, wonder

TROWLE, troll

TROWSES, breeches, drawers

TRUCHMAN, interpreter

TRUNDLE, JOHN, well-known printer

TRUNDLE, roll, go rolling along

TRUNDLING CHEATS, term among gipsies and beggars for carts or coaches (Gifford)

TRUNK, speaking-tube

TRUSS, tie the tagged laces that fastened the breeches to the doublet

TUBICINE, trumpeter

TUCKET (Ital. *toccato*), introductory flourish on the trumpet

TUITION, guardianship

TUMBLER, a particular kind of dog so called from the mode of his hunting

TUMBREL-SLOP, loose, baggy breeches

TURD, excrement

TUSK, gnash the teeth (*Century Dict.*)

TWIRE, peep, twinkle

TWOPENNY ROOM, gallery

TYRING-HOUSE, attiring-room

ULENSPIEGEL. *See* Howleglass

UMBRATILE, like or pertaining to a shadow

UMBRE, brown dye

UNBATED, unabated

UNBORED, (?) excessively bored

UNCARNATE, not fleshly, or of flesh

UNCOUTH, strange, unusual

UNDERTAKER, "one who undertook by his influence in the House of Commons to carry things agreeably to his Majesty's wishes" (Whalley); one who becomes surety for

UNEQUAL, unjust

UNEXCEPTED, no objection taken at

UNFEARED, unaffrighted

UNHAPPILY, unfortunately

UNICORN'S HORN, supposed antidote to poison

UNKIND(LY), unnatural(ly)

UNMANNED, untamed (term in falconry)

UNQUIT, undischarged

UNREADY, undressed

UNRUDE, rude to an extreme

UNSEASONED, unseasonable, unripe

UNSEELED, a hawk's eyes were "seeled" by sewing the eyelids together with fine thread

UNTIMELY, unseasonably

UNVALUABLE, invaluable

UPBRAID, make a matter of reproach

UPSEE, heavy kind of Dutch beer (Halliwell); "— Dutch," in the Dutch fashion

UPTAILS ALL, refrain of a popular song

URGE, allege as accomplice, instigator

URSHIN, URCHIN, hedgehog

USE, interest on money; part of sermon dealing with the practical application of doctrine

USE, be in the habit of, accustomed to; put out to interest

USQUEBAUGH, whisky

USURE, usury

UTTER, put in circulation, make to pass current; put forth for sale

VAIL, bow, do homage

VAILS, tips, gratuities

VALL. *See* Vail

VALLIES (Fr. *valise*), portmanteau, bag

VAPOUR(S) (n. and v.), used affectedly, like "humour," in many senses, often very vaguely, and freely ridiculed by Jonson; humour, disposition, whims, brag(ging), hector(ing), etc.

VARLET, bailiff, or serjeant-at-mace

VAUT, vault

VEER (naut.), pay out

VEGETAL, vegetable; person full of life and vigour

VELLUTE, velvet

VELVET CUSTARD. Cf. "Taming of the Shrew," iv. 3, 82, "custard coffin," coffin being the raised crust over a pie

VENT, vend, sell; give outlet to; scent snuff up

VENUE, bout (fencing term)

VERDUGO (Span.), hangman, executioner

VERGE, "in the —," within a certain distance of the court

VEX, agitate, torment

VICE, the buffoon of old moralities; some kind of machinery for moving a puppet (Gifford)

VIE AND REVIE, to hazard a certain sum, and to cover it with a larger one

VINCENT AGAINST YORK, two heralds-at-arms

VINDICATE, avenge

VIRGE, wand, rod

VIRGINAL, old form of piano

VIRTUE, valour

VIVELY, in lifelike manner, livelily

VIZARD, mask

VOGUE, rumour, gossip

VOICE, vote

VOID, leave, quit

VOLARY, cage, aviary

VOLLEY, "at —," "o' the volée," at random (from a term of tennis)

VORLOFFE, furlough

WADLOE, keeper of the Devil Tavern, where Jonson and his friends met in the *Apollo* room (Whalley)

WAIGHTS, waits, night musicians, "band of musical watchmen" (Webster), or old form of "hautboys"

WANNION, "vengeance," "plague" (Nares)

WARD, a famous pirate

WARD, guard in fencing

WATCHET, pale, sky blue

WEAL, welfare

WEED, garment

WEFT, waif

WEIGHTS, "to the gold —," to every minute particular

WELKIN, sky

WELL-SPOKEN, of fair speech

WELL-TORNED, turned and polished, as on a wheel

WELT, hem, border of fur

WHÊR, whether

WHETSTONE, GEORGE, an author who lived 1544 (?) to 1587 (?)

WHIFF, a smoke, or drink; "taking the —," inhaling the tobacco smoke or some such accomplishment

WHIGH-HIES, neighings, whinnyings

WHIMSY, whim, "humour"

WHINILING, (?) whining, weakly

WHIT, (?) a mere jot

WHITEMEAT, food made of milk or eggs

WICKED, bad, clumsy

WICKER, pliant, agile

WILDING, esp. fruit of wild apple or crab tree (Webster)

WINE, "I have the — for you." Prov.: I have the perquisites (of the office) which you are to share (Cunningham)

WINNY, "same as old word *wonne*, to stay, etc." (Whalley)

WISE-WOMAN, fortune-teller

WISH, recommend

WISS (WUSSE), "I —," certainly, of a truth

WITHOUT, beyond

WITTY, cunning, ingenious, clever

WOOD, collection, lot

WOODCOCK, term of contempt

WOOLSACK (" — pies "), name of tavern

WORT, unfermented beer

WOUNDY, great, extreme

WREAK, revenge

WROUGHT, wrought upon

WUSSE, interjection. (*See* Wiss)

YEANLING, lamb, kid

ZANY, an inferior clown, who attended upon the chief fool and mimicked his tricks